Thinking through Paul is a winning combination of richly illustrated, introductory material on Paul and the Pauline corpus (chaps. 1–10) and discussion of Paul's "theological discourse" (chaps. 11–13). Many up-to-date and judicious discussions of debated issues in Pauline studies are included, studded with illuminating primary and secondary source quotations. The authors stress Paul's "apocalyptic narrative" as providing coherence to the letters, as well as reconstruct other metanarratives—about the covenant people Israel and the Roman imperial order—that help contextualize Paul within Jewish and Roman milieux. Students will be well-served by this up-to-date, expert, and user-friendly textbook, which aims not only to inform but also to foster a christocentric ethos.

—Judith Gundry, Yale Divinity School

For students of the apostle Paul, this is a valuable textbook on several accounts. Not only are Longenecker and Still notable Pauline scholars, but they introduce the life and letters of Paul in a clear manner and with fairness when addressing debated issues. Perhaps most importantly—something that sets this introduction apart from many others—the authors help us to appreciate Paul's rich and complex thought and challenge us to wrestle with his theology for ourselves. Longenecker and Still succeed precisely in their aim, to facilitate "thinking through Paul." The job is never done; it has only begun, but this is a wise place to begin. I look forward to introducing this book to my students!

—Nijay K. Gupta, George Fox Evangelical Seminary

Introducing the apostle Paul is more than a challenge today: not only do historical problems abound but theological debates about the heart of Paul's thinking have become a storm center. Somehow, Longenecker and Still have successfully cleared the ground for students to find Paul. Here is a beautifully produced and efficiently organized introduction to Paul.

—Scot McKnight, Northern Seminary

Written by leading Pauline scholars, *Thinking through Paul* is a reliable and accessible guide both to recent scholarship on the apostle and to the content and context of each of his letters. This is a fine (and richly illustrated) textbook whose use need hardly be confined to the classroom!

—Stephen Westerholm, McMaster University

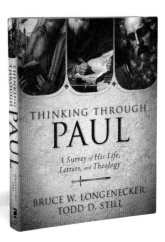

THINKING THROUGH
PAUL

THINKING THROUGH PAUL

An Introduction to His Life, Letters, and Theology

BRUCE W. LONGENECKER
TODD D. STILL

ZONDERVAN

Thinking through Paul

This title is also available as a Zondervan ebook. Visit www.zondervan.com/ebooks.

Requests for information should be addressed to:

Zondervan, *3900 Sparks Dr. SE, Grand Rapids, Michigan 49546*

Library of Congress Cataloging-in-Publication Data

Bruce W. Longnecker.
Thinking through Paul : an introduction to his life, letters, and theology/ Bruce W. Longnecker and Todd D. Still.
pages cm.
Includes index.
ISBN 978-0-310-33086-8 (hardcover)
1. Bible. Epistles of Paul—Criticism, interpretation, etc. 2. Bible. Epistles of Paul—Theology. 3. Paul, the Apostle, Saint. I. Still, Todd D. II. Title.
BS2650.52.L665 2014
227'.06—dc23 2013044552

Cover design: Michelle Lenger
Cover images: (left) Mondadori Portfolio / Electa / Art Resource, NY (center) Scala / White Images / Art Resource, NY (right) National Trust Photo Library / Art Resource, NY (sword and background texture) iStock.com
Interior design: Matthew Van Zomeren and Ben Fetterley

Printed in China

14 15 16 17 18 19 20 /CTC/ 22 21 20 19 18 17 16 15 14 13 12 11 10 9 8 7 6 5 4 3 2 1

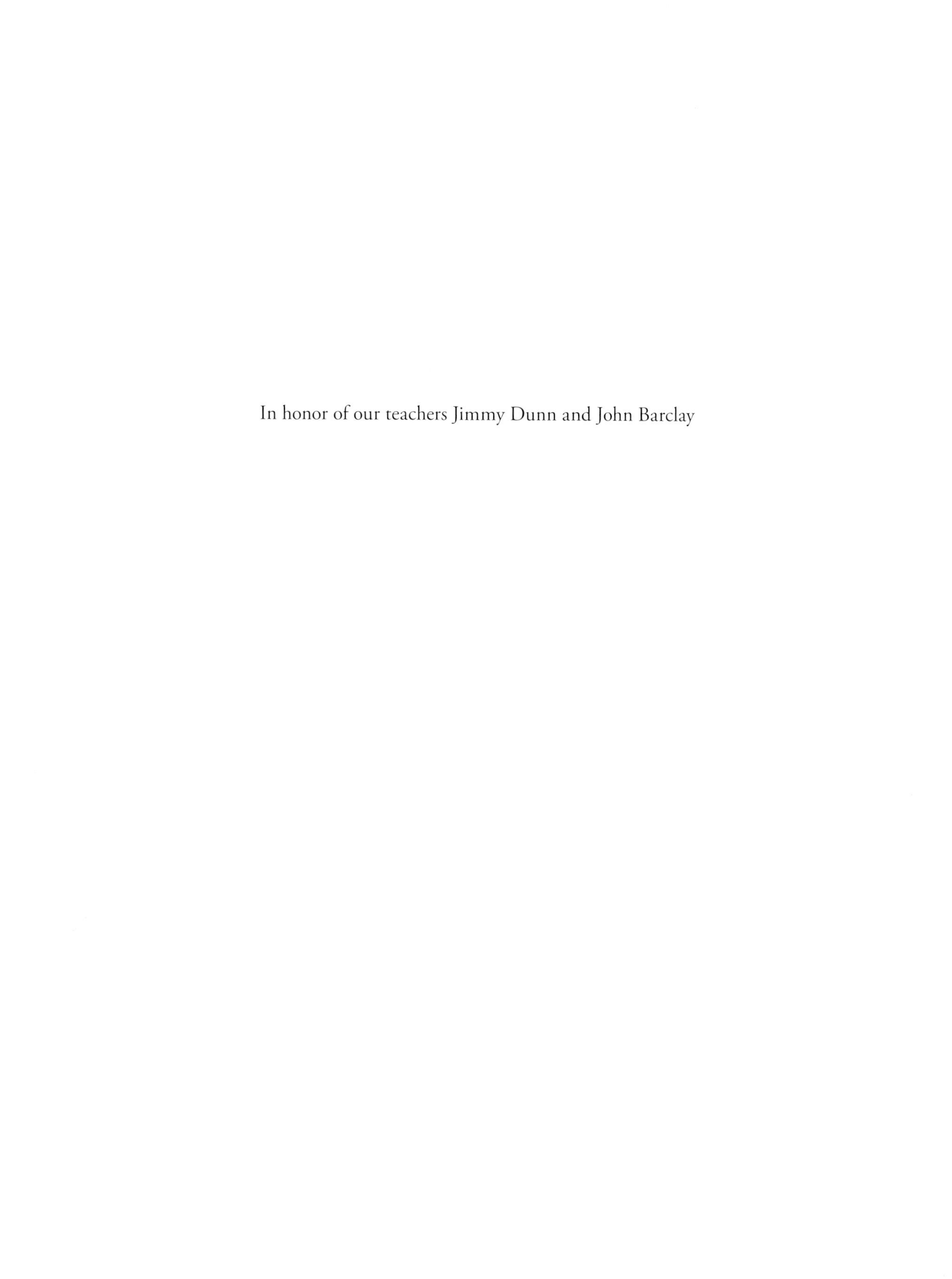

In honor of our teachers Jimmy Dunn and John Barclay

TABLE OF CONTENTS

ABBREVIATIONS

AB	Anchor Bible
ACCS	Ancient Christian Commentary on Scripture
ACNT	Augsburg Commentaries on the New Testament
ANTC	Abingdon New Testament Commentaries
AYB	Anchor Yale Bible
BBC	Blackwell Bible Commentaries
BECNT	Baker Exegetical Commentary on the New Testament
BETL	Bibliotheca ephemeridum theologicarum lovaniensium
BIS	Biblical Interpretation Series
BRev	*Bible Review*
BNTC	Black's New Testament Commentaries
CBQ	*Catholic Biblical Quarterly*
CIL	*Corpus inscriptionum latinarum*
ConBNT	Coniectanea biblica: New Testament Studies
CurBR	*Currents in Biblical Research*
DNTB	*Dictionary of the New Testament Background.* Ed. Craig A. Evans and Stanley E. Porter, 2000.
DPL	*Dictionary of Paul and His Letters.* Ed. Gerald F. Hawthorne, Ralph P. Martin, and Daniel G. Reid, 1993.
ExpT	*Expository Times*
HUT	Hermeneutische Untersuchungen zur Theologie
ICC	International Critical Commentary
JBL	*Journal of Biblical Literature*
JSNT	*Journal for the Study the of New Testament*
JSNTSup	Journal for the Study of the New Testament Supplement Series
LCL	Loeb Classical Library
LNTS	Library of New Testament Studies
NAC	New American Commentary
NCBC	New Century Bible Commentary
NICNT	New International Commentary on the New Testament
NIGTC	New International Greek Testament Commentary
NIVAC	NIV Application Commentary
NovTSup	Novum Testamentum Supplements
NTG	New Testament Guides
NTL	New Testament Library
NTOA	Novum Testamentum et Orbis Antiquus

NTS	*New Testament Studies*
PNTC	Pillar New Testament Commentary
SBLDS	Society of Biblical Literature Dissertation Series
SHBC	Smyth & Helwys Bible Commentary
SJT	*Scottish Journal of Theology*
SNTSMS	Society for New Testament Studies Monograph Series
SP	Sacra pagina
SUNT	Studien zur Umwelt des Neuen Testaments
SwJT	*Southwestern Journal of Theology*
THNTC	Two Horizons New Testament Commentary
WBC	Word Biblical Commentary
WUNT	Wissenschaftliche Untersuchungen zum Neuen Testament
ZECNT	Zondervan Exegetical Commentary on the New Testament

INTRODUCTION

To study Paul well can be exciting. To study Paul well can be challenging. To study Paul well can be life-changing.

If, however, we approach the study of Paul with the goal of acquiring only a superficial familiarity with the basic features of his life and writings, the process is unlikely to be exciting, challenging, or life-changing.

But what if we conceive of the goal in a different fashion? What if we conceive of it as:

1. exploring the complexities of Paul's industrious life and controversial ministry;
2. grappling with the intricacies of his elaborate theological commitments and his rhetorical discourse; and
3. being attentive to the potency of the spirited texts that Paul wrote in ofttimes heated disputes.

When the student of Paul conceives of things in that fashion and commits to undertake diligent study of these issues, the process of studying Paul rarely fails to be exciting, challenging, and life-changing.

WHAT MADE PAUL TICK?

Paul's own encounter with the risen Lord on the road to Damascus was itself life-changing and set in motion a series of exciting and challenging events in his life. He lists some of these in 2 Corinthians 11:23–27, noting that he has been "in prison," "flogged," and "exposed to death again and again"; on five occasions he had been whipped with "forty lashes minus one." He continues:

> Three times I was beaten with rods, once I was pelted with stones, three times I was shipwrecked, I spent a night and a day in the open sea, I have been constantly on the move. I have been in danger from rivers, in danger from bandits, in danger from my own people, in danger from Gentiles; in danger in the city, in danger in the country, in danger at sea; and in danger from false believers. I have labored and toiled and have often gone without sleep; I have known hunger and thirst and have often gone without food; I have been cold and naked. (2 Cor 11:25–27)

If conflict inevitably drives the plot of the best narratives, then a Hollywood filmmaker would have plenty to work with here! Paul's life was anything but ordinary. His ministry was nothing other than provocative. His reputation was contentious. And clearly he suffered much.

Why did he put up with experiences that would have caused most of us to lose heart? What drove him on, despite obstacles of this magnitude? Why did he allow himself to undergo such dreadful hardships? What enabled him to withstand them and yet press on?

Paul offers his readers an answer to those questions. He pressed on out of "concern for all the churches" (2 Cor 11:28), compelled by "the love of Christ" (5:14)—or as he says elsewhere, because of "the love of God that is in Christ Jesus our Lord" (Rom 8:39). That answer may be simple, but it is not simplistic. Paul spent more than thirty years of his life amplifying the inner dynamics of that answer for first-century groups of Jesus-followers who believed Jesus to be the Messiah of Israel and who worshiped him as their Lord. In this textbook, students are invited to explore Paul's answer in its rich complexity and challenging vision.

WHO WROTE WHAT YOU ARE READING?

Just as Paul's writings derive their character and content from their author, so this textbook derives its character and content from the authors who produced it. So, the readers of this book may benefit from knowing something about its authors.

Our friendship extends across twenty years prior to authoring this book. This friendship took root when both of us were living in Britain, where we had the privilege of studying with preeminent Pauline scholars. One of us, Bruce Longenecker, did his PhD research at the University of Durham in England with Professor James D. G. Dunn. The other, Todd Still, did his PhD research at the University of Glasgow in Scotland with Professor John M. G. Barclay, who now serves as the Lightfoot Professor of Divinity at Durham, succeeding Professor Dunn in that post.

We both share a healthy respect for Paul. Paul has had his detractors over the years, and no doubt this will continue to be the case. We hope to continue learning from Pauline scholars long after this textbook has been published, and in that enterprise we will continue to listen to the important voices of those who find Paul to have been flawed as a person, as a theologian, or both. But while Paul may have had limitations (not unlike most of us), he nonetheless demonstrated a strong dose of intellectual rigor, a devotion to the communities he founded, and good intentions for the well-being of others—and these are deserving of respect. We appreciate Paul's love for God and his postmortem importance in nurturing and edifying the faith of the Christian church for nearly two millennia, including his pivotal role in influencing key theologians who themselves have been influential (e.g., Augustine, Luther, Barth).

It is not our intention to extol Paul's virtues too highly—which, as it happens, Paul himself would have opposed, if his comments in 1 Corinthians are anything to go by (1 Cor 1:12; 3:4–9). Rather, our aim is to offer an evenhanded, fair-minded, warmhearted treatment of the person whom the Welch poet and priest R. S. Thomas dubbed "the mountain" whom "theologians have walked round for centuries" but have failed to scale.[1] Although we collectively draw on more than fifty years of personal study about Paul when writing this textbook, we have yet to find him "second rate," "old hat," or "ho-hum." In fact, we feel strongly that Paul's theological vision offers essential resources for the crafting of the Christian mind and Christian practice in our twenty-first-century world.

1. R. S. Thomas, "Covenanters," in *Later Poems: A Selection, 1972–1982* (London: Macmillan, 1984), 170–73.

Furthermore, it is our hope that the readers' intrigue with and appreciation for Paul will grow as they work through this volume. That intrigue and appreciation is not facilitated by watering down Paul's significance into easy sound bites or manageable slogans but, instead, by digging deeply into his richly layered and dynamic theological discourse. At times, this will demand that the reader delve deeply into this process, coming to grips with the more difficult aspects of the Jewish apostle to the Gentiles. But we would prefer rather this than to sell the reader short with a bland concoction that, paraded as the real thing, would verge on a counterfeit.

When grappling with Paul's life and letters, a student may at times feel like concurring with the statement made in 2 Peter 3:16: "There are some things in [Paul's] letters that are hard to understand." But the same canonical author speaks of Paul's having written with "the wisdom that God gave him" (3:15). It would be inadvisable to imagine that Paul's "wisdom" has little relevance to us today. This textbook is undergirded not only by our appreciation for Paul but also by a desire to share what we are learning about that wisdom and its relevance, in our ongoing fascination with Paul's notable life and noteworthy letters.

WHAT WILL YOU FIND IN THIS BOOK?

What, then, will you find as you make your way through this textbook? You will have the textbook that we would have wanted available to us in earlier days — that is, a practical and user-friendly guide to Paul's life, letters, and theological discourse. In a sense, we wrote this for ourselves, and we invite our readers to enter enthusiastically into what we trust will be a rewarding, if at times demanding, study of Paul.

This textbook is comprised of three main parts. In Part 1 (which is comprised of a single chapter), we examine Paul's remarkable life both before and after his encounter with the risen Christ en route to Damascus.

In Part 2 (chapters 2–10), we treat the Pauline letters, where much heavy lifting will be done. The order in which those texts will be explored will not be the same as their order in the New Testament itself. This textbook will study the letters primarily as they fall within subgroups, which themselves largely reflect the order in which the letters were probably written. Beginning with what is probably Paul's earliest letter and its partner text (1–2 Thessalonians), we then consider the "Chief" Letters (Galatians, 1–2 Corinthians, Romans), the Captivity Letters (Philippians, Philemon, Colossians, Ephesians), and the Pastoral Letters (1–2 Timothy, Titus) in turn. Each chapter has three primary tasks:

1. to address historical issues that assist in the interpretation of the Pauline letter(s) studied in the chapter;
2. to sample a selected passage from the letter(s) and illustrate its significance in relation to overarching concerns of the Pauline letter(s) studied in the chapter; and
3. to survey the flow of thought throughout the Pauline letter(s) studied in the chapter.

Put differently, in looking at the letters, we will seek to situate, center, and track each letter's vision.

Throughout this part of the textbook, we will stress the occasional nature of Paul's letters. They were written to particular people in particular places at particular times regarding particular matters. Of course, Paul did not negotiate anew his theological convictions each time he composed a letter, but neither are his letters treatises pulled out from a file of ready-made theological reflections. Instead, Paul's theological discourse was pressed into the service of particular situations, with established theological commitments being unpacked in fresh ways.[2]

After studying the letters in particular, we move to the synthetic task of putting the pieces together, in a sense, to highlight the main strands of Paul's theologizing. Part 3 performs this task by:

1. displaying the key drivers within Paul's theological discourse (see chapter 11 below);
2. outlining the relationship between Paul's theological worldview and other "macro-narratives" of his day (see chapter 12 below)—that is, the "big picture" explanations of how the world operated and where it was going; and
3. probing how Paul sought to shape and inspire the "micro-narratives" (or moral ethos) of Jesus groups (see chapter 13 below)—that is, how Christians are to live their lives in relation to the big picture of what God has done in Christ.

A short conclusion wraps things up.

WHAT IS IN A NAME?

Why have we chosen to entitle this book *Thinking through Paul*? Because it signals two perspectives that characterize its chapters. First, "thinking through Paul" will involve "thinking about Paul," sorting through his letters and considering what he was saying in them. From this vantage point, Paul is the object to be studied, to be "thought through," to be explored. But at times a second sense of the phrase will predominate, in which "thinking through Paul" will involve "thinking in a Pauline manner," seeing things from his perspective, thinking along his thought patterns. From this vantage point, Paul is not the object to be studied but, instead, a catalyst to stir our own thoughts about the things that matter. In our experience, these two senses of "thinking through Paul" reinforce each other. The better we think through Paul (in the first sense), the better we can think through Paul (in the second sense).

When making their way through this textbook, readers might be interested in knowing "who wrote what." Bruce Longenecker was largely responsible for chapters 3–6 and 11–13, while Todd Still was primarily responsible for chapters 1–2 and 7–10 (with introduction and conclusion written jointly). We use "largely" and "primarily" advisedly, since we both have read the other's chapters with critical care and have taken the other's critiques into account when revising those chapters. We have slightly different styles of engaging with the texts, and we have not sought to speak univocally throughout all the chapters, although there is a certain "meeting of the minds" that has animated the project from start to finish.

2. This has been articulated as a relationship between the situational "contingency" of the moment and the "coherence" of Paul's theological worldview in J. C. Beker's important book *Paul the Apostle: The Triumph of God in Life and Thought* (Philadelphia: Fortress, 1980).

We add two notes about citations. First, we will be using the New International Version (published by Zondervan) whenever citing passages of Scripture. Second, the nature of this book does not allow us to cite the work of scholarly peers as much as we are accustomed to do in other venues; it is not our primary task to interact with the amount of secondary literature on Paul but rather to engage students in thinking through Paul based on our sifting through that literature.

The eventful life of the apostle is the subject to which we will turn momentarily, in the first step of this exciting, challenging, and potentially life-changing journey. But before taking that step, the authors would like to offer our thanks to Zondervan Academic for approaching us about writing this textbook, and in particular to Katya Covrett for steering the project through from start to finish. Bruce Longenecker would like to thank his graduate assistants for their invaluable help in commenting on early drafts of his chapters. This includes (in alphabetical order) Grant Edwards, Justin King, Scott Ryan, Lindsey Trozzo, Mike Whitenton, and Nick Zola. Todd Still, along with Bruce Longenecker, would like to thank Baylor University for providing both the time and resources necessary to pursue this project. Even as our appreciation for Paul has grown as we have worked on this volume, so too has our gratitude for Baylor.

Finally, we dedicate this volume to Jimmy Dunn and John Barclay—noted Pauline scholars who became our PhD supervisors and, more importantly, our friends.

Designating Jesus' Followers

The four canonical Gospels (Matthew, Mark, Luke, and John) include twenty instances in which Jesus calls out: "Follow me." Jesus sought to enlist followers who believed him to be the Messiah and who changed their lives to follow him.

One might well think that giving a name to designate those who followed Jesus in the first century should be an easy task. But this is not necessarily the case.

Historically, of course, the followers of Jesus have been referred to as *Christians*. This designation probably arose in the 40s in the Mediterranean city called Antioch of Syria. But there is one weakness that potentially attaches itself to this term when it is used today. That is, it can easily contribute to a misleading impression of historical realities regarding the character of the earliest movement of followers of Jesus. New Testament texts are popularly understood as texts of "Christianity" *over against* "Judaism," as if these two religions were separable and distinct with the coming of Jesus Christ. In past generations, this distorted impression has frequently contributed to the unfair denigration of Judaism, which became the catchall for the things (and the people) that Christians and Christianity surmount and surpass.

But the first-century reality was much different. The early Jesus movement is best understood historically as one form of Judaism under a larger Jewish umbrella in which varieties of Judaism interrelated with each other. Acts 24:5 demonstrates the point well. When Paul returns to Jerusalem in the late 50s, a lawyer for the high priest charges Paul with being a member of "the Nazarene sect." In Luke's presentation of the scene, followers of Jesus were identifiable as one party within Judaism, perhaps like other parties within Judaism, such as the Pharisees, the Sadducees, and the Essenes.

The "partings of the ways" between Judaism and Christianity happened in different ways in different places throughout the second half of the first century and beyond, so that what looks self-evident in hindsight was anything but evident in the first century.

To avoid perpetuating a false perception of this issue, perhaps terms other than *Christians* can be used to foster a more nuanced understanding of how devotion to Jesus was variously configured in relation to first-century Judaism. The term *Christ-followers* presents itself well in this regard. With "Christ" being the Greek word equivalent to the Hebrew word "Messiah," the term *Christ-followers* leaves open the issue of how we should conceive of Jesus' followers in relation to Judaism in any given instance.

But the same useful term can also be historically misleading on another score. It is not uncommon to hear the view that Paul was "the real founder of Christianity," that the historical Jesus of Nazareth illegitimately became "the Lord Jesus Christ" through the preaching and influence of power-hungry people like Paul. Christianity emerged (in this view) a generation after Jesus had died, as Paul turned Jesus into "Christ," twisting the simple Jewish message of Jesus of Nazareth into an elaborate Gentile religion. In this frame of reference, the term *Christ-followers* (like the term *Christians*) can connote "those who were duped by Paul in a religion that had little convergence with the ministry of Jesus." In our view, this reconstruction of things is not historically robust.[3] Consequently, whenever the term *Christ-follower* is used in this textbook, it is not intended with these connotations in mind.

The term *believers* has good merit as a designation of those who followed Jesus, since they believed

3. A case in point, for instance, is the matter of caring for the poor. As a central feature of Jesus' ministry, care for the poor was also an essential feature within Paul's gospel, as surveyed in chapter 13.

in Jesus' message and committed themselves to him as a consequence of that belief. But the term has the potential to skew things somewhat if it were thought to denote those who simply adopted a belief system. Paul's theological discourse ensures that "beliefs" are part of an all-embracing process of transformation in which theological enlightenment is coupled with the enlivenment of new ways of life in practice. When the term *believers* is used in this textbook, it is not intended to highlight merely a cognitive dimension ("beliefs") but should be heard as signaling the "holistic" dimensions of Paul's gospel.

One other term presents itself—that is, *Jesus-followers*. This term has certain advantages. First, it leaves open the matter of how Jesus' followers were positioned in relation to Judaism in any given instance. Second, with the name "Jesus" front and center, it does not lend itself easily to the view that those who had committed themselves to Jesus as Lord were necessarily duped. Third, with the term *follower* front and center, it easily captures the full spread of Paul's holistic gospel, focusing not only on its "doctrinal" theology but also its embodied application in the corporate gatherings and in personal lifestyle. Other useful terms follow in the wake of *Jesus-followers*, such as "Jesus groups," "Jesus devotees," and "the early Jesus movement." But while these terms serve valuable purposes, they nonetheless refer to Jesus only by the name he bore as a Jew of Nazareth in Galilee. In this way, they are less adept at capturing the convictional center of the early Jesus movement—that "God has made this Jesus . . . both Lord and Messiah" (Acts 2:36).

Evidently, then, strengths and weaknesses pertain to each of the various terms that could be used to designate those who followed Jesus in the first century. In order to ensure that the strengths of the various terms cancel out their weaknesses, all of these terms are used virtually interchangeably within this textbook, with the hope that readers will thereby capture the complexities of navigating the study of the early Jesus movement and Paul's place within it.

PART 1

PAUL'S LIFE

INTRODUCTION

While part 2 of this book is devoted to Paul's letters and part 3 devoted to his theology, part 1 explores what we can know of the outline of Paul's life. In fact, the apostle himself frequently builds the theological discourse of his letters from autobiographical elements sprinkled throughout them.

- "Become like me, for I became like you," he says in Gal 4:12.
- "Am I not free? Am I not an apostle? Have I not seen Jesus our Lord? Are you not the result of my work in the Lord?" he says in 1 Cor 9:1.
- "Now I want you to know, brothers and sisters, that what has happened to me has actually served to advance the gospel," he says in Phil 1:12.
- "I will not venture to speak of anything except what Christ has accomplished through me in leading the Gentiles to obey God by what I have said and done," he says in Rom 15:18.

Whether he is calling others to imitate him (as in the first quotation), reminding them that they are the result of his work (second quotation), counseling them that the things that have happened to him have actually benefited the Christian mission (third quotation), or informing them that what he has said and done has been the vehicle for God's activity (fourth quotation)—in these and other instances Paul expects his readers to know something of the story line of his life. Obliging Paul in this expectation turns out to be a sensible way forward, since knowing something about his life will provide much of the historical context within which the study of Paul's letters and theology is best carried out.

CHAPTER 1

A SURVEY OF PAUL'S LIFE AND MINISTRY

CHAPTER GOALS

- To be knowledgeable of and conversant with what can be known about Paul prior to his life-changing encounter with Christ
- To be conversant with texts and issues related to Paul's Damascus experience
- To understand various facets and underlying commitments of Paul's missional strategy and practice
- To be able to describe the make-up of Pauline communities and Paul's commitment to and communication with them
- To be able to summarize how Paul is thought to have died

CHAPTER OVERVIEW

1. From Tarsus to Damascus
2. Paul's Encounter with Christ and Its Immediate Aftermath
3. Paul's Mission to and Ministry in the Mediterranean World
4. Paul's Departure
5. Concluding Remarks
6. Key People, Places, and Terms
7. Questions for Review and Discussion
8. Contemporary Theological Reflection
9. Going Further

KEY VERSES

Philippians 3:4b–6: "If someone else thinks they have reasons to put confidence in the flesh, I have more: circumcised on the eighth day, of the people of Israel, of the tribe of Benjamin, a Hebrew of Hebrews; in regard to the law, a Pharisee; as for zeal, persecuting the church; as for righteousness based on the law, faultless."

1 Corinthians 15:8–11: "And last of all he appeared to me also, as to one abnormally born. For I am the least of the apostles and do not even deserve to be called an apostle, because I persecuted the church of God. But by the grace of God I am what I am, and his grace to me was not without effect. No, I worked harder than all of them—yet not I, but the grace of God that was with me. Whether, then, it is I or they, this is what we preach, and this is what you believed."

Galatians 1:11–17: "I want you to know, brothers and sisters, that the gospel I preached is not of human origin. I did not receive it from any man, nor was I taught it; rather, I received it by revelation from Jesus Christ. For you have heard of my previous way of life in Judaism, how intensely I persecuted the church of God and tried to destroy it. I was advancing in Judaism beyond many of my own age among my people and was extremely zealous for the traditions of my fathers. But when God, who set me apart from my mother's womb and called me by his grace, was pleased to reveal his Son in me so that I might preach him among the Gentiles, my immediate response was not to consult any human being. I did not go up to Jerusalem to see those who were apostles before I was, but I went into Arabia. Later I returned to Damascus."

1 Corinthians 9:19–22: "Though I am free and belong to no one, I have made myself a slave to everyone, to win as many as possible. To the Jews I became like a Jew, to win the Jews. To those under the law I became like one under the law (though I myself am not under the law), so as to win those under the law. To those not having the law I became like one not having the law (though I am not free from God's law but am under Christ's law), so as to win those not having the law. To the weak I became weak, to win the weak. I have become all things to all people so that by all possible means I might save some."

2 Timothy 4:6–8: "For I am already being poured out like a drink offering, and the time for my departure is near. I have fought the good fight, I have finished the race, I have kept the faith. Now there is in store for me the crown of righteousness, which the Lord, the righteous Judge, will award to me on that day—and not only to me, but also to all who have longed for his appearing."

Having met our subject and surveyed our volume in the introduction, we are now ready to "think through" Paul's life, letters, and theology. In this chapter, our aim is to piece together Paul's life. And what a life it was!

Born in **Tarsus** to Jewish parents, Paul (also known as Saul) was a zealous follower of the Lord (Yahweh) and of the law (Torah). Over time, he became both a **Pharisee** and a persecutor of Jesus-followers. A life-altering encounter with the risen Christ while en route to Damascus, however, caused Paul to reevaluate and to alter a number of his convictions and commitments. Having become convinced that Jesus is the living Lord, Paul proceeded to risk life and limb to proclaim the good news of Jesus' death and resurrection to the nations. Like his Lord, Paul was ultimately put to death by Roman hands, but not before his work as an apostle was widely disseminated and well established.

If the above is something of a trailer, below we consider the fuller motion picture of Paul's life. Because we lack the details necessary to trace his life from womb to tomb, the picture that emerges is incomplete. This unfortunate reality will require us to cobble together, with critical care, autobiographical materials from Paul's letters with biographical information found in Acts and other early Christian literature. Yet given the scarcity of our sources and the chronological chasm that separates us from our subject, we are fortunate to know as much about Paul as we do.

A person can examine Paul's life in any number of ways. In this chapter we will treat the apostle's eventful life under the following four headings:

1. From Tarsus to Damascus
2. Paul's Encounter with Christ and Its Immediate Aftermath
3. Paul's Mission to and Ministry in the Mediterranean World
4. Paul's Departure

While Pauline chronology is complicated and controversial, there is a broad scholarly consensus regarding

Todd Bolen/www.BiblePlaces.com, The Archaeological Museum of Delphi

▲ Scholars seeking to date Paul's life consider the Gallio Inscription to be a critical piece of archaeological evidence. This inscription, written by the Roman emperor Claudius ca. AD 52, mentions by name the proconsul Gallio, who served as proconsul of Achaia from 51 to 52 or 52 to 53. According to Acts 18:12–17, Paul appeared before Gallio during his ministry in Corinth. This is the one fixed date in Pauline chronology.

▼ Paul, the subject of this textbook, has also been the subject of many works of art. Artistic geniuses such as Rembrandt, Caravaggio, Michelangelo, El Greco, and Raphael have all turned their creative energies toward Paul. The anonymous mosaic pictured here is one of the earliest preserved artistic portrayals of the apostle. It dates from the late fifth century and is currently housed in a museum in Ravenna, Italy.

Leemage/Universal Images Group/Getty Images

Wikimedia Commons

Wikimedia Commons

▲ During his struggle against Octavian, Marc Antony allied himself with Cleopatra VII in Tarsus. This painting by Sir Lawrence ala-Tadema imagines their meeting.

◀ The well pictured here is known as "St. Paul's Well." It is located in Tarsus, the place of Paul's birth, and dates back to Roman times. It is possible that Paul both drew and drank water from this well. Ancient Tarsus was located in eastern Cilicia in southeastern Asia Minor (modern-day Turkey).

Pivotal Events

Pivotal events with approximate dates in Paul's life include (all dates are AD):

- Birth: about 5 – 10
- Conversion/call: about 35
- Ministry "from Jerusalem to Illyricum" (Rom 15:19): late 30s to late 50s
- The **Jerusalem Conference** (Gal 2:1 – 10; cf. Acts 15:1 – 35): late 40s
- Arrest in Jerusalem and transfer to Caesarea and then to Rome: late 50s/ early 60s
- Death: mid to late 60s

the dating of certain periods and episodes in Paul's life and ministry that we will follow as we proceed with our study.[1]

FROM TARSUS TO DAMASCUS

Birth and Upbringing

Place of birth. Paul does not indicate in his letters where he was born. Acts reports, however, that Paul was born in Tarsus in Cilicia.[2] As it happens, Paul refers to the province of Cilicia in conjunction with Syria in Gal 1:21.[3] Although Pauline and Lukan scholars have questioned the historical veracity of certain claims that Acts makes about Paul, few interpreters doubt that Acts accurately identifies the place of Paul's birth.

Pompey won Cilicia for the Romans in 67 BC. In turn, he named Tarsus the provincial capital. Later

1. For an accessible, valuable introduction, see L. C. A. Alexander, "Chronology of Paul," in *DPL*, 115 – 23.
2. Note Acts 9:11; 21:39; 22:3 (see also 9:30).
3. See, too, Acts 6:9; 15:23, 41; 21:39; 22:3; 23:34; 27:5.

Josephus on the Pharisees

The ancient Jewish historian Josephus (AD 37 – ca. 100), describes the Pharisees as follows in his *Jewish Antiquities*:

▲ Jewish historian Josephus

> The Jews had for a great while three sects of philosophy peculiar to themselves; the sect of the Essenes, and the sect of the Sadducees, and the third sort of opinions was that of those called Pharisees; of which sects, although I have already spoken in the second book of the Jewish War, yet will I a little touch upon them now. Now, for the Pharisees, they live meanly, and despise delicacies in diet; and they follow the conduct of reason; and what that prescribes to them as good for them they do; and they think they ought earnestly to strive to observe reason's dictates for practice. They also pay a respect to such as are in years; nor are they so bold as to contradict them in any thing which they have introduced; and when they determine that all things are done by fate, they do not take away the freedom from men of acting as they think fit; since their notion is, that it hath pleased God to make a temperament, whereby what he wills is done, but so that the will of man can act virtuously or viciously. They also believe that souls have an immortal rigor in them, and that under the earth there will be rewards or punishments, according as they have lived virtuously or viciously in this life; and the latter are to be detained in an everlasting prison, but that the former shall have power to revive and live again; on account of which doctrines they are able greatly to persuade the body of the people; and whatsoever they do about divine worship, prayers, and sacrifices, they perform them according to their direction; insomuch that the cities give great attestations to them on account of their entire virtuous conduct, both in the actions of their lives and their discourses.[4]

Mark Antony made Tarsus a "free city" and exempted it from Roman taxation. Still later, Augustus confirmed and extended these civic privileges. By the close of the first century BC, Tarsus had earned a reputation as a place of culture and learning.[5] Most scholars think that Paul was born in Tarsus near the beginning of the first century AD.

Paul's name. In writing letters in Greek to primarily non-Jewish believers, Paul employs no other name in referring to himself. According to Acts, however, Paul was known also as **Saul** (13:9).[6] Is the name "Saul" a Lukan invention? If not, how was it that Paul could also be known as Saul?

4. Josephus, *Ant.* 18.1.2–3 (trans. William Whiston).
5. On Tarsus, see more fully Calvin J. Roetzel, *Paul: The Man and the Myth* (Columbia, SC: University of South Carolina Press, 1998), 12–16.
6. Although it is widely believed that "Saul" became "Paul" at the time of his "conversion," this is a mistaken notion.

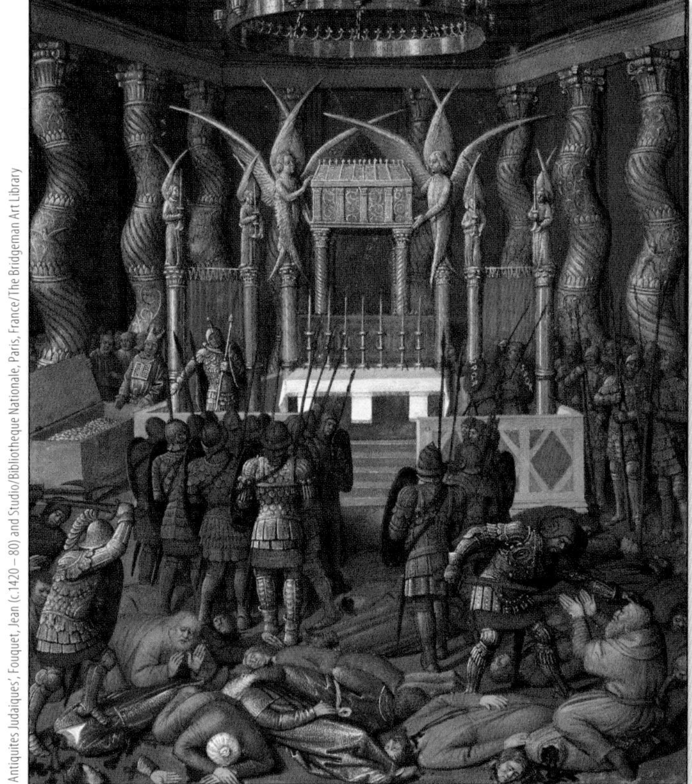

Antiquites Judaiques', Fouquet, Jean (c.1420–80) and Studio/Bibliotheque Nationale, Paris, France/The Bridgeman Art Library

▲ This painting by French artist Jean Fouquet (1420–1481) depicts Pompey the Great's (106–48 BC) entry into and thereby desecration of the Jerusalem temple.

Lawrence OP/Flickr, CC BY-NC 2.0

▲ This stained glass window, in the south transept of St. Mary's Church, Melton Mowbray, England, depicts Saul/Paul learning from Gamaliel.

In Phil 3:5, Paul remarks that he was "a Hebrew of Hebrews" from the "tribe of **Benjamin**" (see also Rom 11:1). In light of his Jewish pedigree, it is unlikely that his parents would have only given him the Roman name "Paul" (which happens to mean "small") from birth. Indeed, it may well be that his Jewish parents named him after Israel's first king, Saul, who was also a Benjamite (1 Sam 9:21). As history would have it, we do not know when, where, or why the Jew "Saul" (*Sha'ul*) began to be called by the Roman name "Paul."[7] So, the man from Tarsus we are studying had two names, one Jewish ("Saul") and the other Roman ("Paul").

Paul's parents. Acts indicates that Paul was "a son of Pharisees" (23:6). This verse *may* suggest that Paul's father was a Pharisee. Whether or not his father was a Pharisee (Paul claims to have been one [Phil 3:5; see also Acts 26:5]), Paul's **circumcision** on the eighth day suggests that his parents were self-respecting, law-abiding Jews (Phil 3:5; note Lev 12:3).

7. Compare Silas in Acts with Silvanus in Paul's letters in the following verses: Acts 15:22, 32, 40; 2 Cor 1:19; 1 Thess 1:1; 2 Thess 1:1 (see NIV text notes for the last three). Silas/Silvanus also appears in 1 Pet 5:12.

How did Paul's parents come to live in Tarsus? There is some suspicion that Paul's parents or ancestors were taken to Tarsus as prisoners of war. The theologian Jerome (late fourth to early fifth century) indicates that Paul and his parents were brought to Tarsus from the region of Gischala in Judea as Roman prisoners of war.[8] Although Jerome does not date their deportation, sometime between 5 BC to AD 5 would be a reasonable inference, when uprisings against Rome were not infrequent.

> The Roman citizen was required to register the birth of his children within thirty days before a Roman official, and he received a wooden diptych recording the declaration, which acted as a certificate of citizenship for the rest of his life.[9]

Because Acts reports, however, that Paul was *born* a Roman citizen (22:28), some have questioned the accuracy of Jerome's account, preferring to place Paul's parents, or more likely his parents' ancestors, in Tarsus at an earlier time. In that view of things, Paul's ancestors could have come to Tarsus as prisoners after Pompey's invasion of Jerusalem (63 BC) or, perhaps even earlier, during the reign of Antiochus IV Epiphanes (175 – 163 BC).

Dual citizenship? According to Acts, Paul was a citizen of both Rome (Acts 22:25) and Tarsus (21:39). Contemporary treatments of Paul reveal skepticism toward both of these Lukan claims. The reasons adduced to counter Luke along these lines are numerous and of varying strength. While the scope of this volume does not afford us the opportunity to enter fully into this ongoing debate, a few points merit mention here.

First, it is certainly possible that Paul could have inherited Roman citizenship from his father or grandfather. Either one could have been granted the status of freedman (through manumission from slavery or distinguished service to the state) and have become a Roman citizen.

Second, when Acts presents Paul as a citizen of Tarsus, Luke may have had in mind something less than full citizenship. The term he uses in Acts 21:39 (*politēs*) can mean "resident" or member of an organization (*politeuma*) as well as a duly recognized citizen. These observations suggest, if all too succinctly, that a case can be made to support Luke's claims with respect to Paul's "dual citizenship."

Citizenship

The important thing for Christians was not the privilege of an earthly citizenship but the fact that they were brothers and sisters. So we can certainly say that Paul did not attach any special value to his citizenship. However, that does not exclude the possibility that he was a Roman citizen who made use of that fact in particular circumstances, especially when he was being threatened.[10]

Place of education and upbringing. Even as many contemporary scholars are wary of Luke's presentation of Paul as a "dual citizen," a number of Paul's modern interpreters also question whether Acts is accurate in maintaining that he was "brought up in [Jerusalem] under **Gamaliel** and was thoroughly trained in the law of our ancestors" (Acts 22:3; see also

8. Jerome, *On Illustrious Men* 5.
9. A. N. Sherwin-White, *The Roman Citizenship* (2nd ed.; Oxford: Clarendon, 1973), 6.
10. Martin Hengel, *The Pre-Christian Paul* (trans. John Bowden; London: SCM, 1991), 8.

26:4). In light of the language, style, and contents of Paul's letters, some specialists regard Tarsus as the more likely location for Paul's education and upbringing.

Whether Paul is best viewed against a Hebraic or Hellenistic backdrop has been a point of ongoing debate among Pauline scholars, despite occasional calls to adopt a moderating position between the two extremes.[11] The degree to which a given scholar judges Paul as more or less Jewish in orientation, cognition, and expression will invariably influence his or her judgment regarding where Paul was educated as he was growing up. Whereas a more Jewish view of Paul lends credence to Acts' claim regarding his education and upbringing, a more Hellenistic understanding of the apostle inclines one to regard Tarsus as a more likely locale for his rearing and training.

For our part, while recognizing the comingling of "**Hellenism**" and "Judaism" as well as the complexity inherent to tracing the relative and various influences on any ancient person's thinking and writing, we are struck by the fact that Paul's autobiographical remarks are a testament to his Jewish past (esp. Gal 1:13–14; Phil 3:5–6). Such statements suggest that Paul was likely a **Diaspora** Jew who valued the ancestral customs and convictions of his people, even if he would eventually radically reevaluate all things Jewish in light of his encounter with the risen Lord and his Gentile mission.

Given Paul's own statements regarding his commitments and concerns prior to becoming a follower of Christ Jesus, it seems altogether plausible that he would have received the lion's share of his religious education in Jerusalem, the epicenter of Judaism and home to at least a few of his relatives, including a sister and a nephew (Acts 23:16). Additionally, if Paul were in fact educated in Jerusalem, it is not beyond the realm of possibility that Gamaliel was his instructor, or one of his instructors, in Pharisaic Judaism.

Paul's social and marital status. If one does not assume that Paul's family paid a handsome price to become citizens of Tarsus and/or of Rome and if one does not presuppose that Paul's education came at a considerable fiscal cost to his family, there is no evidence that would compel one to conclude that he grew up with a silver spoon in his mouth. In fact, if Paul learned his profession as a "tentmaker" or "leatherworker" (Acts 18:3) from his father as a boy, he would not have been a blue blood.[12]

Paul's Pharisaic Education

John M. G. Barclay contends that Paul's "Pharisaic education must have taken place in Jerusalem, in a school of Torah-interpretation, probably in Paul's case in the Greek language. Here Paul acquired his extraordinarily intimate knowledge of the Scriptures, and learned the range of exegetical methods which he was later to display in his letters. Thus the evidence points to a Greek-medium Jewish education, in which the broad spectrum of Hellenism entered Paul's mind only through the filter of his conservative Pharisaic environment."[13]

---

11. So Troels Engberg-Pedersen, ed., *Paul beyond the Judaism/Hellenism Divide* (Louisville: Westminster John Knox, 2001).
12. Justin J. Meggitt, *Paul, Poverty and Survival* (Edinburgh: T&T Clark, 1998), 80, regards the idea that Paul came from an affluent background to be a "myth." Contrast Ronald F. Hock, *The Social Context of Paul's Ministry* (Philadelphia: Fortress, 1980), 35, who maintains that by birth Paul was "a member of the socially elite." Bruce W. Longenecker (*Remember the Poor: Paul, Poverty, and the Greco-Roman World* [Grand Rapids: Eerdmans, 2011], 305) posits "that Paul's upbringing and life prior to his christophanic experience had been marked out by a middling economic profile."
13. John M. G. Barclay, *Jews in the Mediterranean Diaspora: From Alexander to Trajan (323 BCE–117 CE)* (Edinburgh: T&T Clark, 1996), 383–84.

Wikimedia Commons

▲ Augustine (AD 354–430) once posited, "If Stephen had not prayed to God, the church would not have Paul" (*Sermons* 315.7). This famed painting of Rembrandt depicts the stoning of Stephen.

▶ This stained glass in the Norwich Cathedral in Norfolk, England, depicts the stoning of Paul at Lystra.

© Sonia Halliday Photographs

Because we have precious little information about Paul's family of origin and because social structures and status indicators in Greco-Roman antiquity differ considerably from those in contemporary Western cultures, trying to pinpoint Paul's socioeconomic status in today's terms is a tall order. Paul's letters indicate that he was a relatively well-educated and remarkably well-traveled artisan-apostle, who was vulnerable to the vicissitudes of a mobile existence. It may be that prior to becoming a Jesus-follower Paul had achieved some degree of social and/or economic status (Gal 1:14). Perhaps Paul had such markers of success in mind when he states that he had lost all things because of his commitment to Jesus as Lord (Phil 3:8).

It may also be that Paul was married prior to the time that he wrote 1 Corinthians in the mid-50s. In that letter, he indicates he was not married (7:7, 9, 38, 40; 9:4). Some scholars have noted, however, that Paul employs the term *agamoi*, which may be rendered "widowers," in 1 Cor 7:8 and suggest that the apostle included himself among that group. If Paul were at one time married, this would coincide with Jewish traditions that praised and even stipulated marriage. Such an expectation was probably present among Pharisaic Jews in the first century. As a result, Paul might well have thought it both appropriate and prudent to marry.

Paul's Persecutory Activity[14]

Paul's opposition to Jesus-followers. Although uncertainty marks our inquiry into the early Paul, of this we may be sure—prior to his revelatory encounter with Christ en route to or in Damas-

14. For a more detailed treatment, see Todd D. Still, *Conflict at Thessalonica: A Pauline Church and Its Neighbours* (JSNTSup 183; Sheffield: Sheffield Academic, 1999), 165–70.

© Asaf Eliason/Shutterstock

This statue of Elijah, located on Mount Carmel in Israel, portrays a zealous servant of Yahweh slaying the prophets of Baal (see 1 Kings 18).

cus, Paul sought to oppose the church. Paul does not speak frequently or fully about his persecutory activity in his letters, but the passing, retrospective comments he does make allow us some insight into this part of his past.

To begin, in Gal 1:13 Paul describes the action that he took against the "church of God" as ardent persecution intent on destruction (see also 1:23). He does not indicate how he sought to destroy the faith, but the intensity of Paul's language in this verse suggests that he would have taken both sanctioned and unsanctioned action against Jesus-followers. Even though some scholars suspect that Acts dramatizes and formalizes aspects of Saul's persecutory activity,[15] Paul himself reports that during the course of his apostolic ministry he received the maximum number of strokes from synagogal authorities on no less than five occasions (2 Cor 11:24), was driven out of one location by Jewish opposition (1 Thess 2:15), and felt himself consistently endangered by his fellow Jews (2 Cor 11:26; see also Rom 15:31). It may also be that the stoning of which Paul speaks in 2 Cor 11:25 came at the hands of his Jewish compatriots (see also Acts 14:19; 2 Tim 4:11). Paul's apostolic experience of Jewish opposition to which he refers in his letters may well illustrate his own persecution of Jesus-followers before he became one.

From what we can now determine, Paul would have "pulled out all the stops" to thwart "the church of God," which Paul repeatedly identifies as the object of his violent opposition (1 Cor 15:9; Gal 1:13; Phil 3:6). He would have used formal means (e.g., synagogal discipline) and informal means (e.g., mob violence) to effect the obliteration of Jesus groups.[16]

15. See Acts 8:3; 9:1–2; 22:4–5; 26:9–11.
16. Acts 7:58 and 8:1 report that Paul was present at and supportive of the stoning of Stephen.

That Paul was an ardent opponent of believers before his conversion/call is suggested not only by the ongoing regret (guilt?) he experienced over his persecuting past (1 Cor 15:9; see also 1 Tim 1:12–17), but also by what Judean churches were reportedly hearing about Paul a number of years after he had encountered Christ: "The man who formerly persecuted us is now proclaiming the faith he once tried to destroy" (Gal 1:23).

Where did Paul persecute Jesus-followers? In Gal 1:22 Paul indicates that Judean Jesus-followers did not know him by sight for some ten to fifteen years after his Damascus experience. This comment has led some scholars to conclude, in contrast to Acts 8:3; 9:1–2, that Paul did not persecute Jesus-followers in Jerusalem. Before dismissing this particular Lukan claim out of hand, however, a few comments are in order.

First of all, it is possible that Paul is speaking on a general level in Gal 1:22. He could be suggesting that, taken together, those who comprised the Judean churches did not know him by sight. Paul could also be maintaining that, subsequent to his conversion/call, he had next to no interaction with churches in Judea. Therefore, they would not have known him as a Jesus-follower. Additionally, it is worth contemplating where one would find the largest concentration of churches (and, as a result, the largest concentration of Jesus-followers) to persecute in the earliest years of the Jesus-movement. Jerusalem and its immediate environs emerge as the most likely locale.

Why did Paul persecute the church? In Phil 3:6, Paul links his persecutory activity to **zeal** (Acts 22:3; Gal 1:14). His excessive religious devotion and fervor prompted him to take extreme measures to eradicate the nascent Jesus movement. Such zealotism was not uncommon in Jewish tradition (Acts 21:20), and at least in some circles of Second Temple Judaism zealous men like Phinehas, Elijah, and Mattathias were lauded for their passion and devotion to Yahweh and Torah.[17]

Furthermore, in first-century Judea the religio-political environment was a powder keg that would eventually explode in AD 66 as zealous Jews unsuccessfully sought to overthrow their Roman overlords (Acts 5:36–37). Paul has been likened to a vigilante as well as a right-wing militant within Judaism prior to his encounter with the risen Lord.[18] He would live to regret such zeal and regard it as unenlightened (Rom 10:2). However, at the time he was persecuting Jesus-followers, Paul could only see the church as a rapidly growing cancer that had to be removed from the Jewish body. Precisely what it was that these early Christ-followers were doing/saying that Paul found to be so egregious is unclear. It is crystal clear, however, that he wanted to impede them from acting/speaking in ways he regarded as dangerously deviant.

PAUL'S ENCOUNTER WITH CHRIST AND ITS IMMEDIATE AFTERMATH

Pertinent Passages in Paul

Over the course of Christian history, many believers have regarded Paul to be the paradigmatic convert. In addition, Paul's "**Damascus Road**" experience has attracted the attention and fueled

17. See, e.g., Num 25:6–15; Ps 106:28–31; Sir 45:23–24; 1 Macc 2:24, 26, 58.
18. N. T. Wright (*What Saint Paul Really Said* [Grand Rapids: Eerdmans, 1997], 26) depicts the early Paul as a "hard-line Pharisee—what we today would call a militant right-winger."

Planet Art

▲ ▼ Two of the most famous artistic portrayals of the apostle Paul's conversion are a fresco by Michelangelo (1475–1564) and a painting by Caravaggio (1571–1610).

Wikimedia Commons

the imagination of not a few artists. Ironically, Paul speaks sparingly of this pivotal event in his occasional letters.

Most scholars date Paul's encounter with the risen Christ en route to Damascus from AD 32–35 and date his extant letters, which are primarily pastoral rather than autobiographical in nature, from the late 40s/early 50s to the early/mid-60s. Once we consider the passage of time between Paul's "Damascus Road" experience and his earliest preserved correspondence and note the particular reasons for which he wrote to congregations, the fact that he said little about this encounter is not particularly surprising.

There are only two places in his letters where Paul speaks of his conversion/call in any detail: 1 Cor 15:8–11 and Gal 1:11–17.[19] In the first passage, as Paul is seeking to impress on the Corinthians the necessity of Christ's resurrection for their faith and future, he traces his apostolic call to that occasion when the risen Christ appeared to him. Because of his persecution of the church, Paul self-describes as "the least of the apostles" who does "not even deserve to be called an apostle" (1 Cor 15:9). Nevertheless, Paul maintains that "the grace of God" transformed him from a persecutor of the church to a preacher of the gospel (15:10–11).

In seeking to combat a congregational crisis in Galatia, Paul mentions God's revelation (*apokalypsis*) of his Son to/in him on two occasions (1:12, 16). After Paul's departure from Galatia, certain "agitators" arrived and began to call into question his credentials and his gospel. Given the urgent and sometimes strident tone of Galatians, it appears as if his opponents were having some success with their apostolic smear campaign. In fashioning his fiery missive to the Galatian churches (and his detractors), Paul declares in the initial chapter of the letter that the gospel he proclaimed to them came "through a revelation of Jesus Christ," not through human instruction, the apostles in Jerusalem notwithstanding (1:11–12, 16–17).

19. See also 1 Cor 9:1; Phil 3:7; 1 Tim 1:12–14.

Moreover, Paul maintains, the divine call issued him via revelation to proclaim Christ among the nations was an unexpected grace (1:15–16). God's revelation of his Son in/to Paul was not an experience Paul had anticipated; on the contrary, it occurred while he was fully engaged in an effort to destroy the church and to advance in Judaism (1:13–14).

The two autobiographical passages on which we have commented share the following elements in common:

- Both texts refer to Paul's Damascus experience as an appearance (1 Cor 15:8; see also 1 Cor 9:1) or revelation (Gal 1:12, 16).
- Each passage mentions Paul's persecution of the church prior to his revelatory encounter with Christ (1 Cor 15:9; Gal 1:13; see also 1:23).
- Paul speaks of his apostolic work or call in conjunction with his conversion (1 Cor 15:10; Gal 1:15–16, 24).
- Paul emphasizes God's gracious initiative (1 Cor 15:10; Gal 1:15).

James D. G. Dunn explains the differences between 1 Corinthians 15 and Galatians 1 as follows: "What Paul received and preached, and echoed in his letters, was indeed the common Christian conviction that 'Christ died (for us) and was raised (from the dead).' That remained the shared confession and the bond which held together the first Christian churches, despite all of their diversity, in one gospel. What Paul was convinced of on the Damascus road, however, was not simply this central confessional claim but also that this Jesus was now to be preached to the Gentiles."[20]

For all of their similarities, there is one striking difference between these two Pauline texts. In 1 Corinthians 15 Paul stresses that he was but one of many apostolic witnesses, and a Johnny-come-lately at that (vv. 3–11), whereas in Galatians 1 Paul is at pains to establish the divine, not human, origin of his gospel and apostleship (vv. 11–24; compare, however, 2:1–10).

As we read Paul's letters, it is essential to remember that his treatment of any given topic is contingent on context. This is not to suggest that Paul formulates his thought anew every time he faces an issue. We would contend, however, that Paul recognized that different congregational situations necessitated different rhetorical strategies, theological emphases, and pastoral prescriptions.[21]

Sifting through Complex Issues

In the scholarly study of Paul's Damascus experience, there are at least three issues that continue to stimulate dialog and debate:

- the terminology used to describe the event;
- the chronological relationship between Paul's "conversion" and "mission"; and
- the place and role of Acts in gaining a fuller understanding of this event in his life.

20. James D. G. Dunn, *The Theology of the Apostle Paul* (Grand Rapids: Eerdmans, 1997), 177.
21. In his influential book *Paul the Apostle: The Triumph of God in Life and Thought* (Philadelphia: Fortress, 1980), J. C. Beker posited that there is both coherence and contingency in Paul's thought. We regard this proposal to be especially valuable in reading and interpreting the apostle's letters. So also N. T. Wright, "Paul in Current Anglophone Scholarship," *ExpT* 123 (2012): 367–81 (on 378).

The "New Perspective on Paul"

Krister Stendahl (1922–2008), onetime Dean of Harvard Divinity School and Bishop of Stockholm, Sweden, was among the first scholars to contend "that the usual conversion model of Paul the Jew who gives up his former faith to become a Christian is not the model of Paul but of ours."[22] Along with the likes of E. P. Sanders, N. T. Wright, and James D. G. Dunn, Stendahl helped to usher in a "new perspective on Paul" by highlighting the congruity of Paul's theological commitments before and after his Damascus experience and by unveiling the hackneyed, stereotypical portrayal of Judaism as legalism by Christian interpreters of Paul.

Duane Howell, The Denver Post via Getty Images

We will treat these three topics in turn.

Was Paul a convert? To begin, a number of Pauline interpreters have suggested that it is neither appropriate nor accurate to refer to what Paul describes as an "appearance" or "revelation" as a "conversion." These scholars not only note that the word "conversion" is absent from the relevant Pauline texts, but they also maintain that Paul did not imagine himself altering his loyalty to the God of Israel or abandoning key tenets of Jewish monotheistic belief as a result of the "appearance" of which he speaks. Consequently, some scholars prefer to describe Paul's revelatory encounter with Christ not as a "conversion" but as a "call" experience, pointing out that this is the language Paul himself uses in Gal 1:15. The particular nature of Paul's call, they suggest, was to "proclaim [the Son of God] to the Gentiles" (Gal 1:16).[23]

While readily acknowledging that Paul came to conceive and speak of his Damascus experience in terms similar to certain Old Testament call narratives (note esp. Isa 49:1–6; Jer 1:5) and while wholeheartedly affirming a considerable degree of continuity in the pre- and post-Damascus thought and practice of Paul, it seems unnecessarily restrictive to deny the suitability of the term "conversion" to depict the transformation in Paul's life as a result of his encounter with the risen Christ. For starters, he began to proclaim the faith he once sought to destroy (Gal 1:23; see also 2 Cor 11:32–33). Additionally, over time Paul would come to speak of his "former" life in Judaism (Gal 1:13) and of his devaluation of the same in light of his driving desire to know Christ (Phil 3:7–14). Moreover, the Christocentricity of Paul's theology suggests that transformational language ("conversion") may rightly

22. Krister Stendahl, *Paul among Jews and Gentiles*, (Philadelphia: Fortress, 1976), 9.
23. See esp. Stendahl, *Paul among Jews and Gentiles,* 7–23.

be coupled with vocational language ("call") when describing Paul's Damascus experience and subsequent life in Christ.[24]

▲ "Ananias Restoring the Sight of St. Paul" is the work of the Italian painter and architect Pietro da Cortona (1596–1669).

Did Paul's conversion and call occur simultaneously? An additional question with which Pauline scholars grapple is the chronological connection between Paul's conversion on the one hand and his call to be an apostle of the gospel to the Gentiles on the other hand. Stated otherwise, did Paul's conversion and call occur simultaneously or subsequently? When writing Galatians some fifteen to twenty years after his encounter with Christ near or in Damascus, Paul speaks as if his commission to take the gospel to the nations was part and parcel of his conversion (1:16). Be that as it may, nothing Paul says in Galatians or elsewhere precludes one from concluding that it was over an unspecified period of time, perhaps through prayer, reflection on Scripture and his experiences, and encouragement from other believers, that he became convinced that God's call was for him to serve as a herald of the gospel to the Gentiles (Gal 2:2, 9; Rom 15:14–21).

How is Acts best used in the study of Paul's conversion/call? To this point, we have not considered the three accounts of Paul's conversion/call recorded in Acts 9, 22, and 26 respectively. Indeed, as with Acts in general, Pauline scholars debate the extent to which Luke's secondhand reporting of Paul's "Damascus Road" experience should shape our understanding of the event. In comparing the relevant texts in Paul and Acts, one immediately notes certain differences. Some of these emanate from and are explicable by the fact that Luke is writing a narrative regarding the expansion of the Jesus movement whereas Paul is writing occasional, pastoral letters to congregations. The repeated narration and the thicker description of Paul's conversion/call in Acts is in keeping with its theological and literary aims. Additional details we find in Acts with respect to the Damascus Road episode include the following:

- Paul's location and reaction when he encountered the risen Lord
- his subsequent conversation with Jesus
- the presence and response of Paul's traveling companions
- the physical effects of the vision on Paul
- the introduction of **Ananias** through his vision and interaction with Paul
- the restoration of Paul's sight and strength after visiting with and being baptized by Ananias

24. So also Klaus Haacker, "Paul's Life," in *The Cambridge Companion to St Paul* (ed. James D. G. Dunn; Cambridge: Cambridge University Press, 2003), 19–33 (on 24), and Terence L. Donaldson, *Paul and the Gentiles: Remapping the Apostle's Convictional World* (Minneapolis: Fortress, 1997).

An additional wrinkle to note at this point in the discussion is the variation between the three accounts of Saul's conversion in Acts with respect to certain details. For example, the three narratives differ regarding what Paul's companions saw, heard, and did with respect to the light and voice from heaven. Additionally, whereas Acts 9:1 reports that Saul sought letters from the high priest to aid in his interrogation and persecution of believers in Damascus synagogues, Acts 26:12 indicates that he was duly authorized and commissioned to carry out persecutory activity by certain chief priests. Presuming Luke's cognizance of differences such as these, we may conclude that he, an ancient author not a contemporary reporter, did not view these discrepancies as problematic and that his literary and theological goals did not require his accounts of Paul's conversion to mirror one another precisely. It may also be that Luke was the recipient of slightly different versions of what was clearly for him an event of considerable spiritual and strategic importance in the life of the early church.

Differences between the accounts notwithstanding, the three narrations of Paul's conversion in Acts share a common, basic story line: Saul, a dogged opponent of Jesus-followers, encountered the risen Jesus in a vision, and as a result, this most unlikely convert began to share the very message he had desperately sought to silence. What is more, despite the undeniable dissimilarities between Luke's retellings of Paul's Damascus experience and Paul's own accounts, they converge at the following points:

- Paul's early persecution of the church;
- the revelation of Jesus Christ to Paul through a vision; and
- the (eventual) call or commission for Paul to preach the gospel to the nations.

On the Other Side of Damascus

Paul's sojourn in Arabia. In turning our attention to what transpired in Paul's life during those years immediately following his conversion/call, we return to Galatians. After his revelatory encounter with the risen Christ, Paul contends that he did not enter into consultation with any person, including those living in Jerusalem who were apostles before him. Rather, Paul reports that he went to **Arabia**, presumably a part of the Nabatean kingdom located south of Damascus and east of the Jordan River (1:16–17). At this time (about AD 35), **King Aretas IV** (9 BC–AD 40) was the ruler of the Arab kingdom of Nabatea (2 Cor 11:32).

It appears that Paul was forced to leave Damascus subsequent to conversion. Although Paul does not indicate as much, Acts does. Luke states that after his baptism Paul stayed for "some days" with disciples at Damascus until trouble came his way for proclaiming Jesus as the Son of God (Acts 9:19b–22). This conflict, Luke reports, led to a plot upon Paul's life by "the Jews." Although they

▲ Pictured here is a bronze coin of King Aretas IV.

were watching the gates of the city to ambush him, we are told that Paul was able to escape their grasp when certain disciples lowered him over the city wall in a basket (9:23–25). Paul almost certainly refers to the same incident in 2 Cor 11:32–33.[25]

Even if Paul were forced to leave Damascus after his encounter with Christ, as appears to have been the case, we are left to wonder why he went to Arabia and what he did while there. Other remaining questions regarding Paul's sojourn in Arabia include questions such as these: Did Paul know (of) Jesus-followers there? Did he have family and/or friends in Arabia? Did he desire relative isolation to process his recent revelation and his future relative to his past? Was he simply running scared? Did he proclaim the gospel while there? How did he support himself? Was it in Arabia that Paul first learned and/or plied his trade?

Although questions flow freely, answers are elusive. As so often seems to be the case in the study of Paul's biography, this part of his life and ministry is now lost in the mist of history.[26]

Duono, Monreale, Sicily, Italy/Ancient Art and Architecture Collection Ltd./The Bridgeman Art Library

▲ This mosaic, which may be viewed at the Cathedral Church of Monreale in Sicily, Italy, depicts Paul's hasty departure from Damascus.

To Jerusalem and beyond. In our attempt to put together the jigsaw puzzle of Paul's life subsequent to his conversion/call, we now turn to Galatians 1:17b–21, where we find a few additional pieces of information. Firstly, in 1:17b we learn that Paul returned to Damascus after his sojourn in Arabia. Next, Paul tells the Galatians at the outset of v. 18 that "after three years" he went up to Jerusalem. At this point it is unclear whether Paul is tracking time from the point of his conversion/commission or from the time he returned to Damascus (2:1). Either way, we are probably not too far off the chronological mark to date Paul's first trip to Jerusalem after his Damascus Road experience to the late 30s AD.

Paul's stated reason for finally traveling to Jerusalem, a place from which he is at pains to distance himself in Galatians (Gal 1:20), was to visit **Cephas** (1:18). After a

25. This is true even though there are three noticeable differences: (1) Paul does not mention Damascus Jews in connection with the plot upon his life; instead, he speaks of a certain ethnarch under King Aretas [IV] who guarded the city to seize him; (2) Paul does not note why this conflict arose; and (3) Paul states that he "was let down in a basket through [a window in] the wall," thereby escaping King Aretas's underling.

26. N. T. Wright ("Paul, Arabia, and Elijah (Galatians 1:17)," *JBL* 115 [1996]: 683–92) conjectures that when Paul was stopped in his spiritual tracks, he did as his model Elijah did—he headed for Mount Sinai in Arabia.

WikiPaintings

▲ ▼ This well-known painting by the Cretian-born artist El Greco (1541 – 1614) pictures Peter and Paul together, as does this frequently seen icon.

Public Domain

fifteen-day stay in Jerusalem with Cephas (during which time he acknowledges having also seen James, the Lord's brother), Paul left Judea and went to the regions of Syria and Cilicia (1:19, 21). Cilicia, of course, is where Tarsus was located. As for Syria, we learn in Acts that it was home to at least two significant groups of Jesus-followers: one in Damascus (9:19) and another in Antioch (11:26).

Acts also records Paul's movement from Damascus to Jerusalem, though it is silent with respect to Arabia (see Acts 9:26). Additionally, in contrast to Gal 1:18 – 24, Acts maintains that Paul sought to join the band of believers in Jerusalem but was coolly received. Consequently, Acts reports that Barnabas took Paul to the apostles and informed them of his transformation resulting from his vision on the Damascus Road (Acts 9:27). According to Luke, Barnabas's testimony on Paul's behalf enabled him to move freely and to preach boldly in Jerusalem — that is, until such a time as Greek-speaking Jews (so-called Hellenists; cf. 6:1 – 6) turned against him and sought to kill him (9:28 – 29). When certain Jerusalem believers learned of that plan, Acts reports that they ushered Paul out of the city and sent him to Tarsus via Caesarea (9:30). The marked differences between Paul and Acts regarding the apostle's initial journey to Jerusalem after the Damascus event illustrate how difficult it is to reconstruct the life of an ancient figure from incomplete, and at points, tendentious sources.[27]

The "silent years." Such a task becomes even more difficult when there are no details even to consider! This is the fate that befalls Pauline interpreters during the period of the apostle's life sometimes known as the "**silent years**" — that is, the stretch of time between Paul's first visit to Jerusalem after his conversion/call (late AD 30s) and his reemergence in Antioch a number of years later (mid-40s; see Acts 11:25 – 26). When Acts does return to treat Paul's life and ministry, it portrays him as one who assumes a vital spiritual role in the life of the church in Antioch. Indeed, after Barnabas brings Paul from Tarsus to Syrian Antioch, Acts reports that he becomes a teacher and prophet within the church (11:26; 13:1) as well as an authorized messenger and minister of the church, whether in Jerusalem (11:27 – 30; 12:25), Cyprus (13:4 – 12), Pisidian Antioch (13:13 – 50), Iconium (13:51 – 14:5), or Lystra and Derbe (14:6 – 20).

27. Haacker ("Paul's Life," 19 – 20) notes that both the letters of Paul and the Acts of the Apostles are "historically valuable but not free of tendencies to stress certain aspects and to leave out others, paying tribute to the perspective of their authors at the time of their writing."

It is at this point in our treatment of Paul's life, however, that we cross over from his "Damascus Road" experience and its more immediate aftermath to the apostle's missional endeavors in the broader Mediterranean world.

PAUL'S MISSION TO MINISTRY IN THE MEDITERRANEAN WORLD

From Jerusalem to Antioch

In Galatians 2, Paul recounts two episodes that proved to be of monumental importance in shaping his ministry. As it happens, both of these accounts are fraught with interpretive difficulties. One of the chief challenges that scholars encounter when interpreting Gal 2:1–10 and 2:11–14 respectively is the dating and correlating of these reported events with what one finds in Acts, especially Acts 11:27–30 and 15:1–35. While it would be unreasonable to think that we could even begin to unravel this notoriously knotty issue here, we can probe various possibilities as we begin to consider the topic of Paul's apostolic work and witness.

In Gal 2:1 Paul informs the churches of Galatia that he, accompanied by Barnabas and Titus, made another journey to Jerusalem after a period of "fourteen years" had elapsed. Scholars differ in their understanding of the point from which Paul begins counting. Is he marking time from his conversion/call (Gal 1:15–17) or from his initial trip to Jerusalem three years after his encounter with Christ (1:18)? If the former, then it is possible to date the Jerusalem visit of which Paul speaks in 2:1 to the mid-40s and to correlate it with the so-called famine relief visit reported in Acts 11:27–30. This correlation allows one to date Galatians to the late 40s and to identify the recipients of the letter as those assemblies that (according to Acts 13:13–14:23) were founded by Paul in southern or provincial Galatia during his so-called first missionary journey. Moreover, interpreters who espouse this position date Paul's confrontation with Cephas/Peter at Antioch sometime prior to the "Jerusalem Conference" reported in Acts 15:1–35.

▼ Although we are left to wonder about all that Paul did during his so-called "silent years," we do know that he was actively "preaching the faith he once tried to destroy" (Gal 1:23). This painting by the Italian artist Giovanni Paolo Pannini (1691–1765), "Apostle Paul Preaching on the Ruins," dated to 1744 and housed in The Hermitage Museum in St. Petersburg, Russia, envisions Paul's ministry of proclamation.

If, however, the fourteen-year period dates not from his conversion/call but from his initial trip to Jerusalem three years after that experience, then Paul's second visit to Jerusalem occurred in the late 40s. In turn, Paul would have written his Galatian letter sometime after this, somewhere in the time frame of the early to mid-50s and could have written to churches in either South (or provincial) Galatia (Acts 13:13–14:23) or North (or ethnic) Galatia (Acts 16:6; 18:23). On this reading, Gal 2:1–10 would be Paul's version of the so-called Jerusalem Council (Acts 15:1–35), and Paul's confrontation of Peter in Antioch recorded in Gal 2:11–14 would likely have occurred sometime thereafter.

All of this may seem rather cumbersome and complex; nevertheless, it is indicative of the ongoing conversation as to how best to integrate Acts 11 and 15 with Galatians 1–2. Taken together, we think it more likely that Gal 2:1–10 and Acts 15 have the same event in view. As a result, we are also inclined to regard 1 Thessalonians and not Galatians as Paul's earliest surviving letter (see further chs. 2 and 3).

Did Paul Take Missionary Journeys?

As it happens, in his occasional epistles Paul says nothing to indicate that his apostolic ministry was comprised of three missionary journeys (Acts 13:1–14:28; 15:40–18:22; 18:23–21:6) and a final trip from Jerusalem to Rome via Caesarea (23:31–28:16). Indeed, Paul's interpreters sometimes wryly remark that if the apostle had been asked in the midst of his ministry to state the number of the journey he was presently undertaking, he would not even have understood the question. But comments such as this are not entirely fair to Luke's conceptualization of Paul's ministry. Although Luke frames Paul's movements in ways that might well have been foreign to Paul's own understanding, the terminology of "missionary journeys" is not Luke's own terminology; rather, it arises from those who have interpreted Acts.[28]

Indeed, readers of Paul's letters and Acts quickly discover the large number of locations that the two share in common, including Damascus, Syrian Antioch, Philippi, Thessalonica, Athens, Corinth, Ephesus, Troas, Jerusalem, and Rome. Such a striking correspondence at the very least suggests that Luke

▼ French artist Eustache Le Sueur (1617–1655) seeks to capture Acts' portrayal of Paul's ministry in Ephesus (esp. Acts 19:19) in his 1649 painting "The Preaching of St. Paul at Ephesus."

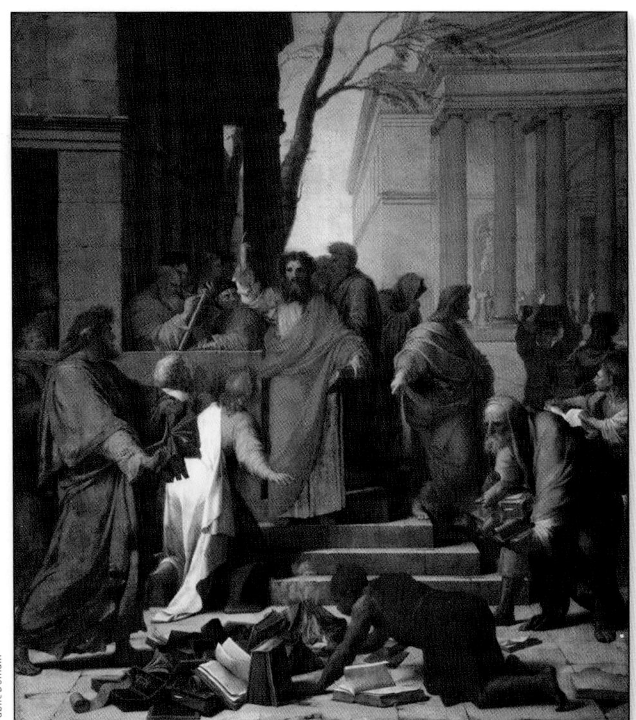

Public Domain

28. Even though we have chosen not to organize this introduction around the three (or even four) missionary journeys discerned by some interpreters of Acts, we would suggest that those who prefer to teach Paul in this way simply place our chapters 2 to 13 where they seem to fit best when utilizing such a schema.

is not inventing a missionary itinerary for Paul from his fertile imagination. What is more, there is an especially strong correlation between Paul and Acts at certain points and in particular places.[29]

Paul's Missionary Travels

Raymond E. Brown helps us to understand better how arduous Paul's missionary travels were with these words:

> Paul was an itinerant artisan who would have had to struggle to get money for food. Horseback travel was difficult . . . [and] Paul would not even have been able or willing to spend money for a donkey to carry his baggage. So we have to picture Paul trudging along the roads, carrying his limited possessions in a sack, at the maximum covering twenty miles a day. Often . . . he had to sleep somewhere near the road, amidst the cold, rain, and snow. As a poor man he would have been easily victimized by brigands, especially in country areas that were less efficiently controlled by police. Sea journeys were not much safer.[31]

Did Paul Have a Missionary Strategy?

Based on remarks that Paul makes in his letters, it does not appear that he conducted his ministry according to a fixed itinerary. Circumstances and forces, whether malevolent or benevolent, sometimes precluded the apostle's ability to move as he willed.[30] In fact, on one occasion Paul's change of plans created considerable tension between him and some members of the Corinthian congregation (2 Cor 1:15–2:4). With this being said, it does not appear that Paul traveled willy-nilly throughout the Mediterranean world with a knapsack on his back wherever the winds and his whims might carry him.

The popular notion of Paul, the wild-eyed apocalypticist, racing indiscriminately around the Roman Empire in a "holy hurry" spouting his missionary message to anyone he could buttonhole does not ring true with the data that we have at hand. According to Acts, Paul spent no less than eighteen months in Corinth (18:11) and some three years in Ephesus (20:31). Moreover, when Paul did have to leave a city prematurely, it was local hostility, not an imminent eschatology, that sent the apostle packing.[32]

On a micro level, Paul appears to have laid rather short-term plans, remaining open to the Lord's intervention and direction all the while. The apostle could well have affirmed the famous line from Robert Burns's 1786 poem "To a Mouse": "The best laid plans of mice and men often go astray." A textual example of Paul's "itinerary elasticity" appears in 1 Cor 16:5–9. There he informs the church of his plan to pay them a protracted visit in the not-too-distant future "if the Lord permits," after having stayed on at Ephesus until Pentecost and after having passed through Macedonia. The apostle's single status (1 Cor 7:8; 9:5) and portable trade afforded him the opportunity to be flexible and to travel lightly, if not swiftly. This is not to suggest, however, that his journeys were necessarily easy (2 Cor 11:25–26). Traveling for a living is not easy now, but it was even harder then!

On a macro level, Paul's overall plan was apparently to traverse a significant swath of the Eastern Mediterranean, carrying the gospel primarily to Gentile city dwellers and

29. For example, compare 1 Thess 2:2; 3:1 with Acts 16:12–18:1 and Rom 15:22–32 with Acts 19:21; 20:16. The traditional interpretation of the "**we sections**" in Acts (i.e., those passages in Acts where the narrative shifts from third person to first person; see 16:10–17; 20:5–15; 21:1–18; 27:1–28:16) places Luke with Paul during portions of his missionary work as well as during his tumultuous trip to Rome.
30. See, e.g., Rom 1:13; 15:22; 2 Cor 2:12–13; 1 Thess 2:18. Note also Acts 16:6–7.
31. Raymond E. Brown, *An Introduction to the New Testament* (New York: Doubleday, 1997), 447.
32. Note 1 Thess 2:2, 15, 17; Phil 1:30. See also Acts 13:50; 14:5–6, 19; 16:35–40; 17:10, 14; 20:1.

▲ Map of a portion of the Mediterranean world

forming converts into Christ-shaped communities. Along the way, Paul added another goal to his ministry, involving the delivery of a monetary collection donated by his largely Gentile churches for impoverished Jesus-followers in Jerusalem.[33] Later still we learn that after preaching the gospel and planting churches from Jerusalem to Illyricum, a Roman province located on the eastern shore of the Adriatic Sea, Paul was preparing to go to Rome and then on to Spain, since there was no longer a room for him to work in the regions and since he was eager "to proclaim the good news" where Christ had not yet been named (Rom 15:20, 23–24).

Whereas Jesus was from the remote village of Nazareth in Galilee and seemingly spent far more time residing in the country than in the city, Paul of Tarsus appears to have carried out the majority of his ministry in strategically located urban centers. It seems anything but happenstance that Paul founded churches in and/or wrote letters to such places as Philippi, Thessalonica, Corinth, Ephesus, and Rome. With the exception of Philippi, all of these were large cities, at least by ancient standards. Furthermore, each of these places was readily accessible by both land and sea.

Just as a stone thrown into a still pond causes a ripple, Paul may well have sought to take the gospel to more densely populated and frequently visited places so that it might not only "make a splash" in the city but also spread out to the surrounding countryside. According to Colossians, Paul had neither founded nor visited assemblies in Colossae, Hierapolis, and Laodicea (Col 2:1; 4:13), cities in the Lycus River valley that were located roughly one hundred miles east of Ephesus. Yet, by virtue of his contact with and influence on Epaphras (Col 1:7; 4:12) and Philemon (Phlm 19), presumably in Ephesus, the gospel that he preached and modeled was able to travel to places he was unable to go.

Paul's Missionary Modus Operandi

Although Paul regarded the gospel as a message more powerful and persuasive than even its most influential messengers (Phil 1:12–18a), he also recognized that people are essential for the proclamation of the gospel (Rom 10:14–17). Although Paul is sometimes presented as a cantankerous, egocentric Lone Ranger, who cut himself off from mutual, meaningful relationships with other believers, this portrait is not accurate. In fact, Paul's letters and

33. See esp. Rom 15:14–32; 1 Cor 16:1–4; 2 Cor 8:1–9:15; see also Gal 2:10.

Acts indicate that the apostle had a cadre of **coworkers** with whom he labored and on whom he depended. The apostle's closest, better-known colleagues were Timothy,[34] Silvanus/Silas,[35] Barnabas,[36] Titus,[37] and the ministry couple Prisca/Priscilla and Aquila.[38]

Baker Photo Archive. The British Museum.

▲ Red-figured cup showing a shoemaker cutting leather (480–470 BC). If Paul were in fact a leatherworker, then he could have "witnessed" just as easily as he could have "whistled" while he worked!

Paul's ongoing association with Prisca/Priscilla and Aquila highlights two additional facets of the Pauline mission. First, despite the fact that Paul's closest ministerial companions were male and that some of his comments can be understood as derogatory to women,[39] Paul's ministry was greatly enhanced by the ministry of a number of women who ministered alongside him. In addition to Prisca/Priscilla, other women involved in ministerial service with the apostle include:

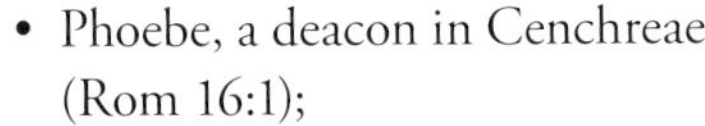

- Phoebe, a deacon in Cenchreae (Rom 16:1);
- Mary, Tryphaena, and Tryphosa, who were "workers" among Jesus-followers in Rome (Rom 16:6, 12);
- Junia, who, along with Andronicus (her husband?), was noteworthy among the apostles (Rom 16:7);
- Euodia and Syntyche, who were "co-laborers" with Paul in Philippi (Phil 4:2); and
- Lydia (Acts 16:14, 40) and Nympha (Col 4:15), who were hosts of Pauline congregations in Philippi and Colossae respectively (see also Apphia in Phlm 2).

Second, Paul worked the same trade as Priscilla and Aquila. According to Acts 18:3, they were *skēnopoioi*. While there is ongoing scholarly debate concerning the meaning of this term and, accordingly, the occupation of Paul and his companions, there is now little

34. Timothy is mentioned in Acts 16:1, 3; 17:14, 15; 18:5; 19:22; 20:4; Rom 16:21; 1 Cor 4:17; 16:10; 2 Cor 1:1, 19; Phil 1:1; 2:19, 22; Col 1:1; 1 Thess 1:1; 3:2, 6; 2 Thess 1:1; 1 Tim 1:2, 18; 6:20; 2 Tim 1:2; Phlm 1; Heb 13:23.
35. Silas is mentioned in Acts 15:22, 27, 32, 40; 16:19, 25, 29; 17:1, 4, 5, 10, 14, 15; 18:5; 2 Cor 1:19; 1 Thess 1:1; 2 Thess 1:1; 1 Pet 5:12.
36. Barnabas is mentioned in Acts 9:27; 11:25; 12:25; 13:2; 15:2, 36–41; 1 Cor 9:6; Gal 2:1, 13.
37. Titus is mentioned in 2 Cor 2:13; 7:6, 13, 14; 8:6, 16, 23; 12:18 [2x]; Gal 2:1, 3; 2 Tim 4:10; Titus 1:4.
38. This couple is mentioned in Acts 18:2, 18, 26; Rom 16:3; 1 Cor 16:19; 2 Tim 4:19.
39. Note 1 Cor 11:2–16; 14:33b–36; 1 Tim 2:11–14 (if written by Paul).

Raphael (Raffaello Sanzio of Urbino) (1483 – 1520)/Victoria & Albert Museum, London, UK/The Bridgeman Art Library

▲ In 1515 the Italian painter and architect Raphael (1483–1520) painted the now-famous "St. Paul Preaching in Athens."

question among Pauline interpreters that his handcraft played an integral role in his missionary work.[40] The fact that Paul plied a trade enabled him to pay his own way and not be a financial burden on his congregations.[41] He could, in his own words, preach the gospel free of charge (1 Cor 9:18; 2 Cor 11:7, 9). Furthermore, it is probable that Paul's workshop served as a place where the apostle shared the gospel while practicing his craft (Acts 17:17).

Paul spoke with people about the crucifixion, resurrection, and coming of the Lord Jesus Christ[42] and taught about the lifestyle of Jesus-followers "until he comes" in a variety of settings:

- Jewish synagogues (2 Cor 11:24; see also Acts 13:14; 14:1; 17:1, 17; 18:4, 19; 19:8);
- private homes (Rom 16:23; 1 Cor 1:16; 14:20–25; 16:5, 19; Col 4:15; Phlm 2; see also Acts 16:15, 40; 17:5; 18:7; 20:20);
- public spaces (Acts 19:9; 20:20); and
- open air settings (Acts 17:22–34).

While Paul declared Christ in all of these places, the homes of those who believed his report seemed to have served as the primary venue for the worship and fellowship of fledgling Pauline assemblies. Believers' homes, whether sprawling villas or Spartan tenements, would have been well suited for intimate gatherings of convinced insiders and intrigued outsiders (1 Cor 14:23). Given that Paul and his message were not always welcomed in Jewish synagogues, public places, and open-air settings, private homes would have been essential for the sharing of the gospel and the building up of communities of Jesus-followers. Moreover, the places where Paul's converts resided would have afforded a degree of privacy to those who met together in Christ's name, even if those gatherings might also have caused unsympathetic outsiders to be suspicious and lodge slanderous accusations against them.

40. Did they make tents exclusively? If so, with what materials did they work (goats' hair, canvas, and/or leather)? Were they leatherworkers in general who made all sorts and sundry of leather goods including tents? Alternatively, were they builders of stage properties for theaters? See further Todd D. Still, "Did Paul Loathe Manual Labor? Revisiting the Work of Ronald F. Hock on the Apostle's Tentmaking and Social Class," *JBL* 125 (2006): 781–95.

41. Note esp. 1 Cor 4:12; 9:6; 1 Thess 2:9; 2 Thess 3:7–8.

42. See 1 Cor 15:3–4 ; 1 Thess 1:9–10; 4:14–15.

Jesus Groups Founded by Paul: A Sketch

Thanks to Paul's letters and to Acts, we know the names of a number of ostensible Pauline converts, including Crispus (1 Cor 1:14; see also Acts 18:8; 19:29), Gaius (Rom 16:23; 1 Cor 1:14), Erastus (Rom 16:23; see also Acts 19:22; 2 Tim 4:20), Stephanas (1 Cor 1:16; 16:15, 17), Onesimus (Phlm 10), Philemon (Phlm 19), Epaphras (Col 1:7; 4:12), Lydia (Acts 17:14), Jason (Acts 17:5–9; see also Rom 16:21), Dionysius (Acts 17:34), and Damaris (Acts 17:34). Furthermore, it is likely that the majority of Paul's coworkers were also his converts (e.g., Euodia, Syntyche, and Clement, named in Phil 4:2–3). Although we know the names of various converts and coworkers of Paul, with few exceptions we know little else about them. This is also true of Paul's churches in general.

In Gal 3:27–28, Paul declares the following, perhaps drawing on a baptismal formula that circulated early on within the Jesus movement: "For all of you who were baptized into Christ have clothed yourselves in Christ. There is neither Jew nor Gentile, neither slave nor free, nor is there male and female, for you are all one in Christ Jesus" (see also 1 Cor 12:13; Col 3:11). While Paul's intention in writing these verses was not to offer a composite portrait of the Galatian churches (or of any other Pauline congregation for that matter), Paul's letters evince there were people drawn from each of these categories in assemblies he founded. Furthermore, the apostle's letters indicate that fellowships that he founded included children, those who were (re)married, the widowed, the divorced, and the single (whether by calling, choice, conviction, and/or circumstance; see especially 1 Corinthians 7).

Because Paul worked and witnessed primarily in cities, the churches he founded were comprised chiefly of urban dwellers. But with the exception of Prisca/Priscilla, Aquila, and the apostle himself, we do not know the occupations of Pauline Jesus-followers, although we are informed in Rom 16:23 that a certain Erastus served within the city treasury (in Corinth?). Based on Paul's admonition to the Thessalonians "to work with [their] own hands," we may infer that at least in Thessalonica the preponderance of the apostle's converts would have been artisans or manual laborers of one sort or another (1 Thess 4:11; see also 2 Thess 3:6–15; cf. Eph 4:28).

Whether or not there were also those of considerable fiscal means and prominent social standing within Pauline congregations remains an open question. At the present time, interpreters of Paul construe the scraps of relevant data in considerably different ways. Whereas some Pauline scholars think it likely that at least a few economically secure patrons would have been present in some or most of Paul's churches, others suggest that Paul and his converts lived a subsistence existence. Paul states in Phil 4:12 that he was well acquainted with both abasement and abundance. What this means in practical terms, however, is as elusive as seeking to pinpoint the social class of the apostle, much less his converts. There is simply too little information and there are too many variables for us to unravel this Gordian knot.

In concluding our précis of Paul's converts and churches, we will consider in turn the ethnic composition and the numerical size of Pauline congregations. Paul was Jewish, a fact in which he sometimes takes pride (Gal 2:15; see also Phil 3:8–9). Nonetheless, the fellowships he helped to found and form were comprised primarily of Gentiles (i.e., non-Jews). When writing to the Thessalonians, for instance, the apostle recollects the assembly's turning to God from idols (1 Thess 1:9). Additionally, he instructs his Thessalonian converts not to live in lustful passion like Gentiles who do not know God (4:5; see also 1 Pet 4:3), so as to imply in context that they had been Gentiles who did know God (1 Thess 2:14).

Similarly, in addressing the Galatian churches, Paul refers to a time when they did not know God and were enslaved to sinister powers (Gal 4:8–9). In Galatians Paul also employs his considerable theological and rhetorical acumen in an attempt to dissuade his male Gentile addressees from being circumcised (see esp. 5:2–12; 6:11–16). In addition, Paul warns his beloved Philippian converts to be on the lookout for interlopers who would encourage them to be circumcised (3:2). And when writing to the Corinthian church, in which there were seemingly at least a few Jews (7:18; see also 12:13), Paul speaks to the assembly as if it were comprised entirely of Gentiles who had previously been beholden to idols (12:2).

The apparent ethnic makeup of Paul's congregations tallies well with his stated apostolic self-understanding and mission. Paul conceived of and described himself as "an apostle to the Gentiles."[43] This is not to suggest that Paul would not and did not preach the gospel to his fellow Jews.[44] In fact, in Rom 1:16 the apostle declares that the gospel is "first to the Jew, then to the Gentile." One may gather, however, from remarks that Paul makes in Romans that his efforts to evangelize his Jewish compatriots were not typically well received (Rom 9:1–3, 6a; 10:1–3; 11:28).

Unfortunately, it is now impossible to determine the size of any given **Pauline** congregation. To complicate matters further, there may well have been multiple Jesus groups in a single city, as was seemingly the case in Rome (cf. Rom 16:5, 10, 11, 14, 15). It is unlikely that any one assembly would have been larger than fifty. Moreover, if the meeting place was an apartment instead of a villa, the numbers may well have been significantly smaller. Even so, we should not assume that the space where Pauline believers met would have been filled to capacity.

It is regrettable that we know so little about the composition, patterns, and practices of Jesus groups founded by Paul. If the Corinthian church is at all indicative, then meetings of believers were lively affairs where men and women prayed, prophesied, taught, sang, spoke in and interpreted tongues, and shared in the Lord's Supper (see esp. 1 Corinthians 11; 14). The Corinthians also practiced baptismal rituals (1 Cor 1:13–17; 12:13; 15:29) and had at least some semblance of local church leadership, even if it was characterized by informality and disunity and was provided by those who hosted gatherings in their homes.[45]

As we study Paul's life, letters, and theology, we need to remember that the apostle worshiped with and worked alongside smallish bands of believers who met in one another's homes. It is anachronistic to think of Pauline congregations as throngs of disconnected people gathering in spaces designed and expressly set aside for the liturgy and ministry of the church.

Staying in Touch

When Paul departed from a town (whether voluntarily or not), he usually left behind a fledgling "church of God" (1 Cor 10:32). His physical separation from a church, however,

43. Rom 11:13; see also 1:13–15; 15:7–27; Gal 1:16; 2:2, 9.

44. Note, e.g., 1 Cor 9:20; 2 Cor 11:24; also Acts 13:15–16; 14:1; 17:2–3, 10; 18:4; 19:8.

45. Note, e.g., 1 Cor 1:10–12; 11:17–22; 16:16; see also Phil 1:1; 4:2–3; 1 Thess 5:12–14.

did not curb his spiritual concern for a church or his desire to be present with its members.[46] Therefore, when Paul could not be with a congregation in person, he would stay in contact with the people through the sending and receiving of envoys and letters. To illustrate the point, Paul tried repeatedly to return to Thessalonica to see how his converts were faring in the faith, but when his attempts were foiled ("Satan blocked our way," 1 Thess 2:18), Timothy went to visit the church in his stead (3:2; see also 1 Cor 4:17; Phil 2:19). In fact, it was the positive report that Timothy brought to Paul regarding the Thessalonians' faith that prompted the apostle to write what appears to be his earliest surviving letter — 1 Thessalonians (see 3:6).

Even as Paul communicated with his churches via messengers and letters, he also received envoys and letters from his churches. Although no correspondence written to Paul survives, in 1 Cor 7:1 the apostle refers to matters about which certain Corinthians had written him. In addition, we learn from Paul's letters of occasions when churches would send representatives to him and of times when believers would travel to be with the apostle of their own accord. For example, when Paul was in Ephesus, certain Corinthian believers came to visit him (16:7, 18; see also 1:11). Additionally, the church in Philippi sent gifts to Paul in his captivity through Epaphroditus (Phil 2:25; 4:18). Apparently, the Philippians sent financial aid to the apostle on a number of occasions throughout his ministry (Phil 4:10, 16; see also 1:5).

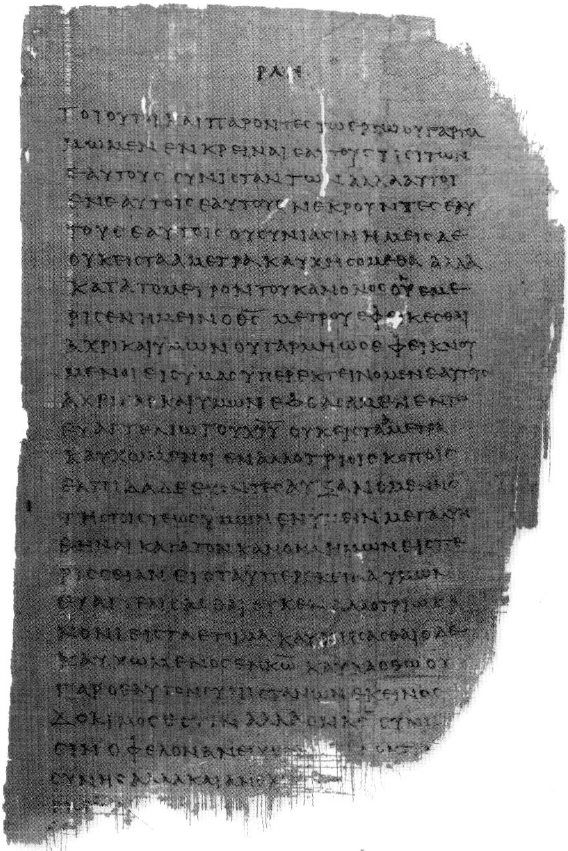

▲ Papyrus 46 (known by the siglum $\mathfrak{P}^{46}$) is among the oldest surviving New Testament manuscripts written in Greek (typically dated to around AD 200). Pictured here is a folio (or sheet) from $\mathfrak{P}^{46}$ containing 2 Cor. 10:11 – 11:2.

PAUL'S DEPARTURE

Paul was a multifaceted person. Among other things, he was a traveler. It is fitting, therefore, that Paul likened his death to a departure (Phil 1:23; 2 Tim 4:6). But the final movements of the apostle's life are sketchy.[47] Moreover, any reconstruction of the end of his life is based on complex interpretive decisions as well as arguments from silence. In concluding this chapter, we will consider how scholars have construed the last chapter of Paul's eventful life.

46. Note 1 Cor 5:3; 2 Cor 11:28 – 29; Phil 1:27; 2:12; Col 2:1; 1 Thess 2:17.
47. Longenecker (*Remember the Poor*, 312) suggests that evidence regarding the end of Paul's life is "precariously patchy."

▲ Spanish artist Enrique Simonet (1866–1927) seeks to capture on canvas Paul's purported execution in his 1887 painting "The Beheading of St. Paul."

When Paul penned Romans, three locations were in the fore of his mind—Rome, where he was writing and was anticipating visiting; Jerusalem, where he was taking an offering from Gentile Jesus-followers to impoverished saints in that city; and Spain, where he was eager to go after having visited with Roman believers (Rom 15:23–25). As it happens, a number of Pauline interpreters regard Romans as the last surviving work of the apostle. These scholars contend that Paul wrote Philippians and Philemon from Ephesus in the mid-50s. Furthermore, they tend to view Colossians, Ephesians, 1 Timothy, 2 Timothy, and Titus to have been written on behalf of Paul instead of by him (an ancient literary phenomenon known as pseudonymity).[48]

Scholars who ascribe all of the Captivity Letters and Pastoral Letters to Paul must also seek to decipher when and where he wrote them. Interpreters have traditionally held that Paul wrote the Prison or Captivity Letters from Rome in the early 60s and the Pastoral Epistles (or at least 2 Timothy) from Rome in the mid-60s. In support of this stance, scholars have:

- followed the ending of Acts, where Paul is arrested in Jerusalem, transferred to Caesarea, and finally transported to Rome (Acts 21:27–28:31);

48. See further below, pp. 80–82.

- suggested that the apostle wrote the Captivity Letters while being detained in Rome (Acts 28:30; 2 Tim 1:17; see also Phil 1:13; 4:22);
- maintained that Paul was subsequently released and traveled to those locales referred to in the Pastorals, including Ephesus, Macedonia, and Crete;
- thought that Paul might even have made it to Spain during this short-lived season of freedom (cf. *1 Clem.* 5.7);
- argued that the apostle was arrested and taken into Roman custody, at which time he wrote 2 Timothy and perhaps 1 Timothy and Titus as well; and
- contended that Paul was executed in Rome in the mid–60s when Nero was using Roman believers as scapegoats.[49]

Although at least some early Jesus-followers considered Paul's martyrdom to be exemplary (*1 Clem.* 5.7; Ignatius, *Eph.* 12), they were not particularly interested in recording the details regarding his death. Fortunately, they did see fit to preserve a number of the letters Paul wrote in the course of his ministry. It is to the study of these documents that we now turn.

CONCLUDING REMARKS

T. R. Glover is credited with saying "that the day was to come when men would call their dogs Nero and their sons Paul."[50] This chapter on the apostle's eventful life offers any number of reasons as to why so many Christians over the sweep of history would name their progeny after Paul of Tarsus. Many Christ-followers have regarded his life-altering encounter with Christ to be exemplary. Others have been been inspired by his abandon for Christ and his far-flung mission to the nations in Jesus' name that ended in an ignominious fashion. Still others have found themselves captivated and instructed by letters he wrote to congregations and persons.

The thirteen Pauline letters preserved for posterity will occupy us in part 2 of this volume. Before we examine Paul's letters in some detail, we do well to see the forest for the trees. These memorable words from Raymond E. Brown help us to do just that: "Our reflections on [the scholarly study of Paul and his letters] . . . must be qualified by the underlying awareness that Paul would grind his teeth if anyone thought any of that was other than dross when compared with experiencing the all-encompassing love of Christ, the goal to which he had devoted every waking hour."[51]

49. See Tacitus, *Annals* 15.44; Suetonius, *Nero* 16. Note also the account of the later ecclesiastical writer Sulpicius Severus, *Chronicle* 2.29, who reports that Paul was beheaded by a sword during the period when Nero was having Roman believers killed.
50. So F. F. Bruce, *Paul: Apostle of the Free Spirit* (Exeter: Paternoster, 1977), 5.
51. Brown, *Introduction*, 450.

» KEY PEOPLE, PLACES, AND TERMS «

Ananias
Arabia
Benjamin
Cephas
Circumcision
Coworkers
Damascus Road
Diaspora
Gamaliel
Hellenism
Jerusalem Conference
King Aretas IV
Pauline
Pharisee
Saul
"Silent years"
Tarsus
"We sections"
Zeal

» QUESTIONS FOR REVIEW AND DISCUSSION «

1. What difference does it make, if any, where Paul was educated?
2. What prompted Paul to persecute "the church of God" prior to his Damascus Road encounter with Christ?
3. How does Paul describe his encounter with Christ en route to Damascus? Is it fitting to refer to this experience as both a conversion and a call? Explain.
4. Respond to the following statement: "Paul's 'pre-Christian' name was Saul."
5. What was Paul's trade? When and from whom might he have learned it? Why did he ply his craft in the midst of his ministry?
6. Why might Paul have traveled to Arabia subsequent to his Damascus Road experience?
7. What appears to have been Paul's missionary *modus operandi*?
8. "Paul preferred to minister by himself or, if necessary, with other males." Respond.
9. What were the various venues in which Paul "preached Christ"?
10. Where did "Pauline churches" meet?
11. Was Paul wealthy? Explain.
12. To whom did Paul think himself called to preach the gospel? Why might this have been the case?
13. What necessitated Paul's writing of letters to various congregations and persons?
14. According to church tradition, when, where, and how did Paul die?

» CONTEMPORARY THEOLOGICAL REFLECTION «

1. Does the contemporary academic debate whether Paul was converted and/or called shed any fresh light on modern notions of conversion/call with which you are familiar? Is either "conversion" or "call" emphasized more than the other in your personal experience or congregational context?
2. Compare Paul's approach to ministry and mission with modern-day missionary efforts about which you know. What are some lessons we might learn from Paul that could inform, if not transform, our perception and practice of missions?

» GOING FURTHER «

Most introductions to Paul will include at least one chapter on his life. For fuller treatments than the one provided here, see:

Bruce, F. F. *Paul: Apostle of the Free Spirit.* Exeter: Paternoster, 1977.

Gorman, Michael J. *Apostle of the Crucified Lord: A Theological Introduction to Paul and His Letters.* Grand Rapids: Eerdmans, 2004.

Murphy-O'Connor, Jerome. *Paul: A Critical Life.* Oxford: Oxford University Press, 1996.

Roetzel, Calvin J. *Paul: The Man and the Myth.* Columbia, SC: University of South Carolina Press, 1998.

Schnelle, Udo. *Apostle Paul: His Life and Theology.* Grand Rapids: Baker, 2005.

Among the volumes seeking to orient students to the scholarly study of Paul, including his life, see especially:

Dunn, James D. G., ed. *The Cambridge Companion to St Paul.* Cambridge: Cambridge University Press, 2003.

Horrell, David G. *An Introduction to the Study of Paul.* 2nd ed. London/New York: T&T Clark, 2006.

Witherington, Ben, III. *The Paul Quest: The Renewed Search for the Jew of Tarsus.* Downers Grove, IL: InterVarsity Press, 1998.

On Pauline chronology, see:

Jewett, Robert. *A Chronology of Paul's Life.* Philadelphia: Fortress, 1979.

Knox, John. *Chapters in a Life of Paul.* Rev. ed. Macon, GA: Mercer University Press, 1987.

Lüdemann, Gerd. *Paul, Apostle to the Gentiles: Studies in Chronology*. Philadelphia: Fortress, 1984.

Riesner, Rainer. *Paul's Early Period: Chronology, Mission Strategy, Theology*. Grand Rapids: Eerdmans, 1998.

On Paul's life before and after the Damascus event in particular, see:

Hengel, Martin. *The Pre-Christian Paul.* Translated by John Bowden. London: SCM; Philadelphia: Trinity Press International, 1991.

Hengel, Martin, and Anna Maria Schwemer. *Paul between Damascus and Antioch: The Unknown Years.* Louisville: Westminster John Knox, 1997.

With respect to Paul's conversion/call, see:

Gaventa, Beverly R. *From Darkness to Light: Aspects of Conversion in the New Testament.* Philadelphia: Fortress, 1986, esp. 17–51.

Kim, Seyoon. *The Origin of Paul's Gospel.* Grand Rapids: Eerdmans, 1982.

Longenecker, Richard N., ed. *The Road from Damascus: The Impact of Paul's Conversion on His Life, Thought, and Ministry.* Grand Rapids: Eerdmans, 1997.

Segal, Alan F. *Paul the Convert: The Apostolate and Apostasy of Saul the Pharisee.* New Haven, CT: Yale University Press, 1990.

Stendahl, Krister. *Paul among Jews and Gentiles.* Philadelphia: Fortress, 1976.

On the social and intellectual milieu of Paul and his churches, see:

Banks, Robert. *Paul's Idea of Community.* Rev. ed. Peabody, MA: Hendrickson, 1994.

Barclay, John M. G. *Jews in the Mediterranean Diaspora: From Alexander to Trajan (323 BCE–117 CE).* Edinburgh: T&T Clark, 1996.

Engberg-Pedersen, Troels, ed. *Paul beyond the Judaism/Hellenism Divide.* Louisville: Westminster John Knox, 2001.

Hock, Ronald F. *The Social Context of Paul's Ministry: Tentmaking and Apostleship.* Philadelphia: Fortress, 1980.

Longenecker, Bruce W. *Remember the Poor: Paul, Poverty, and the Greco-Roman World.* Grand Rapids: Eerdmans, 2011.

Meeks, Wayne A. *The First Urban Christians: The Social World of the Apostle Paul.* New Haven, CT: Yale University Press, 1983.

Meggitt, Justin J. *Paul, Poverty and Survival.* Edinburgh: T&T Clark, 1998.

Sampley, J. Paul. *Paul in the Greco-Roman World: A Handbook.* Harrisburg, PA: Trinity Press International, 2003.

Still, Todd D., and David G. Horrell, eds., *After the First Urban Christians: The Social-Scientific Study of Pauline Christianity Twenty-Five Years Later.* London/New York: T&T Clark, 2009.

With respect to Paul's missionary message and strategy, see:

Bolt, Peter, and Mark Thompson, eds. *The Gospel to the Nations: Perspectives on Paul's Mission.* Downers Grove, IL: InterVarsity Press, 2000.

O'Brien, P. T. *Gospel and Mission in the Writings of Paul: An Exegetical and Theological Analysis.* Grand Rapids: Baker; Carlisle: Paternoster, 1995.

Schnabel, Eckhard J. *Paul the Missionary: Realities, Strategies and Methods.* Downers Grove, IL: InterVarsity Press, 2008.

Stowers, Stanley Kent. "Social Status, Public Speaking and Private Teaching: The Circumstances of Paul's Preaching Activity." *NovT* 26 (1984): 59–82.

On Acts' presentation of Paul, see:

Lentz, John C., Jr. *Luke's Story of Paul.* SNTSMS 77. Cambridge: Cambridge University Press, 1993.

Pervo, Richard I. *Luke's Story of Paul.* Minneapolis: Fortress, 1990.

Porter, Stanley E. *Paul in Acts.* Peabody, MA: Hendrickson, 2001.

Vielhauer, Philipp. "On the 'Paulinism' in Acts." Pages 166–75 in *The Writings of St. Paul.* Ed. Wayne A. Meeks. New York: Norton, 1972.

PART 2

PAUL'S LETTERS

INTRODUCTION

In the midst of his dynamic life and far-flung ministry, Paul wrote a number of letters. Some of his contemporaries described his letters as "weighty and forceful" (2 Cor 10:10; cf. 2 Pet 3:15–16), which testifies to his skill at letter writing. Not all his letters have survived (see 1 Cor 5:9), but the New Testament does contain thirteen letters ascribed to Paul. The first nine letters in the corpus are addressed to congregations, the last four to individuals.

Our task in this part of the book is to work our way through the thirteen Pauline letters. As noted in the introduction, we will begin with 1–2 Thessalonians, sometimes dubbed "The Earliest [or Eschatological] Letters." We will then treat in turn: "The Chief or Capital Letters" (Galatians, 1 Corinthians, 2 Corinthians, Romans) in chapters 3–6; "The Captivity or Prison Letters" (Philippians, Philemon, Colossians, and Ephesians)" in chapters 7–9; and "The Pastoral Letters" (1 Timothy, 2 Timothy, Titus) in chapter 10. If you are familiar with the order of the New Testament documents, you recognize we have opted not to begin with the first text (Romans) and conclude with the last (Philemon). Rather, we have chosen to group the letters and to proceed in more or less a chronological order.

With each of Paul's letters we consider, we will:

1. situate the letter's vision — that is, place the text in its socio-historical context;
2. center the letter's vision — that is, discover what lies near the "nerve center" of the letter; and
3. track the letter's vision — that is, consider the letter's contents.

That we speak of the "vision" of a letter betrays our conviction that Paul's letters had (and have) something significant to communicate to those privileged to receive and read them.

To better "get" and "get around in" these invaluable letters, we offer a few introductory comments regarding the nature and structure of a Pauline letter.

Paul's letters are occasional. Paul wrote to particular people in particular places at a particular point in time about particular matters.

Paul's letters are pastoral. For the apostle, letter writing was not a perfunctory exercise. Rather, his letters served as a surrogate or substitute for his presence. He sought to tell churches on papyrus what he would have told them in person were he present. To say that Paul's letters are pastoral is not to suggest that the apostle was not interested in theology or ideas. He clearly was, but his concern was that of a pastoral theologian. He wanted to see people both grasp the faith and flourish in it.

Paul's letters are mixed in type.[1] Epistolary and rhetorical analyses of Paul's letters have shown them to be a thorough mixture of various types and species. Paul's occasional, pastoral letters do not fit neatly into any single epistolary genre.[2] They do frequently exhibit, however, features of both paraenetic letters (ones that exhort and advise) and friendly letters.

---

1. On this and the following point, see the accessible study of Patrick Gray, *Opening Paul's Letters: A Reader's Guide to Genre and Interpretation* (Grand Rapids: Baker Academic, 2012).
2. One ancient letter handbook, that of Demetrius, identifies twenty-one "types" of letters; another by Libanius specifies forty-one letter "styles." See further ibid., 41–42.

Nor do Paul's letters fit comfortably into any one species of the three types of ancient rhetoric:

- *judicial/forensic rhetoric* (used to convince an audience of the culpability or innocence of a person or a group of people with regard to a wrong done in the past);
- *epideictic/demonstrative rhetoric* (used to celebrate or denigrate people or ideas); and
- *deliberative/hortatory rhetoric* (used to exhort an audience to follow a particular course of action in the future).

Wikimedia Commons

▲ This painting by French artist Valentin de Boulogne (1591–1632) seeks to capture Paul as a letter writer.

Each of these rhetorical types is detectable in Paul's letters, often within the same letter, but no letter conforms perfectly to any one rhetorical type. The same is true of the three styles of argumentation set forth by Aristotle:

- *ethos* ("arguments drawn from the character of the speaker");
- *pathos* ("arguments [that] play on the emotions of the audience"); and
- *logos* ("arguments [that] rely primarily upon reason for their persuasive force").

Finally, *Paul's letters follow a basic structure.* Like other ancient letters, Paul's letters are comprised of an opening, a body, and a closing. Paul typically begins his letters with both a prescript (including the names of the senders, the recipients, and a salutation) and thanksgiving (2 Corinthians, Galatians, 1 Timothy, and Titus are exceptions). As he begins a letter, Paul will often touch on topics to which he will later return. It is in the body of the letter, however, where Paul does the "heavy lifting." Compared to other ancient letters, the body of Paul's letters is expansive. Within it Paul engages in both exposition (teaching an audience in the indicative mood) and exhortation (calling the audience to respond in the imperative mood). In concluding a letter, Paul typically extends a (1) wish-prayer, (2) greetings, and (3) benediction. On occasion, he draws attention to writing in his own hand (see esp. Gal 6:11). Paul can also use the letter closing to reiterate pressing matters within a letter.

With this brief excursus on the order, nature, and structure of Paul's letters behind us, we may now move on to consider those "weighty and forceful" letters themselves.

CHAPTER 2

1 AND 2 THESSALONIANS

CHAPTER GOALS

- To examine the issues that have primary impact on the study of 1–2 Thessalonians
- To highlight the central concerns and basic contents of these letters

CHAPTER OVERVIEW

1. Situating the Vision of 1 Thessalonians: First Things First
2. Centering the Vision of 1 Thessalonians: Perseverance, Purity, and Preparedness until the Parousia
3. Tracking the Vision of 1 Thessalonians: God's Word at Work
4. Situating the Vision of 2 Thessalonians: Take Two
5. Centering the Vision of 2 Thessalonians: "Do Not Let Anyone Deceive You in Any Way"
6. Tracking the Vision of 2 Thessalonians: Consolation and Correction for an Afflicted and Confused Church
7. The Authorship of 2 Thessalonians and Epistolary Pseudonymity
8. Concluding Remarks
9. Key People, Places, and Terms
10. Questions for Review and Discussion
11. Contemporary Theological Reflections
12. Going Further

KEY VERSES

First Thessalonians

1 Thessalonians 1:8–10: "The Lord's message rang out from you not only in Macedonia and Achaia—your faith in God has become known everywhere. Therefore we do not need to say anything about it, for they themselves report what kind of reception you gave us. They tell how you turned to God from idols to serve the living and true God, and to wait for his Son from heaven, whom he raised from the dead—Jesus, who rescues us from the coming wrath."

1 Thessalonians 2:7b–8: "Just as a nursing mother cares for her children, so we cared for you. Because we loved you so much, we were delighted to share with you not only the gospel of God but our lives as well."

1 Thessalonians 4:3–5: "It is God's will that you should be sanctified: that you should avoid sexual immorality; that each of you should learn to control your own body in a way that is holy and honorable, not in passionate lust like the pagans, who do not know God."

1 Thessalonians 4:13–14: "Brothers and sisters, we do not want you to be uninformed about those who sleep in death, so that you do not grieve like the rest of mankind, who have no hope. For we believe that Jesus died and rose again, and so we believe that God will bring with Jesus those who have fallen asleep in him."

1 Thessalonians 5:14–18: "And we urge you, brothers and sisters, warn those who are idle and disruptive, encourage the disheartened, help the weak, be patient with everyone. Make sure that nobody pays back wrong for wrong, but always strive to do what is good for each other and for everyone else. Rejoice always, pray continually, give thanks in all circumstances; for this is God's will for you in Christ Jesus."

Second Thessalonians

2 Thessalonians 1:3–4: "We ought always to thank God for you, brothers and sisters, and rightly so, because your faith is growing more and more, and the love all of you have for one another is increasing. Therefore, among God's churches we boast about your perseverance and faith in all the persecutions and trials you are enduring."

2 Thessalonians 2:1–3: "Concerning the coming of our Lord Jesus Christ and our being gathered to him, we ask you, brothers and sisters, not to become easily unsettled or alarmed by the teaching allegedly from us—whether by a prophecy or by word of mouth or by letter—asserting that the day of the Lord has already come. Don't let anyone deceive you in any way, for that day will not come until the rebellion occurs and the man of lawlessness is revealed, the man doomed to destruction."

2 Thessalonians 3:11–13: "We hear that some among you are idle and disruptive. They are not busy; they are busybodies. Such people we command and urge in the Lord Jesus Christ to settle down and earn the food they eat. And as for you, brothers and sisters, never tire of doing what is good."

"Weighty and forceful" (cf. 2 Cor 10:10) do not spring to mind when reading 1–2 Thessalonians. Nevertheless, these two Pauline letters pack their own appeal. In addition to most likely being the oldest of Paul's surviving letters, 1–2 Thessalonians showcase a caring apostle-pastor encouraging his converts to maintain and to mature in their newfound faith amid external opposition, congregational confusion, and ethical/social challenges. Although often overlooked or given short shrift, it is with these two early and interesting missives that we begin our investigation of Paul's thirteen-letter collection.

SITUATING THE VISION OF 1 THESSALONIANS: FIRST THINGS FIRST

The Arrival of the Gospel in Thessalonica

As Paul reflects on his ministry in **Thessalonica**, he recalls, "We [at least Paul and Silas] had previously suffered and been treated outrageously in Philippi, as you know, but with the help of our God we dared to tell you his gospel in the face of strong opposition" (1 Thess 2:2). What is more, Paul reports that those who eventually comprised the church in Thessalonica welcomed both the message and the messengers "in the midst of severe suffering" (1:6b) as they "turned to God from idols to serve the living and true God, and to wait for his Son from heaven" (1:9–10a).

These statements suggest the following regarding Paul's initial ministry in Thessalonica:

1. Paul and his coworkers, including **Silas or Silvanus** and perhaps **Timothy**, came to Thessalonica after having been "roughed up" in Philippi (cf. Acts 16:16–40; Phil 4:16).
2. Paul and his associates also faced strong opposition in Thessalonica.
3. This fact notwithstanding, the apostles courageously preached the gospel, which a number of Thessalonians readily received.

▲ Paul's travel route from Philippi to Thessalonica

▼ The image of Cassander, founder of Thessalonica, appears on this coin.

▲ This mosaic depicts Alexander the Great riding his horse Bucephalus. Cassander's wife Thessalonike was Alexander's stepsister.

4. The gospel that Paul and his fellow missioners declared to the Gentile Thessalonians entailed their turning to God from idols and hearing about the coming of God's risen Son from heaven.
5. Even as the apostles encountered opposition in proclaiming the gospel in Thessalonica, those who received the message were also opposed.

We will be able to fill out this picture further as we track the vision of the letter, but there are other matters that first require our attention.

The City of Thessalonica

Paul and his ministry companions undoubtedly traveled from Philippi to Thessalonica on the **Via Egnatia**.[1] As they traversed this roughly one-hundred-mile southwesterly trek, they passed through Amphipolis and Apollonia (see Acts 17:1).[2]

When they arrived in Thessalonica in the late 40s AD, they would have discovered a sizeable seaport city strategically located on the Thermaic Gulf with mountains to the north and fertile land to the west.[3] A city that has been in continuous existence since roughly 315 BC, Thessalonica was founded by **Cassander**, the son of Antipater. Cassander named the city after his wife Thessalonike, the daughter of Philip of Macedon and stepsister of Alexander the Great.

In Paul's day, Thessalonica was a "free city" under Roman rule. Among other privileges, this status afforded the city the luxury of governing itself, minting its own money, and

1. Regarding the Via Egnatia, see page 191.
2. On what such arduous travel might have entailed, see Jerome Murphy-O'Connor, "On the Road and on the Sea with St. Paul," *BRev* 1 (1985): 38–47.
3. Estimates regarding the city's population in the middle of the first century range from 40,000 to 100,000.

not having a Roman garrison within its walls.[4] Regarding the religious environment, there were, in Pauline parlance, multiple "idols." In addition to a flourishing imperial cult, it appears that Dionysus and Cabirus had a strong following. Zeus, Heracles, Apollo, Asclepius, Aphrodite, Athene, Serapis, Isis, and the Dioskuri also attracted devotees.[5] It also appears that there were a number of Jews residing in Thessalonica in the middle of the first century; Paul came into contact and conflict with some of them.

www.HolyLandPhotos.org

▲ Acts 17:6, 8 refer to the city authorities in Thessalonica as *politarchs*. The participial form of the verb meaning "to serve as a politarch" appears in the inscription pictured here. This so-called "Politarch Inscription," which dates to the mid-second century AD, was found in Thessalonica in the nineteenth century and is now housed in the British Museum.

Driven from the City, Orphaned from the Church

It is unclear how long Paul's founding visit to Thessalonica lasted. The following considerations suggest a period of several months, perhaps up to half a year:

- Paul forged meaningful, reciprocal relations with the Thessalonian fellowship (note esp. 1 Thess 2:8);
- Paul received aid from the Philippian congregation more than once while stationed in Thessalonica (Phil 4:16); and
- Paul "set up shop" and worked his trade as a leatherworker (1 Thess 2:9).

Whatever the duration of his stay, be it a number of months, as suggested above, or roughly a month, as suggested by some based on Acts 17:1–9 (esp. 17:2), it was not as long as the apostle had hoped. First Thessalonians 2:17–18 suggests as much. There Paul not only speaks of having been "orphaned by being separated" from the Thessalonians, but he also refers to his repeated, if unsuccessful, attempts to return to Thessalonica.

Acts 17:5–9 reports Paul was forced out by an uprising, begun by certain Thessalonian Jews, which was aimed at silencing his proclamation of "another king, one called Jesus" (17:7).[6] Paul may be referring to this event in 1 Thess 2:15, where he speaks of particular Jews who "drove us out."

Wikimedia Commons

▲ This statue of Zeus, the father of the gods and humanity and the ruler of the Olympians, is on display at the Louvre in Paris.

4. It appears that Thessalonica employed a Greek democratic model of government, including a popular assembly (the *dēmos*), a council (the *boulē*), and a group of magistrates (*politarchs*). According to Acts 17:5–9, the Thessalonian believer Jason, along with other unnamed believers, was dragged before the *politarchs* by an upset crowd.
5. On political and religious life in Thessalonica at the time of Paul, see more fully Todd D. Still, "Paul's Thessalonian Mission," *SwJT* 42 (1999): 4–16 (esp. 8–10).
6. On the sometimes politically provocative nature of Paul's gospel proclamation, see chapter 12 below.

▲ Dionysus, pictured here, was the god of the grape harvest and of ecstasy in Greek mythology.

It was Paul's forced, untimely separation from the church of the Thessalonians that prompted him to send Timothy to see how the fledgling fellowship was progressing in the faith (1 Thess 3:2). Paul was fearful that the believers there might become "unsettled" in their newfound faith because of the opposition they were experiencing at the hands of their unbelieving Gentile compatriots (2:14; 3:3, 5). At this point, Paul had moved from Thessalonica to **Athens** (3:1).[7] From there, he traveled on to Corinth, where Timothy brought to him the "good news about [the Thessalonians'] faith and love" (3:6).[8] Buoyed by Timothy's positive report, Paul composes the letter known to us as 1 Thessalonians (around AD 50). A majority of New Testament interpreters, including us, not only regard 1 Thessalonians to be Paul's earliest surviving letter but also think it to be the oldest surviving document in the entire New Testament.[9] It is to this Pauline and New Testament wellspring that we now turn.

CENTERING THE VISION OF 1 THESSALONIANS: PERSEVERANCE, PURITY, AND PREPAREDNESS UNTIL THE PAROUSIA

Near the center of the letter, Paul offers a wish-prayer for the Thessalonian believers (3:11 – 13), the conclusion of which captures his central concerns in this letter. Paul indicates his desire for God to "strengthen [their] hearts so that [they] will be blameless and holy in the presence of our God and Father when our Lord Jesus comes with all his holy ones" (3:13).

Paul's wish that the Thessalonians would be strengthened and encouraged in the faith prompted him to send Timothy to them in his stead (3:2). He was fearful that the afflictions they were experiencing would unsettle them and prompt them to abandon their

7. According to Acts 17, Paul and Silas move from Thessalonica to **Berea**, and then Paul left Berea alone to go to Athens. Those Jews who joined hands with others to force Paul out of Thessalonica are said to have forced him out of Berea as well.
8. See Acts 18:1 – 18 and chapter 4.
9. Some scholars regard both the Letter of James and Galatians to have been written prior to 1 Thessalonians. Although placed first in the New Testament canon, most scholars think that the canonical Gospels were written later, with Mark likely being the earliest, composed around AD 70.

commitment to serve the God to whom they had turned. Indeed, Paul was afraid that the "tempter" might tempt them and render his apostolic labor among them null and void (3:5).

Although the apostle was delighted about the assembly's initial reception of the gospel in the midst of severe suffering (1:6–9; 2:13) and could declare that the missioners' "visit to [them] was not without results" (2:1), he was simultaneously mindful that they were still vulnerable and needed to build spiritual muscles (3:10). While Paul was still in Thessalonica, he instructed them that they "would be persecuted" (3:4). To be told something, however, is one thing; to experience it is another. So Paul writes them a letter to serve as a surrogate and a salve.

The apostle also prayed that the Lord would strengthen the Thessalonians' hearts so that they would be "blameless and holy" (cf. 5:23, where Paul again expresses his desire that God

Sexuality in the Greco-Roman World

What Paul referred to as "sexual immorality" was common in Greco-Roman antiquity. For example, the Platonist philosopher Plutarch (about AD 46–120) instructed would-be brides to turn a blind eye to the sexual peccadillos of their husbands in order to preserve good relations with them (*Moralia* 104B, 144F). Male sexual entitlement is also clear from the remarks of Demosthenes, a fourth-century BC Athenian orator: "Mistresses we keep for our pleasure, concubines for our day-to-day well-being, and wives in order to bear us legitimate children and to serve as trustworthy guardians over our households" (*Orations* 59.122).

Sexual practice in Greco-Roman society was strongly linked to religious and political life, since sexuality and fertility were thought to be vital to a prosperous state. For this reason, prostitution was a widespread and legal phenomenon, often linked to temple worship. Little impeded the sexual impulses of an adult male Roman citizen. He was free to pursue sex with not only his wife but also prostitutes and any socially inferior woman so long as his actions did not offend his peers, that is, other Roman male citizens.

Although male homosexual activity often became fodder for slander, sex with males of inferior status was culturally acceptable. Pederasty was also acceptable as long as proper hierarchy was maintained. (Roman adult males were only to engage younger male partners if they were not free Romans.) The only operative sexual mores were that a male Roman citizen should always be the active partner, not showing any weakness, and that excess should be avoided.

Perceptions of female sexuality differed greatly, since the male-dominated culture objectified women and saw sexual pleasure only from the male perspective. Many exposed and abandoned babies (male and female) were taken into slavery for the sex trade. A female prostitute could not marry. If she did, she was not allowed to continue her business. Married women were expected to be faithful wives, although there were periods of cultural transition where women engaged in uncommon sexual libertinism.

Such movements were often related to certain cults. Some cults, like Bona Dea, were culturally legitimate. Their rites were closed to men, and the details are unknown. Others, like the Cabirus cult, may have taken their practices too far. These cults were often shut down for upsetting the status quo. In response to such movements, Augustus set forth legislation calling for appropriate behavior from Roman women.

Faith, Hope, and Love

The triad of faith, love, and hope appears on two occasions in 1 Thessalonians. In addition to 1:3, Paul calls the Thessalonians in 5:8 to put on "*faith* and *love* as a breastplate, and the *hope* of salvation as a helmet" (cf. Col 1:5). Elsewhere in Paul, love instead of hope appears as the final item in this threefold progression (see Rom 5:1 – 5; Gal 5:5 – 6), most famously in 1 Cor 13:13: "And now these three remain: faith, hope and love. But the greatest of these is love."

Is it possible that Paul ordered these Christian virtues in keeping with congregational needs? A strong argument can be made that this was at least the case in Thessalonica, where believers were in need of hope, and in Corinth, where the church was lacking in love.

"sanctify" and keep them "blameless"). Paul and his coworkers had commanded their Gentile converts in Thessalonica to "avoid sexual immorality" (Greek ***porneia***). Put positively, they called them to learn to control their own bodies (lit., "vessel") in a holy and honorable way (4:3–4). Furthermore, they warned them that the "Lord will punish all those who commit . . . sins" of sexual immorality (4:6b). Ironically, the Jewish apostle to the Gentiles taught his Gentile converts not to live in passionate lust like the Gentiles, who do not know God (4:5). He expected those who comprised the church of God, whether Jew or Greek, to lead exemplary moral lives and insisted that those who failed to live in keeping with such instruction were not guilty of rejecting a human being but God, the very God who gave to them his Holy Spirit (4:8).

If Paul is concerned about perseverance and purity in this letter, he is also committed to impressing on his converts the importance of moral preparedness for the Lord's ***parousia*** (Greek for "coming" or "arrival"). In fact, these concerns coalesce in the verse we are considering. Paul is praying that the Thessalonians will persevere so that they may be found pure in God's presence at the time of Christ's *parousia*.

The coming or *parousia* of the Lord Jesus is a recurring theme in 1 Thessalonians. It features at the conclusion of chapters 1, 2, 3, and 5.

- "You turned to God from idols to serve the living and true God, and to wait for his Son from heaven" (1:9b–10a).
- "For what is our hope, our joy, or the crown in which we will glory in the presence of our Lord Jesus when he comes? Is it not you?" (2:19).
- ". . . when our Lord Jesus comes with all his holy ones" (3:13).
- "May your whole spirit, soul and body be kept blameless at the coming of our Lord Jesus Christ" (5:23).

Moreover, the Lord's *parousia* is the subject of a significant swath of the letter (4:13–5:11). In addressing the Thessalonians' concern about those who have died in Christ, Paul assures them that those "who have fallen asleep in him" will not be left behind or disadvantaged at "the coming of the Lord" (4:14–15). Regarding the timing of his coming, Paul does not prognosticate; rather, he impresses on his converts the importance of preparedness. Regarding children of light and of the day, the day of the Lord (= the Lord's *parousia*) should not catch them by surprise (5:4–5). Until he comes, they are to lead lives of moral excellence and mutual encouragement (5:6, 11).

It would be a mistake to reduce 1 Thessalonians to some kind of Pauline eschatological primer. As important and prevalent a motif as it is, this most ancient of Paul's letters is about far more than perseverance, purity, and preparedness until the *parousia*, as we will now see.

TRACKING THE VISION OF 1 THESSALONIANS: GOD'S WORD AT WORK

Basic Outline[10]

1:1–10	Greeting and Thanksgiving
2:1–16	Paul's Recollection of His Ministry in Thessalonica
2:17–3:13	Paul's Protracted Separation from the Thessalonians
4:1–12	Reinforcing Ethical Instructions
4:13–5:11	Addressing Eschatological Concerns
5:12–22	Congregational Matters
5:23–28	Concluding the Letter

Greeting and Thanksgiving (1:1–10)

Paul commences the letter that one scholar cleverly, if anachronistically, describes as "the birth of the New Testament" with both a brief greeting (1:1) and an expansive thanksgiving (1:2–10).[11] The senders Paul, Silas, and Timothy greet the recipients ("the church of the Thessalonians"). In doing so, they situate the assembly (Greek *ekklēsia*) in "God the Father and the Lord Jesus Christ" and pronounce "grace and peace" on them.

Regarding 1:1, two comments are necessary. (1) Although the letter is sent by Paul, Silvanus, and Timothy, Paul is likely the principal author. This will become clearer as we read further (note esp. 2:18; 3:5) .

(2) We will encounter the greeting "grace and peace" time and again at the outset of Paul's letters.[12] It is commonly suggested that by linking "grace" with "peace" Paul conjoins both the customary Greek and Hebrew greetings—the Greek *chairein* or "greetings" (cf. Jas 1:1) modified as *charis* or "grace," and the Hebrew *shalom* or "peace." This may well be the case. It may also be that Paul employs the theologically rich terms "grace" and "peace" to create "liturgical space" for the reading and hearing of the letter (1 Thess 5:27).

Turning to the thanksgiving, the first of two in 1 Thessalonians (note also 2:13), we immediately encounter the Pauline pillars of faith, love, and hope.[13] In 1:2–3 Paul offers prayerful thanks to God for the Thessalonians' "work produced by *faith*, [their] labor prompted by *love*, and [their] endurance inspired by *hope* in [the] Lord Jesus Christ" (v. 3). There is a theological logic to this ordering of the triad (cf. esp. 1 Cor 13:13). Life in Christ *commences in faith, continues in love, and culminates in hope.*

Paul's recollection of the Thessalonians before God ("we remember," 1:3) leads him to reflect on the arrival of the gospel in Thessalonica. Due to their reception of the gospel, the

10. The outlines we offer in this and subsequent chapters are broad and thematic. More detailed outlines informed by epistolary and rhetorical analysis are both possible and desirable. Consult the various commentaries commended under the heading "Going Further" at the end of each chapter.
11. See Raymond F. Collins, *The Birth of the New Testament: The Origin and Development of the First Christian Centuries* (New York: Crossroad, 1993).
12. Following the order in which we will treat the letters in this text, see 2 Thess 1:2; Gal 1:3; 1 Cor 1:3; 2 Cor 1:2; Rom 1:7; Phil 1:2; Phlm 3; Col 1:2; Eph 1:2; Titus 1:4. Second and First Timothy (considered before Titus in ch. 10) insert "mercy" between "grace and peace," thereby forming the triad "grace, mercy and peace" (2 Tim 1:2; 1 Tim 1:2).
13. Cf. 1 Thess 5:8; also Rom 5:1–5; 1 Cor 13:13; Gal 5:5–6; Col 1:5.

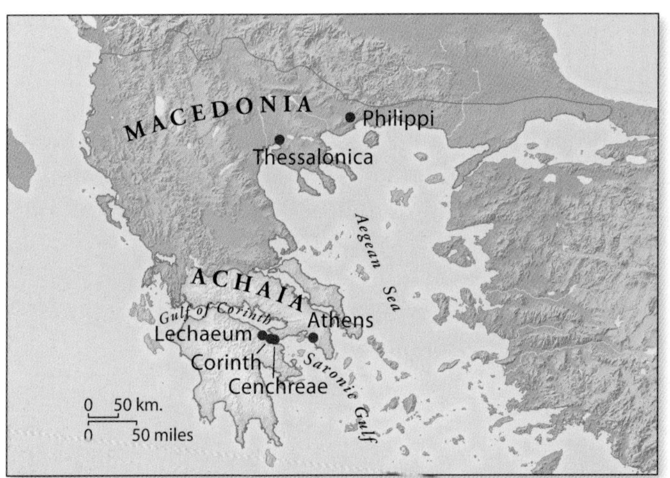

▲ This map shows the Roman provinces of Macedonia and Achaia and pinpoints certain strategic locales within each.

apostle is certain that his brothers and sisters in Thessalonica are loved by and have been chosen by God: "Our gospel came to you not simply with words but also with power, with the Holy Spirit and with deep conviction" (1:5a). Even as Paul recalls the Thessalonians' response to the missioners' proclamation, he reminds them of their way of life among the Thessalonians (1:5b) and how they became "imitators of [them] and of the Lord" by "welcoming [their] message in the midst of severe suffering with the joy given by the Holy Spirit" (1:6).

In so doing, the Thessalonians became an exemplary assembly, a "model" congregation for other believers living in Macedonia (northern mainland Greece, where Thessalonica lies) and in Achaia (southern Greece, from where Paul writes in Corinth; 1:7). From the Thessalonian fellowship, the Lord's word "rang out" like a trumpet. Their "faith in God" flooded Christian news networks in Macedonia, Achaia, and, hyperbolically speaking, "everywhere" (1:8a).

Paul reports with the pleasure of a proud parent how unspecified people were telling him about the missioners' ministry in Thessalonica (1:8b). He makes particular mention of the congregation's positive reception of the "preachers" and of the Thessalonians' conversion, which entailed turning to God, serving this "living and true God," and waiting "for his Son from heaven" (1:9–10). Verses 9–10 have sometimes been understood as a summation of the early church's gospel proclamation to Gentiles. While there are certainly aspects of the gospel that Paul and others propounded in this passage, there is good reason to wonder if this is a satisfactorily full summary of what was declared and embraced.

Paul's Recollection of His Ministry in Thessalonica (2:1–16)

Paul's reflection on the missioners' visit to Thessalonica continues in chapter 2. In 2:1–12 he takes pains to remind the Thessalonians of their ministry among them.[14] Opposition notwithstanding, Paul invites his converts to recall how he and his coworkers proclaimed the gospel boldly among them with demonstrable success (2:1–2). He then launches into a litany of what their ministry in Thessalonica was and was not. Paul declares that the missioners' appeal to the Thessalonians did not "spring from error or impure motives" (2:3). "On the contrary, we [spoke] as those approved by God to be entrusted with the gospel," he insists (2:4a). Furthermore, the apostle contends that while in Thessalonica he and his coworkers were not "trying to please people but God," did not "put on a mask to cover up greed," and "were not looking for praise from people" (2:4b–6). This collection of denials has prompted some people, including us, to think that Paul composed this passage,

14. Note "you know" in 2:1, 2, 5, and 11 as well as "you remember" in 2:9 and "you are witnesses" in 2:10.

at least in part, in response to reported accusations that were being hurled in his direction.[15]

Instead of being slick-talking, people-pleasing, glory-seeking charlatans driven by greed and gain, theirs was a sincere, sacrificial ministry in Thessalonica. In 2:7–12 Paul employs a number of metaphors to capture the nature and character of their Thessalonian mission. Although they could have flexed their apostolic muscles and "asserted [their] authority," they became as *babes* (NIV, "young children"; 2:6c–7a).[16] Indeed, they carried out their ministry with the care of *a nursing mother* (or "wet nurse"). Compelled by love, "we were delighted to share with you not only the gospel of God but our lives as well" (2:8).

Far from making demands and holding out their hands, they "worked night and day [at their trade] in order not to be a burden" (2:9). The Thessalonian believers were witnesses to their commendable behavior as they bore winsome witness (2:10). Their paternal care ("like a *father*") was evident as they dealt with their "*children*," who were also their "*brothers and sisters*" (2:9, 11).

▲ This woodcut by French artist Paul Gustave Doré (1832–1888) seeks to capture Paul's proclamation to the Thessalonians.

Setting aside familial metaphors, at least for the time being (note "were orphaned" in 2:17), Paul enters into another "thanksgiving unit" in 2:13. Here, he again thanks God for the Thessalonians' reception of the gospel as "the word of God" and not merely a human word. As earlier in 1:5–6, Paul links the assembly's embrace of the gospel with suffering. In 2:14, however, he adds an additional wrinkle by comparing the Thessalonian congregation to Judean churches. The Thessalonians "became imitators of God's churches in Judea

15. In other words, we are convinced that 2:1–12 has an apologetic as well as a paraenetic function. Paul is not only commending himself and his companions to the Thessalonians as spiritual models, but he is also, perhaps primarily, defending himself and his coworkers against a smear campaign that has arisen in Thessalonica subsequent to his untimely departure (likely reported to Paul by Timothy). Paul insists that he and his coworkers are not opportunistic hucksters masquerading as third-rate philosophers. Rather, they were and are courageous, conscientious ministers who care deeply for the well-being of the assembly.

16. There is some debate whether the Greek text in 2:7 is best read *nēpioi* ("babes, young children") or *ēpioi* ("gentle"). Regardless, the ministerial character and commitments of Paul and his coworkers stand in stark contrast to egocentric, authoritarian models of leadership.

▲ An icon of Paul's beloved and trusted coworker Timothy

. . . in Christ Jesus" by virtue of their having "suffered from [their] own people the same things that those churches suffered from [certain] Jews." Would that we knew more about the origin and the nature of such suffering.

Paul makes it clearer in 2:15 which "Jews" he has in mind. He only has in view here those particular "Jews who killed the Lord Jesus and the prophets and also drove us out." This is not a blanket indictment of Jews or Jewry; indeed, Jesus and his earliest followers were Jewish, as was Paul himself. Paul then launches a polemical attack on those given Jews "who displease God and are hostile to everyone" by hindering him and his companions "from speaking to the Gentiles so that they may be saved" (2:15–16a). By so doing, Paul maintains, they stockpile sins and invite/incite divine wrath (2:16b-c).

Paul's vituperative outburst against certain Jews in 2:15–16 has troubled contemporary interpreters, so much so that some regard 2:13–16 or portions thereof to be a later scribal insertion, a so-called interpolation.[17] Given that there is not a shred of manuscript evidence to support this view, it is likely that Paul composed this passage at a time when he felt that his Jewish compatriots were impeding his mission of taking the gospel to the nations.[18] Far from a final indictment, 1 Thess 2:15–16 reveals the apostle's frustration with certain Jews who in their opposition to the apostle and the advance of the gospel found themselves, in Paul's perspective and in Lukan parlance, "fighting against God" (Acts 5:39). It may well be—as was clearly the case with Jesus in Jerusalem—that certain influential Jews were colluding with Roman civic authorities in an effort to impede Paul and his mission.

Paul's Protracted Separation from the Thessalonians (2:17–3:13)

If 1 Thess 2:15–16 constitutes a polemical aside, in 2:17 Paul returns to his rehearsal of his relationship with the Thessalonians. The apostle wants them to realize his deep-seated desire to see

17. So similarly 1 Cor 14:33b–36. See further shapter 4.
18. As it happens, Acts reports that certain Jews opposed Paul in both Thessalonica (to where he was writing) and Corinth (from where he was writing). See Acts 17:5–9 (cf. 17:13) and 18:5–6, 12–17.

them again. His having been orphaned from them, albeit for a short amount of time, created an "intense longing" in him to be reunited. Despite repeated attempts, the apostle was unable to return to Thessalonica (2:17–18a). Somehow "Satan blocked" the way and precluded Paul from reconnecting with the Thessalonian church—his "hope," "joy," and "crown" (2:18b–20).

Given this disappointing turn of events, Paul and his companions, when they were no longer able to cope with not knowing how the Thessalonians were faring in the faith in the face of ongoing affliction, "thought it best to be left by [themselves] in Athens" and to send Timothy as an emissary to the assembly (3:1–2). Timothy's remit was to "strengthen and encourage" the Thessalonians in their newfound faith, lest they be unsettled and moved away by the tempter (3:3–5).

Timothy's return and positive report regarding the Thessalonians' faith and love was a great relief and source of encouragement for Paul. His well-being was inextricably linked to theirs (3:6–8). Their "standing firm in the Lord" brought Paul great joy and kindled in him an even greater desire to see them again and to supply what still was lacking in their fledgling faith (3:9–10). Meanwhile, Paul prays that: (1) "our God and Father himself and our Lord Jesus [will] clear the way for us to come to you" (3:11); (2) "the Lord [will] make your love increase and overflow for each other and for everyone else" (3:12); and (3) "[God] may strengthen your hearts" (3:13).

Reinforcing Ethical Instructions (4:1–12)

Having rehearsed and reinforced relations with the Thessalonians, the apostle now turns his attention to "other matters." More specifically, he reminds the assembly that he had instructed them how they ought to live so as to please God. Even though Paul is pleased with their ethical progress, he wants them to continue to grow "more and more" (4:1–2).

In 4:3–12, Paul takes up three topics about which he had previously instructed the Thessalonians in person—sexual purity, brotherly/sisterly love, and civic responsibility. The apostle's aim is transparent—to reinforce that which the assembly already knows and is more or less practicing so that they can "do so more and more" (4:10).

In 4:3–8 Paul reiterates that God's will for the Thessalonians is sexual sanctification. What might this entail?

- avoiding sexual immorality (Greek *porneia*) (4:3);
- controlling their own bodies (lit., "vessel"; Greek *skeuos*) (4:4–5);[19] and
- not wronging or taking advantage of a fellow believer along these lines (4:6a).

It is probable that the Jewish apostle faced a considerable challenge in shaping the sexual scruples of his Gentile converts in Thessalonica and elsewhere.[20] So, he says to them again:

- "The Lord will punish those who commit such sins" (4:6).
- "God did not call us to be impure, but to live a holy life" (4:7).

19. The meaning of *skeuos* in 4:4 is debated. The term *skeuos* ("vessel") is metaphorical. But for what does it stand? Some interpreters render the word "wife." Others, including us, think "body" (perhaps used euphemistically for genitalia) is more likely.
20. This was clearly the case in Corinth. See chapter 4.

- "Anyone who rejects this instruction does not [only] reject a human being but God, the very God who gives you his Holy Spirit" (4:8).[21]

In 4:9–11 Paul continues to address the moral beliefs and behavior of the Thessalonians. With respect to the assembly's commitment to and practice of *philadelphia* (lit., "brotherly love"), the apostle is pleased. Given that the Thessalonians "have been taught by God to love each other" and "do love all of God's family throughout Macedonia," Paul could have dispensed with addressing the matter altogether. By urging the fellowship to practice *philadelphia* "more and more," however, the apostle is able simultaneously to encourage and challenge the assembly.

Before shifting his focus from the ethical to the eschatological, Paul again instructs his converts to:

- "make it [their] ambition to lead a quiet life";[22]
- "mind [their] own business;" and
- "work with [their] hands" (4:11).

By so doing, they may well "win the respect of outsiders." Moreover, they "will not need to dependent on anybody" (4:12). Given the Thessalonians' tense relations with their neighbors because of their conversion and commitment to Christ Jesus, this "code of conduct" makes good sense. "Be productive, not provocative," Paul says. "Be busy, but do not be a busybody," the apostle opines. "This will both enhance social relations and strengthen the congregation," he maintains.

"Tomb markers often carried epitaphs and are a major source of surviving inscriptions. All possible moods in the face of death are reflected. The epitaphs repeatedly emphasize the fact of death, although some feign indifference or trivialize it. The formula 'I was not, I was, I am not, I care not' was common enough that the Latin was simply abbreviated N F F N S N C (*non fui, fui, non sum, non curo*)."[24]

Addressing Eschatological Concerns (4:13–5:11)

If Paul devotes 4:3–12 to reiterating and reinforcing ethical instruction the Thessalonians have already received, in 4:13–18 he sets forth additional instruction for his converts regarding the destiny of their brothers and sisters in Christ who have died.[23] The purpose of such instruction is not to sate their eschatological curiosities; on the contrary, Paul's aim in offering further teaching concerning the end of time is to comfort them (4:18). He wants them to be more fully informed (= not ignorant, Greek *agnoein*) so that they might not grieve like the rest of humanity, that is, non Jesus-followers, who have no hope (4:13).

---

21. Paul commences and concludes his instruction on sexual morality with an emphasis on holiness. The term *sanctification* or *holiness* (Greek *hagiasmos*) occurs in 4:3, and the word *hagios* ("holy") modifies Spirit (Greek *pneuma*) in 4:8.
22. The teaching is oxymoronic: "Be ambitious not to be ambitious."
23. Paul does not indicate either the number or the cause(s) of these deaths. Although some scholars have speculated that they were martyred, the text does not indicate as much.
24. Everett Ferguson, *Backgrounds of Early Christianity* (3rd ed.; Grand Rapids: Eerdmans, 2003), 248.

How does Paul seek to console his converts regarding their deceased loved ones in Christ? He begins with a common confession resulting in a shared conviction: "For we believe that Jesus died and rose again, and so we believe that God will bring with Jesus those who have fallen asleep in him" (4:14). To this shared belief the apostle adds additional information emanating from a "word of the Lord." Paul does not pause to indicate how and from where he received this word (cf. 1 Cor 11:23). Moreover, the precise nature of this word is not entirely clear. It does appear, however, to have included at least the following core message: believers who are still alive when Christ returns will by no means (in Greek the emphatic negation *ou mē*) be given priority over "those who have fallen asleep" (4:15).[26]

"Living in the imminence of Christ's return is the privilege and the proper stance toward life of every generation of Christians."[25]

Paul proceeds in 4:16–17 to offer a picture of what will occur at the Lord's *parousia*.

- "The Lord himself will come down from heaven, with a loud command, with the voice of the archangel and with the trumpet call of God."
- "The dead in Christ will rise first."
- "We who are still alive and are left will be caught up together with them in the clouds to meet the Lord in the air."
- "We [believers whether living or deceased] will be with the Lord forever [subsequent to his coming]."

▼ Michelangelo painted his famed fresco "The Last Judgment" on the altar wall of the Sistine Chapel in Vatican City. It took him four years to complete this masterpiece.

Wikimedia Commons

At least three interpretive comments are necessary here.

1. Paul thought and taught that Jesus *might* well come during his lifetime (note "we who are still alive" in 4:15, 17). That being said, he can also place himself among the living or the dead at the time of the Lord's coming (see "whether we are awake or asleep" in 5:10).
2. Paul depicts Jesus' coming in terms of an ancient ruler's state visit and arrival.

25. E. E. Ellis, *Pauline Theology: Ministry and Society* (Grand Rapids: Eerdmans, 1989), 17 n. 45.
26. In 4:13–18, sleep is a euphemism for death (cf. 1 Thess 5:6–7). That being said, "sleep" suggests rest and signals that believers who have died are under God's watchful eye and in God's providential care (cf. Acts 7:60).

Roman Peace and Security

"The Romans actively and aggressively promoted themselves as those who secured the prized benefit of 'peace' and also, though to a lesser degree, the related blessing of 'security.' The gospel or good news about the *Pax Romana* was spread through a variety of public media. Given the widespread nature of this propaganda, the predominantly Gentile believers in Thessalonica would have immediately recognized in Paul's brief phrase, 'Peace and security' . . . the sloganeering of the Roman state and its claim of providing for its citizens the same two benefactions highlighted by the apostle."[28]

▼ This stone relief depicts a customer in Roman Gaul buying a jug of wine at a bar to take away.

Wine merchant, relief, Roman, 2nd century/Museo della Civilta Romana, Rome, Italy/Roger-Viollet, Paris/The Bridgeman Art Library

3. For Paul, the rapture will occur in conjunction with Christ's coming at the culmination of human history (see again 4:17).[27] The apostle did not envision "rapture" for believers prior to a protracted period of tribulation. Such a message would have seemed both senseless and disingenuous to Thessalonian believers, who were experiencing severe suffering at the hands of outsiders.

Whereas 4:13–18 considers Christ's coming from the perspective of the dead in Christ, 5:1–11 instructs living brothers and sisters regarding "the day of the Lord" (= *parousia*). With respect to the timing of the Lord's coming ("times and dates"), Paul maintains that there is "no need to write to [them], for [they] know very well that the day of the Lord will come like a thief in the night" (5:1–2; cf. Matt 24:43–44/Luke 12:38–39). Not only will the day come unexpectedly like a thief, it will come suddenly "as labor pains on a pregnant woman." For those who are not prepared, the day of the Lord will be a day of judgment. "**Peace and security**," perhaps a Roman imperial slogan that Paul here regards as foolish, will give way to destruction (5:3; cf. 1:10).

Believers, however, ought not to be caught off guard. As children of light and day as opposed to night and darkness, the day of the Lord should come as no surprise. Until that day, however, they are to be wakeful and sober. Slumber and drunkenness are nocturnal activities that are incongruent with their new identity (5:4–7).

As those belonging to the day, they are to don "faith and love as a breastplate, and the hope of salvation as a helmet," being mindful all the while that God's goal for them is salvation, not wrath (5:8–9). The death of the Lord Jesus Christ "for us" enables believers, be they "awake" or "asleep" (i.e., living or dead), to "live together with him" (5:10). Given Paul's ethical and eschatological instruction, the Thessalonians were arguably in a prime position to continue to "encourage one another and build each other up" (5:11).

27. The Greek term (*harpazein*) rendered "caught up" in 4:17 is translated by *rapio* in Latin, from where the English word "rapture" is derived.

28. Jeffrey A. D. Weima, "'Peace and Security' (1 Thess 5.3): Prophetic Warning or Political Propaganda?" *NTS* 58 (2012): 358.

Congregational Matters (5:12–22)

Before concluding the letter, Paul addresses issues that impact the Thessalonians' life together. He begins with the matter of congregational leadership. In particular he implores the "brothers and sisters to acknowledge [or respect] those who work hard among you, who care for you in the Lord and admonish you" (5:12). Not only are leaders to be respected, but they are also to be held in "in the highest regard in love because of their work" (5:13). Peace should prevail among those who serve the "God of peace" (5:23).

Even as believers are to be appreciative of and responsive to congregational leaders, they are also to be committed to each other's well-being (5:14–15). They are to warn the unruly, "encourage the disheartened, help the weak, be patient with everyone" (5:14). Far from marginalizing and ignoring those with needs among them, they are to be one another's keepers. Forgoing retaliation ("pay[ing] back wrong for wrong"), they are to pursue "what is good for each other and for everyone else" (5:15). Such conduct is consistent with the life and ministry of the Lord Jesus.

"No man is an island, entire of itself; every man is a piece of the continent, a part of the main . . . any man's death diminishes me, because I am involved in mankind; and therefore never send to know for whom the bell tolls; it tolls for thee."[29]

Additional instruction follows in 5:16–22 regarding congregational comportment and commitments. In what may be the best-known portion of 1 Thessalonians, Paul enjoins the assembly to "rejoice always, pray continually, give thanks in all circumstances." To do so is "God's will for you in Christ Jesus" (5:16–18). God wants believers to be joyful, prayerful, and thankful. These are marks of Christ's rule and reign amid the nitty-gritty realities of life.

Paul rounds out his instruction of the Thessalonians' congregational life in 5:19–22 with five succinct, yet significant, commands. He begins with two things they are *not* meant to do: "quench [or extinguish] the Spirit" or "treat prophecies with contempt" (5:19–20). Perhaps they could put out the Spirit's fire by discounting prophecies (i.e., Spirit-inspired utterances). The assembly, however, is not to be spiritually gullible. They are to "test" all prophecies and not merely presume that all who declare, "Thus sayeth the Lord," are correct (5:21a). What is and is not from God can be discerned by what is "good" and "evil." The "good" is to be embraced, while the "evil" is to be jettisoned (5:21b–22).

Concluding the Letter (5:23–28)

As Paul prepares to close the letter, he fashions another wish-prayer for the Thessalonians (5:23–24; cf. 3:11–13). He prays that the "God of peace" will "sanctify them through and through" so that every fiber of their being ("spirit, soul and body") might "be kept [and found] blameless at the coming of our Lord Jesus Christ" (5:23). Far from a "human improvement program," it is the faithful Lord who will enable them to be faithful until he comes (5:24).

At this point, Paul winds down his letter with two requests, a command, and a well-wish. First of all, he requests prayer (5:25). What he does for them, he asks of them. He also tells the assembly to greet one another with a "holy kiss." The adjective "holy" is key here.

29. John Donne, "Meditation XVII," in *Devotions upon Emergent Occasions* (1624).

SuperStock

© 1995 by Phoenix Data Systems

▲ Paul most likely wrote 1 and 2 Thessalonians from Corinth around AD 50. The picture displayed here features the Acrocorinth in the background along with various ruins of ancient Corinth in the foreground.

◀ Peter and Paul sharing a "holy kiss" prior to their purported martyrdoms. Because believers sometimes failed to keep holy the "sacred kiss," later church leaders sometimes forbade men and women to greet one another in this manner. See, for example, the third-century AD text the *Apostolic Tradition* 18.2–4.

Prior to extending "grace" to the assembly (5:28), Paul issues one final, solemn imperative. "Before the Lord," he charges the church "to have this letter read to all the brothers and sisters" (5:27). With widespread illiteracy in antiquity and a single copy of the letter, reading it aloud in the context of a worship gathering would not only be desirable or advisable; it would be essential. With this, Paul concludes his "experiment in Christian writing."[30]

SITUATING THE VISION OF 2 THESSALONIANS: TAKE TWO

For the time being, let us presuppose that Paul composed 2 Thessalonians subsequent to 1 Thessalonians. Some scholars suggest that Paul wrote the letter we know as 2 Thessalonians prior to writing what we refer to as 1 Thessalonians. Although this is conceivable because Paul's letters are arranged for the most part according to descending order of length and did not come with titles like "1 Thessalonians" and "2 Thessalonians," we do not think it likely that he would write a letter like 1 Thessalonians after 2 Thessalonians. Few interpreters do. Contemporary Pauline specialists commonly suggest, however, that Paul may not have even written 2 Thessalonians. We will consider this matter, along with issue of **pseudonymity**, as we conclude this chapter.

For now, the following question will occupy our attention: What prompted Paul to compose 2 Thessalonians? We regard the following scenario to be the most plausible one. Not long after Paul composed 1 Thessalonians (around AD 50), he received a report (from

30. So Helmut Koester, "1 Thessalonians—Experiment in Christian Writing," in *Continuity and Discontinuity in Church History: Essays Presented to G. H. Williams* (ed. F. F. Church and Timothy George; Leiden: Brill, 1979), 33–44.

Timothy [or another envoy] upon return to Paul in Corinth?) that things had taken a turn for the worse in Thessalonica. This unfavorable report (contrast the "glad tidings" that gave rise to 1 Thessalonians) appears to have included at least the following three items, each of which Paul seeks to address/redress in the letter.

- The affliction the congregation was experiencing at the hands of outsiders was continuing and perhaps escalating (2 Thessalonians 1).
- There was growing eschatological confusion in the church (2 Thessalonians 2).
- By refusing to work, some within the assembly were proving to be disruptive (2 Thessalonians 3).

This second letter, we gather, was written in relatively close proximity to the first, perhaps even within the same calendar year (AD 50?).

CENTERING THE VISION OF 2 THESSALONIANS: "DO NOT LET ANYONE DECEIVE YOU IN ANY WAY"

Chief among the apostle's concerns when composing 2 Thessalonians was the erroneous claim "that the day of the Lord [had] already come" (2:2). It appears that Paul did not know how and from whom this message had arisen. Perhaps certain Thessalonians with a heightened expectation of the *parousia* while in the throes of affliction misappropriated certain aspects of Paul's previous oral and/or written instruction and equated a now unknown, external calamity with the commencement of the day of the Lord. Regardless of the precise origin of and reason for the claim, the apostle is anxious to counter it, for he is fearful that this erroneous eschatological message might unsettle and even undo the fledgling fellowship. Indeed, he devotes over one-third of the letter seeking to calm, correct, and redirect his Thessalonian brothers and sisters regarding the Lord's coming.

Even as there may have been some correlation between the assembly's protracted afflictions and the intense eschatological expectations plaguing it, it may also be that eschatology played a large role in prompting some within the assembly (the so-called *ataktoi* or "disorderly ones," 1 Thess 5:14) to dispense with work. Perhaps they reasoned that if Jesus' coming were right around the chronological corner, then they did not need to bother with something as inconsequential and temporal as work. Paul will have a fair bit to say about and to these folks near the conclusion of the letter (3:6–15). Indeed, it is the other major issue dealt with in 2 Thessalonians.

TRACKING THE VISION OF 2 THESSALONIANS: CONSOLATION AND CORRECTION FOR AN AFFLICTED AND CONFUSED CHURCH

Basic Outline

1:1–10	Introduction
2:1–12	Eschatological Turmoil and Apostolic Instruction
2:13–3:5	Renewed Thanksgiving and Prayer
3:6–15	Dealing with the Disorderly
3:16–18	Conclusion

▲ This miniature from a twelfth-century illuminated manuscript envisions God surrounded by seraphim.

Introduction (1:1 – 10)

Second Thessalonians commences much as 1 Thessalonians did. "Paul, Silas, and Timothy" address a letter to "the church of the Thessalonians" and extend to the assembly "grace and peace" (1:1 – 2). An expansive thanksgiving follows (1:2 – 10). The missioners indicate that they sense an obligation to God to give thanks for the Thessalonians because of their growing faith and increasing love (1:3). They also report how they boast about the Thessalonians to other congregations because of their steadfast fidelity amid persecution and affliction (1:4).

Far from being inconsequential, Paul regards their steadfastness in the face of suffering for the "kingdom of God" as "evidence that God's judgment is right" (1:5). The apostle contends: "God is just: He will pay back trouble for those who trouble you" (1:6). Tables will turn when the Lord Jesus comes. On that day there will be, on the one hand, punishment (here depicted as "everlasting destruction" and exclusion from the Lord's presence) from God for those who do not know God or obey the gospel (1:8 – 9); on the other hand, God will extend rest to the beleaguered Thessalonian believers (1:7).

Given the Thessalonians' trying, tenuous situation, their apostles pray that God will make them "worthy of his calling" and will empower them both to desire and to do deeds that are good and faithful (1:11). Such prayers are prompted by the missioners' desire for the Lord's glory and grace to be made manifest in the Thessalonians' midst (1:12).

Eschatological Turmoil and Apostolic Instruction (2:1 – 12)

Having sought to offer believers a balm in chapter 1, Paul turns in chapter 2 to address again (remember the first letter) "the coming [*parousia*] of our Lord Jesus Christ and our being gathered to him" (2:1). The apostle is acutely concerned that the assembly not "become easily unsettled or alarmed" by communication that is filtering through the congregation, "asserting that the day of the Lord has already come" (2:2). Whatever the medium ("spirit" [*pneuma*], "word" [*logos*], or "letter" [*epistolē*]), the message is wrong! Therefore, Paul instructs, "Don't let anyone deceive you in any way" (2:3).

Paul propounds, as he had done previously (2:5), that prior to the *parousia* "the rebellion" will occur and the "**man of lawlessness**," who is "doomed to destruction," will be revealed (2:3). Who is this "man" who will seek to establish himself as God? Beyond the sketchy details provided in 2:4 (he will "oppose" God, exalt himself, and take a seat in "God's temple"), Paul does not say. Interpreters, however, have had plenty to say regarding this anti-God figure and the future. Students of Scripture should certainly read and study *scholarly* commentaries on this passage and inform themselves of interpretive options, which have ranged from Roman emperors, to popes, to church reformers, to contemporary political and theological figures and movements. Truth be told, however, it is now impossible to say with surety what Paul meant when speaking of "the apostasy" and "the man of lawlessness."

The same is true with respect to what or who is holding back the man of lawlessness "so that he may be revealed at the proper time" (2:6). Again, interpretive suggestions regarding the identity of what or who is restraining "the man doomed to destruction" are legion (not to mention mind-boggling and sometimes entertaining!). They include:

- the Roman Empire as personified in the Caesar;
- the Jewish state;
- the principle of law and order;
- God and his power;
- the Holy Spirit;
- the proclamation of the gospel by Christian missionaries, particularly Paul;
- an angelic figure restraining evil until the gospel has been preached to all nations;
- Satan; and
- a force and person hostile to God.

Wikimedia Commons

▲▼ Temples were omnipresent in Greco-Roman antiquity. "Herod's temple" in Jerusalem was one of the most renowned and resplendent. The paintings displayed here seek to reconstruct this remarkable temple and its destruction by the Romans in AD 70.

Illustration from 'The Life of Christ', c.1886–94, Tissot, James Jacques Joseph/Brooklyn Museum of Art, New York, USA/The Bridgeman Art Library

Wikimedia Commons

▲ First-century painting of fruit found at Pompeii. In 2 Thess 2:13, Paul describes the Thessalonian believers as "firstfruits."

When faced with the interpretive conundrum that is 2 Thess 2:6–7 (especially the identity of the **restraining force** [*to katechon*] or **restrainer** [*ho katechōn*]), Augustine admitted, "I frankly confess that I do not know what [Paul] means."[31] We do well to join his company.

Even though the nature of the apostasy and the respective identities of the lawless one, the restraining force or restrainer, and "the secret power of lawlessness" (2:7) are now lost on us (as they also were on the Thessalonians [2:5]!), in the final analysis these issues mattered little to Paul. Perhaps such things were as opaque to him as his remarks regarding them now are to us. In any event, when the "lawless one" in collusion with Satan does come, he will "use all sorts of displays of power . . . and all the ways that wickedness deceives those who are perishing" (2:9–10a). Yet, in the words of Luther, "one single word shall fell him," as the lawless one's revelation will be brought to naught by the presence and power of the Lord Jesus at his *parousia* (2:8).

If outsiders who have refused to believe and love the truth subsequently buy the lie and are swept away by such a sinister spiritual charade (2:10–12), this ought not to be the case with the Thessalonians, who have been duly instructed by the apostle both "by word of mouth and by letter" (2:5, 15b). The brothers and sisters, then, are to "stand firm and hold fast to the teachings [or traditions]" (2:15a). In 2:13–15 Paul again offers thanks to God for his beloved Thessalonians (see 1:3–4). He is grateful to God for having chosen the Thessalonians as "firstfruits"[32] (i.e., among the first converts; see also 1 Cor 15:20) and for having called them through the gospel. The apostle is also prayerful (see again 1:11–12) that the Lord Jesus Christ and God the Father will "encourage [their] hearts and strengthen [them] in every good deed and word" (2:16–17).

With respect to prayer, the apostle requests that the assembly be in prayer "that the message of the Lord may spread rapidly and be honored, just as it was with [them]" (3:1). Additionally, he requests that they pray that he and his coworkers might "be delivered from wicked and evil people, for not everyone has faith" (3:2; cf. Rom 15:31). This fact

31. Augustine, *City of God* 20.19.

32. Although a number of textual witnesses read "from the beginning" (*ap' archēs*) instead of "firstfruits" (*aparchēn*), we concur with the decision of the NIV to read *archēs*. See also Bruce M. Metzger, *A Textual Commentary on the Greek New Testament* (2nd ed.; New York: United Bible Societies, 1994), 568.

notwithstanding, Paul assures them that the "Lord is faithful, and he will strengthen you and protect you from the evil one" (3:3). An expression of confidence in the Thessalonians (3:4) leads to another wish-prayer for the Thessalonians — that they will be directed "into God's love and Christ's perseverance" (3:5).

Dealing with the Disorderly (3:6 – 15)

At this point the letter takes an unexpected turn, as commendation gives way to command. As the tone shifts from friendly to forceful, the Thessalonians are enjoined to steer clear of every believer "who is idle and disruptive" (an interpretive gloss for *ataktōs*, lit., "unruly, disorderly") and not in keeping with the traditions (3:6; cf. 2:15). Paul appeals to the missioners' example during their ministry in the city. They were not idle, nor did they eat bread for which they did not pay (3:7 – 8a; cf. 1 Thess 2:9). Instead, they worked night and day so as not to burden the congregation (3:8b). Despite having the right to be supported in the gospel, they did not exercise this right so that they might leave the assembly with an example to follow (3:9; cf. 1 Cor 9:3 – 18; 1 Thess 2:6). The "rule" they offered the fellowship when with them was this: "The one who is unwilling to work shall not eat" (3:10).

It is not until Paul is well into this section of seemingly extraneous instruction that he offers an explanation for it. He has learned that there were those in the congregation who were living *ataktōs* (NIV, "idle and disruptive"; cf. 1 Thess 5:14). Instead of being busy (i.e., working), they were being "busybodies" (that is, gadding about; 3:11). In 3:12 he addresses "such people" directly, commanding and urging them in Christ "to settle down and earn the food they eat" (cf. 1 Thess 4:11 – 12).

Meanwhile, he encourages the rest of the assembly to:

- "never tire of doing what is good" (3:13; cf. Gal 6:9 – 10);
- "take special note of anyone who does not obey our instruction in this letter"; and
- "do not associate with them, in order that they may feel ashamed" (3:14).

That being said, the assembly is not to view the disorderly and disobedient as enemies; rather, they are to warn them as fellow believers (3:15; cf. 1 Cor 5:1 – 12).

Whether the "work stoppage" among some Thessalonians was spawned by eschatological extremism and/or social patterns, Paul perceives and responds to it as a significant congregational problem. In addition to being out of sync with the apostles' example, such unruly behavior was creating tension within the congregation and perhaps in the broader community as well. Instead of sponging off of other believers, Paul calls these "busybodies" to recall his model and to reform their ways.

It is likely that Paul's instructions about being willing to work in order to eat and about not associating with those who do not obey strike some of us as less than gracious. We do well to remember, however, how fragile and close-knit this band of believers was (Did they share most every meal together?) and how deeply Paul wanted to see them not only survive but thrive. With considerable opposition from without, the last thing the Thessalonians needed was unproductive division from within. It is worth pondering how much we care about the well-being of the communities of which we are a part and how we seek to convey such care.

Conclusion (3:16–18)

As Paul concludes the letter, he offers one further wish-prayer: "Now may the Lord of peace himself give you peace at all times and in every way. The Lord be with all of you" (3:16). Paul then signs off on the letter he has composed, drawing attention to his "greeting in [his] own hand" (3:17). He may well have done such here to authenticate and differentiate this letter and the letter purportedly from him (2:2). As with the salutation, the "benediction" of 2 Thessalonians is almost identical to 1 Thessalonians. Paul extends the grace of the Lord Jesus Christ to the church. Given their external and internal struggles, they certainly were in need of grace. So also are we.

THE AUTHORSHIP OF 2 THESSALONIANS AND EPISTOLARY PSEUDONYMITY

In our treatment of 2 Thessalonians above, we have presumed that Paul wrote the letter. This is, in fact, our view. We noted, however, as we began our study of this letter, that many of our academic colleagues do not agree. In fact, at the present time, a modest majority of Pauline scholars regard 2 Thessalonians to be pseudonymous (i.e., written in Paul's name at a later point in time, likely after his death, by someone other than the apostle himself). What has led these biblical interpreters to conclude as much?

1. They regard the letter's authenticating comments and appeals to tradition to signal a pseudonymous author (see esp. 2:2, 15; 3:6, 17).
2. They detect a change in tone between 1 Thessalonians (warm and friendly) and 2 Thessalonians (detached and authoritarian).
3. They consider the "sudden" eschatology of 1 Thessalonians and the "signs" eschatology of 2 Thessalonians to be incompatible.
4. They observe the literary dependence (structural, linguistic, and thematic) of 2 Thessalonians on 1 Thessalonians.

These observations can be countered. For example, one can ask with good reason:

1. If there were a letter circulating in Paul's name (2:2), then do not 2:15 and 3:17 make good sense?
2. If the Thessalonians were in need of instruction and correction, is it unreasonable to think that Paul might change his tack and tone?
3. In light of the Synoptic Apocalypses and the Revelation of John, are suddenness and signs as eschatologically incompatible as some have imagined?
4. If Paul wrote 2 Thessalonians not long after 1 Thessalonians and addressed some of the same issues in both letters, then does it not stand to reason that there would be significant similarities in structure, vocabulary, and content?

Such questions could (do and will) continue. This point should not be lost, however: a number of skilled scholars have concluded that the preponderance of evidence suggests that Paul did not author 2 Thessalonians.

What is more, 2 Thessalonians is but the tip of the iceberg. At present there are five other letters that bear Paul's name that most Pauline specialists do not think he wrote.

In order of descending probability of Pauline authorship, they are: Colossians, Ephesians, 2 Timothy, Titus, and 1 Timothy. (Second Thessalonians is the least disputed of the disputed or **deutero-Pauline** letters.)

We recognize and are appreciative of the fact that not a few readers of this text (along with their teachers and ministers) may be inclined to view pseudonymity as wholly incompatible with canonicity. The argument runs thus: (1) The Bible does not traffic in falsehood. (2) Pseudonymity is tantamount to deceit. (3) Therefore, there are no pseudonymous documents in Scripture. This syllogism is safe, but is it sound?

Many have thought so. For instance, D. A. Carson contends, "The hard evidence demands that we conclude either that some NT documents are pseudonymous and that the real authors intended to deceive their readers, or that the real authors intended to speak the truth and that pseudonymity is not attested in the NT."[33]

It is impossible to know precisely what might have motivated a pseudonymous/allonymous author. Interestingly, the second-century Asia Minor presbyter who authored the *Acts of Paul* and circulated its legendary materials declared that he wrote his text "for love of Paul" (*amore Pauli*; see Tertullian, *On Baptism* 17).

Other scholars who likewise hold to a high view of Scripture and regard it to be authoritative for matters of faith and practice would disagree. For instance, when studying the texts of Jude and 2 Peter (which are commonly thought to be pseudonymous), Richard Bauckham notes, "The pseudepigraphical device is . . . not a fraudulent means of claiming apostolic authority, but embodies a claim to be a faithful mediator of the apostolic message."[34]

Along similar lines, in his commentary on the Pastoral Epistles, I. Howard Marshall has posited the following linguistic solution to this perennial exegetical, historical, and theological problem:

> Since the nuance of deceit seems to be inseparable from the use of the terms "pseudonymity" and "pseudepigraphy" and gives them a pejorative sense, we need another term that will refer more positively to the activity of writing in another person's name without intent to deceive: perhaps "allonymity" [literally 'another name'] and "allepigraphy" may be suggested as suitable alternatives.[35]

For Marshall, as for Bauckham, the aim of the allonymous author was to extend the apostolic voice, not to deceive audiences.

Our aim in this textbook is to help you think through Paul. It is not our intent, however, to tell you what you ought to think about Paul and Pauline studies at every twist and turn. In this introduction, we seek to be good and honest guides. If we were to ignore or deny that a majority of contemporary interpreters of Paul regard certain of his letters to be pseudonymous/allonymous, that would be neither good nor honest. So, as we continue our study, we will continue to grapple seriously with matters pertaining to the purported pseudonymity/allonymity of Pauline letters.

---

33. "Pseudonymity and Pseudepigraphy," in *DNTB*, 857–65 (on 863).
34. Richard Bauckham, *Jude and 2 Peter* (WBC 50; Waco, TX: Word, 1983), 161–62.
35. I. Howard Marshall, *The Pastoral Epistles* (ICC; Edinburgh: T&T Clark, 1999), 84.

Pseudonymity and Percentages

In a recent survey of roughly one hundred attendees at the 2011 British New Testament Conference in Nottingham, England, 100 percent maintained that Paul wrote Romans, 1–2 Corinthians, Galatians, and 1 Thessalonians; 99 percent that he wrote Philippians and Philemon; 57 percent that he wrote 2 Thessalonians; 51 percent that he wrote Colossians; 36 percent that he wrote Ephesians; 24 percent that he wrote 2 Timothy; 23 percent that he wrote Titus; 21 percent that he wrote 1 Timothy; and 0 percent that he wrote Hebrews.[36]

For now we turn to a close reading of four letters (Galatians, 1 Corinthians, 2 Corinthians, and Romans) about which there is little to no debate among scholars regarding Pauline authorship. These letters are known among interpreters of Paul as the Chief or Capital Letters.

CONCLUDING REMARKS

Timothy's glad tidings regarding the Thessalonians' continued *faith* prompted Paul to pen a letter laced with brotherly *love* and infused with eschatological *hope*. This letter, 1 Thessalonians by name, was probably Paul's earliest, and it was soon to be followed by another.[37] Although the Pauline triad of faith, love, and hope appears in 2 Thessalonians, the apostle's concern for the church's well-being in the midst of protracted opposition, end-time confusion, and congregational trouble eclipses all else. These early Pauline missives offer us a fascinating window into the formation, instruction, interaction, and maturation of a community of Christ-followers in northern Greece "in the beginning of the gospel" (Phil 4:15).

36. See Paul Foster, "Who Wrote 2 Thessalonians? A Fresh Look at an Old Problem," *JSNT* 35 (2012): 150–75 (on 170–71).

37. Of the scholars surveyed by Foster, 58 percent maintained that 1 Thessalonians was the first letter written by Paul ("Who Wrote 2 Thessalonians?" 171).

» KEY PEOPLE, PLACES, AND TERMS «

*Atakto*i
Athens
Berea
Cassander
Deutero-Pauline letters
Man of lawlessness
Paraenesis
Parousia
"Peace and security"
Philadelphia
Porneia
Pseudonymity
Restraining force/Restrainer
Silas/Silvanus
Skeuos
Thessalonica
Timothy
Via Egnatia

» QUESTIONS FOR REVIEW AND DISCUSSION «

1. How are Paul's letters arranged in the New Testament?
2. How may one categorize Paul's letters?
3. What is meant by the claim that Paul's letters are occasional and pastoral?
4. How can epistolary and rhetorical analysis assist in studying Paul's letters?
5. What is the basic structure of a Pauline letter?
6. Reconstruct as fully as possible Paul's initial ministry in Thessalonica.
7. How long did Paul's founding visit to Thessalonica last? What factors suggest that it may well have been longer than is sometimes thought?
8. Why did Paul leave Thessalonica? Where did he go after he left the city?
9. What prompted Paul to compose 1 Thessalonians?
10. What do you make of Paul's apparent expectation that Jesus might very well return sooner rather than later?
11. What metaphors does Paul employ to describe his ministry in Thessalonica?
12. What occasioned Paul's polemical outburst in 1 Thess 2:15 – 16?
13. Why was Paul unable to return to Thessalonica?
14. What three ethical issues does Paul raise in 1 Thess 4:3 – 12? Summarize his instruction.
15. What was Paul's intent in writing 1 Thess 4:13 – 18?
16. Paul thought and taught that believers would be raptured away from tribulation. Respond.
17. Why did Paul not think it necessary to write the Thessalonians regarding "times and dates"?
18. If "peace and security" is best understood as a Roman imperial slogan, how do we construe Paul's expressed perspective toward the empire in 1 Thess 5:3?

19. What are the three primary topics that Paul addresses in 2 Thessalonians?
20. In 2 Thessalonians what did Paul envision happening to those who do not embrace and obey the gospel?
21. According to 2 Thessalonians 2, what must take place prior to the *parousia*?
22. Why do a majority of scholars regard 2 Thessalonians to be pseudonymous?

» CONTEMPORARY THEOLOGICAL REFLECTION «

1. Do you think it helpful or healthy to seek to predict when the *parousia* might occur? Why, or why not?
2. If you had been responsible for setting forth instruction in reference and response to the *ataktoi*, what might you have added that Paul omitted and omitted that Paul added?
3. Is "church discipline" like that envisioned and enjoined in 2 Thessalonians 3 possible and desirable today?
4. What if there are pseudonymous documents in Scripture and among the Pauline letters? What if the aim of pseudonymous authors was not to deceive but to honor a master and to extend his instruction (as the authors interpreted it) for another generation of believers? What if Scripture were not weaker but stronger as a result of these works? What if the Pauline legacy were not regarded as tarnished or diminished but as reappropriated through the vehicle of pseudonymity/allonymity?

» GOING FURTHER «

Commentaries

Best, Ernest. *A Commentary on the First and Second Epistles to the Thessalonians.* BNTC. New York: Harper & Row, 1972.

Bruce, F. F. *1 and 2 Thessalonians.* WBC 45. Waco, TX: Word, 1982.

Fee, Gordon D. *The First and Second Letters to the Thessalonians.* NICNT. Grand Rapids: Eerdmans, 2009.

Furnish, Victor Paul. *1 Thessalonians, 2 Thessalonians.* ANTC. Nashville: Abingdon, 2007.

Gaventa, Beverly Roberts. *First and Second Thessalonians.* Interpretation. Louisville: John Knox, 1998.

Green, Gene L. *The Letters to the Thessalonians.* PNTC. Grand Rapids: Eerdmans, 2002.

Holmes, Michael W. *1 and 2 Thessalonians.* NIVAC. Grand Rapids: Zondervan, 1998.

Malherbe, Abraham J. *The Letters to the Thessalonians.* AB 32B. New York: Doubleday, 2000.

Marshall, I. H. *1 and 2 Thessalonians.* NCBC. Grand Rapids: Eerdmans, 1983.

Richard, Earl J. *First and Second Thessalonians.* SP 11. Collegeville, MN: Liturgical, 1995.

Wanamaker, Charles A. *The Epistles to the Thessalonians: A Commentary on the Greek Text.* NIGTC. Grand Rapids: Eerdmans, 1990.

Witherington, Ben, III. *1 and 2 Thessalonians: A Socio-Rhetorical Commentary.* Grand Rapids: Eerdmans, 2006.

Special Studies

Collins, Raymond F., ed. *The Thessalonian Correspondence.* BETL 66. Leuven: Leuven University Press, 1990.

Donfried, Karl P. "The Cults of Thessalonica and the Thessalonian Correspondence." *NTS* 31 (1985): 342–52.

Harrison, James R. *Paul and the Imperial Authorities at Thessalonica and Rome.* WUNT 273. Tübingen: Mohr Siebeck, 2011.

Jewett, Robert. *The Thessalonian Correspondence: Pauline Rhetoric and Millenarian Piety.* Philadelphia: Fortress, 1986.

Luckensmeyer, David. *The Eschatology of First Thessalonians.* NTOA/SUNT. Göttingen: Vandenhoeck & Ruprecht, 2009.

Malherbe, Abraham J. *Paul and the Thessalonians: The Philosophic Tradition of Pastoral Care.* Philadelphia: Fortress, 1987.

Nicholl, Colin R. *From Hope to Despair in Thessalonica: Situating 1 and 2 Thessalonians.* SNTSMS 126. Cambridge: Cambridge University Press, 2004.

Paddison, Angus. *Theological Hermeneutics and 1 Thessalonians.* SNTSMS 133. Cambridge: Cambridge University Press, 2005.

Thiselton, Anthony C. *1 & 2 Thessalonians through the Centuries.* BBC. Chichester: Wiley-Blackwell, 2011.

Still, Todd D. *Conflict at Thessalonica: A Pauline Church and its Neighbours.* JSNTSup 183. Sheffield: Sheffield Academic, 1999.

CHAPTER 3

GALATIANS

CHAPTER GOALS

- To examine the issues that have primary impact on the study of Galatians
- To highlight the central concerns and basic contents of that letter

CHAPTER OVERVIEW

1. Situating the Vision: An Introduction to Galatians
2. Centering the Vision of Galatians: The Apocalyptic Christ Comes Alive
3. Tracking the Vision of Galatians
4. Getting Around in Galatians
5. Key People, Places, and Terms
6. Questions for Review and Discussion
7. Contemporary Theological Reflection
8. Going Further

KEY VERSES

Galatians 1:3–4: "Grace and peace to you from God our Father and the Lord Jesus Christ, who gave himself for our sins to rescue us from the present evil age."

Galatians 2:20: "I have been crucified with Christ and I no longer live, but Christ lives in me. The life I now live in the body, I live by faith [the faithfulness of] the Son of God, who loved me and gave himself for me."

Galatians 3:27–28: "For all of you who were baptized into Christ have clothed yourselves with Christ. There is neither Jew nor Gentile, neither slave nor free, nor is there male nor female, for you are all one in Christ Jesus."

Galatians 4:19: "My dear children, for whom I am again in the pains of childbirth until Christ is formed in you."

Galatians 5:6: "For in Christ Jesus neither circumcision nor uncircumcision has any value. The only thing that counts is faith expressing itself through love."

Galatians 6:14–15: "May I never boast except in the cross of our Lord Jesus Christ, through which the world has been crucified to me, and I to the world. Neither circumcision nor uncircumcision means anything; what counts is the new creation."

SITUATING THE VISION: AN INTRODUCTION TO GALATIANS

The specific issue that stands at the forefront of Paul's letter to Christians in **Galatia** is one that looks to be of little relevance for Jesus' followers of the twenty-first century. Should male non-Jewish Jesus-followers have the foreskin of their penis removed? Today, this issue does not normally foster the heated theological debates that marked out the Galatian crisis.

But if this specific issue is one of a bygone day and will not touch on the interests and concerns of most Christians of the twenty-first century, the way Paul deals with this issue demonstrates much about his understanding of what it means to be a follower of Jesus in any age. The very fact that this is Paul's most "raw" letter, where he exposes his most fundamental theological impulses in their most stark fashion, makes this letter invaluable in recovering the essence of Paul's theological vision.

"The world in which curses and the evil eye are significant is one in which official sanctions to control behaviour are weak. For the daily life of most people, there is no very effective police force or judiciary. As a consequence, threats of punishment for wrongdoing tend to be transferred to the gods: they, rather than the state, are expected to avenge the wrong action that is in view. This is the world of Scripture."[1]

The Contest for the Theological Allegiance of Galatian Followers of the Messiah

Because the Christian communities that Paul addresses in this letter were founded by him, he felt especially protective of their corporate well-being. So his ire was provoked when people from outside those communities began to influence them in ways that Paul imagined were dangerous to their identity as Jesus-followers.

This is precisely what happened to communities of Jesus-followers in Galatia. We do not know exactly who the outsiders were. Paul calls them "**agitators**" (5:12), and he speaks about them (or people like them) or their influence throughout the Galatian letter.

- At the start of his letter, instead of offering his standard thanks to God for his addressees, Paul speaks of his bewilderment that the Galatians are ultimately on course to forfeit the God of grace through their attraction to a mutation of the true **gospel** (1:6–7).
- In 2:4–5, Paul notes that he had already encountered people like the agitators, recounting an earlier occasion when people whom he deemed to be "false believers" maneuvered their way into a position from which to manipulate "the truth of the gospel."
- In 3:1 Paul implies that the agitators have "bewitched" the Galatian followers of Jesus Christ (or better, have "injured them with the **evil eye**," which is the established meaning of the Greek word that Paul uses here, *baskainō*).[2]
- In 4:17, Paul claims that the agitators are seeking to "win over" the Galatians "for no good."
- In the final verses of the letter, Paul contrasts the interests of the agitators (i.e., their own self-interestedness) with his own promulgation of the gospel of "the cross of our Lord Jesus Christ" (6:12–13, 15).

1. Peter Oakes, *Galatians* (Paideia; Grand Rapids: Baker, 2014).
2. On this, see esp. Bruce W. Longenecker, "'Until Christ is Formed in You': Suprahuman Forces and Moral Character in Galatians," *CBQ* 61 (1999): 92–108.

▲ Circumcision tools. The "agitators" in Galatians insist Gentiles devoted to Jesus Christ need to be circumcised.

It is little wonder, then, that in his exasperation Paul speaks his wish that the agitators would simply cut off their own penises if they are so interested in cutting penises (5:12).

Paul's attitude toward the "agitators" is clearly hostile. In his view, they were intruders threatening the salvific well-being of the Galatians by peddling a gospel that runs contrary to the authentic gospel. But even if Paul is antagonistic toward them, it is less clear that they are antagonistic toward him. It is possible that they imagined their message to coincide with Paul's in some fashion, even if its emphasis has been placed on points that differ from Paul's own emphasis. So, for instance, in Gal 3:3 Paul introduces the imagery of "beginning" and "finishing," but that imagery may have initially been introduced to the Galatians by the agitators themselves. They may have maintained that Paul's gospel provided the Galatians with an easy introductory gospel for Gentiles, but his "primer" gospel needs to be supplemented with fuller teaching with which the Galatians need to "finish up." In this scenario, the agitators may have imagined their task as bringing to completion what Paul had started.

Alternatively, we know of episodes when some Christians appear to have been outspoken in their attempts to undermine Paul's authority (as seems to have been the situation behind 2 Corinthians, for instance). This may have been among the agitators' interests too, undermining Paul's credentials and gospel intentionally in order to bring Jesus-followers out from under the influence of one whose reputation was dubious at best.

If the issue capturing the Galatians' interest was whether Gentiles devoted to Jesus Christ need to be circumcised as part of their devotion to Israel's God, for Paul the issue involved more than the issue of **circumcision** alone. At times, for instance, Paul's discourse broadens to address not simply circumcision specifically but law observance in general—as when he speaks of those who "want to be under the law" (4:21). While this might simply be code for "wanting to be circumcised," it might also signal the larger issue that had engulfed Galatian Jesus-followers.

This is suggested also by the likelihood that Deut 27:26, which Paul quotes in 3:10, may have initially been introduced to the Galatians by agitators themselves. A simple reading of that verse would seem to advocate precisely the opposite of Paul's position, since it pronounces a curse on "everyone who does not continue to do everything written" in the **Mosaic Law.** Probably the onus was on Paul to interpret this scriptural passage in accordance with his gospel precisely because it had been brought to the Galatians' attention by the agitators.

If so, it is unlikely that the agitators were simply interested in promoting circumcision. In their theological arsenal was a passage of Scripture that was explicit in its requirement to observe unfalteringly *everything* written in the Mosaic Law. Perhaps the agitators' position resembled a form of "gradualism," in which putting faith in the Messiah was then to be followed up by undergoing circumcision and ultimately observing all the requirements for the people of Israel as stipulated in the Mosaic Law.[3]

In his Galatian letter, Paul exposes the weakness of this viewpoint. In 5:3, for instance, he holds out the prospect of having to obey all the law and insinuates that it is a daunting, unappealing, and errant prospect; and in 6:13 he charges the agitators themselves with not keeping the law, despite their circumcised state.

But if Paul presents the prospect of doing all of the law as wayward, he also knows that his gospel of freedom from the law can all too easily be characterized as theologically dangerous. This emerges, for instance, from his comments in 2:17. There Paul seems intent to repudiate the charge that his gospel transforms Christ into a "servant of the power of sin." In Galatians Paul bats this criticism away briskly. In Romans, he deals with it extensively (see, e.g., Rom 3:7–8; 6:1, 15, as discussed in chapter 6, below).

Moreover, as 1 Corinthians reveals (see next chapter), it is a charge that even his own congregations seem to have toyed with in their interpretation of the ethical implications of Paul's gospel of freedom from the law. For clearly (one might argue), if Jesus-followers are free from the law, then Paul's gospel offers no criteria for moral restraint. To paraphrase Rom 3:8, Paul's gospel might be interpreted to mean that Jesus-followers should behave disgracefully in order to reveal how gracious God really is, since his grace extends (so cheaply) to even the greatest of sinners whose behavior is flagrantly depraved. In order to counter the influence of the agitators in Galatian Jesus groups, Paul's letter would need to demonstrate that his gospel does not degenerate into moral chaos but, in fact, results in a moral life that testifies to the transforming power of the sovereign and righteous God.

Other Galatian Issues

Several things about Paul's Galatian letter are unclear, and scholars are likely to debate them indefinitely. For instance:

1. Where were the addressees of the letter located? For some scholars, they resided in southern **Galatia** (including the cities of Pisidian Antioch, Iconium, Lystra, and Derbe), while for others they resided in northern Galatia (including the cities of Pessinus and perhaps Ancyra). This is important, for instance, when linking Paul's letter to the narrative of Acts.
2. When did Paul write the letter? The suggested dates range from late in the 40s to the mid-50s. This is important when analyzing the possibility of development and differences in Paul's thinking and presentation throughout his extant letter collection.[4]

3. For examples of gradualism of this kind, see Josephus, *Antiquities* 20.38–46; Justin Martyr, *Dialogue with Trypho* 8.2.
4. The absence of any reference to Paul's collection for the poor Jesus-followers in Jerusalem is likely to suggest a date before 53, the year when Paul began his collection efforts. James Dunn proposes a date of 50, writing from Corinth; J. L. Martyn proposes a date of the same year, but written earlier in that year, from Philippi or Thessalonica.

Which Galatia, and When?

It is not wholly clear which Galatia Paul wrote to and, as a consequence, it is not wholly clear when Paul wrote his letter to the Galatians. The area known as "South Galatia" (a Roman territory) includes the cities of Pisidian Antioch, Iconium, Lystra, and Derbe, where Paul founded Jesus groups during the 40s (as recounted in Acts 13:14–15; 14:1; 16:3). But later Paul also seems to have passed through North Galatia (in one prominent reading of Acts 16:6; 18:23).

Scholarly debate will continue as to whether Paul's letter to the Galatians was written to Jesus groups in South Galatia (permitting a date for its composition as early as the late 40s, although later dates would be possible as well) or North Galatia (requiring a date for the letter's composition in the mid-50s or so).

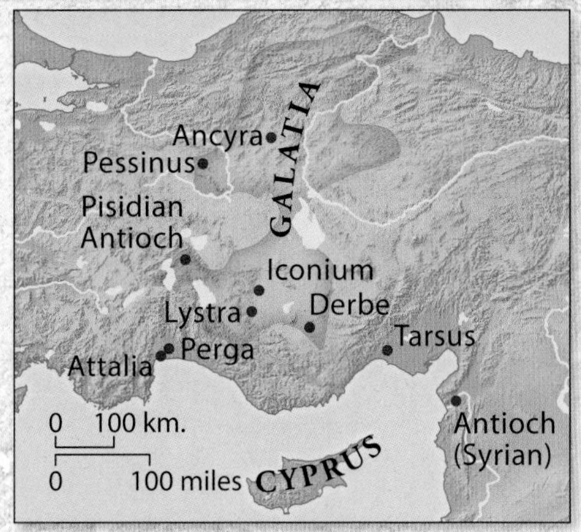

▲ Map showing the location of both North Galatia and South Galatia

3. How does Paul's account of his visit to **Jerusalem** recorded in Gal 2:1–10 relate to the accounts of Paul's visits to Jerusalem found in Acts? For some, the Galatian account corresponds with Acts 11:27–30, while for most it corresponds with Acts 15:1–29. Still others imagine that both accounts in Acts represent traditions about the event described in Gal 2:1–10 and placed in two separate places in Acts. This, too, is important when linking Paul's letter to the narrative of Acts.
4. Regarding the agitators, several issues are outstanding and intertwine. For some, they were local Jews who proposed circumcision and observance of the Mosaic Law so that Gentile Christians, becoming identifiably Jewish, would be relieved of the local expectation to worship the emperor.[5] For others, they were Jewish Christians with connections to Jerusalem-based Jesus groups, who proposed circumcision and observance of the Mosaic Law in order to alleviate Jewish opposition against the early Jesus movement. This is important when considering the complexity of issues that perplexed the early Jesus movement in its nascence.

Each of these issues is important, but attempting to do justice to any one of them in even a superficial overview would require significant amounts of space and, for our immediate purposes, would result in little gain. (They are usually covered in sufficient detail in any good commentary on the letter, where you can dig more deeply into the matter.)

5. The problem with this view is that it leaves Paul's audience without a satisfactory solution to their problem, which is wholly unlike Paul's style. Would Paul really not address the issue (envisaged to be emperor worship) that lay at the heart of the matter? That's not the Paul that emerges from any other letter.

CENTERING THE VISION OF GALATIANS: THE APOCALYPTIC CHRIST COMES ALIVE

"I have been crucified with Christ and I no longer live, but Christ lives in me. The life I now live in the body, I live by faith in the Son of God [or, 'I live by the faithfulness of the Son of God'], who loved me and gave himself for me."

These words from Gal 2:20 have been called the "touchstone" to which "every proposition in theology, every course of action prescribed in ethics, every Christian institution must be brought."[6] Arguably, the role of these words within Galatians itself is no less significant. Throughout this letter Paul demonstrates that when the story of Jesus properly merges with and sculpts the "story" of the lives of Jesus' followers, the problems that perplex the Galatians become manageable in a fashion that would otherwise not be the case. It is little wonder, then, that the story lines of Jesus and his followers fuse together within a concentrated paragraph of major significance in Paul's Galatian letter—namely, 2:15–21, where Paul merges the themes of being "crucified with Christ" and of Christ coming to life "in me."

Within Galatians, Paul often merges the Jesus story with the story lines of both himself and other Christians. The initial point of intersection between Paul's own life story and that of Jesus is tantalizingly hinted at when Paul recounts his first experience of the risen Lord (often referred to as his "**Damascus Road**" experience). In Gal 1:15–16, Paul claims that "God . . . was pleased to reveal his Son *in me* so that I might preach him among the Gentiles." This claim is simply extraordinary. Most translations of Gal 1:16, erring on the side of making good sense in English, speak of Jesus being revealed "to" Paul. This translation gives the impression that Paul underwent *enlightenment* regarding the true identity of Jesus as God's Son. As true as that is, it does not capture the full sense of what Paul originally communicated. Just as Paul speaks in 2:20 of Jesus Christ living "*in* me," so too in 1:16 he speaks of the Son of God being revealed "*in* me" (the Greek in both instances is *en emoi*). This is not simply the enlightenment of the mind; rather, it is the enlivenment of a person in transformed patterns of life.

In Gal 4:19 Paul extends the theme of "Christ in me" beyond his own life to the individual and corporate life of his Galatian addressees, through the imagery of childbirth: "My dear children, for whom I am again in the pains of childbirth until Christ is formed *in you*." The formation of Christ "in" the Galatians is rooted in their having been baptized "into Christ" and having been "clothed . . . with Christ" (3:27). Paul imagines that the lives of the Galatian Christians, and of all Christians, are so altered that Christ himself has been "draped" around them, as if they themselves are involved in an authentic "performance" of Jesus Christ in their own indigenous situations.

Since the story of Jesus incorporates both self-giving and exaltation, Paul imagines the same features to characterize the story of Jesus' followers. But it is self-giving that he highlights predominately in Galatians. In his own case, Paul's ministry of service has included

6. C. K. Barrett, *Freedom and Obligation: A Study of the Epistle to the Galatians* (Philadelphia: Westminster, 1985), 88. In some presentations of the text, the phrase "I have been crucified with Christ" is the final phrase of 2:19.

▲ "The Martyrdom of St. Paul" by Tintoretto. Paul's ministry of service included the giving over of his body to suffering.

the giving over of his body to suffering. He highlights this dimension of "Christ in me" in the second to last verse of his letter: "From now on, let no one cause me trouble, for I bear on my body the marks of Jesus" (Gal 6:17). If the stripes that scarred his own back as a result of his ministry could be perceived as tagging him as a disrupter of society and therefore a man of dishonor, Paul inverts their significance, taking pride in those stripes, the very "marks of Jesus." They are physical imprints of honor and should cause others to think twice about challenging his worthiness as an **apostle** (see 2 Cor 11:21–30). For Paul it is an "enfleshed" example of the theological principle of "Christ in me."

The themes of "crucified with Christ" and "Christ in me," which take pride of place in Gal 2:20, form the axis around which Paul builds his ethical vision in Galatians—and ultimately the axis around which he constructs his rejection of the need for Gentile Christians to be circumcised (and to observe the law). Being crucified with Christ means that Jesus' followers have "crucified" their proclivity toward sinful actions (5:24; see also Romans 6 and 8). The law was not to be the means whereby one's life was ethically controlled, as the "troublers" might have proposed. According to Paul, whenever people are "crucified with Christ" and Christ "comes alive" in them, the sinful "passions and desires" are (to be) replaced by a cruciform pattern of life, for which Paul has no better word than "love"—or more specifically, love expressed in self-giving for the benefit of others.

This is what Paul highlights within Gal 2:20 itself. There Paul expresses the character of the Christ who comes alive in him: that one is characterized by love and self-giving, or perhaps, love defined by self-giving (he "loved" and "gave himself").

This characteristic of Jesus' self-giving love is so significant to Paul's understanding of the situation that he highlights it right at the start of his letter. Noting in the opening verse that God the Father "raised him [Jesus] from the dead," Paul underscores Jesus' crucifixion in the fourth verse of the letter, noting that Jesus "gave himself" (1:4).

There is cause to think that Paul intentionally highlights this cruciform character of self-giving both at the start and the end of his letter (i.e., 1:4 and 6:17). At the start of his letters, Paul often highlights main themes that he will develop later, and at the end of this letter he writes a densely packaged paragraph that compresses and intertwines some major emphases of the letter. Evidently, Paul emphasizes cruciform lifestyle at the start and the end of the Galatian letter because it encapsulates the theological program that Paul lays out for Galatian Christ-followers.

It also lies at the center of his ethical exhortation in the last two chapters of the letter, where, in a sense, the rubber hits the road. So, for instance, in his attempt to undermine an

◀ An icon of a crucified Jesus in the Monastery of St. John. Paul expresses the character of Christ that comes alive in him: "I have been crucified with Christ and I no longer live, but Christ lives in me. The life I now live in the body, I live by faith in the Son of God, who loved me and gave himself for me" (Gal 2:20).

interest in circumcision (which is nonessential) among the Gentile Christians, Paul links faith (which is essential) to practical expressions of love: "For in Christ Jesus neither circumcision nor uncircumcision has any value. The only thing that counts is faith expressing itself through love" (Gal 5:6).

For Paul, then, the characteristic of self-giving that marks out the story of Jesus is intended to mark out the story of Jesus' followers. So Paul exhorts the Galatians to "serve one another humbly in love" (Gal 5:14). It is precisely this characteristic that stands front and center in Paul's list of the "fruit of the Spirit" in 5:22—that list representing the kinds of behaviors, attitudes, and practices that the Spirit brings to life within Jesus' followers. When Paul writes in 5:23 "against such things there is no law," he means that when communities of Jesus-followers are saturated in a character comprised of these spirited attributes, the law becomes irrelevant in its function as a control on behavior. In essence, what the Spirit generates in the life stories of Jesus-followers is the same cruciform, self-giving pattern of life that characterized Jesus' own life story.

"Christian righteousness is, namely, that righteousness by which Christ lives in us, not the righteousness that is in our own person. Therefore when it is necessary to discuss Christian righteousness, the person must be completely rejected. For if I pay attention to the person or speak of the person, then, whether intentionally or unintentionally on my part, the person becomes a doer of works who is subject to the Law. But here Christ and my conscience must become one body, so that nothing remains in my sight but Christ, crucified and risen. By paying attention to myself . . . I lose sight of Christ, who alone is my righteousness and life."[7]

7. Martin Luther, *Luther's Works*, vol. 26: *Lectures on Galatians chapters 1–4* (St. Louis: Concordia, 1962), 166.

This is of critical importance for Paul, since it provides him with what is arguably his most compelling argument against the salvific necessity of circumcision. The Spirit of God stimulates lifestyles of cruciformity that, unlike circumcision, bring Jesus-followers into the arena of Jesus' own intimate sonship. So it is that the Spirit of God cries out in the hearts of Jesus' followers "*Abba*, Father" (Gal 4:6) — repeating (in an Aramaic sound-bite) the very words that characterized Jesus' own prayer life (see Mark 14:36), in intimate obedience to God the Father.

> "Paul does not make faith unformed here [in Gal 5:6], as though it were a shapeless chaos without the power to be or do anything; but he attributes the working itself to faith rather than to love. He makes love the tool through which faith works."[8]

Because a life of self-giving is (to be) the primary characteristic of the lives of those devoted to Jesus Christ, Paul views that pattern of life as itself the means whereby the law given to Israel is ultimately fulfilled. This is his point in Gal 5:14, where he writes: "For the entire law is fulfilled in keeping this one command: 'Love your neighbor as yourself.'"

Here, then, is Paul's ultimate solution to the issue facing the Galatians. Whereas the agitators directed the Galatians' attention to the requirement of circumcision (and perhaps other requirements) within the Jewish Scriptures, Paul directs their attention to the self-giving Lord, and he interprets Scripture in light of his cruciform story. With that story in full frame, the law is interpreted accordingly. The point is made again in 6:2: "Carry each other's burdens, and in this way you will fulfill the law of Christ."[9]

The Fruit of the Spirit

In Gal 5:22 – 23, Paul offers a list of nine attributes that typify the character that the Spirit of God brings to life in Jesus-followers. These include: "love, joy, peace, patience, kindness, goodness, faithfulness, gentleness and self-control." He calls these "the fruit of the Spirit," with the singular word "fruit" probably suggesting that they are part of a "package" of the divine character that progressively imprints itself onto the life of the Christian through the power of the Spirit. Just a few verses earlier, this same character, encapsulated in the word "love," is said to be the fulfillment of the law (5:13 – 14; cf. 6:2).

If Paul's solution to the Galatians' dilemma is about self-giving love, that solution is also placed within a rigorous **apocalyptic** framework. Paul imagines a battle raging between two "systems" (we might say) in competition to regulate the cosmos. The one system he identifies in 5:17 by the term "flesh." This fleshly system fosters actions and attitudes that, when extrapolated into pure forms, induce chaos into the fabric of society. Paul gives examples of the sorts of thing he has in mind in 5:19 – 21, where he provides a list of the "acts of the flesh." So too in 5:15 he calls attention to this system of life, characterizing it in terms of fierce competition ("biting and devouring each other") that leads only to destruction. Paul speaks of this kind of life as enslavement to cosmic forces whose intent is to lead people away from God (4:8 – 11; so also 4:3).

8. Martin Luther, *Luther's Works*, vol. 27: *Lectures on Galatians 5 – 6 (1535) and Galatians 1 – 6 (1519)* (St. Louis: Concordia, 1972), 29.
9. Scholars debate whether the word "law" here refers to the Scriptures, as introduced here, or to something more general (as in "the principle of life demonstrated by the life of Jesus"). The point made in this paragraph is generally unaffected even if the latter is thought to be correct.

The other system of life is that of "love," whose content is defined by Jesus' act of self-sacrifice, which itself is to be replicated in followers of Jesus Christ through the Spirit. Although enough has been said about this already, it is important also to note how Paul places this cruciform self-giving at the forefront of the cosmic battle that is being waged within God's created order. The apocalyptic dimension of Jesus' own cruciform life is highlighted at the start of the Galatian letter, where Paul writes in 1:4 of Jesus "who gave himself for our sins to rescue us from the present evil age."

This present evil age is what some Jewish apocalyptic writers imagined God would rescue the people of Israel from when, at some point in the future, he would invade his own creation to redeem it of chaotic systems and to set it in order—i.e., to set it "right," with "righteousness" pervading the whole of creation. For Paul, that in-breaking of God has already occurred, albeit only in part, in the life, death, and resurrection of Jesus. In opposition to this invasion of self-giving stands the system of "flesh," or competitive self-interestedness at the expense of others (and ultimately, at the expense of one's own self).

Since the significance of Jesus' death and resurrection permeates the depths of the cosmos, participation in the self-giving of Christ has an "apocalyptic" dimension that engulfs the identity of those who follow Christ. Paul states it this way in Gal 6:14: "May I never boast except in the cross of our Lord Jesus Christ, through which the world has been crucified to me, and I to the world." For Paul, it is in this apocalyptic matrix of understanding and power that the Galatians would find the solution to the problem that they were facing. So he writes in the next verse (6:15): "Neither circumcision nor uncircumcision means anything; what counts is the new creation." And that "new creation" is immersed in the ethos and practice of self-giving love. For Paul, whenever communities of Jesus-followers lose that fundamental Spirit-inspired character, they lose the essence of the gospel.

TRACKING THE VISION OF GALATIANS

The basic structure of Paul's letter to Galatian Christians can be outlined as follows:

1:1–5	Letter Opening
1:6–2:21	Paul's Apostleship and the Truth of the Gospel
3:1–5:1	Reading Scripture in Light of the Truth of the Gospel
5:2–6:10	Living Out the Truth of the Gospel
6:11–18	Summarizing the Essentials of the Letter

Galatians 1–2

In the opening (1:1–5), Paul highlights three main features that he will develop in the remaining chapters:

1. his apostolic legitimacy
2. the self-giving of Jesus
3. the apocalyptic schema of two spheres of life (i.e., the present evil age and, by implication, the eschatological age of righteousness)

If these are themes that animate much of Paul's letter, what Paul leaves out of the opening is his standard thanksgiving to God for the good things in his addressees' corporate life. This reflects Paul's state of mind when writing to the Galatians. Being anything but thankful, he is instead astounded that the "foolish Galatians" (3:1) have so easily turned from the gospel to something that parades as the gospel (1:6–9).

This opens up the opportunity for Paul to recount his own life story in relation to the gospel he preaches. This includes a *historical survey* (with theological import) of certain key features and moments of his life (1:10–2:14), and a *theological articulation* of the gospel in light of issues that had faced other Jesus-followers previously and that were now facing the Galatians themselves (2:15–21, which follows directly out of 2:11–14).

There are three main points of the *historical survey*:

1. Paul's gospel ultimately derives its authority from a revelation of the risen Christ given to him by God (1:10–17), not from any institutional authentication.
2. Paul's gospel nonetheless coincides with, and has been confirmed as authentic by, the apostles who knew Jesus and who were currently based in Jerusalem, not least Jesus' own brother James and Jesus' disciples Peter (or Cephas) and John (1:18–2:10).
3. Paul has always affirmed the truth of the gospel and withstood all situations to water it down, even when those situations involved the apostles themselves (2:1–14).

Paul cites two situations of defending the truth of the gospel in which he had already been involved. These were incidents in which some Jesus-followers advocated one of two strategies in relation to preserving the covenant identity of Jewish Jesus-followers. In the first, Paul had fought against those who promoted the circumcision of Gentile Jesus-followers, with whom Jewish Jesus-followers were intimately related in fellowship meals and corporate gatherings (2:1–10). In the second, Paul had fought against the separation of Jewish Jesus-followers from Gentile Jesus-followers in those same corporate gatherings (2:11–14). In Paul's estimate, both cases implied that Gentile Jesus-followers were substandard members of Christian communities. Paul, of course, would have none of it (just as in Romans he would not allow the opposite, with Jewish Jesus-followers being denigrated in relation to Gentile Jesus-followers).

In 2:15–21 Paul gives his *theological articulation* for rejecting both of these attempts (those verses being an extension of Paul's account of 2:11–14). The mainstay of those verses is 2:16: "a person is not justified by the works of the law, but [or 'except'] by faith in [or 'the faith/faithfulness of'] Jesus Christ . . . because by the works of the law no one will be justified." Paul presents all Jewish Christians as being in complete agreement (i.e., "we know," 2:15–16) that the law is not sufficient to effect God's plan of salvation. But after agreeing on this, Paul and other Jewish Christians parted company. For others, despite its insufficiency, observance of the law was nonetheless a necessary part of salvation. For Paul, however, since the law was not sufficient for salvation, neither was it necessary. In 2:17–20, Paul briefly outlines the ethical ramifications of following Jesus without observing the law (much of which has already been discussed above), before repeating his view of the law's insufficiency: "If righteousness could be gained through the law, Christ died for nothing!"

Works of the Law and "the New Perspective on Paul"

The phrase "works of the law" (Gal 2:16, which the NIV 1984 translated "observing the law"; cf. 3:2, 5, 10; also Rom 3:20, 28) has become a focus for scholarly debate regarding the substance of Paul's critique of nomistic observance, or observance of the law ("law" is *nomos* in Greek).

There are two main ways of interpreting the phrase, each of which ascribes different motivations to nomistic observance. In one view, this phrase refers to nomistic observance as motivated by the hope of earning salvation through good works. This equates to a form of legalism. This is the traditional view of the matter, a view that has gained ascendancy since the time of the Reformation.

A more recent view sees the phrase as a reference to nomistic observance as motivated by the desire to maintain the covenant identity of the Jewish people, as commanded by God (especially in Deuteronomy). Since God called the Jewish people to be distinctive, they were responsible to practice the regulations that God had laid out for them in Scripture, thereby differentiating them from all other nations. To compromise on their nomistic observance would be to shun the calling of God. For some, when Paul wrote the phrase "works of the law," he was referring to precisely this covenantal (rather than legalistic) motivation.

This way of perceiving things has come to be called "the new perspective on Paul." The label has become somewhat dated, for two reasons. First, having become popular in the 1980s and beyond, this way of looking at things is no longer "new." Second, its influence has been significant among a wide selection of Pauline interpreters, to the extent that its proponents cannot be said to hold a single interpretive "perspective."

Nonetheless, despite the inadequacies of the label, this way of looking at things has been notably influential among certain circles of Pauline interpreters. (For more on this subject, refer to chapter 12.)

Galatians 3:1 – 5:1

Uniting most of Galatians 3 – 4 is a concentration on the interpretation of Scripture in relation to various theological themes that Paul interweaves throughout the chapters.

Noting the Galatians' experience of receiving the Spirit simply on the basis of their faith in Jesus Christ (3:1 – 3), Paul relates this to Gen 15:6, where Abraham is shown to have been considered "righteous" by God through his faith (Gal 3:6). This is then linked to the scriptural assurances that "all nations will be blessed" through Abraham (3:8) — that is, through their imitation of his faith, through which they can be considered his offspring (3:7 – 9).

Gal 3:10 – 14 comprises a densely populated set of scriptural passages. Gathering various passages together, Paul wants his readers first to probe into the scriptural depiction of observing the law. Scripture promises life to those who observe the law (Lev 18:5, cited in Gal 3:12) and condemns all who do not observe the law (Deut 27:26, cited in Gal 3:10). The agitators would probably have wholly agreed, imagining these Scriptures to validate their concern that Gentile Jesus-followers should be circumcised. In Paul's hands, however, these Scriptures are expected to work in the other direction, probably on the assumption that no one can observe the law worthily enough.

When that assumption is in play, the very passages that Paul cites in Gal 3:10 – 12 should deter one from even trying to observe the law hoping thereby to gain salvation. Instead, Paul highlights a different Scripture that he views as reinforcing the Abraham story already cited in 3:6–9: that is, Hab 2:4. That verse promises righteousness to those who live by faith (Gal 3:11). With the Abraham story acting as the filter for adjudicating diverse scriptural passages, it is faith, rather than law observance, that emerges as the means of enjoying God's righteousness.

Paul then incorporates a supplemental passage to reinforce the point. Since Christ himself was cursed by the law for having "hung on a tree" (Deut 21:23, cited in Gal 3:13) but was raised by God, he liberates others from the curse that the law pronounces on those who do not observe the law — evidently liberating them from having to observe the law so that the promised Spirit of God can be received through faith in Jesus Christ (3:14).

> "Among the key characteristics of Paul's Judaism were precisely critique from within on the one hand and confrontation with paganism on the other. The fact that Paul criticized some aspect of his native Judaism and that he announced a gospel to the Gentiles does not mean that he broke with Judaism in order to do so. On the contrary . . . he claimed to be speaking as a true Jew, criticizing — as did many who made similar claims — those who embraced other construals of Judaism, on the basis that Israel's God had now acted climactically and decisively in Jesus, the Messiah."[10]

The Abraham story comes to the forefront once again in 3:15–18, where it is shown to precede the giving of the law by 430 years. Seeking to dislodge established readings of Abraham as the progenitor of ethnic Israel, Paul argues two things:

- what comes later (i.e., the law) cannot overturn what came earlier (i.e., the promise [of the Spirit] given to Abraham and his seed)
- the "seed" of Abraham is not ethnic Israel but Jesus Christ (since the term "seed" appears in Gen 12:7; 13:15; 24:7 in singular rather than plural form)

But if the law has nothing to do with Abraham and his seed, why was it "added"? Paul gives various reasons for this, usually in terse and undeveloped form. It was added, he says, "because of transgressions" (3:19) — a phrase that has been understood to mean "to enhance transgressions" (as in Rom 5:20), or "to reveal transgressions" (as in Rom 3:20), or "to deal with transgressions" through the sacrificial system. That this purpose (whichever one Paul has in mind) is inferior to what God has done in Christ is evident from the fact that the law was given "through angels" and through "a mediator."

Against this backdrop, Paul enumerates other purposes for the "adding" of the law. Since God's promises operate at a different level of salvation history than the giving of the law, the two cannot be in conflict, since they are intended to achieve different things (3:21–22). The law does not impart life, but instead locks up everything "under the control of sin," or better, the cosmic power of Sin, but only "until the faith that was to come would be revealed" (3:23).

In 3:24–25 Paul seems to put a slightly more positive spin on this notion of the law locking everyone up in sin's control. There he depicts the law as having been added in order to put "us" (probably "the people of Israel") under the supervision of a "**pedagogue**" or,

10. N. T. Wright, "The Letter to the Galatians: Exegesis and Theology," in *Between Two Horizons: Spanning New Testament Studies and Systematic Theology* (ed. Joel B. Green and Max Turner; Grand Rapids: Eerdmans, 1999), 212.

Pedagogue's sarcophagus. Relief. 3rd century AD/Photo © Tarker/The Bridgeman Art Library

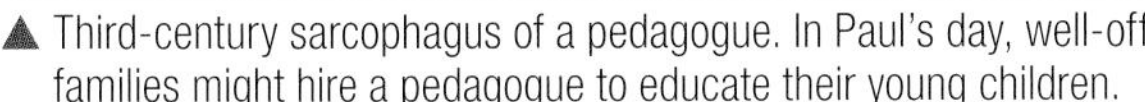

▲ Third-century sarcophagus of a pedagogue. In Paul's day, well-off families might hire a pedagogue to educate their young children.

Wikimedia Commons

▶ This is a funeral monument erected by a father to honor his two sons. In the inscription the father also honors their pedagogue, a young man named Hermes. The inscription reads: "Thrasōn, son of Diogenes, erected this funerary stele for his two sons, Dexiphanes, age 5, and Thrasōn, age 4, and for Hermēs, age 25, who brought them up. In the earthquake collapse, so did he hold them in his arms." Supervisors of young children were often treasured for their skills and care.

perhaps "guardian" (as in the NIV). In Paul's day, well-off families often hired a pedagogue (usually an entrusted slave) to help educate and protect their young children, until such time as the young people had imbibed the ethos of the family and could act responsibly without the pedagogue's direction.[11] Something of the same scenario, Paul suggests, applies to the giving of the law to the people of Israel. Even if the law could not solve the problem of being under the control of the power of sin, it could nonetheless teach them something of what it means to participate in the ethos of the family of God.

In 3:26–4:7 Paul elaborates this in at least three important ways:

1. Those within the family of God, who are "baptized into Christ" and have "clothed" themselves with Christ (3:27), are said to enjoy intimacy with God. This is demonstrated by the Spirit's cry, "*Abba*, Father" (4:6)—the term used by Jesus in his prayers to address God.[12]
2. Those within the family of God are drawn from all parts of humanity, regardless of their subidentities (i.e., both Jews and Gentiles, both slave and free, both male and female, and no doubt the list of 3:28 could go on and on).

---

11. This more positive spin might be evident already in 3:23, when Paul talks about being "in custody under" or perhaps "guarded by" the law.
12. The term "Father" appears on the lips of Jesus to designate God in the following places in the canonical Gospels: Mark 14:36; Matt 6:9/Luke 11:2; Matt 11:25–26/Luke 10:21; Matt 26:42; Luke 23:34; John 11:41; 12:27–28; 17:1, 5, 11, 21, 24–25.

3. Those who "belong to Christ" are themselves incorporated into "Abraham's seed" (3:29), to whom the Spirit had been promised.

In 4:8–11, Paul develops a theme that he first introduced in 4:1–7, imagining in those passages that living under the supervision of the law could also be likened to a form of slavery. With hindsight informed by the intimacy with God that comes from following Jesus, Paul imagines this to be slavery "under the elemental spiritual forces of the world" (4:3)—that is, slavery to "weak and miserable forces" (4:9). In both these phrases, Paul uses a Greek word (*stoicheia*, "elemental forces") whose meaning in this context continues to be debated. But whatever its precise meaning, it hangs ominously over the situation of those who, whether of Jewish or Gentile origins, are not among "God's children" (4:7).

In 4:12–20 Paul surveys his relationship with the Galatians, noting how their own behavior toward Paul is itself a marker of their enlivenment by various spiritual forces. Their early reception of him, despite his threatening weakness, symbolizes their enlivenment by the Spirit of the Son of God, who gave himself for others. By contrast, the Galatians are now in danger of allowing unhealthy spiritual forces to dominate them. Paul tells the Galatians that his eager desire for them is that Christ would be "formed in you" (4:19).

Having contrasted freedom and slavery in 4:1–11, in 4:21–5:1 Paul establishes that contrast as the interpretative lens through which to read another part of the Abraham story, as an allegory to the situation of Jesus-followers. As the slave woman **Hagar** birthed a slave son for Abraham (i.e., Ishmael) and the free woman **Sarah** (not mentioned by name) birthed a free son for him (i.e., Isaac), so Christians are not to enslave themselves to law observance but are to remain free from enslavement, thereby ensuring that they remain the legitimate heirs of Abraham. (For more on this allegory, see the section "Wise Interpretation of Scripture at 'the Culmination of the Ages'" in chapter 13.)

Galatians 5:2–6:18

Paul reinforces his point by prioritizing what really matters for those who worship Jesus as Lord. Determining one's identity with regard to whether one is circumcised or uncircumcised does not matter; the only thing of import is putting one's faith into practice through concrete forms of loving service (5:6). He makes the same point in 5:13–14, this time picking up on the theme of slavery and freedom and linking it to the issue of the law. While Jesus-followers are "free," this does not mean that they are able to do nothing with their faith, or to live irresponsibly. With freedom comes responsibility.

"The criterion of the Spirit's activity is cruciformity, understood as Christ-like love in the edification of others rather than oneself."[13]

The responsibility that Paul highlights is this: "serve one another humbly in love." The Greek is more ironic than English translations permit, since the verb "serve" is the same used to denote "slavery" previously in Galatians. Although he can liken observing the law to a form of slavery, Paul can also liken the freedom of Jesus-followers to a kind of "slavery for the benefit of others." In fact, this kind of slavery-in-freedom or freedom-in-slavery is

13. Michael Gorman, *Cruciformity: Paul's Narrative Spirituality of the Cross* (Grand Rapids: Eerdmans, 2001), 60.

itself the way in which the entire law becomes "fulfilled" among Christians (5:14).

Paul wants his readers to know that they are not expected to lead law-fulfilling lives of love through their own strengths and abilities, but through the power of the Spirit — the Spirit that had been promised to Abraham's seed. The Spirit provides the resources for lifestyles that enhance the well-being of Jesus-followers and their corporate life (5:22–25).

By contrast, the "flesh" promotes ways of life that destroy individual and corporate life (5:15, 19–21, 26). By "flesh," Paul is not referring to human bodies; instead, by this term he describes the human penchant to live self-interested lives. This form of life is engaged in a battle with the Spirit of God that promotes self-giving. Human beings cannot escape the battle, but are inevitably enlisted to enhance one side or the other.

WikiPaintings

▲ Jesus' lowering of himself to serve others was a common theme in the early Jesus movement, as depicted graphically in the story of his washing his disciples' feet (John 13:3–11).

The result is that Jesus-followers are not to do what they are inclined to do (5:16–17), but instead are to be led by the Spirit (5:18), to "live by the Spirit," and to "keep in step with the Spirit" (5:25). Keeping in step with the Spirit is given further elaboration in 6:1–10. Key emphases in that passage include Paul's exhortations for the Galatians to "carry each other's burdens, and in this way you will fulfill the law of Christ" (6:2; see also 5:13–14), and to not grow weary in doing good to all people (6:9–10).

"Following the Spirit (5.25) is no mere passive act of 'being led by the Spirit' (5.18), but requires also a resolute intention to 'walk by the Spirit' (5.16); the balance between passive and active will be deliberate."[15]

The fact that almost every verse of 6:11–18 has been discussed in the introductory section to Galatians above serves to reinforce this section's significance within the letter. At the close of the letter, Paul, now taking the stylus from his secretary, highlights its main themes for all to see. (Paul speaks of how he writes with "large letters" [6:11] in much the same way that we would use bold or italic font to highlight emphases.) Since moral character plays a role in Paul's theological inventory in Galatians, it is not surprising that he demonstrates within this section the questionable character of those who are agitating the Galatians (6:12–13). What matters is not circumcision but a life lived in cruciform conformity

To have the Spirit is to spend oneself."[16]

14. James D. G. Dunn, *The Theology of Paul's Letter to the Galatians* (Cambridge: Cambridge University Press, 1993), 110.
15. Frances Young and David F. Ford, *Meaning and Truth in 2 Corinthians* (London: SPCK, 1987), 175.

The Life Blood of Paul's Galatian Letter

The Apocalyptic Emphasis in the Letter's Frame

Gal 1:4: "[the Lord Jesus Christ] gave himself for our sins to set us free from the present evil age, according to the will of our God and Father."

Gal 6:14–15: "May I never boast except in the cross of our Lord Jesus Christ, through which the world has been crucified to me, and I to the world. Neither circumcision nor uncircumcision means anything; what counts is the new creation."

The Apocalyptic Overspill into Christian Moral Ethos (and Discourse on Law)

Gal 5:6: "For in Christ Jesus neither circumcision nor uncircumcision has any value. The only thing that counts is faith expressing itself through love."

Gal 5:13–14: "You, my brothers and sisters, were called to be free. But do not use your freedom to indulge the flesh; rather, serve one another humbly in love. For the entire law is fulfilled in keeping this one command, 'Love your neighbor as yourself.'"

Gal 6:2: "Carry each other's burdens, and in this way you will fulfill the law of Christ."

The Apocalyptic Embodiment of Christ as the Basis for Christian Ethos and Unity

Gal 2:20: "I have been crucified with Christ and I no longer live, but Christ lives in me. The life I now live in the body, I live by the faithfulness of the Son of God [or less likely, 'faith in the Son of God'], who loved me and gave himself for me."

Gal 3:27–28: "All of you who were baptized into Christ have clothed yourselves with Christ. There is neither Jew nor Gentile, neither slave nor free, nor is there male and female, for you are all one in Christ Jesus."

Gal 4:19: "My dear children, for whom I am again in the pain of childbirth until Christ is formed in you."

Gal 5:22–25: "But the fruit of the Spirit is love, joy, peace, forbearance, kindness, goodness, faithfulness, gentleness and self-control. Against such things there is no law. Those who belong to Christ Jesus have crucified the flesh with its passions and desires. Since we live by the Spirit, let us also keep in step with the Spirit."

to Christ (6:14–15). That Paul himself leads such a life is testified to by the scars on his own body, the very "marks of Jesus" (6:17) that legitimate his apostleship and his gospel.

SUMMARY REFLECTION

Paul's letter to the Galatians offers us a glimpse of "raw Paulinism." Nowhere else in the corpus of his letters do we find him so challenged, and perhaps so challenging—both as a rhetor making his case and as a theologian hoping to instruct others. Finding himself on the defensive and having to make up substantial ground in the wake of the agitators' influence, Paul pulled out all the stops in this letter, attempting to ensure that Galatian Jesus-followers continued "obeying the truth" (Gal 5:7). The result is a cascading mix of autobiographical reconstruction, scriptural interpretation, and moral exhortation within a rich theological package and a singularly focused rhetoric that pulls no punches. If there is a single letter that most defines Paul, Galatians is an obvious contender for that title.

» KEY PEOPLE, PLACES, AND TERMS «

Agitators	Damascus Road	Gospel	Mosaic Law
Apostle	Flesh	Jerusalem	Pedagogue
Circumcision	Galatia		

» QUESTIONS FOR REVIEW AND DISCUSSION «

1. How would you articulate "the essence" of Paul's theological vision? What are his most fundamental theological impulses?
2. In Paul's mind, what was it about the agitators that made them so dangerous?
3. Do you find Paul's violent imagery in Gal 5:12 troubling? For what reasons do you think Paul adopted this language?
4. What, beyond circumcision, might have been the real agenda of the agitators?
5. What about Paul's "Gospel of Freedom" might be theologically dangerous?
6. What are the unresolved issues regarding the background of Galatians? In what ways do the various interpretive options affect interpretation?
7. What event from Paul's life is hinted at in Gal 1:15 – 16? How does this event affect the way we understand Paul's claim that "God . . . was pleased to reveal his Son in me so that I might preach him among the Gentiles"?
8. What two themes form the axis around which Paul builds his ethical vision in this letter? To what specific issue does Paul apply these themes, and what is his conclusion on the issue?
9. What, according to Paul, should be the primary characteristic of the lives of Christians?
10. What are the two "systems" at war in Paul's apocalyptic framework?
11. What three main themes does Paul highlight at the opening of the letter (Gal 1:1 – 5)? What typical feature does Paul not include here?
12. What hero from Israel's history does Paul discuss at length? What function does this story/character have for Paul's argument?

» CONTEMPORARY THEOLOGICAL REFLECTION «

1. If Paul were here today, what issues do you think he would address (given that the issue of circumcision has fallen out of relevance in the twenty-first century)?
2. What contemporary influences threaten Christian identity today?
3. In Gal 6:10 Paul discusses "doing good." What sorts of actions do you think he envisions for his first-century readers? What sorts of actions are implied for followers of Jesus today?

» GOING FURTHER «

Galatians Commentaries

De Boer, Martinus, *Galatians*. NTL. Louisville: Westminster John Knox, 2011.

Dunn, James D. G. *The Epistle to the Galatians*. BNTC. London: Black, 1993.

Longenecker, Richard N. *Galatians*. WBC. Dallas: Word, 1990.

Martyn, J. L. *Galatians*. AB. New York/London: Doubleday, 1997.

Oakes, Peter. *Galatians*. Paideia. Grand Rapids: Baker Academic, 2014.

Witherington, Ben, III. *Grace in Galatia: A Commentary on St. Paul's Letter to the Galatians*. Edinburgh: T&T Clark, 1998.

Galatians Studies

Barclay, John M. G. *Obeying the Truth: A Study of Paul's Ethics in Galatians*. Edinburgh: T&T Clark, 1988.

Barrett, C. K. *Freedom and Obligation: A Study in the Epistle to the Galatians*. London: SPCK, 1985.

Dunn, James D. G. *The Theology of Paul's Letter to the Galatians*. Cambridge: Cambridge University Press, 1993.

Longenecker, Bruce W. *The Triumph of Abraham's God: The Transformation of Identity in Galatians*. Edinburgh: T&T Clark, 1998.

Nanos, Mark. *The Irony of Galatians: Paul's Letter in First-Century Context*. Minneapolis: Fortress, 2002.

Nanos, Mark, ed. *The Galatians Debate: Contemporary Issues in Rhetorical and Historical Interpretation*. Grand Rapids: Baker Academic, 2002.

Silva, Moisés. *Interpreting Galatians: Explorations in Exegetical Method*. Grand Rapids: Baker Academic, 2001.

CHAPTER 4

1 CORINTHIANS

CHAPTER GOALS

- To examine the issues that have primary impact on the study of 1 Corinthians
- To highlight the central concerns and basic contents of that letter

CHAPTER OVERVIEW

1. Situating the Vision: An Introduction to 1 Corinthians
2. Centering the Vision of 1 Corinthians: Nothing but Christ Crucified
3. Tracking the Vision of 1 Corinthians
4. Summary Reflection
5. Key People, Places, and Terms
6. Questions for Review and Discussion
7. Contemporary Theological Reflection
8. Going Further

KEY VERSES

1 Corinthians 2:1–2: "When I came to you, I did not come with eloquence or human wisdom as I proclaimed to you the testimony about God. For I resolved to know nothing while I was with you except Jesus Christ and him crucified."

1 Corinthians 6:11: "You were washed, you were sanctified, you were justified in the name of the Lord Jesus Christ and by the Spirit of our God."

1 Corinthians 11:1: "Follow my example, as I follow the example of Christ."

1 Corinthians 13:13: "And now these three remain: faith, hope and love. But the greatest of these is love."

1 Corinthians 15:17: "And if Christ has not been raised, your faith is futile; you are still in your sins."

SITUATING THE VISION: AN INTRODUCTION TO 1 CORINTHIANS

Above any other writing in the New Testament, 1 Corinthians provides the most intricate and extensive window on the life of early communities of Jesus devotion in an urban context. This is for two main reasons.

1. In sixteen chapters, Paul deals with a dozen or so topics that were complicating the corporate life of Corinthian Jesus-followers.
2. The topics he deals with resonate markedly with what is known to us about the first-century city of **Corinth**.

The combination of these two factors results in a portrait of Corinthian Jesus groups that has greater depth than portraits of Jesus groups in other locations. For this reason, studying Paul's Corinthian correspondence (both 1 and 2 Corinthians) often opens up exciting aspects in understanding the spread of the early Jesus movement within urban contexts.

The Context of Paul's Addressees

Knowing something about the first-century city of Corinth helps us to understand certain dimensions of the corporate life of Corinthian Christians. The first thing to note about Corinth is its prime location in relation to the flurry of activity of ancient civic life in the Roman province of Achaia. Situated some fifty miles (eighty kilometers) almost due west of Athens and sitting virtually under the canopy of the impressive uplift of the **Acrocorinth,** Corinth sat at the hub of a popular road network, on a narrow strip of land connecting the southern peninsula of Greece (the Peloponnese) and mainland Greece to the north.

From that route, and located on the coast of the Gulf of Corinth, it had easy access to the shipping lanes to the west (the port of Lechaeum), while only five miles (eight kilometers) to the southeast the port city of Cenchreae accessed the shipping lane to the east. If in the ancient world all roads led to Rome, a good number of routes passed through

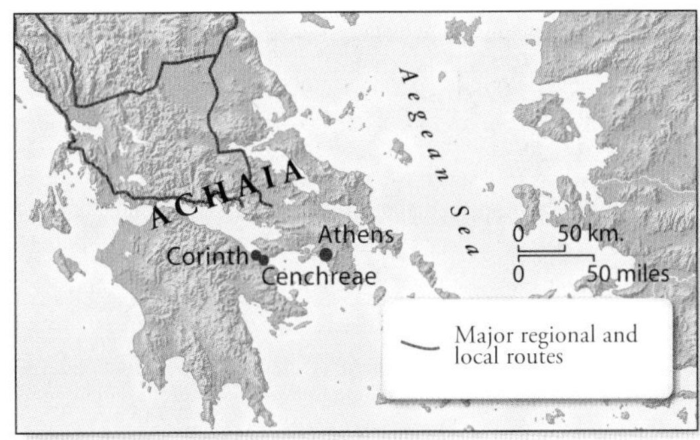

▲ Province of Achaia in ancient Greece

▼ The Temple of Apollo in Corinth, with the Acrocorinth uplift dominating the skyline behind it.

Matt O'Brien

▲ Ruins of Corinth overlooking the Gulf of Corinth

▼ These are the ruins of a public toilet in the heart of Corinth. Paul must have made use of these premises during the eighteen months that he resided in Corinth.

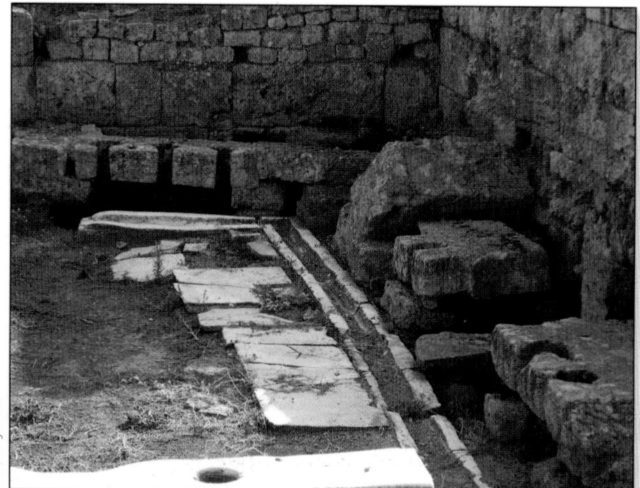

Bruce Longenecker

Corinth. Consequently, for those who could benefit from Corinth's strategic location, the material benefits were plentiful.

Not surprisingly, then, first-century Corinth was a thriving metropolis of perhaps a quarter of a million people. Archaeological excavations have uncovered much of what Paul would have known of the city, including various temples (including statues and monuments to the gods Apollo, Asclepius, Athena, Demeter, Serapis, and others), shops and workshops, the marketplace, the civic *bema* or "judgment seat" (see Acts 18:12, 16–17), public baths, and even the public toilets. There was probably a notable Jewish population in Corinth (see Acts 18:4–8, 12–17), but the pagan environment clearly predominated. Paul taps into the religious ethos of the day, which Corinth exemplifies, when he speaks of "many 'gods' and many 'lords'" (1 Cor 8:5).[1]

Those "gods" and "lords" played a role in a much larger quest for personal, corporate, and civic honor. This honor quest was engrained deeply in the Corinthian way of life, stretching back at least as far as the city's recent founding as a Roman colony. Having been destroyed by Rome in 146 BC, Corinth was reestablished by Julius Caesar in 44 BC, when its years of dormancy came to an end, becoming engulfed by a wave of pro-Roman sentiment and benefits.

The colonists sent to rebuild the city were not members of the elite, but were hungry for socioeconomic and religio-political advancement in a new city that was coming alive under Rome's auspices. By the time Paul arrived in the city, Corinth had established itself as the chief city of Achaia, one of the shining jewels in the crown of the Roman imperial order. Characteristic of most urban centers of the Roman world, the capture of honor for personal and civic benefit was the order of the day.

This aspect of the Corinthian civic ethos has its effect throughout Paul's Corinthian correspondence. The honor quest at times stands behind the pages of his letters, helping to

1. It is often said that sexual immorality was rampant in first-century Corinth. This reputation marked out Corinth a few centuries earlier, as part of the intercity polemic between the neighboring cities of Corinth and Athens. According to an Athenian slur, "to play the Corinthian" was to be sexually immoral. But it is not obvious that the slur had the same currency in the first century.

explain problems that Paul deals with time and time again. At other times, dimensions of Corinthian civic honor bleed onto the page itself. This is the case, for instance, with Paul's extended metaphors of athletic competition in 1 Cor 9:24–27. One of Corinth's main pillars of civic pride was the fact that it had hosted the prestigious **Isthmian Games** since 40 BC. This was not simply an athletic event; it was a biennial occasion that brought together vast swaths of spectators in one of the primary festivals that celebrated the spirit of all things progressive. Consequently, it bestowed incredible honors on Corinth, while at the same time ensuring that the service industries of Corinth (including, of course, leatherworkers/tentmakers such as Paul) were granted an enormous economic boost on a regular basis.

What Do We Know about Corinthian Followers of Jesus Christ?

Besides knowing something about the city of Corinth, we also know a few things about Corinthian Jesus-followers themselves. Some members of Corinthian Jesus groups seem to have enjoyed a certain degree of wealth and status. Although members of the civic elite were few and far between within Christian communities, some Corinthian believers in Jesus seem to have been relatively well placed in socioeconomic terms. Paul has them in view when speaking of the "not many" among the Corinthian Christians who were "influential" and "of noble birth" (1 Cor 1:26).

Among this number seem to be Corinthians whom Paul mentions specifically by name. One of them is **Gaius**, identified in Rom 16:23 as hosting "the whole church" of Corinth (i.e., all of the Jesus groups simultaneously) in his own home on occasion. **Stephanas** was another Corinthian householder who probably enjoyed at least comfortable means, with Paul commending him and his household for having "devoted themselves to the service of the Lord's people" (1 Cor 16:15–16). If the **Crispus** mentioned in 1:14 is the same Crispus mentioned in Acts 18:8, not only can we surmise that he became a Jesus-follower as a result of Paul's ministry but that, as the leader of the Corinthian synagogue, he may have had more than subsistence resources to draw upon.[2] The same is true of Phoebe, a woman whom Paul identifies as "the benefactor of many people" (Rom 16:2), especially those Christian communities in nearby Cenchreae.

There continues to be significant debate over whether the **Erastus** of Corinth whom Paul identifies as being involved in organizing the city's public works (Rom 16:23) is the same person honored on a Corinthian inscription for having paid for a city pavement as a consequence of having been appointed to a one-year administrative position that brought him much honor within the city. Clearly this inscriptional Erastus was a man of notable civic esteem, probably one of the civic elite. Nonetheless, the inscription may well date from the late first century or early second century, making it unlikely that the Erastus of the Corinthian inscription is the same as the Erastus of Rom 16:23.

All we really have, then, of the Corinthian Jesus-follower named Erastus is his profile in Rom 16:23. The NIV's translation of Paul's description of him in that verse (namely, "the city's director of public works"; Greek *ho oikonomos tēs poleōs*) will not please everyone,

2. Compare also the Sosthenes of Acts 18:7, a leader of the Corinthian synagogue. Is he the same person who is listed as the coauthor of 1 Corinthians (1 Cor 1:1)?

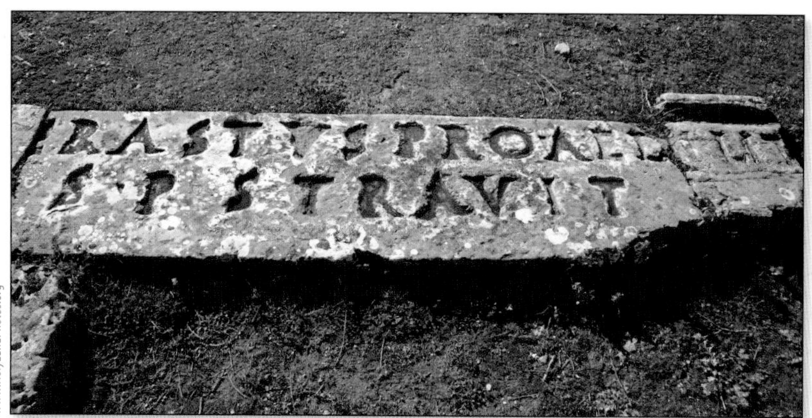

www.HolyLandPhotos.org

▲ The "Erastus Inscription" of Corinth, now lying on the ground. The name "Erastus" can be found in the top left corner of the inscription.

since the Greek term lying behind this translation seems to have had currency at a number of different civic levels, from the elite freemen down to servile civic functionaries whose public profile would not have risen above a middling status. Nonetheless, it is likely that, one way or another, the Corinthian Jesus-follower known to us as Erastus from Rom 16:23 would have had some public profile, even if he may not have been a civic "director" per se.

It would be wrong to give the impression from this that Corinthian Christians were notably prosperous. Some of the individuals named in Paul's texts seem to have been economically comfortable to an extent that would have differentiated them from most other Jesus-followers. But many Jesus-followers would have been in economically vulnerable situations—the kind of people Paul has in mind when speaking of "those who have nothing" (1 Cor 11:22). Although we don't know any of them by name, they probably comprised the backdrop against which to contrast not only the public image and civic ethos of Corinth but also of some of the better-off Corinthian Jesus-followers themselves.

Paul probably took great joy in seeing communities of Jesus-worshipers in which those with relatively secure economic means worshiped God alongside of those who were economically vulnerable. For him, where relationships of that sort resulted in models of fellowship and support, those relationships were unashamed testimonies and concrete advertisements of the in-breaking of God's reign.

This was a remarkable conviction on Paul's part, not least when we keep in mind the relatively small size of the Christian communities that he founded. Whereas churches today often have memberships reaching into the hundreds and, at times, thousands, the Jesus groups to which Paul was writing (several in each city) were each comprised of small numbers of people. It might be best to imagine several groups of Corinthian Jesus-followers, the average size of the groups being, say, twelve to twenty members, depending on their physical context (i.e., the size of the meeting place) and their resources. However we envision things, we are ultimately prevented from imagining a sizeable number of Corinthian Jesus-followers by Paul's comment about Gaius having hosted "the whole church" of Corinth in his home.

We cannot be sure that all communities of Jesus-followers met within household contexts. Some (in Corinth but also in other urban contexts) may have met in small shops (or in rooms behind or above them) or in small tenement apartments on higher floors above ground level. Most of these would not have been places of comfortable surroundings. Even those groups that met in larger households might have found themselves in the midst of

The House of the Bicentenary

Tyler Bell/Flickr

This picture is of a fairly large house in the first-century city of Herculaneum—the so-called House of the Bicentenary. The house is entered from a doorway that leads to a fairly large atrium (a open square area) that served a variety of purposes. A conglomeration of bedrooms and dining rooms adjoin the atrium. Beyond them is a peristyle that is open to the sky, with various rooms adjoining it (kitchens, perhaps slave accommodations). There were stairs in the middle that led up to separate apartments on the next level of the house, where approximately three separate residences existed.

A house of this kind might provide the background to Paul's comments in 1 Cor 14:23–24. There he seems to imagine people other than Jesus-followers simply walking into a corporate gathering of Jesus-followers that is already in progress. Space was largely shared in the ancient world, and people would have passed through open spaces when undertaking their various duties.

activity, since households were not merely "houses" for a single family unit (as is common in Western cultures today) but were hives in which familial, patronal, servile, and commercial relationships intersected.

Paul and the Corinthians, Thus Far

By the time Paul wrote 1 Corinthians, the Christian communities in Corinth had probably become used to the arrival and departure of people who were influential in the Jesus movement or who had proven their effectiveness in its mission. Paul, their founding father, was only the first of these. Also involved was **Apollos** of **Alexandria** in Egypt, who seems to have been a brilliant orator in defense of the message of the early Jesus movement. Acts recounts how Apollos left Ephesus to visit Corinth and reside there for a time (Acts 18:27–19:1). By the time Paul composed 1 Corinthians, however, Apollos was again back in Ephesus (1 Cor 16:12).

Similarly, **Prisca** (or **Priscilla**) and **Aquila**, who probably arrived in Corinth in AD 49 or early 50, seem to have left Corinth in 51 to take up residence in Ephesus. That they were an impressive team in ministry is suggested by three things.

- Most likely they went to Ephesus in AD 51 at Paul's request in order to prepare the way for his later Ephesian ministry, which he began there in 52 or perhaps 53.

▲ Map of Asia with Ephesus as the hub of Paul's churches

- Acts recounts that they themselves had been influential in instructing Apollos (Acts 18:24–26).
- After they had relocated to Rome again, Paul sends them greetings in a way that suggests that they had been steadfast leaders, identifying them as "my co-workers in Christ Jesus" and noting that they had "risked their lives for me" and that "all the churches of the Gentiles are grateful to them" (Rom 16:4–5).

It is even possible (in light of Paul's discussion in 1 Corinthians 1–4) that the apostle Simon Peter, the disciple of Jesus, had visited Corinthian Jesus groups at some point (he is named "Cephas" in 1 Cor 1:12; 3:22; 9:5; 15:5; Gal 1:18; 2:9; 11, 14).[3]

These arrivals and departures of relatively impressive and/or important people within the early Jesus movement would have taken place within the five years before Paul wrote 1 Corinthians. After he wrote 1 Corinthians, Paul's relationship with Corinthian Christians became bitter, stormy, and precarious. But in the letter known as 1 Corinthians, written half a year or so prior to 2 Corinthians (or at least, prior to its earliest section, 2 Corinthians 10–13; see the next chapter for details), those storm clouds are only on the horizon.

After residing in Corinth from early AD 50 to mid-50s, Paul eventually settled in Ephesus for several years (perhaps from 52 to 54/55). This provided him with an ideal location not only for planting Christian communities in another thriving metropolis of the Greco-Roman world, but also for keeping in touch with the fledgling Jesus groups for which he felt responsibility. Ephesus was situated at the hub of those communities that he had already founded, arcing as they did from Galatia to the east or northeast (depending on whether he wrote to communities in south Galatia or north Galatia, respectively), through Macedonia to the northwest (specifically, Philippi and Thessalonica), and down to Achaia to the west (specifically, Corinth and Cenchreae).

It was from Ephesus that Paul wrote 1 Corinthians (see 16:8), perhaps in the spring of AD 54 (although the following spring is also a strong contender). While the letter is known to us as *First* Corinthians, it was not the first letter that Paul had written to Corinthian Christians. Paul had sent them at least one earlier letter (see 1 Cor 5:9), probably from Ephesus in the second half of AD 53. Although this "previous letter" has not

3. This would help to explain some of the dispute reflected in 1 Cor 1:10–17 (cf. 3:21–23). Moreover, there is a strong tradition that Peter visited Rome (and died there), suggesting an apostle who traveled some distances in his mission.

survived,[4] we nonetheless can surmise that among Paul's exhortations was his counsel to avoid sexually immoral people. By this, Paul had meant that Jesus-followers should shun *other Jesus-followers* who engaged in immoral sexual behavior. But from Paul's comments in 5:9–13, we learn that the Corinthians understood him to suggest that Jesus-followers should avoid engaging with *outsiders* to Corinthian Jesus groups. As Paul understood all too well, this would only shut them off from opportunities to influence others with the good news of the early Jesus movement.

"One of the most obvious facts about the movement associated with Paul and his fellows was the vigor of its missionary drive, which saw in the outsider a potential insider and did not want to cut off communication with him or her."[5]

Paul must have been prompted to write the "previous letter" because of news he had heard about the Corinthian Christians. More news was yet to follow, and in a double dose. After sending the "previous letter," Paul was visited by two groups of people who brought news about and questions from Corinthian Jesus groups. The first group is easily designated as "**Chloe**'s people" (1 Cor 1:11)—probably a woman's servants who were traveling from Corinth to Ephesus.[6] They informed Paul about the rise of a serious rupture in the social fabric of Corinthian Jesus groups, brought about by allegiances to different leaders. About the same time, perhaps just a little bit later, Paul received a letter from some other Corinthian Christians (who may also have delivered oral reports of their own). This letter, probably carried by Stephanas, **Fortunatus**, and **Achaicus** (1 Cor 16:17; see also 7:1), asked Paul to comment on several issues that had arisen in Corinthian Christian communities.

The structure of 1 Corinthians is largely determined by Paul's successive responses to the matters brought to his attention by these two groups of people. Paul's letter begins with a lengthy engagement on the matter of allegiance and affiliation within Christian communities (1 Corinthians 1–4)—a matter registered by Chloe's people. Most of chapters 7 through 16 deal with matters mentioned in the letter carried by Stephanas and others, including:

- sexual conduct and marriage (which Paul addresses in ch. 7)
- meals and worship issues (which Paul addresses in chs. 8–10)
- heavenly speech (which Paul addresses in chs. 12–14)
- the funds that Paul was collecting for members of Jerusalem Jesus groups (which Paul addresses at the start of ch. 16)

It is not clear whether the issues dealt with in 1 Corinthians 5–6 (regarding specific sexual practices and legal relationships), 1 Corinthians 11 (regarding women in worship

4. Some imagine that part of the letter is now contained within 2 Cor 6:14–7:1, but this is unlikely.
5. Wayne A. Meeks, *First Urban Christians: The Social World of the Apostle Paul* (New Haven, CT: Yale University Press, 1983), 101.
6. We do not know whether Chloe was based in Corinth or Ephesus. Nor can we be sure that she was a Jesus-follower. Probably her servants were Jesus-followers. This might suggest that she was as well, although masters often allowed their servants to worship deities with relative freedom.

and the **Lord's Supper**), and 1 Corinthians 15 (regarding the resurrection) were brought to Paul by Chloe's delegation or by Stephanas and his associates.[7]

The portrait of Corinthian Jesus groups that emerges from 1 Corinthians is one in which some Corinthian Christians had become enamored with a spirituality of empowerment, enrichment, and enlightenment that, while stemming from the power of the gospel, nonetheless was in danger of undermining that gospel. Their spiritual power was impressive (1:5–7), not least in the ecstatic speech that they shared with the heavenly angels (chs. 12–14). They imagined themselves to be among the spiritual elite, those who have all the spiritual manifestations of salvation already. The spiritual power that comes from being "in Christ" was theirs already and completely, and they needed nothing further. They were free, enlightened, and empowered (see, e.g., 4:8–10, where Paul employs some biting criticism).

Paul saw things much differently. He saw Corinthian Jesus groups enthralled by the allure of spiritual power but blinded to the cancers that were eating away at their corporate life and their theological understanding in a number of ways. And with this in mind, we turn now to a sample passage that demonstrates Paul's preferred approach to the matter of spiritual formation appropriate to Christians.

CENTERING THE VISION OF 1 CORINTHIANS: NOTHING BUT CHRIST CRUCIFIED

> And so it was with me, brothers and sisters. When I came to you, I did not come with eloquence or human wisdom as I proclaimed to you the testimony about God. For I resolved to know nothing while I was with you except Jesus Christ and him crucified. I came to you in weakness with great fear and trembling. My message and my preaching were not with wise and persuasive words, but with a demonstration of the Spirit's power, so that your faith might not rest on human wisdom, but on God's power. (1 Cor 2:1–5)

The true force of Paul's comments here can be easily missed, with the practical implications and outworking of his claims becoming converted into mere religious platitudes. But Paul's resolve "to know nothing" except "Jesus Christ and him crucified" is not simply an expression of heartfelt piety. Nor does it introduce a new option for jewelry ornamentation (and who today hasn't seen the cross worn as a mere fashion item?). As Paul unpacks the phrase "Jesus Christ crucified," he shows that it involves a radical redefinition of life and a sweeping reconfiguration of lifestyle. If "Jesus Christ crucified" is something of a slogan for Paul,[8] it is a slogan that informs the repatterning of whole sectors of life—individual and collective, ethical and ecclesial, political and religious.

These words from 2:1–5 exemplify what Paul does throughout much of this letter. That is, he highlights a strand of the gospel that subverts the Corinthians' cultural norms

---

7. It seems most likely, however, that the matters raised in 1 Corinthians 5–6 were first reported to Paul by Chloe's people. This does more justice to the phrase that introduces chapter 7 ("Now for the matters you wrote about," 7:1), and might explain why issues about sexuality tend to gravitate to chapters 5–7, as if providing a hinge between the issues reported by Chloe's people (chs. 1–6) and those issues raised by Stephanas and his associates (predominantly throughout chs. 7–16).
8. Both 1 Cor 1:17–18 and Gal 3:1 also offer a slogan-like effect to the phrase "Christ crucified." Also, 1 Cor 15:3 ("For what I received I passed on to you as of first importance: that Christ died for our sins according to the Scriptures") demonstrates that this part of Paul's gospel was fully embedded within the earliest formulation of the early Jesus movement's gospel proclamation.

and expectations and applies it to their situation in ways that reorient them along the path of the gospel's outworking.

In 1 Corinthians 1–4, for instance, Paul offsets Corinthian disputes about who is the most impressive among various leaders by contrasting the gospel's configuration of honor with the things that enhanced status within Greco-Roman culture (see, e.g., 1:17–2:5; 3:18–23; 4:8–13). When addressing issues about eating meat sacrificed to idols and participating in civic meals in chapters 8–10, Paul inserts into the Corinthians' deliberations the notion of forfeiting one's own benefits in order to enhance the well-being of others (esp. 8:9–9:27). In 11:17–34, Paul identifies the Corinthians' observance of the Lord's Supper as running contrary to the ethos of the gospel because their practices had become infected by conformity to honor codes of the day; in contrast, Paul calls on them to align their practices with the ethos of self-giving care for the vulnerable. And whereas some of the Corinthians were imagining certain of the more "impressive" spiritual gifts to be badges of honor and prestige, in chapters 12–14 Paul is forced to redefine "impressive" and to reconstruct the quest for spiritual gifts by (1) offsetting the quest for personal enhancement through spiritual gifts and (2) foregrounding the enhancement of the body of Christ through gifts that build up others.

At the heart of all this is what Paul calls "the message of the cross." As he readily recognizes, that message is "foolishness" when analyzed in reference to the quest for honor that enraptured the Corinthian ethos. Paul calls the Corinthians to look beyond that perception of foolishness in order that they might be empowered with "the power of God" (1 Cor 1:18; also 2:4–5), enabling them to be reoriented to the story of the cross and resurrection of Jesus.

In this regard, however, it is important to notice that what Paul brings to the table in his application of "the message of the cross" is a focus on the corporate dimension of following Jesus. If some Corinthian Jesus-followers imagined that their spiritual empowerment could be used to augment their own status, Paul harnesses their expectations by ensuring that they will imagine themselves to be (and therefore act accordingly as) those fully embedded within and responsible to the corporate "body of Christ." In this, slogans that the Corinthians probably attributed to Paul's gospel of "freedom" become reprocessed, with Paul disinfecting them and setting them back in play with a new spin.

For instance, if some Corinthians thought Paul's gospel could be encapsulated in the slogan "I have the right to do anything," Paul qualifies this with "but not everything is beneficial," and with "but not everything is constructive" (1 Cor 6:12–13; 10:23).[9] In their context, these qualifications introduce a corporate mindedness into the Corinthian mix. When insisting that not everything is beneficial or constructive, he means for the well-being of the community of Jesus-followers. For Paul, acting for the well-being of others involves a cross-centered posture toward others. So he writes, "no one should seek their own good, but the good of others" (10:24). While that directive might sound like foolishness in a world engulfed in the quest for honor capture, it is nothing less than the corporate application of the "message of the cross."

9. For other occasions in which Paul seems to register and then qualify slogans that, although having truth to them, need nonetheless to be qualified, see 1 Cor 8:1, 4–6.

When individuals and communities align themselves aright with the message of Christ crucified, they will find themselves engulfed in nothing less than "God's power"—power that transforms people for service and frees them from the endless quest for culturally defined honor.

TRACKING THE VISION OF 1 CORINTHIANS

The basic structure of 1 Corinthians can be outlined as follows:

1:1–9	Opening Greeting (1:1–3) and Thanksgiving (1:4–9)
1:10–4:21	On Corporate Divisions: God's Wisdom Confounds Cultural Codes of Honor
5:1–6:20	On Sexual and Litigious Practices: The Sanctified Life
7:1–40	On Marriage and Celibacy: God's Gifting of Various Lifestyles
8:1–11:1	On Food Sacrificed to Idols: Individual Freedom and Corporate Responsibility
11:2–16	On Women in Prayer and Prophecy: Gender Matters
11:17–34	On the Lord's Supper: The "Have-Nots" within the Body of the Lord
12:1–14:40	On Spiritual Gifts: Individual Gifting and Corporate Roles
15:1–58	On Resurrection: Redemption Includes the Created Order
16:1–24	Letter Closing

1 Corinthians 1–4

A gospel of the crucified Jesus that frees his followers from the endless quest for culturally defined honor is the topic of 1 Corinthians 1–4. In the ancient world, honor was ascribed in different quantities depending on any number of components of one's identity: gender, ethnicity, family background, educational opportunities, servile or nonservile status, occupation, relationships, financial well-being, rhetorical eloquence, and on and on. As a consequence, the ancient world was highly attuned to differences in identity, in order to ensure that its social mechanisms ran like clockwork.

In Paul's view, however, whenever those mechanisms invaded Christian communities, more often than not they dissembled the proper workings of those groups. For Paul, followers of Jesus Christ were to relate to each other not by heightening their identity differences but by heightening their sense of corporate unity despite those differences.

Paul gets right to the point in chapters 1–4, appealing to the Corinthian Christians that "there be no divisions among you" (1:10). But they are a long way from that goal. Instead, some of the Corinthians have fallen into the trap of allowing the gospel to be clouded by a zealous attachment to a personality whose rhetorical prowess they favor—whether that be Paul, Apollos, or Cephas (i.e., Peter; 1:12; see also 3:4).[10] The rhetorical question makes the point, "Is Christ divided?" (1:13). In Paul's view, the ways of society had permeated the corporate structures of Corinthian Christian communities. So, the "jealousy and quarreling" among them indicated only that they remained "worldly" and were acting "like mere human beings" (3:3) in their various attachments to leading personalities in the early Jesus movement.

Bruce Longenecker

▲ An ancient inscription that places the names of Paul and Peter together; from the Roman catacomb of Saint Sebastian

This deficit in their practice and understanding was itself part of their complicity with the social mores of honor and prestige. Paul depicts these Corinthians in a way that probably resonated with their own perception of things, even if he intends these words to be heard with a note of ironic burlesque: "Already you have all you want! Already you have become rich! You have begun to reign" (4:8). This depiction might suggest that some of the Corinthians were imagining that they already experienced the fullness of the reign of God in its totality—often called "realized" or (better) "over-realized" **eschatology**. After all, marvels brought about by the Spirit of God were in their possession.[11] Other places in this letter seem to suggest that this same perception led to other deficiencies as well, as if there were nothing left for God to do with them, either in the present or the future.

But Paul contrasts that view of things with another one—one that is sometimes called "**inaugurated** (but not yet fully realized) **eschatology**." In this view of things, God's plan of salvation has not yet been fully completed and involves patterns of lifestyle that run contrary to the way of "honor" defined by those who benefit from established societal structures. So Paul outlines how the "wisdom of God" in the gospel of the crucified Messiah clashes with "the wisdom of this age" (2:6; see his full discussion in 1:18–2:16).

Ironically, the "leading personalities" that the Corinthian Christians so much admire but bicker about are not in competition with each other but are serving different purposes for

10. Paul also mentions "Christ" in this context, but this is unlikely to reflect the allegiance of a particular subgroup. More probably, it represents Paul's ironic exaggeration of the situation—as if to say, "If you start down this track, you'll be likely to relegate even Jesus Christ to the position of a cult personality."
11. See, e.g., the way Paul characterizes the Spirit in ways that address this Corinthian problem in 2:10–3:4.

A Small Bakery Apartment from Pompeii[13]

This is the ruins of a small bakery apartment in the first-century city of Pompeii. A cross was found on one of the walls of the storefront, although it is disputed whether this represents the presence of early Jesus devotion within the city of Pompeii prior to its destruction in the eruption of Mount Vesuvius in AD 79. If this cross was an artifact of Jesus devotion, it was perhaps the earliest Christian artifact ever uncovered. Unfortunately the cross has been demolished by the processes of nature.

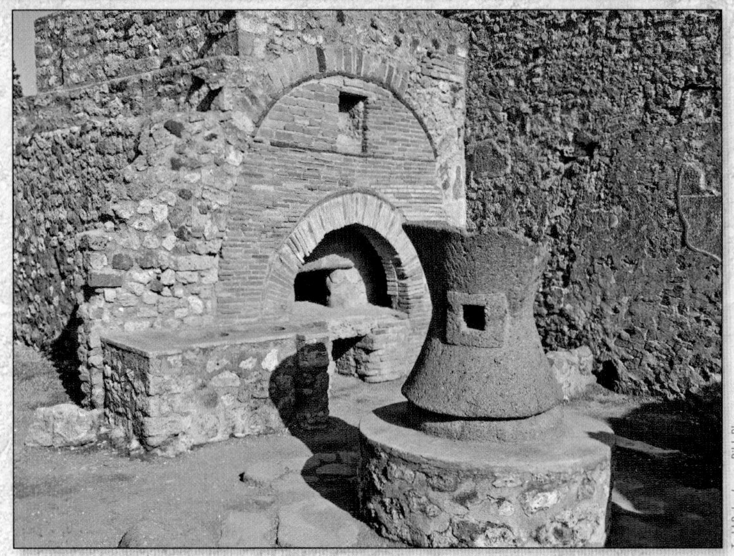

Todd Bolen/www.BiblePlaces.com

▲ The oven in the bakery

"It was characteristic of Paul's preaching that he focused on the fact that Jesus had died by crucifixion. He had made his hearers believe that they were present at the cross. No mere rhetorical tricks could achieve such an effect. Paul had to have the imagination to re-create the event for himself, and relive the appropriate emotions, before he could achieve the verbal vividness that he claims in Galatians 3:1. Paul's compulsion to replicate the crucifixion [in his public preaching] is explicable only if it made a huge impact on him."[12]

the same goal (3:5–10)—that is, to enhance the gospel foundations within the Corinthians' individual and corporate lives (3:10–17; see also 4:6). The apostolic pattern of Paul's ministry itself demonstrates that God's wisdom runs against the grain of culturally constructed systems of honor. So Paul characterizes his ministry as, among other things, foolish, weak, and dishonorable by cultural standards (4:9–13), concluding that he has "become the scum of the earth, the garbage of the world."

Having dealt harshly with this form of Corinthian complicity with cultural codes of honor, Paul concludes the section without pulling his punches. He speaks of the arrogance of those Corinthians who have gone wrong in this regard and threatens the prospect of disciplining them when he next comes to Corinth (4:18–21). Paul feels he had a right to speak severely to them, just as a father has cause at times to speak severely to his children (4:14–16). It may be, however, that some of the Corinthians took great offense

12. Jerome Murphy-O'Connor, *Paul: His Story* (Oxford: Oxford University Press, 2006), 34.

at Paul's stern comments (see, e.g., 3:1–4, 18; 4:8–10, 14, 19–21), and that their offense led to further problems between Paul and the Corinthian Jesus groups (as evidenced by what Paul will later write in 2 Corinthians).

Bruce Longenecker

▲ A wall painting of wise Hellenistic philosophers from the ancient city of Ostia

1 Corinthians 5–6

In these two chapters, Paul engages with three topics that have been reported to him (probably by Chloe's people). The first (5:1–13) and third (6:12–20) deal with sexual issues, but these are separated by an issue that has nothing to do with sexual relations, dealing instead with Christians in lawsuit situations (6:1–11).

Although this "sandwiching" of topics may simply be incidental, the fact that it corresponds to a patterning technique of Paul's day suggests that there may have been intentionality in this structure. When used effectively, the A-B-A structure that these chapters exhibit (with A-sections dealing with sexual matters and the B-section dealing with a nonsexual matter) would have suggested to the audience that the B-section holds the interpretative key that underlies even the A-sections.[13] Paul goes on to use precisely this same structure in 1 Corinthians 8–10 (with chapter 9 as its centerpiece) and 1 Corinthians 12–14 (with chapter 13 as its centerpiece). If the same pattern is evident in chapters 5–6, then what Paul writes in 6:9–11 (the end of the middle topic) probably qualifies as the centerpiece of the section. There he speaks of the sins (including especially sexual sins) that exclude people from the kingdom of God; he contrasts that by reminding the Corinthian Jesus-followers: "you were washed, you were sanctified, you were justified in the name of the Lord Jesus Christ and by the Spirit of our God" (6:11).

As a consequence of that status, Corinthian Jesus-followers should not be taking each other to court (6:1–11). For Paul, if Christians seek compensation for perceived wrongs done by other Christians, they are in danger of compromising the missionary witness of Christian communities. If the gospel of the self-giving Christ has come alive among them, how feeble it would be for them to try to assert their individual rights or to seek their own benefits over against other Jesus-followers. Instead, Paul makes a proposal that runs against the grain of every culture throughout the ages: "Why not rather be wronged? Why not rather be cheated?" (6:7, resonating with his words in 4:7: "What do you have that you did not receive [from God]?").

13. The gospel of Mark often exhibits this form of structure, for precisely this purpose.

As a consequence of their "sanctified" status, Corinthian Jesus-followers should not be reveling in the sin of one of their (prominent?) members, who is now living (and having sexual relations) with his father's wife (i.e., the person's stepmother, not his mother; 5:1–13). Paul despises both the sin itself and the attitude that seems to have predominated in some circles of Corinthian Christians toward that sin. Perhaps the attitude of pride that was transpiring emerged as a consequence of a view that, as "sanctified" people who were not restrained by "the law," they could adopt even the most morally dubious lifestyle without compromising God's great pleasure toward them. But Paul sees no reason to be proud. Instead, he instructs them to exclude the sinner from among their fellowship. This exclusion (i.e., handing the sinner "over to Satan") will serve two purposes. First, it may result in the repentance of the sinner (i.e., his sinful way of life will be destroyed, 5:5). Second, it will stop the contagion of sin from spreading further within Corinthian Christian communities (5:6–8).

"Paul [denies] to the higher status members of the Corinthian church one of the important means by which they defended and promoted their prestige and status, at least if it involved another believer. The practice of civil litigation, intended as a way of upholding honour, is described as shameful for a believer. The values of the dominant social order are reversed and opposed."[14]

Finally, as a consequence of their "sanctified" status, Corinthian followers of Christ should not be having sexual relations with prostitutes (6:12–20). Once again an **antinomian** or **libertine** attitude may have been used to justify this practice among Corinthian Christians, as in their slogan of 6:12: "I have the right to do anything." Some Corinthian Christians probably compared sexual appetite to hunger (6:13). They may have imagined that, just as hunger is satisfied by eating, so too the sexual appetite is to be satisfied by indulging it in whatever way, even with a prostitute outside of marriage.

But Paul qualifies their "rights" with the important qualifications that "not everything [within one's rights] is beneficial," and "I will not be mastered by anything" that compromises my faithfulness before God. For Paul, one's sexuality is bound up with one's spirituality, rather than being separate from it. Sexual union is not just an inconsequential physical act; instead, it involves the essence of one's identity. For Paul, damaging sexual practices emerge from and perpetuate a fractured spirituality.

1 Corinthians 7

The issue of sexual relations carries over into this section of the letter, being driven by a Corinthian slogan that "it is good for a man not to have sexual relations with a woman" (7:1). How they arrived at this view is not certain, although it may be another feature of an "over-realized eschatology." That is, already living fully in the new age, some may have thought that they needed to deny their physical bodies all sexual appetites (in contrast to others, who may have thought that the body was irrelevant and they could do anything with it at all).

---

14. David G. Horrell, *The Social Ethos of the Corinthian Correspondence: Interests and Ideology from 1 Corinthians to 1 Clement* (Edinburgh: T&T Clark, 1996), 141.

This topic gets Paul started on a series of issues (including a short paragraph on slavery, 7:21–24). He advocates having sexual relations only within a marriage between husband and wife in order to avoid sexual immorality (and this is advice he gives to both married and single people). He notes that his own preference is for singleness and celibacy over against marriage, but he recognizes also that God calls people to different kinds of lifestyles, whether married or celibate. So married couples are not to separate in order to adopt a celibate lifestyle, but instead should maintain the marriage. Likewise, when one marriage partner becomes a Jesus-follower and the other partner does not, the marriage is not to be dissolved but maintained, not least in the hope of converting the one who is not a follower of Jesus. In general, says Paul, with regard to their choice for marriage or celibacy, Christians are to remain on the course to which God has called them.

▲ This is one of the rooms in a brothel at Pompeii, where women (usually slaves) serviced customers in the sex trade.

1 Corinthians 8:1–11:1

The contents of these chapters revolve around the issue of eating, an issue comprised of two subparts. The first has to do with the eating of meat. In the ancient world, most people could not afford to purchase meat. The main exception to this was meat that, having first been offered to idols but now being surplus to temple and priestly requirements, was sold in meat markets in connection with pagan temples. The second subpart of the issue is related to the first, but specifically involves the question of whether Jesus-followers should take part in dinners held in local pagan temples, where meat of this kind would have been part of the meal. Not surprisingly, the connection between meat and idolatry put these issues squarely on the moral radar of some Corinthian Christians.

Paul's discussion reveals that there were two views on these matters among his audience, who are identified (by him?) as "the strong" and "the weak." Those identified as "the strong" seem to have thought that, since an idol was nothing but an inanimate object, the meat involved in idol sacrifices was in no way contaminated; consequently, neither eating the meat

▼ The Macellum in Pompeii seems to have served as the central food market for this Greco-Roman town. Perhaps much of the meat offered to the local gods in nearby temples was moved to this market area to be sold to local residents.

nor participating in banquets could compromise the identity of a Jesus-follower. Those identified as "the weak," however, were not so sure.

Paul's position does not coincide fully with either of these two groups. On the matter of whether idol meat is contaminated, he agrees with "the strong" that it is not. But that is not the end of the matter for him. The fact that "the weak" struggle with the issue means that "the strong" cannot simply think and do what they like and then leave "the weak" to be scandalized by their behavior. While "the strong" may have the proper "knowledge," that knowledge must be fed through a corporate filter in order to assess whether or not to act on it.

"One of the most interesting things about [1 Corinthians 8:1 – 11:1] is that Paul seems to agree with the theological principles upon which the strong base their freedom to eat idol-food. He could, presumably, have developed and strengthened their point of view. However, Paul emphasizes a different value which must inform and direct the actions of the Corinthians: limitations of one's own rights and freedom in deference to the other. For Paul this seeking the benefit of others is the fundamental ethical maxim."[15]

If this is Paul's main point in chapter 8, he reinforces it in chapter 9 with an example from his own apostolic ministry. For any number of reasons, Paul had the right to receive economic support for his ministry among Corinthian Jesus groups. But Paul insisted on not receiving financial reimbursement from them, giving up his right for the benefit of others. With regard to forfeiting entitlements, then, Paul does not expect anything of "the strong" that he has not already implemented in his own life and ministry. Paul expects cruciform morality both in himself and in Christian communities—and all of this flows from the pattern of Jesus Christ's own self-giving (cf. 1 Cor 11:1: "Follow my example, as I follow the example of Christ").

If Paul provides Corinthian Jesus-followers with a positive example for dealing with the matter of food sacrificed to idols in chapter 9, a narrative from the Old Testament provides him with a negative example in 10:1–13. The story of the people of Israel falling into idolatry (see Exodus 14–34 and Numbers 11–20) demonstrates just how easy it is for those who have enjoyed God's favor to be overcome by dangers that, when left unaddressed, undermine their enjoyment of God's grace among them.

Having registered both an example and a warning, Paul returns to the practical issues facing Corinthian worshipers of Jesus in 1 Cor 10:14–11:1, elaborating on his instruction in chapter 8. Although idols themselves are nothing other than brute matter, there are nonetheless spiritual realities involved in meals hosted at idol shrines or pagan temples. Those suprahuman forces might appear to be innocuous enough, but in reality they are dangerous to the identity of those who worship Jesus as Lord. For Paul, physical acts (such as having sexual relations outside of marriage, or participating in the Lord's Supper, or eating a meal with others at a pagan shrine) have spiritual components to them, and the danger of participating in a pagan meal is that one unintentionally becomes bound to and enslaved in a situ-

15. Horrell, *The Social Ethos of the Corinthian Correspondence*, 149.

ation where the spiritual atmosphere compromises one's relationship with God (10:14–22).

In 10:23–11:1 Paul again returns to the issue first addressed in chapter 8, summarizing his position (and repeating once again Corinthian freedom slogans in 10:23–25). Meat bought in the marketplace can be eaten without cause for concern regardless of whether it had previously been part of a pagan sacrifice. However, if some Jesus-followers are scandalized by the prospect of eating such meat, then other Jesus-followers should graciously forfeit their right to eat it. Paul's gospel of "freedom" is tempered by a concern to take into account the good of one's neighbors, to build them up (10:23–24). While Paul himself models this kind of practice (as outlined in chapter 9), he is only following the pattern established by Jesus Christ himself (11:1).

Bruce Longenecker

▲ The Temple of Isis in Pompeii, one of the smaller of the many temples of that Greco-Roman town. Temples to Greco-Roman gods characterized towns and cities throughout the Mediterranean basin.

1 Corinthians 11:2–16

In this part of Paul's letter, both the situation he addressed and the particulars of his instruction are mired in dispute, due to a lack of clarity in each case. One thing seems clear, however—that women were among the ones who led Corinthian Jesus groups in corporate prayer and prophecy (11:5, 13).[16] Paul has no qualms about this, but only about how it is being practiced among Christians. The problem may simply have been that women prayed and prophesied without veils, or it may have been that female prophetesses within Corinthian Jesus groups were loosening their hair completely like wild female pagan prophetesses. Regardless of how the situation is reconstructed, Paul thinks that some dimension of propriety and decorum was being transgressed in their habits.

When taken together at face value, Paul's instructions may exhibit some fragility. For instance, in 11:7–8 Paul interprets the Genesis story of humanity's creation in ways that can easily be read as suggesting that women are in a position of inferiority to men, as was commonly thought in Paul's day. But in 11:11–12, Paul argues just the opposite with regard to how things are to be for those "in the Lord." Perhaps what we are witnessing, then,

16. While prayer might be carried out in corporate or individual contexts, Paul imagines prophecy to be carried out solely within situations of corporate worship. In 14:1–5, for instance, he characterizes prophecy as involving edificatory words spoken to other people within the church for the purpose of strengthening the church. The assumption that prophecy operates within corporate worship contexts is evident also in Paul's comments in 14:24, 31.

is Paul going through the process of assembling a series of arguments, some of which are more informed by the gospel than others (e.g., arguments in vv. 5 and 14–15 are informed by cultural convention; the argument in vv. 2 and 16 invokes ecclesiastical tradition), but all of which are serving a single point.

What is that point? The common denominator to most of his arguments is that men and women are different. No matter how you look at it, this is incontrovertible: God created male and female differently; despite equality between male and female in Christ, differentiation between the sexes still remains; cultural values are built on an assumption of sexual differentiation. Indicators such as these reinforce the sole point that sexual differentiation is not to be contaminated or confused within Corinthian Christian communities.

However the issue was specifically configured in Corinth (and it may have had a complexity that is hard to pin down on the basis of Paul's letter), Paul seems to view the issue through this matrix of sexual differentiation, expecting that Corinthian women will take account of its implications for proper cultural decorum (e.g., wearing a veil). Paul argues that it is inappropriate for women to pray and prophecy in corporate gatherings without covering their heads, but he seems to argue the point not primarily because a hierarchy of the sexes applies to Christians but because the differences between women and men need to be preserved in a fashion that is sensitive to the cultural habits of the first-century world.[17] The fact that he does not allow those habits to completely overrun the gospel is evidenced in the fact that, when writing these words, he has no qualms about women praying and prophesying in gatherings of male and female followers of Jesus Christ.

1 Corinthians 11:17–34

Paul again discusses an issue that included identity differences among Jesus-followers, but this time he advocates a position that ran contrary to the norms of cultural propriety. Again the specifics of the situation are not wholly transparent, except that they involved the observance of the Lord's Supper among Corinthian Christians. Here socioeconomic factors seem to be in play. Evidently some Christians were having their fill of food and drink while others in their Jesus group were going hungry. Perhaps the more affluent members (whose houses were the likely context in which the Lord's Supper was being observed) were enjoying among themselves a meal that was superior in both quantity and quality to the meals of those "who have nothing." Because of this inequity, Paul chastises the Corinthians, saying, "It is not the Lord's Supper you eat" (11:20). Instead, by "humiliating those who have nothing," the more affluent members can be said to "despise the church of God" (11:22).

Probably what we are seeing is the influx of cultural values of honor within the value system of Corinthian Jesus-followers in their observance of the Lord's Supper. Much like his case in chapters 1–4 and elsewhere, Paul imagines this influx of culturally defined honor to undermine the proclamation of the good news about Jesus Christ (i.e., the proclamation of the Lord's death, 11:26). This meal is not simply a meal for the building up of one's own

17. Notice too how Paul, when discussing corporate unity in 1 Cor 12:13, repeats two of the contrasting terms of reference of Gal 3:28 (Jews/Greeks, slaves/free) but omits the third (male/female). It seems as if, in Paul's view, things were going wrong in Corinth with regard to sexual differentiation, with the theme of corporate unity being interpreted in problematic ways among some Jesus-followers there.

The Institution of the Lord's Supper

Jesus' words at "the institution of the Lord's Supper" are remembered in the gospels of Matthew, Mark, and Luke, and in Paul's letter of 1 Corinthians.

Matthew 26:26–29	Mark 14:22–25	Luke 22:15–20	1 Cor 11:23–26
While they were eating, Jesus took bread, and when he had given thanks, he broke it and gave it to his disciples, saying, "Take and eat; this is my body." Then he took a cup, and when he had given thanks, he gave it to them, saying, "Drink from it, all of you. This is my blood of the covenant, which is poured out for many for the forgiveness of sins. I tell you, I will not drink from this fruit of the vine from now on until that day when I drink it new with you in my Father's kingdom."	While they were eating, Jesus took bread, and when he had given thanks, he broke it and gave it to his disciples, saying, "Take it; this is my body." Then he took a cup, and when he had given thanks, he gave it to them, and they all drank from it. "This is my blood of the covenant, which is poured out for many," he said to them. "Truly I tell you, I will not drink again from the fruit of the vine until that day when I drink it new in the kingdom of God."	And he said to them, "I have eagerly desired to eat this Passover with you before I suffer. For I tell you, I will not eat it again until it finds fulfillment in the kingdom of God." After taking the cup, he gave thanks and said, "Take this and divide it among you. For I tell you I will not drink again from the fruit of the vine until the kingdom of God comes." And he took bread, gave thanks and broke it, and gave it to them, saying, "This is my body given for you; do this in remembrance of me." In the same way, after the supper he took the cup, saying, "This cup is the new covenant in my blood, which is poured out for you.	For I received from the Lord what I also passed on to you: The Lord Jesus, on the night he was betrayed, took bread, and when he had given thanks, he broke it and said, "This is my body, which is for you; do this in remembrance of me." In the same way, after supper he took the cup, saying, "This cup is the new covenant in my blood; do this, whenever you drink it, in remembrance of me." For whenever you eat this bread and drink this cup, you proclaim the Lord's death until he comes.

body with nutrients (if that's their attitude, they should simply eat at home on their own time; 11:22, 34). Instead, the Lord's Supper should be an instantiation and reflection of the values of the gospel itself, an ongoing memorial of remembrance for all time of what Jesus died for.

To offset the problem, Paul simply recites the countercultural story of Jesus, who, as recounted in the tradition of the Lord's Supper, gave himself for others. Paul expects the narrative ethos of that story to pave the way for a revised moral ethos among the Corinthian Christ-followers. Accordingly, he calls them all to "examine themselves" in their attitude to their corporate gatherings in order that they might "discern the body of Christ" in a worthy manner (11:27–29; cf. also 10:16–17). By this Paul probably means primarily that they should examine the health of their relationships to others within the corporate gathering, ensuring that those relationships testify to the cruciform character of the gospel rather than the Greco-Roman honor code. When those relationships are overrun by the quest for social honor rather than corporate support, God's judgment is inevitable (11:29–34).

1 Corinthians 12–14

These three chapters cover much ground, being driven in the first instance by the issue of speaking in tongues, "tongues . . . of angels" as Paul refers to them (perhaps echoing a Corinthian point of view, 13:1).

People of the ancient world were not unfamiliar with forms of spiritual ecstasy. It was not altogether uncommon for a spirit-person to allow himself or herself to be caught up in the grip of a possessing spirit, uttering garbled babbling as a sign and by-product of being enraptured by that spirit. Corinthian Jesus groups had among their number some Jesus-followers whose own enrichment in Christ Jesus included "all kinds of speech" (1:5). While this was notable, Paul thought that Corinthian Jesus-followers understood those manifestations of the Spirit incorrectly. By using their spiritual gifts to enhance their own personal status, the Corinthians were using the Spirit as a mechanism in the cultural game of honor-capture, resulting in individualistic one-upmanship characterized by competitiveness and, perhaps, conflict. They seem to have ranked the gifts of the Spirit and prioritized speaking in tongues as the greatest of all spiritual gifts.

Although Paul himself spoke in tongues (14:18), his view of that gift was much different than that of some Corinthians. On the assumption that spiritual rapture can look much the same in pagan contexts and in Christian communities, Paul insinuates that spiritual manifestations themselves need to be tested for their authenticity. Authentic spirituality needs to comply with the affirmation that "Jesus is Lord" (12:1–3). That affirmation is not, however, some verbal utterance that otherwise has little significance. Instead, it is connected to a full-bodied theology of community. Consequently, much like his discussion of the Lord's Supper in 11:17–34, here Paul argues that an authentic spirituality among those who believe in Jesus Christ must be associated with a proper understanding of "the body of Christ" (12:27).

The whole of Paul's discussion in 12:4–31 amplifies this point. Two main points run throughout this section. In 12:4–11, Paul points out that all spiritual gifts derive from a common source, namely, the Spirit who bestows gifts differently among the community. While the Corinthians might well have agreed with this, Paul filters the whole of his discussion through a corporate lens through the phrase "for the common good" (12:7).

That lens itself becomes the focal point in the second half of the chapter (12:12–31), where Paul emphasizes that the gifts are part of a program whereby the Spirit resources Christian communities for corporate edification and corporate service. As such, the gifts are not meant as advertisements of one's spiritual celebrity but, instead, are to enhance the corporate resources of Christian communities. Just as a body would be a monstrosity if it had only one component or would be defective if it despised parts of itself, so too the body of Christ is to be characterized by an appreciation of the mutual interdependence of its corporate gifting.[18]

With the Corinthians in the habit of prioritizing spiritual gifts, Paul decides to set out his own hierarchy of gifts, in which the gift of tongues is placed last (12:28). But his bet-

18. See also Paul's emphasis on building up the body in 14:4, 5, 12, 17, 26, where his focus is on a similar issue.

ter strategy is to get them to move beyond gift hierarchies in order to understand and put into practice "the most excellent way" (12:31b). With this phrase as its interpretative prism, Paul's extended tribute to love is set out in 13:1–13—one that has long been embedded within the standard liturgy for ecclesiastical wedding ceremonies. The love that Paul has in mind, however, is characterized less by emotional feelings than by deep commitment to others. This is why it is "the more excellent way," precisely because it is a manifestation of what is everlasting.

Gifts of the Spirit are only a temporary phenomenon; once God's eschatological reign is fully implemented, there will no longer be a need for the Spirit to resource Christian communities with spiritual gifts. But what will continue on into that eschatological reign of God is the excellent way of love that benefits others (13:8–12). Notably, in 13:13 Paul ranks the three exceptional attributes of faith, hope, and love. Of those three, Paul emphasizes for the Corinthians' benefit that love should be the primary soil to nourish the exercising of spiritual gifts in corporate gatherings of Christians (14:1). Giftedness without agape-love is vacuous.

"1 Corinthians 13 reflects the continuing influence of [Jesus'] spirit of self-sacrificial love. Jesus wrote nothing to the Corinthians, but without him 1 Corinthians 13 would not have been written."[19]

Returning to the issue of speaking in tongues, in chapter 14 Paul contrasts that gift with the gift of prophecy (which he has already ranked more highly than tongues in 12:28, right under the gift of apostleship). Paul considers prophecy to be more edificatory than tongues for several reasons. Unless they are interpreted, the gift of tongues tends to edify merely the individual, whom no one can otherwise understand. The gift of prophecy, however, edifies the group by exercising the mind. The gift of tongues runs the risk of outsiders imagining that Christians are "out of their minds," whereas the gift of prophecy, with its power to convict members and offer guidance to the community, will give rise to outsiders worshiping God as a result of their observation that "God is really among you." In exercising their gifts, Corinthian Christians are to ensure that they do all things "in an fitting and orderly way" (14:40).

An instruction about women in corporate meetings appears within this context (14:34–35). It appears here because the person who penned these words imagined that the injunction that "women should remain silent in the churches" and "are not allowed to speak, but must be in submission, as the law says," is itself a feature of ecclesiastical order, with everything being done "in a fitting and orderly way."

But who is the person who penned these two verses? The point is disputed. It is, in fact, possible that Paul did not write these verses at all, but that they crept into the letter through other means. As noted in a footnote in the NIV, these verses also appear in some manuscripts after 14:40 instead of after 14:33. The placing of the same words in different places in different manuscripts can signal that those words first originated not in the text itself but in the margin of the text, where a scribe of a later generation took it upon himself to add a further thought to what the author had originally written. The next scribes who

19. Dale Allison, *The Historical Christ and the Theological Jesus* (Grand Rapids: Eerdmans, 2009), 28.

then copied from that manuscript imagined that the words in the margin had originally been in the text itself and needed only to be put back into the text. But they didn't put the marginal gloss into the text in the same fashion; instead, one scribe placed it after 14:33 and another scribe placed it after 14:40. Because the views expressed in 14:34–35 are difficult to harmonize with what Paul expresses in 11:1–16 about women exercising public roles in Christian communities, and because in 14:36–40 Paul picks up on the discourse that 14:34–35 interrupts, the scribal insertion theory has a notable degree of plausability.[20]

If the scribal insertion theory is not accepted, how is it possible to relieve what looks to be an outright contradiction between Paul's statements about women in 14:34–35 and 11:1–16, where he assumes that women are free to exercise roles of public prayer and prophecy among Christians? Perhaps in 14:34–35 he meant only to address a particular case that had arisen within Corinthian groups of Jesus-followers, in which certain women were disrupting the meeting inordinately by chattering among themselves while the meeting was in progress (although if this were the case, we might wish that Paul had made the point more carefully).

David Parker, a prominent analyst of ancient manuscripts, writes: "Variation in positioning [as in the case of 14:34–35] is often a sign of an interpolation. That is why the evidence concerning the location of the verses is so important. Perhaps the sentence [of 14:34–35] was first written in the margin as a comment or addition and then found its way into the text in two different places."[21]

Or perhaps the advice about women in 14:34–35 is driven by the concern that Jesus-followers should avoid offending others unnecessarily. In this option, Paul has already advocated letting go of certain "freedoms" that Christians might normally enjoy in order that others might benefit (see 9:8; 10:32). And he advertises his own pattern of life as involving the endurance of anything "rather than hinder[ing] the gospel of Christ" (9:12). Moreover, he has already advised Jesus-followers to regulate their eating practices in order to avoid offending or shocking someone (1 Corinthians 8–10), and encouraged women to ensure that their freedom in Christ is not used flagrantly in matters where culturally sensitive issues suggest they should act with propriety—that is, covering their heads, as they would in a Jewish synagogue (11:2–16).

In 1 Corinthians 14, Paul then addresses the propriety of exercising spiritual gifts within the community, mentioning the prospect of nonbelievers coming into the midst of Jesus-followers during their corporate worship. In that scenario, Paul wants everything to be done in such a way as to impress and encourage unbelievers, even to the extent that they will join in with the worship of Jesus themselves (14:24–25). Worship must be conducted wholly with a view to building up the community in its worship (14:26), so that unnecessary offense will be minimized, permitting only the offense of the gospel (e.g., 1:23) to transpire within corporate meetings. Consequently, Paul emphasizes the need for orderly worship, saying: "For God is not a God of disorder but of peace—as in all the congrega-

20. For defense of this view, see Gordon D. Fee, *God's Empowering Presence* (Peabody, MA: Hendrickson, 1994), 272–81.

21. David Parker, *An Introduction to The New Testament Manuscripts and Their Texts* (Cambridge: Cambridge University Press, 2008), 276.

tions of the Lord's people" (14:33).[22] He says the same in 14:39–40, where he encourages Jesus-worshipers to "be eager to prophesy, and do not forbid speaking in tongues. But everything should be done in a fitting and orderly way."

This is the theological context that surrounds the two verses under consideration. Regardless of who authored the instructions about women in 14:34–35, those verses seem to be articulated in relation to these concerns for the welfare of the gospel—concerns that seem uppermost in Paul's mind in the context of 1 Corinthians 14 and are articulated earlier as well. Paul was eager to remove unnecessary offenses from the process of promulgating the gospel, and perhaps something similar is evident in 14:34–35.

Perhaps the potential offense that lies behind these verses was simply one of charismatic excess, with female Jesus-followers being particularly vulnerable to the problem of unruly charismatic enthusiasm. Or perhaps the offense involved the role of women in public meetings. In the Jewish synagogue, for instance, women were relegated to a separate section of the meeting place, where they participated quietly in worship without exercising leadership roles. For women to exercise a more public and vocal role within worship meetings might have been a point of offense for some unbelievers (especially those concerned with what "the law says"). In situations such as this, if there is a risk of seriously offending someone, it is better for women to remain silent and not to speak but to be submissive, as the law instructs, because (for some people who prioritize what the law says) it is a shameful thing for a woman to speak in worship meetings.

If verses 34–35 were authored by Paul (rather than having been written into the margin by a scribe and later becoming incorporated into Paul's text), it is probably best to read those verses along lines such as these, against the backdrop of the cultural sensitivities of unbelievers who might visit a Jesus group, rather than taking them as a general principle applicable in all cultural situations. (Otherwise there would be far too much tension between what he says here and what he says in 11:2–16, where he seems to have no issue with women praying and prophesying within corporate worship.) The concern of these verses is to guard the gospel message from unnecessary offense, keeping the lines of communication as uncluttered as possible in situations where cultural customs dictated certain expectations regarding the place of women in worship meetings.

Arguably, if this is the principle to derive from these verses, it is possible to imagine different instruction being applicable in situations where different customs and expectations predominated within a culture. Might it be that, contrary to the cultural norms of Paul's day, unbelievers in many contexts today would be offended by a worship meeting that prohibited women from speaking or from taking a full part in the worship proceedings?

Such matters need to be considered carefully by any worshiping community today, while taking into account the full spread of biblical material. In any attempt to do justice to the biblical material, worshiping communities will need to form an opinion on three

22. If Paul (rather than a later scribe) wrote the phrase "as in all the congregations of the Lord's people" in 14:33, it is important to note that the phrase must refer not to the injunction that women should be silent (14:34–35, assuming that he wrote those verses) but to the fact that God is a God of order (14:33). Paul used the phrase at the end of discussions to confirm points he has already made, not at the beginning of new topic; see, for instance, his use of similar phrases in 1 Cor 4:17 and 7:17.

matters pertaining to 1 Corinthians 14 before considering other passages beyond that letter. These are:

- Were verses 34–35 authored by Paul or by a later scribe?
- How do verses 34–35 relate to 11:2–16?
- Are verses 34–35 to be taken prescriptively or descriptively? That is, are they universal prescriptions for all Christians, or are they illustrative of how early Jesus-followers were expected (by Paul or by a scribe) to negotiate features of their identity in a specific cultural context, without being binding on Christians in other cultural contexts?[23]

1 Corinthians 15

Fifty-eight verses are dedicated to issues pertaining to the resurrection. At the heart of the problem is a Corinthian denial about the necessity of the resurrection, whether it be the resurrection of Jesus Christ or their own resurrection. We cannot be completely sure what their denial entailed, whether there were various forms of it, or what motivated it. Perhaps it was the result of thinking that the body had no real significance; all that matters is the spirit or soul that lives on after shedding "this mortal coil." Perhaps it was a corollary of the view that some of them held that they "already" had everything, they already were "rich," they already "reigned" as kings (4:8)—being "spiritual" people who "possess knowledge" (8:1) and speak with "angelic tongues" (13:1). What else would they need, and why would they need a resurrected body?

▼ A first-century mosaic depicting the vulnerability of life (a butterfly on a wheel) before "The Great Leveler" that equalizes all things—Death itself. Whether the fragility of fate tips life toward wealth (left) or poverty (right), Death comes to all.

Bruce Longenecker

For Paul, this is a betrayal of the whole of their identity in Christ. Jesus Christ has been raised, as hundreds of eyewitnesses have testified, some of whom are still alive at the time Paul writes this (15:3–8). If he had not been raised, then there is no reason to continue being Jesus-followers, who would deserve to be "pitied more than all others" (15:19). But instead, Christ has been raised, not only as a single individual but, more significantly, as the first in a long line of those who, as his followers, will be raised with him in eschatological glory, to the demise of the power of Death and to the ultimate glory of God (15:20–28).

Most of the second half of chapter 15 is dedicated to the issue of how one's mortal body is related to one's eschatological body (15:29–58). For

23. For additional biblical, theological, and practical reflection on this topic, see the pamphlet by Todd D. Still at www.baylor.edu/content/services/document.php/144245.pdf.

Paul, although there is continuity, there is also discontinuity. Just as the body of a seed gives way to the body of a plant or tree, so too the mortal body is like a seed that gives way to the immortal body. Whereas some Corinthian Christians thought it absurd to imagine that our present bodies would be of value beyond the here and now, Paul basically agrees; but whereas some Corinthians imagined that this meant that there would be no need for bodies beyond the here and now, Paul insisted that there would be resurrected bodies that were splendidly transformed to match the eschatological matrix of the fully realized kingdom of God.

On two occasions, Paul's discussion of the resurrection expands to take on the grandest of narrative and theological proportions. In the middle of his discussion of the resurrection of Jesus Christ (15:24–28 within 15:1–34) and at the climax of his discussion of the resurrection body (15:54–56 within 15:35–58), Paul draws his audience's attention to the ultimate narrative within which the resurrection plays a critical role. In each of these places, he elongates the resurrection story so that Jesus-followers can see what they are participating in—that is, the final defeat of suprahuman powers that run contrary to and battle against the will of God.

Some Corinthians had "pushed aside the apocalyptic coordinates of the resurrection of Christ and the final resurrection of the dead, with the result that the triumph of God through Christ has become solely the triumph of Christ over our personal death, and the kingdom of Christ as present in the church has displaced the expectation of the coming triumph of God over his creation."[24]

Ultimately, then, the death and resurrection of Jesus Christ are in no way merely to be the platform for pyrotechnic spiritual experiences reserved for those who imagine themselves to be fully enriched "kings" in the present. Neither are the death and resurrection of Jesus Christ framed in solely sacrificial terms, resulting in the forgiveness of people's sins (although sins are clearly part of the problem, as in 15:3). Instead, the death and resurrection of Jesus Christ are two parts of an apocalyptic event in the ongoing drama of salvation history, ultimately shattering the coalition of spiritual forces intent on wrestling God's good creation out of his hands and dissolving it into chaos and nonexistence.

The death and resurrection of Jesus address the cosmic powers of Sin and Death that are attempting to usurp God's sovereignty over his creation. For the Corinthians to deny the resurrection of Jesus, or to deny the futurity of the resurrection story, is to deny that God is indeed the cosmic sovereign, thereby denying his ultimate triumph over every power that seeks to undermine his reign. Jesus' resurrection is not merely the revivification of a single individual, but the inauguration of the process whereby the whole of the created order is to be restored by the God who created it. For Paul, a narrative of salvation that was divorced from a full-bodied narrative of God's creational involvement was tantamount to a rejection of the gospel itself.

1 Corinthians 16

Paul covers several issues in his concluding chapter of this letter. Although only four verses are dedicated to the collection of funds for poor Christians in Jerusalem (16:1–4), this

24. J. C. Beker, *Paul the Apostle: The Triumph of God in Life and Thought* (Philadelphia: Fortress, 1980), 157–58.

issue is not simply mundane. The collection carried much more significance to Paul than a simple count of verses might otherwise suggest. This will become evident from the way he discusses the matter in 2 Corinthians 8–9 and then again in Rom 15:25–33. Here, his instructions are short and to the point: Corinthian Christians are instructed to minimize the financial burden of Paul's collection initiative by putting a little bit of money aside each week.

With these instructions Paul seems to be addressing neither those whose economic situation was perilous nor those who were relatively secure financially; the first were probably not expected to contribute much, and the latter were no doubt expected to contribute more than the relatively little amounts that Paul seems to have in mind here. Instead, these instructions were probably directed to those who could save a small amount every week and still manage to get by. This may seem innocuous enough, but as 2 Corinthians indicates, the issue of Paul's collection was soon to become a problematic issue in Paul's ongoing relations with the Corinthians.

The same is true for the next issue Paul discusses—his travel plans. Whereas Paul lays out one itinerary in 16:5–9, that itinerary never came to fruition. Instead, other itineraries came into play as circumstances necessitated. Paul undoubtedly had no reason to suspect that giving the Corinthians his travel plans would later be used against him, but 2 Corinthians indicates that this was, in fact, what transpired during a turbulent phase in Paul's relationship with the Corinthian Christians.

The Collection

As noted in chapter 1 above, during the mid–50s (probably from AD 53–57) Paul spent much of his time and energy assembling a "collection" (i.e., a donation of money) from members of the Christian communities he had founded. This collection was intended to benefit those identified in Romans as "the poor among the Lord's people in Jerusalem" (Rom 15:26). This initiative was driven by concerns to offset the needs of Jewish Jesus-followers by a gift from Gentile Jesus-followers (with the prospect that the roles might be reversed at any time; see 2 Corinthians 8–9). This gesture of assistance ultimately spoke to the essential unity of Jesus-followers across all divides, with care flowing across those traditional divides, as a testimony to the transforming grace of God.

Paul felt the need to commend a young Timothy to the Corinthians (16:10–11). He also wanted to assure them that he himself was not preventing Apollos from coming to them (16:12). He lauds those members of the delegation who had brought word to him about the situation of Jesus groups in Corinth (16:15–18), probably since the delegation may have been looked upon with suspicion by some Corinthians. Greetings from Jesus-followers in Ephesus are then mentioned, along with various closing points, including Paul's assurance that he loves the Corinthians in Christ Jesus. Judging from what was to come, this assurance did little to endear some Corinthian Jesus-followers to Paul and his apostolic ministry.

SUMMARY REFLECTION

First Corinthians was written by a confident, powerful author whose theological dexterity enabled him to grapple with a variety of challenging issues and showed him to be a towering force to contend with—perhaps a bit like an epic hero batting away challenges coming at him from the left and the right in quick succession.

But Paul's goal was not to enhance his own status; instead, his primary interest was to enhance his Corinthian addressees in their Christian thought and practice. These Jesus groups had been founded only five or so years earlier, and their burgeoning but inexperienced Christian spirituality required discipline, balance, and focus. Sometimes Paul tipped the scales in the direction of the corporate, sometimes toward the individual; sometimes he tipped them in the direction of the cross, sometimes toward the resurrection; sometimes he tipped them in the direction of the Spirit, sometimes toward tradition; sometimes he tipped them in the direction of the novel and the new, sometimes toward the ancient and the established.

Throughout, Paul exudes confidence that the corporate and individual lives of Jesus-followers are subject to the transformation that results whenever God is encountered "in the name of the Lord Jesus Christ" (1 Cor 6:11) by means of "the Spirit [who] searches all things, even the deep things of God" (1 Cor 2:10).

» KEY PEOPLE, PLACES, AND TERMS «

Achaicus
Acrocorinth
Alexandria
Antinomian
Apollos
Aquila
Chloe
Corinth
Crispus
Erastus
Fortunatus
Gaius
Inaugurated eschatology
Isthmian Games
Libertine
Lord's Supper
Realized eschatology
Prisca (or Priscilla)
Stephanas

» QUESTIONS FOR REVIEW AND DISCUSSION «

1. What is it about 1 Corinthians that makes it such a good window into the life of early urban Jesus groups?
2. Describe the urban landscape of Corinth with attention to its physical location, economic position, civic life, political life, and religious life.
3. What pursuit, which characterized Corinthian life, provides the backdrop for Paul's letters to this community? What related pursuit problematically emerges within the spiritual lives of the Corinthians?
4. What caused the social rupture that prompted Paul's letters to Corinth?
5. What phrase becomes a slogan for Paul (see 1 Cor 2:1 – 5), and what does it mean? What Corinthian slogans is Paul countering here (see 1 Cor 6:12 – 13 and 10:23)?
6. What is "inaugurated eschatology"? What view does this perspective combat?
7. What is the "sandwiching pattern" present in this letter, and how does it influence interpretation?
8. Describe Paul's position on celibacy, sex, singleness, and marriage.
9. From what controversy did Paul's categories "the strong" and "the weak" emerge? Describe the stance of each group — and Paul's position on the matter.
10. Explain why Paul instructs the Corinthian women to cover their heads in worship. What else do we learn about the participation of women in the Corinthian church through this letter? How does the picture given here relate to the instructions in 14:34 – 35? Further, what makes this particular instruction so complex?
11. How were the issues of the Lord's Supper and speaking in angelic tongues related to the Corinthian honor system?
12. Why, according to Paul, is the resurrection so vitally important?

» CONTEMPORARY THEOLOGICAL REFLECTION «

1. Much of the discussion in this letter deals with personal honor and corporate versus individual values in an ancient honor-shame culture. In what ways are these issues still relevant today? How have the terms changed? How have they remained the same?
2. In Gal 3:28 Paul writes that in Christ there is neither male nor female. Does this not hold true in 1 Corinthians? What does it mean that Paul's instructions in 1 Corinthians are "culturally bound"? How have you seen gender distinctions maintained in Christian communities in ways that are harmful? In ways that are healthy? How do you define those terms?
3. In 1 Cor 9:22, Paul makes the following claim: "I have become all things to all people, that by all possible means I might save some." Describe, in practical terms, how Christians should be flexible and accommodating to culture while maintaining their Christian identity. How does this relate to the oft-discussed "slippery slope"?
4. Paul had a vision about the unity of Christians and about the building up of the diverse body of Christ. To what extent is that vision successfully reflected in contemporary forms of Christianity?

» GOING FURTHER «

Commentaries on 1 Corinthians

Fee, Gordon. *The First Epistle to the Corinthians.* NICNT. Grand Rapids: Eerdmans, 1987.

Fitzmyer, Joseph. *1 Corinthians.* AYB. New Haven, CT: Yale University Press, 2008.

Garland, David. *1 Corinthians.* BECNT. Grand Rapids: Baker Academic, 2003.

Keener, Craig. *1 and 2 Corinthians.* NCBC. Cambridge: Cambridge University Press, 2005.

Thiselton, Anthony C. *The First Epistle to the Corinthians: A Commentary on the Greek Text.* NIGTC. Grand Rapids: Eerdmans, 2000.

Witherington, Ben, III. *Conflict and Community in Corinth: A Socio-Rhetorical Commentary on 1 and 2 Corinthians.* Grand Rapids: Eerdmans, 1995.

Studies of Corinth and 1 Corinthians

Adams, Edward, and David G. Horrell, eds. *Christianity at Corinth: The Quest for the Pauline Church.* Louisville: Westminster John Knox, 2004.

Chow, John K. *Patronage and Power: Studies in Social Networks in Corinth.* Sheffield: Sheffield Academic, 1992.

Horrell, David G. *The Social Ethos of the Corinthian Correspondence: Interests and Ideology from 1 Corinthians to 1 Clement.* Edinburgh: T&T Clark, 1996.

Meeks, Wayne. *The First Urban Christians: The Social World of the Apostle Paul.* New Haven, CT: Yale University Press, 1983.

Still, Todd D., and David G. Horrell, eds. *After the First Urban Christians: The Social-Scientific Study of Pauline Christianity Twenty-Five Years Later*. London: T&T Clark, 2009.

Theissen, Gerd. *The Social Setting of Pauline Christianity: Essays on Corinth*. Philadelphia: Fortress, 1982.

Winter, Bruce W. *After Paul Left Corinth: The Influence of Secular Ethics and Social Change*. Grand Rapids: Eerdmans, 2001.

Theological Dimensions of 1 Corinthians

Chester, Stephen J. *Conversion at Corinth: Perspectives on Conversion in Paul's Theology and the Corinthian Church*. London: T&T Clark, 2003.

Furnish, Victor Paul. *The Theology of the First Letter to the Corinthians*. Cambridge: Cambridge University Press, 1999.

Hay, David M., ed. *Pauline Theology*. Volume 2: *1 and 2 Corinthians*. Atlanta: Society of Biblical Literature, 1993.

CHAPTER 5

2 CORINTHIANS

CHAPTER GOALS

- To examine the issues that have primary impact on the study of 2 Corinthians
- To highlight the central concerns and basic contents of that letter

CHAPTER OVERVIEW

1. Situating the Vision: An Introduction to 2 Corinthians
2. Centering the Vision of 2 Corinthians: Foolish Appearances, Glorious Gospel
3. Tracking the Vision of 2 Corinthians
4. Summary Reflection
5. Key People, Places, and Terms
6. Questions for Review and Discussion
7. Contemporary Theological Reflection
8. Going Further

KEY VERSES

2 Corinthians 3:18: "We all, who with unveiled faces contemplate the Lord's glory, are being transformed into his image with ever-increasing glory, which comes from the Lord, who is the Spirit."

2 Corinthians 4:5: "For what we preach is not ourselves, but Jesus Christ as Lord, and ourselves as your servants for Jesus' sake."

2 Corinthians 5:17: "If anyone is in Christ, the new creation has come: The old has gone, the new is here!"

2 Corinthians 8:9: "For you know the grace of our Lord Jesus Christ, that though he was rich, yet for your sake he became poor, so that you through his poverty might become rich."

2 Corinthians 12:9: "He said to me, 'My grace is sufficient for you, for my power is made perfect in weakness.' Therefore I will boast all the more gladly about my weaknesses, so that Christ's power may rest on me."

SITUATING THE VISION: AN INTRODUCTION TO 2 CORINTHIANS

The text we know as 2 Corinthians does not resemble the checklist approach of 1 Corinthians, where Paul worked through issues of concern to him and his audience one by one. Instead, 2 Corinthians is more like a lengthy theological analysis of Paul's relationship to the Corinthians over a stormy period of general animosity and distrust. Within the full corpus of Paul's texts, it is in 2 Corinthians that we see Paul at his most vulnerable, that we learn about some of his most demoralizing experiences, and that we hear some of his most moving rhetoric on the power of Christ to work in and through our own weaknesses. It is also a text that soars to elevated heights at times (see his discourse on glory in 3:1–4:6) and earths itself in matters of practical importance at other times (see his discussion about the collection in chs. 8–9). Along the way, the reader recognizes the grand canvas on which Paul paints his theological interpretation regarding the contours of his rocky relationship with Corinthian Jesus-followers.

It is also one of the hardest of Paul's letters to get right—the result of a number of factors pertaining to its structure and the occasion(s) that facilitated it. We could take a number of approaches to sidestep the relatively complicated historical issues that surround the writing of 2 Corinthians. We could take a thematic approach to the text, for instance, or we could sit light to the historical complexities and simply appreciate the letter's contents. But if we want to come to grips with the text and its contents, we must initially grapple with issues pertaining to the text's structure and compositional history.

This may make for a rougher path than in most other chapters of this textbook, but in taking this path, we will be able to better recognize the strategies Paul employed in his handling of a complicated situation. That situation was one of the most disconcerting situations in Paul's apostolic ministry. Accessing that situation allows us to witness him in one of the most embattled points in his life. If heavy lifting is required in the process, it is worth the effort, especially if the historical and theological dimensions of 2 Corinthians are to be correctly interpreted.

After 1 Corinthians, Before 2 Corinthians

Second Corinthians is full of details regarding Paul's relationship to the Corinthian Christians and theological reflection on that relationship. This might appear to be a welcome aspect of the text, but because of the complicated compositional history of this letter (see below), sorting out the events that transpired after Paul wrote 1 Corinthians is not an easy thing.

In 2 Cor 1:8–11 Paul recounts a traumatic experience that he had undergone in which his life itself seemed to be at its end. This event may have happened at some point after the writing of 1 Corinthians (although it might correspond instead with Paul's fighting "the wild beasts in **Ephesus**" mentioned in 1 Cor 15:32). It is notable that Paul refers to this experience having been "in the province of Asia." If 1 Corinthians was written in Ephesus, itself located in Asia, it seems that Paul is writing these verses at the beginning of 2 Corinthians in a location other than Ephesus, since the phrase "in the province of Asia" distances him from that location. We will consider Paul's new location below.

A few verses later Paul speaks of having been grieved by one Corinthian man (2 Cor 2:5–8). This seems to have been on the occasion implied by 2:1, where Paul speaks of his decision not to make "another painful visit to you." Prior to writing these words, then, Paul seems to have made a personal visit to **Corinth** that caused him anguish, arising in relation to one man in particular (but not necessarily exclusively).

Others were also causing trouble for Paul. At some point after Paul wrote 1 Corinthians, some people arrived in Corinth who claimed to be legitimate apostles (in 2 Cor 11:5 and 12:11 Paul sarcastically calls them "**super-apostles**"). Although it is unclear who these people were (and they were not "apostles" in the strict sense of that term), their interest in the pneumatic or "spiritual" probably lay at the heart of their program. The gospel of these "Spirit people" differed significantly from Paul's, but probably meshed nicely with the views that Paul had already sought to undermine in 1 Corinthians.

These "super-apostles" were probably Jewish Christ-followers (11:22) who could boast of having experienced exalted states of spiritual existence, such as visions and the performance of miracles, and could probably enhance their boast by ornate speech, inspiring rhetoric, and elaborate scriptural interpretation. If some Corinthian Christ-followers were lacking in their allegiance to Paul and his gospel, these "super-apostles" appear to have benefitted as a consequence. The combination of anti-Paul sentiment from outside and inside the Corinthian Jesus groups was a merger that, at least for a certain period of time, threatened the legitimacy of Paul and his gospel within Corinthian communities of Jesus devotion.

▼ Paul's "Travel Plan 1"—1 Corinthians 16:5–7

After writing 1 Corinthians, Paul's travel plans became a point of tension between Paul and the Corinthians. Paul seems to have advocated two different travel plans at different times, and the travels that he eventually undertook corresponded with neither of them.

In 1 Corinthians 16:5–7, for example, Paul expressed his intention to visit Jesus groups in **Macedonia** (i.e., in **Philippi** and **Thessalonica**) before arriving in Corinth (perhaps for the winter).[1] This might be called "Travel Plan 1." In 2 Corinthians 1:15–23, however, Paul outlines a different travel plan (the first phase of which he had already initiated when he made a "painful visit" to Corinth but which, as it transpires, he failed to fulfill completely). Instead of leaving Ephesus and traveling northwest to Macedonia before heading south to Corinth (as in Travel Plan 1, outlined in 1 Corinthians 16), Paul left Ephesus and traveled directly to Corinth (his second visit to them, the first being his eighteen-month residency there from AD 50 to 51). Instead of doing two sides of a triangle in order to get to Corinth (via Macedonia), Paul chose the quicker one-sided route right to Corinth. So he says in 2 Cor 1:15–16: "I wanted to

1. Christians in Macedonia (esp. Philippi?) were apparently supportive of Paul (cf. 2 Cor 8:1; Phil 4:10–19), and this may have influenced Paul when imagining that he would travel there.

visit you on my way to Macedonia and [then] to come back to you [again] from Macedonia," in order that "you might benefit twice." This is a different travel itinerary than the one outlined in 1 Cor 16:5–7 and might be called "Travel Plan 2."

Both Travel Plan 1 and Travel Plan 2 differ, however, from the travels that Paul seems ultimately to have undertaken. As 2 Cor 2:1 reveals, after his second visit to Corinth Paul did not return to that city in the short term (as laid out in Travel Plan 2, outlined in 2 Corinthians 1). The painful experiences of his second visit resulted in his decision not to return to Corinth for the time being. Instead, he returned to Ephesus once again (instead of going to Macedonia, as expected). This might be called "Paul's Travel Route 1" in order to distinguish it from the two Travel Plans that were successively aborted.

It may seem odd to us that Paul's shifting travel plans proved to become a point of tension between Paul and the Corinthians. But the tone of Paul's words in 2 Cor 1:15–23 seems to suggest that. In that passage, despite feeling that his relationship with the Corinthians is on the mend after an exceedingly rough patch, Paul seems nonetheless to be on the defensive even now, as reflected in 1:17: "Was I fickle . . . ? Or do I make my plans in a worldly manner?" Perhaps some in Corinth (who might already have been disenchanted with Paul) portrayed him as unreliable. Was he telling the Corinthians one thing but doing something else altogether? And if his integrity was at stake, why should Corinthian Jesus-followers be raising funds to support his collection for Jerusalem Jesus-followers? Was he pocketing the money himself? For those already predisposed to find fault with him, Paul's seemingly ad hoc travel plans could be used to enhance any lingering questions as to whether Paul was, in fact, worthy of the affections of the Corinthian Jesus-followers.[2]

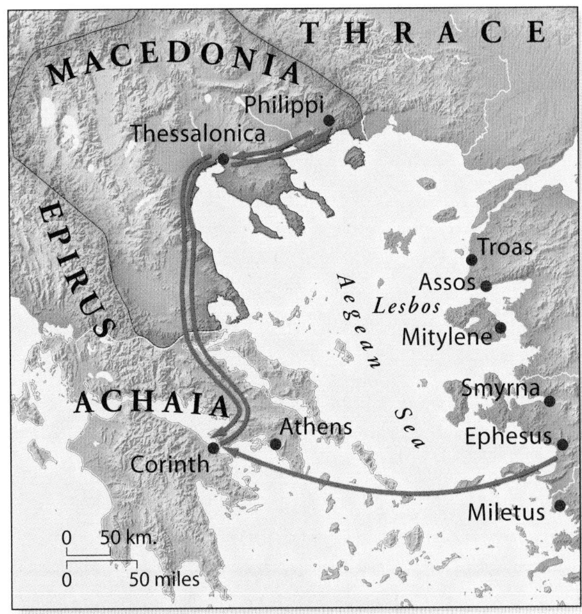

▲ Paul's "Travel Plan 2"—2 Corinthians 1:15–16
▼ Paul's "Travel Route 1"—2 Corinthians 2:1 (cf. 12:18; 13:2)

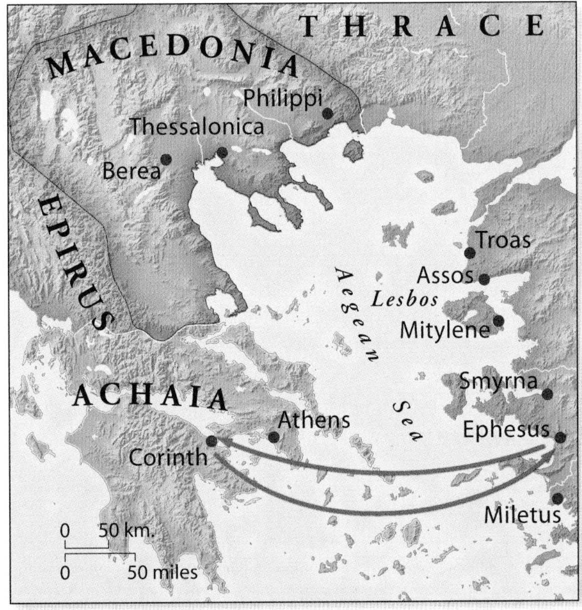

2. The whole thing may have resulted from a misunderstanding about the nature of the various travel plans. Travel Plan 1 was the scenario whereby Paul intended to collect funds for "the poor among the Lord's people in Jerusalem" (as he describes things in Rom 15:26, and something that seems to have been delayed several more years, for some reason), whereas Travel Plan 2 was the result of reports that Paul had received about the desperate situation that had arisen within Corinth since writing 1 Corinthians.

For Paul, however, it wasn't a matter of his predictability and reliability that was at stake. If Paul had abandoned the second half of Travel Plan 2, it was not because of a character flaw on his part but on the part of some of the Corinthians. So he writes in 2 Cor 1:23: "I call God as my witness — and I stake my life on it — that it was in order to spare you that I did not return to Corinth." Something similar emerges from 2:1 – 2, where Paul imagines that his return to Corinth (after the envisioned trip to Macedonia that itself may never have transpired) would have resulted in nothing short of causing them extreme grief. Paul intimates there that the final part of his second travel itinerary was not enacted because returning to Corinth would have resulted in Paul vigorously chastising the Corinthian Christians. What would he have chastised them for? Presumably for the things that had transpired during the "painful visit" mentioned in 2:1. The grief Paul experienced during that visit seems to have cast a long shadow over his relationship with the Corinthians that Paul is only now emerging from at the time of writing.

Choosing not to revisit the Corinthian Christians for a third time, Paul decided instead to send another letter (which we may or may not have; see next section), with the hopes of restoring his relationship with them, after which he would return to them again (2:3). Based in Ephesus, Paul sent **Titus** to Corinth, who probably carried (and interpreted) this letter, with Paul having given him hopeful assurances that the letter would serve its intended purposes (7:6 – 7, 13 – 16).

Paul refers to this letter in 2:4, where he depicts it as having been written "out of great distress and anguish of heart and with many tears." Paul depicts this "**tearful letter**" as having been written in order to call the Corinthian Christians to obedience (so 2:9: "to see if you would stand the test and be obedient in everything"). Paul knew that their obedience would not be won easily. Instead, it would only be won by inflicting "sorrow" and "hurt" among them (7:8 – 12) — and this was by means of the "tearful" letter itself. That same letter also seems to have been an occasion in which Paul was forced to commend himself to them (3:1) — an issue to which we will return below.

▼ Paul's "Travel Route 2" — 2 Corinthians 2:12 – 13; 7:5 – 7

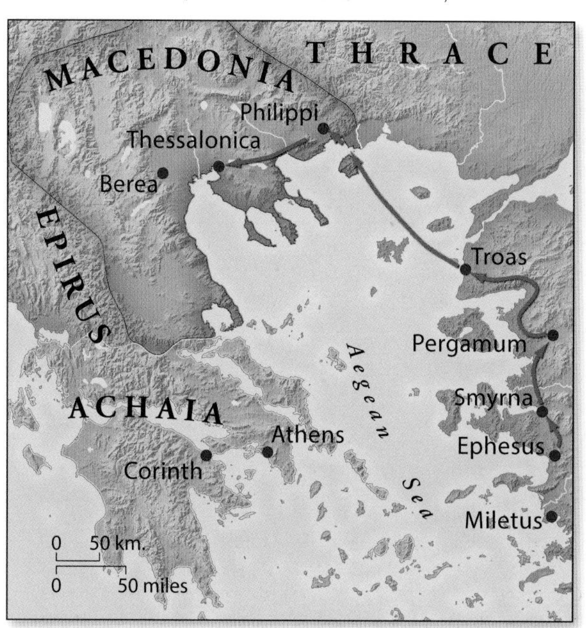

With Paul "in tears" during the letter's composition and the Corinthians being targets of Paul's severe reprimand, the reception of this letter by the Corinthians occasioned great anxiety for Paul. With Titus's departure to Corinth, Paul moved north to **Troas** (2:12 – 13). His ministry there was fleeting because of his fears about the Corinthians' reaction to the letter (presumably fears that he did not divulge to Titus prior to sending him to Corinth). Instead of staying in Troas, Paul went west, basing himself among Jesus groups in Macedonia (Philippi or Thessalonica) in the hopes of meeting Titus all the sooner on his return trip to Ephesus from Corinth. Even then, Paul was deeply distressed as he waited for news about how the Corinthians had responded to the "tearful" letter (7:5). This might be called "Paul's Travel Route 2."

There is a happy ending to this episode. Paul met Titus as he traveled through Macedonia (probably through a "Christian" network in Philippi or Thessalonica) and learned from him that the tearful letter had achieved its desired affect. If one man had caused Paul intense pain previously and had undermined the Corinthians' confidence in Paul, the Corinthian Christians had once again reaffirmed their allegiance to Paul (7:6–16).

It is against this background that Paul decides to write yet again to the Corinthians, in order to shore up his relationship with them and to move it along to the next stage. That new letter is contained within 2 Corinthians. But the question that continues to be debated is whether 2 Corinthians is itself a single letter or is composed of two or more letters (see next section).

Is 2 Corinthians a Single Text?

The text known as 2 Corinthians comprises thirteen chapters. But those thirteen chapters exhibit various chops and changes in their flow of reasoned discourse and rhetorical tone.

Second Corinthians 1–7 is largely self-contained, but within it the discourse about travel plans appears toward the start (1:8–2:13) and end (7:5–16) of those chapters. Tucked in between that travel discourse is an extended sermonic reflection on the nature of Paul's apostolic ministry (2:14–7:4). Might that be evidence of a separate text finding its way into the flow from 2:13 to 7:5? And even within 2:14–7:4, the argument of 6:14–7:1 seems to interrupt the discursive flow from 6:13 to 7:2. (For some, 6:14–7:1 does not even sound like Paul and is thought to be a later interpolation into the text.)

Beyond 2 Corinthians 1–7, chapter 8 introduces the topic of Paul's collection for "the poor among the Lord's people in Jerusalem," but chapter 9 addresses the same topic afresh along somewhat different lines.[3]

Furthermore, chapters 10 through 13 introduce a much harsher tone into the letter. Paul has been accused, it seems, of being timid and unimpressive (10:1, 10). Consequently, Paul is forced to commend himself in the most rigorous of ways (much beyond his comfort zone for self-commendation; see 12:11). Moreover, he bitterly chastises the Corinthians for lack of allegiance to him and for being so easily swayed against him. (Contrast the pride, encouragement, and joy that Paul expresses regarding the Corinthians in 7:4.) Paul claims he is writing harshly in order to spare them from his wrath should he come to them in person (13:10). In fact, he does intend to come to them, which he says will be his "third time" to Corinth (12:14).

These literary twists and turns make 2 Corinthians enormously difficult to negotiate, both in relation to the composition of the text and the historical situation behind it. For this

3. In 2 Cor 8:1–8 Paul boasts to the Corinthian Christians about the dedication of Macedonian Christians; in 9:1–5, however, he tells the Corinthian Christians that he has boasted about them to Macedonian Christians. In 8:16–18 Paul says that he is soon to send Titus and another "brother" to help administer the collection; in 9:3–5, however, he says that he is sending "the brothers" to do this task. Is this simply a reference to Titus and the "brother," or do the two passages reveal different strategies for administering the collection? Is the sentence of 9:1 really what we would expect to find midway through an exhortation to dedicate themselves to the collection effort, or is it the start of a self-contained letter (2 Cor 9)?

reason, it is frequently postulated that 2 Corinthians is a composite text. Many hold the view that, for whatever reason, separate letters have been fused together to form what we now know of as 2 Corinthians. But the number and sequence of the various parts is disputed.

In the most widely held "partition" theory, only two letters have been merged, one comprising chapters 1–9 and the other comprising chapters 10–13. But those who advocate this division within the text are themselves divided on the issue of whether chapters 1–9 precedes or postdates chapters 10–13.

Much more complicated partition theories have also been proposed, some involving as many as five different letters. In one recent reconstruction, those five are as follows, listed in sequential order:[4]

Letter A: chapter 8

Letter B: 2:14–7:4

Letter C: 10:1–13:10

Letter D: 1:1–2:13 along with 7:5–16 and 13:11–13

Letter E: chapter 9

The five-letter proposal highlights the primary issues that continue to be disputed and will probably never be fully resolved.

- Is the shift of tone from 2 Corinthians 1–9 to 2 Corinthians 10–13 significant enough to warrant postulating that the final four chapters originally derived from a single and separate text?
- Are the differences in chapters 8 and 9 enough to suggest distinct textual origins for each?
- Do chapters 1 through 7 really flow smoothly enough to be considered a single discursive unit?

Theological estimates about Scripture will not resolve this matter, and neither does simple historical acumen. Interpreters of various theological persuasions align themselves with each of the general options. Textual interpretation is as much an art as it is a science, and this issue provides an obvious case in point. It is simply unwise to hold to any position on this matter with firm insistence.

With that said, however, if partition theories have been suggested for some other Pauline letters (e.g., Philippians), they are not nearly as compelling in those instances as in the case of 2 Corinthians. If there is a text within the Pauline corpus that is comprised of more than one letter, it is 2 Corinthians.

Adopting a View

It would be possible to proceed to the interpretation of 2 Corinthians while sitting lightly to partition theories. We might simply be interested in the form of the text as it has been handed down through generations and in how Paul's words are configured within that

4. Margaret M. Mitchell, "The Corinthian Correspondence and the Birth of Pauline Hermeneutics," in *Paul and the Corinthians: Studies on a Community in Conflict* (ed. T. J. Burke and J. K. Elliott; Leiden: Brill, 2003), 17–53.

form. We might not want to concern ourselves with deciding whether that form was the result of authorial crafting or of the later compilation of two or more texts.

Taking that route, however, gives a misleading impression of Paul's relational roller coaster with the Corinthian Christian communities and skews our understanding of Paul's rhetorical strategy. Moreover, since Paul's theological discourse arises out of historical situations, understanding those situations helps to facilitate an understanding of that discourse. Consequently, it is necessary to take a stance on the issue of partition within 2 Corinthians in order to earth Paul's discourse in a historical scenario that is most plausible.

We will work with the understanding, then, that 2 Corinthians is best understood to comprise two separate letters. Loosely joined at the textual hinge, 2 Corinthians 1–9 and 10–13 are testimonies to Paul's relationship with the Corinthians at two distinct stages, demonstrating different pastoral strategies employed at different moments in a tense relationship. Moreover, it is likely that 2 Corinthians 10–13 is, in fact, the main part of the "tearful letter" (which now lacks only its brief opening and perhaps its closure). That being the case, chapters 10–13 would have preceded the writing of 2 Corinthians 1–9. This sequence suggests that Paul's extremely fractious and fraught relationship with the Corinthians when writing 2 Corinthians 10–13 gave way to a stage in which he began to enjoy a fragile but hopeful reconciliation with them.

When 2 Corinthians is read in this way, things that are said in the earlier text (chs. 10–13) resonate well with things said in the later text (chs. 1–9). Several examples demonstrate the point.

In 10:2 Paul implies that the Corinthians themselves should take disciplinary measures toward anyone who challenges Paul's apostolic authority (as outlined in 10:10–11). In 2:5–10, Paul now commends them for having done just that (although he adds that their strident discipline now needs to give way to forgiveness). Accordingly, what Paul hoped for when writing chapters 10–13 has become a reality by the time he wrote chapters 1–9.

In 10:6 Paul encourages the Corinthians to demonstrate their "obedience" in this matter, and in 2:9 Paul notes that one of the purposes of the (formerly written) "tearful letter" was to test whether the Corinthians would "be obedient in everything." The way Paul talks about the Corinthian "obedience" in these two passages is strongly suggestive that 2 Corinthians 10–13 is (part of) Paul's earlier "tearful letter."

When Paul asks in 3:1, "Are we beginning to commend ourselves again?" and declares in 5:12, "We are not trying to commend ourselves to you again," he has in mind a prior occasion in which he did commend himself (probably in the "tearful letter"). Not surprisingly, the whole of 2 Corinthians 10–13 reads like an exercise (albeit an unwilling one) in self-commendation, with Paul using the verb "to commend" four times in those chapters (10:12, 18 [2x]; 12:11).

Paul seems to put the collection for Jesus-followers in Jerusalem on hold among the Corinthians in chapters 10–13, in view of the allegations of financial impropriety leveled against him (11:7–15; 12:14–18). But the collection initiative is gingerly advanced in chapters 8–9 (cf. 1 Cor 16:1–4). It is fairly simple to imagine a crisis having arisen in the situation addressed by 2 Corinthians 10–13, a situation that has passed by the time Paul wrote 2 Corinthians 1–9.

One advantage of this approach to 2 Corinthians is what it avoids. If 2 Corinthians 10–13 had been composed *later* than 2 Corinthians 1–9 (as opposed to earlier, as we maintain), we would need to imagine Paul engaged in a four-stage narrative of "self-commendation" that, in its later stages, is less than likely. In the first stage, Paul resorts to a strategy of self-commendation in the (now-lost) tearful letter. Second, by the time he wrote 2 Corinthians 1–9, that strategy of self-commendation seems to have had some positive effect, with Paul's relationship with the Corinthians now gingerly back on track. Third, that relationship went terribly wrong yet again, with Paul's previous efforts to reconcile himself to the Corinthians (including self-commendation) coming undone. Fourth, in writing 2 Corinthians 10–13, Paul yet again resorts to the technique of self-commendation, the strategy that had already proved only temporarily effective. If the strategy did not have long-term success initially, it is hard to see how Paul could have hoped it would be more effective the second time. Such a reconstruction is possible, of course, but it appears less likely than the alternative reconstruction, with 2 Corinthians 10–13 being the tearful letter that preceded 2 Corinthians 1–9.

It is best to imagine, then, that at some point these two letters to Corinthian believers were linked together by an editor (if not Paul himself, then one of his coworkers). Placing longer texts before shorter ones was a common practice when grouping texts together in single collections.[5] Perhaps the editor followed the same principle when assembling the two surviving letters to Corinthian Christians, privileging length over chronology, and putting the longer text (2 Corinthians 1–9) prior to the shorter one (2 Corinthians 10–13).[6]

If 2 Corinthians comprises two texts, and if Paul is based in various locations throughout this period (including Ephesus, Troas, and Macedonia, not to mention Corinth itself), can we decipher the location that the two texts were written from? The best estimate is that 2 Corinthians 10–13 was written from Ephesus, during the time that Paul returned there after his painful visit to Corinth.[7] But as noted above, 2 Cor 1:8–11 suggests a location other than Ephesus for this portion of the letter. If Paul was in Macedonia when Titus brought him the good news about the Corinthians, the location for the writing of 2 Corinthians 1–9 is most likely to have been Macedonia (i.e., either Philippi or Thessalonica). In conclusion, we estimate that 2 Corinthians 10–13 was written in either late 54 or early 55, and 2 Corinthians 1–9 was written in early to mid-55.

What Else?

Some readers might imagine a different historical situation to stand behind 2 Corinthians. Some might prefer to envisage it to be a single, unified text; others might think of it as a fivefold composite text, or a twofold composite with chapters 10–13 being written in a situation *after* chapters 1–9. Anyone who holds to these views will inevitably need to make

5. The Pauline letter collection itself testifies to this, which runs from the longest text through to the shortest in both the letters to communities (i.e., Romans to 2 Thessalonians, with the exception of Ephesians, which is longer than Galatians) and the letters to individuals (1 Timothy to Philemon).
6. There may have been an additional attraction in assembling the letters in this fashion, if Galatians was also a part of the editor's letter collection. Placing the highly charged rhetoric of 2 Cor 10–13 at the end of the Corinthian correspondence allows for a smooth transition from that correspondence to the Galatian correspondence, itself being markedly harsh in rhetorical tone.
7. 2 Cor 10:16 might support this. There Paul expresses his desire to "preach the gospel in the regions beyond you"—that is, to the west of Corinth. That geographical "point of view" works best if written from the east (i.e., Ephesus) rather than if written from the north (i.e., Macedonia).

adjustments to the reading of the material offered below, where chapters 10–13 are deemed to have been the "tearful" letter that preceded chapters 1–9.

But despite these differences, all readers can agree that Paul's relationship with the Corinthians was ultimately repaired. That Paul wrote his letter to the Christians in Rome from the city of Corinth testifies to the fact that what had proved to be an enormously fractious relationship in AD 54–55 had been repaired by AD 57. If 2 Corinthians 10–13 was written *after* 2 Corinthians 1–9 (as a few have suggested), that repair might have been accomplished only late in the period between 55 and 57. But if 2 Corinthians 10–13 was written *before* 2 Corinthians 1–9 (as advocated above), then that repair in their relationships had already been in place by AD 55, as testified to by the later of those two letters.

If we notice how Paul made use of the theme of his love for Corinthian Christians, we can see how he urgently sought this repair in their relationship already in the "tearful" letter of 2 Corinthians 10–13. At the end of 1 Corinthians, Paul highlighted his love for each and every Corinthian Jesus-follower. Paul had spoken harshly to (some of) them at times in that letter, and so he took the initiative to remind them of his love for them in 1 Cor 16:24: "My love be with all of you in Christ Jesus."[8] This motif springboards into Paul's tearful letter. Whereas he mentioned his love for them only once in the sixteen chapters of 1 Corinthians, he recalls his love for them three times in the four chapters of the "tearful" letter of 2 Cor 10–13 (11:11; 12:15, 19 ["beloved"]). The motif reappears four times in the nine chapters of Paul's final letter to the Corinthians (2 Cor 2:4; 6:6; 7:1; 8:7).

In other words, when writing 2 Corinthians 1–9, Paul seems confident in his relationship with the Corinthian Jesus-followers, to the point that he speaks not only of his love for them but of their love for others as a means to encourage their support of his collection for the poor among Jewish Jesus-followers in Jerusalem (8:8, 24)—itself having been a point of antagonism at an earlier phase in Paul's relationship with Corinthians Jesus-followers. For Paul, self-giving love is the salve that heals wounds.

CENTERING THE VISION OF 2 CORINTHIANS: FOOLISH APPEARANCES, GLORIOUS GOSPEL

> Whatever anyone else dares to boast about—I am speaking as a fool—I also dare to boast about. Are they Hebrews? So am I. Are they Israelites? So am I. Are they Abraham's descendants? So am I. Are they servants of Christ? (I am out of my mind to talk like this.) I am more. I have worked much harder, been in prison more frequently, been flogged more severely, and been exposed to death again and again. (2 Cor 11:21–23)
>
> For what we preach is not ourselves, but Jesus Christ as Lord, and ourselves as your servants for Jesus' sake. For God, who said, "Let light shine out of darkness," made his light shine in our hearts to give us the light of the knowledge of God's glory displayed in the face of Christ. (2 Cor 4:5–6)

Of these two excerpts, the first is from the earlier tearful letter and the second is from its successor. Each captures something of the flavor of its respective letter and demonstrates

8. Whereas the phrase "the grace of the Lord Jesus (Christ)" appears as the final benediction at the end of three other letters of Paul (2 Cor 13:13; Phil 4:23; Phlm 25), in this instance he shifts the focus in the final frame from the grace of Jesus to his love for the Corinthian Jesus-followers.

Paul's Relationship with the Corinthians: The Story from AD 53 – 57

The sources for this reconstruction are as follows. Stages 1 through 3 derive from 1 Corinthians; stages 4 through 9 derive from 2 Corinthians 10 – 13; stages 10 through 13 derive from 2 Corinthians 1 – 9; and stage 14 derives from Romans. The dates listed are only approximations.

1. Paul writes a letter to Corinth (the "previous" letter written in late 53), advising the Corinthians to avoid people who are impure (1 Cor 5:9 – 11).
2. Chloe's people (1 Cor 1:11 – 12) and Stephanas and his entourage (7:1, 25; 8:1; 12:1; 16:1, 12) bring reports and questions to Paul in Ephesus.
3. Paul writes 1 Corinthians (sent from Ephesus in early 54), addressing the things that he had heard of and been asked about.
4. Paul hears (from **Timothy**, whom Paul had sent to Corinth in between the arrival of Chloe's people and Stephanas and his entourage?) that things had started to go very wrong with the Corinthians' allegiance to Paul, because of the arrival of outsiders questioning the legitimacy of Paul's apostleship (cf. Galatians).
5. Paul leaves Ephesus and goes (by boat) straight to Corinth (mid-54), where he hadn't been since the late summer of 51.
6. While in Corinth, instead of being bold against the one particular person who was stirring up trouble against Paul (cf. 2 Cor 2:5 – 8, 10; 7:12), Paul held back, contrary to his bold posturing in 1 Cor 4:18 – 21.
7. Paul's reticence is taken by some Corinthians to be a sign that, although his letters are weighty, he himself is weak and ineffectual. Thus, he is not worthy to be an apostle (2 Cor 10:1 – 11).
   - Other people who have recently come to Corinth and who appear to be "super-apostles" seem far more impressive than Paul in knowledge and speech (2 Cor 11:5, 12 – 15; 12:11).
   - Moreover, for some Corinthians, Paul's attitude toward money shows that something is wrong with his apostleship. Either he doesn't accept Corinthian money (showing that he isn't good enough to be an apostle, or he thinks he's better than the Corinthians), or he is using the collection itself as a means for him to line his own pockets. Is he simply a **charlatan** (see 2 Cor 11:7 – 11; 12:16 – 17)?
   - Further, in 1 Cor 16:5 – 6 Paul had said that he would go first to Macedonia and then travel to Corinth, although in reality he simply arrived in Corinth without first passing through Macedonia. Some Corinthians wonder whether Paul is simply undependable (2 Cor 1:15 – 17) and therefore unworthy to be an apostle.
8. Paul returns to Ephesus and writes the painful letter of 2 Corinthians 10 – 13 (probably in late 54), asserting his own authority and engaging in uncomfortable self-praise. This included:
   - legitimating his integrity with regard to the collection (implied: 2 Cor 11:7 – 11; 12:16 – 17);
   - explaining why he failed to chastise the main offender (2 Cor 10:5 – 6);
   - stating that he could in fact trounce the offender, if required to (10:1 – 6; 13:1 – 4, 10);
   - claiming (subtly) that, if visions and revelations are important for an apostle, then his own visions and revelations were superior to those of anyone (2 Cor 12:2 – 4).

   The letter is carried to Corinth by Titus (2 Cor 7:13 – 14).
9. Paul leaves Ephesus, establishes a brief ministry in Troas, but he is so troubled by the Corinthian situation that he fails to operate effectively there (2 Cor 2:12 – 13).
10. Hoping to connect with Titus upon his (Titus's) return from Corinth, Paul moves to Macedonia (probably Thessalonica). There he and Titus meet (2 Cor 7:6).

11. Titus informs Paul that the painful letter did its work. The Corinthian community had reaffirmed its loyalty to Paul and had disciplined the offender (2 Cor 7:6–13; 2:5–11).
12. Paul writes 2 Corinthians 1–9 (probably from Thessalonica in early 55) to establish a cautiously conciliatory relationship with them. In the letter, he defines lifestyle and apostleship "in Christ" in terms of cruciformity, reserving the final two chapters (i.e., 2 Corinthians 8–9) to enlist the Corinthians fully in the collection for Jerusalem Jesus-followers. The letter was delivered to the Corinthians by Titus in early 55 (2 Cor 8:1–6, 17).
13. After preaching the gospel in Illyricum (see Rom 15:19), Paul returns to Corinth, where he writes Romans (probably in AD 57). His relationship with the Corinthians has been positive, and they are full participants in his collection efforts (Rom 15:26).

something of that letter's situation in Paul's relational roller-coaster ride with the Corinthian Christians. But the two also merge together harmoniously. This owes to the fact that Paul's understanding of his ministry remained stable despite the unstable shifts in his relationship with Corinthians.

The first excerpt begins a long litany of boastful entries that are intended to demonstrate Paul's credentials as one who excels in his task—that is, his task as an apostle (11:21–29).[9] Roughly two dozen entries are listed there. Most notable in the list are those moments when Paul's life was in extreme danger. Even after this list, Paul continues to boast—boasting in an escape from danger (11:32–33) and in visionary revelations that he had received (12:1–4).

But Paul wants it to be known that he is uncomfortable with such boasting, ultimately because boasting of this kind runs contrary to the grain of the gospel itself. For Paul, boasting exhibits a misplaced trust in one's self and one's own accomplishments. Accordingly, it testifies to a person's attachment to the never-ending quest for honor and self-aggrandizement. Consequently, Paul lets it be known that he is being forced by the Corinthian situation to play the fool ("I have made a fool of myself, but you drove me to it," 12:11).[10] His boasting is wholly out of step with the gospel that he proclaims.

Why was Paul forced to resort to self-praise? Because his apostolic legitimacy was being vociferously challenged by some in Corinth. His detractors were most

▼ Rembrandt's famous painting of Paul in prison.

SuperStock/Getty Images

9. The Greek root-word for "boast" (*kauch-*) occurs nineteen times in the four short chapters of 2 Corinthians 10–13, while it occurs only ten times in the sixteen chapters of 1 Corinthians (if "boast" is original to 1 Cor 13:3; if not, then only nine times), and ten times in 2 Corinthians 1–9.
10. The Greek word for "fool/foolish" (*aphrōn/aphronsyne*) appears ten times in the undisputed letters of Paul (eleven times if Ephesians is included in the count), eight of which appear in 2 Corinthians 10–13.

likely the "super-apostles" in combination with a man (and his entourage?) who stirred up trouble for Paul locally.[11] For them, Paul could easily be disparaged as unimpressive. Paul did not dispute them on that score. Instead, whatever truth there might be to that characterization of him Paul places it in a completely different context—a context in which service, no matter how unimpressive or lacking in honor, lies at the heart of what it means to be a Jesus-follower. It is Paul, ironically, whose apostolic ministry (even when unimpressive) is in line with the gospel, unlike the "super-apostles."

Regardless of their impressiveness, in Paul's view the proclamation of the "super-apostles" does not enhance the glory of God. Instead, it serves only to enhance their own vain glory. Accordingly, Paul considers them to be "false apostles, deceitful workers, masquerading as apostles of Christ . . . [and] as servants of righteousness" (11:13, 15). In Paul's eyes, they preach "a Jesus other than the Jesus we preached . . . a different spirit [and] a different gospel" (11:4) than the authentic gospel. Ultimately, for Paul the self-commendation of the "super-apostles" is little other than self-condemnation: "It is not the one who commends himself who is approved, but the one whom the Lord commends" (10:18; cf. 10:12).

By contrast, the gospel that Paul preaches, even in its lack of "worldly" credentials, is the vehicle through which the power of the creator God (the very one who said, "Let light shine out of darkness") is made accessible. God's wisdom is actuated even and especially within Paul's allegedly lackluster ministry, on the basis of his assurance to Paul that his "power is made perfect in weakness"; consequently, and ironically, Paul is content to "boast all the more gladly about my weaknesses, so that Christ's power may rest on [or perhaps 'dwell in'] me" (2 Cor 12:9).

Public Domain

▲ One of the things that Paul feels he could boast about (if the Corinthians needed to examine his credentials) is a mystical journey of being "caught up to the third heaven" (2 Cor 12:1–5). Paul describes this as having happened to "a man," by which he seems to mean that it happened to himself (even though he seeks to deflect attention away from himself by using this strategy).

▼ This raised platform was the "bema" or "place of judgment" in Corinth. Paul stood before Gallio, the proconsul of Achaia, when defending himself from charges laid against him (Acts 18:12–16), much like he found himself engaging in self-defense in 2 Corinthians. The Acrocorinth rises up in the background.

Bruce Longenecker

11. Although this man is referred to in 2 Cor 2:5–11, he may also be the one that Paul had already spoken harshly against in 1 Cor 5:1–11, as in 5:5: "hand this man over to Satan." He may also be the one whom Paul has primarily in mind in the earlier "tearful letter," when Paul imagines that when he returns to the Corinthians, he "will be grieved over many who have sinned earlier and have not repented of the impurity, sexual sin and debauchery in which they have indulged" (2 Cor 12:21). The plural focus of this passage matches the pluralized culpability of the man's sin that Paul expressed in 1 Cor 5:2, 6.

If Paul's apostleship could appear to be weak and uninspiring in the sight of others, it was not ineffectual in the sight of God. Knowing how to interpret what one experiences is a key to proper discipleship. So Paul writes in 2 Cor 5:16: "From now on we regard no one from a worldly point of view." For Christians, status evaluation is transformed by the power of the God of creation, in alignment with the gospel Paul preaches: "If anyone is in Christ, the new creation has come: The old has gone, the new is here!" (5:17). Despite all the trouble that Paul has had with the Corinthian Jesus-followers, by the time he writes 2 Corinthians 1–9 he is confident that, even in their fragile allegiance to Paul's gospel, the Corinthian Jesus-followers "are being transformed into his [Jesus'] image with ever-increasing glory" (3:18).

TRACKING THE VISION OF 2 CORINTHIANS

2 Corinthians 10–13

Because the text of 2 Corinthians is judged here to be composed of two letters (an earlier "tearful" letter and a later letter of reconciliation), the overview of 2 Corinthians will follow the temporal sequence of its two components.

The Basic Structure of the (Earlier) Tearful Letter:
2 Corinthians 10–13

10:1–18	Paul Declares War
11:1–12:13	Paul Speaks as a Fool (His Enforced but Inverted Boasting)
12:14–13:13	Paul's Final Defense and Warning

Because 2 Corinthians 10–13 has been discussed in some detail in the previous section, it will be only briefly outlined here, without subsections.

A coalition of Christians was putting Paul's apostolic credentials in dispute—a coalition comprised of some Corinthians and some recent "infiltrators" of the Corinthian Christian communities. Paul places their characterization of him solidly on the page of the letter—that is, he is said to be bold in his letters but timid in person (as was evidently the case during his recent visit to Corinth). But Paul asserts that, when judged in light of the gospel, his arguments demolish those who undermine his authority (10:3–5). Should he be required to, he will be forced to punish the Corinthians, in case they fail in their allegiance to his ministry and gospel (10:6; cf. 12:19–13:4, 10). Paul has plenty to boast about, he says, but his is a boast in the things that God has been doing through him. By contrast, those who have recently arrived in Corinth do plenty of boasting, but only in things that do not measure up to the promotion of faith (10:12–18).

Paul warns the Corinthians that ultimate realities are at stake in their decision about what to believe and with whom they should align themselves (11:1–6, 12–15). Not only was Paul's rhetorical ability in dispute, but so too was his pattern of financing his ministry. There were two sides to this coin. On the one hand, Paul was criticized for not accepting financial contributions from Corinthian Christians (11:7–11). Judged by the honor codes of his day, this could have been interpreted in one of two ways: either (1) as a sign of his apostolic inferiority, with an underlying lack of confidence resulting in his failure to command financial support; or (2) as a snub, as if he deemed himself superior to them, unwilling to accept their money. Paul himself interpreted it as a sign of his apostolic legitimacy, demonstrating that he was not benefitting financially from his ministry and that he was embodying the power of the gospel (11:7–11; Paul had highlighted much the same in 1 Corinthians 9).

On the other hand, Paul became suspect of being a charlatan. After all, he and his coworkers were collecting funds from Corinthian Jesus-followers. Could they be sure that Paul's motives were proper? Could they be sure that the collection would end up benefitting poor Jesus-followers in Jerusalem and not in Paul's coffers? Paul has to assert his integrity in the hope of assuring the Corinthians of his sincerity in this matter (12:14–18).

In the meantime, if the Corinthians force Paul into it, he will oblige them in an exercise of boasting. But Paul inverts the boast, so that he boasts not in things that are impressive, but in things that advertise weakness (11:16–12:13). Ironically, of course, it is that weakness that demonstrates God's strength and power, since God uses weakness to accomplish his purposes.

With the tearful letter (2 Corinthians 10–13) dispatched to Corinth, Paul waited anxiously to hear of its effectiveness. Eventually the news from Titus was that the letter had in fact done what it was intended to do (7:5–16). The Corinthian Christians had aligned themselves with Paul, disciplining the main troublemaker in their midst. Overjoyed that reconciliation was established, Paul writes 2 Corinthians 1–9. In it, he does everything he can to reinforce the fragile reconciliation and to set the record straight regarding matters he had not addressed previously.

The Basic Structure of the (Later) Letter of Reconciliation:
2 Corinthians 1–9

1:1–2	Opening Greeting
1:3–2:13	Paul Assesses the Rift between Him and the Corinthians
2:14–6:10	Paul Outlines the Character of His Apostolic Ministry
6:11–7:16	Paul Rejoices in His Reconciliation with the Corinthians
8:1–9:15	Paul Endears the Corinthians to His Collection Effort

2 Corinthians 1:1–2:13

Paul begins this letter by noting that his own life had been severely threatened but that God had rescued him for further ministry. This section could almost be thought to pick up from the inverted fool's speech of the tearful letter, demonstrating once again that Paul's weakness can be used by God to demonstrate God's great power (1:3–11).

Paul then wants to set the record straight about his travel itinerary. The changes in his travel plans had evidently resulted in accusations that he vacillated too much and was therefore unreliable and unworthy as an apostle. Paul wants to let it be plainly known that his travel plans changed according to the needs of the changing situation, as a wise and discerning minister of God. To have kept to an initial itinerary despite the situational changes would have caused unnecessary heartache to one and all (1:12–2:4).

Glad that the Corinthians have disciplined the one among them who had caused so much trouble (both for Paul and for them), Paul nonetheless wants them not to be overly harsh on him. In the task of discipline, those who discipline need to exercise care and caution lest the situation should backfire and they get caught up in the satanic grip of establishing themselves as moral superiors (2:5–11).

(Note: This person, who had been influential among the Corinthians, may have been the one whom Paul directly challenged in 1 Corinthians 5, although this is not certain. In 1 Corinthians 5 Paul had urged the Corinthian Christians to expel the man from their midst, in view of his extremely aberrant moral behavior. The Corinthians, however, seem to have done nothing initially, allowing this man to inflame the situation among them, with the help of the "super-apostles" who had been eager to criticize Paul. Now, as a result of Paul's "tearful" letter, they have acted in accordance with his wishes.)

2 Corinthians 2:14 – 7:16

This lengthy section exhibits notable twists and turns in its discursive focus, but it is unified by an underlying theme of the glory of the gospel regardless of the apparent inadequacy of those who bring the gospel message. Paul has emphasized this point on various occasions already in his letters to the Corinthians. Repeating it here serves to establish their reconciliation with him around this central axis, banning once and for all the cancer of judging his apostleship on the basis of cultural codes of honor that run contrary to the gospel's own matrix of honor.

"Dissension in the church is deeply worrisome to Paul, for the aim of his apostolic labors has been to build community, not just to save souls."[12]

Paul's comments in chapter 3 are a particularly dense part of this discourse. Introducing that chapter is the claim that Paul should never need to commend himself before the Corinthians. The Spirit of God is operative in their midst, by way of Paul's ministry, so that their transformed hearts are all that Paul should need by way of having a letter of recommendation (3:1 – 3).[13] Through the Spirit, Paul is a minister of the new covenant, a covenant that gives life (3:3 – 6).

With the notion of a new covenant in play, Paul pivots into a complex interpretation of Scripture, involving the interweaving of Jer 31:31 – 34 and Exod 34:29 – 35 (along with an echo of Ezek 36:26). If those who had infiltrated the Corinthian Jesus groups had themselves been skilled (but unwise) interpreters of Scripture, Paul demonstrates that he too can engage in masterful (i.e., both skilled and wise) interpretations of Scripture that edify the Jesus groups properly.

Christian theology "has no more exalted or profound word — essentially, indeed, it has no other word — than this: that God was in Christ reconciling the world unto Himself (2 Cor 5:19)."[14]

In an interpretative exercise that is perhaps unsurpassed in the Pauline corpus in both its extent and complexity, Paul finds Scripture itself to differentiate between the covenantal ministry of Moses and the ministry of the new covenant, for which Paul himself is working (3:7 – 18). While the former covenant was glorious, its glory has been outstripped by the new covenant, in which the Spirit of freedom is operative, allowing Scripture to be understood in a new configuration in its application to Christian communities, whose members "are being transformed into his [the Lord's] image with ever-increasing glory" (3:18).

12. Richard B. Hays, *The Moral Vision of the New Testament: A Contemporary Introduction to New Testament Ethics* (San Francisco: HarperSanFrancisco, 1996), 34.
13. Here Paul is probably contrasting himself with the "super-apostles," who might have had impressive letters of recommendation from other Christians.
14. Karl Barth, *Church Dogmatics* (ed. and trans. G. W. Bromiley and T. F. Torrance; Edinburgh: T&T Clark, 1957), II/2 88).

That glory partakes in the glory of God's all-powerful act of creation. Both the primordial event of creation and the enlightenment of Jesus-followers involve light penetrating the deep recesses of darkness. For the followers of Jesus, this involves recognizing the glory of God in the very face of Christ (4:6). But the god who oversees "the world" (i.e., the god who perpetuates cultural honor codes that dictate a person's worth) can blind people's minds to the ways of the true God (4:3–4). What they will see is weakness, but the power of God emerges from and through that weakness (4:7–12).

Throughout his ministry Paul constantly appeals "to the supreme critical instance, the death and resurrection of Jesus Christ. That is a drastic critique of all tradition and signifies a new freedom and the breaking in of a new and hopeful future. It is a 'dangerous memory,' and its content forbids any past-oriented, antiquarian retrieval. Paul has an apocalyptic hope for the future in relation to which the tradition is interpreted."[15]

Consequently, weakness is not shameful and, even when taken to the point of death, it is not fearful. Instead, the Corinthian Christians are to know that the full manifestation of glory lies in the future (4:16–5:10). As a result of all this, Paul presses on in his apostolic ministry, even though it may seem unimpressive when judged by the cultural standards of his day (6:3–10). He is compelled to serve God by setting up communities whose moral ethos runs contrary to the honor codes of the world (5:11–15). In those communities are found Christians who "no longer live for themselves but for him who died for them and was raised again" (5:15).

The perspective of those communities does not derive from a "worldly point of view" (5:16). Instead, overturning the massive weight of the age-old codes of honor, the perspective of those transformed and transformative communities is nothing other than a "new creation" itself: "The old has gone, the new is here!" (5:17). The new creation that Paul's ministry enhances is magnificent, with the sinfulness that runs rampant throughout God's world being replaced by the righteousness of God (5:21).

▼ The glory of God in the self-giving of Jesus Christ

The Holy Trinity, Semitecolo, Nicoletto/Padua Cathedral, Italy/Alinari/The Bridgeman Art Library

Consequently, Paul encourages the Corinthians to be "yoked" to his cruciform apostolic ministry rather than to the ministry of others whose gospel does not conform to the truth (6:11–7:4).[16] From this, Paul makes a transition to recount his ongoing relationship with the Corinthian Christ-followers, emphasizing his great pleasure that the period of difficulty is behind them and that they have been reconciled to each other in a relationship of harmony (7:5–16).

15. Frances Young and David F. Ford, *Meaning and Truth in 2 Corinthians* (London: SPCK, 1987), 159.
16. This passage is popularly interpreted to discuss the unsuitability of marriage partners who are not Christians. In its context, however, the passage serves much different purposes.

2 Corinthians 8:1–9:15

The final sentence of the previous section sets the tone for the final two chapters of this letter: "I am glad I can have complete confidence in you" (7:16). With the previous chapters working to enhance the new but fragile reconciliation between Paul and Corinthian Jesus-followers, Paul now moves to the practical matter that was of notable concern to him—that is, his collection for impoverished Jesus-followers in Jerusalem. In various strands of discourse throughout 2 Corinthians 8–9, Paul expresses his "complete confidence" that the Corinthian communities of Jesus devotion will participate wholeheartedly in that initiative.

Although the collection had been a point of contention between Paul and some Corinthian Jesus-followers (so 2 Cor 12:16–18), Paul cannot fail to address the matter once again (even though he must do so with notable delicacy, see 8:20–21). Were Paul to lose Corinthian support, the resources of the collection would be notably reduced, since some Corinthian Jesus-followers seem to have enjoyed a comfortable level of economic security (perhaps in a higher concentration than in Christian communities based elsewhere).

Paul makes use of a number of different strategies to motivate the Corinthians in this initiative, some of which lie more closely at the heart of his gospel than others. The motivating factors Paul cites for participating in the collection effort include the following items, in roughly sequential order.

1. Since Paul had boasted about the Corinthian Christians to Christians in Macedonia, the Corinthians need to live up to that boast, not least because the less-affluent Christian communities in Macedonia have already expressed their generosity diligently (8:2–5, 8, 10–12; 9:2–4).
2. Paul appeals to the Corinthians' sense of self-importance (notable already in

Humility in Ethical Traditions

A study of humility in ethical traditions (carried out by researchers at Macquarie University) included within its conclusions two important things. First, humility was not a treasured commodity in most sectors of the ancient world. Second, a seismic shift in ethical tradition is notable in the aftermath of a certain Jewish rabbi, who was perceived as a great man and who gave himself up willingly to a shameful death on a Roman cross in about the year 30 or so; his followers then had two choices—either he was not as great as they thought or greatness consists in something other than honor. We know what they concluded.[17]

"Paul never romanticized or idolized authority. He suffered too much at the hands of religious and political authorities to do that. His chief concern in 2 Corinthians might be described as theological purification of authority through the gospel. Is it possible to have a specifically Christian concept of authority which, in community, unites the freedom 'where the Spirit is' (3.17) with 'the love of Christ constraining us' (5.14)? Only, Paul suggests, if the vision informing that is of the authority of God, his glory known 'in the face of Christ' (4.6)."[18]

17. For a general treatment of this theme, see John Dickson *Humilitas* (Grand Rapids: Zondervan, 2011), esp. ch. 5 ("*Philotimia*: Why the Ancient World Didn't Like Humility") and chapter 6 ("Cruciform: How a Jew from Nazareth Redefined Greatness").
18. Young and Ford, *Meaning and Truth in 2 Corinthians*, 231.

1 Corinthians), noting that "since you excel in everything" else, so you should excel in this too (8:7).

3. Corinthian participation in Paul's collection will be a prudent way for them to build up their own "insurance" for the future, in the event that they come to experience a time of difficulty and require assistance from others (8:14–15).
4. Paul's collection initiative is informed by scriptural injunctions (8:15; 9:9; see Exod 16:18 and Psa 111:9).
5. Corinthian participation in the collection will be one way in which they can be of service to others (9:1, 12).
6. God looks with favor upon the giving of one's resources, and he will reward the generous giver (9:6, 8, 10–11).
7. Participating in Paul's collection is a means for Corinthian Christians to express their thankfulness to God, who himself has been generous to them (9:12).
8. Through Paul's collection, Corinthian Christians will establish fellowship with other Christians (*koinōnia*, translated as "sharing" in the NIV; 9:13)
9. Donating resources to Paul's collection offers a witness to others that Corinthian Christians have been transformed (9:13), as Gentiles (who were not known to care for the poor) exhibit behavior that characterizes God's people (i.e., the ethnic people of Israel, who traditionally were know for their care for the poor).

Two further features of Paul's discourse in 2 Corinthians 8–9 deserve special mention.

10. Notice that Paul embeds the story of the self-giving Jesus within his motivational splattergun approach. So he writes: "For you know the grace of our Lord Jesus Christ, that though he was rich, yet for your sake he became poor, so that you through his poverty might become rich" (2 Cor 8:9). In 1 Corinthians Paul already emphasized the importance of imitating Christ (1 Cor 11:1); here he simply reiterates the point in an economic frame of reference.
11. Notice too that the whole of Paul's discussion about the collection is framed in terms of "the grace that God has given" (8:1, 6–7, 9, 19; 9:8, 14), God's own "indescribable gift" (9:15). For Paul, divine grace is not something merely to benefit from, but something that inspires obedience in patterns of generosity among Jesus-followers.

"For Paul, the collection itself was intricately associated with the very gospel that he proclaimed, a gospel about the righteousness of Israel's deity that sets the world to order."[19]

It is little wonder, then, that his discussion about the collection is infused with highly theological terminology. He speaks of Corinthian involvement in the collection as being a demonstration of "the obedience that accompanies your confession of the gospel of Christ" (9:13). Or he can speak of it in terms of "service" (8:4; 9:1, 12, 13) and "righteousness" (9:9–10)—both the righteousness of God and of those obedient to him. For Paul, the collection initiative was itself a hard copy of the very gospel he proclaimed—a gospel about

19. Bruce W. Longenecker, *Remember the Poor: Paul, Poverty, and the Greco-Roman World* (Grand Rapids: Eerdmans, 2010), 188.

The Word *Charis* and Its Meaning in 2 Corinthians 8–9

In the Greco-Roman world of Paul's day, the Greek word *charis* could refer to one of several things in any given instance: (1) a gift, (2) generosity motivating a gift, or (3) gratitude for a gift received. Interestingly, Paul employs all three uses in 2 Corinthians 8–9. In fact, *charis* occurs with a higher frequency in these two chapters than in any other consecutive chapters in the Pauline corpus. The following chart is devised to overview Paul's various uses of *charis* in 2 Corinthians 8–9. For each verse in which *charis* occurs, the chart identifies the giver of *charis*, the recipient of *charis*, the semantic sense Paul has used, and the NIV's English translation.[20]

Verse	Giver of *charis*	Recipient of *charis*	Sense of *charis*	NIV Translation
2 Cor 8:1	Macedonians	Jerusalem saints	Benefaction	"grace"
2 Cor 8:4	Paul and coworkers	Macedonians	Benefaction	"privilege"
2 Cor 8:6	Corinthians	Jerusalem saints	Benefaction	"act of grace"
2 Cor 8:7	Corinthians	Jerusalem saints	Benefaction	"grace of giving"
2 Cor 8:9	Jesus	Jesus-followers	Generosity	"grace"
2 Cor 8:16	Paul	God	Gratitude	"thanks"
2 Cor 8:19	The churches	Jerusalem saints	Benefaction	"offering"
2 Cor 9:8	God	Corinthians	Benefaction	"bless . . . abundantly"
2 Cor 9:14	God	Corinthians	Generosity	"grace"
2 Cor 9:15	Paul	God	Gratitude	"thanks"

the righteousness of God in which the self-giving lives of Christians is part of the process of setting the world to right.

SUMMARY REFLECTION

Second Corinthians reveals two sides of Paul: the Paul at his most embattled and besieged (chs. 10–13), and the Paul seeking to salvage and consolidate a healthy relationship with Jesus groups that included within their number some people who had wounded him badly (chs. 1–9). In the midst of this torturous period, Paul was disheartened to the point of tears about the situation of the Corinthian Jesus groups, but he did not fail in his fight to help them correct the errors of their ways. Against this backdrop, it is stunning to hear him say to those with whom he had been dissociated and now enjoyed a fragile reconciliation: "God made him who had no sin to be sin for us, so that in him we might become the righteousness of God" (5:21).

20. The chart was devised by Grant G. Edwards.

» KEY PEOPLE, PLACES, AND TERMS «

charlatan
Corinth
Ephesus
Macedonia
Philippi
Super-apostles
Tearful letter
Thessalonica
Timothy
Titus
Troas

» QUESTIONS FOR REVIEW AND DISCUSSION «

1. How is the tone of 2 Corinthians 1 – 9 different from that of 1 Corinthians? Why do these chapters have this distinct tenor?
2. Describe the points of tension between Paul and the Corinthians. What caused these points of tension to arise? How did Paul respond to them?
3. How does the two-part partition theory affect how we understand 2 Corinthians and its background?
4. What is Paul's problem with the "super-apostles," and why does he call them by this name?
5. Sketch the "story" of Paul's relationship with the Corinthians, tracing the major events and movements.
6. What practical matter concerned Paul in 2 Corinthians 8 – 9, and why is it so important to him?

» CONTEMPORARY THEOLOGICAL REFLECTION «

1. Why do you think Paul experienced so much opposition during his ministry? Should his response and his commitment to reconciliation shape conceptions of conflicts within twenty-first-century communities of Christians?
2. How do Paul's bold self-affirmations strike you as a twenty-first-century reader? What might be gleaned for twenty-first-century ministry from Paul's sensitivity to boasting, his humility, and his opinion of the "super-apostles"?
3. What is the import of Paul's instructions concerning "yoking" in 2 Corinthians 6:11 – 7:4? How has this section often been interpreted/applied in modern churches? What do you think has led to such an interpretation?
4. What do we make of Paul's bold requests for financial support in this letter? What distinctive elements of Paul's requests could serve as guidelines by which to compare today's numerous requests for financial support?

» GOING FURTHER «

Many of the books and commentaries listed at the end of chapter 4 on 1 Corinthians are pertinent to the study of 2 Corinthians as well.

Further Academic Commentaries on 2 Corinthians

Barnett, Paul. *The Second Epistle to the Corinthians.* NICNT. Grand Rapids: Eerdmans, 1997.

Furnish, Victor Paul. *2 Corinthians.* AB. New Haven, CT: Yale University Press, 2007.

Garland, David E. *2 Corinthians.* NAC. Nashville: Broadman & Holman, 1999.

Harris, Murray J. *The Second Epistle to the Corinthians.* NIGTC. Grand Rapids: Eerdmans, 2004.

Matera, Frank. *Second Corinthians: A Commentary.* NTL. Louisville: Westminster John Knox, 2003.

Thrall, Margaret. *The Second Epistle to the Corinthians.* 2 vols. ICC. Edinburgh: T&T Clark, 1994, 2000.

Theological Dimensions of 2 Corinthians

Carson, D. A. *A Model of Christian Maturity: An Exposition of 2 Corinthians 10–13.* Grand Rapids: Baker Books, 2007.

Murphy-O'Connor, Jerome. *The Theology of the Second Letter to the Corinthians.* Cambridge: Cambridge University Press, 1991.

———. *Keys to Second Corinthians: Revisiting the Major Issues.* Oxford: Oxford University Press, 2010.

Savage, Timothy B. *Power through Weakness: Paul's Understanding of the Christian Ministry in 2 Corinthians.* Cambridge: Cambridge University Press, 1996.

CHAPTER 6

ROMANS

CHAPTER GOALS

- To examine the issues that have primary impact on the study of Romans
- To highlight the central concerns and basic contents of that letter

CHAPTER OVERVIEW

1. Situating the Vision: An Introduction to Romans
2. Centering the Vision of Romans: Revealing the Righteousness of God
3. Tracking the Vision of Romans
4. Key People, Places, and Terms
5. Summary Reflection
6. Questions for Review and Discussion
7. Contemporary Theological Reflection
8. Going Further

KEY VERSES

Romans 1:16–17: "I am not ashamed of the gospel, because it is the power of God that brings salvation to everyone who believes: first to the Jew, then to the Gentile. For in the gospel the righteousness of God is revealed—a righteousness that is by faith from first to last, just as it is written: 'The righteous will live by faith.'"

Romans 5:5, 8: "God's love has been poured out into our hearts through the Holy Spirit, who has been given to us. God demonstrates his own love for us in this: While we were still sinners, Christ died for us."

Romans 8:38–39: "For I am convinced that neither death nor life, neither angels nor demons, neither the present nor the future, nor any powers, neither height nor depth, nor anything else in all creation, will be able to separate us from the love of God that is in Christ Jesus our Lord."

Romans 11:25–26: "I do not want you to be ignorant of this mystery, brothers and sisters, so that you may not think you are superior: Israel has experienced a hardening in part until the full number of the Gentiles has come in, and in this way all Israel will be saved."

Romans 12:1–2a: "Therefore, I urge you, brothers and sisters, in view of God's mercy, to offer your bodies as a living sacrifice, holy and pleasing to God—this is true worship. Do not conform to the pattern of this world, but be transformed by the renewing of your mind."

SITUATING THE VISION: AN INTRODUCTION TO ROMANS

The longest of Paul's extant texts, Paul's letter to Jesus-followers in **Rome** is also his most influential literary enterprise. It has impacted people who have influenced the course of history, even centuries after it was originally written. By their own admission, such notable figures as Augustine, Martin Luther, John Wesley, and Karl Barth have credited this letter with either their initial conversion or the subsequent renewal of their Christian commitment. And through such people, vast numbers of others have also been influenced. If a short list were to be drawn up of the most influential of ancient documents, Romans would likely be somewhere toward the top.

Paul, of course, would know nothing about how significant his late-50s letter to Roman Christians would eventually become in the broader course of human history. But it would probably not have surprised him to learn of its enduring and widespread importance. Its sixteen chapters are, after all, an expression of "the gospel of God," the very "power of God that brings salvation to everyone who believes" (Rom 1:16).

The Text of Romans

But how many of the sixteen chapters of Romans were originally part of his letter? Much of what we say about this document depends on where we imagine the letter originally to have ended (which is why this issue needs to be addressed before we can say much else about it).

Although the text appears to be composed of material that was later demarcated within sixteen chapters, some have maintained that the letter sent to Rome did not include one or two of the final chapters. Chapter 16 has often been vulnerable to this suspicion. That last chapter of Romans, which largely comprises greetings to people evidently known to Paul, has occasionally been deemed to have made its way into the letter only when Paul sent a copy of this letter to Christians in Ephesus. On this view, since Paul had not yet been to Rome, he is unlikely to have composed the greetings of Romans 16 with residents of Rome in mind; instead, since Paul had already resided in Ephesus for almost three years (from ca. AD 52 to 55), the extensive greetings of Romans 16 were only tacked onto the end of the copy that was sent to Ephesus in order to greet Christians there. The view is interesting, but it suffers from the fact that no ancient manuscript of Romans lacks chapter 16. Accordingly, there is a strong consensus that Romans 16 is, in fact, the final chapter in Paul's letter to the Christians at Rome.[1]

But other features toward the end of the letter also require comment. The end of Romans 16 includes a **doxology** that seems fitting for the whole of the letter.[2] Although this appears at Romans 16:25–27 in most manuscripts, in some later manuscripts it appears at the end of Romans 14 or, as in one case, at the end of Romans 15.

1. Some later manuscripts omit the phrase "in Rome" from the two occasions in Romans 1 when Paul identifies his readers as being located there (Rom 1:7, 15). This omission seems to have been motivated by pastoral concerns of later centuries, enabling this ancient letter to be better read by Christians in any location.
2. While some imagine this doxology to have been added by a later editor, it is more likely to have been authored by Paul. In either scenario, however, it captures much of the theological dynamics of the letter.

Order of Contents in Various Ancient Manuscripts

ℵ, B, C, D	1:1–14:23		15:1–33	16:1–23		16:25–27	
A	1:1–14:23	16:25–27	15:1–33	16:1–23		16:25–27	
Majority	1:1–14:23	16:25–27	15:1–33	16:1–23	16:24		
F, G	1:1–14:23		15:1–33	16:1–23	16:24		
Some Vulgate	1:1–14:23				16:24	16:25–27	
$\mathfrak{P}^{46}$	1:1–14:23		15:1–33			16:25–27	16:1–23

What is going on here? Probably what we are witnessing in this situation has resulted from the influence of **Marcion**.[3] Living in the middle of the second century, Marcion sought to denude the New Testament of anything suggesting that the God of salvation was covenantally related to the Jewish people, so he removed anything promoting a favorable attitude toward the Jews. Thus, he sought to restrict the Christian canon to contain Luke's gospel only and the letters of Paul, and even then he excised certain parts of those texts. Romans 15 seems to have been problematic for Marcion, with its mention of Jesus Christ having been the occasion for God to confirm the promises that he made to the patriarchs of Israel (15:8), and its mention of Gentiles sharing in the spiritual blessings of the Jewish people (15:27). Accordingly, Romans 15 seems to have been omitted from Marcion's canon, and with it went most of Romans 16, except for the final doxology.

▲ The book of Romans could be considered one of the most influential ancient documents. This papyrus from P46 contains Romans 16:4–13.

It is possible that Marcion's considerable influence in the late second century caused many to believe that Romans 14 was the end of Paul's letter, onto which the doxology of 16:25–27 was then appended. But this situation was not stable, with Romans 15 and 16 making their way back into most of the manuscripts that we can now consult. In fact, precisely because Paul's argument in Romans 15 flows so organically from Romans 14 and because most of the ancient manuscripts contain all of Romans 14 through 16 in one order or another, there is no reason to think that Paul's text ended at Romans 14 or even at the end of chapter 15.

The last two chapters of Paul's letter reveal much about the situation of both Paul and his addressees at the time that the letter was written—two issues that are addressed in the next two sections of this chapter.

Indicators of Paul's Situation

The final chapters of Romans indicate that it was written from Corinth. Just as Paul identifies a man called "Gaius" in 1 Cor 1:14, so too in Romans 16:23 he gives greetings from

3. In one of the earliest manuscripts ($\mathfrak{P}^{46}$) the dexology appears at the end of Romans 15.

Gaius as if he were known to some among Roman Christians (i.e., Prisca [or Priscilla] and Aquila, who had previously lived in Corinth). Although the name Gaius was common, these remarks in two of Paul's letters likely refer to the same Corinthian person. That the letter originated from Corinth is further supported by Paul's mention of Phoebe in 16:1. Presumably the carrier (and perhaps the first interpreter) of the letter to Rome, Phoebe had her home base in **Cenchreae**, a port city adjacent to the east of Corinth.

If Paul wrote the letter of Romans from Corinth, his comments in Romans 15 allow us to learn something of how he regarded his apostolic ministry up to that point. Paul presents his ministry as having infiltrated the eastern part of the Mediterranean basin to a sufficient extent ("there is no more place for me to work in these regions," 15:23), and this enabled him to devise plans for ministry further afield in the western Mediterranean (15:17–24).

But prior to undertaking that expansion of his ministry to the west, Paul wanted to do something that would take him once again back to the east. Having already collected a sizeable fund for "the poor among the Lord's people in Jerusalem" (15:26), Paul is now transitioning to the point of delivering that fund from predominantly Gentile Jesus-followers in urban cities of the Greco-Roman world to predominantly Jewish Jesus-followers in Jerusalem.

Although money is normally favorably received by those who receive it, in this case Paul suspects that things might be different. In view of the controversy that had already plagued his ministry, Paul knows that the delivery of this collection is itself controversial, to the point of being dangerous. Paul seems even to fear for his own life. So he writes: "I urge you, brothers and sisters . . . to join me in my struggle by praying to God for me. Pray that I may be kept safe from the unbelievers in Judea and that the contribution I take to Jerusalem may be favorably received by the Lord's people there" (15:30–31).

This helps us to date Romans fairly accurately, since it seems that Paul delivered the collection funds in the spring of AD 58. Consequently, working backward and allowing for travel restrictions (e.g., the closure of seaports during the rough winter months), Romans is likely to be dated to the autumn of 57 or so, just prior to his final journey back to Jerusalem.

Women in the Greco-Roman World

Although the Greco-Roman world was thoroughly patriarchal in its structures, on rare occasions women slipped through the androcentric configuration and rose to civic prominence. Although women were not allowed to hold public office or even to vote, we sometimes find them at the heart of public benefaction, donating vast sums of wealth to enhance the civic environment and acting as financial patrons to Greco-Roman associations. Such women exist in the literary and material record and testify to the manner in which embedded values (the prioritizing of maleness over femaleness) could at times be trumped by other values (i.e., the injection of resources into society).

This might provide a bit of a background (although on a much less grandiose scale) to the way that Paul mentions Phoebe in Rom 16:2: "I ask you to receive her in the Lord in a way worthy of his people and to give her any help she may need from you, for she has been the benefactor of many people, including me."

Why Did Paul Write to Followers of Jesus in Rome?

If we can delineate much about the text of Romans (its extent, its date, its place of composition, its author's conceptualization of his ministry's future), we still need to ask why Paul would have written this lengthy letter at this point in his ministry and, in particular, why he would write to Jesus-followers in Rome.

Some have suggested that Paul intended this letter to serve as his "last will and testament," in a sense. Cognizant of the dangers that potentially awaited him in Jerusalem, Paul may have written the letter in order to bequeath to others a literary landmark of and memorial to his gospel. In this view, the letter witnesses to and demonstrates the full contours and scope of his message. Along these lines, Melanchthon, a great figure from the Reformation period, once called Romans a "compendium of Christian doctrine."

Of course, Romans cannot be considered a complete compendium of Christian doctrine (and Melanchthon himself does not seem to have imagined that it was).[4] In Romans Paul does not deal in any detailed and developed way with certain key issues, such as resurrection, eschatology, Christology, and the Lord's Supper. For those matters, other letters provide many more theological resources than Romans does. So this letter is not in any sense analogous to, say, Karl Barth's multivolume *Church Dogmatics*, which (when completed) addressed all the key topics of Christian theology in extensive coverage.

Consequently, the "last will and testament" scenario is less satisfactory than other explanations. The fact that Paul addressed this letter to Christians *at Rome* must itself give us pause for thought. His addressees were Christians whose communities had been founded by others and whom Paul had never been able to visit in their local context (see Rom 15:20–24). If he had written this letter intending only to bequeath a literary testament to his gospel, he would probably have preferred to send it to Christians in, say, Ephesus—where he had been based for approximately three years from about AD 52 to 55, in fruitful relationships with other Christians. The decision to send a letter to Jesus-followers *in Rome* suggests that Paul had something else in mind, something that pertained particularly to them, when he authored his longest extant letter.

There was likely a variety of situational factors motivating Paul to write Romans. But the focal point to them all likely lies in what he writes in Rom 15:23–32. There, interspersed with reflections on the necessity of taking his collection to Jerusalem, Paul speaks of his hope "to do so [i.e., to visit them] when I go to **Spain**" and of his desire "to see you while passing through and to have you assist me on my journey there, after I have enjoyed your company for a while" (15:24). Paul sends this letter to believers in Rome precisely because he has his eyes set on preaching the gospel in "Spain" (the word "Spain" probably serving to designate the territory to the west of Italy in broad terms). But why should Jesus-worshipers in Rome be key to his interest in taking the gospel to Spain?

The answer seems to lie in the little phrase that Paul uses in Romans 15:24, "to have you assist me on my journey." With that phrase Paul is planting a seed that he hopes to harvest in the future, should all go well in Jerusalem in the meantime. While such assistance might certainly involve noneconomic means of support (such as prayer and encouragement), the

4. See Robert L. Plummer, "Melanchthon as Interpreter of the New Testament," *WTJ* 62 (2002): 257–65.

primary reference in this phrase is economic. Paul is intimating that Christians in Rome might find it in their hearts to back his plans to take the gospel to Spain by offering him the finances necessary to undertake such an enterprise.

Paul does not wait until he gets to Rome to put this idea in their minds. He is thinking several steps ahead. With this letter to the Christians in Rome, he starts the ball rolling, in order to benefit from its momentum when he arrives. Just as the funds for "the poor among the Lord's people in Jerusalem" took a while to be raised before they could be delivered, so too the funds to support Paul's mission to Spain would be more substantial if the Roman Christians caught the vision of his ministry prior to his arrival.

But this meant that Paul had to introduce his gospel to them in order to gain their (financial) support. After all, he had a controversial reputation within (certain circles of) the early Jesus movement. He knew it, and he knew that Christians in Rome knew it (cf. Rom 3:8). If he was to succeed in his goal of extending the gospel message into parts where no one had yet taken it, he would need the financial support of those Christians; but he would first need to convince them that his gospel message was one that they should indeed support. It is for this reason that he introduces the gospel message that he preached with the words, "I am not ashamed of the gospel, because it is the power of God that brings salvation to everyone who believes" (1:16).

Some people thought that Paul should, however, be ashamed of his gospel. The crux of the matter seems to have involved Paul's view (shared by others, but with him at the lead) that being a follower of Jesus did not require observing the stipulations that God had given to the people of Israel. As Paul will argue in this letter, Jewish Christians should continue to observe the Mosaic law if they feel that such observances are a part of their identity before God, but observance of the Mosaic law per se was not something that was to mark out the identity of each and every follower of Jesus and should not be imposed on Gentile Christians as a requirement (see Romans 14–15).

As we have seen from our survey of the Galatian and Corinthian letters, there were two issues that sprang immediately from this. One involved the people of Israel themselves. If God had given the law to Israel, but if the law was not required of all followers of Jesus, what was the current status of God's **covenant** with the people of Israel? This issue of salvation history arises from Paul's severe letter to the Galatians. Without much of a stretch of imagination, that letter could almost be construed to imply that the covenant with Israel is now to be seen as, at best, relatively unimportant to God (although that would be a misreading of Paul's true intent).

The second issue pertains to ethics. If followers of Jesus are not required to observe the law and in fact can consider themselves to be "free" from the law, does it follow that Jesus-followers have no ethical constraints on their behavior? This interpretation of Paul's gospel had already taken root in Corinth, where some Jesus-followers imagined that "I have the right to do anything" (1 Cor 6:12; 10:23).

That these two issues are intertwined is evidenced within Paul's own presentation in Romans. In Romans 3:1–8, he brings them both to the table through a series of rhetorical questions that articulate each issue in quick succession. The issue of salvation history is raised at the start of the section, where Paul asks: "What advantage, then, is there in being a

Jew, or what value is there in circumcision?" (To this, his initial response in 3:2 is "Much in every way!") Or he asks in 3:3, "What if some [Jews] were unfaithful? Will their unfaithfulness nullify God's faithfulness?"

The issue of ethics is raised at the end of the section (Rom 3:7 – 8), where Paul puts the matter this way: "Someone might argue, 'If my falsehood enhances God's truthfulness and so increases his glory, why am I still condemned as a sinner?'" After all, if the failures of ethnic Israel do not overturn God's faithfulness to them, why should it be any different for anyone else? Paul elaborates this view further: "Why not say — as we are being slanderously reported as saying and as some claim that we say — 'Let us do evil that good may result?'" With this slogan, Paul has crystallized the position of others in the early Jesus-movement who credited him with the view that the more immoral we are, the more we demonstrate how gracious God is to us. According to Paul, those who continue to attribute that view to him do a disservice to the gospel that he proclaims (or as he says, "their condemnation is just!").

Much of what we find in Romans is dedicated to addressing these two issues, each of which derives from his view about the law. Paul's full engagement with these issues is not found within Rom 3:1 – 8, however. In that concentrated passage, he merely lays down the topics that he addresses later in the letter. The issue of salvation history (specifically, is God unfaithful to Israel?) arcs over into Romans 9 – 11, where Paul offers three heartfelt and protracted chapters on the issue of God's faithfulness to ethnic Israel. And the issue about ethics (specifically, are we free to do as we like?) arcs over into Romans 6 (and beyond), where Paul raises the point directly and asks on two occasions: "What then are we to say? Should we continue in sin in order that grace may abound?" (6:1); "Should we sin because we are not under law but under grace?" (6:15). In each instance, Paul vehemently undermines the view.

So it looks like one of the reasons why Paul wrote Romans is to set the record straight (for those whose support he is seeking) about how his gospel is to be understood. With regard to the people of Israel, his gospel does not undermine God's faithfulness. And with regard to ethics, his gospel does not perpetuate behavioral immorality. In fact, Paul wants Jesus-followers in Rome to understand that rather than wreaking havoc in Christian communities, his gospel (when properly understood) enhances those communities, since it is "the power of God that brings salvation to everyone who believes" (1:16).

And judging from what he writes in Romans 14 – 15, Paul wants the full extent of that power to be experienced by Jesus-followers in Rome. In those two chapters, Paul addresses an issue that seems to be causing some tension within (certain sectors of) Roman Jesus groups. That issue involved how Christians of different lifestyles (specifically, those who observe the Mosaic law and those who do not) can activate Paul's vision of corporate lifestyle in the body of Christ in a way that coheres with fundamental principles of the gospel. That discussion itself builds on much that Paul says about living as Jesus-followers in Romans 12 – 13.

All this, it seems, is an effort to demonstrate that, rather than being dangerous, the gospel that Paul preaches, of which he is not ashamed, and for which he seeks the financial support of Jesus-followers in Rome, is a gospel that inspires "the obedience of faith" among communities that he plants. To accentuate the point, Paul identifies the goal of his ministry as calling "all the Gentiles to the obedience that comes from faith." That this phrase occurs at the start and end of the letter (1:5; 16:26, if the latter is original to the letter) suggests that Paul wants it to serve as a kind of thematic frame to the whole of the intervening chapters.

Why, then, did Paul see the need to write to those devoted to Jesus Christ *at Rome*, whose communities he had not founded and most of whose members he had never met? Seeking to capture their appreciation of his gospel and their support for his mission to Spain, he wrote in advance of that mission in order to demonstrate the power of the gospel for the promotion of "righteousness"—that is, right relationships of all kinds and dimensions. Rather than being problematic and defective, his gospel message was praiseworthy and principled, enhancing the corporate life of Jesus groups not only from Jerusalem through to **Illyricum** (so 15:19), not only in Spain (should Paul's plans come to fruition), but also in Rome itself—probably the last major outpost of the Jesus movement in the west at that time.

What Do We Know about Followers of Jesus Christ in Rome?

It seems that Christians in Rome met in similar circumstances to those of other Jesus groups throughout the Mediterranean basin. Most likely they met in small groups, either in small apartments, workshops, or houses (see Rom 16:5, 14–15). According to one extensive study, some of these Jesus groups were probably based in the "workers' quarter" of the city, accommodating people of rather meager income, such as warehouse porters, sailors, brickyard workers, shopkeepers, craftsmen of small shops, millers, and tanners.[5] From the list of names in Romans 16, it seems that Paul's addressees included Jews and Gentiles, slaves and freeborn, male and female.

We know that Paul did not found any of the communities of Jesus-devotion in Rome. The origins of those groups are murky. It is possible that they go as far back as the **Pentecost** incident described in Acts 2, where Jewish pilgrims to Jerusalem became followers of Jesus before returning to their homeland. Acts 2:10 specifically mentions "visitors from Rome" being present there. Intriguing in this scenario is Paul's reference to **Andronicus** and **Junia** in Romans 16—a husband and wife team whom Paul refers to not only as "outstanding among the apostles" but also as "in Christ before I was" (16:7).[6] Were they instrumental in bringing the message of Jesus Christ to Rome? We cannot tell for sure, but it is possible.

It also seems that the lives of most of these Christ-followers were dramatically affected by two emperors: **Claudius** (emperor from AD 41 to his death in 54) and **Nero** (emperor from 54 to his death in 68). In about the year 49, Claudius initiated the "expulsion" of Jews from Rome. The historian **Suetonius** claims that this was in reaction to the incessant rioting among the Jews by the instigation of someone called "**Chrestos**" (*Claudius*

---

5. Peter Lampe, *From Paul to Valentinus: Christians at Rome in the First Two Centuries* (trans. M. Steinhauser; Minneapolis: Fortress, 2003), 50.
6. There is some debate about the interpretation given here. First, some manuscripts assume that the name in 16:7 is the masculine Junias rather than the feminine Junia. Second, some have argued that the phrase that describes the two figures of 16:7 is best interpreted to mean "held in high regard by the apostles." The authors of this textbook, along with the majority of scholars, find the most persuasive arguments to support the reading "Andronicus and Junia [feminine] . . . outstanding among the apostles." In defense, see Eldon Jay Epp, *Junia: The First Woman Apostle* (Minneapolis: Fortress, 2005).

The Fire of Rome, Robert, Hubert/Musee des Beaux-Arts Andre Malraux, Le Havre, France/Giraudon/The Bridgeman Art Library

▲ An artist's depiction of the burning of Rome

25). It is commonly thought that this does not refer to the actions of a synagogue Jew based in Rome (*Chrestos* is not a Jewish name) but is instead a muddled reference to disputes among Jews in Rome regarding Christ. *Chrestos* and *Christos* (the Greek for "Christ") would have been pronounced almost identically, resulting in Christ-followers occasionally being known as "Chrestians" (or "Chrestianoi").[7]

This interpretation for the cause of the expulsion is debated, and we are likewise unclear about how the expulsion was enforced and how many Jews it included. But it seems probable that the disturbance had something to do with Christians in Rome and that Jewish Christ-followers were included in the expulsion. In Acts 18:1–2, for instance, we read of Aquila and Priscilla (or Prisca, as Paul refers to her) as having relocated from Rome to Corinth in view of Claudius's expulsion order. The order lapsed with the death of Claudius in 54, however, with some Jews and Jewish Christ-followers returning to Rome at that point (as in the case of Prisca/Priscilla and Aquila; see Rom 16:3–4). That Paul writes his letter in 57, not long after the expulsion orders lapsed, may have something to do with the return of these Jewish Christians to communities of Jesus-devotion in Rome.[8]

We next hear of these same Christians in Paul's letter to the Philippians. If that text was written from Rome in the early 60s (see chapter 7 below), it is notable that Paul can speak of them as fervent in their proclamation of the gospel, emboldened by their association with the imprisoned Paul. So he writes: "Most of the brothers and sisters have become confident in the Lord [by my imprisonment] and dare all the more to proclaim the gospel without fear" (Phil 1:14). Although Paul is under house arrest, Jesus-followers in Rome are taking the initiative to make the Christian message heard in the streets of Rome.

But the situation was soon to take a disastrous turn. No more than seven years after Paul wrote to these Christians, the emperor Nero targeted them to be scapegoats in a vicious and sadistic pogrom. In AD 64, much of the city of Rome burned down. Rightly or wrongly (probably the latter), popular opinion was that Nero himself had instigated the destruction

7. Tacitus, *Ann.* 15.44; Tertullian, *Apol.* 15.3; *Ad nationis* 1.3. See also the textual variants for 1 Pet 2:3.
8. See especially Paul's comments about Jews and Gentiles in Romans 11, and again in Romans 14–15, although the ethnic distinction in the latter two chapters needs to be nuanced somewhat.

The Persecution of Roman Christians by Nero as described by Tacitus, *Annals* 15.44.

"But all human efforts, all the lavish gifts of the emperor, and the propitiations of the gods, did not banish the sinister belief that the conflagration was the result of an order [from Nero himself]. Consequently, to get rid of the report, Nero fastened the guilt and inflicted the most exquisite tortures on a class hated for their abominations, called Christians by the populace. Christus, from whom the name had its origin, suffered the extreme penalty during the reign of Tiberius at the hands of one of our procurators, Pontius Pilatus, and a most mischievous superstition, thus checked for the moment, again broke out not only in Judaea, the first source of the evil, but even in Rome, where all things hideous and shameful from every part of the world find their center and become popular. Accordingly, an arrest was first made of all who pleaded guilty; then, upon their information, an immense multitude was convicted, not so much of the crime of firing the city, as of hatred against mankind. Mockery of every sort was added to their deaths. Covered with the skins of beasts, they were torn by dogs and perished, or were nailed to crosses, or were doomed to the flames and burnt, to serve as a nightly illumination, when daylight had expired. Nero offered his gardens for the spectacle, and was exhibiting a show in the circus, while he mingled with the people in the dress of a charioteer or stood aloft on a car. Hence, even for criminals who deserved extreme and exemplary punishment, there arose a feeling of compassion; for it was not, as it seemed, for the public good, but to glut one man's cruelty, that they were being destroyed."[9]

of the city (if only to gain acreage for a newly positioned palace). In order to squelch the view and to distract attention from himself, Nero set upon the Christians, blaming them for anti-imperial subversion and the burning of the city. He ensured that many Christians experienced prolonged and excruciating deaths in the public arena (see textbox above). Perhaps as they were dying from their torture, some Christians recited words of comfort from Paul's letter to them (e.g., phrases from Rom 6:8, or 8:11, 17, 23, 37–39; 12:1)—although this, of course, is mere speculation.[10]

The decimated and vastly depopulated groups of Christians in Rome may be referred to in 2 Tim 4:16 (written perhaps in the late 60s), which reads: "At my first defense, no one came to my support, but everyone deserted me. May it not be held against them." In one reconstruction of the last stages of Paul's life, this passage is understood as referencing Paul's appearance in the halls of Roman justice in 66/67 or thereabouts, and demonstrating that Christians who survived Nero's pogroms

▼ An artist's depiction of the killing of Christians in the arena at Rome

Christian Martyrs in the Roman Arena, c.1865/Private Collection/Ken Welsh/The Bridgeman Art Library

9. Taken from Alfred John Church, William Jackson Brodribb, Sara Bryant, ed., *The Complete Works of Tacitus* (New York: Random House, 1942), 15.44.
10. If the surviving Christians in Rome returned to Paul's text and reread Rom 13:1–7 in the aftermath of Nero's persecution, it is anyone's guess how they might have received Paul's words at that point.

found it necessary to keep their head down and maintain a low profile, even when Paul himself was being tried before the emperor.

CENTERING THE VISION OF ROMANS: REVEALING THE RIGHTEOUSNESS OF GOD

> I am not ashamed of the gospel, because it is the power of God that brings salvation to everyone who believes: first to the Jew, then to the Gentile. For in the gospel the righteousness of God is revealed—a righteousness that is by faith from first to last. (Rom 1:16–17)

▼ An ancient inscription invoking Paul's name in a prayer to God, from the Roman catacomb of Sebastian.

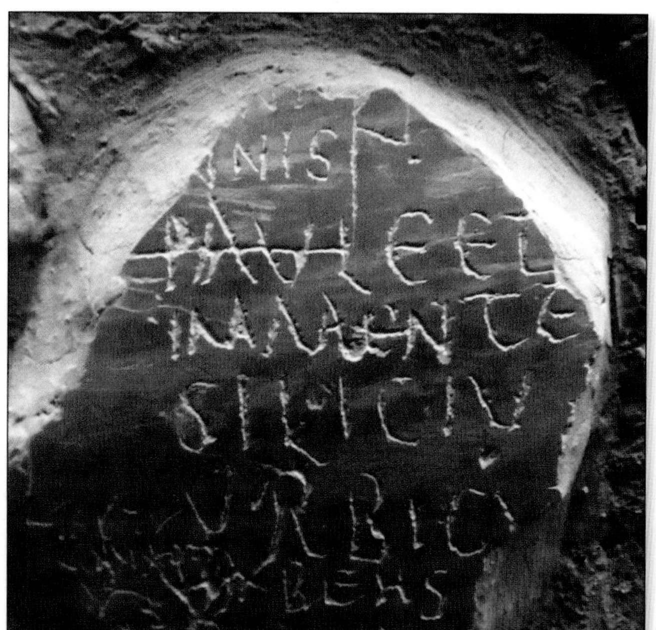

Bruce Longenecker

The heart of Paul's theology in Romans is contained in the phrase "the righteousness of God." Paul himself emphasizes its importance even in the way he structures his letter. Not only is the righteousness of God introduced in the "thesis statement" of 1:16–17 (most of which is cited above), but it also frames the key passage of Rom 3:21–26 (in both 3:21–22 and 3:26), where the thesis statement is expanded upon extensively.[11] In both of these passages, Paul packages some of the primary themes of his letter in rich and concentrated fashion, and in each, the righteousness of God takes pride of place.

But the phrase "the righteousness of God" has been understood to signify different things at different points in the history of interpretation. In the period just prior to the Reformation, for instance, the phrase was largely understood to refer to the justice that God possesses and demonstrates in his role as the just and scrupulous judge of sinful humanity.

While this notion is indeed a part of what the phrase signifies, it all too easily can (and did) foster a perception of God as an exacting, aloof accountant who determines the eternal state of individuals solely on the basis of whether the eschatological scales of justice tip more in the direction of good deeds or bad deeds. In this perception of things, the Christian religion can almost imperceptibly slip into a kind of arid legalism, with salvation being little more than behavioral accountancy and God being little more than a great rubber-stamper in the sky.

With the Reformation, the interpretation of "the righteousness of God" began to change. Martin Luther found the phrase to signal something much grander than he had been raised to imagine. Reacting to the legalism of the church of his day, Luther came to understand "the righteousness of God" to be strongly aligned to the notion of God's lov-

11. See also Rom 3:5 and 10:3.

ing grace. Without jettisoning the sense of God's justice, Luther understood "the righteousness of God" to signal God's merciful gift of righteousness that is bestowed on all those who believe in Jesus Christ. This is righteousness that:

- emerges from God's own righteousness
- is imparted to those who have faith
- God himself reckons as righteousness when he considers the standing of those who believe in Jesus Christ

In some ways, the full force of the Reformation dates to the time when Luther's eyes were opened to this understanding of the phrase, interpreting it in parallel with God's love and grace, accessed by faith in Jesus Christ. This was quite a transformation in Luther's worldview, since he had been taught to fear Jesus and to seek the benevolent intervention of the saints on his behalf before a hawkish God.

In the mid-twentieth century, one of the heavyweights of Pauline interpretation proposed a further adjustment. For the German scholar Ernst Käsemann, the phrase "the righteousness of God" connotes God's active sovereignty over the whole of his cosmos, as evidenced in acts of power whereby he invades the created order to set it right. For Käsemann, "the righteousness of God" signifies God's powerful saving *activity* (i.e., the righteousness that he causes to come about) in order to rectify the whole of creation (not just an "imputation" of righteousness upon believing individuals, as predominated in Luther's view). The "righteousness of God" is shorthand for talking about God's act of cosmic rectification, in which God is exercising his victory over the forces of chaos that roam through his creation and set it in disrepair. That victory is evident already in the people of faith, who have been grasped by a loving God restoring right relationships throughout every sector of his creation.[13] In short, righteousness is not something that

"For God does not want to save us by our own righteousness but by an extraneous righteousness which does not originate in ourselves but comes to us from beyond ourselves, which does not arise on our earth but comes from heaven. Therefore, we must come to know this righteousness which is utterly external and foreign to us. That is why our personal righteousness must be uprooted."[12]

"[The righteousness of God is] that faithfulness with which the Creator persists in his work of creation in spite of, and beyond, the falling away of his creatures, and with which he preserves his creation and gives it a new foundation. The righteousness of God is . . . God's victory amid the opposition of the world. It is God's sovereignty over the world revealing itself eschatologically in Jesus. It is the rightful power with which God makes his cause to triumph in the world which has fallen away from him and yet, as creation, in his inviolable possession. God's power reaches out for the world, and the world's salvation lies in its being recaptured for the sovereignty of God."[14]

12. Martin Luther, *Luther: Lectures on Romans* (W. Pauck, ed.; Philadelphia: Westminster, 1961), 4.
13. Ernst Käsemann, "'The Righteousness of God' in Paul," in his *New Testament Questions of Today* (Philadelphia: Fortress, 1969), 168–82.
14. Käsemann, *New Testament Questions of Today*, 180, 182.

The "Righteousness of God" at Qumran

This second-century BC text from the **Qumran** literature (1QS 11.10 – 15) illustrates how the "righteousness of God" was linked in Paul's day to God's merciful deliverance, his power, and his sovereignty:

> As for me, I belong to wicked mankind, to the company of unjust flesh. My iniquities, rebellions, and sins, together with the perversity of my heart, belong to the company of worms and to those who walk in darkness. For mankind has no way, and man is unable to establish his steps, since *justification* is with God and perfection of way is *out of His hand* [or "by his power"]. All things come to pass by His knowledge; He establishes all things by His design and *without Him nothing is done.* As for me, if I stumble, *the mercies of God* shall be my eternal salvation. If I stagger because of the sin of flesh, my *justification* shall be *by the righteousness of God* which endures for ever. When my distress is unleashed, He will *deliver* my soul from the Pit and will *direct* my steps to the way. He will *draw* me near *by His grace*, and *by His mercy* he will bring my *justification.* He will judge me *in the righteousness of His truth* and *in the greatness of His goodness* He will pardon all my sins. *Through his righteousness* he will cleanse me of the uncleanness of man and of the sins of the children of men, that I may confess to God *His righteousness*, and *His majesty* to the Most High.[15]

God simply dispenses or downloads. Instead, it is something that God is present within each and every moment, with relationships of all kinds being set to right through the powerful righteousness of God that is actively reclaiming the world.

A good number of Paul's modern interpreters stand in Käsemann's wake in their understanding of the phrase. This is because Käsemann's understanding of "the righteousness of God" as salvific power:

- coheres well with instances of the term in the Old Testament;
- correlates with the way first-century Jews probably understood the term (see sidebar on Qumran); and
- resonates with Paul's emphasis elsewhere in Romans on God's powerful recapturing of his creation.[16]

"That God's grace and righteousness relate to the world and intend a new creation, not merely a number of believing individuals, seems to me an irrelinquishable truth if the Christian proclamation is to be the foundation of anything more than merely private piety."[17]

Moreover, Käsemann's view coheres well with recent interest in the "narrative shape" of Paul's theology (see chapter 11 below). As one interpreter has recently commented,

15. Geza Vermes, *The Dead Sea Scrolls in English: Revised and Extended* (Sheffield: Sheffield Academic, 1995), 87 – 88.
16. Note also that Käsemann's perceptive insights emerged from the failure of most forms of Christianity in Germany to speak truth to German Nazism and the evils that transpired under its "lordship." The quotations from Käsemann in this section take on an added poignancy when read in that light.
17. Ernst Käsemann, *Perspectives on Paul* (Philadelphia: Fortress, 1971), 78.

"Käsemann's understanding of the theme fits well into a general understanding of Romans (or at least of Romans 1–8) as strongly influenced by a 'story of God and creation.'"[18]

One feature of Käsemann's work has not withstood the test of time, however. In Käsemann's view, "the righteousness of God" was primarily interpreted in Paul's day with regard to God's fidelity to Israel; but Käsemann argues that Paul stripped the term of its ethnic focus in order to broaden it out to its full cosmic proportions. For many recent interpreters the two must not be seen as alternatives. Instead, the saving power God has unleashed through the good news is, in its first instance, an expression of his covenant faithfulness to ethnic Israel.

In his analysis of the motif of the righteousness of God in the Psalms, Geoffrey Turner notes that "the dominant issue [in the Psalm material] is whether God will prove his righteousness by vindicating his righteous ones in times of persecution and suffering. The question raised by the Psalmist is, 'How long, O Lord, will you turn away for ever?'"[19]

So, for instance, Ps 98:2–3 speaks of God making known "his victory" and revealing "his righteousness" in the sight of all the nations to all the ends of the earth, but this is accomplished in conjunction with God's "steadfast love and faithfulness to the house of Israel." Numerous other instances could be added to make the point, which one interpreter summarizes in this way: "The reason why these texts (Isaiah and the Psalms) call God's vindication of his oppressed people his 'righteousness' is that it is an act of faithfulness to his covenant promise to them."[20]

Paul's own discussion of the righteousness of God keeps this issue of God's faithfulness to Israel firmly in view throughout Romans 9–11. It is also evident in 3:3 and 15:8–9. In 3:3, Paul raises the issue of whether unfaithfulness within the people of Israel ultimately undermines "God's [covenant] faithfulness." In 15:8–9, he claims that what God has done in Christ pertains in the first instance to "the truth/truthfulness of God." For reasons of this sort, the phrase "the righteousness of God" in Romans "firmly retains its Jewish and covenantal associations. The 'righteousness of God' is the divine covenant faithfulness, which is both a quality upon which God's people may rely and something visible in action in the great covenant-fulfilling actions of the death and resurrection of Jesus and the gift of the Spirit."[21]

Understanding Paul's notion of "the righteousness of God" puts us in position to unpack much of his presentation in Romans. Probing its significance helps to establish the theological parameters of Paul's thought in this, his most extended of letters.

18. Edward Adams, "Paul's Story of God and Creation: The Story of How God Fulfils His Purposes in Creation," in Bruce W. Longenecker, ed., *Narrative Dynamics in Paul: A Critical Assessment* (Louisville: Westminster John Knox, 2002), 38.
19. Geoffrey Turner, "The Righteousness of God in Psalms and Romans," *SJT* 63 (2010): 290.
20. J. I. Packer, "Justification," in *New Bible Dictionary* (ed. J. D. Douglas; London: Inter-Varsity Press, 1962), 683.
21. N. T. Wright, "On Becoming the Righteousness of God," in *Pauline Theology*; vol. 2: *1 & 2 Corinthians* (ed. David M. Hay; Minneapolis: Fortress, 1993), 207.

TRACKING THE VISION OF ROMANS

The basic structure of Paul's letter to Jesus-followers in Rome can be outlined as follows:

1:1–15	Letter Opening: Greetings and Thanksgiving
1:16–17	God's Power in the Gospel (Letter Theme)
1:18–4:25	God's Righteousness in a Cosmos under the Power of Sin
5:1–8:39	God's Triumph in Life and Salvation History
9:1–11:36	God's Exceptional Dealings with Israel and the Nations
12:1–15:13	God's People in Community and the World
15:14–16:27	Paul's Mission Plans and Commendations

Romans 1–4

Most of the Christians in Rome knew of Paul only by reputation (and a controversial one at that). Little wonder, then, that 1:1–7 offers a densely packed introduction that functions almost like a prospectus of what he stands for. Bound to a "gospel of God" that accords with the Scriptures of Israel and is centered on the resurrected Son of God who is Lord, Paul's apostleship is specifically for the purpose of bringing the Gentile nations to "obedience that comes from faith" (lit., "the obedience of faith"). A brief "prayer-report" (1:8–15) sets the letter in the context of Paul's desire that he and the Roman Jesus-followers be mutually edified.

▼ Paul describes idolatrous worship as part of a life dominated by the power of Sin. The worship of Isis is depicted in this wall-painting from Herculaneum. The high priest stands at the entrance to the temple and looks down on the ceremony beneath him, which is supervised by priests with shaven heads. One priest tends the sacred fire and another behind him leads the faithful in worship. In the foreground of the painting can be seen two ibises, sacred to Isis, and to the right is a flautist.

Ceremony of the Cult of Isis, from Pompeii/Museo Archeologico Nazionale, Naples, Italy/De Agostini Picture Library/The Bridgeman Art Library

For Paul, that edification is rooted firmly in the gospel he preaches. It is a gospel that he was not ashamed of, contrary to the view of some others who seem to have thought that he should be ashamed of it. According to the thesis statement of 1:16–17 (discussed briefly above), that gospel incorporates the power of God that brings salvation, precisely because the righteousness of God (whereby the cosmos is being reassembled in proper relationship) is effective within the gospel. Paul emphasizes faith as a condition for this salvation, so that righteousness is "by faith from first to last," with Hab 2:4 cited to demonstrate the point ("The righteous will live by faith").

Before displaying the effective power of the gospel (as of 3:21), Paul first paints a portrait of what the gospel's power is offsetting. Romans 1:18–3:20 contributes to that goal. The best way to understand what

Habakkuk 2:4 in Romans 1:17

Paul cites Hab 2:4 in Rom 1:17. The first chapter of that OT book puts salvation against the backdrop of problems that are rampant within societies and God's apparent lack of concern:

> How long, LORD, must I call for help,
> but you do not listen?
> Or cry out to you, "Violence!"
> but you do not save?
> Why do you make me look at injustice?
> Why do you tolerate wrongdoing?
> Destruction and violence are before me;
> there is strife, and conflict abounds.
> Your eyes are too pure to look on evil;
> you cannot tolerate wrongdoing.
> Why then do you tolerate the treacherous?
> Why are you silent while the wicked
> swallow up those more righteous than themselves? (Hab 1:2, 3, 13)

Is the context of Hab 2:4 important for understanding Paul's citation of that verse in Romans? Richard Hays writes: "When Paul quotes Hab. 2:4, we cannot help hearing the echoes — unless we are tone-deaf — of Habakkuk's theodicy question [specifically, is God really up for the job?]. By showcasing this text . . . at the beginning of the letter to the Romans, Paul links his gospel to the Old Testament prophetic affirmation of God's justice and righteousness."[22]

Paul is doing there is to look toward the end of that section, where in 3:9 he explicitly states what the focus of that section has been: "We have already made the charge that Jews and Gentiles alike are all under the power of sin." By this Paul means much more than simply that everyone is a sinner. Here, and predominantly throughout the first eight chapters of Romans, sin (or better, Sin) is conceived of as a cosmic power, a suprahuman force with intentionality that seeks to work its way within God's world by enslaving persons for its own purposes, reducing them to mere manipulated puppets operated by its overpowering control and thereby rendering them incapable of serving God.

Accordingly, as Paul catalogues a series of "sins" that characterize the Gentile world (in 1:18–32) and the Jewish world (with exaggeration in 2:21–24), he is working to this goal. These very misdeeds testify beyond themselves to the fact that the whole world is under the power of Sin — that is, in the clutches of powers that run contrary to God's ways.

Paul offers a register of some of the manifestations of life dominated by the power of Sin, including things like idolatrous worship and the skewing of sexual behavior. But the feature that he showcases at length is the proclivity toward self-centeredness, resulting in its most pronounced forms in disdainful arrogance and contempt for others. This corrosive

22. Richard B. Hays, *Echoes of Scripture in the Letters of Paul* (New Haven, CT: Yale University Press, 1989), 40.

cancer has the power to engulf even God-given things and God-entasked people groups. This is a world that, apart from divine intervention of a radical kind, stands under "the wrath of God" (1:18), with the law revealing the culpability of all people within this "sin-full" matrix of existence (3:10–20).

Because of the interlock of human sin with the cosmic power of Sin, whatever else the gospel does, it must empower restored right(eous)ness within relationships at every level of God's created order.

"The 'rabbinic' language of sacrifice and atonement is unsatisfactory for Paul. Although it expresses judgment and forgiveness, it is incapable of stating the new ontological state of life that succeeds the judgment of God in the death of Christ. Forgiveness means acquittal of punishment but not the destruction of the power of sin or the 'new creation' of the Christian's participation in the resurrection mode of life."[23]

Paul's claim that God has "presented Christ as a sacrifice of **atonement**" (3:25, within the context of 3:21–26) stands at the heart of God's cosmos-redeeming initiative. The single Greek word behind the translation "sacrifice of atonement" is more specific than the translation might suggest, as noted in the NIV marginal note: "The Greek for *sacrifice of atonement* refers to the atonement cover on the **ark of the covenant** (see Lev. 16:15, 16)." The atonement cover of the ark of the covenant is the place where the sins of Israel piled up throughout the year before God in the Most Holy Place until, on the **Day of Atonement**, the high priest sprinkled blood over it, which resulted in the cleansing of the people before God.

In an astoundingly bold move, Paul (perhaps echoing a theological claim of the early Jesus movement) depicts Jesus as that atonement cover. But in the context of Paul's presentation of Romans, the sins Jesus dealt with were the sins of all those caught up in the grip of "the power of Sin"—that is, both Jews and Gentiles. Unstated but implied is the conviction that the Day of Atonement has been configured anew, in relation to all ethnic groups (not just Israel) and in relation to the power of Sin (along with other cosmic powers) that operate within God's good creation for ungodly purposes. Redemption or "liberation" (3:24) from that destructive matrix has now come "by Christ Jesus" and is available "to all who believe" (and perhaps "through the faithfulness of Jesus Christ," as in the NIV's marginal note at 3:22), through God's gracious initiative.[24]

Since God is the God of all people groups and since faith is the means of participating in liberation from the tyranny of the power of Sin, no single people group (not even God's people Israel, who perform "works of the law" in response to God's grace on them) can boast in anything (3:26–31). This is critical for Paul to establish. Accordingly, he offers an extended demonstration of his claims in 4:1–25, enlisting the story of Abraham and confirming that his gospel does not nullify the law but upholds it (3:31).

Framing Romans 4 are quotations from Gen 15:6 (in Rom 4:3, 22; so too in 4:9, 23), the full citation being "Abraham believed God, and it was credited to him as righteous-

23. J. C. Beker, *Paul the Apostle: The Triumph of God in Life and Thought* (Philadelphia: Fortress Press, 1980), 197.

24. On "the faithfulness of Jesus Christ," see chapter 11 below.

ness." Paul wants to show that this story has significance not only for "the circumcised" Jew but also for "the uncircumcised" Gentile (as in 4:9). This is because Abraham is to be seen as the father of both groups of people (4:16), just as God promised to make Abraham "a father of many nations" (Gen 17:5 cited in Rom 4:17; see also Gen 15:5 cited in Rom 4:18).

Here's how. Abraham believed in God when he was uncircumcised, making him to be father in faith to the Gentiles who have faith; and he continued to believe in God after he had been circumcised, making him to be father in faith to the Jews who have faith (see esp. 4:11–12). In fact, this family of faith, embracing all the nations, is itself the "reward" that God had promised Abraham (Gen 15:1; LXX *misthos*). Paul seems to expand on this motif in 4:4–5 when he establishes the principle that rewards (*misthos*, often translated "wages") are usually given on the basis of what one does, but in this instance the reward (of the worldwide family) was awarded to Abraham on the basis of faith.

The correspondence between Abraham and other believers extends further still, with regard to the one in whom faith is properly exercised—that is, the creator God (see 1:20, 25). Abraham believed him to be the one "who gives life to the dead and calls into being things that were not" (4:17), just as God has "raised Jesus our Lord from the dead" (4:24).

"The Old Testament refers to two people being justified . . . by some act: Abraham (Gen 15:6; 1 Macc 2:52) and Phinehas (Ps 106). Abraham was justified by faith; he believed the promise of God: 'And he [Abraham] believed the LORD; and the LORD reckoned it to him as righteousness.' According to Psalm 106, Phinehas was justified by his violent zeal: it was and is 'reckoned to him as righteousness' [Ps 106:31]. Is this antithetical parallel between Abraham and Phinehas, and Paul's quotation of the former rather than the latter, merely coincidental? Or does Paul know full well that justification has two paradigms in the Scriptures, one based on violent zeal for the Law and the purity of Israel, the other on faith?"[25]

Romans 5–8

Since Jesus' death was "for our sins" and his resurrection was "for our justification" (4:25), Paul proclaims that "we have peace with God through our Lord Jesus Christ" (5:1).[26] This confident assertion sharply contrasts with Paul's depiction of God's wrath standing over the arena of life dominated by the "power of Sin" (1:18–3:20). Now Paul strings together four chapters that unpack what "peace with God" looks like, without abandoning his depiction of a desperate world under the domination of suprahuman forces. That Romans 5–8 form a single text-unit is indicated by the repeated use of the phrase "through/in our Lord Jesus Christ" (and its variants) at key structural points throughout those chapters (5:1, 11, 21; 6:23; 7:25; 8:39).

25. Michael Gorman, *Inhabiting the Cruciform God: Kenosis, Justification, and Theosis in Paul's Narrative Soteriology* (Grand Rapids: Eerdmans, 2009), 147.

26. A strong tradition within some early Greek manuscripts reads *echōmen* instead of *echomen*, rendering the meaning "let us have peace with God" instead of "we have peace with God." All mainstream translations currently advocate the reading "we have peace," but a good case can also be made for "let us have peace."

akg-images/Pirozzi

▲ A fourth-century Christian artist depicted Adam and Eve in the garden the moment before they sinned by eating the apple.

Paul's tone of confident assurance extends throughout 5:1–11, where he constructs a mini-essay on divine love. This love is demonstrated in the self-giving of God, offering hope for all those in Christ and overspilling from their lives in love for God and for others.[27]

After those overwhelmingly powerful verses, Paul sets out a contrast between the entrenched problem that engulfs the whole of creation and the salvific solution that overwhelms the problem (5:12–21). In overviewing the problem, Paul draws on the story of **Adam**. In this discussion of the problem that needs rectifying, Adam's sin is depicted not simply as the first in a never-ending line of sins replicated by Adam's offspring, but as the occasion for suprahuman powers to get a solid foothold within God's creation (Greek *kosmos*, 5:12).

Paul has already introduced one of these powers in 3:9: the power of Sin. In 5:12–21, he couples that with another, the power of Death. At times in this section, Paul seems to have human sinfulness and human death in view, while at others he seems to have the cosmic powers in view—not least when speaking of them as "reigning" or being the overlords of the sphere of influence in which sin and death are human inevitabilities (5:14, 17, 21). For Paul, the cosmic and the personal are intertwined dimensions of the same problem.

"The prime commitment of theology is seen to be the understanding of God's *kenosis* [self-giving], a grand mysterious truth for the human mind, which finds it inconceivable that suffering and death can express a love which gives itself and seeks nothing in return."[28]

The resources for solving that problem are not found in the God-given law (5:13–14, 20), but only in the events proclaimed in the gospel. Whatever has been accomplished with the death and resurrection of Jesus, it operates not only in relation to the human inevitabilities of sin and death but also in relation to the cosmic powers of Sin and Death. Against this catastrophic

27. The phrase "the love of God" in Rom 5:5 is best understood as a polyvalent phrase that references God's love for us, our love for God, and our love for others. This view is defended in Bruce W. Longenecker, "The Love of God (Romans 5:5): "Expansive Syntax and Theological Polyvalence," in *Interpretation and the Claims of the Text: Resourcing New Testament Theology* (ed. Jason Whitlark et al.; Waco, TX: Baylor University Press, 2014), 145–58.
28. Pope John Paul II, *Fides et Ratio: On the Relationship between Faith and Reason* (Boston: Pauline Books & Media, 1998), 115–16.

backdrop, Paul proclaims another power to be operative—that is, "grace," which reigns "through righteousness to bring eternal life through Jesus Christ our Lord" (5:21).

With this established, Paul brings to the table one of the issues that seem to have plagued his ministry: the relationship between sin and the Jesus-follower. Paul has already indicated in 3:8 that this problem has dogged his ministry: "Why not say—as we are being slanderously reported as saying and as some claim that we say—'Let us do evil that good may result'?" Evidently Paul's gospel was being misrepresented as promoting what might be called an immoral "**libertinism**"—living without any kind of restraint, and all to the glory of God. After all, if Paul's gospel is that righteousness comes graciously and "apart from law" (3:21), and if law places moral constraints on those who follow it, then perhaps followers of Jesus can do just about anything they want to do without worrying about being condemned as sinners. All this fosters God's own reputation as one who overflows in graciousness by not counting sins against those who follow Jesus. Paul says about those who misunderstand his gospel in this way that "their condemnation is just" (3:8, which suggests they may have been willfully misrepresenting his gospel).

But Paul does more than disown the charge against him. He demonstrates why it is false. On two occasions in Romans 6 he voices the issue directly: "Shall we go on sinning so that grace may increase? . . . Shall we sin because we are not under the law but under grace?" (6:1, 15). On each occasion he gives a most vociferous reply (along the lines of "that must not be the case!"). Having contrasted two spheres of influence in 5:12–21, Paul now shows the disconnect with imagining that human sinfulness can have a proper place within the sphere of grace and righteousness.

For Paul, the point is simple and the key is baptism. Followers of Jesus have been baptized into Christ Jesus and have been united with him in death; as a consequence, the power of Sin is duped, since it gets no inevitable traction in the lives of Jesus-followers. When people die, the power of Sin no longer has a foothold in their lives; since Jesus-followers have died with Christ (in baptism), the power of Sin has thereby been hoodwinked. But these "died-with-Christ people" are not trophies for the power of Death. Instead, they have come alive in a new "sphere of lordship"—a sphere in which their lives are instruments of God's grace and righteousness.

▲ A third-century painting of Christian baptism, from the Saint Calixte Catacomb in Rome

Catacombs of San Callisto, Rome, Italy/Index/The Bridgeman Art Library

For Paul, Sin is no longer the controlling overlord of those who follow Jesus, and those who follow Jesus are no longer "slaves" to the power of Sin. So he writes: "do not let [the power of] Sin reign [or be the lord] in your mortal bodies . . . for [the power of] Sin shall no longer be your master [or overlord]" (6:12, 14). But Paul recognizes nonetheless that Jesus-followers may improperly "offer" their bodies to the power of Sin, allowing that power to influence their lives. Instead, Jesus-followers are exhorted to offer themselves to the power of God, "as those who have been brought from death to life" (6:13), thereby confounding the powers of Sin and Death.

In Romans 7, this scenario of cosmic powers in conflict is applied specifically to the issue of "the law." Paul's main point is clearly articulated in 7:1–6, where he outlines that dead persons (like those who have died with Christ) are not bound to laws that bind others, suggesting that there is no salvific necessity to observing the Mosaic law.

"The law says 'Do this' and it is never done. Grace says 'Believe in this' and everything is already done."[29]

But in 7:5 Paul registers another point that spills over throughout the rest of the chapter: that is, the law itself shares some complicity in Sin's project. Almost immediately he qualifies this by excluding the inference that the law itself is sinful (7:7) and by affirming that the law is "holy" and "spiritual" (7:12, 14; so too the "commandment" is "holy, righteous and good," 7:12).

Paul amplifies this in several ways. First, the law can identify sinfulness (7:7). Second, a legal commandment can actually multiply sinfulness; being told not to do something can itself stir up the desire to do that very thing (7:8–11). This is one way in which the law shares some complicity in Sin's program. If the assumption is that greater sinfulness demonstrates the glory of God's grace all the more, Paul shows the irony in all this, in that the power of Sin is undermining itself. Using the good law to perpetuate sinfulness makes the power of Sin recognizable as "utterly sinful" (7:13), and this is the backdrop against which Paul paints the good news of redemption in Christ throughout the glorious overview of Romans 8. Outside of that redemption, Paul depicts a tragic situation in which even God-given instruments of goodness and holiness and righteousness can be conscripted by the power of Sin to perpetuate its tragic purposes.

The experiences of the "I" who speaks in Romans 7 have been variously interpreted. Throughout the centuries, they have frequently been interpreted as descriptive of Paul's experience of struggling with sin even after deciding to follow Jesus. In fact, however, Paul probably meant the experiences outlined in Romans 7 to be indicative of the experiences of those outside of Christ who link their salvific hope to the law.[30] That is, Rom 7:7–25 is probably Paul's description of the situation of Jews who are not (yet) followers of Jesus—a description heavily influenced by Paul's own perspective as one already "in Christ."

The use of the first person singular ("I") conforms to the ancient practice of offering "speech in character"—that is, allowing another person's views to be articulated as if by the person itself. (Paul has already used this device in Rom 3:7.) To add to the texture of this description of those outside of Christ who link their salvific hope to the law, Paul seems to

29. Martin Luther, *Luther's Works*; vol. 25: *Lectures on Romans* (St. Louis: Concordia, 1972), 36.
30. See, for instance, the temporal contrast that Paul sets up in 7:5–6 and 8:1 between (1) the eschatological "now" that those "in Christ" participate in and (2) the former "then" of which they are no longer (to be) a part. See also the phrase "sold as a slave to sin" in 7:14; as Paul has demonstrated repeatedly throughout Rom 6, this is not the situation of Jesus-followers.

recount their situation with some echoes of the story of Adam thrown in.[31] What emerges from Romans 7, then, is a portrait of the desperate circumstance of those outside of Christ, including even the people of Israel. If being caught in the clutches of the power of Sin is true even of the ethnic people of Israel (i.e., those who "know the law," 7:1), then it certainly must be true for all other people groups (i.e., Gentiles) as well.

The liberation that Paul elaborates throughout Romans 8 is already anticipated in 7:25, where he writes, "Thanks be to God through Jesus Christ our Lord!"[32] The climax of Romans 8 is found in Paul's confident assurance that absolutely nothing "will be able to separate us from the love of God that is in Christ Jesus our Lord" (8:39). Highlighting that divine love toward the start of Romans 5–8, Paul there characterized it as demonstrable in Christ's self-giving death for us (5:8). Here too Jesus' death takes center stage as the means whereby the domination of the power of Sin is shattered in its combination with the human propensity toward sinfulness (8:1–4). As powerful as they are, even the powers of Sin and Death cannot undo the salvific effect of bringing God's love to a creation in bondage, through Jesus' death and resurrection.

"It is God rather than ourselves who initiates prayer, and . . . it is God's power, not ours, that answers to the world's needs. We are always preceded in intercession. God is always already praying within us. When we turn to pray, it is already the second step of prayer. We join with God in a prayer already going on in us and in the world."[33]

With nineteen references to the Spirit in this chapter alone, what emerges in Romans 8 is an essay on the role of the Spirit.[34] At its heart lies Paul's confidence that "the Spirit of God lives in you" (8:9 and elsewhere). This has a number of implications.

1. The Spirit's residency within Jesus-followers results in patterns of lifestyle that are themselves the fulfillment of "the righteous requirement of the law" (8:4).
2. The Spirit is the means whereby Jesus-followers enter into intimate familial relationship with God, replicating something of Jesus' own intimacy with God; note the correspondence to Jesus' own prayer address to God as "*Abba*, Father" (8:15; see Mark 14:36).
3. The Spirit assists Jesus-followers, uttering prayers to God on their behalf (8:26–27),

"Now having the Spirit of Christ ([Rom] 8:9), humans experience any sufferings as a participation in the first phase of Christ's own trajectory. To participate in the Son's suffering and death is to be guaranteed participation in his resurrection and glorification."[35]

31. In the Edenic garden Adam was once alive without a law/commandment, and he was deceived in relation to the commandment not to eat of the tree; see then Rom 7:9, 11.
32. The phrase "who delivers me" in the NIV's rendering "Thanks be to God, who delivers me through Jesus Christ our Lord!" does not appear in the Greek text.
33. Walter Wink, *Engaging the Powers: Discernment and Resistance in a World of Domination* (Minneapolis: Fortress, 1992), 304.
34. This is the count in Greek, excluding the reference to "our spirit" in 8:16.
35. Douglas A. Campbell, *The Deliverance of God: An Apocalyptic Rereading of Justification in Paul* (Grand Rapids: Eerdmans, 2009), 66–67.

especially as they continue to live in a world out of joint, characterized by suffering and groaning (8:18, 23).

4. Just as God raised Jesus, so too the presence of the Spirit in the lives of Jesus-followers ensures that he will do the same for them in the future (8:11).

"The Holy Spirit is the 'forward' which majestically awakens, enlightens, leads, pushes, and impels, which God has spoken in the resurrection of Jesus from the dead, which he has spoken and still speaks to the world of humanity: forward to the new coming of Jesus and the kingdom."[36]

"The fewer the words, the better the prayer."
Quotation attributed to Martin Luther

Paul's vision is not simply about the redemption of individuals, however. For Paul, God's redemption cannot fail to engulf the whole of creation (8:18–23), not least because God is the creator God who, in a sense, wants his creation back. The rightful king of creation is not content to leave his handiwork in the hands of usurpers (i.e., the powers of Sin and Death) while he and his followers huddle away blissfully in heavenly enclave or exile. A scheme of that kind verges on salvation through resignation and abandonment. For Paul the sphere of God's redemptive reign is not restricted merely to some "heavenly" arena, to the exclusion of the created order. Instead, Paul envisions the hopeful day when "the creation itself will be liberated from its bondage to decay and brought into the freedom and glory of the children of God" (8:21). On that day, the powers of Sin and Death that have been eating away at every bit of God's good creation will finally be confounded.

Romans 9–11

If the God of redemption is also the creator God, he is also the God who covenanted himself to the people of Israel. But Paul's story of redemption has not put Israel within the parameters of the redemptive solution but within the parameters of the ruinous problem, along with the rest of humanity. How can that be? Has God been unfaithful to ethnic Israel? If this is the outcome of Paul's gospel, then the whole thing threatens to tumble down like a house of cards. If God can be seen as unfaithful in his dealings with Israel, then there's no reason to believe that he would be faithful in his dealings with Christians and with the whole of his creation. Perhaps, then, having come this far with Paul, his readers are now in a position to find his gospel to be theologically defective, promoting an ethically deficient God.

Paul addresses these matters throughout Romans 9–11—three chapters that rank among the hardest to interpret consistently within the Pauline corpus. What is clear is Paul's sense of heartfelt concern for the salvation of the ethnic people of Israel (9:1–3; 10:1). Similarly, although it is not altogether obvious how this will come about, Paul holds out the assurance that ultimately "all Israel will be saved" (11:26). Although some want to interpret this to mean all *Christians* will be saved, what precedes and follows this simple statement suggests that, more likely, it is the ethnic people of Israel whom Paul has in mind here. Paul

36. Karl Barth, *The Christian Life* (G. W. Bromiley, trans.; Grand Rapids: Eerdmans, 1981), 256.

imagines ethnic Israel to be in a double state, as he makes clear in 11:28–29: "As far as the gospel is concerned, they are enemies for your sake; but as far as election is concerned, they are loved on account of the patriarchs, for God's gifts and his call are irrevocable."

With regard to ethnic Israel, then, Paul ultimately excludes any suggestion that God has been unfaithful to his covenant people, and he does this by drawing back, in a sense, to survey the future contours of salvation history. With that larger (eschatological) picture in view, God is shown to be unshakeable in his gracious initiatives for his people—gracious initiatives that have also characterized his dealings with ethnic Israel earlier in the salvation-historical narrative (9:4–5; so too 3:1–2). Salvation (which for Paul involves faith in Jesus Christ) is ensured for both "parts" of ethnic Israel, when the eschatological deliverer (Jesus Christ) comes from the heavenly Zion (11:25–27).[37] In that eschatological event, any lack of faith among the people of Israel will be transformed by the covenant-making God into faithful allegiance, as one manifestation of his mysteriously awe-inspiring ways (11:33–36).

If the past and future of God's covenant with Israel are relatively straightforward, the current state of affairs is much more complicated, and most of Romans 9–11 is dedicated to teasing out its complexity. At the heart of that complexity lie the two "parts" of Israel that ultimately will be joined in allegiance to Jesus Christ. Paul introduces these two parts in 9:6–24. There Paul's primary interest is not in advocating a theology of the predestination of individuals but, more to the point, in demonstrating something about how God has always worked throughout history. As a careful reading of Scripture shows, God's initiatives in raising some people to prominence (e.g., Pharaoh) have never been ends in themselves but have always served larger purposes within history. The same, suggests Paul, is true of God's election of Israel, which itself falls within God's freedom to choose a part of Israel for one purpose and a part of Israel for another purpose, and all within God's larger purposes within history.

But Scripture also shows that God has not only elected the ethnic people of Israel (specifically, to play various roles in salvation history), but has also called Gentiles to be among his people (9:24–29). With this, Paul sets out a discourse on the nature of obedience to God, in which faith lies at the heart of everything, regardless of ethnic identity (9:30–10:31). So while Gentiles have submitted themselves to God through their allegiance to Jesus Christ, those of ethnic Israel who have not aligned themselves to God's ways in Jesus Christ have proved themselves to be "a disobedient and obstinate people" (10:31). Throughout all this, Paul interweaves scriptural citations that reinforce his understanding of the gospel, including the emphasis already set out in Romans 3:21–4:25: "there is no difference between Jew and Gentile—the same Lord is Lord of all and richly blesses all who call on him" (10:12).

But even if the means of right relationship with God is the same for all people (i.e., faith in or allegiance to Jesus Christ), God's covenant relationship with ethnic Israel is a central issue that Paul simply cannot jettison. This is the case in Paul's assertion about the continuing existence of a "remnant" within Israel (11:1–6)—a proportionately small group of Jews whom God has "chosen by grace" from within the ethnic people of Israel. They represent the believing "part" of ethnic Israel who do not rely on their covenant works in order to find acceptance with God.

37. In a sense, then, Paul's "Damascus Road" christophany has resemblances to what awaits the nonbelieving part of ethnic Israel in the future.

▲ This coin depicts the two emperors who reigned during the most active period of Paul's ministry: Claudius (41–54) and Nero (54–68).

But God has also "hardened" others within ethnic Israel (11:7–10). Why would God do this? Paul has a double-barreled answer to this, each part of which he interweaves with the other through 11:11–25. One part of the answer operates on the assumption that the hardening of a part of Israel permits "space" for Gentiles to be brought into the fold. The other part of the answer builds on this—that is, when seeing Gentiles brought into proper relationship with God, some from among disbelieving Israel will become "jealous" of what Gentile Jesus-followers have and will align themselves with Jesus Christ (11:14; see also 10:19).

Along the way, Paul takes great pains to undermine any opportunity for the Gentiles to become haughty over the Jewish people. For Paul, even if many Jews are among the disbelieving "part" of Israel, that does not mean that God has foresworn his allegiance to ethnic Israel. Instead, the Gentile Jesus-followers are to see themselves as having been included in something that has involved ethnic Israel from the beginning.

He makes this point by likening Gentile Jesus-followers to "unnatural branches" that have been grafted into an olive tree (11:17–24). Much of Paul's point in this analogy of the olive tree is restated later in 15:27: "the Gentiles have shared in the Jews' spiritual blessings." If much of Romans is dedicated to offsetting Jews' overconfidence in their covenant relationship with God, here Paul shows himself to be just as concerned about Gentile smugness over the Jewish people. The situation of both people groups is summarized by Paul in 11:32: "God has bound everyone [or all nations] over to disobedience so that he may have mercy on them all."

Romans 12–16

In light of "God's mercy" (12:1) that Paul has discussed throughout Romans 1–11, Paul now gives an overview of what living by God's mercy looks like in practice. First and foremost, it requires "offering" oneself to God (the same verb appears five times in Romans 6), and this results in a pattern of life that contrasts with the kind of sinfulness Paul outlined in 1:18–32 in relation to the power of Sin (3:9). This "transformed" lifestyle is showcased at the start and finish of Romans 12–13 (12:1–2; 13:11–14).

Between those two sections, Paul establishes a basis for transformed living that runs contrary to the quest for honor that marked out the ancient world (much like today). A diverse community of Christians is to be characterized, then, not by ranking its members according to their social importance and stature. Instead, its members are to be encouraged to play whatever role they have been called to play, with each being appreciated as integral to the whole and contributing to its well-being (12:3–8). Individual members are called to live lives of sincere love (12:9), which Paul unpacks both in relation to Christians (12.10–16) and to those beyond the boundaries of Jesus groups (12:14–21).[38]

This leads Paul to consider the relationship of Jesus-followers to the "governing authorities" (13:1–7). He presents those authorities as having been established in their positions by God as his servants for bringing about goodness within society, commending those who do good and punishing those who do wrong. Accordingly, the governing authorities are to be obeyed, and, to support them in their God-given role, taxes are to be paid. This passage will be discussed further in chapter 12 below.

▲ A denarius with the face of Tiberius Caesar.

Jay King

Having proposed earlier that the differing spiritual gifts of Jesus-followers contribute to the well-being of Christian communities (12:3–8), in 14:1–15:13 Paul again discusses differences among Jesus-followers, but now moves into more difficult waters. What happens when certain Jesus-followers believe that God has called them to live in ways that, on the face of things, seem to erect obstacles prohibiting a viable corporate life? Paul entertains a scenario that may well have resembled a real-life tension within some sectors of his Roman audience. He depicts two main groups, which he identifies by the labels "the strong" and "the weak." The weak consider it proper to adopt a more rigorous form of lifestyle than the strong, at least in matters of dietary practices and calendar observances (traditional practices of Jewish identity). If they judged the strong to adopt a deficient way of life, the strong tended to despise the weak as adopting an unnecessary way of life.

Against the backdrop of this scenario, Paul constructs a notable solution of sorts, ensuring that each group's integrity is maintained. He does this by aligning himself with the view of the strong while also protecting the right of the weak to live in a manner to which God has called them. Differences are affirmed, while solidarity is ensured. Paul's solution culminates in adopting the story of Jesus Christ to make the point. Just as he gave himself for others, accepting them in a sense, they too should be accepting of each other in order to enhance their corporate relatedness.

It is almost astonishing, while at the same time utterly predictable, that Paul sees healthy relationships among Christians who overcome their differences and support one another to be among the primary manifestations of the power of the gospel that facilitates the righteousness of God on the stage of world history. Accordingly, his discussion of corporate

38. On the structural overlap of these two topics within 12:14–16, see Bruce W. Longenecker, *Rhetoric at the Boundaries: The Art and Theology of New Testament Chain-Link Construction* (Waco, TX: Baylor University Press, 2005), 95–101.

solidarity moves directly into discussion of giving glory and praise to God (15:6–7), with Gentiles joining the chorus in fulfillment of God's faithfulness to Israel (15:8–13).

This makes for a fitting occasion for Paul to highlight his own ongoing mission to the Gentiles "so that the Gentiles might become an offering acceptable to God" (15:16). In particular, Paul features his plans (1) to deliver the collection to Jerusalem, and (2) to take the gospel to Spain, through the support of Christians in Rome (15:24), many of whom he commends in closing.

SUMMARY REFLECTION

Romans is Paul's calling card, in a sense. Desiring support for his Spanish mission, Paul sends to Jesus-followers in Rome a discursive elaboration of the gospel he preaches. In the process, they will get to know him and what he stands for, directly "from the horse's mouth" rather than by word of mouth along a communications grapevine.

But Romans is not a theological tractate untouched by the situation of Christians on the ground. Paul is aware that the gospel inevitably embeds itself within indigenous situations, drawing health out of dysfunction as it goes. As "the power of God that brings salvation" (1:16), the gospel preached in this letter will inescapably shape the lives of Roman Christ-followers to enhance their patterns of discipleship. As they experience that transforming power within their own individual and corporate lives, so they will "assist me [Paul] on my journey there, after I have enjoyed your company for a while" (15:24). In this way, Paul hopes that believers in Rome will assist him in his "priestly duty of proclaiming the gospel of God, so that the Gentiles might become an offering acceptable to God, sanctified by the Holy Spirit" (15:15).

» KEY PEOPLE, PLACES, AND TERMS «

Andronicus	Claudius	Libertinism	Rome
Ark of the covenant	Day of Atonement	Marcion	Spain
Atonement	Doxology	Nero	Suetonius
Cenchreae	Illyricum	Pentecost	
Chrestos	Junia	Qumran	

» QUESTIONS FOR REVIEW AND DISCUSSION «

1. Why does it matter where the letter to Christians in Rome originally ended?
2. What proposals have been suggested as to why Paul wrote Romans? Which are the most compelling proposals? Is there a single reason why Paul wrote this letter, or is it better to think that a variety of reasons were in play?
3. What are the different interpretations suggested for "the righteousness of God" throughout the history of interpretation?
4. At times in Romans, Paul seems to imagine the law operating in two different spheres of influence with two different effects. How do you understand his differentiation between "the law that requires works" and "the law that requires faith" in 3:27; or between "the law of the Spirit who gives life" and "the law of sin and death" in 8:2?
5. Why does Paul quote Habakkuk 2:4? How might the context of Habakkuk help us understand the purpose of this quotation for Romans?
6. Describe the "libertinism" that some supposed Paul to be promoting. How does Paul combat this idea in Romans?
7. Explain why God's relationship with ethnic Israel is such an important topic for Paul. How does he explain God's plan for ethnic Israel, and how does that relate to his plan for the Gentiles?
8. Early on in Romans Paul speaks of Jewish priority (1:16; 2:10; 3:1 – 2; see also 9:4 – 5) as well as divine impartiality (2:11). How does Paul clarify the relationship between these two phenomena in Romans?

» CONTEMPORARY THEOLOGICAL REFLECTION «

1. Why do you think Paul's letter to the Romans came to be one of the most influential ancient texts of all time?
2. Does Romans 8 (see esp. 8:19–22) provide resources for an environmental theology? Explain.
3. What theological advantages does the "weaker brother" principle offer to a group of Christians? Are there instances in which the principle needs to give way to other principles?

» GOING FURTHER «

Academic Commentaries on Romans

Fitzmyer, Joseph A. *Romans*. AB. New Haven, CT: Yale University Press, 1993.

Hultgren, Arland. *Paul's Letter to the Romans: A Commentary*. Grand Rapids: Eerdmans, 2011.

Jewett, Robert. *Romans: A Commentary*. Hermeneia. Minneapolis: Fortress, 2008.

Longenecker, Richard N. *The Epistle to the Romans*. NIGTC. Grand Rapids: Eerdmans, 2015.

Matera, Frank J. *Romans*. Paideia. Grand Rapids: Baker Academic, 2010.

Moo, Douglas. *The Epistle to the Romans*. NICNT. Grand Rapids: Eerdmans, 1996.

Witherington, Ben, III, and Darlene Hyatt. *Paul's Letter to the Romans: A Socio-Rhetorical Commentary*. Grand Rapids: Eerdmans, 2004.

Helpful Studies of Romans

Campbell, Douglas A. *The Deliverance of God: An Apocalyptic Rereading of Justification in Paul*. Grand Rapids: Eerdmans, 2009.

Donfried, Karl P., ed. *The Romans Debate*. Rev. and expanded. Peabody, MA: Hendrickson, 2005.

Hay, David M., ed. *Pauline Theology*. Vol. 3: *Romans*. Atlanta: Society of Biblical Literature, 1995.

Longenecker, Richard N. *Introducing Romans: Critical Issues in Paul's Most Famous Letter*. Grand Rapids: Eerdmans, 2011.

Oakes, Peter. *Reading Romans in Pompeii: Paul's Letter at Ground Level*. Minneapolis: Fortress, 2010.

Wagner, J. Ross. *Heralds of the Good News: Isaiah and Paul in Concert in the Letter to the Romans*. Boston: Brill Academic, 2003.

Wedderburn, A. J. M. *The Reasons for Romans*. Edinburgh: T&T Clark, 1988.

CHAPTER 7

PHILIPPIANS

CHAPTER GOALS

- To examine the issues that have primary impact on the study of Philippians
- To highlight the central concerns and basic contents of Philippians

CHAPTER OVERVIEW

1. Situating the Vision: An Introduction to Philippians
2. Centering the Vision of Philippians: The Mind of Christ
3. Tracking the Vision of Philippians: The Progress of Christ's Gospel and the Partnership of Christ's People
4. Concluding Remarks
5. Key People, Places, and Terms
6. Questions for Review and Discussion
7. Contemporary Theological Reflections
8. Going Further

KEY VERSES

Philippians 1:6: Being confident of this, that he who began a good work in [or among] you will carry it on to completion until the day of Christ Jesus.

Philippians 1:21: For to me, to live is Christ and to die is gain.

Philippians 4:4: Rejoice in the Lord always. I will say it again: Rejoice!

Philippians 4:6–7: Do not be anxious about anything, but in every situation, by prayer and petition, with thanksgiving, present your requests to God. And the peace of God, which transcends all understanding, will guard your hearts and your minds in Christ Jesus.

Philippians 4:13: I can do all things through him who gives me strength.

Philippians 4:19: And my God will meet all your needs according to the riches of his glory in Christ Jesus (4:19).

Although not numbered among the "Chief" or "Capital" Pauline Letters (see chapters 3–6 above), Philippians, one of four so-called "Captivity" Letters (see, too, chapters 8 and 9 below), is no less loved. In fact, Philippians is laced with some of the most memorable lines the apostle ever penned.

Indeed the seven stirring verses cited above are typically thought to pale in comparison to the seven verses cited below. Indeed, Philippians 2:5–11 is frequently viewed as one of the most profound poetic passages not only in Paul but also in the whole of Scripture.

> In your relationships with one another, have the same mindset as Christ Jesus:
> Who, being in very nature God,
> did not consider equality with God something to be used to his own advantage;
> rather, he made himself nothing
> by taking the very nature of a servant,
> being made in human likeness.
> And being found in appearance as a man,
> he humbled himself
> by becoming obedient to death—even death on a cross!
> Therefore God exalted him to the highest place
> and gave him the name that is above every name,
> that at the name of Jesus every knee should bow,
> in heaven and on earth and under the earth,
> and every tongue acknowledge that Jesus Christ is Lord
> to the glory of God the Father.

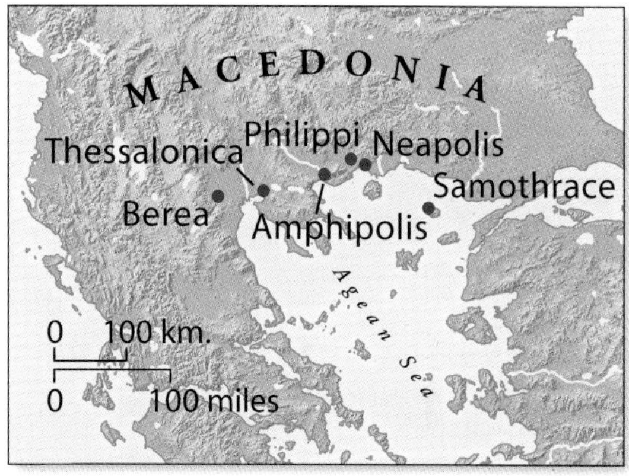

▲ This map of Macedonia indicates where Philippi was located.
▼ A contemporary mosaic of Paul's Macedonian vision located in modern-day Veria (ancient Berea).

Of course, Philippians is not simply a collection of Paul's "greatest hits." Rather, like the Chief Letters treated above and the other Captivity and the Pastoral Letters examined below, Paul wrote Philippians to address particular needs and concerns, not to showcase his epistolary style or poetic prowess. As we begin our examination of Philippians, then, we first need to attend to a number of introductory issues that bear upon a careful study of the letter.

SITUATING THE VISION: AN INTRODUCTION TO PHILIPPIANS

"From the First Day until Now" (1:5)

In the late AD 40s, Paul traveled to the Roman province of Macedonia in northern Greece. There he founded fellowships of Christ-followers in (at least) Philippi and Thessalonica. Whereas Paul wrote to the Thessalonians not long after he was forced out of that city, a number of years had elapsed between the apostle's initial visit to

© William D. Mounce

▲ Remains of the Via Egnatia

▼ An early first-century AD marble statue of Augustus portrayed as the Roman god Jupiter/Jove (Greek, Zeus) holding a scepter and an orb.

Saiko/Wikimedia Commons, CC BY-SA 3.0

Philippi and his writing of the letter we now know as Philippians. While 1 Thessalonians is replete with reminiscences of a recent past, Philippians evinces a protracted partnership in the gospel over a significant stretch of time, probably the better part of a decade.

Wikimedia Commons

▲ A marble head of Philip II of Macedon

According to Acts 16, Paul's Macedonian ministry commenced in response to a vision (16:9–10), the so-called **Macedonian vision**. Taking leave of the seaside city of Troas in northwestern Asia Minor (modern-day Turkey), Paul and his traveling companions came to Philippi via the Aegean island of Samothrace and the Macedonian seaport city of **Neapolis** (present-day Kavala). Paul and his coworkers likely made the ten-mile, southwesterly trek from Neapolis to Philippi by foot on the Via Egnatia, a Roman road that ran through the city.[1] Named after **Philip II of Macedon** (the father of Alexander the Great), Philippi, which was best known in antiquity for battles waged near the city by would-be Caesars, became a Roman colony in 42 BC.

Paul and his fellow missioners arrived in Philippi over one hundred years after those battles. At that time (the late AD 40s) Philippi had yet to experience its building boom. Nonetheless, there were approximately 10,000 to 15,000 residents of Philippi in the middle of the first century AD, not a few of whom were Roman military veterans. Additionally, the archaeological record indicates no shortage of religions on offer when the missioners came to call. It appears that the Roman imperial cult (centered upon the veneration of the Caesar) was especially prominent at that point in the city's history. The gospel of the once-crucified, now-exalted Lord whom Paul and his coworkers proclaimed and certain Philippians embraced would have stood in stark contrast to the imperial ideology of the day, which was passionately promulgated throughout the vast Roman Empire.

Once in Philippi, Luke reports that Paul was able lead a certain **Lydia** "from the city of Thyatira . . . a dealer in purple cloth,"

1. The road itself, eventually 700 miles long, bore the name of Gnaios Egnatios, the Roman proconsul who commissioned its construction. Begun in 146 BC, when completed in 120 BC it ran from Byzantium in the east to Dyrrachium in the west.

Matt O'Brien

Michael Goltz, www.michaelgoltzicons.biz

▲ A photograph of the place where Paul and Silas are said to have been imprisoned in Philippi

▶ An icon of Lydia, a convert of and host for Paul in Philippi

along with her household, to belief and baptism in Christ (Acts 16:14–15). Conflict arising from the exorcism of a "Pythic spirit" from a "slave girl," however, resulted in Paul and Silas being beaten with rods (cf. 2 Cor 11:25) and thrown into prison (16:16–24). Their stay in stocks, short-lived because of an earthquake, led to the conversion of the Philippian jailor and his family (16:25–34). The missioners' presence in the city, however, was not welcomed, and Paul and Silas were sent packing by Philippian magistrates (16:35–40).

Shortly thereafter, Paul and his coworkers arrived in Thessalonica with a view to carrying out a similar ministry (1 Thess 2:2). Then and there, Paul recollects, the Philippians sent him aid more than once when he was in need (Phil 4:16). Furthermore, when Paul left Macedonia, no other church supported him financially except the Philippians (4:15). Although Paul left their province, he did not escape their loving thoughts, prayers, and care.

Staying in Touch

Over the years and miles, the church in Philippi maintained consistent contact with and expressed tangible concern toward Paul. In fact, it appears that Philippians itself was occasioned, at least in part, by a gift that the Philippian church sent to Paul through a man named **Epaphroditus** (4:18; cf. 2:25–30). At that point in time, Paul was "in chains" (1:7, 13, 14, 17). There has been a fair amount of discussion regarding where Paul was imprisoned when he wrote Philippians, and it is to this matter that we now turn our attention.

The provenance of Philippians. In the course of his "fool's speech" in 2 Cor 11:16–12:10, Paul declares that he had been "in prison more frequently" than his "superlative" opponents (11:23). Unfortunately, neither the apostle nor Luke gives specific details regarding his frequent imprisonments.[2] In addition to Philippi, Acts indicates that Paul was also in Roman

2. Writing near the end of the first century AD, the writer of *1 Clement* reports that Paul wore chains on seven occasions. This claim, however, almost assuredly has more to do with numerical symbolism (the number seven signaling completion or perfection) than with actual history.

Louvre, Paris, France/The Bridgeman Art Library

▲ This second-century AD marble bas-relief discovered in Rome portrays members of the Praetorian Guard of Augustus.[3]

custody in Jerusalem (21:33), Caesarea (23:33), and Rome (28:16). Based on certain statements Paul makes in his Corinthian correspondence (esp. 1 Cor 15:32; 16:9; 2 Cor 1:8–13), Pauline interpreters have also posited an Ephesian imprisonment for the apostle. Such observations, however, beg the question of where Paul actually was in chains when writing Philippians (and the other **Captivity Letters** for that matter).

Traditionally, the letter of Philippians has been linked to Rome and correlated with the ending of Acts, which portrays Paul under house arrest awaiting trial before Caesar (28:16–31). This fact notwithstanding, a number of interpreters have suggested other locations for the writing of Philippians, including Corinth, Ephesus, and Caesarea. Contemporary commentators are divided on the matter. At present, a greater number of Anglophone writers are opting for Rome, while a majority of German scholars are leaning toward Ephesus.

For our part, we incline to Rome as the place where Paul was in chains when writing to his beloved fellow believers in Philippi. We favor this position for two primary reasons:

1. The **"palace guard"** and "Caesar's household," to which Paul refers in Philippians 1:13 and 4:22 respectively, fit most naturally in Rome.
2. Philippians 1:18a–26 tallies remarkably well with the ending of Acts. Paul is awaiting a hearing before Caesar and is pondering the potential outcomes.

The primary objections to our position are also two:

1. The distance between Philippi and Rome (roughly 800 miles) is thought to be too great for the various trips between the two locations suggested by the letter.
2. Paul anticipated further ministry in the Roman West (not least Spain) when writing Romans ca. AD 57; therefore, an earlier date for Philippians (about 55–56 from Ephesus) is preferable, since Paul envisions taking another trip to Philippi (see esp. 2:24) in the Roman East.

To our mind, the mobility of believers in the "Pauline circle" and the apostle's desire to return eastward adequately address these concerns. Additionally, we would note that

3. On this famed guard, see further Sandra Bingham, *The Praetorian Guard: A History of Rome's Elite Special Forces* (Waco, TX: Baylor University Press, 2013).

although Paul's purported Ephesian imprisonment is a responsible scholarly construct, it is not an actual Pauline or Lukan claim. To be fair, the arguments are finely divided, and the provenance of Philippians is far from being the letter's most pressing interpretive issue.

Opponents in Philippians. Another matter that interests interpreters of Philippians is the identity of the various opponents who appear in the lines of the letter. The following passages pertain to the identity of these opponents:

> It is true that some preach Christ out of envy and rivalry, but others out of goodwill. The latter do so out of love, knowing that I am put here for the defense of the gospel. The former preach Christ out of selfish ambition, not sincerely, supposing that they can stir up trouble for me while I am in chains. But what does it matter? The important thing is that in every way, whether from false motives or true, Christ is preached. And because of this I rejoice. (1:15–18a)

> Whatever happens, conduct yourselves in a manner worthy of the gospel of Christ. Then, whether I come and see you or only hear about you in my absence, I will know that you stand firm in the one Spirit, striving together as one for the faith of the gospel without being frightened in any way by those who oppose you. This is a sign to them that they will be destroyed, but that you will be saved—and that by God. For it has been granted to you on behalf of Christ not only to believe in him, but also to suffer for him, since you are going through the same struggle you saw I had, and now hear that I still have. (1:27–30)

> Watch out for those dogs, those evildoers, those mutilators of the flesh. (3:2)

> For, as I have often told you before and now tell you again even with tears, many live as enemies of the cross of Christ. Their destiny is destruction, their god is their stomach, and their glory is in their shame. Their mind is set on earthly things. (3:18–19)

What is true of Paul elsewhere is no less the case here—the apostle tells us precious little about those who oppose him and his converts. In 1:15–18a it appears that Paul is referring to fellow believers (and missioners?) who are also preaching Christ, likely in the place of his captivity (note 1:14). From Paul's perspective, however, some of them are doing so "out of envy and rivalry," "out of selfish ambition, not sincerely" (1:15, 17). Why? Paul thinks that they are doing so to compound his troubles and to exacerbate his affliction in captivity. In 1:30 Paul again refers to the conflict in which he finds himself. By so doing, he could have in view the same struggle of which he speaks earlier in the chapter. He may also be referring, however, to his present captivity and the charge (seemingly of sedition) hanging over his head, as he waits for his "day in court."

As Paul seeks to encourage the Philippians in the face of their own conflict, the cause and nature of which he does not indicate, he alludes to his own difficulty in the city, about which we learn a little in Acts 16. Recent scholarship on the letter suggests that the church's trouble was with unbelieving outsiders and centered on civic concerns. It may well be that the Philippian believers had to endure social ostracism, economic deprivation, and even physical suffering as a result of their dedication to Christ and to each other.[4]

Turning to chapter 3, most contemporary interpreters concur that Paul had his Jewish, Christ-following competitors in view when he enjoined the Philippians to "beware of the dogs,

4. See further Todd D. Still, *Philippians & Philemon* (SHBC 27b; Macon, GA: Smyth & Helwys, 2011), 44; Peter Oakes, *Philippians: From People to Letter* (SNTSMS 110; Cambridge: Cambridge University Press, 2001), 77–102.

beware of the evil-workers, beware of the mutilation" (3:2, trans. TDS). Arguably, given that such detractors had dogged his trail elsewhere, not least in Galatia and Corinth, the apostle wanted the Philippian assembly to be on guard against and wary of what Paul regarded to be their harmful spiritual influence. With respect to those people whom Paul depicts as "enemies of the cross of Christ" in 3:18 and whom he continues to defame in 3:19, they are either one and the same with those whom Paul excoriates in 3:2 or are some now unidentifiable group of people whom the apostle regarded as seriously and dangerously misguided.

The unity of Philippians. As with 2 Corinthians, scholars have sometimes treated canonical Philippians as a composite document, comprised of two or three letters. Those who espouse the two-letter theory maintain that Paul wrote in the following sequence:

The First Letter: 3:1b–4:20

The Second Letter: 1:1–3:1a along with 4:21–23

Interpreters who argue for three letters envision the following literary progression:

The First Letter: 4:10–20

The Second Letter: 1:1–3:1a + 4:4–7, 21–23

The Third Letter: 3:1b–4:3 + 4:8–9

▼ Philippians 2:9 exclaims, "God exalted [Jesus] to the highest place and gave him the name that is above every name." The "Christ Pantocrator ('Almighty')" icon pictured here is from the Deesis Mosaic, located within the Hagia Sophia in Istanbul, Turkey. This iconic type seeks to extol Christ as all-powerful Lord.

Both of these theories require later editorial emendation.

There are two primary reasons as to why interpreters have thought it necessary to propose compilation theories for Philippians. First, the sudden shift both in subject and in tone at the outset of chapter 3 has caused a number of scholars to detect the hand of a later editor. Additionally, commentators have contended that the appearance of a thanksgiving near the conclusion of Philippians reveals editorial work. To support further the case that canonical Philippians is a composite document, appeal is frequently made to a remark of Polycarp, Bishop of Smyrna in the first half of the second century. In a letter he penned to the Philippians, Polycarp speaks of *letters* that the apostle had written to them.[5]

A multiple-letter scenario is increasingly seen to be unsatisfactory, even though the transition at the outset of chapter 3 is admittedly abrupt. Proponents of the letter's unity also maintain that a thanksgiving at the end of the letter is not as problematic as some have imagined, especially given the gratitude Paul expresses at the outset of the letter. As to Polycarp's remark, it may well be that Paul wrote multiple letters to the Philippian church, but this would not require canonical Philippians to be a collage of the same. In brief, more and more interpreters—including us—are inclined to see Philippians

5. Polycarp, *To the Philippians* 3.2.

as a single letter. Granted, there are a few less-than-smooth transitions within the letter; however, as it stands, canonical Philippians is far from a hodge-podge of random musings. In fact, recurring themes and vocabulary within Philippians signal a single letter, and it is from this perspective we will conduct our study.

CENTERING THE VISION OF PHILIPPIANS: THE MIND OF CHRIST JESUS

As noted at the outset of this chapter, Philippians is a letter chock-full of well-known verses. No passage, however, is better known than Philippians 2:5–11. The poetic profundity of this portion of Philippians has inspired and encouraged both ancient and modern believers the world over. Along with John 1, Colossians 1, and certain portions of Revelation, Christ-followers have poured over this passage to garner christological insights and to praise the Lord extolled therein. Taken together, these verses tell the story of Jesus' humility, fidelity, agony, and victory. They speak of Christ Jesus' incarnation as a man, crucifixion on a cross, and exaltation to the highest place. It is easy to see why so many Christians have valued, indeed have loved, Philippians 2:5–11 and have viewed it as something of the letter's "nerve center."

Scholars have also been arrested by 2:5–11 and have examined these verses with painstaking care. Among other things, they have considered their origin, background, form, vocabulary, theology, and function. In the course of study, not a few interpreters have proposed that vv. 6–11 comprise an early church hymn that Paul more or less cites here. Such inquiries and theories are to be welcomed, as they have aided our understanding of this programmatic passage immeasurably. That being said, 2:5–11 is not a textual island cut off from the letter, and we do well to consider this text in its context.

> Gordon D. Fee remarks on Phil 2:5–11: "Here is the epitome of God-likeness: the pre-existent Christ was not a 'grasping, selfish' being, but one whose love for others found its consummate expression in 'pouring himself out,' in taking on the role of a slave, in humbling himself to the point of death on behalf of those so loved. No wonder Paul cannot abide triumphalism — in any of its forms. It goes against everything that God is and that God is about."[6]

This passage, which shines like a supernova on the letter's landscape, is sandwiched between calls to unity enabled by humility (2:1–4) and fidelity characterized by purity (2:11–18). The selfless regard for others and joyful obedience to which Paul calls the Philippians is clearly displayed by the Lord lauded in the "hymn." What is more, Paul admonishes the church in their "relationships with one another" to "have the same mindset as Christ Jesus" (2:5). That is, they are to become "Christ-minded," to think as Jesus thought, so that in turn they might live as he lived. This, of course, does not reduce the Lord to a moral example, but it does place before the fellowship a model to emulate. Human models— whether Timothy (2:19–24), Epaphroditus (2:25–30), or Paul himself (3:17)— pale in

6. Gordon D. Fee, *Paul's Letter to the Philippians* (NICNT; Grand Rapids: Eerdmans, 1995), 197.

Christ's *Kenōsis* or Self-Emptying

The NIV renders the Greek verb *kenoō* in Phil 2:7 "made himself nothing." Other versions (e.g., NRSV) translate the term "emptied himself." Theologians have struggled to understand Christ's *kenōsis* or self-emptying. Of what did Christ empty himself when he took on human likeness, they wonder? Some have answered that the incarnate Christ divested himself of certain divine attributes, while others have contended that he forfeited the independent exercise thereof.

The ancient Alexandrian theologian Origen (AD 182–254) maintained, "In emptying himself he became a man and was incarnate while remaining truly God. Having become a man, he remained the God that he was. He assumed a body like our own, differing only in that it was born from the Virgin by the Holy Spirit." Relatedly, the early commentator on Paul's letters known as Ambrosiaster notes, "He is said not to have taken the form of God but to have been in the form of God. What he is said to have taken is the form of a slave when he was humbled like a sinner. His taking the form of a slave was not simply becoming human but his profound identification with sinners, voluntarily taking the form of a slave."[8]

comparison to the incomparable Christ, the exemplar par excellence, and it is he whose habit of mind that they are to possess and express.

One interpreter has posited that the letter's "most comprehensive purpose is the shaping of a Christian *phronēsis*, a practical moral reasoning that is 'conformed to [Christ's] death' in hope of his resurrection."[7] It is both interesting and instructive to note how terms related to thinking, knowing, considering, regarding, and the like permeate Philippians. But this only begs the question: Of what does Paul want the assembly to be mindful so that they might be Christ-minded?

As indicated, the apostle enjoins the Philippians *to be mindful of their models*, both (1) Christ the Lord and (2) those who live exemplary lives in Christ. Paul writes in 3:17, "Join together in following my example, brothers and sisters, and just as you have us as a model, keep your eyes on those who live as we do." Even as the Philippians are to keep their eyes on Jesus and those who follow in his train, such as Paul, Timothy, and Epaphroditus, they are also to resist emulating those who are not worthy of imitation. Paul paints those who he thinks oppose and distort the gospel in dark hues in order to dissuade believers in Philippi from thinking as such people think and doing as they do. There are types and antitypes, models to embrace and examples to eschew. Part of having the "mind of Christ" is to know whom to listen to and follow after and whom not. The apostle does not want the Philippians to succumb to the influence of those who seek "their own interests, not those of Jesus Christ" (2:21).

Indeed, Paul longs for "God's holy people in Christ Jesus at Philippi" (1:1) *to be mindful of and committed to the gospel and to koinōnia ("close mutual relationship") in Christ.* The apostle shared a rich, reciprocal relationship with the Philippians in the gospel, and for such he was grateful (1:5). The fellowship had stood with Paul over the long haul through thick and thin, and the assembly's dogged devotion to the mobile apostle was not lost on him (1:7; 4:15). Timothy had also proven to be a faithful companion to Paul as one who "served" alongside him "in the work of the gospel" (2:22).

---

7. Wayne A. Meeks, "The Man from Heaven in Philippians," in *The Future of Early Christianity* (ed. Birger A. Pearson; Minneapolis: Fortress, 1991), 333.
8. These quotations are drawn from Mark J. Edwards, ed., *Galatians, Ephesians, Philippians* (ACCS 7; Downers Grove, IL: InterVarsity Press, 1999), 243, 245.

Paul desired for the Philippians to partner with one another as they had with him. Were such *koinōnia* to occur, however, the assembly would have to live more fully "in a manner worthy of the gospel of Christ" and would have to "strive together" more ardently "as one for the faith of the gospel" (1:27). This, in turn, would require the congregation to "do nothing out of selfish ambition or vain conceit." On the contrary, in humility they would have to value others above themselves, not looking to their own interests but to the interests of others (2:3–4). Such a habit of mind is neither easy nor natural, but it is in keeping with the one who "made himself nothing by taking the form of a slave" (2:7).

Instead of grumbling, arguing, and competing with one another, Paul's vision for the Philippians was one of concord and contentment in Christ borne of sacrificial, mutual, joyful service in the gospel (2:1–2, 14, 29; 4:1–9). To this end, the Philippian Epaphroditus (2:25–30) served as a concrete example for the assembly, including **Euodia and Syntyche**, who were in conflict with each other (4:2).

All the while, Paul encouraged the Philippians both by example and by precept *to be mindful of their spiritual future in the present by not living in the past.* Despite his pedigree and performance in Judaism (3:5–6), Paul came to consider everything a loss (indeed garbage) because of the surpassing worth of knowing Christ Jesus his Lord (3:8). The apostle's ambition was "to know Christ—yes, to know the power of his resurrection and participation in his sufferings" (3:10). How did Paul aim to arrive at this end? The answer he offers in 3:12–14 is by pressing on "toward the goal." To "take hold" and "win the prize," the apostle forgets that which is behind and strains toward that which is ahead with a view to that which is above. At various places throughout the letter, he reminds his "beloved" in Philippi of the coming day of Christ (1:6, 10) and of their heavenly, not earthly, citizenship (1:27; 3:20; 4:3). What is true of him should be no less true of them—"to live is Christ and to die is gain" (1:21).

TRACKING THE VISION OF PHILIPPIANS: THE PROGRESS OF CHRIST'S GOSPEL AND THE PARTNERSHIP OF CHRIST'S PEOPLE

The Basic Structure of Philippians

1:1–11	Letter Opening
1:12–30	Preaching and Living the Gospel
2:1–3:21	Embodying, Extolling, and Exemplifying Christ
4:1–20	Instructions to and Gratitude for the Church
4:21–23	Closing Greetings

The Reasons for the Writing of Philippians

In this section, we will track the vision of Philippians by noting seven possible reasons for the letter's composition. We will treat these purported purposes by working our way through the letter, beginning with chapter 1. Put differently, here we will overview Philippians by asking and seeking to answer the question of what prompted Paul to write the letter in the first place. As we will see, some reasons for the apostle's communication with the assembly were more pressing than others. While some interpreters have sought to discover a single overarching macro-purpose for the letter (e.g., it is a letter of friendship or a letter of consolation, etc.), we would like to set forth seven discernible, overlapping reasons for the writing of Philippians.

First of all, Paul writes *to inform the Philippians of his present circumstances and future desires*. The assembly is aware that the apostle is in chains (1:30), but Paul wants them to understand that his captivity is not in vain. He assures them that his shackles are in service of the gospel (1:7, 16). At the time of writing, Paul's circumstances were tenuous. As he waited for his "day in court" on capital charges, his life hung in the balance.

Yet Paul did not hang his head. Instead, he crafted a letter wherein he is joyful about life and defiant about death. On the one hand, the apostle relished life and the opportunity it afforded him to exalt Christ and to engage in fruitful gospel service (1:20, 22). On the other hand, had Paul his druthers, he would have preferred to depart to be with Christ, which he regarded as "better by far" (1:23). When writing to the Philippians, Paul was confident he would continue to live, in no small measure due to the church's prayers and "God's provision of the Spirit of Jesus Christ" (1:19). Moreover, the apostle was convinced that his ongoing presence would enable the assembly to grow in the faith and to rejoice in the Lord (1:25–26; 2:24). Whether he lived or whether he died, however, it was Paul's eager expectation and hope to "have sufficient courage" so that Christ might be "exalted" through him. For the apostle, "to live is Christ and to die is gain" (1:21).

Paul also composes the letter *to express his joy in the progress of the gospel in spite of his present peril*. Paul is joyful (i.e., grateful to God for the grace of the gospel) and enjoins the congregation to be joyful too (1:18; 2:18; 3:1; 4:4). Given the Philippians' partnership with Paul in the gospel "from the first day until now" (1:5; cf. 4:15–16), the "advance of the gospel" (1:12) becomes a ground for shared joy. As a result of Paul's captivity, it had become clear throughout the palace guard and to everyone else that he was in chains for Christ (1:13). What is more, other believers, for reasons both noble and narcissistic (1:15–17), were emboldened in the Lord "to proclaim the gospel without fear" (1:14). Whatever the motivation, Paul rejoiced that Christ was being preached. He recognized and wanted the Philippians likewise to realize that the one preached (i.e., Christ), and not the ones doing the preaching, was "the important thing" (1:18).

Two additional reasons Paul arguably composes Philippians are *to call the assembly to steadfastness in the face of suffering as well as to unity through humility*. In 1:27, Paul enjoins the congregation to live life as gospel citizens and not merely as Roman citizens (cf. 3:20) so that they might stand firm in the one Spirit and strive together as one for the faith, whether he was or was not with them. Furthermore, the apostle wants to impress on his brothers and sisters in Christ in Philippi that they need not fear those who presently oppose them (1:28), whoever they might be, for both salvation and destruction belong to God. Far from an unexpected blight, Paul encourages the Philippians to see suffering as an anticipated privilege for Christ-followers (1:29). Their "struggle" for the sake of the gospel is, the apostle maintains, the same struggle they saw Paul had and now hear that he still has (1:30).

The circumstances surrounding the Philippians' suffering are unclear. The same is true regarding the fissures in the church's fellowship. Whatever the reasons for dissension, however, Paul is at pains in the letter to draw the congregation together. In 2:1–4, he reminds them of their common life and love and implores them to set aside selfish ambition, vain conceit, and their own self-interests. Instead, he calls them in their "relationships with one another" to "have the same mindset as Christ Jesus" (2:5). On the heels of this admonition, Paul composes or includes a most majestic meditation on Christ's humble obedience to God as an example for the Philippian believers to embrace and emulate (2:6–11).

Wikimedia Commons

▲ "The Starry Night" is one of the most readily recognizable works of the Dutch post-Impressionistic painter Vincent van Gogh (1853–1890). In Phil 2:15, Paul enjoins the Philippians to "shine . . . like stars in the sky" (cf. Dan 12:3).

If Euodia and Syntyche (4:2–3) were to have the same habit of mind that led Christ to cross-death, would they persist in being at cross-purposes with one another? Paul hopes not, and he charges the church in Philippi to repair the breaches. They are, with or without him, "to work out [their] own salvation with fear and trembling" (2:13) and to "do everything without grumbling or complaining" (2:14), so that they might be "blameless and pure" and "shine . . . like stars in the sky" (2:15) as they "hold firmly to the word of life" (2:16). The concord Paul experiences with the Philippians is what he envisions for the Philippians (2:16a–17). The path to unity that Paul prescribes is the way of Christlike humility, obedience, and service.

Another discernible reason Paul wrote to the Philippians was *to commend to the assembly Timothy, Epaphroditus, and himself as models worthy of emulation.* To be sure, Paul regarded Jesus as the ultimate exemplar (2:5–11). Nonetheless, the apostle thought that human models of Christ-following were invaluable. In 3:7–14 Paul sets forth his passionate, ongoing pursuit of Christ, especially his desire to know the power of Christ's resurrection and participation in his sufferings (3:10), as exemplary and as evidence of spiritual maturity. Albeit ironic, maturity in Christ is marked by the realization that this side of heaven perfection is unattainable (3:12–13). Yet, like a track athlete, Paul, and those who would follow in his train, strain toward what is ahead (3:13). To move forward, Paul is determined to forget what is behind and to press on toward the goal to win the prize for which God called him heavenward in Christ Jesus (3:14).

Paul did not fancy himself to be wholly unique, however. There were other believers who were no less capable of serving as examples of the Lord's selfless, sacrificial life of service, including Timothy (2:19–24) and Epaphroditus (2:25–30). As for Timothy, who was like a "son" to and a surrogate for Paul, the apostle reminds the Philippians of how he has proven his spiritual mettle by slaving alongside him in the gospel (2:22). In fact, Paul maintains that he has no one else like him, who will show genuine concern for the Philippians' welfare (2:20). If others look out for "their own interests, not those of Jesus Christ" (2:21), this was patently not the case with Timothy. Therefore, he represents in his person that to which Paul has called the congregation — a regard for others that mirrors the Christ who "made himself nothing" (2:7).

Wikimedia Commons

▲ In Phil 3:13–14, Paul likens his pursuit of Christ to a race (cf. 1 Cor 9:24–27). This ancient Greek vase depicts a running contest.

Regarding the otherwise unknown Philippian Epaphroditus, Paul lavishes him with praise and lifts him up as a spiritual model. In delivering the church's gift to Paul, he risked life and limb. Indeed, "he almost died for the work of Christ" (2:30), the apostle reports. Once with Paul, Epaphroditus fell ill and nearly died. But God was merciful, both to him and the apostle. The Lord spared Epaphroditus's life and spared Paul "sorrow upon sorrow" (2:27). In sending Epaphroditus from his side back to Philippi, Paul instructs the church "to welcome him in the Lord with great joy, and honor such people like him" (2:29). And what was Epaphroditus like? He was Christlike. By caring for others, even at great personal cost, he exhibited and exuded Christ.

Not all people, however, live that way, not even others who claim to be Christ-followers. "Many," the apostle laments, "live as enemies of the cross of Christ" (3:18). Instead of having the mind of Christ (2:5), these people, against whom Paul polemicizes, set their minds on earthly things, not heavenly ones (3:19). In so doing, they become negative models or antitypes for the fellowship. Paul writes to "all God's holy people in Christ Jesus at Philippi" (1:1), therefore, *to warn them of potential opponents and to remind them that their citizenship is in heaven.*

It is not only those against whom Paul rails in 3:19 that the assembly is to be wary of, however. They are also to "watch out for those dogs, those evildoers, those mutilators of the flesh" (3:2). The vast majority of interpreters understand, rightly to our mind, those of whom Paul speaks so negatively in 3:2 to be law-observant Jesus-followers who were also missioners. The apostle regarded these largely, if not entirely, Jewish Jesus-followers to be mistaken regarding the place and role of the Jewish law in the lives of Gentile believers. Believing that to be forewarned was to be forearmed, Paul seeks to cut these interlopers off at the pass by alerting the Gentile Philippians to what he regarded to be their deleterious influence.

As an apostle of Christ to the Gentiles, Paul thought and taught that those who "serve God by his Spirit, who boast in Jesus Christ, and who put no confidence in the flesh" constitute "the circumcision" (3:3). He who had been "circumcised on the eighth day, of the people of Israel, of the tribe of Benjamin, a Hebrew of Hebrews; in regard to the law, a Pharisee; as for zeal, persecuting the church; as for righteousness based on the law, faultless" (3:5–6), had not always embraced and espoused the view that "righteousness . . . comes from God on the basis of faith," that is, faith in Christ or perhaps the faithfulness of Christ (3:9).

Having become convinced of such, however, Paul came to regard his pedigree and past performance as a Jew, as well as every other thing he had previously viewed as gain, to be loss, even garbage (Greek *skybala*), that he might gain Christ (3:7–8). Paul puts it this way: "I want to know Christ—yes, to know the power of his resurrection and participation in his sufferings, becoming like him in his death, and so somehow, attaining to the resurrection of the dead" (3:10–11). As one who had been captivated and called by Christ, Paul came to view knowing Christ Jesus his Lord to be of "surpassing worth" (3:8).

Given that Paul regarded full and final knowledge of Christ to be a future hope, not a present possession (note also 1 Cor 13:12), he reminds the Philippians in 3:20–21: "Our citizenship is in heaven. And we eagerly await a Savior from there, the Lord Jesus Christ, who, by the power that enables him to bring everything under his control, will transform our lowly bodies so that they will be like his glorious body" (cf. 1:6, 10, 28). Until the culmination of all things in Christ, the assembly should live steadfastly in unity (4:1–3). What is more, they should be marked by joy and gentleness, being mindful all the while of the Lord's nearness and God's peace, experienced in no small measure through prayer (4:4–7). In sum, Paul desired for them to dwell on things that are "excellent or praiseworthy" (4:8) and to "put into practice" what they had learned or received or heard from Paul, or seen in him (4:9; cf. 3:17).

Finally, Paul sent a letter to his beloved brothers and sisters in Philippi in order *to thank them for their partnership in the gospel, including their most recent gift to him*. If other congregations partnered with Paul in fits and starts, a steady stream of commitment, encouragement, and support appears to have flowed to the apostle from Philippi. This had been the case "from the first day until now" (1:6; cf. 4:15–16). If the apostle had wondered if this would be true even in his chains, then such concerns were allayed by Epaphroditus's arrival, replete with gifts from the Philippian fellowship (4:18).

One gathers, however, that the coming of Epaphroditus to Paul in his captivity was none too soon. As Paul commences what is sometimes called his "thankless thanks" (4:10–20), he seems to be as relieved as he is joyful that the Philippians had at last renewed their concern for him. Not that they were unconcerned, Paul hastens to add, but they had not had the "opportunity to show it" (4:10). Although the apostle appears to be genuinely grateful for the church's most recent gift (which he depicts in 4:17–18 as a spiritual credit and as a "fragrant offering, an acceptable sacrifice, pleasing to God"), he did not think of himself to be in need. Rather, he had learned to be content whatever the circumstances (4:11) and stood convinced that he could do all things through Christ who gave him strength (4:13).

Indeed, the "secret" of Paul's contentment, "whether well fed or hungry, whether living in plenty or in want," was his trust in the Lord's strength and provision. He did not regard this perspective and response to life's vicissitudes, however, to be an apostolic preserve. Rather, he seeks to impress on the Philippians his deep-seated belief (shaped in the cauldron of deprivation and affliction and rescue from the same) that God will supply all their needs according to the riches of his glory in Christ Jesus (4:19). Such confidence in Christ was and remains both contagious and transformative and is good reason, indeed sufficient reason, to read and to reflect on Philippians time and again.

CONCLUDING REMARKS

In the midst of captivity, whether in Rome or elsewhere, a certain Epaphroditus paid Paul a visit. He came bearing gifts from the church in Philippi. It was not uncommon for the Philippian assembly to help Paul financially in the course of his apostolic ministry. Indeed, the shackled apostle had a protracted, reciprocal relationship with this fellowship, and Epaphroditus's timely delivery only heightened his profound appreciation for the Macedonian congregation.

As the once ill Epaphroditus was preparing to return home, Paul composed a letter for his beloved brothers and sisters in Philippi. In this missive the apostle couples deep joy with abiding gratitude and prayerful peace as he informs the Philippians of his present circumstances and his future desires. He also encourages and instructs them regarding their shared life in the gospel. Moreover, in the lines of the letter Paul challenges them to embrace and to exemplify the "mind of Christ." Even as all else pales in comparison to Christ's incomparable person, all else is to pale in comparison to the pursuit of the one who has taken hold of believers and "will transform [their] lowly bodies so that they will be like his glorious body" (3:21).

» KEY PEOPLE, PLACES, AND TERMS «

Captivity Letters
Epaphroditus
Euodia and Syntyche
Koinōnia
Lydia
Macedonian vision
Neapolis
Palace guard
Philip II of Macedon

» QUESTIONS FOR REVIEW AND DISCUSSION «

1. From where (and when) might Paul have written Philippians (and other "Captivity Letters")?
2. Where may one turn to learn of the "founding" of the Philippian church? Roughly how much time had elapsed between the assembly's beginning and the writing of Philippians?
3. Discuss the unity of Philippians.
4. Why was Paul being detained "in chains" (1:13)? How did Paul view and want the Philippians to see his captivity?
5. Why was Paul so fond of the Philippian congregation?
6. Compare Paul's attitude toward his opponents in Philippians 1:15–18a with Philippians 3:2, 18–19.
7. How does Paul seek to address the seeming disunity among the Philippian congregation?
8. Is Paul's admonition for the Philippians to follow his example (3:17; 4:9) an example of egotism? Why or why not?
9. Why might Paul's expression of thanks for the Philippians' gifts be somewhat tempered and restrained?
10. Note six possible reasons that Paul wrote Philippians and elaborate briefly upon each.

» CONTEMPORARY THEOLOGICAL REFLECTION «

1. What might Paul mean when he says, "For to me, to live is Christ and to die is gain" (1:21)? How might contemporary believers seek to live similarly?
2. In 1 Cor 2:16, Paul maintains that certain believers "have the mind of Christ." In Phil 2:5, the apostle enjoins the Philippians to "have the same mindset as Christ Jesus." Based on Phil 2:6–11, the so-called *kenōsis* hymn, how might those in Christ cultivate the mind of Christ?

3. It has been said of certain Christians that "they are so heavenly-minded that they are no earthly good." Do you think this was true of Paul? Might this be true of you?

» GOING FURTHER «

Philippians is well served by a number of fine commentaries and special studies. We would commend the following resources written in (or translated into) English. For a fuller discussion of the scholarly literature on Philippians through 2008, see Todd D. Still, "An Overview of Recent Scholarly Literature on Philippians," *ExpT* 119 (2008): 422–28.

Commentaries on Philippians

Barth, Karl. *The Epistle to the Philippians: 40th Anniversary Edition.* Trans. James W. Leitch. Louisville/London: Westminster John Knox, 2002.

Bockmuehl, Markus. *The Epistle to the Philippians.* BNTC 11. Peabody, MA: Hendrickson, 1998.

Fee, Gordon D. *Paul's Letter to the Philippians.* NICNT. Grand Rapids: Eerdmans, 1995.

Hooker, Morna D. "Philippians." *The New Interpreter's Bible.* Nashville: Abingdon, 2000, 11:497–549.

Silva, Moisés. *Philippians.* 2nd ed. BECNT. Grand Rapids: Baker Academic, 2005.

Still, Todd D. *Philippians & Philemon.* SHBC 27b. Macon, GA: Smyth & Helwys, 2011.

Special Studies on Philippians

Holloway, Paul A. *Consolation in Philippians: Philosophical Sources and Rhetorical Strategies.* SNTSMS 112. Cambridge: Cambridge University Press, 2001.

Oakes, Peter. *Philippians: From People to Letter.* SNTSMS 110. Cambridge: Cambridge University Press, 2001.

Portefaix, Lillian. *Sisters Rejoice: Paul's Letter to the Philippians and Luke-Acts as Seen by First-Century Philippian Women.* ConBNT 20. Stockholm: Almqvist & Wiksell, 1988.

Sumney, Jerry. *Philippians: A Greek Student's Intermediate Reader.* Peabody, MA: Hendrickson, 2007.

Wansink, Craig S. *Chained in Christ: The Experience and Rhetoric of Paul's Imprisonments.* JSNTSup 130. Sheffield: Sheffield Academic, 1996.

Ware, James P. *The Mission of the Church in Paul's Letter to the Philippians in the Context of Ancient Judaism.* NovTSup 120. Leiden/Boston: Brill, 2005.

CHAPTER 8

PHILEMON AND COLOSSIANS

CHAPTER GOALS

- To examine the issues which have primary impact on the study of Philemon and Colossians
- To highlight the central concerns and basic contents of these letters

CHAPTER OVERVIEW

1. Situating the Vision of Philemon: Introductory Questions
2. Centering the Vision of Philemon: Neither Slave nor Free
3. Tracking the Vision of Philemon: Praising, Persuading, and Expecting
4. Philemon: The Rest of the Story
5. Situating the Vision of Colossians: Introductory Issues
6. Centering the Vision of Colossians: "Christ Is All"
7. Tracking the Vision of Colossians: Fullness and Faithfulness in Christ
8. Concluding Remarks
9. Key People, Places, and Terms in Philemon and Colossians
10. Questions for Review and Discussion on Philemon
11. Contemporary Theological Reflection on Philemon
12. Going Further with Philemon
13. Questions for Review and Discussion on Colossians
14. Contemporary Theological Reflection on Colossians
15. Going Further with Colossians

KEY VERSES

Philemon

Philemon 8–9a: "Therefore, although in Christ I could be bold and order you to do what you ought to do, yet I prefer to appeal to you on the basis of love."

Philemon 15–16a: "Perhaps the reason he was separated from you for a little while was that you might have him back forever—no longer as a slave, but better than a slave, as a dear brother."

Philemon 17–18: "So if you consider me a partner, welcome him as you would welcome me. If he has done you any wrong or owes you anything, charge it to me."

Colossians

Colossians 1:15–18: "The Son is the image of the invisible God, the firstborn over all creation. For in him all things were created: things in heaven and on earth, visible and invisible, whether thrones or powers or rulers or authorities; all things have been created through him and for him. He is before all things, and in him all things hold together. And he is the head of the body, the church; he is the beginning and the firstborn from among the dead, so that in everything he might have the supremacy."

Colossians 2:13–15: "When you were dead in your sins and in the uncircumcision of your flesh, God made you alive with Christ. He forgave us all our sins, having canceled the charge of our legal indebtedness, which stood against us and condemned us; he has taken it away, nailing it to the cross. And having disarmed the powers and authorities, he made a public spectacle of them, triumphing over them by the cross."

Colossians 3:1–4: "Since, then, you have been raised with Christ, set your hearts on things above, where Christ is, seated at the right hand of God. Set your minds on things above, not on earthly things.

For you died, and your life is now hidden with Christ in God. When Christ, who is your life, appears, then you also will appear with him in glory."

Colossians 3:15–17: "Let the peace of Christ rule in your hearts, since as members of one body you were called to peace. And be thankful. Let the message of Christ dwell among you richly as you teach and admonish one another with all wisdom through psalms, hymns, and songs from the Spirit, singing to God with gratitude in your hearts. And whatever you do, whether in word or deed, do it all in the name of the Lord Jesus, giving thanks to God the Father through him."

As you begin reading this chapter, you may be wondering why we have chosen to pair a brief letter to a slave owner (**Philemon**) with a letter of instruction to a congregation (Colossians). Beyond the fact that both are Captivity Letters, scholars tend to treat Philemon with either Philippians or Colossians (or, on occasion, Ephesians) because of its length (only 335 words in Greek).

Why, then, have we chosen Colossians instead of Philippians? Interpreters have tended to link Philemon with Colossians because of the Pauline associates mentioned in both letters, not least of whom **Onesimus**. It is typically thought that the Onesimus who features in Philemon (see v. 10) is one and the same as the Onesimus described in Col 4:9 as "our faithful and dear brother, who is one of you." The phrase "who is one of you" is usually taken to mean that Onesimus, Philemon's slave, had been living in Colossae with his master. Since Philemon and Colossians were both written to Colossian believers, it makes eminently good sense to treat them together—or so the logic has run.

At present, however, such logic has lost at least some of its luster for those Pauline scholars who think that Paul did not write Colossians. It is not uncommon, therefore, for contemporary interpreters of Paul to pair Philemon with Philippians, which is more commonly seen as a genuine Pauline letter. Although we are pairing Philemon with Colossians, we will consider Philemon first, presupposing with virtually all other Pauline scholars that it is an authentic Pauline letter. Thereafter, we will examine Colossians. In doing so, we will take up the matter of authorship. But let us first turn our full attention to the fascinating letter of Philemon.

Steven Enich Serbian Orthodox Church Cultural Slide Collection/Hilandar Research Library/The Ohio State University

▲ One may view this mosaic of Onesimus at the St. Petka Chapel in Belgrade, Serbia.

SITUATING THE VISION OF PHILEMON: INTRODUCTORY QUESTIONS

Who Are the Letter's Main Characters, and How Do They Interrelate?

Albeit a short letter by Pauline standards, Philemon includes a number of characters. Many are minor, and Paul ushers them on and off of the epistolary stage rather quickly: Timothy, Apphia, Archippus, Epaphras, Mark, Aristarchus, Demas, Luke, and the assembly who meets in Philemon's home (see vv. 1–2, 23–24). The major players are three—Paul, a shackled and aged apostle (vv. 1, 9–10, 13); Philemon, a slave-owner and believer, who apparently was led to faith by Paul in Ephesus, some one hundred miles west of Colossae, where Paul spent some three years in the early to mid-50s; and Onesimus, Philemon's slave, who became a Jesus-follower through Paul's influence.

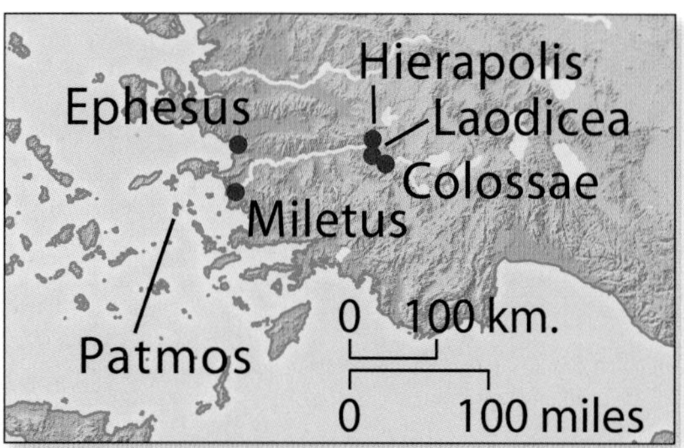

▲ Colossae was roughly one hundred miles east of Ephesus.

> **What Was the Situation of Onesimus?**
>
> How did Onesimus happen to come to meet Paul? In addition to the runaway slave and aggrieved slave hypotheses discussed in the text, scholars have posited that the Colossian church sent Onesimus as a messenger to Paul (the commissioned slave hypothesis); or perhaps Onesimus was wandering from his home when he encountered Paul (the wandering slave hypothesis); or Onesimus had a falling out with Philemon, his biological brother, and sought out Paul for help (the estranged brother hypothesis).

How Did Onesimus Come to Be with Paul, and Where Was Paul "in Chains"?

It is commonly thought that Onesimus and Paul crossed paths when the former, having stolen something from his owner (as implied by v. 18; see also v. 11), proceeded to run away from Colossae and somehow met up with Paul in Rome. Such a scenario, while not impossible, is not provable and is by no means the only scholarly proposal. In fact, although the "runaway slave hypothesis" has long held sway, it has begun to give way to the "aggrieved slave hypothesis." On this reading, Onesimus had some kind of falling out with Philemon (as implied by v. 18; see also v. 11). In response, Onesimus sought out Paul, a friend of his master whose whereabouts he knew or discovered, to mediate the conflict. Whatever this case (and these are but the two most widely held theories), the chained apostle leads Onesimus to faith in Christ (v. 10). Paul then composes a letter on behalf of "his son" before reluctantly sending him back (along with a letter of mediation/recommendation) to Philemon (vv. 12–13).

As to where the apostle might have been in chains when Onesimus became his son, three options are usually suggested: Rome, Caesarea, and Ephesus. For any number of reasons, few interpreters have opted for Caesarea. This leaves Rome (in the early 60s) and Ephesus (in the mid-50s) as the locations most commonly espoused for the composition of Philemon. Although we incline to Rome, our reading of the letter would not differ much, if at all, if it were demonstrated that the provenance of this letter were other than Rome.

Pliny the Younger to Sabinianus

Scholars often compare Philemon to the following letter from Pliny the Younger to Sabinianus on behalf of a freedman:

> Your freedman, whom you lately mentioned to me with displeasure, has been with me, and threw himself at my feet with as much submission as he could have fallen at yours. He earnestly requested me with many tears, and even with all the eloquence of silent sorrow, to intercede for him; in short, he convinced me by his whole behaviour that he sincerely repents of his fault. I am persuaded he is thoroughly reformed, because he seems deeply sensible of his guilt. I know you are angry with him, and I know, too, it is not without reason; but clemency can never exert itself more laudably than when there is the most cause for resentment. You once had an affection for this man, and, I hope, will have again; meanwhile, let me only prevail with you to pardon him. If he should incur your displeasure hereafter, you will have so much the stronger plea in excuse for your anger as you shew yourself more merciful to him now. Concede something to his youth, to his tears, and to your own natural mildness of temper: do not make him uneasy any longer, and I will add, too, do not make yourself so; for a man of your kindness of heart cannot be angry without feeling great uneasiness. I am afraid, were I to join my entreaties with his, I should seem rather to compel than request you to forgive him. Yet I will not scruple even to write mine with his; and in so much the stronger terms as I have very sharply and severely reproved him, positively threatening never to interpose again in his behalf. But though it was proper to say this to him, in order to make him more fearful of offending, I do not say so to you. I may, perhaps, again have occasion to entreat you upon his account, and again obtain your forgiveness; supposing, I mean, his fault should be such as may become me to intercede for, and you to pardon. Farewell.[1]

CENTERING THE VISION OF PHILEMON: NEITHER SLAVE NOR FREE

In Gal 3:28, Paul, perhaps citing a baptismal confession, declares that for those who have been baptized and clothed in Christ (Gal 3:26–27), "There is neither Jew nor Gentile, neither slave nor free, nor is there male and female, for you are all one in Christ Jesus." Paul's letter to Philemon may be valuably read as a real-life application of the declaration that there is "neither slave nor free" in Christ.

Paul does not think that the epithet "slave" best describes or captures Onesimus's deepest identity. Rather than a useless slave (or in the words of Aristotle a "living tool"),[2] the apostle regarded and referred to Onesimus as a useful son and desired for his master Philemon to see him likewise (vv. 10–11). Indeed, as Paul ponders Onesimus's return to Philemon and pleads for him, he calls on Philemon to perceive and receive him "no longer as a slave, but better than a slave, as a dear brother" (v. 16).

Furthermore, Paul says to Philemon, his beloved coworker and brother in Christ (vv. 1, 20), "If you consider me a partner, welcome [or receive] him as you would welcome [or receive] me" (v. 17). This admonition begs the question: How would Philemon receive Paul? The letter suggests an answer—he would receive him with joy and honor (cf. v. 22). Paul's

---

1. Pliny the Younger, *Letters* 9.21 (trans. William Melmoth).
2. Aristotle, *Nichomachean Ethics* 8.11.

request is bold, even outrageous. "Treat your slave Onesimus as you would treat me," he implores. What might this entail? Let us track the vision of the letter in search of an answer.

TRACKING THE VISION OF PHILEMON: PRAISING, PERSUADING, AND EXPECTING

The basic outline of Philemon is as follows:

1–3	Address and Greeting
4–7	Thanksgiving and Appreciation for Philemon
8–18	Paul's Appeal to Philemon on Behalf of Onesimus
19–25	Concluding the Letter

Paul commences his shortest preserved letter by depicting himself as a "prisoner" (cf. vv. 9, 13) and by mentioning Timothy as "our brother" (v. 1). Although a personal letter, it is by no means a private one. To be sure, Philemon, addressed and described in v. 1 as "our [i.e., Paul and Timothy's] beloved coworker" (trans. TDS), is the letter's primary recipient. But others are greeted: "Apphia, our sister," "Archippus our fellow soldier," and "the church that meets in [Philemon's] home." Furthermore, others join Paul and Timothy (v. 1) in sending greetings to the letter's recipients at the end of the letter: Epaphras, Paul's fellow prisoner, as well as Mark, Aristarchus, Demas, and Luke, Paul's fellow workers (vv. 23–24).

We highlight this point because of its import in interpreting the letter—the letter to Philemon was neither written nor received in a relational vacuum. It is not only Paul who knows Philemon's and Onesimus's "business," nor is Paul the only person who is interested in and will be impacted by Philemon's reception of Onesimus. By mentioning other believers by name at both the beginning and the end of this letter, Paul is seeking to impress on Philemon, albeit subtly, that they "were all baptized by one Spirit so as to form one body—whether Jews or Gentiles, slave or free—and . . . were all given the one Spirit to drink. Even so the body is not made up of one part but of many" (1 Cor 12:13–14).

Slavery in the Ancient World

In Paul's day, slavery was not based on race. Additionally, slaves had any number of duties and responsibilities, ranging from farming, mining, and milling to cooking, teaching, and managing. Furthermore, slaves were not infrequently freed from the shackles of slavery (a process known as manumission).

There is no mistaking the fact, however, that slavery in the Greco-Roman world was degrading, dehumanizing, and downright disgusting. Taken together, slaves were perceived and treated as property and were frequently subject to unimaginable punishments based on their masters' malevolent whims. Indeed, Roman historian Cassius Dio tells of an especially cruel slave owner, Vedius Pollio, who had slaves who displeased him thrown into a pool of flesh-eating eels (*Roman History* 54.23).

Paul continues his subtle, skillful communication to Philemon in vv. 4–7 by reporting his thanksgiving to God for Philemon. The apostle is grateful to God for the love and faith Philemon demonstrates toward "the Lord Jesus" and "all the saints" (among whom Onesimus would now be numbered) and prays that Philemon's "partnership in the faith" will "promote the knowledge of all the good that is ours in Christ" (vv. 5–6, RSV).

Paul also indicates that he has derived "great joy and encouragement" from the fact that the hearts [lit., 'bowels' or 'entrails'; Greek ***splanchna***] of the saints had been refreshed through Philemon (v. 7).[3] As we continue reading this letter, we will pay special attention to how Paul employs both the noun "heart" and the verb "refresh." His strategic repetition and placement of these terms is seemingly part of his delicate, yet deliberate, rhetorical strategy.

▲ Pictured here is a theater mask from the second century BC representing a slave.

Having praised Philemon, Paul begins in v. 8 to set forth his appeal for Onesimus, whom he does not mention by name until v. 10, after he is well into the letter. He begins his appeal by maintaining that he is sufficiently bold in speech to command Philemon what he ought to do vis-à-vis Onesimus (v. 8). That being said, Paul's preference is to give all due deference to Philemon and "to appeal to [him] on the basis of love" (v. 9). In doing so, Paul pours on the *pathos*, depicting himself as both an "old man" and as a "prisoner of Christ Jesus" (v. 9; cf. v. 1).

Having sufficiently "primed the pump," the apostle appeals to Philemon on behalf of "my son Onesimus," whose name we ought to note means "useful." It is not Philemon's slave for whom Paul appeals; rather, it is Paul's "son." What does Paul mean by this term? This fictive kinship language conveys an all-important, relationship-altering development—the imprisoned Paul had led the slave Onesimus to faith in Christ (v. 10). Although the apostle is willing to grant, perhaps for the sake of argument, that Onesimus was formerly "useless" to Philemon, he hastens to add that he is now "useful" not only to Philemon but also to himself (v. 11). In so doing, Paul serves up a delicious pun on Onesimus's name. In the past, Paul concedes, Onesimus did not live up to the meaning of his name. What may well have been truth then, however, is no longer the case. Onesimus is now decidedly and demonstrably useful.

Beginning in v. 12, Paul begins to support this bold assertion. The apostle indicates that he is sending Onesimus to Philemon. The decision to do so, however, was painful, for in doing so Paul was sending his "very heart." Even as Philemon had refreshed the *splanchna* of the saints (v. 7), by sending his very *splanchna* (i.e., Onesimus) to Philemon, the apostle is offering him refreshment. To part with one's heart is by no means easy and is not to be taken lightly.

Just as Paul labored to give birth to Onesimus (v. 10), he labored to let him go. Had he done what he wanted to do, he would have kept Onesimus at his imprisoned side so that he could take Philemon's place in helping him while he was in chains for the gospel (v. 13). Nevertheless, Paul thought it best to ask for Philemon's permission instead of his forgiveness—he did not want to do anything without his consent, so that any favor Philemon might do "would not seem forced but would be voluntary" (v. 14). Paul may not want to coerce Philemon, but he clearly wants to cajole him!

3. The Greek word *splanchnon* (sing.)/*splanchna* (pl.) literally refers to a person's "guts." Realizing that Paul is employing the term metaphorically in vv. 7, 12, and 20, the NIV rightly renders the term "heart(s)." By doing so, translators of the NIV do not, of course, have in mind the muscle that pumps blood through our bodies; rather, they employ "heart" to suggest a person's inmost self or feelings.

In fact, Paul goes so far as to wonder whether Onesimus's separation from Philemon was part of a larger divine plan (cf. Rom 8:28).[4] Although Onesimus was, for whatever unstated reasons, away for a while (lit., "for an hour"), it may well be, Paul muses, that Philemon could have him back for good (lit., "forever") (v. 15). Onesimus's return, however, will not be "business as usual." Neither will it be a mere interruption of the status quo. Rather, as he returns to Colossae, he will do so, the apostle declares, no longer as a slave, but more than a slave, as a beloved brother (v. 16). If Onesimus is a "beloved brother" who is "very dear to me," Paul maintains, he should be "even dearer to you," Philemon. The apostle propounds that this should be true for Philemon with respect to Onesimus, both as a fellow human being (lit., "in the flesh") and as a "brother in the Lord" (v. 16).

Having deftly set the literary stage, in v. 17 Paul finally sets forth his appeal. "If you consider me as a partner," the apostle commences, then "welcome [Onesimus] as you would welcome me," he concludes. If, perhaps, "he has done you any wrong or owes you anything," Paul states, then put it on my tab, "charge it to me," Paul requests (v. 18). Unsure of how Philemon will respond to Onesimus's return, the apostle seeks to leverage his relationship with Philemon for the sake of Onesimus.

If Paul has employed a scribe or **amanuensis** until now, in v. 19 the apostle takes over in the actual writing of the letter. Taking up the pen, he scrawls what amounts to an IOU. He assures Philemon that he is good for any and all debts that he might accrue relative to Onesimus. That being said, the apostle does not pass up the opportunity to remind Philemon of his profound indebtedness to him. He wryly writes, as it were: "I will pay it back, that is, anything you place on my bill because of Onesimus — not to mention [just to mention!] that you owe me your very self" (v. 20). Most interpreters figure that Paul is alluding here to the fact that he had at an earlier point in time also led Philemon to faith in Christ, perhaps in Ephesus, where Paul spent at least three years in ministry (Acts 20:31).

Referring to Philemon as "brother" (cf. vv. 7, 16), he expresses his desire that Philemon would give to him "some benefit . . . in the Lord" (v. 20). The term rendered "benefit" is *onaimēn* (from *oninamai*). We tell you this to alert you to the possibility of yet another Pauline pun (recall v. 11). Could it be that Paul is playing upon Onesimus's name (Greek *Onēsimos*) here, too? If so, then the apostle would be making a (not so) veiled request that Philemon send Onesimus back to him. This would be in keeping with what Paul said in v. 13: "I would have liked to keep him with me so that he could take your [i.e., Philemon's] place in helping me while I am in chains for the gospel." Such a reading would also be congruent with the final phrase of v. 20, where Paul asks Philemon to "refresh [his] heart [*splanchna*] in Christ." What Philemon has done for other believers — that is, refreshed their *splanchna* (v. 6) — Paul now asks him to do for him. How so? Paul does not say. But he seems to suggest that his *splanchna* would be refreshed if Philemon were to send back to him the one who is his *splanchna* (v. 12), none other than Onesimus.

Before the apostle sends greetings from coworkers and extends grace to Philemon, **Apphia**, **Archippus**, and unnamed others (vv. 23–25; the "your" in v. 25 is plural in

4. Note Paul's use of the innocuous phrase "he was separated" in v. 15, where the passive voice attempts to minimize Onesimus's culpability in departing from his owner.

Greek), he expresses confidence in and makes a final request of Philemon (vv. 21 – 22). Of what is Paul confident with respect to Philemon? He is "confident of [his] obedience." This is part of what prompted Paul to write in the first place (see v. 21). Given that Paul has not clearly and explicitly ordered Philemon to do anything (v. 8), it would seem that the obedience that the apostle has in view is not primarily to himself but to God (cf. Phil 2:12). Paul is so confident in Philemon that he knows that he will do even more than he asks.

In v. 22 the apostle makes an additional, final request of Philemon. He asks him to prepare a guest room for him, because he hopes "to be restored" [or "granted"] by God to Philemon and the church that meets in his home in answer to their prayers. This request serves as a none-too-subtle reminder that he is not simply dashing off a letter and washing his hands of this all-too-delicate matter. He cares about the outcome of this relational struggle even as he cares for all parties involved — Philemon, Onesimus, and the church to which they both now belong. Even if there is no easy answer to the problem that has arisen, Paul is mindful that the God who answers prayer can also reconcile relationships.

"The central meaning and purpose of the Letter to Philemon concern the difference the transforming power of the gospel can make in the lives and relationships of believers, regardless of class or other distinctions. Close study of the text [of Philemon] makes clear that Paul's primary focus is not on the institution of slavery but on the power of the gospel to transform human relationships and bring about reconciliation."[5]

PHILEMON: THE REST OF THE STORY

Having situated, centered, and tracked the vision of Philemon, two pertinent questions remain:

- What is it that Paul actually asks of Philemon?
- What became of Onesimus?

Although it is clear that Paul finds himself on the horns of a dilemma in writing to Philemon regarding Onesimus, beyond asking him to welcome Onesimus as he would welcome Paul (v. 17), it is not immediately clear what the apostle wanted and expected Philemon to do. Did he want him to accept Onesimus back as both a slave and a brother? Did he think that Philemon should receive Onesimus as a brother but no longer as a slave? While both readings are possible, we are inclined to think that Paul is less concerned with Onesimus's status whether "slave or free" (note also 1 Cor 7:21 – 25) and more concerned that Philemon send Onesimus back to Paul's imprisoned side as soon as possible, which may or may not result in his **manumission**.

In this little letter Paul does not offer us a treatise on ancient slavery. Nor does he unequivocally denounce this pervasive, systemic, ancient practice as evil. There is no shortage of explanations as to why the apostle does not do so. It is suggested, for example, that:

5. Cain Hope Felder, "The Letter to Philemon," in *The New Interpreter's Bible* (12 vols.; Nashville: Abingdon, 2000), 11:885.

Renowned Reformer Martin Luther (1483 – 1546) on Philemon

The epistle gives us a masterful and tender illustration of Christian love. For here we see how St. Paul takes the part of poor Onesimus and, to the best of his ability, advocates his cause with his master. He acts exactly as if he were himself Onesimus, who had done wrong. Yet he does this not with force or compulsion, as lay within his rights; but he empties himself of his rights in order to compel Philemon also to waive his rights. What Christ has done for us with God the Father, that St. Paul does also for Onesimus with Philemon. For Christ emptied himself of his rights (Phil. 2:7) and overcame the Father with love and humility, so that the Father had to put away his wrath and rights, and receive us into favor for the sake of Christ, who so earnestly advocates our cause and so heartily takes our part. For we are all his Onesimus's if we believe.[6]

▲ Martin Luther

- Paul did not/could not view slavery as sinister per se.
- Paul's conviction that Christ would return sooner rather than later caused him to be less concerned about altering social structures and practices.
- Paul did not think it his place to stipulate to believing masters (like Philemon) that they manumit or release believing slaves (like Onesimus).

The letter of Philemon is less about ancient slavery and more about an ancient slave's relationship with a master and subsequently with a master's friend. So, what became of Onesimus? The short answer is that we do not know. Whatever the outcome, however, the preservation of the letter suggests it was well received, and consequently, so too was Onesimus. Some have speculated that it was Onesimus himself who preserved the letter, along with the others that are now part the Pauline Letter corpus. Sometimes truth is stranger than fiction.

It would be no less remarkable if the Onesimus who served as bishop in Ephesus in the late first/early second century AD[7] were none other than the one-time "useless" slave of Philemon! Such a development would be consonant with the Pauline gospel, where the slave is regarded as brother and the master is called to sacrificial, Christlike service.

SITUATING THE VISION OF COLOSSIANS: INTRODUCTORY ISSUES

Frequently paired with Philemon and compared to Ephesians, Colossians is sometimes given short shrift. It is a letter, however, that has much to offer, not least its compelling vi-

6. Martin Luther, "Preface to the Epistle of Saint Paul to Philemon, 1546 (1522)," in *Luther's Works: American Edition* (ed. E. Theodore Bachmann; 55 vols.; Philadelphia: Fortress, 1960), 35:390.
7. Ignatius, *To the Ephesians*, 1 – 2.

▲ Lycus River

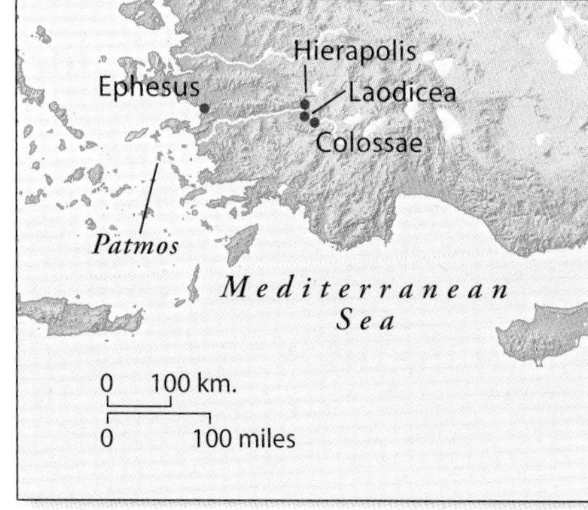

▲ Map showing the location of Colossae, where Philemon lived, as well as Hierapolis, Laodicea, and Ephesus

sion of Christ and life in him. We do well to dwell on it and on the One in whom "God was pleased to have all his fullness dwell" (Col 1:19; see also 2:9). As we continue this chapter, let us turn to consider this christological jewel of the Pauline corpus.

The City of and Church in Colossae

The city that Philemon and Onesimus appear to have called home no longer exists. Before it was reduced to rubble, probably by an earthquake, **Colossae** lay in the Lycus River valley. A one-time thriving market city, known for the purple hue of its wool, Colossae was located close to **Laodicea** and **Hierapolis** (Col 4:13). By Paul's time, Colossae was smaller and less influential than its Lycus River valley neighbors.

▼ Lycus River valley

Colossians indicates that someone other than Paul carried the gospel to Colossae. **Epaphras** was seemingly the individual who introduced the Colossians both to Christ and to Paul (1:7–8). It is possible that Paul had introduced Epaphras to the gospel, perhaps during the apostle's Ephesian ministry in the early to mid-50s. In any event, Colossians depicts Epaphras as a "dear fellow servant" and a "faithful minister of Christ," "who is one of you," that is, from Colossae (1:7; 4:12). The letter also places Epaphras with Paul at the time of writing (4:12; cf. Phlm 23, where Epaphras is said to be Paul's "fellow prisoner").

From Where, When, and by Whom Was Colossians Written?

According to Colossians, Paul was in chains when he wrote the letter (4:3, 18; note also 4:10). As to where and when the apostle was being held captive, the options are the same as they were for Philippians and Philemon and will be for Ephesians—Ephesus (mid-50s), Caesarea (late 50s), and Rome (early 60s).[8]

With Colossians (and Ephesians), however, there is an additional wrinkle. A number of contemporary scholars maintain that a Pauline disciple wrote Colossians after Paul's death, perhaps around AD 80. Interpreters who regard the letter to be pseudonymous have noticed differences in style and vocabulary between Colossians and the less-disputed letters of Paul. They have also detected christological, eschatological, ecclesial, and ethical variation. It is suggested that Colossians contains a more consistently exalted Christology, a more thoroughly realized eschatology, a decidedly expanded ecclesiology, and an accommodating ethic.[9] A number of interpreters also view a greater focus on Paul's apostolic office in Colossians to be a mark of inauthenticity (see esp. 1:24–2:5). Arguments against the letter's authenticity are complex, cumulative, and compelling to many and must be carefully weighed.

It needs to be noted, however, that a respectable case can still be made for the authenticity of Colossians. Some would seek to establish the case on theological grounds alone, contending that epistolary pseudonymity is incompatible with biblical canonicity.[10] Others who affirm the letter's authenticity have argued:

- The theological developments detectable in Colossians are not as drastic as some have imagined.
- The correlation between Philemon, an undisputed Pauline letter, and Colossians in terms of Pauline personnel is real, not contrived (cf. Phlm 1, 23–25 with Col 4:7–17).
- The differences between syntax and vocabulary are explicable, at least in part, by rhetorical conventions and contextual concerns.

---

8. If Paul were released from Roman captivity in the early 60s and rearrested (and beheaded) in the mid to late 60s, then it is possible that he could have written Colossians from Rome during his second imprisonment. Perhaps Paul could also have written Ephesians and (one of) the Pastoral(s) at this point in time.
9. For example, Colossians envisions Christ, "the head of the body, the church," as supreme, and as "the fullness of the Deity . . . in bodily form" (2:9). It also presents believers as "raised" and "seated" with Christ (3:1), tends to refer to the church trans-locally (see 1:24; cf. 4:15), and sets forth a "household code" akin to Greco-Roman ones of the time (3:18–4:1). While an interpreter can view all of these elements as logical developments of the theology Paul espouses elsewhere, it is the concentration of such detectable differences in Colossians that has given many scholars cause for pause.
10. See our more detailed discussion in chapter 2.

For our part, we think it probable (though not provable) that Paul penned Colossians from Roman captivity in the early (or perhaps mid) AD 60s.[11] Colossians was occasioned, it appears, by Epaphras's arrival in Rome. In coming to Paul, he shares with him both his ministerial successes and challenges in Colossae and in Laodicea and Hierapolis (4:13). Chief among Epaphras's concerns seems to have been the so-called "**Colossian philosophy**." It is this "hollow and deceptive philosophy" (2:8) on which Paul sets his sights and to which we now turn as we conclude our introduction to Colossians.

▲ The unexcavated tel of ancient Colossae

The "Colossian Philosophy"

What was the nature of the "philosophy" against which Paul rails in Colossians, and why was it such a source of concern to him? Let us consider these two questions in turn.

Interpreters of Colossians have construed the "Colossian philosophy" (sometimes pejoratively described as a "heresy" or "error") in various ways. Scholarly proposals regarding the nature of the "philosophy" include:

- Jewish Gnosticism
- Jewish apocalypticism and/or mysticism
- Hellenistic philosophies and religions[12]

While most scholars concur that there was in fact a "philosophy" Paul was seeking to combat, they disagree how best to understand and label the spiritual phenomenon against which the apostle polemicizes.

The first order of interpretive business is to note how Paul, less than objectively, describes the "philosophy," which comes into clear view in Colossians 2. In addition to deriding this movement as "hollow and deceptive," he contends that it "depends on human tradition and the elemental spiritual forces of this world rather than on Christ" (2:8; see also 2:20). Based on Christ's person and work (2:9–15), Paul enjoins the Colossians not to "let anyone judge you by what you eat or drink, or with regard to a religious festival, a New Moon celebration or a Sabbath day" (2:16). Furthermore, the apostle admonishes

11. Readers who are inclined to think otherwise can substitute "Paul" (or the more cumbersome "author of Colossians") for Paul in what follows. See more fully Todd D. Still, "Colossians," in *The Expositor's Bible Commentary* (rev. ed.; 12 vols.; Grand Rapids: Zondervan, 2006), 11:268–70.
12. See further Troy W. Martin and Todd D. Still, "Colossians," in *The Blackwell Companion to the New Testament* (ed. David E. Aune; Chichester: Wiley-Blackwell, 2010), 490–91.

the assembly not to "let anyone who delights in false humility and the worship of angels disqualify" them (2:18).

Lastly, Paul questions the Colossians regarding their willingness to submit to rules regarding handling, tasting, and touching (2:20–21). "Such regulations have an appearance of wisdom," he states, "but they lack any value in restraining sensual indulgences" (2:23). Given that they are in league with "elemental spiritual forces of the world" (2:20) and "are based on merely human commands and teachings" (2:22), such rules are to be eschewed, not embraced. Taken together, Paul thinks the purveyors of this "philosophy" are guilty of:

- "false humility" (2:18, 23);
- being "puffed up with idle notions by their unspiritual minds" (2:18); and
- having "lost connection with the head," that is, Christ (2:19).

The next order of business is to seek to determine more objectively the nature of the "philosophy." It appears that those whom Paul opposed for promoting a "hollow and deceptive philosophy" were advocating:

- certain Jewish religious observances linked to "diet and days" (2:16);
- visionary experiences involving angelic worship (2:18);
- a form of asceticism in conjunction with various regulations (2:18, 20–21); and
- procurement and promotion of a certain kind of spiritual wisdom (2:23).

While the precise background and nature of this "philosophy" remain unclear, it is manifestly clear that Paul is acutely concerned about the harmful effects it might have on the Colossians' commitment to Christ and to his body, the church. Whatever these "teachers" were selling, Paul says in effect, "Do not buy it!" Why does he say this? It seems that Paul thought that whatever they were peddling devalued and deprecated Christ, who must not be supplemented lest he be subverted. This explains in no small part why Christ's supremacy and sufficiency is so thoroughly woven throughout the fabric of Colossians.

CENTERING THE VISION OF COLOSSIANS: "CHRIST IS ALL"

Colossians 3:11 maintains that in the image of Christ "there is no Gentile or Jew, circumcised or uncircumcised, barbarian, Scythian, slave or free, but Christ is all, and is in all." It would be difficult to imagine a more suitable summation of Colossians than the declaration, "Christ is all, and is in all." Such christological claims and confessions suffuse Colossians. This is due in no small measure to the "philosophy" that the letter is seeking to combat.

Near the outset of Colossians the recipients are told that God "has rescued [them] from the dominion of darkness and brought [them] into the kingdom of the Son he loves" (1:13). This Son, through whom believers have redemption (further described as "the forgiveness of sins" [1:14]), is lauded as "the image of the invisible God, the firstborn over all creation" (1:15). It is in, through, and for him that *all things* were and have been created (1:16). What is more, "He is before *all things*, and in him *all things* hold together" (1:17, italics added). Little wonder that 3:11 affirms "Christ is all, and is in all."

But that is not all; the poetic meditation on Christ, frequently thought by scholars to be an early church "hymn," continues in 1:18 – 20.[13] There, the Son is said to be "head of the body, the church," as well as "the beginning and the firstborn among the dead." As God's "fullness," he brooks no spiritual rivals. The divine design was for the Son to have supremacy in *all* things (1:18 – 19). Through him and his bloody cross, God effects the reconciliation of *all things*, including Gentiles such as the Colossians (1:20, 22).

Wikimedia Commons

▲ This painting by Peter Paul Rubens (1577 – 1640), entitled "Descent from the Cross," captures one aspect of the rich Christology set forth in Colossians.

If previously concealed, the mystery that is Christ and his presence in the church is "now disclosed to the Lord's people" (lit., "his saints"; 1:27; 2:2). More than a mystery, however, "in Christ all the fullness of the Deity lives in bodily form" (2:9). No mere shadow, he is the "reality," the substance (2:17). Furthermore, the once-crucified, now-risen Christ is "seated at the right hand of God," and "the hope of glory" will appear in glory (1:27; 3:4).

For a rather small letter, at least by Paul's standards (4 chapters with 95 verses), Colossians makes a substantial christological contribution to the Pauline letter collection as well as to the NT canon. In addition to the well-known and oft-treated "hymn" of 1:15 – 20, wherein, as we have seen, the Son is extolled as the divine "image," "firstborn over all creation," "head of the . . . church," "the beginning," "the firstborn from among the dead," Colossians also proclaims Christ as God's fullness and mystery "in whom are hidden all treasures of wisdom and knowledge" (2:3). Furthermore, it is he, "the fullness of the Deity . . . in bodily form" (2:9), who has "disarmed the powers and authorities, [making] a public spectacle of them, triumphing over them by the cross" (2:15). In Colossians, Christ is all-encompassing. There is no aspect of reality (past, present, or future) that he does not touch and transform by his self-giving, death-defying reign.

As we track the vision of Colossians, we will discover the aim of such large, lavish christological claims. To anticipate Paul's purpose in composing this most christological letter, we might note in passing a pivotal, transitional verse: "So then, just as you received Christ as Lord, continue to live your lives in him" (2:6). Paul did not fashion Colossians as an academic exercise in Christology — as meaningful and valuable as such exercises can be.

13. Compare Col 3:16, where the Colossians are instructed "to teach and admonish one another . . . through psalms, hymns, and songs from the Spirit." See also our treatment of Phil 2:6 – 11 in chapter 7 above.

Rather, he wrote this pastoral missive to call the Colossian church to "firm" up her faith in Christ (2:5), a faith that Paul feared was in jeopardy.

The conflict in Colossae was not yet as acute as the crisis Paul had faced in Galatia, but he wanted to nip in the bud this pernicious influence before it bloomed into a full, less-than-fragrant flower. Having been informed by Epaphras of the serious situation confronting the assembly vis-à-vis the philosophy, the captive Paul issues a clarion call: recall and reclaim Christ as the One who is all and is in all, and allow him to undergird and guide every facet of existence. We now turn to see more fully how this call unfurls in the lines of the letter.

TRACKING THE VISION OF COLOSSIANS: FULLNESS AND FAITHFULNESS IN CHRIST

The Basic Structure of Colossians

1:1 – 14	Address, Greeting, Thanksgiving, and Prayer Report
1:15 – 23a	The Son's Supremacy
1:23b – 2:5	The Apostle's Ministry
2:6 – 3:4	Christ's Lordship over the Philosophy's Lure
3:5 – 4:6	Living as Christ's in the World
4:7 – 18	Concluding Instructions and Greetings

▼ The first page of Colossians from a twelfth-century manuscript known as Codex Harleianus 5557 or minuscule 32

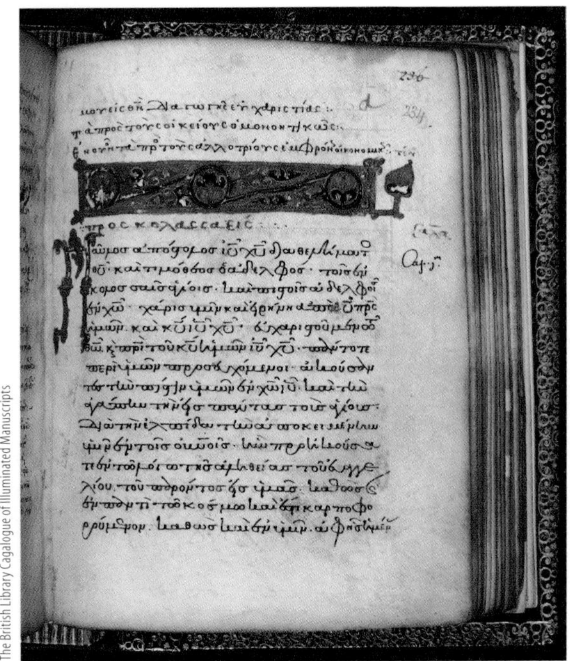

Address, Greeting, Thanksgiving, and Prayer Report (1:1 – 14)

Paul, "an apostle," commences Colossians by referring to his cosender Timothy, "our brother," by greeting the holy and faithful brothers and sisters in Christ in Colossae and by extending to the letter's recipients: "Grace and peace from God our Father" (1:1 – 2).

Greeting segues into thanksgiving, as Paul informs the Colossians of his prayers to God on their behalf. His gratitude springs from that which he has heard about their "faith in Christ Jesus" and their "love for all God's people." Such faith and love emanate from a heavenly hope, about which they heard in the gospel (1:3 – 5).

The gospel, grounded in and vivified by faith, love, and hope (cf. Rom 5:1 – 5; 1 Cor 13:13; Gal 5:5 – 6; 1 Thess 1:3), continues to bear fruit and grow, the apostle reports, not only in Colossae but also "throughout the whole world" (Col 1:6). Upon hearing and truly understanding the grace of God in the gospel, he knows that growing and fruit-bearing occur. Epaphras, whom Paul depicts as a "fellow slave" and "faithful minister of Christ," was responsible for teaching the gospel to the Colossians and for telling Paul of their "love in the Spirit" (1:7).

Despite the fact that the Colossians were not directly Paul's spiritual children, this did not lessen his sense of spiritual responsibility for them.[14] The apostle reports in 1:9 that from the time he learned of the "Colossian saints" he had not stopped praying for them. Even as he was thankful to God for the Colossians, he was prayerful to God on their behalf. Paul and his coworkers continually ask God to "fill [them] with the knowledge of his will through all wisdom and understanding that the Spirit gives" (1:9). Given the artificial wisdom and pseudo-understanding on offer in Colossae through the presence and influence of the "philosophers," such prayer would be apt, timely, and necessary.

The knowledge Paul covets for the Colossians is decidedly practical and ethical. The apostle's prayerful hope for the Colossian believers is that they would "live a life worthy of the Lord and please him in every way" (1:10). Leading lives worthy of and pleasing to God would result in their:

- "bearing fruit in every good work";
- "growing in the knowledge of God";
- "being strengthened . . . so that [they might have] great endurance and patience"; and
- "giving joyful thanks to the Father" (1:10–12).

There is much for which to give God thanks, and Paul will call the Colossians to be thankful later in the letter (3:15, 17; 4:2). Here, he offers the fellowship three reasons to be grateful "to the Father." He has:

- "qualified [them] to share in the inheritance of his holy people in the kingdom of light";
- "rescued [them] from the dominion of darkness"; and
- "brought them into the kingdom of the Son he loves" (1:12–14).

As we have already observed above, Paul proceeds in 1:15–20 to extol "the Son [God] loves, in whom we have redemption, the forgiveness of sins" (1:14). Before we pay additional attention to this majestic poetic meditation on the person and work of Christ, we do well to pause and note that there are a number of matters that Paul touches on at the outset of this letter that he will return to in due course. A representative list with corresponding verses continued later in the letter includes: faith (2:5, 12), hope (1:27), love (3:14, 19), the gospel (1:23), grace (4:6, 18), peace (1:20; 3:15), Epaphras (4:12–13), wisdom (2:3, 23; 3:16; 4:5), and knowledge (2:3; 3:10). One of the apostle's literary propensities is to "telegraph" at the outset of a letter various topics within a letter.

The Son's Supremacy (1:15–23a)

Mention of the Son's kingdom and redemption in 1:13–14 gives rise to an extended meditation on the Son, which is then applied to the Colossians (1:15–23). In what many scholars regard to be an early church "hymn," the Son's priority, power, and supremacy are stressed. Not only is he said to be the "image of the invisible God" (1:15a) and "the beginning" (1:18b), in whom God's fullness was pleased to dwell (1:19), but he is also described as "the firstborn

14. Note 2 Cor 11:28: "Besides everything else, I face daily the pressure of my concern for all the churches."

over all creation" and as "the firstborn from among the dead" (1:15b, 18b). The poem propounds that in, through, and for him "all things have been created" and that he who "is before all things" holds all things together (1:17). The cosmic Christ is also the church's Christ; the church's Lord is a crucified, reconciling, peacemaking Lord (1:18a, 20).

> In commenting upon Colossians 1:17, H. G. C. Moule made this memorable remark: "[Christ] keeps the cosmos from becoming a chaos."[15]

This Lord Christ turns foes into friends by means of his reconciling and life-giving death. Although the Colossians were once "alienated from God" and "enemies in [their] minds," through "Christ's physical body" God has enabled them to be "holy in his sight, without blemish, and free from accusation" (1:22). The recipients are responsible, however, for continuing in the faith and for holding to the hope of the gospel (1:23). Saving faith is continuing faith.

The Apostle's Ministry (1:23b–2:5)

The gospel embraced by the Colossians and served by the apostle is a gospel with universal reach (1:23b). Paul's suffering in Christ's stead is said to be for the sake of "his body, which is the church" (1:24); his service was occasioned by a divine commission to present God's word in its fullness (1:25). What was once concealed as a mystery is now revealed to those who receive the gospel, even to (or especially to) Gentiles by means of Paul's ministry (1:26).

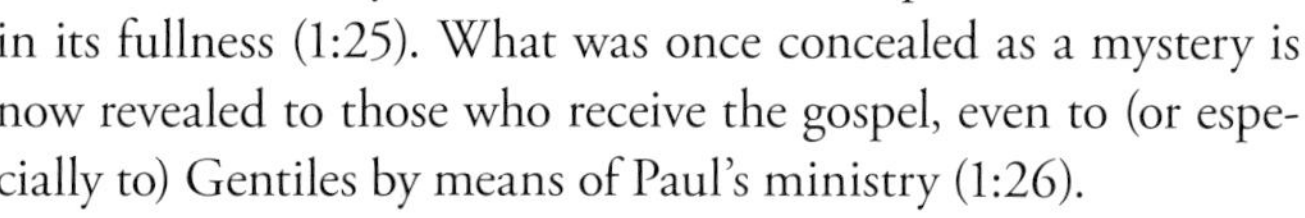

What is this mystery? That Christ's presence in the church's midst is the hope of glory (1:27). Paul's proclamation to the nations centers on the person of Christ (1:28). His admonition and instruction, bathed in wisdom, is aimed at presenting "everyone fully mature in Christ" (1:28). Paul dispenses this ministry (not infrequently marked and marred by difficulty) with all the energy that Christ enables (1:29; cf. Phil 4:13).

Paul informs the Colossians that his struggle in the gospel is for them, the Laodiceans, and all the other assemblies who have not met him personally (2:1). His ministerial aim is for both believers and outsiders (4:5) to know Christ, "the mystery of God" (2:2). For it is in Christ that "all the treasures of wisdom and knowledge" are hidden and may be more fully revealed and discovered (2:3). Paul highlights this point because he is both informed about and wary of the "fine-sounding arguments" that the "philosophers" are whispering in the Colossians' ears (2:4). Unable to be with them in person, the apostle regards himself as present in spirit (by means of the Spirit?) and rejoices in advance regarding the discipline and stability of their faith in Christ (2:5).

▼ The Chi Rho, one of the earliest christograms, is formed by superimposing the first two (capital) letters chi (X) and rho (P) of the Greek word ΧΡΙΣΤΟΣ = *Christ*. The Chi Rho pictured here, surrounded by a wreath, is on a lidless sarcophagus and signifies both Christ's crucifixion and resurrection. Colossians 1:18b–20 lauds the crucified and resurrected Christ.

Wikimedia Commons

15. H. G. C. Moule, *Colossians Studies* (London: Doran, 1898), 78.

Christ's Lordship over the Philosophy's Lure (2:6–3:4)

Having extoled Christ (1:15–20) and reflected on the Colossians' reconciliation to Christ as well as his ministry for Christ (1:21–2:5), Paul now turns his epistolary attention to combatting the "philosophy" directly. By means of this letter, the apostle "strenuously contends" against the "philosophy" for the spiritual stability and well-being of the assembly. We will not repeat here what we said above regarding the ostensible origin and particular nature of the philosophy. Rather, we will consider how Paul seeks to counter this movement. We do well to remember that the apostle is condemning a "hollow and deceptive philosophy" afoot in Colossae and not philosophical inquiry in general.

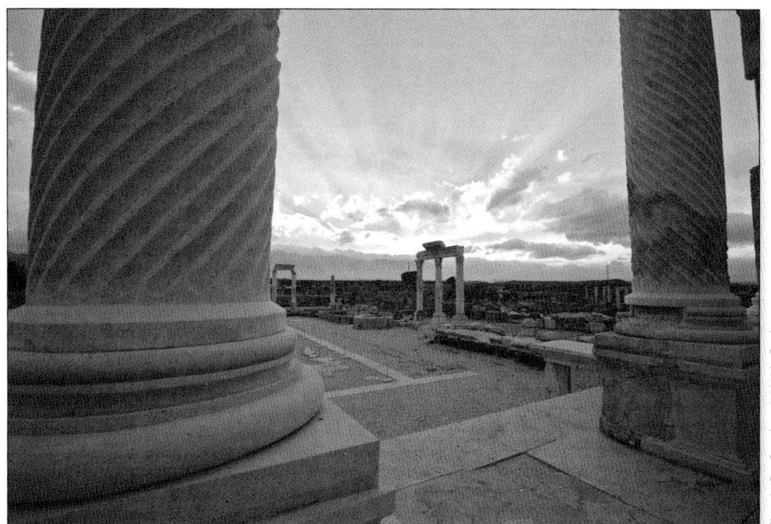
Photo by Ben Greenhoe, © 2012 by Zondervan

▲ Paul refers to Laodicea in Colossians 2:1 as well as in 4:13, 15, 16 (cf. Rev 1:11; 3:14). This photograph is of ruins in Laodicea.

At the outset of this section, Paul admonishes the Colossians to continue living their lives in Christ, whom they have "received" (2:6). A fourfold description of what typifies such a life follows. It is "rooted [in him]," "built up in him," "strengthened in the faith" that they were taught by Epaphras, and "overflowing with thanksgiving" (2:7).

Next, the apostle issues a pastoral warning: "See to it that no one takes you captive through [a] hollow and deceptive philosophy" (2:8). Not grounded in and focused on Christ, this "philosophy" runs the risk of leading the Colossians astray, that is, away from Christ. This would be a dreadful spiritual mistake. Not only does all of the fullness of Deity dwell in Christ in bodily form, and not only is Christ the head over every power and authority—including those being promulgated by the "philosophy"—but it is in Christ that the Colossians have been brought to fullness in life (2:9). It was in him that these Gentiles had been "circumcised," so to speak (cf. Rom 2:25–29), via baptism (2:11–12).

What is more, it was in Christ that they, once dead in their sins and in the uncircumcision of their flesh, had been made alive and forgiven (2:13). As a result of Christ's triumphant cross (an oxymoron to be sure), the spiritual indebtedness they had accrued and by which they stood condemned had been canceled, taken away, nailed to the cross. Moreover, Paul insists that at and through Christ's cross God both disarmed and shamed the "powers and authorities" (2:15).

Given the cosmic, apocalyptic reverberations and repercussions of the cross (see chapter 11 below), it is senseless and needless to slink back into the spiritual shadows. "The reality is found in Christ" (2:17). Paul pleads with the Colossians not to let the practitioners of the "philosophy" judge them relative to diet and days (2:16) or to seek to disqualify them based on their preferred angelic worship practices (2:18). The apostle regards the "philosophers" to be falsely humble and unspiritual (2:18). He goes so far as to contend, "They have lost connection with the head" (2:19).

Beginning in 2:20 and continuing through 3:4, Paul tells the Colossians, in so many words, to use their heads. It makes little to no spiritual sense, the apostle contends, for those who have "died with Christ to the elemental spiritual forces of the world" to live as if they "still belonged to the world" (2:20; cf. Rom 12:2). To be sure, regulations regarding handling, tasting, and touching "have an appearance of wisdom." They are, however, "destined to perish with use." Moreover, "they lack any value in restraining sensual indulgence" (2:21–23).

In his classic work *Christus Victor*, Swedish bishop and theologian Gustav Aulén (1887–1977) contended, "The work of Christ is first and foremost a victory over the powers which hold mankind in bondage: sin, death, and the devil." Colossians 2:15 lends biblical support to the so-called "Christus Victor" theory of the atonement.[16]

Instead of focusing on "earthly things" such as these, Paul enjoins the Colossians, who "have been raised with Christ," to seek and to "set [their] minds on the things above" (3:1–2). It is there where Christ dwells at God's right hand, and the Colossians dwell in Christ, who is their life. Indeed, having died with Christ, they are now "hidden with Christ in God." In God's good time, Christ will appear; when he does, they "also will appear with him in glory" (3:3–4).

Although Paul assures the Colossians that they have been raised with Christ (2:12; 3:1) and that their lives are "hidden with Christ in God" (3:3), he tempers the "eschatological already" (so-called "realized eschatology") with the "eschatological not yet" (so-called "future eschatology") by reminding the assembly that Christ has not yet come fully and finally in glory (3:4; cf. 3:6; 3:24–25).[17]

How should the Colossians live in the meantime? Paul will now turn his attention to this question. To anticipate the apostle's answer, although he calls the assembly to seek and to set their minds on the things above, he does not advocate a retreatist mentality or morality. Rather, he challenges the Colossians to be distinct in and different from their ambient culture.

LIVING AS CHRIST'S IN THE WORLD (3:5–4:6)

Negatively, Paul enjoins the assembly to "put to death" that which is earthly or unholy. To illustrate, he enumerates five vices they are to avoid. Sexual sins feature in this fivefold list, and greed is described as tantamount to idolatry (3:5). Such reckless disregard for God and the good incites God's wrath or judgment of sinfulness. In the past, the Colossians' lives were characterized by such patterns and practices. As those who have died and been raised in Christ, however, they must now rid themselves of attitudinal and verbal sins as well as sexual ones. A second five-item list of sins to avoid includes "anger, rage, malice, slander, and filthy language" (3:8). Furthermore, they are told not "to lie to each other," for dishonesty is not consonant with their new identity in Christ (3:9–11).

16. Gustav Aulén, *Christus Victor: An Historical Study of the Three Main Types of the Idea of Atonement* (trans. A. G. Herber; London: SPCK, 1931; New York: Macmillan, 1969), 20.

17. See further Todd D. Still, "Eschatology in Colossians: How Realized Is It?" *NTS* 50 (2004): 125–38.

Positively, Paul instructs the recipients to live out their new life as "God's chosen people, holy and dearly loved" (3:12). Five illustrative virtues follow: "compassion, kindness, humility, gentleness and patience" (3:13). Interestingly, the central quality of this catalog, humility, is juxtaposed to the "false humility" that is said to have characterized the "philosophers" (2:17, 23). Additionally, these Gentile converts in Colossae are to "bear with each other" and "forgive one another." Their model is none other than their Lord (2:13). Vivifying these seven virtues is love, for it is the tie that binds the virtues together in perfect unity (3:14).

Even as the Colossians' life together was to be grounded in forgiveness and bonded in love, the peace of Christ was to rule and the message of Christ to dwell in their midst. Their relationships were to be peaceful, and their fellowship and worship marked with gratitude in their teaching one other and singing to God "with all wisdom through psalms, hymns, and songs from the Spirit" (3:16). In sum, whatever they were to do, "whether in word or deed," they were to "do it all in the name of the Lord Jesus, giving thanks to God the Father through him" (3:17).

The *Paterfamilias*

The oldest living male, referred to as the *paterfamilias* or "father of the family," was the head of the Roman family. He had absolute authority over family members (including wife, children, and sometimes relatives) and over the household's business affairs, property, and religious practices.

Christ's holy and loving lordship was to be operative in every nook and cranny of the Colossians' lives, including home life. In what is likely the earliest "**household table or code**" in both Paul and the NT,[18] three pairings within an ancient Greco-Roman household are addressed: wives/husbands, children/fathers, and slaves/masters. In each instance a different "subordinate" is instructed first. Wives are enjoined to submit, whereas children and slaves are to obey. To whom are they to submit or obey? They are to submit to and obey one person with three distinct roles: the "head of the family" or "owner of the estate," the so-called *paterfamilias.*

Wives are to submit themselves to their husbands "as [it] is fitting *in the Lord*" (3:18). The phrase rendered "as it is" is ambiguous. Does it mean "because it is" or "to the extent that it is"? Regardless, one does well to note the christological orientation of their voluntary submission. Similarly, *children* are instructed to "obey [their] parents in everything" and are informed "this pleases *the Lord*" (3:20). *Slaves* are also told to "obey [their] earthly masters in everything" and are to do so "with sincerity of heart and reverence *for the Lord*" and "as working *for the Lord*." Their work is *for* and their future inheritance is *from the Lord.* Thus, they are to serve *the Lord Christ* (3:22–25). *The Lord (Christ)* clearly features in the instructions given to wives, children, and slaves. He is to be the ultimate object of submission and service.

As for husbands/fathers/masters, they are told to:

- "love [their] wives and [to] not be harsh with them" (3:19);
- "not embitter [their children lest] they become discouraged" (3:21); and
- "provide [their] slaves with what is right and fair" (4:1a).

18. See also esp. Eph 5:21–6:9; compare 1 Pet 2:18–3:7.

Procession, south wall of the Ara Pacis, Roman, (1st century BC)/Ara Pacis (Altar of Peace), Rome, Italy/The Bridgeman Art Library

▲ This processional frieze from the *Ara Pacis* ("Altar of Peace") in Rome shows Augustus as high priest of Rome accompanied by his family members.

At the conclusion of the "code," the masters (husbands/fathers) are reminded that they also have a *Lord in heaven* to whom they are subject and are to obey (4:1b).

Although this "household table" is understandably disconcerting to many contemporary Christians (not least because of calls for wifely submission), at the time it was written it afforded "subordinates" a degree of dignity (at least they are addressed) and a fresh interpretive frame through which to view their social/familial lot. Simultaneously, "superordinates" are reminded that they are not independent moral agents who can act indiscriminately with next to no accountability. On the contrary, they are called to cultivate a Christlike character (note again 3:19, 21; 4:1, where they are told to "love," "not embitter," and "provide . . . what is fair and right") and to remember that they are responsible for their actions both in the here and in the hereafter.

On the heels of instructions for households, Paul calls the Colossians to devote themselves to watchful, thankful prayer, including prayer for the apostle and the advance of the gospel through his clear proclamation of the "mystery of Christ" (4:2–4). As he concludes the body of the letter, he also admonishes the recipients to be wise in their interaction with outsiders and in their conversation with everyone (4:5–6).

Concluding Instructions and Greetings (4:7–18)

Paul concludes by informing the Colossians that one **Tychicus**, whom he positively describes as "a dear brother, faithful minister, and fellow servant in the Lord," will tell them about him (4:7).[19] Indeed, Paul is sending him, along with Onesimus (presumably the same person who featured in Philemon, here referred to as a "faithful and dear brother, who is one of you") to inform them about the apostle and to encourage them in the gospel (4:8–9).

Paul continues his conclusion by extending greetings on behalf of Aristarchus, his "fellow prisoner," and Mark, "the cousin of Barnabas," about whom the congregation had already received instructions and were meant to welcome (4:10).[20] Along with the otherwise unknown Jesus Justus, Aristarchus and Barnabas were "the only Jews among [Paul's] co-workers for the kingdom of God" who were with Paul. They had proven to be a comfort for Paul in the midst of his ministry and as he languished in prison (4:11).

19. Cf. Eph 6:21; 2 Tim 4:12; Titus 3:12; also Acts 20:4.
20. On Aristarchus, cf. Acts 19:29; 20:4–5; 27:2; on Mark, see Phlm 24; cf. Acts 12:12, 25; 13:5, 13; 15:36–41; 2 Tim 4:11; on Barnabas, see, e.g., Acts 4:36–37; 9:27; 11:22–30; 13:1–3; Gal 2:13; 1 Cor 9:6.

Epaphras, about whom we commented in 1:7–8, also extends greetings to the assembly. Paul assures the Colossians of Epaphras's prayers for their spiritual stability and maturity and of his industry on behalf of them, as well as for the fellowships in Laodicea and Hierapolis (4:12–13). Well-wishes in Christ are also extended from Luke, the doctor, and Demas (4:14).[21]

Paul then makes a few requests himself. He asks the Colossians to greet "the brothers and sisters at Laodicea," including a certain Nympha and the church that gathered in her house (4:15; cf. Lydia in Acts 16:40). Paul also instructs the church to make sure that once the letter he has written to them has been read, that it also be read to "the church of the Laodiceans." Furthermore, he tells them to read the letter that is coming their way from Laodicea, a letter that is sometimes identified with canonical Ephesians (see chapter 9 below). Such instruction signals that Paul regarded what he wrote for one congregation to be generally applicable and relevant to all of the churches. As we read Paul's letters over ancient believers' shoulders, we concur with this principle in practice.

A final "see to it" follows in 4:17, where Paul instructs the Colossians to tell Archippus (Phlm 2) to "complete the ministry [he had] received in the Lord." Paul's admonition to Archippus was the apostle's aspiration for all who named and claimed Christ. The apostle concludes Colossians by picking up the stylus and scrawling: "Remember my chains. Grace be with you" (4:18). Arguably, the Colossians needed to remember others, in this case Paul, lest they succumb to self-absorption; they needed grace to face their circumstances and challenges with freshness and wisdom from on high. We need no less.

Wikimedia Commons

▲▼ In concluding Colossians, Paul mentions Mark (top) and Luke (bottom) by name (4:10, 14). Pictured here are icons of these two leading figures in early Christianity.

WikiPaintings

CONCLUDING REMARKS

Commentators on Philemon and Colossians routinely observe that the letters share a number of names, not least Onesimus. Connections between these two Pauline Captivity Letters go deeper than this, however. Consider, for example, the christological link. Even as Christ is the common denominator between the various characters in Philemon, Christ stands at the center of Colossians. In fact, Christology radiates from the core of Paul's theology and animates his letter corpus. If Colossians articulates that "Christ is all, and is in all" (3:11), Philemon illustrates how this profound confession impinges on Christian interaction. In the memorable words of Col 3:17, "whatever [believers] do, whether in word or in deed," they are to "do it all in the name of the Lord Jesus, giving thanks to God the Father through him."

21. On Luke, see 2 Tim 4:11 and the so-called "we sections" in Acts (16:10–17; 20:5–15; 21:1–18; 27:12–8:16); on Demas, cf. 2 Tim 4:10.

» KEY PEOPLE, PLACES, AND TERMS IN PHILEMON AND COLOSSIANS «

Amanuensis
Apphia
Archippus
Colossae
"Colossian philosophy"
Epaphras
Hierapolis
"Household Code"
Laodicea
Manumission
Onesimus
Philemon
Splanchna
Tychicus

» QUESTIONS FOR REVIEW AND DISCUSSION ON PHILEMON «

1. What prompted Paul to write Philemon?
2. How did Onesimus come to be with Paul?
3. What do you think Paul wanted Philemon to do with respect to Onesimus?
4. What does the name *Onesimus* mean? How does Paul play upon his name and its meaning in the course of the letter? How does Paul describe his relationship with Philemon?
5. It is sometimes suggested that Paul seeks to manipulate Philemon. If this were true, would it bother you? Why or why not?
6. In Philemon, Paul does not explicitly denounce the institution of slavery. What are some possible reasons for his not doing so?
7. If you had written to Philemon, what, if anything, would you have done differently than Paul?
8. If you were Philemon, how would you have responded to Paul's letter?
9. How might Philemon be employed to combat the myth of the autonomous self?

» CONTEMPORARY THEOLOGICAL REFLECTION ON PHILEMON «

1. Why were subsequent generations of Christians so slow and reluctant to condemn slavery as inhumane?
2. Why do you think that the church preserved and should continue to read Philemon?
3. If you could write an ending to Philemon, how would it go?

» GOING FURTHER WITH PHILEMON «

In addition to the commentaries on Philemon that are conjoined with Colossians (see further below), we would recommend the following commentaries and special studies.

Commentaries

Arzt-Grabner, Peter. *Philemon.* Papyrological Commentary on the New Testament. Göttingen: Vandenhoeck & Ruprecht, 2003.

Barth, Markus, and Helmut Blanke, *The Letter to Philemon.* Eerdmans Critical Commentary. Grand Rapids: Eerdmans, 2000.

Hope Felder, Cain. "The Letter to Philemon." In *The New Interpreter's Bible* (12 vols.; Nashville: Abingdon, 2000), 11:881–905.

Osiek, Carolyn. *Philippians, Philemon.* ANTC. Nashville: Abingdon, 2000.

Still, Todd D. *Philippians & Philemon.* SHBC 27b. Macon, GA: Smyth & Helwys, 2011.

Special Studies

Barclay, John M. G. "Paul, Philemon and the Dilemma of Christian Slave-Ownership." *NTS* 37 (1991): 161–86.

Callahan, Allen Dwight. *Embassy of Onesimus: The Letter of Paul to Philemon.* Valley Forge, PA: Trinity Press International, 1997.

De Vos, Craig S. "Once a Slave, Always a Slave? Slavery, Manumission and Relational Patterns in Paul's Letter to Philemon." *JSNT* 82 (2001): 89–105.

Harrill, J. Albert. *Slaves in the New Testament: Literary, Social, and Moral Dimensions.* Minneapolis: Fortress, 2006.

Marshall, I. Howard. "The Theology of Philemon." Pages 177–91 in *The Theology of the Shorter Pauline Letters.* Cambridge: Cambridge University Press, 1993.

» QUESTIONS FOR REVIEW AND DISCUSSION ON COLOSSIANS «

1. What are some reasons that prompt a majority of contemporary scholars to conclude that someone other than Paul wrote Colossians? How cogent do you think their arguments are?
2. Based on Colossians, describe the "Colossian philosophy." Can you think of contemporary analogies to this "philosophy"?
3. Colossians is often thought of as a christological letter. Why is this the case? How does Colossians describe Christ? What impact might the letter's occasion have on the description?

4. How does Paul seek to counter the "Colossian philosophy"?
5. Do you regard the ethical instruction of Colossians to be "otherworldly"? Why or why not?
6. Summarize the instructions set forth in the "household code."
7. In conclusion, Paul mentions eleven other individuals by name. What, if anything, does this indicate about the Pauline mission?

» CONTEMPORARY THEOLOGICAL REFLECTION ON COLOSSIANS «

1. How much does it matter to you whether or not Paul wrote Colossians? Why?
2. Reflect on the contemporary (in)applicability of the "household codes."

» GOING FURTHER WITH COLOSSIANS «

Commentaries

Dunn, James D. G. *The Epistles to the Colossians and to Philemon*. NIGTC. Grand Rapids: Eerdmans, 1996.

Garland, David E. *Colossians/Philemon*. NIVAC. Grand Rapids: Zondervan, 1998.

Lincoln, Andrew T. "The Letter to the Colossians." In *The Interpreter's Bible* (rev. ed.; 12 vols.; Nashville: Abingdon, 2000), 11:551–669.

MacDonald, Margaret Y. *Colossians and Ephesians*. SP 17. Collegeville, MN: Liturgical, 2000.

Moo, Douglas J. *The Letters to Colossians and to Philemon*. PNTC. Grand Rapids: Eerdmans, 2008.

O'Brien, Peter T. *Colossians, Philemon*. WBC 44. Waco, TX: Word, 1982.

Pao, David W. *Colossians & Philemon*. ZECNT 12. Grand Rapids: Zondervan, 2012.

Still, Todd D. "Colossians." In *The Expositor's Bible Commentary* (13 vols.; Grand Rapids: Zondervan, 2006), 12:263–360.

Sumney, Jerry L. *Colossians: A Commentary*. NTL. Louisville: Westminster John Knox, 2008.

Thompson, Marianne Meye. *Colossians and Philemon*. THNTC. Grand Rapids: Eerdmans, 2005.

Wilson, R. McL. *A Critical and Exegetical Commentary on Colossians and Philemon*. ICC. London/New York: T&T Clark, 2005.

Wright, N. T. *The Epistles of Paul to the Colossians and to Philemon*. TNTC. Grand Rapids: Eerdmans, 1996.

Special Studies

Arnold, Clinton E. *The Colossian Syncretism: The Interface between Christianity and Folk Belief in Colossae*. Grand Rapids: Baker, 1996.

Barclay, John M. G. *Colossians and Philemon*. NTG. Sheffield: Sheffield Academic, 1997.

Beetham, Christopher A. *Echoes of Scripture in the Letter of Paul to the Colossians.* BIS 96. Leiden/Boston: Brill, 2008.

Bevere, Allan R. *Sharing in the Inheritance: Identity and the Moral Life in Colossians*. JSNTSup 226. Sheffield: Sheffield Academic, 2003.

Smith, Ian K. *Heavenly Perspective: A Study of the Apostle Paul's Response to a Jewish Mystical Movement at Colossae*. LNTS 326. London/New York: T&T Clark, 2006.

Wilson, Walter T. *The Hope of Glory: Education and Exhortation in the Epistle to the Colossians*. NovTSup 88. Leiden: Brill, 1997.

CHAPTER 9

EPHESIANS

CHAPTER GOALS

- To examine the issues that have primary impact on the study of Ephesians
- To highlight the central concerns and basic contents of Ephesians

CHAPTER OVERVIEW

1. Situating the Vision of Ephesians: In Search of a Setting
2. Centering the Vision of Ephesians: Gentiles as Heirs with Israel
3. Tracking the Vision of Ephesians: "Sit, Walk, Stand!"
4. Concluding Remarks
5. Key People, Places, and Terms
6. Questions for Review and Discussion
7. Contemporary Theological Reflections
8. Going Further

KEY VERSES

Ephesians 1:3: "Praise be to the God and Father of our Lord Jesus Christ, who has blessed us in the heavenly realms with every spiritual blessing in Christ."

Ephesians 2:8–10: "For it is by grace you have been saved, through faith—and this is not from yourselves, it is the gift of God—not by works, so that no one can boast. For we are God's handiwork, created in Christ Jesus to do good works, which God prepared in advance for us to do."

Ephesians 2:14–16: "For he himself is our peace, who has made the two groups one and has destroyed the barrier, the dividing wall of hostility, by setting aside in his flesh the law with its commands and regulations. His purpose was to create in himself one new humanity out of the two, thus making peace, and in one body to reconcile both of them to God through the cross, by which he put to death their hostility."

Ephesians 3:17b–21: "And I pray that you, being rooted and established in love, may have power, together with all the Lord's holy people, to grasp how wide and long and high and deep is the love of Christ, and to know this love that surpasses knowledge—that you may be filled to the measure of all the fullness of God. Now to him who is able to do immeasurably more than all we ask or imagine, according to his power that is at work within us, to him be glory in the church and in Christ Jesus throughout all generations, for ever and ever! Amen."

Ephesians 4:4–6: "There is one body and one Spirit, just as you were called to one hope when you were called; one Lord, one faith, one baptism; one God and Father of all, who is over all and through all and in all."

Ephesians 6:10–12: "Finally, be strong in the Lord and in his mighty power. Put on the full armor of God, so that you can take your stand against the devil's schemes. For our struggle is not against flesh and blood, but against the rulers, against the authorities, against the powers of this dark world and against the spiritual forces of evil in the heavenly realms."

© Ewa Studio/Shutterstock

▲ Ephesians has been called the Switzerland of the New Testament. The famed Swiss Alps are pictured here. With the probable exception of Romans, Ephesians has exercised more influence on Christian thought and spirituality than any other Pauline letter.[1]

If Christology animates Colossians, ecclesiology energizes Ephesians. In Ephesians the church is presented and celebrated as the body and bride of Christ. God has exalted Christ to be "head over everything for the church, which is his body," a body that Christ is said to love, feed, and care for (1:22–23; 5:29).

Frequently regarded and treated as a larger, later companion to Colossians, Ephesians has been lauded as "one of the divinest compositions of man," "the Bach of the Bible," "the Switzerland of the New Testament," and "the crown and climax of Pauline theology."[2] In this chapter, the third and final one on Paul's Captivity Letters, we will situate, center, and track the vision of Ephesians.

SITUATING THE VISION OF EPHESIANS: IN SEARCH OF A SETTING

The Occasion for Ephesians

Thus far in our study of Paul's letters we have emphasized the importance of knowing as much as possible about the circumstances surrounding the writing of a particular letter. In fact, the first characteristic of Paul's letters we noted in our introduction to part 2 of this textbook was their occasional nature. Ephesians, however, is an exception to the rule.

Besides Paul's captivity as a prisoner (3:1; 4:1; 6:20) and Tychicus's ministry as an envoy (6:21–22), the letter offers no concrete data regarding either the author or the audience. As a result, Ephesians is frequently regarded as the least occasional and the most general of the Pauline letters. This, however, is as strange as it is surprising. It is, to be sure, atypical for a Pauline letter to lack contextual details. But it is all the more unusual given that the letter is

1. So Raymond E. Brown, *An Introduction to the New Testament* (New York: Doubleday, 1997), 620.
2. See Klyne Snodgrass, *Ephesians* (NIVAC; Grand Rapids: Zondervan, 1996), 17.

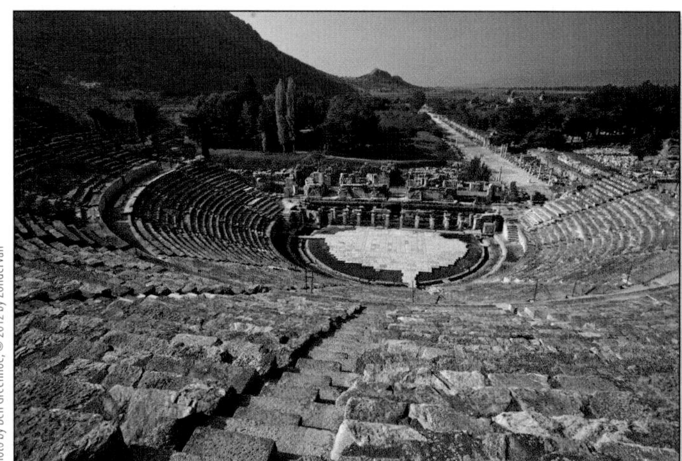

Photo by Ben Greenhoe, © 2012 by Zondervan

▲ Ruins of the Ephesian theater
▼ Library of Celsus

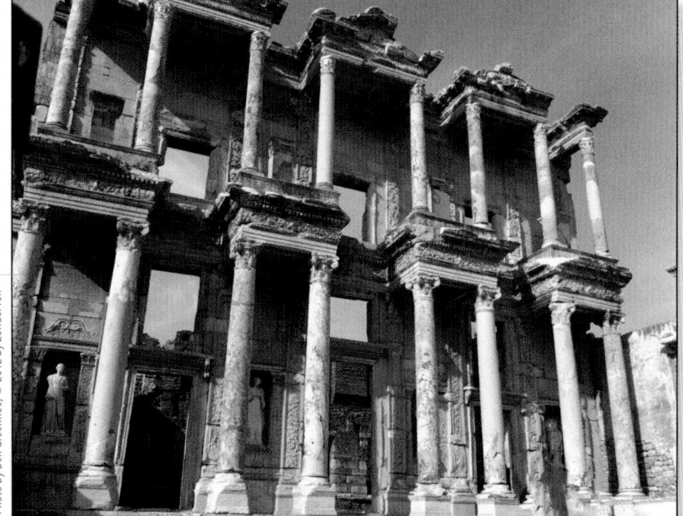

Photo by Ben Greenhoe, © 2012 by Zondervan

addressed to a place where Paul purportedly spent three years engaged in ministry (Acts 20:31).

As it happens, in the letter of Ephesians the writer and the audience do not even appear to know one another (1:15; 3:2). How might this be explained?

The Recipients of Ephesians

Ostensibly, Ephesians was written to "God's holy people in Ephesus, the faithful in Christ Jesus" (1:1b). Upon closer investigation, however, this may not have been the case. To be sure, the letter is known by the title "To the Ephesians," and the words "in Ephesus" appear in the vast majority of ancient witnesses. But "in Ephesus" is not found in several of the earliest and most important manuscripts.[3] It is probable, then, that we should follow the marginal reading in the NIV (which eliminates "in Ephesus") and read Eph 1:1b as "to the holy and faithful who are in Christ Jesus."

If Ephesians was not written to the Ephesian church, then to whom was it written? Perhaps the letter was initially addressed to the Laodiceans. As it happens, Col 4:16 encourages the church in Colossae to "read the letter from Laodicea." Additionally, in the second century, Tertullian's archrival Marcion referred to "Ephesians" as "Laodiceans."[4] Or perhaps, and more likely, Ephesians was written as a **circular letter** (an encyclical) for believers in western Asia Minor, and over time, it became associated with **Ephesus**, the leading metropolis in that region and one of the places where the letter was circulated and preserved.[5] In this chapter we sometimes refer to the letter's recipients as the Ephesians. It is conventional among Pauline interpreters to do so and less cumbersome than a number of other possible expressions.

3. These include the all-important Chester Beatty Papyrus II ($\mathfrak{P}^{46}$, dating to around 200) as well as the fourth-century Codices Sinaiticus and Vaticanus.
4. Tertullian, *Against Marcion* 5.17.
5. Ephesus is the first of the seven churches in Revelation (Rev 2:1–7).

The Authorship of Ephesians

If the audience of Ephesians is debated, so too is the authorship of the letter. Although purportedly from Paul (1:1; 3:1), a number of the letter's features have given scholars cause for pause. These include:

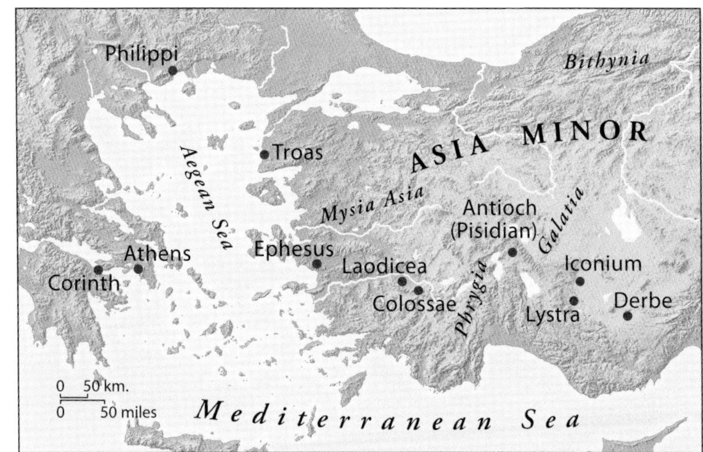

▲ This map locates Ephesus as well as other significant ancient locales in the Eastern Mediterranean.

1. the general, impersonal nature of the letter;
2. a concentration of un-Pauline vocabulary in Ephesians, as well as typical Pauline terminology employed in non-Pauline ways;
3. the expansive style of Ephesians, replete with long sentences including numerous clauses, phrases, and synonyms;
4. Ephesians' demonstrably close relationship to Colossians, suggesting dependence amid difference;[6]
5. the development of thought, particularly detectable along christological (more exalted than cruciformed), eschatological (more realized than imminent), and ecclesiological (more cosmic than local) lines; and
6. an apparently later setting than Paul's time, when the apostle's struggle with his fellow Jews over his **Gentile** mission was over and Paul's role within salvation history is described in retrospect.

So what is one to make of such observations? Whatever one's predilections regarding the authorship of Ephesians, it seems foolhardy to try to deny the decided differences between this letter and the nine other Pauline letters studied thus far.[7] Neither should such differences, however, be exaggerated. In truth, there is both an underlying unity and a rich diversity in the collection of all the twenty-seven documents we know as the New Testament.[8]

Once the smoke clears and the dust settles, there are two basic options regarding the authorship of Ephesians:

1. Paul composed or authorized the epistle during his lifetime.
2. A Pauline disciple wrote the letter in Paul's name after his death.

---

6. It is sometimes suggested that what Romans is to Galatians, Ephesians is to Colossians. For any number of reasons, this comparison is imprecise, not least because Romans, unlike Ephesians, is still a decidedly contextual letter. Recall chapter 6 above.
7. We also noted substantive differences between Colossians and the undisputed Pauline letters in chapter 8 above, as well as the differences in 2 Thessalonians in chapter 2.
8. See further James D. G. Dunn, *Unity and Diversity in the New Testament: An Inquiry into the Character of Early Christianity* (3rd ed.; London: SCM, 2006); also Richard B. Hays, *The Moral Vision of the New Testament: Community, Cross, New Creation; A Contemporary Introduction to New Testament Ethics* (San Francisco: HarperOne, 1996).

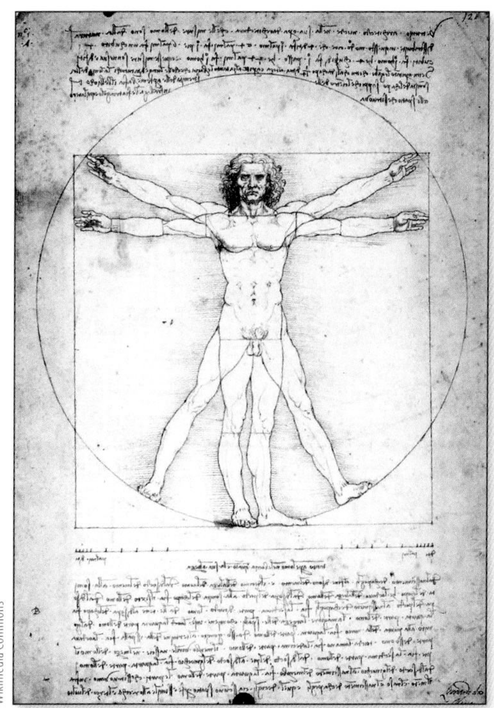

Wikimedia Commons

Todd Bolen/www.BiblePlaces.com

▲ In the Jewish temple rebuilt by Herod the Great, "a low balustrade separated the Court of the Gentiles from the temple proper. Placed in the wall were stones bearing the inscription, 'No man of another nation is to enter within the barrier and enclosure around the temple. Whoever is caught will have himself to blame for this death which follows.'"[9]

◀ Ephesians speaks of the church, comprised of both Jews and Gentiles, as one body in Christ. Pictured here is Leonardo da Vinci's (1452–1519) famous pen and ink drawing on paper known as "The Vitruvian Man."

If (1) were the case, then it is possible that Paul could have written Ephesians from any of his various captivities. By now, we know the options well: (1) Ephesus (mid-50s); (2) Caesarea (late 50s); and (3) Rome (early to late 60s, if Paul were twice a prisoner in Rome; if only once in Roman captivity, early 60s). If (2) were the case, then we do not know when or where Ephesians might have been written, though it is commonly suggested that a close companion of Paul (Timothy? Tychicus? Luke?) crafted the letter from or near Ephesus around AD 90.

As to our mind on the matter, a recent commentator captures well our present thinking when he writes: "I genuinely do not know whether Paul wrote Ephesians. I understand when others find that the evidence speaks more clearly one way or another; I am less certain. As an interpreter of this text, however, I am not disturbed by this situation." He goes on to note, "This sort of agnosticism . . . is made much easier to accept by the fact that the letter does not reveal a great deal about the occasion of its writing."[10] Whoever the author of Ephesians may have been, he refers to himself as Paul. In what follows, we will refer to the "author of Ephesians" in any number of ways, including "Paul."

---

9. See Everett Ferguson, *Backgrounds of Early Christianity* (3rd ed.; Grand Rapids: Eerdmans, 2003), 562.
10. Stephen E. Fowl, *Ephesians: A Commentary* (NTL; Louisville: Westminster John Knox, 2012), 27–28, 29. Were we forced to decide between (1) and (2) above, we would simply note that the preponderance of evidence in this complex, cumulative case presently appears to point toward (2).

CENTERING THE VISION OF EPHESIANS: GENTILES AS HEIRS WITH ISRAEL

Whereas Romans contemplates the grafting in of Gentiles and the mystery of Israel's salvation (Rom 11:11–32), Ephesians celebrates the unity of Jew and Gentile through Christ and considers the mystery of Christ to be "that through the gospel Gentiles are heirs with **Israel**, members together of one body, and sharers together in the promise in Christ Jesus" (Eph 3:6). While Paul was, of course, a Jewish believer and among those "who were the first to put [their] hope in Christ" (1:12), the letter's audience, comprised almost exclusively of Gentiles (2:11; 3:1), had more recently heard the gospel and believed in Christ (1:13). Ephesians exults in this mystery revealed to Paul and made manifest in his ministry, namely, that in Christ "we" (primarily Jewish believers) and "you" (largely Gentile believers) have become "us" (one body in Christ).[11]

Indeed, Ephesians envisions and exclaims a Christ who is and has effected peace between Israelite insiders and Gentile outsiders. "He himself is our peace," Eph 2:14 declares, "who has made the two groups one and has destroyed the barrier, the dividing wall of hostility."[12] Christ's purpose "to create in himself one humanity out of the two" and "to reconcile both of them to God" was brought about through his bloody cross. Through his death he has "put to death" hostility and enabled unity between the two parties (2:15–16). Jews and Gentiles are now one through the One who "came and preached peace to you [Gentile believers] who were far away and peace to those [Jewish believers] who were near. For through [Christ] we both have access to the Father by one Spirit" (2:17).

Through Christ's life-giving, peace-producing ministry and the apostle's pronouncement of this mystery, believing Gentiles are not only part of a new humanity and of one body (2:15–16), but they are part of a new family and are "members of [God's] household" (2:19). The "uncircumcised" (2:11) are "no longer foreigners and strangers, but fellow citizens with God's people" (2:19). If "the apostles [of the church] and prophets [of Israel?]" are foundational to this new temple hewn by and holy to the Lord, it is Christ Jesus who is the "chief cornerstone," in whom "the whole building is joined together and rises to become a holy temple" (2:20–21).

Although Gentiles have been swept into this stunning soteriological story authored by a God who loves greatly and is rich in mercy (2:4), their spiritual plight had not been bright. Indeed, in Ephesians' perception and portrayal, it was dim—no, dark (4:18)—for they "were dead in their transgressions and sins" (2:1). In this sinful state, they "followed the ways of this world and of the ruler of the kingdom of the air [presumably

▼ Ephesians 2:20 refers to Jesus as the "chief cornerstone."

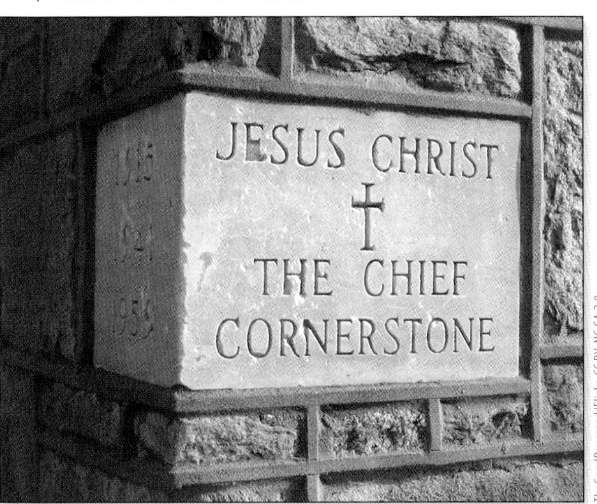

11. See this progression of pronouns in Eph 1:12–14.
12. On peace in the letter, see also 1:2; 2:17; 4:3; 6:15.

the devil]" (2:2; cf. 4:27; 6:11). Additionally, they, like the rest of wayward humanity, were bedeviled, led by fleshly cravings and deserving of wrath (2:3).

Despite having been in this sin-sickened and terminal spiritual state ("dead in transgressions" [2:5; note again 2:1]) in which they "were separate from Christ, excluded from citizenship in Israel and foreigners to the covenants of the promise, without hope and without God in the world" (2:12), they were "made alive" and "raised up" by God with Christ (2:5–6). This mind-bending, world-altering development is God's doing, a divinely ordained act of grace, a supernatural expression of kindness in Christ Jesus. Even as saving grace comes from God, it is to be embraced by faith and embodied by works (2:7–10).

In Ephesians, God's transformative work through Christ is cosmic in sweep and scope. Far from a special preserve or a tribal idol for a few, by virtue of his resurrection and session at God's right hand Christ is "above all rule and authority and power and dominion, and above every name that is named, not only in this age but also in the age to come" (1:21). The cosmic reign of Christ over all things is said to be for the church, which Ephesians presents as "his body, the fullness of him who fills everything in every way" (1:22–23). Far from being insular, smug, and self-congratulatory, however, Ephesians insists that the church's vocation is to make known "the manifold wisdom of God . . . to the rulers and authorities in the heavenly realms" (3:10).[13] Those raised and seated with Christ in the heavenly places are to show "the incomparable riches of [God's] grace, expressed in his kindness to [believers] in Christ Jesus" (2:7).

To be sure, all of this is rather "heady stuff." Ephesians is eager, however, that its Gentile recipients realize and actualize the hope to which they had been called, the riches of God's glorious inheritance in his holy people, and his incomparably great power for those who believe (1:18–19). The apostle wants the people to translate this lofty theology into lived reality, to both inculcate and incarnate these transformative truths.

How does the letter seek to aid its auditors in achieving this aim? In the first instance, as we have seen, Paul calls the Ephesians *to remember their new identity in Christ*. Formerly, as uncircumcised Gentiles, they were "without God in the world" and were following "the ways of this world" (2:2, 12). "But now in Christ Jesus" they "have been brought near" (2:13, 17). The Isaianic promise was coming to pass in the Prince of Peace (Isa 9:6). Through his blood and by his cross, Christ was in effect proclaiming, "'Peace, peace, to those far and near,' says the LORD. 'And I will heal them'" (Isa 57:19).[14]

By virtue of their new identity in Christ, Gentile believers were "no longer foreigners and strangers, but fellow citizens with God's people and also members of his household" (Eph 2:19). As "heirs together with Israel, members together of one body, and sharers together in the promise" (3:6), in Christ and through faith in him they, along with Jewish believers, may approach God with freedom and confidence (3:12). Blessed, chosen, adopted, redeemed, and forgiven in Christ, theirs is a great inheritance, one sealed by the Holy Spirit (1:3, 4, 5, 7, 13–14). Until the "day of redemption" for which they were sealed by the Holy Spirit (4:30), they are to strive to "reach unity in the faith and in the knowledge of the Son

13. For the expression "heavenly realms or places," see also 1:3, 20; 2:6; 6:12.
14. In its original context, "the far" referred to those still in exile and "the near" those in Judah.

of God and become mature, attaining to the whole measure of the fullness of Christ" (4:13).

▲ Roman period seal impression bearing an eagle's head and five emperor's profiles. Ephesians envisions believers as sealed by the Holy Spirit (1:13; 4:30).

Wikimedia Commons

Given their new identity and destiny as part of a new humanity and family called to unity and maturity, grounded in love,[15] Paul enjoins his Gentile audience *to embrace and exhibit a new morality for Christ.* Albeit ironic, he tells them emphatically, insisting in the Lord, that they "must no longer live as the Gentiles do, in the futility of their thinking" (4:17). To do so would be to both misapprehend and betray their new character and commitments, for from a decidedly pessimistic Jewish perspective the Gentiles (lit., "the nations" [Greek *ta ethnē*]) writ large are "darkened in the understanding and separated from the life of God" (4:18; cf. Rom 1:21, 24). Gentile outsiders are benighted and cut off because of their hard-hearted ignorance. Spiritually adrift and insensitive, these unbelieving Gentiles have no moral compass. They "have given themselves over to sensuality" and unbridled impurity (cf. Rom 1:24, 26, 28). What is more, "they are full of greed" (Eph 4:19).

In the not too distant past, this is who the Gentile believers addressed by Ephesians were and how they lived. They caved in to fleshly cravings, yielding to the "desires and thoughts" of the sinister power that is the Flesh (2:3). Uncircumcised in the flesh, they led lives controlled by the Flesh. Once dead and "darkness," they became alive and "light" in the Lord (2:1, 5; 5:8). Ephesians enjoins these "former Gentiles" who are now "dearly loved children of God" (5:1) to "live as children of light . . . and find out what pleases the Lord" (5:8b, 10). The "prisoner for the Lord" (4:1), an "ambassador in chains" (6:20), reminds them that the way of life they had learned as believers required them to jettison their former way of life, to put off their old self, to be made new in the attitude of their minds (cf. Rom 12:1–2), and to put on the new self (4:20–23).

To summarize, Ephesians aims to assist more recent Gentile converts to live a life worthy of the calling they had received (4:1). Given that such a "resocialization process" is fraught with sometimes confounding and always demanding challenges, the letter (which may be usefully thought of and instructively read as a catechesis of sorts) is meant to assist the audience in finding out what pleases the Lord (4:10).[16] To do so, it seeks to impress upon the recipients their new identity in Christ and does so, we might add, with significant rhetorical skill and profound theological insight. As those who have been incorporated into

15. John Paul Heil ("Paul and the Believers of Western Asia," in *The Blackwell Companion to Paul* [ed. Stephen Westerholm; Chichester: Wiley-Blackwell, 2011], 79–92 [on 87]) maintains, "Christian love is the theme central to the overall purpose of Ephesians." Heil goes on to note that in Ephesians the noun "love" occurs ten times, the verb "love" ten times, and the adjective "beloved" two times.
16. J. Paul Sampley ("Ephesians," in *The HarperCollins Study Bible* [New York: HarperCollins, 1993], 2192) suggests that the letter "is designed to guide [Gentile readers] from their baptism (4:5, 22, 24, 31; 6:11) toward their presentation as the unblemished bride of Christ (5:32–33)."

Christ and his church, it is now incumbent on them to abandon their "pagan" past and to walk in a way consonant with their new selves. Their new identity in Christ is to issue forth a new morality for Christ.

Ephesians 1–3, the so-called "indicative" or doctrinal section, focuses on the recipients' new identity in Christ. Ephesians 4–6, the so-called "imperative" or paraenetic section, concentrates on the recipients' new morality for Christ. Let us now turn to tracking the vision of the letter that we have just sought to situate and to center.

TRACKING THE VISION OF EPHESIANS: "SIT, WALK, STAND"[17]

The Basic Structure of Ephesians

1:1–2	Address and Greeting
1:3–23	Benediction, Thanksgiving, and Prayer Report
2:1–22	The Saving, Unifying Work of God in Christ
3:1–13	Paul's Ministry of the Mystery
3:14–21	Prayers to and Blessing of God
4:1–5:20	Unity, Maturity, and Purity in the Body of Christ
5:21–6:9	Mutual Submission in Familial Relations
6:10–20	The Spiritual Struggle and the Prayers of God's People
6:21–24	Tychicus's Mission and a Pauline Pronouncement of Peace, Love, and Grace

Address and Greeting (1:1–2)

At the outset of his letter to "God's holy people . . . the faithful in Christ Jesus," Paul describes himself as "an apostle [lit., "one sent"] of Christ Jesus by the will of God" (1:1). Later in Ephesians, Paul will reflect on his apostolic ministry to the Gentiles (3:1–13). Here, he claims that his apostleship was in keeping with the divine plan and purpose.[18] Paul's brief introduction concludes with a pronouncement of grace and peace upon the recipients (1:2).

Benediction, Thanksgiving, and Prayer Report (1:3–23)

As with 2 Corinthians and 1 Peter, Ephesians begins with a benediction. Commencing with the common Jewish prayer form "Blessed be" (NIV, "Praise be"), the apostle praises God for blessing believers with "every spiritual blessing in Christ" (1:3). Divine benefactions for the author and the audience include being chosen by God in Christ to be "holy and blameless" (1:4) and being predestined by God for "adoption to sonship through Jesus Christ" (1:5). What is more, believers have "**redemption**" in Christ as a result of God's prodigal grace (1:8).[19] Ephesians views "redemption through [Christ's] blood" (further described as "the forgiveness of sins") to be in keeping with the revealed will of God purposed

---

17. These three verbs are sometimes thought to capture "the basic dynamic in the thought of Ephesians." See Andrew T. Lincoln, "Ephesians," in *The Cambridge Companion to St Paul* (ed. James D. G. Dunn; Cambridge: Cambridge University Press, 2003), 133–40 (on 140). Believers are seated with Christ (2:6), are called to walk in Christ (5:1), and are equipped to stand for Christ (6:13).
18. The phrase "will of God/the Lord" or "his will" occurs elsewhere in Ephesians at 1:5, 9, 11; 5:17; 6:6.
19. On "redemption" (in historical context meaning the buying back of a slave or the freeing of a prisoner) in Ephesians, see also 1:14 and 4:30.

in Christ that in the fullness of time "all things in heaven and on earth" would be brought to unity under Christ (1:10). In addition, believers (whether Jew or Greek) have been blessed with "the promised Holy Spirit," who is depicted as "a deposit guaranteeing [believers'] inheritance until the redemption of those who are God's possession" (1:11 – 14).[20]

A succinct thanksgiving follows Ephesians' expansive benediction (1:15 – 16) and segues into a powerful, lengthy prayer (1:17 – 23). The apostle implores "the God of our Lord Jesus, the glorious Father" to give the Ephesians the Spirit (or a spirit) of "wisdom and revelation" so that they might know God better (1:17). Such divine enlightenment will enable them to know the hope to which God has called them and "his incomparably great power for [those] who believe" (1:18 – 19).[21] The power for which Paul is praying is the same power God exercised in the resurrection and session of Christ (1:20). As the resurrected, reigning One, Christ rules over (or is head over) all things for all time for the sake of the church (1:21 – 22), "his body, the fullness of him who fills everything in every way" (1:23).

Stated differently, the apostle is prayerful that the letter's Gentile recipients will realize and actualize God's enabling power made manifest in Christ and Christ's church. Paul wants them to recognize that the Spirit of him who raised Jesus from the dead is living in and among them (Rom 8:11).

The Saving, Unifying Work of God in Christ (2:1 – 22)

Far from being alive and empowered, at one time the Gentile Ephesians were spiritually impotent; indeed, they were "dead in [their] transgressions and sins" (2:1). In this state, they "followed the ways of the world and of the ruler of the kingdom of the air" and were subject to sinister powers and forces that hold sway over those who disobey (2:2). Despite the fact that these lesser lights darken instead of illumine and pale in comparison to the incomparable power of God, they are able to exercise a certain dominion over disobedient humans (cf. 6:11 – 12). Both Jew ("us") and Gentile ("you") believers once lived among the sons of disobedience, gratifying and following the will and desires of the Flesh as opposed to God. Both Jew and Gentile are "by nature deserving of wrath," sinful and powerless mortals in the presence of a pure, all-powerful, eternal God (2:3).[22]

Driven by "great love" for believers, and by extension outsiders, the God who is "rich in mercy" (2:4):

- "*made us alive* with Christ even when we were dead in transgressions" (2:5; cf. Rom 5:8);
- "*raised us up* with Christ" (2:6a); and
- "*seated us* with him [i.e., God] in the heavenly realms in Christ Jesus" (2:6b).

Why would God do such for sons of disobedience and children of wrath? Eph 2:7 answers: "in order that in the coming ages [God] might show the incomparable riches of his grace, expressed in his kindness to us in Christ Jesus."

---

20. On the Holy Spirit as "deposit," "pledge," "guarantee," and "seal," see also Eph 4:30; 2 Cor 1:22; 5:5. On salvation as inheritance, see also, e.g., Col 1:12.
21. The word "power" appears in Ephesians eight times (1:19 [2x], 21; 3:7, 16, 18, 20; 6:10).
22. Compare Rom 3:22b – 23: "There is no difference between Jew and Gentile, for all have sinned and fall short of the glory of God."

▲ Found in April 2010 near Frome in Somerset, England, the Frome Hoard contains 52,503 Roman coins. Ephesians 2:7 speaks of the "incomparable riches" of God's grace shown to us in the kindness of Christ Jesus.

Turning to Eph 2:8–10, a passage well known to and deeply loved by many, one encounters what might be thought of as the Pauline gospel in miniature. Here, salvation is said to be: (1) by grace through faith, and (2) a gift of God not from oneself, that is, not earned by works or through human striving. As a result, "no one can boast" (cf. Rom 3:27; 1 Cor 1:29–31). Following on from faith, believers come to recognize that "we are God's handiwork, created in Christ Jesus to do good works." This is in keeping with the divine design (2:10). According to Paul, humans are not to work for salvation, but believers are to continue to work out their own salvation with fear and trembling (Phil 2:12).

If Paul's Gentile audience now stands in a place of grace, this had not always been the case. In 2:11 he calls them to recall the time that they as uncircumcised Gentiles were:

- "separate from Christ";
- "excluded from citizenship in Israel and foreigners to the covenants of the promise"; and
- "without hope and without God in the world" (2:12).

But that was then; this is now. Now, once faraway Gentiles, who have heard the message of truth, the gospel of their salvation, and believed (1:13), "have been brought near by the blood of Christ" (2:13; cf. 1:7).

Christ has not only enabled salvation through his atoning death, but through the cross he has also eradicated the barrier, "the dividing wall of hostility," between uncircumcised Gentiles and circumcised Jews (2:11, 14, 16). Jesus came and announced peace to both Gentiles who were far away and Jews who were near (2:17). Furthermore, through his death he set aside "the law with its commandments and regulations" and reconciled Jew and Gentile to God and to one another (2:15). By creating "one new humanity out of two," the one who is peace made peace (2:14–15). Now, through Christ, both Jew and Gentile "have access to the Father by one Spirit" (2:18).

In 2:19, Ephesians reiterates that Gentiles are "no longer foreigners and strangers"; rather, they are "fellow citizens with God's people" and "members of his household." This household is "built on the foundation of both apostles and prophets, with Christ Jesus himself as the chief cornerstone" (2:20). Christ brings together the church and those who comprise it so that it/they might be "holy," a place and a people among whom God by his Spirit lives and dwells (2:21).

Paul's Ministry of the Mystery (3:1–13)

The thought of Gentiles being united with Jews to become a "holy temple in the Lord" prompts Paul to offer prayer and praise to God (3:1). Before doing so, however, the prisoner for the sake of the Gentiles reflects on his ministry to the Gentiles. Here, the apostle speaks of his ministry of the "mystery," both in terms of commission and revelation.[23] This mystery, heretofore hidden but now made known by God's gracious disclosure to Paul and other "holy apostles and prophets," is "that through the gospel the Gentiles are heirs together with Israel" (3:5–6).[24]

Even as Paul understood salvation as a gift of God's grace (2:8), he construed his role as a servant of the gospel to be a grace-gift, one for which he, as "less than the least" of all the saints, was unworthy.[25] Despite Paul's unworthiness, God grasped him and graced him "to preach to the Gentiles the boundless riches of Christ, and to make plain to everyone the administration of this mystery" (3:7–9). In so doing Paul was able to make known God's intent to use the church to make known "the manifold wisdom of God to the rulers and authorities in the heavenly realms" (3:10). Although recently revealed, this was in keeping with God's "eternal purpose that he accomplished in Christ Jesus our Lord" (3:11). Paul concludes this reflection on his ministry to the Gentiles by reminding his Gentile audience that in Christ and through faith in him believers can come to God "with freedom and confidence" and by asking them not to lose heart because of his sufferings on their behalf (3:12–13).

Baker Photo Archive. Istanbul Archaeological Museums.

▲ Relief on a sarcophagus depicting a sculptor's workshop. From Ephesus, Roman, second century AD. Ephesians 2:10 refers to believers as God's "handiwork" (Greek *poiēma*).

▼ The church is "to become a holy temple in the Lord" (Eph 2:21). Pictured here are remains of a second-century AD temple built in Ephesus to honor the Roman emperor Hadrian (ruled AD 117–138).

© William D. Mounce

Prayers to and Blessing of God (3:14–21)

Having apprehended and articulated his revelatory commission in decidedly apocalyptic terms,[26] the apostle now proceeds to pray for his

23. On Paul's ministry as a commission, see especially 1 Cor 9:17 and Col 1:25. On Paul's ministry as a revelation, note particularly Gal 1:12, 16; 2:2.
24. Cf. Rom 11:25; 1 Cor 15:51; Col 1:25–27.
25. See similarly 1 Cor 15:9 and 1 Tim 1:15.
26. Terms such as "mystery," "revelation," "power," "kept hidden," "wisdom," "ruler and authorities in the heavenly realms," "eternal purpose," and "sufferings."

Gentile audience on bended knee "before the Father, from whom every family in heaven and on earth derives its name" (3:15). He prays:

- that God might *strengthen* their inner being through his Spirit (3:16);
- that Christ might *dwell* in their hearts through faith (3:17);
- that they might *comprehend* the width, length, height, and depth of God's purposeful plan (3:18); and
- that they might *know* that Christ's love surpasses knowledge (3:19a).

Were such prayers to be answered, the Ephesians would "be filled to the measure of all the fullness of God" (3:19b).

Paul concludes his prayer for his audience with a doxological flourish. He extols God as "able to do immeasurably more than all we [i.e., believers] ask or imagine" (3:20a). God does so by empowering the church to do his work and will in the world (3:20b). This active, transformative God is to receive glory in the church and in Christ Jesus "throughout all generations" for all time. With the "Amen," the first major part of Ephesians ends. The benediction of 3:20–21 functions as a summation of chapters 1–3 and as a transition to chapters 4–6. God's cosmic, salvific, eternal work through Christ and the church is to continue through believers who live lives worthy of the one who called them.

"What is meant when Paul speaks of length and breadth and depth and height? Think of a sphere. The length is the same as the breadth and the height the same as the depth. So too all is proportional within the immeasurable infinity of God. A sphere is enclosed in a definite manner. God, being unenclosed, not only fills all things but exceeds all things. God is not confined but has everything within himself, so that he is the only one to be reckoned infinite. We cannot sufficiently thank him for the fact that, being so great, he deigned through Christ to visit human beings when they were subject to death."[27]

Unity, Maturity, and Purity in the Body of Christ (4:1–5:20)

Paul begins the "imperative" or "paraenetic" section of Ephesians (chs. 4–6) by urging or begging his Gentile audience to "live a life [lit., 'walk'] worthy of the calling" to which they had been called (4:1). They are to carry out this call with all humility, gentleness, and patience. Additionally, as they bear with one another in love, they are to strive to preserve the "unity of the spirit in the bond of peace" (4:3). As believers they are "one body" and share "one Spirit," even as they were "called to one hope." They also hold in common "one Lord, one faith, one baptism, [and] one God and Father of all" (4:4–6). Given that the number seven can signal perfection and completion, these seven "ones" may signify the full and total unity to which they were called and were meant to aspire.[28]

---

27. Ambrosiaster, *Epistle to the Ephesians* 3.18.2.
28. Cf. Phil 3:5–6, where Paul lists his sevenfold Jewish credentials. See further Todd D. Still, "(Im)Perfection: Reading Philippians 3:5–6 in Light of the Number Seven," *NTS* 60 (2014): 139–48.

To enable unity and maturity and thereby attain to "the whole measure of the fullness of Christ" (4:13), the once-descended-in-incarnation, now-ascended-in-exaltation Christ gave his followers gifts (4:7–10).[29] A smattering of such gifts, focusing on church leadership, appears in 4:11.[30] The express purpose of these gifts is "to equip [Christ's] people for works of service" (4:12a). Service for Christ and the fullness of Christ are linked. Furthermore, spiritual maturity leads to spiritual stability. Moving beyond infancy and its accompanying vulnerability to unsound teaching and deceitful scheming, mature believers grow collectively and individually in love into Christ, who is head, both as authority and source, of the body (4:14–16).

© William D. Mounce

▲ Growing up in Christ enables believers not to be like a boat, "tossed back and forth by the waves, and blown here and there by every wind of teaching" (4:14).

Having called his Gentile audience to unity and maturity in Christ, Paul next calls them to purity. In contrast to the past, they are to live the way of life they learned when they heard about Christ and were taught in him (4:20–21). They were taught to:

- "put off [their] former way of life, to put off [their] old self . . . corrupted by its deceitful desires" (4:22);
- "be made new in the attitude of [their] minds" (4:23); and
- "put on the new self, created to be like God in true righteousness and holiness" (4:24).

On a practical level, 4:25–5:20 addresses what putting off the old self and putting on the new self entails. Among other things, it involves putting off various vices. Verbal vices are especially singled out. Falsehood is to be put away (4:25). In addition, no "unwholesome talk is to come out of [their] mouths" (4:29). Furthermore, slander is to be set to one side (4:31), as is "obscenity, foolish talk [and] coarse joking" (5:4). The Ephesians are also instructed not to be deceived by "empty words" (5:6). Along with verbal vices, the recipients are to avoid attitudinal sins, including anger, bitterness, malice, and greed (4:26, 31; 5:3). Stealing (4:28), sexual immorality (5:3), and "any [other] kind of impurity" (5:3) are additional vices to be avoided. Such acts "are improper for God's holy people" (5:3), and "no immoral, impure or greedy person . . . has any inheritance in the kingdom of Christ and of God" (5:5).

A number of prohibitions are also woven throughout this section of Ephesians. For example, believers are enjoined not to:

29. Ephesians cites Ps 68:18 in 4:8 to support this point and proceeds to offer a christocentric interpretation of "he ascended" in Eph 4:9–10.

30. "Christ himself gave the apostles, the prophets, the evangelists, the pastors and teachers" (4:11). Cf. Rom 12:6–8 and 1 Cor 12:28–30.

- "let the sun go down while [they] are still angry" (4:26);
- "give the devil a foothold" (4:27);
- "grieve the Holy Spirit of God" (4:30);
- let even "a hint of sexual immorality" be among them (5:3);
- "be partners with [idolaters]" (5:7);
- have anything to do "with the fruitless deeds of darkness" (5:11);
- live "as unwise but as wise" (5:15);
- "be foolish" (5:17); and
- "get drunk on wine, which leads to debauchery" (5:18).

Coupled with this considerable list of prohibitions and vices to avoid, however, are various virtues to exhibit, commitments to keep, aspirations to realize, and values to embrace. Believers are instructed to speak truthfully because "we are all members of one body" (4:25). Those who steal are to do so no longer. Instead, they "must work, doing something useful with their own hands, that they may have something to share with those in need" (4:28). Unwholesome talk must not occur so that those who listen to what is spoken might be built up and benefited (4:29). The Holy Spirit must not be grieved, for the Spirit is the one who seals believers for the "day of redemption" (4:30). Believers are enjoined to "be kind and compassionate to one another, forgiving each other, just as in Christ God forgave you" (4:32).

What is more, as beloved children they are to imitate God (5:1) and "walk in the way of love, just as Christ loved us and gave himself up for us" (5:2). Sexual immorality, any kind of impurity, and greed are to be rejected out of hand, "because these are improper for God's holy people" (5:3). Thanksgiving is to replace "obscenity, foolish talk or coarse joking," for these are entirely out of place for God's people (5:4).

Furthermore, they are not to be partners with idolaters, described as "immoral, impure or greedy" people (5:5, 7). To do so would be to betray their new identity. They are not to be the darkness they once were (5:8) and are not to do the "fruitless deeds of darkness" they once did (5:11). Instead, as "light in the Lord," they are to expose deeds of darkness (5:11) and are to "live as children of light" and produce the fruit of light, which "consists in all goodness, righteousness and truth" (5:9). Such commitments are captured and inculcated by what may be a snippet of an "early Christian hymn" of unknown origin:

> Wake up, sleeper,
> rise from the dead,
> and Christ will shine on you. (5:14)

Ephesians enjoins believers to speak to one another "with psalms, hymns, and songs from the Spirit"; they are to "sing and make music from [their] heart to the Lord, always giving thanks to God . . . in the name of our Lord Jesus Christ" (5:19–20). They are to live carefully and wisely, "making the most of every opportunity, because the days are evil" (5:15–16). Forgoing foolishness, they are to "understand what the Lord's will is" (5:17). In short, they are to be filled with and to live by the Spirit (5:18).

Although it might be tempting to reduce this expansive section of ethical instruction (4:25–5:20), replete with "dos and don'ts," to some sort of checklist, it is far more than that.[31] The new morality that Gentile recipients are to embrace and exhibit as Christ-followers coalesces with and reinforces the new identity that is theirs in Christ Jesus. Being may well precede doing, but what believers do or fail to do reveals and reflects who they are or are not becoming. "Everything exposed by the light becomes visible—and everything that is illuminated becomes a light" (5:13). Believers are "to be made new in the attitude of [their] minds; and to put on the new self, created to be like God in true righteousness and holiness" (4:23–24).

Wikimedia Commons

▲ Ephesians 5:19 enjoins, "Sing and make music from your heart to the Lord." This tempera on paper shows the prophetess Miriam and other women celebrating the crossing of the Red Sea.

Mutual Submission in Familial Relations (5:21–6:9)

Ephesians continues by instructing that true righteousness and holiness are to be displayed in household relations, grounded in mutual submission "out of reverence for Christ" (5:21). The Ephesians "household code," set forth in 5:21–6:9 and labeled by the German Reformer Martin Luther as a *Haustafel* ("house table"), bears a number of similarities to the table we treated in Colossians (see chapter 8, above). "Subordinates" (wives, children, and slaves) are told to submit or to obey to their "super-ordinates." Wives are to submit to their own husbands, children to obey their parents, and slaves to obey their masters. Husbands/fathers/masters, who are one and the same (the *paterfamilias*), are also addressed and instructed to love their wives, to not exasperate their children, and to reward their slaves for doing good and to stop threatening them. The christological texture of the code in Colossians is also found in Ephesians.[32]

There are also, however, a number of differences between the household code in Colossians and the one in Ephesians. We would like to note three.

First, unlike Colossians, the code in Ephesians commences with a command for believers to "submit to one another out of reverence for Christ" (5:21). Although interpreters sometimes interpret 5:21 in conjunction with 5:20 and the preceding verses, we think it more likely that 5:21 serves as a suitable segue between 5:20 and 5:22, not only concluding 5:15–20 but also introducing 5:22–6:9. This view becomes all the more likely when it is recognized that 5:22 does not have a verb and is thereby dependent on 5:21 to supply one (i.e., "submit").

Second, the household code in Ephesians is considerably longer than the one in Colossians (twenty-one verses as opposed to nine verses). The greater length does not stem so

31. As we will note in chapter 13 below, Paul is not simply concerned with ethics (matters of morality), he is also concerned with *ethos* (fostering a Christlike community).
32. "Lord" occurs five times (5:22; 6:1, 4, 7, 8), and "Christ" appears seven times (5:23, 24, 25, 29, 32; 6:5, 6).

Goddess Vesta blesses a Roman wedding ceremony, Roman, (2nd century AD)/Ancient Art and Architecture Collection Ltd. /The Bridgeman Art Library

▲ Ephesians 5:25–33 likens the relation between husbands and wives to that between Christ and the church. The statue displayed here depicts an ancient Roman wedding ceremony.

▼ Third-century Roman relief showing a family meal. Ephesians 6:4 instructs fathers to "bring them [children] up in the training and instruction of the Lord."

Relief depicting a family meal, Roman, (3rd century AD)/Museo della Civilta Romana, Rome, Italy/ Giraudon/The Bridgeman Art Library

much from additional commands as it does from the rationale given to support the commands set forth.

Wives and husbands. Wives are told to submit themselves to their husbands not only because it "is fitting in the Lord" (Col 3:1; cf. Eph 5:22: "as you do to the Lord"), but also because the "husband is head of the wife as Christ is the head of the church," and even "as the church submits to Christ, so also wives should submit to their husbands in everything" (5:23–24). *Husbands* are told not only to "love [their] wives" and "not be harsh with them" (Col 3:19), but they are also told to "love [their] wives, just as Christ loved the church" (Eph 5:25). Furthermore, Ephesians contends that Christ "gave himself up," or "handed himself over," for the church so that he might make her holy and present her to himself as a "radiant church" (5:25–27). In the same way, husbands are to love their wives even as they do their own bodies. Even as they love their own bodies by feeding and caring for them, Christ feeds and cares for his body, the church (5:28–30). The citation from Gen 2:24 precedes a conclusion.[33] Christ's care for and union with his church is said to be a "profound mystery" (5:32; cf. 3:4, 6, 9; 6:19). Husbands who love their wives and wives who respect their husbands, however, are not meant to be a mystery or an oddity but a lived reality (5:33).

Children and parents/fathers. In Colossians, children are told to "obey [their] parents in everything, for this pleases the Lord" (3:20). Ephesians instructs *children* to "obey [their] parents in the Lord, for this is right" (6:1). Furthermore, Ephesians cites Deut 5:16, the fifth commandment—"the first commandment with a promise" (6:2–3).[34] As for *fathers*, they are simply told to "not exasperate [their] children" or provoke them to anger; rather, they are to "bring them up in the training and instruction of the Lord" (6:4).[35]

Slaves and masters. Instructions to slaves and masters are of similar length and substance in Colossians and Ephesians. In Ephesians, *slaves* are told to obey their "earthly masters" with respect, fear, and sincerity of heart "just as [they] would obey Christ" (6:5). They are to obey them not simply to win their favor but "as slaves of Christ, doing the will of

33. "For this reason a man will leave his father and mother and be united to his wife, and the two will become one flesh" (Gen 2:24 as cited in Eph 5:31).
34. "Honor your father and mother so that it may go well with you and that you may enjoy long life on the earth" (Deut 5:16 as cited in Eph 6:2–3).
35. In Col 3:21 fathers are told not to "embitter" their children lest they become "discouraged."

God from [their] heart" (6:6; cf. Col 3:22, 24b). Their wholehearted service is to be rendered to the Lord, for it is Lord who rewards those who do good, be they slave or free (6:7–8; cf. Col 3:23–24a). The comparatively truncated instruction to *masters* calls on them to reward their slaves for the good they do and not to threaten them. Such treatment of their slaves is to be informed by their knowledge of the fact that the heavenly Lord is the Master of them both and that he is not party to favoritism (6:9; cf. Col 3:25b; 4:1).

▲ A second-century AD Roman mosaic of four slaves serving two masters.

Third, the final difference to note between the Ephesian code and its Colossian counterpart is Ephesians' focus on the church. While the term "church" (Greek *ekklēsia*) does not appear in the Colossian code, it permeates the instruction given to wives and husbands in Ephesians. In fact, the word appears no less than six times in twelve verses. This is in keeping with the ecclesial vision and instruction in the letter (see esp. 1:22–23; 3:10, 20–21).[36]

We conclude our discussion of the Ephesian household code with a perceptive remark from one of the leading commentators on the letter.

> Justified twenty-first century sensitivities about the [code's] accommodation to patriarchy and slavery ought not to lead to an overlooking of the fact that this household code challenges the Graeco-Roman notion of household management as a constituent part of the state, replacing the rationale of loyalty to the state with that of submission in Christ.[37]

The Spiritual Struggle and the Prayers of God's People (6:10–20)

In conclusion ("Finally"), Ephesians enjoins its recipients to "be strong in the Lord" and to "put on the full **armor of God**" (6:10–11a). To put on the divine armor enables believers to "stand against the devil's schemes" (6:11b). Here, the apostle reminds the letter's auditors that their struggle is cosmic in scope. As Christ-followers, their battle is not with mere mortals ("flesh and blood"); rather, they are now engaged in an ongoing conflict with suprahuman, sinister powers—against rulers, authorities, powers of this dark world, and the spiritual forces of evil in the heavenly realms (cf. 1:20–21; 3:10; 4:9–10).[38]

Given the anticipated onslaught of evil intimated in their ongoing struggle, they are to "put on the full armor of God" and are to "stand firm" (6:13–14; cf. 6:11).[39] Pieces of the spiritual armor include: the belt of truth, the breastplate of righteousness, gospel-of-peace

36. The term "church" (*ekklēsia*) appears nine times in Ephesians (1:22; 3:10, 21; 5:23, 24, 25, 27, 29, 32).
37. Lincoln, "Ephesians," 139.
38. On the apocalyptic perspective that gives rise to a passage like 6:10–17, see chapter 11 below.
39. On the "armor of God" elsewhere in Paul, see 1 Thess 5:8 (cf. 2 Cor 6:7). Note also Isa 11:5; 59:17.

Model of Trajan's Column (Rome)/De Agostini Picture Library/A. Dagli Orti/The Bridgeman Art Library

▲ This panel from Trajan's column shows a Roman auxiliary troop. Ephesians 6 calls believers to "put on" and to "take up" the "full armor of God" (vv. 11, 13).

shoes, the shield of faith, the helmet of salvation, and the sword of the Spirit. How are they to overcome evil with good? How are they to win the spiritual battle? They are to do so by embracing and exhibiting truth, righteousness, peace, and faith and by leaning into and living out salvation and God's word.

Furthermore, they are to pray "in the Spirit with all kinds of prayers and requests" (6:18). They are to pray vigilantly and continually for other believers as well as for the shackled apostle so that he might fearlessly proclaim the "mystery of the gospel" (6:19–20). Once spiritually disobedient and impotent, these Gentile believers are now equipped and empowered to live confidently and fruitfully in a world where darkness impinges upon and seeks to snuff out light.

Tychicus's Mission and Paul's Pronouncement of Peace, Love, and Grace (6:21–24)

Ephesians ends with a commendation of Tychicus and his mission. Tychicus, who is similarly commended in Col 4:7–9 (cf. Acts 20:4; 2 Tim 4:12; Titus 3:12), is described as a "dear brother and faithful servant in the Lord" and is meant to tell the recipients how and what Paul is doing. Furthermore, he is being sent to encourage the Ephesians. Scholars who think that Paul wrote Philemon, Colossians, and Ephesians about the same time and from the same place—Rome in the early 60s being the leading candidate—sometimes suggest that Tychicus served as the courier for all three letters and delivered them at the same time.

Even as love laces this letter, it features in the final greetings. Love is linked with peace and faith in 6:23 and with grace in 6:24. Peace and grace are to reside with all believers "who love our Lord Jesus Christ with an undying love" (6:24).

CONCLUDING REMARKS

We conclude our introduction to Ephesians with a brief reflection. If Paul authored Ephesians, then he had thought through some issues afresh and anew prior to doing so—not least the nature of the church, the church's relation to Israel, his strategic apostolic role, and the problem and pervasiveness of "the powers." If Paul inspired but did not compose Ephesians, then one of his erstwhile followers and most gifted disciples had carefully and sufficiently thought through various works of his master—not least Colossians and Romans—in order that he might pen "one of the divinest compositions of man."[40] Either way, it has been our privilege to think the thoughts after the author and myriads of other interpreters. We now turn to do the same with one additional bundle of letters, the so-called Pastoral Epistles: 1 Timothy, 2 Timothy, and Titus.

40. Snodgrass, *Ephesians*, 17.

» KEY PEOPLE, PLACES, AND TERMS «

Armor of God
Circular letter
Ephesus
Gentile(s)
Israel
Redemption

» QUESTIONS FOR REVIEW AND DISCUSSION «

1. Why do a majority of contemporary Pauline scholars think that a Pauline disciple wrote Ephesians?
2. How important to you is it that Paul composed Ephesians himself? Why?
3. Who is the implied audience of Ephesians?
4. Why might Ephesians have been written?
5. What is a broad, twofold outline for Ephesians?
6. How does Ephesians describe its recipients prior to their conversion?
7. How does Paul describe his apostolic role in Eph 3:1 – 13?
8. For what does Paul pray for the Ephesians in Eph 3:16 – 19?
9. What are the seven "ones" set forth in Eph 4:4 – 6?
10. What is the nature of the gifts set forth in Eph 4:11?
11. What differentiates the household code in Ephesians from the one in Colossians?
12. What constitutes the "armor of God" according to Eph 6:14 – 17?

» CONTEMPORARY THEOLOGICAL REFLECTION «

1. How and in what ways do you regard the moral instruction of Eph 4:25 – 5:20 to be applicable today?
2. To what extent do you embrace the apocalyptic worldview espoused in Ephesians (and elsewhere in Paul)?

» GOING FURTHER «

Commentaries

Arnold, Clinton E. *Ephesians.* ZECNT 10. Grand Rapids: Zondervan, 2010.

Best, Ernest. *Ephesians.* ICC. Edinburgh: T&T Clark, 2001.

Fowl, Stephen E. *Ephesians: A Commentary.* NTL. Louisville: Westminster John Knox, 2012.

Hoehner, Harold W. *Ephesians.* Grand Rapids: Baker Academic, 2002.

Lincoln, Andrew T. *Ephesians.* WBC 42. Waco, TX: Word, 1990.

MacDonald, Margaret Y. *Colossians, Ephesians.* SP. Collegeville, MN: Liturgical, 2000.

Muddiman, John. *The Epistle to the Ephesians.* BNTC 10. Peabody, MA: Hendrickson, 2004.

O'Brien, Peter T. *The Letter to the Ephesians.* PNTC. Grand Rapids: Eerdmans, 1999.

Perkins, Pheme. *Ephesians.* ANTC 10. Nashville: Abingdon, 1997.

Slater, Thomas B. *Ephesians.* SHBC 27a. Macon, GA: Smyth & Helwys, 2012.

Snodgrass, Klyne. *Ephesians.* NIVAC. Grand Rapids: Zondervan, 1996.

Talbert, Charles H. *Ephesians and Colossians.* Paideia. Grand Rapids: Baker Academic, 2007.

Thielman, Frank. *Ephesians.* BECNT. Grand Rapids: Baker Academic, 2010.

Special Studies

Arnold, Clinton E. *Ephesians, Power and Magic: The Concept of Power in Ephesians in Light of its Historical Setting.* SNTSMS 63. Cambridge: Cambridge University Press, 1989.

Brannon, M. Jeff. *The Heavenlies in Ephesians: A Lexical, Exegetical, and Conceptual Analysis.* LNTS 447. London/New York: T&T Clark, 2011.

Darko, Daniel K. *No Longer Living as the Gentiles: Differentiation and Shared Ethical Values in Ephesians 4.17–6.9.* LNTS 375; London/New York: T&T Clark, 2008.

Dawes, Gregory W. *The Body in Question: Metaphor and Meaning in the Interpretation of Ephesians 5:21–33.* BIS 30. Leiden/Boston: Brill, 1998.

Gombis, Timothy G. *The Drama of Ephesians: Participating in the Triumph of God.* Downers Grove, IL: InterVarsity Press, 2011.

Heil, John Paul. *Ephesians: Empowerment to Walk in Love for the Unity of All in Christ.* Atlanta: Society of Biblical Literature, 2007.

Moritz, Thorsten. *A Profound Mystery: The Use of the Old Testament in Ephesians.* NovTSup 85. Leiden/New York: Brill, 1996.

Mitton, C. Leslie. *The Epistle to the Ephesians: Its Authorship, Origin, and Purpose.* Oxford: Clarendon, 1951.

Smith, Julien. *Christ the Ideal King: Cultural Context, Rhetorical Strategy, and the Power of Divine Monarch in Ephesians.* WUNT 313. Tübingen: Mohr Siebeck, 2011.

Yee, Tet-Lim N. *Jews, Gentiles and Ethnic Reconciliation: Paul's Jewish Identity and Ephesians.* SNTSMS 130. Cambridge: Cambridge University Press, 2005.

Yoder, Neufeld. *"Put On the Armour of God": The Divine Warrior from Isaiah to Ephesians.* JSNTSup 140. Sheffield: Sheffield Academic, 1997.

CHAPTER 10

THE PASTORAL LETTERS

CHAPTER GOALS

- To examine the issues that have primary impact on the study of the Pastoral Letters (Titus, 1–2 Timothy)
- To highlight the central concerns and basic contents of these letters

CHAPTER OVERVIEW

1. Situating the Vision of the Pastorals: Critical Concerns
2. Centering the Vision of Titus: The Epiphany of Grace and Glory
3. Tracking the Vision of Titus: Order for Cretan Congregations
4. Centering the Vision of 1 Timothy: Conduct in God's Household
5. Tracking the Vision of 1 Timothy: A Good Minister of Jesus Christ
6. Centering the Vision of 2 Timothy: Sharing in Suffering
7. Tracking the Vision of 2 Timothy: Passing the Faith Along
8. The Authorship and Contribution of the Pastoral Letters
9. Key People, Places, and Terms
10. Questions for Review and Discussion
11. Contemporary Theological Reflections
12. Going Further

KEY VERSES

Titus

Titus 2:11–14: "For the grace of God has appeared that offers salvation to all people. It teaches us to say 'No' to ungodliness and worldly passions, and to live self-controlled, upright and godly lives in this present age, while we wait for the blessed hope—the appearing of the glory of our great God and Savior, Jesus Christ, who gave himself for us to redeem us from all wickedness and to purify for himself a people that are his very own, eager to do what is good."

Titus 3:4–7: "But when the kindness and love of God our Savior appeared, he saved us, not because of righteous things we had done, but because of his mercy. He saved us through the washing of rebirth and renewal by the Holy Spirit, whom he poured out on us generously through Jesus Christ our Savior, so that, having been justified by his grace, we might become heirs having the hope of eternal life."

1 Timothy

1 Timothy 1:15–17: "Here is a trustworthy saying that deserves full acceptance: Christ Jesus came into the world to save sinners—of whom I am the worst. But for that very reason I was shown mercy so that in me, the worst of sinners, Christ Jesus might display his immense patience as an example for those who would believe in him and receive eternal life. Now to the King eternal, immortal, invisible, the only God, be honor and glory for ever and ever. Amen."

1 Timothy 2:5–6: "For there is one God and one mediator between God and mankind, the man Christ Jesus, who gave himself as a ransom for all people. This has now been witnessed to at the proper time."

1 Timothy 4:8–10: "For physical training is of some value, but godliness has value for all things, holding promise for both the present life and the life to come. This is a trustworthy saying that deserves full acceptance. That is why we labor and strive, because we have put our hope in the living God, who is the Savior of all people, and especially of those who believe."

1 Timothy 6:6–10: "But godliness with contentment is great gain. For we brought nothing into the world, and we can take nothing out of it. But if we have food and clothing, we will be content with that. Those who want to get rich fall into temptation and a trap and into many foolish and harmful desires that plunge people into ruin and destruction. For the love of money is a root of all kinds of evil. Some people, eager for money, have wandered from the faith and pierced themselves with many griefs."

2 Timothy

2 Timothy 1:9b–12: "This grace was given us in Christ Jesus before the beginning of time, but it has now been revealed through the appearing of our Savior, Christ Jesus, who has destroyed death and has brought life and immortality to light through the gospel. And of this gospel I was appointed a herald and an apostle and a teacher. That is why I am suffering as I am. Yet this is no cause for shame, because I know whom I have believed, and am convinced that he is able to guard what I have entrusted to him until that day."

2 Timothy 3:16–17: "All Scripture is God-breathed and is useful for teaching, rebuking, correcting and training in righteousness, so that the servant of God may be thoroughly equipped for every good work."

2 Timothy 4:6–8: "For I am already being poured out like a drink offering, and the time for my departure is near. I have fought the good fight, I have finished the race, I have kept the faith. Now there is in store for me the crown of righteousness, which the Lord, the righteous Judge, will award to me on that day—and not only to me, but also to all who have longed for his appearing."

In our introduction to part 2 of this volume, we noted one feature that characterizes a Pauline letter is its pastoral nature. It is appropriate to ask, therefore, why scholars label 1 Timothy, 2 Timothy, and Titus in particular as "The Pastoral Letters." Interpreters have referred to these three letters as "pastoral" for roughly four hundred years now because they focus on the care for and organization of churches.[1] In this chapter we will conclude our study of Paul's letters by examining these three letters addressed to two of his most faithful and capable coworkers—Timothy and Titus.

Timothy was one of Paul's closest coworkers (Phil 2:19–24). The cosender of six Pauline letters,[2] he was integral to the apostle's work in Philippi, Thessalonica, and Corinth.[3] The son of a Greek father and Jewish mother (Acts 16:1), Timothy is ostensibly in Ephesus when he receives both letters that bear his name.[4] As for Titus, he too was a valued Pauline companion. A Gentile, Titus was present with Paul at the "Jerusalem Conference"[5] and

1. The German scholar Paul Anton (1661–1730) is most often credited for being the first to employ the title "Pastoral Letters" to describe 1 Timothy, 2 Timothy, and Titus in 1726. Others had previously employed similar epithets to depict one of the three letters. Thomas Aquinus (1225–1274) referred to 1 Timothy as a "pastoral rule," and D. N. Berdot spoke of Titus as a "Pastoral Epistle" in 1703.
2. Namely, 2 Corinthians, Philippians, Colossians, 1 and 2 Thessalonians, and Philemon.
3. Note 1 Cor 4:17; 2 Cor 1:19; Phil 2:19–24; 1 Thess 3:1–6.
4. See 1 Tim 1:3; 2 Tim 1:18; 4:12–13.
5. See Gal 2:1–10; cf. Acts 15:1–29.

St Timothy, originally from Neuwiller (Lr. Rhine), French School, (12th century)/Musee National du Moyen Age et des Thermes de Cluny, Paris/The Bridgeman Art Library

Orthodox Church in America, www.oca.org

▲ Icon of Titus
◀ Stained glass of Timothy

played a pivotal role in the "Jerusalem Collection."[6] Titus was also instrumental in helping Paul to patch up ruptured relations with the Corinthians.[7] According to Titus 1:5, he receives Paul's letter while serving as a Pauline emissary in Crete.

Although written to Timothy and Titus, the Pastoral Letters are not about Timothy and Titus (any more than Philemon is about Philemon per se). Rather, these three personal Pauline letters are given over to instructions regarding "sound doctrine," church organization and offices, and ministerial and ecclesial practices. In each letter, Paul functions as a "senior minister" of sorts, taking "junior ministerial associates" under his aged, apostolic wing. While these three letters are unique among the Pauline corpus, we will approach them as we did the other ten we have studied thus far, namely, by situating, centering, and tracking their vision. While we will center and track the Pastoral Letters individually, we will situate them collectively.

SITUATING THE VISION OF THE PASTORALS: CRITICAL CONCERNS

We have discovered time and again in our study that there are decided differences of opinion among Pauline scholars. (This is also the case in other academic disciplines.) As we will see, this is no less true with respect to the Pastoral Letters. That being said, there are two significant issues about which almost all interpreters of Paul tend to agree relative to the Pastorals:

6. So 2 Cor 8:6, 16–24.
7. See 2 Cor 2:13; 7:6–7, 13–15; 8:6, 16–23; 12:18.

1. Paul's movements in the Pastoral Letters differ from what one finds in Acts and his other letters. That is to say, taken together the Pastorals present a "second career" for Paul, which is sometimes unhelpfully described as a "fourth missionary journey," in the Roman East subsequent to his captivity in Rome.
2. Second Timothy differs considerably from 1 Timothy and Titus in both context and contents.

These two observations lead to two related questions we will address below:

1. Was Paul released from a first Roman captivity in the early 60s?
2. Is it possible that Paul wrote at least one of the Pastoral Letters, perhaps 2 Timothy?

Acts concludes by reporting that Paul remained in Roman captivity "in his own rented house" for "two whole years" and "welcomed all who came to see him" (28:30). What happened to Paul after these two years? Scholars differ in answering this pertinent question, and their answers make a difference in how they construe and reconstruct the end of Paul's life.

On the one hand, a fair number of contemporary interpreters contend that Paul was never released from the captivity reported in Acts and was executed by Roman authorities in the capital city in the early 60s. Relatedly, these scholars regard the Pastorals as pseudonymous/allonymous documents written in the late first century or early second century AD[8] by a sympathetic Pauline disciple, or disciples, in his name after his death. On the other hand, other interpreters propound that the apostle was released from the Roman captivity of which Acts speaks. Thereafter, they posit, Paul continued his ministry by returning to some of the places referred to in the Pastorals before he returned or was taken

▼ Timothy pictured here with Paul

8. Other reasons scholars consider the Pastoral Letters to be pseudonymous include:

- late (second half of the second century) and less-than-universal attestation
- a concentration of terms and expressions not found in Paul's other letters and an absence of other terms and expressions that do occur
- the nature of the views purportedly espoused by opponents
- a more advanced form of church leadership and order than found in the other letters of Paul

As with 2 Thessalonians, Colossians, and Ephesians, there are multiple considerations that lead scholars to conclude that the Pastoral Letters are pseudonymous—that is, the case is cumulative. That being said, if Paul was dead at the time these documents were presumably written, then from a historical perspective these other observations—astute though they may be—only "gild the lily."

to Rome for a second period of captivity, which ended in his execution in the mid to late 60s. These scholars remain open to the possibility that Paul composed at least one of the Pastorals.

Although the second scenario is sometimes dismissed out of hand as "sheer speculation,"[9] such out-of-hand dismissiveness fails to take into account the evidence at hand. There are at least two pieces of textual evidence that should be placed on the table for consideration and closer inspection. The first is found in a document known as *1 Clement*, which was likely written in Rome and sent to the church in Corinth near the close of the first century. The pertinent passage runs as follows:

> After [Paul] had been seven times in chains, had been driven into exile, had been stoned, and had preached in the east and in the west, he won the genuine glory for his faith, having taught righteousness to the whole world and having reached the farthest limits of the west. Finally, when he had given testimony before the rulers, he thus departed from the world and went to the holy place, having become an outstanding example of patient endurance. (*1 Clement* 5.6–7)[10]

For our purposes, the pressing interpretive question arising from this text is what *1 Clement* meant by "the farthest limits of the west." While some scholars are inclined to think that Clement has Rome in view, others regard Spain to be the more likely referent.[11] If *1 Clement* can be trusted and if *1 Clement* did in fact have Spain in view, this is early evidence suggesting that Paul traveled to Spain after his first Roman imprisonment.

The other text is both later and clearer than *1 Clement* 5.7. In *History of the Church* 2.22, Eusebius of Caesarea (about AD 263–339) wrote the following:

> There is evidence that, having been brought to trial, the apostle again set out on the ministry of preaching, and having appeared a second time in the same city found fulfillment in his martyrdom. In the course of this imprisonment he composed the second Epistle to Timothy.[12]

While a number of scholars regard both of these texts to be tendentious, at the least they raise the possibility of Paul having been released from an initial Roman captivity and of having written 2 Timothy.

Where does this discussion lead and leave us? It puts us in position where we may now center and track the vision of each Pastoral Letter. Before doing so, however, two other prefatory remarks are in order. (1) We will treat the Pastoral Letters in the following sequence: Titus, 1 Timothy, and 2 Timothy. In addition to there being a particular logic to discussing the letters in this order, such an arrangement appears to have antiquity on its side.[13]

(2) For the time being, we will leave open the question of authorship. As with Ephesians, in centering and tracking a given Pastoral Letter's vision, we will refer to the author variously,

---

9. Jouette M. Bassler, "The First Letter of Paul to Timothy," in *The HarperCollins Study Bible* (New York: HarperCollins, 1993), 2229.
10. See Michael W. Holmes, trans. and ed., *The Apostolic Fathers in English* (3rd ed.; Grand Rapids: Baker Academic, 2006), 45.
11. Jerome Murphy-O'Connor (*Paul: A Critical Life* [Oxford: Oxford University Press, 1997], 361) insists, "From the perspective of someone writing from Rome [as was Clement], 'the boundary of the setting (of the sun)' [= 'the farthest limits of the west'] can only mean Spain."
12. Eusebius, *History of the Church* 2.22 (trans. G. A. Williamson; London: Penguin, 1989).
13. The logic is this: In Titus there is a less-developed church structure than in 1 Timothy, and in 2 Timothy Paul is near death. The Muratorian Fragment orders the Pastorals as follows: Titus, 1 Timothy, and 2 Timothy. See more fully Raymond E. Brown, *An Introduction to the New Testament* (New York: Doubleday, 1997), 640.

not infrequently as Paul. Having "tasted and seen" (note Ps 34:8; cf. 1 Pet 2:3) the Pastorals on their own terms (after all, the "proof is in the tasting"), we will be in a better position to deal with the sticky wicket of authorship. We will return to this matter as we conclude the chapter.

CENTERING THE VISION OF TITUS: THE EPIPHANY OF GRACE AND GLORY

Matters of church order, orthodoxy ("right belief"), and orthopraxy ("right behavior") mark the Pastoral Letter of Titus. Woven into the various instructions that will occupy our attention, however, are two liturgical-like texts that offer a theological foundation and orientation for the letter's manifold exhortations. The first of the two follows instructions that Titus is supposed to give to older men and women, younger men and women, and slaves (2:1 – 10). Paul instructs Titus to teach slaves in such a way that "they will make the teaching about God our Savior attractive" (2:10), and then he writes:

> For the grace of God has appeared that offers salvation to all people. It teaches us to say "No" to ungodliness and worldly passions, and to live self-controlled, upright and godly lives in his present age, while we wait for the blessed hope — the appearing of the glory of our great God and Savior, Jesus Christ, who gave himself for us to redeem us from all wickedness and to purify for himself a people that are his very own, eager to do what is good. (2:11 – 14)

The "grace of God" made manifest in Jesus Christ is both to instruct and inspire believers as they await the second manifestation ("the blessed hope") of the one who gave himself to save people from themselves and for himself.

A second creedal-like saying that is said to be sure (3:8; cf. 1:13) appears in 3:4 – 7:

> But when the kindness and love of God our Savior appeared, he saved us, not because of righteous things we had done, but because of his mercy. He saved us through the washing of rebirth and renewal by the Holy Spirit, whom he poured out on us generously through Jesus Christ our Savior, so that, having been justified by his grace, we might become heirs having the hope of eternal life.

The "kindness and love of God our Savior" made manifest in Christ (3:4) stand in stark contrast to the sinful enslavement in which the author and audience once lived (3:3). So, too, such divine kindness and love mingled with grace enable salvation. This salvation, depicted as justification by grace, is a testament of divine mercy, not human activity (3:5, 7). What is more, God's generous provision of the Holy Spirit through Jesus Christ allows for rebirth, renewal, and (as heirs) the hope of eternal life (3:5 – 7).

TRACKING THE VISION OF TITUS: ORDER FOR CRETAN CONGREGATIONS

The Basic Structure of Titus

1:1 – 4	Letter Opening: Address and Greeting
1:5 – 16	Appointing Elders and Opposing Disruptive Teachers
2:1 – 10	Teaching Sound Doctrine and Offering Pastoral Instruction
2:11 – 3:11	Grace and Good Works
3:12 – 15	Final Instructions and Greetings

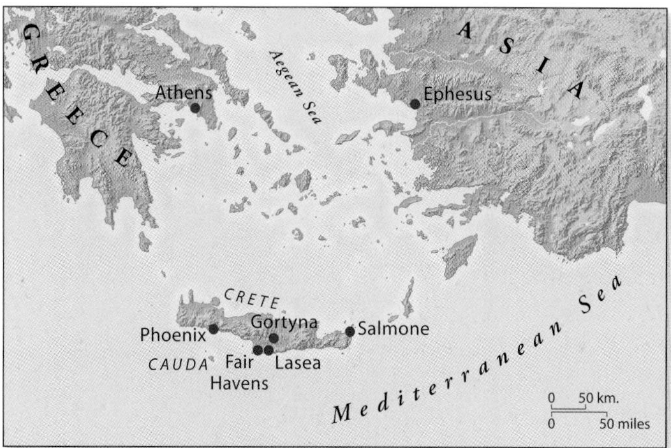

▲ The island of Crete is located at the bottom of this map.

Letter Opening: Address and Greeting (1:1–4)

Titus begins with a description of Paul as both a "servant of God" and "an apostle of Jesus Christ." His apostolic service has a purpose: "to further the faith of God's elect and their knowledge of the truth that leads to godliness in the hope of eternal life" (1:1–2a). Such hope is not a new development, for God, who does not lie, promised eternal life before time began. Through the proclamation entrusted to Paul, this long-concealed promise has been "brought to light" (1:2b–3). Titus is addressed as a loyal child in a common faith and is greeted with "grace and peace" (1:4).

Appointing Elders and Opposing Disruptive Teachers (1:5–16)

Dispensing with thanksgiving (cf. Galatians), Paul tells Titus that he left him in **Crete** so that he might (1) "put in order" unfinished business and (2) "appoint elders in every town," as instructed (compare Acts 14:23). He then proceeds in 1:6–9 to set forth various qualities that elders and overseers are to possess. It is not clear whether an **elder** (*presbyteros*) was one and the same as an overseer or bishop (*episkopos*), or if a singular **overseer/bishop** arose from council of elders. Given that *presbyteros* appears in the plural (1:5) and *episkopos* in the singular (1:7), probably two ecclesial offices are in view.[14] If a congregation or cluster of assemblies had a number of elders, they seemingly had only one overseer/bishop.

▼ This picture is of the Psiloritis mountains in western Crete.

Elders. Although the letter does not indicate what an elder was to do, it does specify three things an elder was to be:

- "blameless" (not sinless, but above reproach);
- "faithful to his wife" (lit., "a one-woman man"); and
- an individual whose "children believe" (or are faithful) and "are not open to the charge of being wild and disobedient".

14. That is to say, while an overseer/bishop may also be an elder, it does not appear that the pastoral office of elder is equivalent to that of an overseer.

Before proceeding, we offer three interpretive suggestions for reading this and the following list regarding church offices/officers (cf. similarly 1 Tim 3:1 – 13; 5:17 – 22).

1. This "virtue list for church officials" and others akin to it in the Pastorals is illustrative, not exhaustive. These are but a few of the qualities the Pastoral Letters consider necessary for ministry.
2. Such catalogs are best employed as guides for the selection of ecclesial officers, not as litmus tests, far less as a "club" to ensure compliance. The Lord and his church call fallible individuals, not "ideal candidates." (If Titus 1:6 were used as a litmus test, for example, Paul would not be qualified to serve as an elder, for we know that he was not married at the time he wrote 1 Corinthians 7.)
3. These ancient lists are both descriptive of initial contexts and prescriptive for eventual contexts. Careful exegesis and principled hermeneutics are essential in interpreting and applying such passages in the church today.

Bishops. As God's steward an overseer/bishop, like an elder, was to be "blameless" (1:7; cf. 1:6). A bishop was not to be arrogant, quick-tempered, given to drunkenness, violent, or greedy for gain (1:7). Rather, he was to be hospitable, a lover of goodness, prudent, upright, devout, and self-controlled (1:8). Additionally, an overseer was to "hold firmly to the trustworthy message as it had been taught." By doing so, the bishop would be able both to encourage and to refute with "sound doctrine" or "healthy teaching" (1:9).[15]

▲ An image of Epimenides, a Cretan philosopher-poet.

In 1:10 the author tells Titus that refutation with sound doctrine is necessary because there are "many rebellious people" who are "full of meaningless talk and deception" (cf. Rom 16:18), particularly those "out of the circumcision group" (apparently Jewish Christ-followers; cf. Col 4:11). These idle talkers and deceivers are said to have been "disrupting whole households" by teaching wrong doctrine ("Jewish myths," 1:14) for the wrong reason ("dishonest gain,"1:11). This deleterious development is thought to be in keeping with a "true saying" (1:13a) from one of Crete's own prophets, presumably Epimenides (around 600 BC): "Cretans are always liars, evil brutes, lazy gluttons."

If this is who wayward Cretan believers had become, this is not who they were meant to be. Titus is enjoined, therefore, "to rebuke them sharply" so that they will stop being swayed by "commands of those who reject the truth" and will become "sound in the faith" (1:13 – 14). As it stands, far from being pure, these unbelieving people are "corrupted in mind and conscience." What is more, they are "detestable, disobedient, and unfit for doing anything good" (1:15 – 16). Would that we knew more about this movement regarded as deviant.

15. Compare Titus 1:13; 2:1. See also 1 Tim 1:10; 4:6; 6:3; 2 Tim 1:13; 4:3. As we will see, the Pastorals perceive "sound doctrine" to be invaluable for the church's ongoing well-being.

Teaching Sound Doctrine and Offering Pastoral Instruction (2:1–10)

Whatever its precise nature, this movement was thought to be particularly disruptive to households, to whom Titus "must teach what is appropriate to sound doctrine" (2:1).

Beginning with "older men" (A),[16] Titus must teach them to be "temperate, worthy of respect, self-controlled, and sound in faith, in love and in endurance" (2:2). Turning to "older women" (B), he must teach them to live reverent lives free from slander and addiction to wine, so that they in turn can "teach what is good" (2:3), especially to "younger women" (B′), urging them (2:4–5):

A "to love their husbands and children,"
  B "to be self-controlled and pure,"
    C "to be busy at home,"
  B′ "to be kind,"
A′ "to be subject to their husbands."

Younger women are to live in such a manner "that no one will malign the word of God" (2:5).

Similarly, Titus must "encourage the young men (A′) to be self-controlled" (2:6; cf. 2:2). Titus, possibly a younger man himself (cf. 1 Tim 4:12), is then enjoined in 2:7 to be an example in all respects by "doing what is good." Furthermore, in his teaching he is to display "integrity, seriousness and soundness of speech that cannot be condemned." By excelling in both practice and proclamation, Titus can shame those who oppose him "because they [will] have nothing bad to say" (2:7–8).

Prior to a "liturgical interlude" (2:11–14), one other group within the household is singled out for instruction (2:9–10). Titus must teach slaves to:

- "be subject to their masters in everything";
- "try to please them";
- not "talk back to them"; and
- not "steal from them".

Were slaves to behave in this manner, they would "make the teaching about God our Savior attractive" (2:10).

Before we transition to the next section of Titus, a few reflections on 2:1–10 are in order. First, many of character qualities that Titus is to teach a given group of people are arguably applicable to all believers, both then and now. This is particularly true of the virtues commended to older men and older women (2:2–3).

It is also worth noting that instructions intended for younger women (2:4–5), younger men/Titus (2:6–8), and slaves (2:9–10) conclude with a "so that." These groups are to comport themselves in such a way *so that* "no one will malign the word of God" (younger women, 2:5); "those who oppose you may be ashamed because they have nothing bad to say about us" (younger men/Titus, 2:8); and "in every way they will make the teaching about God our Savior attractive" (slaves, 2:10). We do well to wonder if such noble ends justify what we now regard as such ignoble means, not least unquestioned patriarchy and slavery.

16. Note the progression from older men (A) to older women (B) to younger women (B′) to younger men (A′). Notice also below the movement in the instructions that older women are to offer younger women (A-B-C-B′-A′) (2:4–5). The central element encourages good household management, which is a fitting summation of 2:1–10.

We also do well to note the asymmetrical nature of the instructions Titus is to offer younger women/wives and slaves. As we saw in chapters 8 and 9 above, the household codes in both Colossians and Ephesians admonish husbands and masters as well. That being said, it is our contention that the church in any given generation needs to grapple with how best to interface with ambient culture in ways that are faithful to the gospel and attractive to outsiders.[17]

Grace and Good Works (2:11 – 3:11)

In the midst of Paul's instructions to Titus, one encounters creedal-like materials intended to undergird and guide the church's profession and performance (2:11 – 14; 3:3 – 7). Because "the grace of God has appeared" offering "salvation to all," believers are to embrace godliness and are to be "eager to do what is good" (2:11 – 14). Titus is to teach such doctrine and "encourage and rebuke with all authority," allowing no one to look down on him (2:15).

Before the next liturgical panel (3:3 – 7), Paul instructs Titus to remind the people of seven shared commitments (3:1 – 2):

1. "to be subject to rulers and authorities" (cf. 1 Tim 2:1 – 2; Rom 13:1 – 7);
2. "to be obedient" (to these rulers and authorities?);
3. "to be ready to do whatever is good" (cf. Titus 2:7, 14; 3:8, 14; 1 Tim 2:10; 5:10, 25; 6:18);
4. "to slander no one" (cf. Titus 2:3);
5. "to be peaceable";
6. "to be . . . considerate"; and
7. "to be gentle toward everyone."

Unlike their past behavior, also illustrated with a seven-item list (3:3),[18] such conduct is seen as congruent with the salvation God had kindly, lovingly, mercifully, generously, and graciously given them through "Jesus Christ our Savior" and the Holy Spirit (3:4 – 7). Titus is to impress this "trustworthy saying" on "those who have trusted in God," would-be heirs living in hope of eternal life, so that they might "be careful to devote themselves to doing what is good . . . excellent and profitable for everyone" (3:7 – 8).

In contrast, Titus is told to avoid "foolish controversies and genealogies and arguments and quarrels about the law" (3:9; cf. 1 Tim 4:7; 2 Tim 2:16, 23). Such tomfoolery is said to be "unprofitable and worthless" (3:9). In fact, after warning a divisive person once and again, Titus is to "wash his hands," recognizing that such an individual is "warped and sinful [and] self-condemned" (3:10 – 11).

Final Instructions and Greetings (3:12 – 15)

Paul concludes his letter to Titus by making a number of requests, exchanging greetings, and extending grace. In the first instance, he asks Titus, subsequent to the arrival of Artemas or Tychicus,[19] to do his best to come to Paul at Nicopolis, where he had decided to

---

17. A good way to begin thinking through this important issue is by reading the classic volume by H. Richard Niebuhr, *Christ and Culture* (New York: Harper & Row, 1951).
18. "At one time we too were 1. foolish, 2. disobedient, 3. deceived and enslaved by all kinds of passions and pleasures. We lived in 4. malice and 5. envy, 6. being hated and 7. hating one another."
19. Artemas is an otherwise unknown Pauline associate. On Tychicus, see Acts 20:4; Eph 6:21; Col 4:7 – 9; and 2 Tim 4:12.

▲ Nicopolis is identified on this map.
▼ Ironically, Nicopolis, which means "city of victory," now lies in ruins.

▼ Reconstructed ruins of one of the so-called "terrace houses" in Ephesus, illustrating wealthy family life during the Roman period

spend the winter (3:12).[20] The apostle also instructs Titus to do everything he can to provide Zenas the lawyer and Apollos with what they need in their coming to and going from Crete (3:13).[21]

Prior to extending greetings to Titus on behalf of unnamed others and asking Titus to "greet those who love us in the faith" (3:15a), Paul admonishes Titus to instruct people "to devote themselves to doing what is good." By doing good, they could "provide for urgent needs" and live productive lives (3:14). The letter closes with a grace-wish (3:15b). Far from an abstract theological concept or construct, the letter of Titus teaches that the "grace of God has appeared," offering salvation to all and justifying those who trust in God (2:11; 3:7–8).

CENTERING THE VISION OF 1 TIMOTHY: CONDUCT IN GOD'S HOUSEHOLD

Near the center of 1 Timothy, one encounters a passage that reveals the letter's purpose. Paul, whose location is not given, tells Timothy, who is in Ephesus (1:3), that he hopes to come to him soon (3:14; cf. Phil 2:19, 23–24). As a stopgap measure, however, he is writing him a letter so that even if he is delayed, Timothy "will know how people ought to conduct themselves in God's household" (3:15).

Over the course of our study, we have seen how Pauline churches typically met in households. Here, "household" serves as a metaphor for the church (see also Gal 6:10; Eph 2:19). Given that the Pastorals are replete with instructions to those who comprise households (1 Tim 2:8–15; 5:1–2; 6:1–2; recall Titus 2:1–10), this image is apropos and functions as something of a master metaphor.

20. Nicopolis was a seaport city on the western coast of Greece. Sea travel was not possible in the winter (cf. 2 Tim 4:21).
21. While Zenas is only mentioned here, Apollos is a well-known figure in Acts and in Paul's letters (see, e.g., Acts 18:24–28; 1 Cor 3:4–9; 16:12).

In 1 Tim 3:14 "the church of the living God" is also depicted as "the pillar and foundation of the truth."

As with Titus, 1 Timothy seeks to combat "false teaching" and inculcate "sound doctrine."[22] When one puts together all of the textual puzzle pieces, the aberrant instruction against which the Pastorals polemicize appears to have been an amalgam, as was arguably the "Colossian philosophy." It likely conjoined various Jewish elements and emphases with gnostic proclivities, ascetic practices, and realized eschatology.[23] The Pastorals perceive and present this movement as a real and present danger. By worming their way into homes of believers (2 Tim 3:6), these teachers are seen as having a disruptive and corruptive influence on "the household of God."

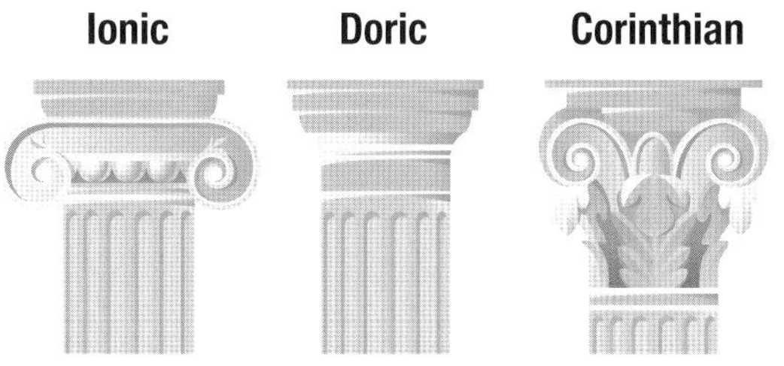

© mart/Shutterstock

▲ There were three basic types or orders of Greek columns or pillars: Ionic, Doric, and Corinthian.

▼ Today, only a single, reconstructed Ionic column remains of the Temple of Artemis in Ephesus, one of the seven wonders of the ancient world.

© Goldika/Shutterstock

How does 1 Timothy go about "home security and home repairs"? As is true with Titus, 1 Timothy stresses right belief and right behavior with a good dose of instruction on church order and offices thrown in for good measure. A primary way that 1 Timothy attempts to effect the doctrinal reorientation of the audience is through the incorporation of liturgical/creedal materials (cf. Titus 2:11–14; 3:4–7). On the heels of a statement revealing the letter's purpose (3:15), one encounters a hymnic fragment wherein the "mystery from which true godliness springs" is stated and celebrated:

> He appeared in the flesh,
> was vindicated by the Spirit (or in spirit),
> was seen by angels,
> was preached among the nations,
> was believed on in the world,
> was taken up in glory.

This confession is decidedly christological and missiological. The incarnate, risen, and glorified Jesus is to be proclaimed and believed on in the world. Other liturgical materials in 1 Timothy praise the mediating, sacrificial work of Christ (2:5b–6), "who made the good confession before **Pontius Pilate**" (6:13), and laud the God-who-is-one as eternal, immortal, invisible, life-giving, and sovereign (1:17; 2:5a; 4:10; 6:13, 16).[24] Additionally, Timothy

22 See, e.g., 1 Tim 1:3, 10; 4:6; 6:3; Titus 1:9, 13; 2:1–2; cf. 2 Tim 1:13; 4:3.

23 On Jewish features, see 1 Tim 1:6–11; Titus 1:10, 12; on gnostic tendencies, note 1 Tim 1:4; 6:20; 2 Tim 3:7; on ascetical elements, see 1 Tim 4:3; and on the resurrection as having already occurred, note 2 Tim 2:18.

24. In countering teachers (labeled "hypocritical liars") who "forbid people to marry and order them to abstain from certain foods," 1 Timothy insists that matrimony and foodstuffs are divine gifts from God and asserts that "everything God created is good, and nothing is to rejected if it is received with thanksgiving" (4:2–4).

© blickwinkel/Alamy

▲ A model of the first temple of Artemis
▶ A first-century AD Roman copy of the cult statue of the temple of Artemis. On devotion to this goddess in the first century, see Acts 19:23–41.

Bruce Longenecker

and other believers are called to live a life marked by purity until the future epiphany of the Lord Jesus Christ (6:14).

Accordingly, Timothy is to live life in conformity with the glorious gospel (cf. 1:11); so, too, are the bishops, deacons, and elders appointed to serve the church (see 3:1–13; 5:17–22). This entails fighting "the good fight" (6:12; cf. 1:18) by having "faith and a good conscience" (1:19). Prayer, godliness, contentment, and good works are also commended to Timothy (2:1–2; 4:5, 7–8; 6:3–10, 17–19), as are love, faith, purity, and a little wine (!) (4:11; 5:23). Though youthful, Timothy is to be a model of speech and conduct to his charges as he leads and feeds, guards and guides, instructs and inspires them in faith (4:12). And by all means, he is to practice what he preaches, for in so doing he will save both himself and his hearers (4:15–16).

TRACKING THE VISION OF 1 TIMOTHY: A GOOD MINISTER OF JESUS CHRIST

A Basic Outline of 1 Timothy

1:1–2	Address and Greeting
1:3–10	Timothy's Ministry in Ephesus
1:11–20	The Lord's Grace to Paul and Paul's Charge to Timothy
2:1–3:14	Worship and Leadership in the Church
4:1–16	Godliness and Its Antithesis
5:1–6:2	Instructions to Groups within the Congregation
6:3–19	"The Good Fight of Faith"
6:20–21	Letter Closing

Address and Greeting (1:1–2)

Paul begins this so-called first letter to Timothy by describing himself as an apostle by divine command and by speaking of his junior associate as a true child in the faith (cf. 1 Cor 4:17; Phil 2:22). In his salutation, Paul pronounces grace, mercy, and peace on Timothy (cf. 2 Tim 1:2) and refers to God as their Savior and Father and to Christ Jesus as their hope and Lord.[25]

Timothy's Ministry in Ephesus (1:3–10)

Forgoing a thanksgiving (cf. Titus), Paul charges Timothy, even as he did prior to his departure to Macedonia in northern Greece,[26] to remain in Ephesus to combat the teaching of false doctrines, myths, and endless genealogies by "certain people."[27] Such teachings "promote endless speculations" that retard instead of advance the plan and purposes of God (1:3–4).

In countering "false teaching," Timothy must be guided by love springing from a "pure heart and a good conscience and a sincere faith" (1:5). Having departed from such, the opponents have resorted to "blowing smoke"—meaningless, vacuous chatter confidently proclaimed. Although their points are weak, they preach loudly (1:6–7). Despite their desire to be "teachers of the law," they fail to comprehend the law, which is "good" when used "properly" (1:8).[28] The law is not really intended for the righteous; rather, it is meant to combat sinful acts (cf. Gal 3:19, 23–25) that are incongruent with the "sound doctrine that conforms to the gospel" (1:8–11).[29]

The Lord's Grace to Paul and Paul's Charge to Timothy (1:11–20)

In 1:12–17 Paul expresses gratitude to "Christ Jesus our Lord," who strengthened him (cf. Phil 4:13) for "appointed [him] to his service." Despite the fact that he was once a blasphemer, persecutor, violent man, and sinner (cf. Gal 1:13, 23), the Lord showered grace, faith, love, mercy, and patience on him. Albeit once "the worst of sinners," Paul became a prime example of the "trustworthy saying that deserves full acceptance: Christ Jesus came into the world to save sinners."[30] That the blessed God would entrust to a sinful individual the glorious gospel prompts Paul to erupt in joyful, doxological praise.

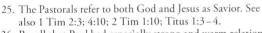

▼ A map showing, among other things, the province of Macedonia and the city of Ephesus

25. The Pastorals refer to both God and Jesus as Savior. See also 1 Tim 2:3; 4:10; 2 Tim 1:10; Titus 1:3–4.
26. Recall that Paul had especially strong and warm relations with the Macedonian churches in Philippi and Thessalonica.
27. With the exception of Hymenaeus and Alexander (1 Tim 1:20), these opponents are left nameless. This is typical for Paul.
28. On the law as good, see Rom 7:12, 16.
29. In 1:9–10, representative lawless acts (including sodomy and slave-trading) are set forth in a vice list.
30. For other "sure sayings" in the Pastorals, see 1 Tim 3:1; 4:9; 2 Tim 2:11; Titus 3:8.

© The Art Archive/Alamy

▲ To date, the oldest known underwater shipwreck discovery is the so-called Dokos shipwreck, which took place near the Grecian island of Dokos in the Aegean Sea around 2200 BC. A painting of a Greek trireme (lit., "three-oarer") appears here.

Paul returns in 1:18 to renew his charge to Timothy, telling his "son" that the command he is giving him (1:3) is in keeping with the "prophecies" spoken over him when he was set apart for ministry (cf. 4:14). To recall these prophetic words will not only help him to "fight the battle well," but will also help him to not to suffer "shipwreck" in the faith like Hymenaeus and Alexander, whom Paul had "delivered over to Satan" so that they might be "taught not to blaspheme" (1:19–20; cf. 1 Cor 5:3–5).

Worship and Leadership in the Church (2:1–3:14)

Having stated and reiterated Timothy's basic task, at the outset of chapter 2 Paul impresses on Timothy the necessity of engaging in prayer for all people, including "kings and all those in authority" (2:1–2). Such prayer is said to be good and pleasing to "God our Savior, who wants all people to be saved and to come to a knowledge of the truth" (2:3–4). As a divinely appointed herald and apostle, "a true and faithful teacher of the Gentiles" (2:7), Paul bears witness to this timely, timeless message of salvation, especially that Christ Jesus, who died "as a ransom for all people," is the one mediator between God and the human race (2:5–6). The theme of universality in these verses stands out—prayers are to be offered for *all* people (including *all* in authority); God desires for *all* people to be saved; and Christ Jesus died as a ransom for *all* people.

If all believers in all places are to pray for all people, in the context of the church's worship it is the *men* who are to pray, "lifting up holy hands without anger or disputing" (2:8). Meanwhile, *women* are to dress modestly and to adorn themselves with good deeds, for such is said to be fitting for "women who profess to worship God." In this context for women to dress "with decency and propriety," they are required to forgo elaborate hairstyles (= braided hair), exquisite jewelry (gold and pearls), and expensive clothes (2:9–10; cf. 1 Pet 3:3–6).

What is more, Timothy is instructed that a *woman* (or perhaps a *wife*) "should learn in quietness and full submission" (2:11). She is not to be permitted "to teach or to assume authority over a man" (or husband); she is to "be quiet" or keep silent (2:12). The rationale given for womanly (or wifely) submission is twofold: the order of creation ("Adam was formed first, then Eve") and Eve's vulnerability to and culpability arising from deception ("Adam was not the one deceived . . . the woman was deceived and became a sinner")

(2:13–14). Yet, Timothy is told that women (lit., "she") "will be saved through childbearing—if they [the women or the children?] continue in faith, love and holiness with propriety" (2:15).

If 1 Tim 2:8–15 is difficult exegetically (and it is), it is no less challenging hermeneutically. Allow us to offer three brief observations regarding this perplexing, problematic passage.

▲ Detail of wooden sarcophagus of well-adorned Roman woman, Ptolemaic and Roman periods, from excavations in the Fayum necropolis, Egypt 305 BC–AD 395.

1. Certain biblical texts support the injunction that a woman/wife "should learn in quietness and full submission" and the notion that a woman/wife ought not to teach or assume authority over a man (see esp. Gen 2:4–25; 3:1–7, 13). Indeed, strong readings of such texts can result in Adam/man being prioritized and Eve/woman being demonized (cf. Gen 1:27; 2:20b–25; 2 Cor 11:3).
2. The instructions given to women in 1 Tim 2:8–15 are decidedly contextual. For example, if 1 Timothy's scruples regarding women's hairstyles, jewelry, and clothing were once thought to be normative, these particular concerns are regarded and treated as irrelevant by most congregations in most locations today. Furthermore, it is altogether likely that the presence and influence of "false teachers" in the assemblies shaped the perception of and instructions to women in 1 Timothy. To illustrate, if "deceivers" were duping certain women addressed by the letter (cf. 2 Tim 3:6–7), then it makes eminently good pastoral sense to prohibit their teaching and preaching within the gathered community. Additionally, if the "false teachers" were forbidding marriage, as 1 Tim 4:3 indicates, then 2:15 makes better (if not complete) sense. One wonders if the salvation of which the author speaks in this verse relative to women is salvation from false teaching through (marrying and) childbearing and by continuing in "faith, love and holiness with propriety."
3. The instructions in 1 Tim 2:8–15 regarding the familial, ecclesial, and social life of women are partial in that they are patently and demonstrably patriarchal. (See further the discussion of 1 Cor 14:33b–36 in chapter 4 above.) They are also partial to the extent that they are incomplete; they are far from the only canonical voice or Pauline perspective on the issue. As we have noted elsewhere in this study, not a few women played pivotal ministerial and pastoral roles in the Pauline circle and churches.

Following instructions on prayer and the comportment of women in worship, 1 Timothy addresses qualifications for overseers/bishops (3:1–7; cf. Titus 1:7–9) and **deacons** respectively (1 Tim 3:8–13).[31] After stating that the one who "aspires to be an overseer desires a noble task" (3:1), the letter lists seven representative virtues an overseer is to possess (3:2) and four illustrative vices he is to avoid (3:3).[32] It is then stipulated that an overseer/bishop must "manage his family well" and "see that his children obey him," for it is thought that a person who cannot manage his own family will also be unable to care for "God's church" (3:4–5). Two other guidelines for the selection of overseers appear in 3:6–7. An overseer "must not be a recent convert" lest he become conceited and be judged like the devil (!), and "he must have a good reputation with outsiders" lest he fall into disgrace and the devil's trap.

With respect to deacons (here, as in Rom 16:1 and Phil 1:1, denoting a particular role or office within the church), they are to be "worthy of respect" and "sincere" and are to embrace the mystery or deep truths of the faith with a clear conscience (3:8–9). They, too, are to be husbands of one wife and good managers of their children and household (3:12). Meanwhile, they are not to indulge in much wine or pursue dishonest gain (3:8). Deacons are to be "tested" prior to being appointed for service, and those who serve well as deacons "gain an excellent standing and great assurance in their faith in Christ Jesus" (3:10, 12).

What about 3:11? This verse stipulates that "women" are to be "worthy of respect," "temperate," and "trustworthy" and are not to be "malicious talkers." It is unclear whether the women referred to here are women deacons or wives of deacons. Although Paul refers to Phoebe as a "deacon of the church in Cenchreae" (Rom 16:1),[33] given both the immediate literary context and the overall ecclesial/liturgical commitments of this letter we think it more likely that 1 Tim 3:11 has deacons' wives in view.

Godliness and Its Antithesis (4:1–16)

First Timothy 3:14–16, replete with a christological confession (3:16), precedes a chapter where "false teachers" (4:1–5) are juxtaposed to what "a good minister of Christ Jesus" like Timothy is meant to be (4:6–16).[34] At the outset of chapter 4, Timothy is informed that the Spirit has indicated (through the ministry of prophecy?) that in the "later times" some believers "will abandon the faith and follow things taught by demons" (4:1). As it happens, the "later times" have arrived in the form of teachings being peddled by "hypocritical liars, whose consciences have been seared as with a hot iron" (4:2). These opportunists without moral moorings are promoting asceticism (prohibiting marriage and certain foodstuffs), a position that is said to stand in stark contrast with the goodness of God's creation (4:3–5).

31. Overseers and deacons also appear together in Phil 1:1.

32. The virtues are as follows: above reproach, faithful to his wife (= a one-woman man), temperate, self-controlled, respectable, hospitable, and able to teach. An overseer is not to be given over to drunkenness, violence, quarrelling, or the love of money. The topics of hospitality (5:10; cf. Titus 1:8) and love of money (1 Tim 3:8; 6:9–10, 17–19) recur latter in the letter.

33. Cf. also Phil 1:1. Did Euodia and Syntyche serve in this capacity or as "overseers/bishops" in Philippi? Might it be that they along with Lydia (Acts 16:11–15) were among the founding leaders of the Philippian church?

34. On 1 Tim 3:14–16, see above, pp. 273–74.

For Timothy's part, as a "good minister of Christ Jesus" he is to "point . . . out" to believers such deviation and is to be "nourished" by "truths of the faith" and "good teaching" (4:6). Rejecting "godless myths and old wives' tales" promoted by the false teachers excoriated above, Timothy is to train himself in godliness. Whereas physical training is temporally profitable, spiritual training has eternal value (4:7–9). Spiritual labor and striving is driven by "hope in the living God, who is the Savior of all people, and especially of those who believe" (4:10).

Furthermore, as "a good minister of Christ Jesus," Timothy is told in 4:11–16 to:

- "command and teach" such truths;
- "set an example for the believers in speech, in conduct, in love, in faith and in purity," despite his youth;
- give attention to the "public reading of Scripture," to exhorting, and to teaching;
- not neglect the gift of ministry given him through prophecy at the time of his "ordination" when "the body of elders laid their hands on him" (5:17–21); and
- "be diligent," wholly devoted, vigilant, and steadfast with respect to both life and doctrine so that others might see his progress and so that both he and his hearers might be saved.

▲ Given that illiteracy was widespread in Greco-Roman antiquity, the "public reading of Scripture" was altogether necessary. This first-century AD bronze statuette is of a young woman reading. She would have been exceptional in her day.

Instructions to Groups within the Congregation (5:1–6:2)

Throughout 1 Timothy 5 and into chapter 6, Timothy receives instructions regarding additional groups within the church (cf. 3:1–12). Following general advice as to how best to relate to various age groups (5:1–2; cf. Titus 2:1–8), considerable counsel is set forth regarding widows (5:3–16). The church is to care for widows in need (5:16b), but given the extent of the need, guiding principles are required.

1. If a widow has believing children or grandchildren, they should support her (5:3–8). Failure to put one's "religion into practice" along these lines is regarded as a denial of the faith and as being "worse than an unbeliever."
2. If a believing woman "has widows in her care," she should continue to care for them in order that they might not be a fiscal burden on the church (5:16a).
3. Only widows left all alone and over sixty years of age are to be placed on the list.[35] Even then, they are to be paragons of piety, fidelity, hospitality, purity, and generosity (5:5–6, 9–10).

---

35. Some scholars suggest that certain widows (those "on the list of widows") served as church officers (not unlike overseers/bishops, elders, and deacons) and that the qualifications for the office of widow are set forth in 5:9–10. Given 5:11 (which refers to a list with respect to younger widows), we think this intriguing theory to be unlikely.

Tertullian on Widowhood

The early Christian theologian Tertullian (ca. AD 160–225, pictured here), wrote the following regarding widows: "For, concerning the honours which widowhood enjoys in the sight of God, there is a brief summary in one saying of His through the prophet: 'Do thou justly to the widow and to the orphan; and come ye, let us reason, saith the Lord' [cf. Isaiah 1:17–18]. These two names, left to the care of the divine mercy, in proportion as they are destitute of human aid, the Father of all undertakes to defend. Look how the widow's benefactor is put on a level with the widow herself, whose champion shall 'reason with the Lord!'"[36]

Special Collections Library, University of Michigan

4. Given their reported propensity to want to remarry and to become "busybodies," younger widows (i.e., those sixty years of age and younger) are not to be placed on the list at all. Instead, they are to remarry, have children, and manage their homes lest they give outsiders grounds for slander and Satan a foothold to deceive (5:11–15). (The harsh language employed in these verses with respect to younger widows not only suggests a certain bias against them but also reveals a significant problem that was taxing the resources and challenging the goodwill of the church.)

Regarding elders (5:17–20; cf. Titus 1:5–6), those who serve well as such, especially in the ministry of preaching and teaching, are said to be worthy of "double honor," that is of financial support (5:17). Scripture maintains as much (5:18).[37] Additionally, Timothy is instructed not to casually entertain an accusation against an elder; "two or three witnesses" are necessary (5:19). He must also "reprove before everyone" any elders who persist in sin, as a "warning" to others (5:20).

Before addressing the subject of slavery (6:1–2), additional instructions are given to Timothy (5:21–25). He is to:

- show no partiality or favoritism in doing as he has been told;
- be circumspect in the ordaining of others ("the laying on of hands");
- not share in the sin of others, but to keep himself pure;
- drink wine along with water because of stomach upset and frequent illness; and
- realize that both sinful acts and good deeds will be revealed sooner or later.

36. Tertullian, *To His Wife* 1.7.1; *Ante-Nicene Fathers*, vol. 4; trans. S. Thelwall. Available at http://www.tertullian.org/anf/anf04/anf04–12.htm#TopOfPage.
37. See Deut 25:4 ("Do not muzzle an ox while it is treading out the grain") and Luke 10:7 ("The worker deserves his wages"). That 1 Timothy would cite Luke 10:7 as Scripture is of considerable historical and theological interest.

Speaking of slavery, but not to slaves (contrast Eph 6:5–8; Col 4:22–25), 1 Timothy maintains that slaves should "consider their masters worthy of full respect, so that God's name and our teaching may not be slandered" (1 Tim 6:1; cf. Titus 2:9–10). What is more, slaves who have believing masters, far from showing them disrespect, are to serve them all the more (6:2).

"The Good Fight of Faith" (6:3–19)

As the letter nears its end, the true teaching and leadership that Timothy must offer are once again contrasted with those of the "false teachers." Because the teaching entrusted to and exhibited by Timothy is sound and godly, those who fail to embrace it are said to be conceited and to understand nothing (6:2b–4a). Additionally, these "deviants" are described as having an "unhealthy interest in controversies and quarrels about words," resulting in unhealthy ways of living and relating (6:4b–5a). Corrupt in mind, these "malcontents" have been "robbed of the truth" and duped into thinking that "godliness is a means to financial gain" (6:5b).

When coupled with contentment, godliness is indeed a means of "great gain" (6:6), but it is a boon of another kind. Godly contentment enables a perspective that espouses, "We brought nothing into the world, and we can take nothing out of it" (6:7). The contented person, it is said, is grateful for food to eat and clothes to wear (6:8). Those desiring to get rich, however, "fall into temptation and a trap and into foolish and harmful desires that plunge people into destruction and ruin" (6:9). Indeed, "the love of money is a root of all kinds of evil" (6:10a).

Given that some believers eager for money have lost their way, "wandered from the faith and pierced themselves with many griefs" (6:10), Timothy is charged to command rich believers not to be "arrogant or to place their hope in wealth, which is so uncertain." On the contrary, the rich are to place their hope in God, whose provision is as constant and abundant as his character (6:17). Moreover, Timothy is to command wealthy believers "to do good, to be rich in good deeds, and to be generous and willing to share" (6:18). By so doing, they are paying forward to the future, for a coming age where the currency is categorically different and life is truly life (6:19).

▼ A mosaic of two female slaves attending their mistress

Fabien Dany, www.fabiendany.com

Polycarp, Bishop of Smyrna

In his letter *To the Philippians* 1 – 4, Polycarp (AD 69 – 155), bishop of Smyrna, laments that one Valens, a former presbyter of the church in Philippi, succumbed to avarice:

> I am deeply grieved for Valens, who once was a presbyter among you, because he so fails to understand the office that was entrusted to him. I warn you, therefore: avoid love of money, and be pure and truthful. Avoid every kind of evil. But how can someone who is unable to exercise self-control in these matters preach self-control to anyone else? Anyone who does not avoid love of money will be polluted by idolatry and will be judged as one of the Gentiles, who are ignorant of the Lord's judgment. Or do we not know that the saints will judge the world, as Paul teaches?
>
> But I have not observed or heard of any such thing among you, in whose midst the blessed Paul labored, and who are praised in the beginning of his letter. For he boasts about you in all the churches — the ones who at that time had come to know the Lord, for we had not yet come to know him. Therefore, brothers and sisters, I am deeply grieved for him and for his wife; may the Lord grant them true repentance. You, therefore, for your part must be reasonable in this matter and do not regard such people as enemies, but, as sick and straying members, restore them, in order that you may save your body in its entirety. For by doing this you build up one another.[38]

▼ Russian painter Nikolai Ge's (1831 – 1894) "What Is Truth?" See further John 18:33 – 38, where Jesus makes the "good confession."

What is Truth? (Christ and Pilate), Ge (Gay), Nikolai Nikolaevich/Tretyakov Gallery, Moscow, Russia/The Bridgeman Art Library

Sandwiched between instruction and reflection on money are admonitions to Timothy, addressed as "man of God," to flee ministry for money and to pursue "righteousness, godliness, faith, love, endurance and gentleness" (6:11). In addition, he is admonished to "fight the good fight of faith" and to "take hold of eternal life" (6:12). Timothy is called in the sight of God and Christ Jesus, who made the "good confession" before Pontius Pilate, to hold fast his "good confession" in purity until the epiphany of the Lord Jesus Christ (6:13 – 14). The manifestation of Christ will come about in God's own time, who is praised for being immortal and transcendent and is lauded as "the blessed and only Ruler, the King of kings and Lord of lords" (6:15 – 16).

Letter Closing (6:20 – 21)

First Timothy concludes with a charge to Timothy to "guard what has been entrusted to [his] care" and with an admonition for him to "turn away from godless chatter" and "false knowledge" (6:20). The profession of such knowledge has caused some to depart from the faith (6:21a). The letter closes with a grace-wish to "you all" (i.e., "you" is plural, 6:21b). This signals

38. Michael W. Holmes, trans. and ed., *The Apostolic Fathers in English* (3rd ed.; Grand Rapids: Baker Academic, 2006), 139 – 40.

that the letter, albeit addressed to Timothy, has other believers in view throughout. The closing also indicates that the "false teaching," replete with its "meaningless speech" and "faux wisdom" and frequently on the letter's surface, is never far from the fore of the writer's mind.

CENTERING THE VISION OF 2 TIMOTHY: SHARING IN SUFFERING

"False teachers/teaching" are also a primary concern in 2 Timothy.[39] Absent, however, are various instructions regarding church offices as well as admonitions to particular groups within the church. To this extent, 2 Timothy differs from its Pastoral partners. It is also different by virtue of the fact that Paul is pictured as captive in Rome undergoing trial and contemplating death.[40] Feeling abandoned and all but alone in Rome, Paul writes to his "dear son" Timothy (1:2), who is seemingly still in Ephesus.[41] As he composes something akin to a "last will and testament," Paul instructs and implores Timothy on any number of ministerial matters. One such matter that leaves an indelible mark on the letter is Paul's repeated call for Timothy to join him in "suffering for the gospel."

We have had occasion to note throughout our study that Paul was "a man of suffering, and familiar with pain" (Isa 53:3). In 2 Tim 3:11 Paul recalls in particular the persecutions that he endured in Antioch, Iconium, and Lystra.[42] Furthermore, when writing to Timothy, he is suffering for the gospel, "even to the point of being chained like a criminal" (2 Tim 2:9). From Paul's perspective, he is "already being poured out like a drink offering" (cf. Phil 2:17), and the time for his departure (i.e., death) is near (4:6).

Although Paul was suffering because of his appointment to be a herald, apostle, and teacher of the gospel (1:11–12a), he did not regard suffering to be an apostolic preserve. Indeed, 2 Tim 3:12 propounds that "everyone who wants to live a godly life in Christ Jesus will be persecuted." In 2 Timothy, Paul takes pains to impress on Timothy the necessity of suffering. "Join with me in suffering for the gospel, by the power of God," Paul writes (1:8a). Then again, "Join with me in suffering, like a good soldier of Christ Jesus" (2:3). Even as Paul suffers and endures hardship for the sake of the gospel (2:8–10), he calls Timothy to endure suffering as the latter carries out his ministry (4:5).

The theological rationale for the Christian vocation of shared suffering is enshrined in one of the hymnic fragments, a so-called "trustworthy saying," that adorn the Pastoral Letters:

> If we died with him,
> we will also live with him;
> if we endure,
> we will also reign with him.
> If we disown him,
> he will disown us;
> if we are faithless,
> he remains faithful,
> for he cannot disown himself. (2:11–13; see also 1:9b–10)

---

39. See, e.g., 1:13; 2:14, 16–18, 23–25; 3:1–9, 13; 4:3–4, 14–15.
40. See 1:8, 16–17; 2:9; 4:6–8, 16–18.
41. Note 4:10–11, 16, 21; see also 1:2, 18; 4:15, 21; 1 Tim 1:3.
42. See Acts 13:13–14:20. Acts suggests that it was in Lystra where Paul and Timothy first met (see 16:1–3).

TRACKING THE VISION OF 2 TIMOTHY: PASSING THE FAITH ALONG

A Basic Outline of 2 Timothy

1:1–5	Address, Greeting, and Thanksgiving
1:6–18	Timothy's Responsibility and Paul's Plight
2:1–24	Timothy Admonished
3:1–9	Opponents Denounced
3:10–4:8	Timothy's Tasks and Paul's Departure
4:9–18	Instructions and Information
4:19–22	Greetings and Grace

Address, Greeting, and Thanksgiving (1:1–5)

Second Timothy commences with an address from Paul, an "apostle," to Timothy, a "dear son." Even as Paul pronounces "grace, mercy and peace" on Timothy from "God the Father and Christ Jesus our Lord," he describes his apostleship as God's will "in keeping with the promise of life that is in Christ Jesus" (1:1–2).

This succinct salutation is followed by a brief thanksgiving, in which Paul thanks God "night and day" as he constantly remembers Timothy in his prayers. As Paul thanks the God he serves with a "clear conscience," as did his ancestors, he recalls Timothy's tears, perhaps when they last parted, and he longs to see him in order to be filled with joy (1:3–4).[43] Furthermore, as Paul thinks about and gives thanks for his own spiritual ancestors, he is reminded that the "sincere faith" now residing in Timothy first lived in Timothy's grandmother **Lois** and mother **Eunice** (1:5).

▼ Stained glass windows of the boy Timothy with his mother Eunice and of Timothy's grandmother Lois

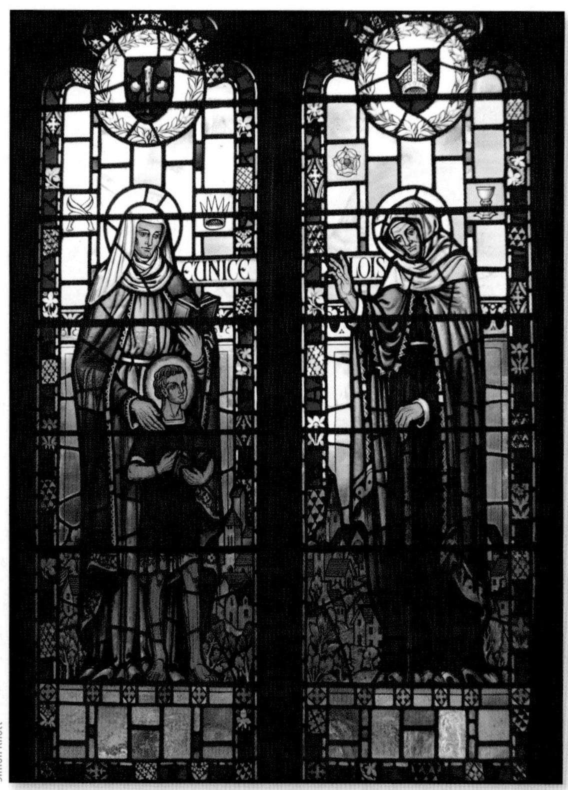

Simon Knott

Timothy's Responsibility and Paul's Plight (1:6–18)

Lest Timothy lose sight of his spiritual legacy and giftedness, Paul calls him to fan into flame the gift of God that was in him through the laying on of Paul's hands (1:6). Hoping to inspire courage in his younger associate, Paul instructs Timothy that "the Spirit God gave us does not make us timid, but gives us power, love and self-discipline" (1:7). As a result,

43. In the Pastorals, the term "conscience" also appears in 1:5, 19; 3:9; 4:2. On Paul's spiritual ancestry, see Phil 3:5–6. On Paul's "clear conscience," see also Rom 9:1; 1 Cor 4:4; and 2 Cor 1:12. Cf., too, Acts 23:1; 24:16.

Timothy is not to shrink back from suffering or to shirk his God-given responsibilities.[45] Far from being ashamed of the testimony about the Lord or of Paul as the Lord's prisoner, he is to join the apostle in suffering for the gospel as God enables and empowers (1:8).

In concert with God's purpose and because of God's grace, believers have been saved and called to holiness. Although God showered this grace on believers before time began, only recently was it revealed (1:9). Through his epiphany, "our Savior, Christ Jesus . . . destroyed death and brought life and immortality to light through the gospel" (1:10). It is this gospel that Paul serves fervently and for which he suffers unashamedly (1:11 – 12).

Wikimedia Commons

▲ Ring depicting a Roman soldier. Timothy is called to be "like a good soldier of Christ Jesus."

Paul's suffering was ongoing. Not only had he suffered desertion by believers in Asia (Ephesus?), including the otherwise unknown Phygelus and Hermogenes (1:15), but he has also experienced desertion in Rome (4:10, 16), where he was suffering "even to the point of being chained like a criminal" (2:9). One person, however, a certain **Onesiphorus**, was not ashamed of Paul's chains. He searched for Paul in Rome until he found him, and having done so, refreshed him (1:16). Paul requests two times over that the Lord would show mercy to both Onesiphorus and his household for having found and refreshed Paul in Rome and for having helped the apostle in "many ways" in Ephesus (1:16, 18).

Timothy Admonished (2:1 – 24)

Second Timothy 2 is comprised of some twelve admonitions with varying degrees of elaboration. Paul instructs Timothy, who is Paul's child in the ministry.

1. "Be strong in the grace that is in Christ Jesus" (2:1; see again 1:9 – 10).
2. "Entrust to reliable people who will also be qualified to teach others" what he had heard Paul say "in the presence of many witnesses" (2:2; cf. 1 Tim 6:12).
3. "Join with [Paul] in suffering, like a good soldier of Christ Jesus" (2:3), and do not get "entangled in civilian affairs." Instead, he should seek to "please his commanding officer" (2:4). Moreover, like an athlete competing for "the victor's crown," Timothy must compete by the rules (2:5). Employing yet a third analogy, Paul likens Timothy to a "hardworking farmer" who "should be the first to receive a share of the crops" (2:6).
4. "Reflect on what [Paul] is saying," that is, on the metaphors employed, "for the Lord will give you insight into all this" (2:7).
5. "Remember Jesus Christ." More specifically, that he was "raised from the dead" and "descended from David" (2:8; cf. Rom 1:3 – 4). Paul labels these core beliefs "his gospel," for which he suffers like a chained criminal, though "God's word is

45. Timothy is to keep "the pattern of sound teaching" that he learned from Paul and is to guard the good treasure of the gospel entrusted to him (1:13 – 14).

not chained." Indeed, he endures all things for the sake of believers ("the elect") so that they might obtain "the salvation that is in Christ Jesus" (2:9–10).

6. "Keep reminding" believers of the truths encapsulated and articulated in the "trustworthy saying" of 2:11–13 (2:14a).
7. "Warn [believers] before God against quarreling about words," since "it is of no value, and only ruins those who listen" (2:14b-c).
8. "Do your best to present yourself to God as one approved," an unashamed worker who "correctly handles the word of truth" (2:15).
9. "Avoid godless chatter," for those who engage in it only become increasingly ungodly as their talk spreads like gangrene, the death and decay of body tissue (2:16–17a). Two "chatterers" have swerved from the truth by declaring "the resurrection has already taken place"—Hymenaeus and Philetus (2:17b–18b; cf. 1 Tim 1:20). Although they have subverted the faith of some (2:18c), "God's solid foundation" stands firm; it is sealed with an inscription and comprised of quotations from Num 16:5 and another unclear source (see Job 36:10 and Isa 26:13, however). It stands written, "The Lord knows those who are his," and "Everyone who confesses the name of the Lord must turn away from wickedness" (2:19).

   In 2:20–21 an analogy is employed to contrast faithful ministers (like Paul and Timothy) with "false teachers" (like Hymenaeus and Philetus). In a large house there are utensils made for "special purposes" (utensils of "honor" made of gold and silver) and for "common use" (utensils of "dishonor" made of wood and clay; 2:20). Those who reject the "false teachers" and their "godless chatter" can become "instruments for special purposes, made holy, useful to the Master and prepared to do any good work" (2:21).
10. "Flee the evil desires of youth" (2:22a).
11. "Pursue righteousness, faith, love and peace," with others "who call on the Lord out of a pure heart" (2:22b-c; cf. 1 Tim 1:5).
12. Have nothing "to do with foolish and stupid arguments," for they only produce quarrels (2:23; see again 2:14). Timothy is told that "the Lord's servant" is not to be "quarrelsome" or "resentful," but is to be "kind to everyone [and] able to teach" (2:24). Furthermore, opponents are to be corrected with gentleness and in hope that "God will grant them repentance" and that they "will come to their senses" and thereby escape the devil's snare and sway (2:25–26).

Opponents Denounced (3:1–9)

Albeit a new chapter,[46] the topic remains the same—"false teachers." In a passage akin to 1 Tim 4:1–5, Timothy must understand that in the "last days" terrible times will come (3:1). Eighteen vices are cataloged to illustrate these distressing days, which encroach on the present (3:2–4). The picture is anything but pretty. Timothy is to avoid such people, who hold to a "form of godliness" while "denying its power" (3:5).

46. Chapter and verse divisions were not original to the text. They were added in the early thirteenth and the mid-sixteenth century respectively.

In the context in which he finds himself, Timothy is to have nothing to do with those people "who worm their way into homes and gain control over gullible women" (3:6a), who are said to be "loaded down with sins" and "swayed by all kinds of evil desires" (3:6a, 8a). These depraved opportunists denounced here are so muddle-minded that despite continual instruction, they are unable to arrive at a "knowledge of the truth" (3:7). What is more, like **Jannes and Jambres**, who opposed Moses,[47] these teachers are described as those who "oppose the truth" (3:8). Because of their counterfeit faith, they (also like Jannes and Jambres) will have little success. Instead, their folly will be clear to everybody (3:9). The amount of space devoted to and the harshness of the polemic employed against the "false teachers" in the Pastorals strongly suggests that their presence and influence was regarded as a real threat.

Timothy's Tasks and Paul's Departure (3:10–4:8)

While Timothy was to avoid the so-called knowledge of the "false teachers," he "knew all about Paul's teaching, [his] way of life, [his] purpose, faith, patience, love, endurance, persecutions, [and] sufferings" (3:10). In fact, he was knowledgeable of particular persecutions Paul had experienced in Antioch, Iconium, and Lystra and how the Lord had rescued him from them all (3:11). What was true for Paul is true for all who seek "to live a godly life in Christ Jesus"—they "will be persecuted" (3:12).

As "evildoers and impostors . . . go from bad to worse" (3:13), deceiving others even as they themselves are deceived, Timothy is to continue in his received faith as informed by the Holy Scriptures (= Jewish Scriptures), which "are able to make [people] wise for salvation through faith in Christ Jesus" (3:14–15). Indeed, God-breathed Scripture—that is, the Hebrew Bible/Old Testament and by way of extension the New Testament (note 1 Tim 5:18; 2 Pet 3:16)—is invaluable as it enables God's servants to be "thoroughly equipped for good work" (3:16).[48]

Paul concludes his final charge to Timothy in chapter 4 by striking a particularly solemn note. In the presence of the divine, both God and Christ Jesus,[49] and in view of Christ's epiphany and kingdom, Timothy is charged to "preach the word," that is, the gospel message. He must be prepared and persistent at all times ("in season and out of season") and conduct his preaching ministry with all due patience and care (4:2). For the time was to come—and indeed had come with the "opponents"—when people would have no appetite for "sound doctrine" (cf. 1:13). Instead, they will search for teachers who will say what they want to hear, and in so doing, turn from "truth" to "myths" (4:3–4; cf. 1 Tim 1:4; 4:7; Titus 1:14). In this den of confusion and deviation, Timothy is to stay the course by keeping his head, enduring hardship, doing the work of an evangelist, and discharging his ministerial duties, even as Paul had done (4:5).

Speaking of Paul, in one of the most memorable passages in the Pastorals (if not the whole of Paul), the following lines appear:

---

47. According to later Jewish sources, Jannes and Jambres were the names of Pharaoh's magicians (Exod 7:11, 22).
48. Scripture is said to be "useful for teaching, rebuking, correcting and training in righteousness" (3:16). It is to be part and parcel of Timothy's ministry (note 1 Tim 4:13; cf. 2 Tim 4:2).
49. "Christ Jesus" is further described as the one who will "judge the living and the dead" (4:1).

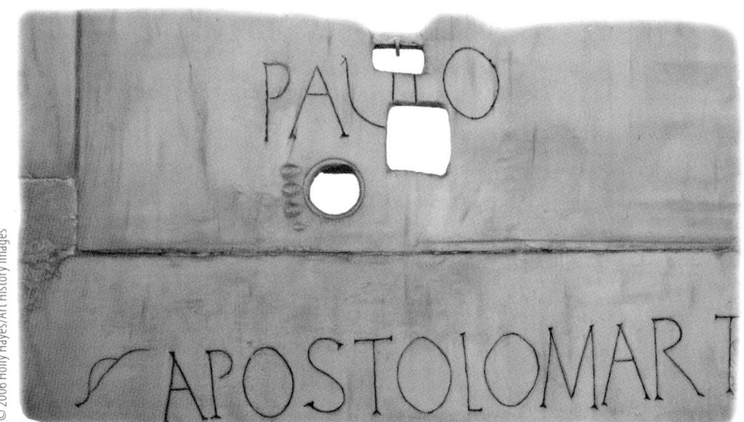

▲ Replica of the marble slab placed over the purported tomb of Paul in the Constantinian period (early fourth century), inscribed "PAULO APOSTOLOMART" ("Paul, Apostle, Martyr").

▼ This map identifies the cities mentioned at the conclusion of 2 Timothy.

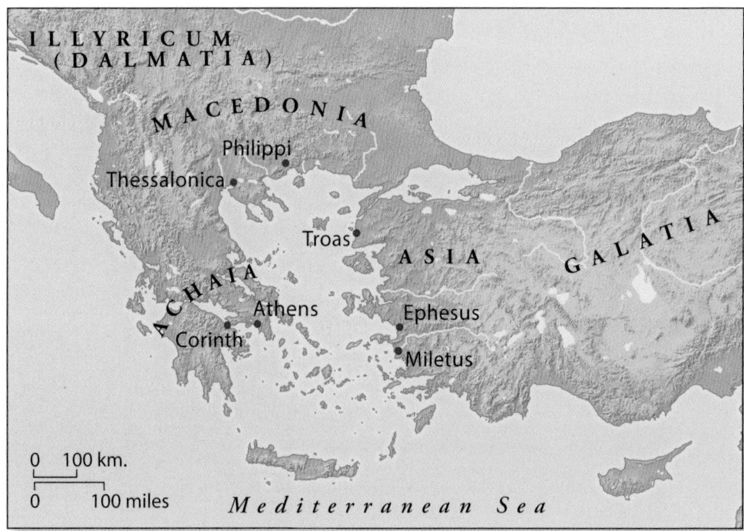

For I am already being poured out like a drink offering, and the time of my departure is near. I have fought the good fight, I have finished the race, I have kept the faith. Now there is in store for me the crown of righteousness, which the Lord, the righteous Judge, will award to me on that day—and not only to me, but also to all who have longed for his appearing. (4:6–8)

Ostensibly, Paul composed this passage, likening his life to a libation and an athletic contest, when he thought himself to be at death's door (cf. Phil 1:19–26). Traditionally, it has been thought that he did so near the end of a second Roman captivity. In any event, Paul's life and death are regarded as paradigmatic for Timothy and others who follow in his apostolic train.

Instructions and Information (4:9–18)

Given Paul's impending death, Timothy is instructed to come quickly (4:9). Paul finds himself all but alone in Rome; only Luke is with him (4:11a). Demas, Crescens, and Titus have all "flown the coop," abandoning the apostle for "greener pastures" in Thessalonica, Galatia, and Dalmatia respectively (4:10).[50] Additionally, Paul has dispatched Tychicus to Ephesus (4:12; note also Acts 20:4; Eph 6:21; Col 4:7; Titus 3:12). Meanwhile, Timothy is told to "get" and "bring along" Mark when he comes (cf. Col 4:10). Timothy, who must do his best to get to Paul before winter, when ships do not sail (4:21a), is also to bring Paul's cloak he left with Carpus at Troas and his "scrolls, especially the parchments," when he comes to Rome (4:13).

Until he comes, Timothy would do well to be on his guard against "Alexander the metalworker" (cf. Acts 19:33; 1 Tim 1:20). When Paul was in Ephesus, this named op-

50. On Demas, see also Col 4:14; Phlm 24. Crescens is otherwise unknown. On Titus, see above. Dalmatia is the region also known as Illyricum (see Rom 15:19).

ponent did him a "great deal of harm" and "strongly opposed [his] message." Here, vigilance is viewed as the best defense, and judgment is thought as best left to the Lord (4:14–15).

▲ Remains of the Miletus theater, which are still impressive

© Valery Shanin/Shutterstock

In 4:16–18 Paul reports that at his "first defense," perhaps during his present captivity, he was left deserted, not supported (4:16). Although he received no support from fellow believers, he did not grow embittered. Rather, he was mindful that the "Lord stood at [his] side and gave [him] strength"—strength sufficient to proclaim the gospel to Gentiles. The Lord had delivered Paul "from the lion's mouth" (cf. 1 Cor 15:32), and the apostle was confident that the Lord would continue to "rescue [him] from every evil attack" so as to "bring [him] safely to his heavenly kingdom" (4:17–18).

Greetings and Grace (4:19–22)

By way of conclusion, Paul tells Timothy to greet Priscilla and Aquila as well as the household of Onesiphorus (4:19).[51] Additionally, he informs Timothy that Erastus remained in Corinth, and Trophimus, who was sick, stayed in Miletus (4:20).[52]

Prior to wishing Timothy God's presence and pronouncing grace on "you all" (4:22; cf. 1 Tim 6:21), Paul pleads with his beloved coworker to come before winter and sends him greetings from "all the brothers and sisters" in Rome, particularly Eubulus, Pudens, Linus, and Claudia.

THE AUTHORSHIP AND CONTRIBUTION OF THE PASTORAL LETTERS

Although we already covered a good bit in this chapter, we must close by considering two questions: (1) Who wrote the Pastorals? (2) What contribution do these three letters make to the Pauline corpus? Let us consider these two important matters in turn.

Regarding the first question, there are a number of options. They include the following five scenarios:

1. Paul was never released from Roman captivity in the early 60s, so he could not possibly have written the Pastorals, which presuppose Pauline ministry in the East in the mid-60s.[53]

51. On Priscilla (= Prisca) and Aquila, see Acts 18:2, 18; Rom 16:3; 1 Cor 16:19. On Onesiphorus, see 2 Tim 1:16–18.
52. On Erastus, see also Acts 19:22; Rom 16:23. On Trophimus, note Acts 20:4; 21:29. Miletus was a seaport city of Caria, located on the southwestern coast of Asia Minor (modern-day Turkey). See also Acts 20:15, 17.
53. A few scholars have argued that Paul authored 2 Timothy even though he was never released from Roman captivity. They maintain that 2 Timothy can be correlated with Acts.

2. Paul was released from the Roman captivity reported in Acts 28, but did not travel to the places purported by the Pastorals. Neither did he write the Pastorals.
3. Even though Paul was released and traveled to the West and East, he did not author the Pastorals. It is possible, however, that Paul's "fingerprints" may be on the Pastorals as a result of a later author or authors incorporating genuine notes or fragments into the letters.
4. Paul was released, traveled both West, as far as Spain, and East to the places the Pastorals purport, and wrote at least one of the Pastorals, most likely 2 Timothy from Rome prior to his execution (about AD 67).
5. In addition to the view outlined in (4), both 1 Timothy and Titus are best attributed to Paul, perhaps written by the apostle en route to Rome or in Rome itself at a time earlier than 2 Timothy.

While sympathetic to (3) and (5), we presently think (4) most likely. It is, of course, possible that Paul did not write 2 Timothy or that he did so without ever having been released from Roman captivity. At the very least, however, we think that many, if not most, of the personal elements in 2 Timothy (see esp. 4:9–21) are best explained as historical rather than fictional, realizing all the while that 2 Timothy differs considerably from the so-called authentic Pauline letters and fits rather neatly into the frequently pseudepigraphical literary category of a final testament.

"[First Tim 2:11 – 15] is one of the passages in the letter that could hardly have come from the pen of Paul. The assertion that women will be saved through child bearing clashes flagrantly with Paul's profound conviction that all human beings are saved by virtue of the death of Christ. The lame exoneration of Adam (2:13 – 14) also sits oddly in conjunction with Paul's portrayal in Romans 5:12 – 21 of Adam as the source of sin and typological representative of sinful humanity."[54]

It is also possible that Paul wrote 1 Timothy and Titus. Were he to have done so, however, he would have had to adjust some of his views and to alter some of his vocabulary. Perhaps there was a time when circumstances were such that Paul, for example, instructed only men/husbands to pray publicly and for younger widows to marry (cf. 1 Tim 2:8 with 1 Cor 11:5 and 1 Tim 5:14 with 1 Cor 7:8–9). There may also have been a time when Paul could write, "For Adam was formed first, then Eve. And Adam was not the one deceived; it was the woman who was deceived and became a sinner" (1 Tim 2:13–14). It is not special pleading to point out, however, that this perspective stands in considerable tension with 1 Cor 11:11–12: "Nevertheless, in the Lord woman is not independent of man, nor is man independent of woman. For as the woman came from man, so also man is born of woman. But everything comes from God."

More than a matter of modern taste, such statements seem to reveal a real difference in ancient thought. As F. F. Bruce once noted, "It is difficult to square the passage from

54. Richard B. Hays, *The Moral Vision of the New Testament: Community, Cross, New Creation; A Contemporary Introduction to New Testament Ethics* (San Francisco: HarperSanFrancisco, 1996), 67.

1 Timothy [2:8–15] with the undoubtedly genuine Pauline affirmation that in Christ there is neither male nor female. But if the passage from Timothy . . . is post-Pauline, there is no need to try to square the passages with each other."[55]

So, should we then throw the Pastorals under the canonical bus, dismissing them out of hand, pretending they do not exist, or explaining away the objectionable parts, especially the polemic against the "false teachers" and the instruction regarding women/wives?[56] This would not be our recommendation. Rather, we would concur with Arland J. Hultgren, with whose wise words we conclude our treatment of Paul's letters in general and the Pastorals in particular:

> Like other books in the New Testament, the Pastorals exist within a constellation of claims, exhortations, and instructions concerning Christian faith and life. Study of the New Testament in depth exposes the differences among them and poses the question, then, of what is of first importance. The Pastorals do not stand alone, and few would grant them the last word on all matters they take up. But for the beauty of their expressions concerning God, their strong affirmations of divine love, will, and grace for human redemption in Christ, and their passion for sound teaching and honourable living in the world, they have won their acceptance, and their importance, within the canon of Christian literature.[57]

---

55. F. F. Bruce, "The Enigma of Paul: Why Did the Early Church's Great Liberator Get a Reputation as an Authoritarian?" *BRev* 4 (1988): 32–33 (on 33).
56. The writer of this chapter had a former colleague who euphemistically remarked that the Pastorals were the least functional part of the biblical canon for him.
57. Arland J. Hultgren, "The Pastoral Epistles," in *The Cambridge Companion to St Paul* (ed. James D. G. Dunn; Cambridge: Cambridge University Press, 2003), 154.

» KEY PEOPLE, PLACES, AND TERMS «

Bishop/Overseer
Crete
Deacon
Elder
Jannes and Jambres
Lois and Eunice
Onesiphorus
Pontius Pilate

» QUESTIONS FOR REVIEW AND DISCUSSION «

1. What three Pauline letters comprise the Pastorals? Why are they so labeled?
2. What can one learn about Timothy and Titus from the Pauline letters and Acts?
3. About what two matters do scholars generally agree regarding the Pastorals?
4. For what reasons do most contemporary Pauline scholars regard the Pastoral Letters to be pseudonymous?
5. Where is Paul at the end of Acts? According to Eusebius, what happened to Paul after the close of Acts?
6. In what order are the Pastorals treated in this chapter? Why?
7. Identify and discuss the two creedal-like texts in Titus.
8. In Titus, instructions to younger women, younger men, and slaves concludes with a "so that" statement. What are these statements? Do you think the desired ends justify the stated means?
9. What was the nature of the "false teaching" the Pastorals attempt to combat?
10. What three suggestions are offered regarding the interpretation of 1 Tim 2:8 – 15?
11. According to 1 Timothy 5, what principles are to be employed when caring for widows?
12. Summarize 1 Timothy's instructions regarding money.
13. What differentiates 2 Timothy from 1 Timothy and Titus?
14. According to 2 Timothy, from whom did Timothy learn the faith?
15. What three metaphors does Paul employ in his instruction of Timothy in 2 Timothy 2?
16. According to 2 Timothy 4, what was Paul's mind-set regarding the future?
17. What are five interpretive options on offer regarding authorship of the Pastorals?

» CONTEMPORARY THEOLOGICAL REFLECTION «

1. Note the three interpretive suggestions we offer for reading qualifications set forth for church offices/officers in the Pastorals. In what ways might these texts be best appropriated in a twenty-first-century church context?
2. How might the church today better care for the elderly, including widows/ widowers, in its midst?
3. According to 2 Timothy 3, what kind of behavior will presage the last days? Do you think that we are living in the last days? Why or why not?
4. Reflect on the nature and purpose of Scripture according to 2 Timothy 3:16–17.
5. Respond to the following statement that the author of this chapter once heard: "If Paul did not write the Pastorals, then they either need to be removed from the canon or be completely ignored."

» GOING FURTHER «

Commentaries

Barrett, C. K. *The Pastoral Epistles.* Oxford: Oxford University Press, 1963.

Bassler, Jouette. *1 Timothy, 2 Timothy, Titus.* ANTC. Nashville: Abingdon, 1996.

Gloer, W. Hulitt. *1 & 2 Timothy-Titus.* SHBC. Macon, GA: Smyth & Helwys, 2010.

Hultgren, Arland J. *1–2 Timothy, Titus.* ACNT. Minneapolis: Augsburg, 1984.

Johnson, Luke Timothy. *1–2 Timothy.* AB 35A. New York: Doubleday, 2001.

Marshall, I. Howard. *A Critical and Exegetical Commentary on the Pastoral Epistles.* ICC. Edinburgh: T&T Clark, 1999.

Mounce, William D. *Pastoral Epistles.* WBC 46. Nashville: Nelson, 2000.

Quinn, Jerome D. *The Letter to Titus.* AB 35. New York: Doubleday, 1990.

Towner, Philip H. *The Letters to Timothy and Titus.* NICNT. Grand Rapids: Eerdmans, 2006.

Wall, Robert W., with Richard B. Steele. *1 and 2 Timothy and Titus.* THNTC. Grand Rapids: Eerdmans, 2012.

Special Studies

Aageson, James W. *Paul, the Pastoral Epistles, and the Early Church.* Peabody, MA: Hendrickson, 2007.

Donelson, Lewis R. *Pseudepigraphy and Ethical Argument in the Pastoral Epistles.* HUT 22. Tübingen: Mohr, 1986.

Harding, Mark. *What Are They Saying about the Pastoral Epistles?* New York: Paulist, 2001.

Kidd, Reggie M. *Wealth and Beneficence in the Pastoral Epistles: A "Bourgeois" Form of Early Christianity?* SBLDS 122. Atlanta: Scholars, 1990.
Pietersen, Lloyd. *The Polemic of the Pastorals: A Sociological Examination of the Development of Pauline Christianity.* JSNTSup 264. London/New York: T&T Clark, 2004.
Towner, Philip H. *The Goal of Our Instruction: The Structure of Theology and Ethics in the Pastoral Epistles.* JSNTSup 34. Sheffield: JSOT Press, 1989.
Twomey, Jay. *The Pastoral Epistles through the Centuries.* BBC. Chichester: Wiley-Blackwell, 2009.
Van Neste, Ray. *Cohesion and Structure in the Pastoral Epistles.* JSNTSup 280. London/New York: T&T Clark, 2004.
Verner, David C. *The Household of God: The Social World of the Pastoral Epistles.* SBLDS 71. Chico, CA: Scholars, 1983.
Wilson, Stephen G. *Luke and the Pastoral Epistles.* London: SPCK, 1979.

PART 3

PAUL'S THEOLOGY

INTRODUCTION

If the previous ten chapters have outlined Paul's life and sunk exploratory probes into parts of his extant letters, the next three chapters work "higher up," in a sense—seeking to gain more of an "aerial perspective" of Paul's theological landscape.

The task is challenging, since Paul's theological discourse is less like a set of tidy propositions and more like a lion on the loose, intent on its task and refusing to be caged or tamed. But even lions have personalities and patterns of life that characterize them individually, allowing researchers to get to know their habits, their preferences, and their lifestyles. So although we cannot hope to tame the lion that is Paul's theological discourse, we can nonetheless hope to spot some of its main characteristics and get a sense of what makes it roar.

In the hope of glimpsing what holds Paul's theological discourse together, these three chapters dedicated to that task will not unpack every issue that Paul's discourse engages throughout his letters. The task, instead, will be to foreground key features of Paul's theological discourse, to see something of the character of those features, and to spot the theological connective tissue that coordinates them.

To that end, our task is divided into three parts, with a chapter dedicated to each one.

- Chapter 11 catches sight of the "apocalyptic narrative" animating Paul's theological discourse.
- Chapter 12 analyzes how that narrative engages with grand "macro-narratives" of Paul's day, in particular, the narratives about the covenant people of Israel and the Roman imperial order.
- Chapter 13 offers a series of case studies in which the apocalyptic narrative impacts the "micro-narratives" of the lives of Jesus-followers and the ethos of Jesus groups.

CHAPTER 11

THE APOCALYPTIC NARRATIVE OF PAUL'S THEOLOGICAL DISCOURSE

CHAPTER GOALS

The goal of this chapter is to come to grips with some primary components within Paul's theological worldview. This will serve to foster a better understanding of the theological narrative that generated Paul's theological discourse and motivated his pastoral concerns.

CHAPTER OVERVIEW

1. What Kind of Thinker Was Paul?
2. Did Paul Think Jesus Was Divine, and How Does the Answer to That Question Have Relevance?
3. Did "the Jesus of History" Really Matter to Paul?
4. Did Paul Advocate Faith in Jesus Who Himself Was Faithful?
5. Did Paul Think That Faith Is All There Is to It?
6. Key People, Places, and Terms
7. Questions for Review and Discussion
8. Contemporary Theological Reflection
9. Going Further

WHAT KIND OF THINKER WAS PAUL?

Having traversed the Pauline corpus letter by letter, we are now in a position to reflect on the mind behind those letters. What kind of thinker was Paul? Since we know what he left behind in his extant texts, what do those texts reveal about how he articulated his theological discourse?

Some have viewed Paul as if he were an armchair systematic theologian. In the deep recesses of his penetrating mind, Paul delved into intricate theological issues, emerging from his passionate cogitations with rigorously considered ideas that he bequeathed to the church as systematically robust articulations of Christian theology.

Clearly this view has some merit, since Paul's theological discourse repeatedly demonstrates a notably resourceful and ingenious mind that demands respect. But Paul was not an academic systematic theologian; instead, he was more of an expert missionary and a devout pastor who, in fulfilling his commission, exercised a keen vision that was fed by deep theological resources. He spent many years on the road traveling from place to place, carrying his tent, his garb, and his gear. When he settled in a city for any period of time, he was busy engaging people in discourse about his gospel, all the while working with his hands and shepherding fledgling communities of Jesus devotion. His letters to Jesus groups of other cities were not systematic treatises per se, but were pastoral letters occasioned by specific situations and intended to influence the thinking and behavior of localized groups of people who required correction or instruction on selected matters.[1]

So we might ask: Are Paul's letters emblematic of systematic logic? Many have thought not. For instance, toward the beginning of the twentieth century, the influential Pauline interpreter Wilhelm Wrede claimed: "It is no great feat to unearth contradictions, even among his [Paul's] leading thoughts."[2] Toward the end of the twentieth century, Heikki Räisänen was similarly influential in proposing that "contradictions and tensions" are "constant features of Paul's theology."[3]

▼ A fourth-century fresco of the apostle Paul preaching

1. This is true even of Romans, as discussed in chapter 6 above.
2. Wilhelm Wrede, *Paul* (Boston: American Unitarian Association, 1908), 77. Similar estimates have been registered for many ancients, including the Jewish philosopher and exegete Philo of Alexandria. See, for instance, David T. Runia, "Flight and Exile in Philo of Alexandria," in *The Studia Philonica Annual* 21 (2009): 1–24 (esp. 6–7); Gregory Sterling, "How Do You Introduce Philo of Alexandria?" in *The Studia Philonica Annual* 21 (2009): 63–72 (esp. 68).
3. Heikki Räisänen, *Paul and the Law* (Tübingen: Mohr Siebeck, 1983), 11.

Paul's Brilliant Mind

"No other religion enjoys anything like the combination of a charismatic figure like Jesus and a first-class intellectual like St. Paul. If you're wanting omnipotence to set up a religion, it seems to me that this is the one to beat!"

These are the words of Anthony Flew, the leading atheist philosopher of the twentieth century, who later changed his mind and accepted the existence of God. The account of his transformation in thinking is explained in his intriguing little book *There Is a God: How the World's Most Notorious Atheist Changed His Mind* (San Francisco: HarperOne, 2007). This quote is on page 157, though the thought is repeated (with slight changes) on pages 185–86, with the additional note that Paul "had a brilliant philosophical mind."

▲ Paul writes to communities that he founded.

Räisänen was not intending to criticize Paul per se but primarily to cause interpreters to think long and hard about what they expect to find in Paul's letters. Instead of anticipating robust **systematic theology**, Räisänen proposed that we should expect from Paul what we would expect of any other preacher, missionary, or community builder. For Räisänen, Paul's theological articulations in any given instance are not primarily intended to satisfy the requirements of logical coherence so much as to shape the lives of their auditors through rhetorical urgency. So, according to Räisänen, Paul was simply "a man of practical religion who develops a line of thought to make a practical point, to influence the conduct of his readers; in the next moment he is quite capable of putting forward a statement which logically contradicts the previous one when trying to make a different point or, rather, struggling with a different problem."[4]

While Räisänen goes too far in his estimate that inconsistency lies at the heart of Paul's theological articulations, he does successfully raise the issue as to what kind of thinker we imagine Paul to have been. Should we expect Paul to have had a fully articulated theological system or package "in his back pocket," in a sense, from the moment he encountered the resurrected Christ? Did he carry around with him a theological box full of goodies that he simply tilted in this direction or that on any given occasion, with helpful theological nuggets spilling out to edify his audience? Is there a central concept that gives coherence to Paul's thinking across the spectrum of his letters, such as "justification by faith," "reconciliation with God," "Jesus is Lord," or being "in Christ"?

4. Ibid., 267 (also p. 12). Views of this sort are not uncommon when considering the intricacies of Paul's discourse on matters such as the law, the people of Israel, or the Roman imperial order—all of which will be considered in chapter 12 below.

Moreover, when thinking of the problem that redemption in Christ solves, does Paul think "from solution to plight," so that his analysis is already predetermined by an indebtedness to the conviction that salvation is found exclusively "in Christ"?[5] Or does his thinking move instead "from plight to solution," so that a predetermined view of the salvific problem informs his view of salvation in Christ?[6] Or are things more complicated than either of these views, with "solution" and "plight" being held in a dialogical loop within Paul's mind, as they mutually inform each other in an ongoing discovery of dimensions within each of them?

With issues of this kind proving enormously difficult to resolve, many Pauline scholars prefer to speak less about Paul's "theology" and more about his "theologizing" in any given instance. This avoids imagining that Paul's theology comes readily "prepackaged" and does better justice to the situational dimension of his thinking.

"Paul's ad hoc arguments do not add up to a system, whether one treats the letters individually or collectively. If Paul, the letter writer, is a contextual theologian rather than a systematic one, then one expects literary and conceptual untidiness."[7]

Along with this goes a recognition of the **socio-rhetorical** dimension of Paul's theologizing. While logical coherence clearly plays a role within Paul's discourse, it may nonetheless become subordinate to Paul's rhetorical goals in certain instances. That is to say, Paul's distinct arguments are rhetorically targeted to serve their purposes within particular situations, being driven primarily by canons of rhetorical urgency rather than logical consistency across the whole of what would later become the Pauline corpus.

But Paul's texts should not be thought of simply as a hodgepodge of discombobulated theological expressions that came into being through Paul's knee-jerk reactions to varying situations. Understanding Paul's letters and theology properly involves getting the balance right between contingency and coherence. At any given point, attention must be given to both the situational dimension of Paul's theologizing (i.e., its contingency) and the larger matrix of Paul's theological convictions (i.e., its coherence).

"I regard Paul as a coherent thinker, but not a systematic theologian. His letters are much more interesting, exciting, and in fact glorious than that."[8]

Instructive in this matter is the magisterial work of one of Paul's most insightful interpreters, J. C. Beker. In his magnum opus *Paul the Apostle: The Triumph of God in Life and Thought* (published in 1980 but still worth careful consideration today), Beker proposed that behind Paul's contingent theologizing lay not a

5. This position is advocated by E. P. Sanders, *Paul and Palestinian Judaism* (Philadelphia: Fortress, 1977).
6. This position is advocated by Frank Thielman, *From Plight to Solution: A Jewish Framework for Understanding Paul's View of the Law in Galatians and Romans* (Leiden: Brill, 1989).
7. Gregory Tatum, *New Chapters in the Life of Paul: The Relative Chronology of His Career* (Washington, DC: Catholic Biblical Association, 2006), 11.
8. E. P. Sanders, "Did Paul's Theology Develop?" in *The Word Leaps the Gap: Essays on Scripture and Theology in Honor of Richard B. Hays* (ed. J. Ross Wagner et al.; Grand Rapids: Eerdmans, 2008), 330.

A mighty fortress is our God, a bulwark
never failing;
Our helper He, amid the flood of mortal
ills prevailing:
For still our ancient foe doth seek to
work us woe;
His craft and power are great, and armed
with cruel hate,
On earth is not his equal.
—Martin Luther, "A Mighty Fortress is Our God"

single theological nugget contained in a simple slogan but a coherent "macro-symbol" of the sovereign triumph of Israel's God over competing forces that threatened to unravel the cosmic order of creation. According to Beker, this "**apocalyptic**" matrix, or "the apocalyptic interpretation of the Christ-event,"[9] is the filter through which Scripture, tradition, and situation were fed whenever Paul analyzed a situation's full dimensions.

The preceding chapters have repeatedly highlighted features of Paul's letters that tend to corroborate Beker's view on the "apocalyptic" coherence within Paul's contingent theological articulations. But it also needs to be noted that a narrative dimension lies within the heart of the apocalyptic matrix of Paul's thought. Although Paul did not write stories in his extant letters, the apocalyptic matrix that undergirds those letters seems itself to be narratively configured.

Many leading Pauline scholars are now advocating "narrative" as the nexus that gave rise to Paul's contingent articulations at any given point. One cannot get far into the writings of prominent interpreters like Richard Hays, Tom Wright, Ben Witherington III, or Michael Gorman without reading about the narrative substructure to Paul's theologizing. So, for instance, Tom Wright articulates the point in this way:

> Within all his letters . . . we discover a larger implicit narrative [than Paul's explicit discourse articulates]. Paul presupposes this story even when he does not expound it directly, and it is arguable that we can only understand the more limited narrative worlds of the different letters if we locate them at their appropriate points within this overall story-world.10

That story world, itself comprising the apocalyptic thrust of Paul's theologizing, might best be articulated in the following fashion:

> The God of Israel has created a good creation that is currently under the influence of cosmic forces that run contrary to the ways of the creator God. These forces include the powers of Sin and Death, who have conscripted the human race (as evidenced in Adam) in their efforts to denude God of his creation. Through the death and resurrection of Jesus Christ, God has acted to redeem his good creation from the clutches of those powers. Being "in Christ" and living within the story of Jesus, Jesus-followers are participants in that process of divine triumph, whose lives are continually to be transformed by the Spirit as miniature advertisements and embodiments of the eschatological rectification of the whole of the created order, to the glory of God.[11]

9. J. C. Beker, *Paul the Apostle: The Triumph of God in Life and Thought* (Philadelphia: Fortress, 1980), 135.
10. N. T. Wright, *The New Testament and the People of God* (London: SPCK, 1992), 405. On the narrative approach to Paul, see Bruce W. Longenecker, "The Narrative Approach to Paul: An Early Retrospective," *CurBR* 1 (2002): 88–111 (reprinted in *New Testament Studies: Benchmarks in Religious Studies* [ed. Paul Foster; London: Sage, 2010]); also the collection of essays in Bruce W. Longenecker, ed., *Narrative Dynamics in Paul: A Critical Assessment* (Louisville: Westminster John Knox, 2002).
11. This way of constructing the undergirding narrative of Paul's theologizing is much different than the one proposed by Rudolf Bultmann and many others, who extracted a narrative that complied with the Gnostic Redeemer Myth that came into full existence only in the second century AD.

An apocalyptic narrative along lines such as this basic outline (which requires significant amplification at almost every turn) seems to provide the fertile soil that fed most of Paul's most profound theological articulations.

A final word about the adjective *apocalyptic* is called for here. Since the term can have a number of connotations, it might fail to connote distinct meaning. Moreover, clearly at times the word has been used controversially within Pauline scholarship.[12] But the choice is made here not to throw the baby out with the bathwater, especially since there is no better term currently on offer to carry the full weight of Paul's theologizing.

"Paul sees the community of faith being caught up into the story of God's remaking of the world through Jesus Christ. Within this world shaped by the story of Jesus Christ, the community wrestles with the constant need for spiritual discernment to understand and enact the obedience of faith. In so doing, the community discovers *koinōnia* with one another in the sufferings of Christ and in the hope of sharing his glory."[13]

"Paul's eschatology locates the Christian community within a cosmic, apocalyptic frame of reference. The church community is God's eschatological beachhead, the place where the power of God has invaded the world."[14]

Taking our cues from Gal 1:16, the verbal form of the word group ("to apocalypse" [NIV "reveal"]) is used there to connote transformation—a transformation that is all-encompassing. Claiming in Gal 1:16 that God was pleased to "apocalypse" his Son "in" him, Paul is referring to much more than a disclosure of divine revelation (see chapter 3 above on Galatians). Paul is, in effect, presenting himself here as a microcosm of the cosmos under the control of cosmic forces at odds with God. His point is that what God is doing in the world has already happened in him. Paul presents himself, in a sense, as a case study in a much larger narrative of God's reclamation of the cosmos from the grip of competing forces. It is a reclamation of the world in which God transforms what is opposed to him and rechannels it in new directions, according to his purposes. Later in Galatians Paul goes on to speak of this as his dying with Christ so that Christ lives in him (2:19–20) and likens it to "new creation" (6:15). All this is transpiring despite the entrenched grip of the elemental forces that have sought to enslave the world (4:8–9). But in Jesus Christ, God has "set us free from the present evil age" (1:4).

All this breathes the air of **Jewish apocalypticism**, with God ultimately reclaiming his creation from the "cosmos grabbers" (Eph 6:12, trans. BWL) who seek to wrestle it from him. Or as Eph 6:12 more fully states, the larger struggle that Jesus-followers have been drafted into is "not against flesh and blood, but against the rulers, against the

12. Both authors of this textbook have sought to avoid the approach that divorces "apocalyptic" from "covenant." See for instance the *Journal for the Study of Paul and His Letters* 2 (2012), wherein Bruce W. Longenecker's article "Salvation History in Galatians and the Making of a Pauline Discourse" is found on pages 65–87, and Todd D. Still's article "'Once Upon a Time': Galatians as an Apocalyptic Story" is found on pages 133–41.
13. Richard B. Hays, *The Moral Vision of the New Testament: A Contemporary Introduction to New Testament Ethics* (San Francisco: HarperSanFrancisco, 1996), 45–46.
14. Hays, *The Moral Vision of the New Testament*, 27.

Job's Evil Dreams, Blake, William/Pierpont Morgan Library, New York, USA/The Bridgeman Art Library

▲ "Job's Evil Dreams" by William Blake. Paul states in Ephesians 6:12 that Jesus-followers will struggle against the spiritual forces of evil.
▼ For Paul, the triumph of God over competing forces is assured by means of the death and resurrection of Jesus Christ.

Ms 139/1363 fol.30v Christ running through the Leviathan, from 'Le Miroir de l'Humaine Salvation', Flemish School, (15th century)/Musee Conde, Chantilly, France/Giraudon/The Bridgeman Art Library

authorities, against the powers of this dark world and against the spiritual forces of evil in the heavenly realms." If the struggle is not yet complete, the victory is nonetheless assured, as Paul notes simply in 1 Cor 15:24: "Then the end will come, when he hands over the kingdom to God the Father after he has destroyed all dominion, authority and power." These passages encapsulate the main foci of Paul's apocalyptic perspective — the subjection of all things under the control of the God who long ago called Israel to be his covenant people. For Paul, the triumph of God over competing forces is assured by means of the death and resurrection of Jesus Christ.

DID PAUL THINK JESUS WAS DIVINE, AND HOW DOES THE ANSWER TO THAT QUESTION HAVE RELEVANCE?

It is clear that both the God of creation and Jesus Christ are foregrounded within Paul's narratively configured theological discourse. But how are we to imagine their relationship? How is Jesus to be understood in relation to God's restoration of the cosmos? Is the notion of divine **incarnation** appropriate to Paul's view of Jesus Christ and his role in the apocalyptic drama?

In the 1970s and early 1980s, a variety of theologians and biblical scholars dedicated themselves to exploring the so-called "Myth of God Incarnate." They considered what Christian theology would be like if it could shed its commitment to God becoming incarnate in Jesus. Can that doctrine be extracted from Christian theology without undermining the core of Christianity itself?

In the study of Paul's theology, it became pressing to ask whether a doctrine of the incarnation of God in Christ was even present in Paul, and if so, to what extent. It was not uncommon to hear that instead of understanding Jesus as preexistent, Paul imagined simply that Jesus had fulfilled the human program, incarnating what it means to live "authentically" before God, in contrast to the rest of the human race before and apart from him. Whereas Adam had thrown the human race into sinfulness through his act of self-aggrandizement, Jesus, the "authentic human being," had lived in such a distinctive way as to offset the effects of human sinfulness through his act of heroic self-giving, thereby effecting a new situation and introducing a new option for humankind to follow in his wake.

While all this sounded fresh and stimulating, it resulted in the severe curtailment of certain features of Paul's gospel, greatly diminishing the full narrative contours of his worldview.

To demonstrate this, it is important first to note that Paul evidences moments of extremely high **Christology**, to the point of almost trinitarian disclosure. It is true, of course, that a fully developed view of the **Trinity** was not available to Paul, since it took Christian theologians several centuries to craft a fully nuanced and balanced theology of the Trinity. But there are, nonetheless, notable trinitarian "resources" within Paul's letters. They are not the only building blocks within Paul's theological discourse, and they frequently intertwine with others that are "less developed."[15] But they do have a foothold in Paul's letters.

Altar frontal depicting the Trinity between St. Sebald and Archangel Michael, from Nuremberg, German School, (15th century)/Germanisches Nationalmuseum, Nuremberg, Germany/The Bridgeman Art Library

▲ Fifteenth-century art of the Trinity. A fully developed view of the Trinity was not available to Paul, but there are notable Trinitarian "resources" within Paul's letters.

This is especially true for the way that Paul includes Jesus within the focus of worship of the divine. In this regard, notice the way that the **Shema** (the single confession that lay at the very heart of Jewish **monotheism**) is found in reworked fashion in 1 Cor 8:4–6. A prayer recited morning and evening by pious Jews, the Shema begins with the words of Deut 6:4: "Hear, O Israel: The LORD our God, the LORD is one." While Paul builds his discourse on the oneness of God in Rom 3:29–30 and Gal 3:20, it is 1 Cor 8:4–6 that reveals the extent to which Jesus Christ has invaded and qualified Paul's monotheism. Addressing the issue of idolatry (specifically, the issue of food sacrificed to idols), Paul first affirms (as Corinthian Christians seem to have accepted) that "there is no God but one"—echoing the Jewish Shema (8:4). But he goes on to place a christological spin on that same confession that lay at the heart of Jewish monotheistic affirmation. So he writes: "There is one God, the Father, from whom all things came and for whom we live; and there is but one Lord, Jesus Christ, through whom all things came and through whom we live" (8:6).

15. In this regard, some point to the threefold division of Father, Son, and Spirit at various points in Paul's letters. The issue of whether Paul actually called Jesus "God" is more difficult. He usually differentiates Jesus and "God," as in 1 Cor 15:27–28 and in many other places. Some think Paul called Jesus "God" in Rom 9:5 (as in the NIV), although that interpretation is not beyond dispute (as in the NIV note to Rom 9:5). The author of Titus (whether an elderly Paul or, more likely, a disciple writing in his name) is explicit in calling Jesus "God" (Titus 2:13).

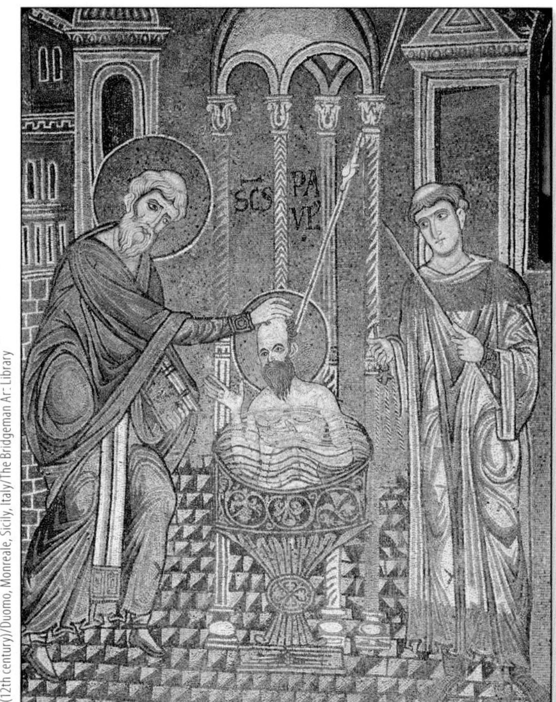

▲ A mosaic of Paul being baptized by Ananias. Early Jesus-followers had a very Jesus-centered focus. They prayed to Jesus, invoked his name at their meals, and baptized new members in his name.

Here the traditional portrait of the one, sovereign, and covenant God is refashioned in the light of Christ. Prior to his **Damascus Road** experience, Paul would have prayed the Shema twice a day, understanding both "God" and "Lord" as referring to Israel's sovereign and covenant God. At some point after that experience, however, Paul began to understand the Shema differently. For Paul, the term "God" now refers to "the Father" and the term "Lord" now refers to "Jesus Christ."

In effect, Paul has split the Shema into two parts, one of which is focused on Jesus Christ. If the Shema had the practical effect of bolstering commitment to Israel's sovereign and covenantal God, Paul dramatically revised the Shema, placing Jesus Christ at the heart of his understanding of that God. In the span of three short verses, then, Paul has introduced a striking modification of a cardinal tenet of the Jewish understanding of God. The text of 1 Cor 8:4–6 demonstrates how a Judean itinerant teacher of humble origins, who died a humiliating and disgraceful death (in the year AD 30), is referred to only twenty-four years after his crucifixion in a fashion that puts him at the center of traditional Jewish devotion to the sovereign God—albeit in a wholly "untraditional" fashion.

It is hardly surprising, then, to see Paul doing much the same with monotheistic Scriptures. In Phil 2:9–11 Paul elaborates the exaltation of Jesus in this way:

> Therefore God exalted him to the highest place
> and gave him the name that is above every name,
> that at the name of Jesus every knee should bow,
> in heaven and on earth and under the earth,
> and every tongue acknowledge that Jesus Christ is Lord,
> to the glory of God the Father.

This daring articulation employs terminology used in Scripture to describe Israel's God. In Isa 45:23, Yahweh is cited as saying, "Before me every knee will bow; by me every tongue will swear." The theological vision of Isaiah imagines a day when the God of Israel will triumph over forces competing for control over God's good creation, with all the world offering worship to the one true God of all. In Paul's letter to Philippian Christians, the prophet's vision is now refracted so that it now incorporates Jesus Christ at the heart of the worshipful adoration properly offered to Israel's God.[16]

16. So too, in Rom 10:13 Paul interprets Joel 3:5 christologically; whereas within its literary context the "Lord" of Joel 3:5 is Yahweh, the God of Israel, Paul now reads it in reference to Jesus Christ.

Similarly, aspects of Jewish worship that were normally part of the worship of Israel's God were practiced in Jesus groups, with Jesus Christ as their focus. So, Jesus-followers prayed to Jesus, sang reverential hymns about God's redemptive action through him, met in his name, invoked his name at their meals ("the **Lord's Supper**"), and expected his imminent appearance ("**maranatha**," which best translates as "our Lord, come" [1 Cor 16:22]). Feeling his presence among them in worship, they baptized new members into his name and performed healings and exorcisms in his name. These features of the corporate worship of the early Christian communities testify to an overwhelming devotion to Jesus that is astoundingly bold in comparison to the monotheistic parameters that were standard within first-century Judaism.[17]

The Eucharist (fresco), Paleo-Christian, (2nd century)/Catacombs of Priscilla, Rome, Italy/ The Bridgeman Art Library

▲ A second-century fresco of the Eucharist. This meal was part of corporate worship in the early communities of Jesus-followers.

While this is significant in relation to Paul's understanding of God, it is also significant in relation to his understanding of the human predicament and the means whereby God is acting to redeem his creation. In Paul's view, humanity apart from Jesus Christ is under the domination of suprahuman powers that shape human choices and human patterns of life, with the result that sinfulness permeates every level of creation, which is caught in the clutches of death. In the context of Romans 7, for instance, Paul depicts the power of Sin as dominating even the well-intentioned Jewish lover of God whose respectable goal is to please God by obeying the life-giving Torah; even in that promising scenario, however, the power of Sin seizes even the Torah so that it cannot perform its God-given purposes and produces sinfulness, despite the best of one's intentions. If this is true for members of God's elect people, what hope is there for the rest of humanity!

The gospel "is not a doctrine about our nature, about our authentic existence as human beings, but rather is the proclamation of this liberating act of God, of the salvation occurrence that is realized in Christ."[18]

This all-encompassing situation of despair cannot be redeemed simply through the heroic appearance of a human being who manages against all odds to live out some imagined, ideal human program. To hope that "authentic humanity" might somehow emerge from such a scenario involves underestimating the desperate condition that has engulfed the whole of creation, thereby allowing the powers of Sin and Death to maintain their sovereignty but disguising the depths of hopelessness within this situation.

17. On this, see especially Larry Hurtado, *Lord Jesus Christ: Devotion to Jesus in Earliest Christianity* (Grand Rapids: Eerdmans, 2005).
18. Rudolf Bultmann, *The New Testament and Mythology* (Minneapolis: Fortress, 1986), 26.

If redemption is to transpire, it cannot be achieved through the emergence of some exceptional human being; the conglomeration of powers is too dominant and controlling to permit that to ever happen. Instead, redemption requires the invasion of a force more commanding, more prevailing, and more sophisticated than the suprahuman powers of destruction, in order to undo their devastating grip over God's good creation. For Paul, God himself initiated the rectification of the cosmos by sending his preexistent and divine Son in the "likeness" of humanity-in-bondage-to-Sin (Rom 8:3). Only in that incarnation of divine power are the suprahuman forces that run contrary to God being dismantled.

"Paul's view of Sin-dominated Flesh has as its counterpart a notion of the Incarnation that is crucial to his theology, though it has been greatly underemphasized by critical scholarship. When humanity is at a dead end, God takes the initiative."[19]

When speaking of Jesus Christ as being in the "likeness" of humanity-in-bondage-to-Sin, Paul did not mean that Jesus Christ was only partially human. That would take us to the other end of the spectrum from those who imagined that Jesus might be thought of as the full embodiment of "authentic humanity." Instead, Paul meant only that Jesus' humanity had not been abducted by the power of Sin, unlike the rest of humanity. So it is that Paul thinks of Jesus Christ as one "who had no sin" (2 Cor 5:21). Jesus did not simply manage to evade Sin's clutches, as a human who fulfilled the human program. Instead, he overcame Sin's power precisely because, as the preexistent one in whom God is most manifestly evident, he neutralized the power of Sin in his life of self-giving love. In a sense, then, it took an authentic incarnation of the authentic God to incarnate the authentic humanity evident within the person of Jesus. To diminish any part of this equation is to allow Paul's theology to unravel irredeemably.

"The human being can never escape from a state of dependency on things and relationships. The question then is simply whether it is a dependency which binds us closer to sin, flesh and death; or a dependency on a higher power, the power which makes it possible for us to be what we were made to be and which little by little moulds us into what we were made to be, the image of God in Christ."[20]

It is here that we find Paul's most fertile theological articulations about the processes of salvation, involving the transfer of the Jesus-follower from one realm of power to another—from enslavement to the power of Sin on the one hand, to the freedom that arises through power of the Spirit that permeates the sphere of being "in Christ." This central feature of Paul's theologizing has been dubbed "**participationistic eschatology**" by E. P. Sanders, who describes it as follows:

> God has sent Christ to be the savior of all, both Jew and Gentile (and has called Paul to be the apostle to the Gentiles); one participates in salvation by becoming one person with Christ, dying with him to sin and sharing the promise of his resurrection; the transforma-

19. George W. E. Nickelsburg, "The Incarnation in Paul: Paul's Solution to the Universal Human Predicament," in *The Future of Early Christianity: Essays in Honor of Helmut Koester* (ed. Birger A. Pearson et al.; Minneapolis: Fortress, 1991), 349, 356.
20. James D. G. Dunn, *Christian Liberty: A New Testament Perspective* (Eugene, OR: Wipf & Stock, 2005), 70.

tion, however, will not be completed until the Lord returns; meanwhile one who is in Christ has been freed from the power of sin and the uncleanness of transgression, and his behavior should be determined by his new situation; since Christ died to save all, all [humanity] must have been under the dominion of sin, "in the flesh" as opposed to being in the Spirit.[21]

In light of what we have seen at various points in the chapters above, two other components could helpfully be added to this condensed version of what lies at the heart of Paul's theologizing:

- a cosmic scope, involving the rectification not simply of all humanity (and certainly not simply of individual souls escaping to a heavenly resort in the sky), but the rectification of the whole of God's created order
- a salvation-historical perspective, involving what God had been doing in and through Israel (on this, see chapter 12 below)

DID "THE JESUS OF HISTORY" REALLY MATTER TO PAUL?

But what did Paul really know about the one who embodied both authentic divinity and authentic humanity? How much did Paul know about Jesus' life, and how much did he care about what Jesus taught and how he had lived? Was Paul's apocalyptic gospel simply a grand metanarrative that had little or nothing to do with Jesus of Nazareth, whom he proclaimed as Lord?

We will never know whether Paul had already known anything about Jesus prior to his crucifixion in AD 30. Paul may have known something about Jesus prior to that date, since Paul seems to have been highly attentive to issues of Jewish covenant identity (Gal 1:14; Phil 3:5–6) at much the same time when Jesus was publicly active and entangled in controversy with leaders of the Jewish people (roughly AD 27–30).[22] But even if Paul may have had some knowledge about Jesus prior to his crucifixion, it would have come to him secondhand, from others who had encountered Jesus; if Paul himself had encountered Jesus prior to the crucifixion, there would probably be some mention of that fact within Paul's extant letters (an argument from silence that, nonetheless, carries some weight).[23]

Whatever Paul may have known about Jesus before his crucifixion was supplemented further after Jesus' resurrection. The earliest preaching of Jesus' transformed apostles may have afforded Paul some basic data about Jesus' life, even prior to Paul's own christophany on the Damascus Road in the year 32 or so. After that experience, a visit to Jerusalem in about the year 35 would have provided Paul with an invaluable opportunity to learn about Jesus' life; spending more than two weeks with Peter on that occasion would have enabled Paul to hear about the life of the resurrected Messiah directly from Peter, one of Jesus' closest and most significant disciples (Gal 1:18).

21. Sanders, *Paul and Palestinian Judaism*, 549.
22. Paul might have been in his late teens at the time of Jesus' public ministry, if we take into account the reference to "Saul" as a "young man" (perhaps twenty years old) at the time of Stephen's stoning (Acts 7:58).
23. When Paul speaks of once having regarded Jesus Christ from "a worldly point of view" but of doing so no longer (2 Cor 5:16), he is speaking not about having known Jesus prior to his crucifixion. Instead, Paul's transformed relationship with Jesus Christ is being used merely as an example of how he no longer evaluates the worth of others in any way other than through the lens of the gospel.

St. Peter and St. Paul, Italian School, (15th century)/Chiesa di Santa Maria Maddalena, Gressan, Italy/Seat Archive/Alinari Archives/The Bridgeman Art Library

▲ A fifteenth-century depiction of Peter and Paul

When laying the foundations on which communities of Jesus devotion were built, Paul seems to have instructed new Jesus-followers in the key moments in the story of Jesus' life. In his directives to Corinthian Christians concerning Jesus' resurrection, for instance, Paul speaks of their early initiation into this story, with the phrase "what I received I passed on to you as of first importance" (1 Cor 15:3). The words Paul chose here to depict transmission of the story ("receive" and "pass on") were established terms that indicated how someone learned a body of teaching from established authority figures and then conveyed that teaching to others. The same terms are used in 1 Cor 11:23 when Paul speaks of his instruction regarding Jesus' Last Supper with his disciples (although there Paul adds the phrase "from the Lord" when indicating how he had received the tradition).

Paul seems also to have known of the notable character of Jesus' own prayer life. This is suggested by the fact that Paul makes use of the term "*Abba*" when writing to recently converted Gentiles in communities he founded (Gal 4:6) and to others (Rom 8:15). The term "*Abba*" is Aramaic for "father" and did not have strong currency in Jewish prayers of Jesus' day. Evidently, the term was retained by Paul and other early Jesus-followers as having been characteristic of Jesus' prayer life, in remembrance of one who prayed intimately to God, as a loving Son to a loving Father (see Mark 14:36). For Paul, Christians have been brought into the sphere of Jesus' own intimate and obedient relationship to God, so that they can share the same prayer address that Jesus used when addressing God in prayer: "*Abba*, Father." Evidently, then, Paul instructed Gentile converts in a synopsis of Jesus' own life of obedient sonship to God, a synopsis complete with Aramaic sound bites.

▲ The extent of first-century Christianity

Moreover, echoes of Jesus' ethic seem to pepper Paul's instruction at times. This is the case, for instance, in 1 Cor 7:10–11, where Paul seems cognizant of Jesus' attitude toward divorce (see Mark 10:11 – 12). Similarly in 1 Cor 9:14 (see also Gal 6:6; 1 Tim 5:18), Paul knows of a Jesus-saying instructing that those who preach should receive support for that service (see Luke 10:7; cf. Matt 10:10).

Paul's knowledge of the Jesus tradition seems especially evident in Romans 12, where he discusses the issue of relationships within and beyond Jesus groups (Rom 12:14; see also 1 Cor 4:12 – 13). The overlap of Paul's instructions in Romans with those attributed to Jesus in Matt 5:44 (see also 5:11) and Luke 6:28 is significant, since Paul seems simply to assume that echoes of Jesus' social ethic will be recognized among Jesus groups hundreds of miles away that Paul had not founded.

Rom 12:14	Bless those who persecute you; bless and do not curse.
Matt 5:44	Love your enemies and pray for those who persecute you.
Luke 6:27 – 28	Love your enemies, do good to those who hate you, bless those who curse you, pray for those who mistreat you.

Parallels of this kind suggest not only that Jesus' social ethic was part of the moral world of newly formed Jesus groups as the Jesus movement spread across the Mediterranean basin in the 40s and 50s, but also that Paul himself was similarly cognizant of Jesus' social ethic, along with the Jesus groups he founded.[24] Through the Jesus movement and Paul's own efforts, the social ethic that Jesus taught in **Galilee** and **Judea** was extending to pagan cities of the Greco-Roman world.[25]

Despite these significant pieces of data, however, it is nonetheless true that in his extant texts Paul rarely alludes to a Jesus saying. It seems that what mattered most to Paul were not so much the pronouncements of Jesus but, instead, his actions — or better, the model of life that Jesus' actions depicted. If Jesus' striking social ethic was a fundamental component in the teaching of the emergent Jesus movement, Paul seems to have focused his attention more on the way that Jesus himself embodied that social ethic within his own life, by giving of himself in order to benefit others. Accordingly, it is the model of Jesus' self-giving life that Paul foregrounds repeatedly. To have concentrated only on the social ethic

"In rarely citing JT [Jesus Tradition] explicitly Paul does not represent a special case, but is typical of what we find in early Christianity. The view that he was uninterested in JT rests primarily on the flimsy foundation of a faulty exegesis of 2 Cor. 5.16, an argument from silence based on unjustified expectations, and a reading of Paul through the distorted lens of Gal. 1.11 – 12, an affirmation made in the heat of his most polemical letter and balanced by 1 Cor. 15.3 – 7. The proper question is not why does Paul not quote or directly refer to JT more often, but why he does so at all."[26]

24. Another echo of a Jesus saying might be evident in Gal 6:1; compare Matt 18:15.
25. It is worth considering Richard Bauckham's speculative suggestion (*Jesus and the Eyewitnesses: The Gospels as Eyewitness Testimony* [Grand Rapids: Eerdmans, 2008], 270) that the gift of teaching among Jesus followers (Rom 12:7) may have included the preservation, retelling, and handing on of stories about Jesus' public ministry in Galilee and Judea.
26. Michael Thompson, *Clothed with Christ: The Example and Teaching of Jesus in Romans 12.1 – 15.13* (Sheffield: Sheffield Academic, 1991), 239.

of Jesus' teachings would be to obstruct the way that those teachings were embodied within Jesus' own life. In a sense, Paul is most interested in the fact that the Son of God himself practiced what he preached, and with cosmos-shifting effect.

DID PAUL ADVOCATE FAITH IN JESUS WHO HIMSELF WAS FAITHFUL?

If Jesus lived according to the ethic that he preached (and if he died, we might say, because he lived according to that ethic), does his model life have much traction in Paul's theological discourse?

When telling others of the self-giving life of the Son of God, Paul exhorted them to have faith in Jesus Christ. If this much is clear, less clear is whether Paul also spoke of Jesus Christ as himself exhibiting a kind of faith, or faithfulness. (The two concepts, "faith" and "faithfulness," were expressed by the same word in Greek, *pistis* — a word that needs to be incorporated into the discussion in the following paragraphs). If Jesus-followers have *pistis* in Jesus, did Paul also imagine that Jesus' life was itself characterized by *pistis*? If so, how do the two relate?

At the heart of the issue is a Greek phrase that Paul uses on several occasions, *pistis Iēsou Christou* (and its variants; see Rom 3:22, 26; Gal 2:16, 20; 3:22–23; Phil 3:9; Eph 3:12). In Greek, the phrase can signal either "faith *in* Jesus Christ" or "faith(fulness) *of* Jesus Christ." If this phrase simply means "faith in," then Gal 2:16 should read as follows:

> a person is not justified by works of the law, but by *faith in* Jesus Christ. So we, too, have put our faith in Christ Jesus that we may be justified by *faith in* Christ and not by works of the law.

But if the phrase means "faith(fulness) of," then the same verse would read as follows (as it appears in the NIV note for this verse):

> a person is not justified by works of the law, but through *the faithfulness of* Jesus Christ. So we, too, have put our faith in Christ Jesus that we may be justified on the basis of *the faithfulness of* Christ and not by works of the law.

Scholars are divided as to which of these translations is preferable. While "faith in" has predominated throughout much of Christian history, many today are finding "faith of" to be the more compelling translation and interpretation. If so, the phrase "the faith/faithfulness of" Christ may signal one or both of the following:

- Jesus' faithful obedience to God's call (see also Rom 5:18–21: Phil 2:6–8)
- Jesus' faith in God's own trustworthiness (in particular, perhaps, God's trustworthiness to raise Jesus from the dead)

For many interpreters, certain passages within Paul's letters take on a much fuller theological dimension when they are seen to include a reference to the faith(fulness) of Jesus Christ. In a passage like Rom 3:21–26, for instance, the inbreaking of God's faithful righteousness is not simply "to all who believe," but is to all who believe "through the faithfulness of Jesus Christ" (3:22); and God has put Jesus forward to be the "mercy seat" (or "sacrifice of atonement") not merely "to be received by faith" (although that is true) but "through [his] faithfulness" (Rom 3:25). In a sense, then, Paul's theologizing operates within a triangulation of faith/faithfulness:

- God's *pistis* or faithfulness (as in Rom 3:3)[27]
- Jesus' *pistis* or faithfulness (as in Rom 3:22, 25–26)
- the *pistis* or faith of Christians (as in Rom 4 esp.; see also 9:30–32; 10:4, etc.)

Moreover, the faith(fulness) of Jesus Christ would contrast with the unfaithfulness of the people of Israel (Rom 3:3), with God's righteousness flowing to all the nations through faithfulness (i.e., Jesus') rather than unfaithfulness (i.e., Israel's). In this way, as Rom 1:17 might be translated, Paul's gospel is about a righteousness that is "by faith from first to last."

Similarly in Galatians, the faith(fulness) of Jesus Christ is said to have "come" with the apocalyptic turning of the ages, thereby initiating the new era of God's salvation (Gal 3:23). Accordingly, it is Jesus' unprecedented, unique, and "enlivened" faith(fulness) before God that serves as the vehicle through which the righteous benefits of God's promises flow to those who believe in Jesus (Gal 2:16; 3:22)—in contrast to covenantal "works of the law" that the Galatians were interested in performing.

If "the faith(fulness) of Jesus Christ" is the correct interpretation of the phrase *pistis Iēsou Christou* and its variants, then central strands of the apocalyptic narrative of Paul's gospel run right through that weighty characteristic of Jesus' own life.

"In Romans 3:1–8 the problem that faces God, as well as the whole human race, is that Israel has been 'faithless' to the commission to be the light of the world (cf. 2:17–24). How then is God to reveal his own covenant faithfulness? Paul's answer is that God's faithfulness is revealed in and through the faithfulness of Jesus the Messiah. Paul also says, sometimes in the same breath, as in Romans 3:22 and Galatians 2:16; 3:22, that the beneficiaries of this covenant faithfulness of the Messiah are precisely those who in their turn 'believe' or 'are faithful.'"[28]

DID PAUL THINK THAT FAITH IS ALL THERE IS TO IT?

If God's power operates within the sphere of those who are in "Jesus Christ," is that power also operative in and through the lives of Jesus-followers?

One way of addressing this is through the motif of the faithfulness of Jesus Christ (assuming that interpretation is correct). If the faith(fulness) of Jesus Christ is the vehicle through which divine righteousness flows (Gal 2:16), it also becomes the ethical matrix animating Jesus-followers in their everyday lives. If the faith(fulness) of Jesus Christ enlivens the faith of his followers and if they become incorporated into his faithfulness, Paul envisions that Jesus' faithfulness demarcates (or should demarcate) the lives and loves of his

27. See also Rom 15:8, where the notion of God's faithfulness is conveyed through the Greek phrase *alētheia theou*, "the truthfulness of God."
28. N. T. Wright, "The Letter to the Galatians: Exegesis and Theology," in *Between Two Horizons: Spanning New Testament Studies and Systematic Theology* (ed. Joel B. Green and Max Turner; Grand Rapids: Eerdmans, 1999), 218.

own followers—or as Paul says in Gal 2:20, "the life I now live in the flesh I live by the faithfulness of the Son of God." Faith immerses Christians into a reservoir of faithfulness that engulfs their lives and animates their lifestyle.

But regardless of whether it is right to read passages of this kind as referring to the "faith(fulness) of Christ," we come out at much the same place with regard to how Jesus-followers are to live no matter where we start in Paul. Contrary to popular opinion, Paul never talks about "salvation through faith *alone*," since the word "alone" is absent from his formulations of "by faith" and "through faith."[29] The view that salvation is by "faith alone" has at times been taken to imply that Paul only wanted Christians to hold to a set of right convictions about Jesus, and that anything beyond the holding of those deeply held beliefs would be tantamount to a form of Christian legalism or salvation by works.

Taken independently, some of Paul's statements might be read in this way, as in the affirmation of Rom 10:9: "If you declare with your mouth, 'Jesus is Lord,' and believe in your heart that God raised him from the dead, you will be saved." But Paul also held that such affirmations had a life-changing DNA about them, so that confessions of faith were themselves wrapped within cosmos-transforming power. Paul wanted Christ-followers to hold to a set of convictions about Jesus that consequently transformed their lives in practical ways through the power of God. If righteousness is "through faith," it is also the case that Paul expected faith to be expressed in practical terms and evidenced in obedient forms of lifestyle.

Consequently, at both the start and finish of his letter to Christians in Rome, Paul speaks of his mission as a vehicle for inducing "faith and obedience" among the nations (Rom 1:5; 16:26). The Greek for this phrase is somewhat ambiguous: *hypakoē pisteōs* (lit., "the obedience of faith"). This phrase could either mean that faith itself equates to obedience, or that faith is the source of practical obedience (or perhaps the ambiguity was intentional, with both meanings subtly implied). The balance of probability suggests that the second is more likely, with the phrase connoting something like "the obedience that faith inspires," or "produces," or "awakens." Paul wants Roman Christians to regard his ministry not as a ministry that inspires sinfulness through faith (as some seem to have depicted it; see Gal 2:17 and Rom 3:8) but as inspiring obedience through faith.

The foil for this, of course, was some among the Corinthian Christians. They came to imagine that Paul's gospel permitted them ethical freedoms precisely because it foregrounds so centrally the grace of God, making everything else pretty much irrelevant. For these Christians, "obeying the truth" (as Paul puts it in Gal 5:7) was extraneous, since "knowing the truth" was all that mattered.

Theological convictions and beliefs were not enough for Paul, however. They were to overspill into concrete forms of lifestyle. Accordingly, whatever differences we might perceive in the way that Paul and the author of the letter of James constructed their theological arguments, Paul would not have protested the point that "faith by itself, if it is not accompanied by action [Greek: *erga*, 'works'], is dead" (Jas 2:17). We hear Paul say the same thing

29. For example, Rom 1:17; 3:28, 30; 4:13; 9:30, 32; 5:1; Gal 3:26; Eph 2:8; 3:12, 17; 2 Tim 3:15. The only biblical writer to use the phrase "faith alone" is James, and he uses it in a negative fashion! See Jas 2:24 in its context.

in his own way in his own letters, such as in 2 Cor 9:13, where he lauds the Corinthian Christians for what he calls "the obedience that accompanies your confession of the gospel of Christ."

In a sense, this concern to enhance "the obedience that accompanies your confession of the gospel of Christ" is what animates Paul's letters from start to finish. To document the point would be to repeat the commentary summaries of previous chapters unnecessarily. But we must underscore that whenever Paul saw faith separated from patterns of life and lifestyle, he took it upon himself to place patterns of life firmly back on his audiences' radar screens. This had nothing to do with "salvation by works" and everything to do with "the only thing that counts," as Paul calls it in Gal 5:6: faith working practically in lives of self-giving love, with those lives advertising the triumph of the sovereign God who, through Christ, is restoring right relationships throughout his created order.

> "Nothing good can arise out of our will until it has been reformed; and after its reformation, in so far as it is good, it is so from God, not from ourselves."[30]

It is noticeable that in Gal 5:6 Paul intentionally speaks of faith "working practically" (Greek *energeō*). Faith works. Faith works itself out in practice. The lifestyle of the Jesus-follower is the arena in which one's faith becomes active. Much the same is evident in Phil 2:12, where Paul urges the Philippian Christians to "continue to work out your salvation with fear and trembling," and where the verb is based on the same primary stem of "work" (Greek *katergazomai*).

But that verse is indicative of Paul's view of the obedience of Jesus-followers, since it continues, "for it is God who works in you to will and to act in order to fulfill his good purpose." Once again the verb "work" emerges from Paul's pen (Greek *energeō*), this time with the subject of the verb being God. Elsewhere Paul might speak of the Spirit as the power that animates the transformed lifestyle of Jesus-followers (Rom 8:4–16; Gal 3:2–5; 4:6; 5:16, 18, 25), or of being enslaved "to obedience" (Rom 6:16) or "to righteousness" (6:18–19). But whatever the motif in any given context of thought, Paul consistently depicted lifestyle as intricately connected to the identity of those who follow Jesus, as God's transforming power animates their lives, often in culturally transgressive ways.

SUMMARY REFLECTIONS

In this chapter we have attempted to track the habits of "the lion on the loose"—that is, we have canvassed Paul's theological discourse and captured something of its organic coherence, its inner connectivity, and its dynamic compulsion. In the process we have explored the heights of a grand narrative of cosmic conflict and seen how that macro-narrative engulfs the micro-narratives of the lives of Jesus-followers in groups of devotion to their Lord.

Perhaps nothing characterizes Paul's theologizing more than his adept ability to move from the micro-narrative of people's lives to the macro-narrative of the cosmic triumph of God through Jesus Christ. Paul excelled at teaching Jesus groups to situate their micro-level issues within that much larger macro-level context. His theological discourse was targeted

30. John Calvin, *Institutes of the Christian Religion*, 3.3.8 (from the McNeil/Battles translation).

to bring solutions to indigenous issues, with those solutions emerging from and being embedded within a staunch vision of the narrative of God's triumphant reclamation of the cosmos.

For Paul, theological solutions to corporate and individual issues were to flow from the narrative of God's invasion in Christ into a world being torn apart by dark forces that conspire to reduce God's good creation to chaos through the imposition of self-interest in a battle of the survival of the fittest. In Paul's view, the individual and corporate lives of Jesus-followers are the arena in which the sovereignty of God is advertised, enlivened, and embodied, with the self-giving love of Jesus Christ engulfing the lives of his followers and reconstituting right relationships among them—all this as a result of "God's love," which "has been poured into our hearts through the Holy Spirit, who has been given to us" (Rom 5:5).

» KEY PEOPLE, PLACES, AND TERMS «

Apocalyptic
Christology
Damascus Road
Galilee
Incarnation
Jewish apocalypticism
Judea
Lord's Supper
Maranatha
Monotheism
Participationistic eschatology
Shema
Socio-rhetorical
Systematic theology
Trinity

» QUESTIONS FOR REVIEW AND DISCUSSION «

1. What kind of a thinker was Paul? What are the merits of the "systematic theologian" portrait, and what are its problems? What other images might be more accurate for conveying the personality presented in Paul's letters?
2. Explain the socio-rhetorical dimension of Paul's theology. How does this affect the way we should approach Paul and his letters?
3. What are the "trinitarian resources" in Paul's letters, and how do they help answer the question of whether Paul thought Jesus was divine? How does the answer to that question have relevance for our view of Paul's overall theology?
4. What is Paul's view of "the human predicament," and how does this affect our understanding of Paul's view of Jesus?
5. What did Paul know about the Jesus of history? What aspects of Jesus' teaching appear most clearly in Paul's writings?
6. Explain the "triangulation of faith" in Pauline writings.
7. Explain the concept "faith alone." Where do we find this idea in Paul's letters? What other concern animates his letters?

» CONTEMPORARY THEOLOGICAL REFLECTION «

1. What might be the danger in viewing Paul's thinking as systematic theology?
2. Does it matter if Paul thought (or taught) that Jesus was divine? Why or why not?
3. If the "faithfulness of Jesus" plays a role in Paul's theologizing along with "faith in Jesus," does this change the theological impact of Paul's discourse in practical terms?
4. If the phrase "faith alone" is not actually in Paul's writings, why do you think so much theological discussion has focused on this understanding?

» GOING FURTHER «

Paul's Theologizing in General

Campbell, Constantine R. *Paul and Union with Christ: An Exegetical and Theological Study*. Grand Rapids: Zondervan, 2012.

Dunn, James D. G. *The Theology of Paul the Apostle*. London: T&T Clark, 2003.

Gorman, Michael. *Inhabiting the Cruciform God: Kenosis, Justification, and Theosis in Paul's Narrative Soteriology*. Grand Rapids: Eerdmans, 2009.

Matera, Frank J. *God's Saving Grace: A Pauline Theology*. Grand Rapids: Eerdmans, 2012.

Schnelle, Udo. *Apostle Paul: His Life and Theology*. Grand Rapids: Baker Academic, 2005.

Wright, N. T. *Paul in Fresh Perspective*. Minneapolis: Fortress, 2009.

———. *Paul and the Faithfulness of God*. Minneapolis: Fortress, 2013.

The Apocalyptic Character of Paul's Theologizing

Beker, J. Christian. *Paul the Apostle: The Triumph of God in Life and Thought*. Philadelphia: Fortress, 1980.

Gaventa, Beverly Roberts. "The Singularity of the Gospel." Pages 101–11 in idem, *Our Mother Saint Paul*. Louisville: Westminster John Knox, 2007.

Longenecker, Bruce W. "The Narrative Approach to Paul: An Early Retrospective." *CurBR* 1 (2002): 88–111; repr. in *New Testament Studies: Benchmarks in Religious Studies*. Edited by Paul Foster. London: Sage, 2010.

Martyn, J. L. *Theological Issues in the Letters of Paul*. Edinburgh: T&T Clark, 1997.

Jesus and God in Paul

Bauckham, Richard. *Jesus and the God of Israel: God Crucified and Other Studies on the New Testament's Christology of Divine Identity*. Grand Rapids: Eerdmans, 2008.

Dunn, James D. G. *Did the First Christians Worship Jesus? The New Testament Evidence*. Louisville: Westminster John Knox, 2010.

Hurtado, Larry. "Early Pauline Christianity." Pages 79–154 in idem, *Lord Jesus Christ: Devotion to Jesus in Earliest Christianity*. Grand Rapids: Eerdmans, 2005.

Paul and the Jesus of History

Barclay, John M. G. "Jesus and Paul." Pages 492–503 in *Dictionary of Paul and His Letters*. Edited by G. F. Hawthorne, R. P. Martin, and D. G. Reid. Downers Grove, IL: InterVarsity Press, 1993.

Barnett, Paul. *Paul, Missionary of Jesus: After Jesus*. Volume 2. Grand Rapids: Eerdmans, 2008.

Thompson, Michael B. *Clothed with Christ: The Example and Teaching of Jesus in Rom 12:1–15:13*. Sheffield: Sheffield Academic, 1991.

Wenham, David. *Paul: Follower of Jesus or Founder of Christianity?* Grand Rapids: Eerdmans, 1995.

The Faithfulness of Jesus

Bird, Michael F., and Preston M. Sprinkle, eds. *The Faith of Jesus Christ: Exegetical, Biblical and Theological Studies*. Grand Rapids: Baker Academic, 2010.

Hays, Richard B. *The Faith of Jesus Christ: An Investigation of the Narrative Substructure of Galatians 3:1–4:11*. 2nd ed. Grand Rapids: Eerdmans, 2002.

Lives Enlivened by Faith and Obedience

Furnish, Victor Paul. *Theology and Ethics in Paul*. Louisville: Westminster John Knox, 2009.

Hays, Richard B. *The Moral Vision of the New Testament: Community, Cross, New Creation*. San Francisco: HarperOne, 1996 (esp. pp. 16–72).

CHAPTER 12

PAUL'S THEOLOGICAL NARRATIVE AND OTHER MACRO-NARRATIVES OF HIS DAY

CHAPTER GOALS

The goal of this chapter is to situate Paul's theological narrative in relation to two of the primary "macro-narratives" of his day. This will serve to enhance an appreciation of how Paul's theological contributions would have been heard in distinction from those competing macro-narratives.

CHAPTER OVERVIEW

The previous chapter began by considering what kind of thinker Paul was, and we considered rich textures of an undergirding apocalyptic narrative in some detail. A fuller consideration of the matter would also reveal that Paul's theologizing was often marked by convictions and ways of reasoning that fall within the breadth of Jewish conviction and reasoning. In a sense, Paul often shows himself to be a thoroughly Jewish thinker.

This is evident in his emphasis on abandoning the worship of the pagan gods (e.g., 1 Thess 1:9) and abandoning pagan ways of life (e.g., Rom 1:18–32; 1 Cor 6:9–11; 1 Thess 4:3–7). The same is true of his reasoning regarding the resurrection (1 Corinthians 15), the proper use of the body in sexual relations (e.g., 1 Corinthians 6), and a number of other issues (including the use of Scripture and caring for the poor—issues discussed in the chapter 13 below).

But if his theological discourse was immersed in the resources of Jewish Scripture and tradition, Paul was also adept at drawing new dimensions out of those resources (cf. Jesus' analogy in Matt 13:52 of the householder who "brings out of his treasure what is new and what is old"). As a missionary spreading the good news of the early Jesus movement, Paul often thought fresh thoughts about issues old and new (although usually within certain fixed theological parameters).

Often Paul's thoughts are freshest when he was forced to interact with other macro-narratives of his day. This is especially true with regard to the story of the **covenant** people of Israel. It is a story that, despite its many variations in Jewish tradition and literature, has its roots in the scriptural account at least as far back as **Abraham** in Genesis 15; it is a story that, in its traditional retelling, yokes Abraham to the ethnic people of Israel on whom God's favor would be poured out in the day when he restores right relations throughout the created order.

Among the early Christians, it was Paul who excelled in considering the story of God's action in Jesus Christ in relation to the story of the covenant people of Israel. In fact, this was a wholly pressing task for Paul in particular, since his call was to preach to the Gentiles the good news about the reclamation of the world by Israel's God. The first half of this chapter will explore ways in which he theologized about them. (See too the section entitled "The Wise Interpretation of Scripture" in chapter 13 below.)

But there was another macro-narrative that pervaded the Greco-Roman world that sits tantalizingly nearby to Paul's own macro-narrative — the narrative undergirding **Roman imperial ideology**. In essence, it is a narrative of the dawning of a new age in which right relationships transpire under the beneficent rule of Rome and its gods. Whereas human efforts to keep chaos at bay had come to nothing, new forces for good had been unleashed into society with the dawning of the **Augustan era** (beginning in the last quarter of the first century BC); peace and prosperity had taken hold and would benefit all those who align themselves with Rome's gracious, triumphant, and eternally divine reign.

Paul did not spend much time addressing the relationship of his gospel to the imperial gospel, and where he does articulate matters pertaining to Roman rule his statements seem to derive from different sentiments (as will be evident when discussing 1 Thess 5:1 – 11 and Rom 13:1 – 7 below). But there are tantalizing aspects of Paul's discourse that intertwine with the "imperial gospel," leaving us in the situation of having to nuzzle into Paul's convictional world to see whether there is more to the matter than is explicitly recounted in Paul's letters.

In a sense, then, the task in the first half of this chapter is much different than that of the second half. In the first half, we will consider the macro-story of the people of Israel and Paul's explicit engagement with it. In the second half, we will consider the macro-story of the **Roman imperial order** and whether, despite his general lack of engagement with it, we can spot what his general posture might have been toward the good news of Rome that had taken Paul's world by storm.

DID PAUL THINK THAT HIS GOSPEL PERTAINED TO THE ETHNIC PEOPLE OF ISRAEL?

If God's love was now being poured out on Gentile nations in ways that went beyond the traditional understandings of God's covenant with the ethnic people of Israel, how could God's election of Israel be understood? Had the covenant between God and Israel been broken, whether by the ethnic people of Israel or by God himself? Was Israel intricately involved in what God was doing in and through Jesus Christ? Or was the good news irrelevant to ethnic Israel?

Paul's view on issues of this sort can be teased out in relation to two views that have had some currency among Paul's interpreters, each of which has some interpretive deficiencies. These are the "two ways" view and the "replacement" view.

"Two ways view." Interpreters who adopt the "two ways" view maintain that Paul did not think that there was any kind of "salvific deficit" within traditional forms of **Judaism**, since (so the interpretation goes) Paul did not imagine that his gospel was in any way applicable to the Jewish people, being a gospel for the Gentiles only. For instance, when speaking in Romans about "the obedience of faith" that his ministry promoted he speaks as if his ministry was focused exclusively on Gentiles (Rom 1:5, "to call all the Gentiles [lit., 'nations'] to the obedience that comes from faith"; 16:26, "so that all the Gentiles [again, 'nations'] might come to the obedience that comes from faith"). Perhaps, then, Paul understood salvation to operate in two different ways, with the Jewish people enjoying one way of salvation (i.e., by their elect status through God's covenant with ethnic Israel) and the Gentile nations enjoying another (i.e., by being brought into relationship with Israel's God through Jesus Christ).

In this view, Paul's only complaint against the Jewish people was that they often failed to recognize that his "law-free" gospel was a legitimate way for Gentiles to enjoy relationship with Israel's God. Paul's negative comments regarding "works of the **Torah**" pertain to occasions when Gentile Christ-followers were intimidated into thinking that they had to perform "works of the Torah" in order to gain the appreciation of Israel's God. For Paul (the interpretation goes), "works of the Torah" were to remain in the domain of the Jewish people, not Gentile Christ-followers, just as faith in Jesus Christ was to remain in the domain of Gentile Christ-followers, not the Jewish people. It was only when the "two ways" got confused in people's minds that Paul's discourse took on a harsh and uncompromising tone.

The Survival of the Jews

The famous author of vampire novels Anne Rice points to "the survival of the Jews" as "a mystery without a solution, a mystery so immense that I gave up trying to find an explanation because the whole mystery defied belief." She notes how this ancient people group continues to live on, despite hardship and oppression over the millennia. "These people had endured as the great people who they [are]." It was this mystery that prompted her renunciation of atheism and her acceptance of theism; in her view, their very survival as a people-group testifies to the existence of God.[1]

A "two ways" interpretation of Paul's letters offers a stimulating opportunity to rethink traditional interpretations of Paul's theology, lest they should be based on misreadings of his letters. Ultimately, however, this approach to Paul's letters involves too many instances of special pleading and interpretative sleight of hand to be convincing. Texts like Romans 9–11, Galatians, and 2 Corinthians 3, for instance (and others beyond them), are comprised of many features that seem most naturally to run along different lines than those proposed by "two ways" interpreters.

Replacement view. But other readings of Paul's view of ethnic Israel are just as problematic. These include the "replacement theologies" that have characterized so much of the history of the Christian church. In this view of things, Christians have replaced the Jewish people in the affections of God, with the Jewish people no longer being God's chosen people and no longer having a special place in the unfolding plan of God. Instead, they have been rejected by God because they rejected Jesus. Consequently, God now favors the non-Jewish "new Israel"—that being the Christian church.

Views such as these run roughshod over a variety of remarks in Paul's letters. Paul frequently contends that God's saving initiative in Jesus Christ does nothing to sever his relationship with the people of Israel, even when the majority of ethnic Israel have not aligned themselves with the good news of Jesus Christ. Notice, for instance, that Paul does not trivialize the fact that Jesus himself was a Jew; instead, he takes it as a given that Jesus was "born under the law" (Gal 4:4). This itself feeds into another dimension of Paul's discourse: Jesus was a "servant to the circumcised" (Rom 15:8), and through Jesus Christ God has sought in the first instance "to redeem those under the law" (Gal 4:5). The gospel itself is said to be "to the Jew first and also to the Greek" (Rom 1:16; cf. also Rom 2:9–10).

In Paul's mind, God could do no other, in a sense, than to desire the redemption of "those under the law" because he was constrained by his own "truth" or faithfulness to his covenant commitments "so that the promises made to the patriarchs might be confirmed" (Rom 15:8). In

1. Anne Rice, *Lord Jesus Christ: Out of Egypt* (New York: Knopf, 2005), 308–9.

the end, Paul expects that "all Israel will be saved"—a verse that, taken in its most natural sense, refers to the salvation of ethnic Israel when the Redeemer comes from the heavenly Zion and takes away the sins of ethnic Israel, precisely because "they are beloved, for the sake of their ancestors" (Rom 11:28; see 11:25–31).

▲ New shoots grafted into the stump of an olive tree. Paul discusses how Gentiles can be grafted in among the "natural branches."

Ferrell Jenkins/www.BiblePlaces.com

Although Jewish unbelief complicates things, Paul never concludes from it that God's covenant with Israel has simply been abrogated and annulled. In Romans, in fact, he goes so far as to insist that Gentile Jesus-followers "have shared in the Jews' spiritual blessings" (Rom 15:27).[2] God's saving power is operative first in relation to the covenant people of Israel in order that, as a consequence of God's faithfulness to his covenant people, the Gentiles might "receive adoption to sonship" (Gal 4:5) and "glorify God for his mercy" (Rom 15:9). A full appreciation of passages of this kind (see also Gal 3:13–14) suggests that the covenant people of Israel is the location in which God's cosmic salvation has, in a sense, its initial foothold, from which to progressively engulf the Gentile nations and the whole cosmic order.

The main problem with enlisting Paul in the service of a "replacement theology," however, is that replacement theology runs contrary to the only passage in which Paul engages significantly with the issue of replacement theology. In Romans 11, the fact that many Jews do not share a christocentric faith with Gentile Jesus-followers is not used by Paul as an indicator that God has excluded ethnic Israel from his purposes and has renounced their call as his covenant people. Instead, Paul demonstrates that God has in fact chosen to make use of their lack of faith for his own salvific purposes, thereby working his will within the world specifically (albeit ironically) through his covenant people.

Paul's words in Rom 11:25–26 cannot be neglected in this regard: "Israel has experienced a hardening in part until the full number of the Gentiles has come in, and in this way all Israel will be saved." Paul wants to show that it is precisely because the Jews are the covenant people of God that a part of them has experienced hardening, since God works now, as God always has worked, through both hardening and enlivenment. For Paul, if God's calling is an honor, it does not always have a glorious outcome for the ones called. For just as he did not spare his own Son in order that others would be benefited (8:32), so too he did not spare his own people (11:21), some of whom he has called to be hardened in order that Gentile Jesus-followers might benefit by being grafted into the cultivated olive tree among the "natural branches" (thereby "sharing in their spiritual blessings").[3] Paul maintains that

2. A similar conviction seems to undergird Paul's comments in 1 Cor 10:1–13.
3. The fact that Paul uses the same verb "did not spare" when speaking of both Jesus and (some within) ethnic Israel (8:32 and 11:21) does not, of course, mean that the two situations are analogous in terms of their salvific significance. But it does testify to an overlap in Paul's theologizing, with a similar narrative pattern being applied to each, and with a shared salvific goal in view—that is, the offer of God's salvation to and beyond ethnic Israel, through what God has done in Christ, for the benefit of all within God's good creation.

both the enlivened and the hardened "parts" within the chosen people of Israel are playing a role in the extension of God's salvation to universal proportions.

Here, there is not a trace of replacement theology in the divine reclamation of the world. Instead, ethnic Israel remains central to the whole of God's complex work of redeeming the whole of his fallen creation. (For more on this issue, see the comments on Romans 11 in chapter 6 above).[4]

WHAT WAS IT ABOUT OBSERVING THE LAW THAT PAUL FOUND TROUBLING?

Paul did not conceive of ethnic Israel's relationship to the good news in terms of either a "replacement" schematization or a "two ways" schematization. Paul sought to maintain two principles simultaneously:

1. The ethnic people of Israel occupy a central position within the story of God's reclamation of his good creation.
2. "The law" that defined that ethnic group was not ultimately central to the story of God's reclamation of creation.

The inevitable tension within these two convictions is something that he sought to deal with repeatedly in his letters.

To articulate that tension, we can ask a series of questions. What did Paul think was the salvific deficiency that engulfed ethnic Jews who did not align themselves with Jesus Christ? Why did Paul think that participating in God's righteousness had no necessary connection with observing the law? If (as we have seen repeatedly, not least in chapter 11 above) Paul's gospel promoted the practical "working out" of one's convictions, what did he find to be the problem with traditional forms of Judaism? After all, the Jewish people performed works as expressions of their convictional world in much the slame way that Paul expected the convictions of Christians to find concrete expression in the "out-workings" of their lives.

These have been issues of notable debate among modern Paul's interpreters for more than a hundred years, but especially since the late 1970s. To generalize, there tended to be two main lines of thinking regarding the issue of "Paul and the law"—that is, the "traditional perspective" and the so-called "new perspective."

In the *traditional view*, Paul imagined that human sinfulness has rendered the law ineffective since the law is incapable of overturning the condition of human sinfulness. Observance of the law is not involved in God's fundamental solution since, whatever purposes it might have served, it does not get to the heart of the problem.

Moreover, in this traditional view of things, it is thought that those who imagined their law observance to be crucial to their status before God must have assumed one of two things:

4. We might ask whether Paul was supersessionistic in his theology. The answer, quite simply, is yes, although he did not advocate a replacement theology. The two have sometimes been intertwined in Christian thought, but unnecessarily so. Supersessionism describes the fact that Paul thought his religious convictions and practice superseded those of those in traditional forms of Judaism because God's promises had found fulfillment in Christ; replacement theologies wrongly imagine this to mean that God has abandoned his covenant with the Jewish people. For more on this matter, see Bruce W. Longenecker, "On Israel's God and God's Israel: Assessing Supersessionism in Paul," *JTS* 58 (2007): 26–44.

either (1) that there is little hope of salvation, since they were all too cognizant of their inability to do the law perfectly, or (2) that they stood a pretty good chance of salvation, since their own efforts of observing the law were sufficient for the task. In the traditional view of Paul and the law, both of these assumptions are thought to emerge from a fundamentally "legalistic" form of religion, in which one sought to amass good works within the account books of heaven. Legalistic religion of any day is little more than a form of mathematics, with good works and bad works being added up and the verdict of salvation or damnation being pronounced justly on the basis of whether the final total is a positive or a negative number.

Although this view is best described simply as the "traditional" view of things, it has often been called the "Lutheran" view, since it has some semblance to Luther's application of Paul's theology to counter the "legalism" of the Christian church of his day. Luther imagined that the Christian legalism of the sixteenth century was replicating the Jewish legalism of the first century, with both forms of religion perpetuating the problem and, consequently, obstructing the course of salvation.[5]

Luther may have been an expert interpreter of Paul for the needs of the sixteenth-century Christian church,[6] but it is not wholly clear that his capable application of Paul's theology should largely determine our understanding of Paul's theology itself. This, at least, is the view of those who hold to what has been termed the "new perspective" on Paul.

> "The Reformers interpreted Paul by equating the problem of the Judaizers and the Torah in Paul with the problem of work-righteousness in late medieval piety. This ingenious translation or application of Pauline theology may be 80 per cent correct but [it] left 20 per cent of Paul inexplicable."[7]

New perspective on Paul. The term "new perspective" was devised in the early 1980s to denote interpretations of Paul that were in general agreement with Ed Sanders's 1977 portrait of first-century Judaism (or better, Judaisms) as undergirded by what Sanders called "**covenantal nomism**." Advocates of the new perspective find that most forms of Judaism in Paul's day are not worthy of the attribute "legalistic" (especially when that term is thought to connote a sterile and arid religion). Instead, most forms of first-century Judaism were animated by a robust awareness that God had elected the people of Israel through his gracious mercy.

As a consequence of this, observance of the law was not considered to be "action" undertaken in order to gain salvation by good works of one's own initiative; instead, at the very least, it was considered "reaction" to God's prior initiative of grace upon his chosen covenant people. In the Judaism of Paul's day, keeping the law was not thought to be an impossibility, despite human weakness; instead, God had taken account of human weakness within the law itself so that the notion of keeping the law includes within itself the

5. E. P. Sanders (*Paul and Palestinian Judaism* [Philadelphia: Fortress Press, 1977], 57): "We have here a retrojection of the Protestant-Catholic debate into ancient history, with Judaism taking the role of Catholicism and Christianity taking the role of Lutheranism."
6. This is true in some respects more than others. His denouncement of the Jews, for instance, is something that Paul would have censured.
7. Krister Stendahl, "Contemporary Biblical Theology," in *Interpreter's Dictionary of the Bible* (ed. G. A. Buttrick; Nahsville: Abingdon, 1962), 1:420.

God's Power Manifested in Lifestyle 1

The conviction that one's ethical life was itself the arena in which God's power becomes manifest is evident throughout a variety of texts from the Judaism of Paul's day, as illustrated by these selected texts:

Prayer of Manasseh 14: "May you [God] demonstrate your goodness in me [or 'in me you will manifest all your grace']; For although I am unworthy, you will deliver me by your great mercy."

Wisdom of Solomon 15:1 – 3: "To know your power is the root of immortality."

Letter of Aristeas 231: "It is the gift of God to be able to do good actions" — actions described in paragraph 255 as being "by the power of God."

Jubilees 1:23 – 24: "I [says God] will create for them a holy spirit . . . and their souls will cleave to me and my commandments, and they will do my commandments."

1QS 4.4: The covenanter in the Dead Sea community claims that his everyday life is "sustained by his [God's] constant faithfulness."

4Q 521:6 (f2ii+4:1): "Over the humble His spirit hovers, and He renews the faithful in His strength."[8]

repentance of the transgressor who seeks forgiveness from a merciful God, not least by way of sacrifices that atone for infractions of the law. That, itself, is part of what it means "to do the law."

"God's sovereignty does not limit or reduce human freedom, but is precisely what grounds and enables it. The two agencies thus stand in direct and not inverse proportion: the more a human agent is operative, the more (not the less) may be attributed to God."[9]

The bedrock of first-century Judaism, then, was not an arid, individualistic legalism but a vibrant, corporate covenantalism, undergirded by a stout confidence in the grace of God on his covenant people. Sanders presented this by distinguishing between "getting in" (i.e., by divine covenant grace) and "staying in" (i.e., by responsive obedience to God's commands).

Of course, from one view of things, individualistic legalism and corporate covenantalism might not look all that different from each other, if we conceive of them as two versions of "contractualism" between God and Israel

8. See also Wisdom of Solomon 9:6; 7:15; 12:16; *Letter of Aristeas* 17 – 18; Baruch 2:31 – 33; 3:7; 2 Maccabees 1:2 – 4; *Jubilees* 5:12; 12:20; and most notably 1QS 11:1 – 17, as noted in the sidebar entitled "God's Power Manifested in Lifestyle 2." See also *Hellenistic Synagogal Prayers* 12.65.

The importance of the texts like the *Prayer of Manasseh*, the Wisdom of Solomon, the *Letter of Aristeas*, Baruch, and 2 Maccabees cannot be overemphasized, since these are texts of mainstream Jewish discourse. And the convictions evident in these texts are comparable to much the same in some of Paul's texts, not least Phil 2:12 – 16 (although Paul's convictions are thoroughly embedded within his Christotheocentrism, as in the phrase "on the day of Christ" in Phil 2:16).

Relatedly, the whole of *Psalms of Solomon* 16 is dedicated to pleading for God's "everlasting mercy" to continue to support the speaker (i.e., Solomon), to come to his aid "for salvation," to restrain him from "sordid sin," to "direct the works of my hands . . . and protect my steps" in order that ultimately the speaker might "receive mercy from the Lord" on the eschatological day.

9. John M. G. Barclay, "Introduction," *Divine and Human Agency in Paul and His Cultural Environment* (ed. Simon J. Gathercole and John M. G. Barclay; New York/Edinburgh: T&T Clark, 2008), 7.

God's Power Manifested in Lifestyle 2

The conviction that one's ethical life was itself the arena in which God's power becomes manifest is strikingly evident in this passage from 1QS or the "Community Rule" of the Qumran community (11:2–17), a community which lived on the shore of the Dead Sea at the time of Paul.

Baker Photo Archive

▲ Here are part of the remains of the community of Jews that lived on the shore of the Dead Sea, who attempted to replicate the purity of the ideal temple within their midst. Their "Community Rule" offers a window onto their worldview.

> 2As for me, my justification lies with God; In His hand are the perfection of my walk and the virtue of my heart. 3By His righteousness is my transgression blotted out. 4He who is eternal is the staff of my right hand, upon the Mighty Rock do my steps tread; before nothing shall they retreat. For the truth of God—5that is the rock of my tread, and His mighty power, my right hand's support. From His righteous fount comes my justification, the light of my heart from His wondrous mysteries. Upon the eternal 6has my eye gazed—even that wisdom hidden from men, the knowledge, wise prudence from humanity concealed. The source of righteousness, gathering 7of power, and abode of glory are from fleshly counsel hidden. 10Surely a man's way is not his own; neither can any person firm his own step. Surely justification is of God; by His power 11is the way made perfect. All that shall be, He foreknows, all that is, His plans establish; apart from Him is nothing done. As for me, if 12I stumble, God's lovingkindness forever shall save me. If through sin of the flesh I fall, my justification will be by the righteousness of God which endures for all time. 13Though my affliction break out, He shall draw my soul back from the Pit, and firm my steps on the way. Through His love He has brought me near; by His lovingkindness shall he provide 14my justification. By His righteous truth has He justified me; and through His exceeding goodness shall He atone for all my sins. By His righteousness shall He cleanse me of human 15defilement and the sin of mankind—to the end that I praise God for His righteousness, the Most High for His glory. Blessed are you, O my God, who has opened to knowledge 16the mind of your servant. Establish all of his works in righteousness; raise up the son of your handmaiden—if it please You—to be among those chosen of mankind, to stand 17before You forever. Surely apart from You the way cannot be perfected, nor can anything be done unless it please You.[10]

(soft contractualism = covenantalism; hard contractualism = legalism). But we also need to be cognizant of the extent to which some Jews of Paul's day imagined even their observance of the law to be a manifestation of God's empowerment, in which case all traces of contractualism fall away. So overwhelming was their sense of God's grace on them that some Jews conceived of their works of obedience to be expressions of God's gracious power within their lives (see "God's Power Manifested in Lifestyle" sidebars). Although it is common to view

10. Michael Wise, Martin Abegg, and Edward Cook, eds., *The Dead Sea Scrolls: A New Translation* (San Francisco: HarperCollins, 1996), 142–43.

agency as an "either-or" situation (either the individual or God empowers works of obedience), Jewish texts from early Judaism often testify to an altogether different conceptualization of obedience, in which divine and human initiative are directly proportionate.

In this light, the confident assurance of Deut 30:11 is wholly in keeping with the covenantal context out of which observing the law emerges. In that verse the people of Israel are assured that obeying the law of God "is not too difficult for you or beyond your reach." And we might interpret Paul's statement in Phil 3:6 in the same light. Looking back on his life in Pharisaic Judaism, Paul speaks there of having been "blameless" with regard to "righteousness under the law." This cannot mean that Paul had imagined himself to be sinless or completely without error in his lifestyle; instead, his point is simply that throughout his earlier life he was mindful of his responsibility to practice the stipulations of the law, including seeking forgiveness through sincere repentance and through the offering of atoning sacrifices.

Jubilees 22.16: "Separate yourself from the Gentiles, and do not eat with them, and do not perform deeds like theirs. And do not become associates of theirs. Because their deeds are defiled, and all of their ways are contaminated, despicable, and abominable."

Consequently, the question needs to be posed afresh: If most forms of first-century Judaism were marked out primarily by various forms of covenantalism rather than by legalism per se, and if many Jews even imagined their own covenant obedience to be animated by divine empowerment, how is Paul's critique of life under the law to be understood?

For advocates of the new perspective, the answer is that Paul was opposed to the ethnocentricity that had taken hold in many sectors of first-century Judaism. The law, as a means of keeping the people of Israel distinct from other nations, generated the separation of Jews and Gentiles at the most intimate level of social interaction. This was nowhere more pronounced than in the case of the practice of circumcision and Jewish dietary observances (e.g., the eating of kosher foods alone). This "social function" of the law proved to be diametrically opposed to how Paul, the apostle to the Gentiles, understood God's plan of salvation in Christ. For Paul, the diversity of Christians within loving and supportive communities was itself an advertisement of God's triumphant power in a world characterized by monochrome self-interestedness.

Looked at through this prism, Paul's letters appear somewhat different than they do when examined through the traditional prism. The backdrop to the Galatian letter, for instance, snaps into place. Paul recounts with heavy emphasis how some Jewish Christians (whom Paul calls "the circumcision group," Gal 2:12) had already been promoting law observance within the ranks of the early Jesus movement, especially advocating circumcision (see 2:1 – 10; 6:12 – 13) and dietary purity (see 2:11 – 14). The motivation behind their action does not appear to be legalistic but covenantal. That is, they were not encouraging Gentile Jesus-followers to earn salvation by their works per se, but were trying to preserve the purity of Jewish Jesus-followers, either by having them withdraw from the intimacy of table fellowship with Gentile Jesus-followers (as in the Antioch episode of 2:11 – 14) or by having Gentile Jesus-followers adopt the practices of mainstream Judaism (as in the Jerusalem episode of 2:1 – 10).

Something similar might emerge from Paul's letter to Jesus groups in Rome. In that letter, Paul depicts his Jewish dialog partner as one who boasts in being especially related to God over against the Gentile nations (Rom 2:17). Or having registered that God's righteousness manifests itself to all who believe, the contrast seems not to be legalism but ethnocentrism, as in Paul's posing of the question of 3:29: "Is God the God of Jews only? Is he not the God of Gentiles too?" Paul's answer keeps the focus on the distinction between Jews and Gentiles: "Yes, of Gentiles too, since there is only one God, who will justify the circumcised by faith and the uncircumcised through that same faith" (3:29–30).

In the same light, when Paul attributes Jewish lack of belief to the fact that "they sought to establish their own righteousness" (Rom 10:3), he is not describing a posture of legalistic works righteousness (as in the traditional view) but of ethnocentric covenantalism. In this light, the phrase signifies that their lack of faith in Christ is bound up with their attempt to establish a righteousness that pertains to "their own" race primarily or exclusively.

What can we say about the "traditional" and "new" perspectives? Four points are important to note.

First, the terminology to differentiate them is not adequate. This is because advocates of both perspectives have differing emphases that cannot be simply reduced to a single "perspective," and because the "new perspective" can hardly qualify as new any longer. Nonetheless, these terms have become standard when framing the main contours of the issue. The day is coming when new terms will overtake these failing and ailing descriptors, and that day will not be too early in coming.

Second, advocates of both perspectives have sometimes expressed their views as if the legitimacy of one perspective rules out the legitimacy of the other. The "either-or" of scholarly discourse has been unhelpful. In fact, both perspectives may have their own strengths, which become weaknesses when the issue is pressed into a polarized "either-or."

For instance, on the one hand, it is arguable that the traditional perspective is right in finding Paul's critique of the law to involve the conviction that people are unable to keep the law because of the radical extent to which sin fundamentally marks out the human condition. On the other hand, the traditional perspective is less successful in its view that a pessimism regarding human ability lay at the heart of Judaism in Paul's day.

Conversely, it is arguable that the new perspective is well placed to highlight both the covenantal motivation behind Jewish observance of the law and Paul's concern about the "social function" of the law in separating Jews and Gentiles.[11] For the apostle to the Gentiles, the law's demarcation of Jews over against Gentiles was an impediment to the corporate embodiment of the gospel, which promoted the unity of Christians through the invading power of God within this fragmented world.[12] The new perspective is keenly attuned

11. Arguably, for instance, Paul's depiction of the law as a guide for ethnic Israel prior to the coming of Christ, in Gal 3:23–25 and 4:1–3, works better in the new perspective than in a more traditional frame of reference.

12. Although the new perspective keeps social relationships in clear focus, it is not simply a "sociological" reading of Paul's theology; instead, it involves the recognition that Paul's theology pressed deeply into issues regarding the corporate and social identity of Christians. But if the issue of the corporate identity of Christians in relation to God's dealings with ethnic groups ran deeply within Paul's theological narrative of God's salvific dealings throughout the ages, this is a far cry from being simply a sociological reading of Paul.

to this "particularistic" dimension that lay at the heart of any broader attempts to obey the Torah that God had revealed to Israel.[13]

On the other hand, while it might be true that early Judaism is better characterized as a "covenantal" religion than a legalistic one, the adjective "covenantal" itself might too easily cloak a diversity of views regarding the relationship of divine grace and human obedience to the law. At times, Jewish texts of Paul's day seem to place a heavy emphasis on obedience to the law as a matter of personal choice and obligation, as a means to life, without any neighboring discussion of divine graciousness or empowerment. In this fashion, an emphasis on obedience to the law seems to overshadow a covenantal cradle. It is probably fair to say that the texts of early Judaism testify to a vigorous conversation about precisely how the divine grace corresponds to human obligation and obedience.

"It is striking that Paul's theology is both *so like* the structure of Judaism in his understanding of grace and works and *so unlike* the structure of covenantal nomism in his participatory pattern of salvation."[14]

Moreover, advocates of the new perspective have been less successful in doing full justice to some of Paul's most profound statements concerning the law. Despite all that he has to say about the law in connection with God's covenantal election of the people of Israel, Paul says some other, far more radical things about the law that reveal how much he has come to understand the human situation in a way that was radically different from what many of his Jewish contemporaries would have accepted. So, for instance, Paul speaks in Rom 8:3 of God doing in Christ "what the law was powerless to do" because the law had been weakened by the human proclivity toward sinfulness under the power of sin. In more than just its christological focus, then, Paul's theologizing moves beyond understandings of divine initiative that were typical within mainstream forms of Judaism.

In short, then, the new perspective helpfully highlights the social and corporate dynamics of Paul's theology against the backdrop of the varieties of covenant theology that pervaded Judaism in the first century, but its advocates have tended to undervalue or leave unarticulated Paul's radical conviction that the law is not able to be kept because of a fundamental problem residing in the human heart. It is this problem that James Dunn (himself a leading proponent of the new perspective) unmasks as "the self in its various manifestations—self-gratification, self-assertion, self-justification, self-pity, and so on."[15]

Third, and arising from the second, it is important to recognize that Paul often depicts Jewish observance of the law in ways that other Jews of his day would barely recognize. So, for instance, foreign to most Jewish covenant theology of Paul's day is his conviction that it

13. Even Rudolph Bultmann, who handed on the view that the Judaism of Paul's day was an arid "legalism," nonetheless recognized that the debates in the early Jesus movement followed along different lines; for one segment of the early Jesus movement as opposed to another, "the condition for sharing in salvation is belonging to the Jewish People" (*Theology of the New Testament* [2nd ed.; Waco, TX: Baylor University Press, 2007], 1:55).

14. John M. G. Barclay, "Grace and the Transformation of Agency in Christ," in *Redefining First-Century Jewish and Christian Identities: Essays in Honor of Ed Parish Sanders* (ed. F. E. Udoh; Notre Dame, IN: University of Notre Dame Press, 2008), 374.

15. James D. G. Dunn, *Christian Liberty: A New Testament Perspective* (Carlisle, UK: Paternoster, 1993), 70.

is impossible to observe the law because of the inadequacies of the human heart.[16] It is likely that Paul himself did not hold this conviction prior to his encounter with the risen Lord. He seems to have developed it only as a consequence of his conviction about the essential unity of Jewish and Gentile Jesus-followers. This is one reason why some have suspected that Paul's essential theologizing may have moved "from solution to plight"—that is, from a realization about what God has done in Christ to a new realization about the desperate state of the human condition.

Similarly, it seems likely that Paul sometimes depicts covenantally motivated Jewish observance of the law in terms that are not a world away from a legalistic frame of reference (see Rom 9:11–12, 32; 11:5–6; on Rom 4:4–5, see comments in chapter 6 above). This is neither surprising nor arbitrary, but follows on from theological first principles. Since Paul finds God's saving grace to be operative among Jesus-followers, Jews beyond Jesus groups who imagine their covenantal acts to be responses to (and perhaps enlivened by) God's grace are actually, and contrary to their own self-understanding, doing little other than acting legalistically. For this reason, Paul can set divine grace and human works in bare antithetical relationship, even when thinking about the "works" of covenantally motivated Jews.

Tolkien's Depiction of Gollum

In J. R. R. Tolkien's books *The Hobbit* and *The Lord of the Rings*, the memorable character Gollum becomes caught in a spiral of self-referentiality. As Gollum's world shrinks to encompass little other than himself, he becomes the center of his own affections, as indicated by the fact that he is said to have "always called himself 'my precious.'"[17]

Tolkien's depiction of Gollum may well have similarities to Paul's analysis of the human condition in all spheres of life, including corporate identities.

Fourth, it needs to be noted that in one respect the traditional and new perspectives are wholly complementary. In Paul's Galatian letter, for instance, the agitators who advocated the salvific necessity of law observance are depicted as wholly self-interested (Gal 4:17; 6:13). No doubt they imagined themselves as operating on the basis of a far nobler motivation, with Gentile Christ-followers becoming fully Jewish in order to participate in the covenantal blessings of Israel. But Paul, knowing that God's plans to bless the Gentiles lay along different lines, considered the agitators to be using the gospel to promote their own reputation and profile.

In this way, the covenantalism that motivated the agitators was unmasked by Paul to be little other than a form of human self-interestedness. For Paul, national ethnocentrism and individual egocentrism are two forms of the same fundamental problem of the human heart. That problem is antithetically mirrored in the gospel, in which God is shown to be working through the One who gave himself and through the Spirit who inspires similar patterns of self-giving in those who follow Jesus. Little wonder Paul can say that God has accomplished "what the law was powerless to do" because of the inadequacies of the self-interested human heart. In Paul's view, even the "holy, righteous and good" law of God

16. The Jewish author who composed the text of *4 Ezra* did stumble (in a sense) on this view, but only as a consequence of the destruction of Jerusalem in AD 70, and even then he recognized that his view was not shared by the masses. On this, see Bruce W. Longenecker, *2 Esdras* (Sheffield: Sheffield Academic, 1994).
17. J. R. R. Tolkein, *The Hobbit* (Boston: Houghton Mifflin Harcourt; Kindle ed.), 69.

(Rom 7:12) could be swept away into the matrices of unhealthy self-referentiality, both at individual and national levels.

WAS PAUL UNBOTHERED BY THE IDEOLOGY SUPPORTING THE ROMAN IMPERIAL ORDER?

To move from Paul's engagement with the macro-narrative of God's dealings with Israel to Paul's engagement with the macro-narrative of the Roman imperial order might look artificial to modern eyes. But there was no artificiality about the move in Paul's day. In a day when the "separation of church and state" was not even on the radar, the issue of what God was doing with his people was intricately embedded with the issue of how God was managing the world. In Paul's day, one could not speak about management of the world without speaking about Rome.

> "It seems clear . . . [from Jewish texts of Paul's day] that, however zealous and holy a first-century Jew might be, there was still a 'problem': not Martin Luther's personal problem, but the national problem of Jews under Roman rule, with Scripture unfulfilled. Israel was unredeemed; Israel's God had not returned in glory and power. This is the kind of quarry that Sanders's net was not designed to catch. A further weakness: Sanders assumed not only a sixteenth century view of 'grace,' but also an eighteenth century view of 'religion.' First-century Judaism embraced land, family, politics, and above all Torah and Temple, not because it was 'works-righteousness' but because of the God of the Bible, whose 'righteousness' meant, among other things, his faithfulness to covenant and promise."[18]

The point has not always been appreciated among Paul's interpreters. This is glaringly evident in Sanders's formulation of "covenantal nomism" as simply a "pattern of religion" that involves "getting in" by divine grace and "staying in" by obedience to the law. The formulation itself seems to derive from modern constructions of what "patterns of religion" are supposed to look like. It fails to appreciate that Jewish covenant theology in Paul's day was at the center of a grand theological discourse with no self-determined boundaries as to its relevance in any area of life. Jewish covenant theology inevitably had the theological resources to tackle the substantial issues that pressed themselves on the Jewish people. Front and center was the issue of God's covenant promises to the people of Israel: Had God not promised to bless his people? Had Rome and its gods usurped the place of Israel and her God? Was God up for the job of being faithful to his people and in control of the world, the nations, and their people? Was Rome's imperial reign an affront to the reign of Israel's sovereign God, or a feature within it, or what?

Paul himself had much to say on these matters—matters about God's faithfulness to his covenant people, about his sovereignty, about his working on the world stage, most dramatically and climactically in Jesus Christ. So the question arises: Did Paul have the theological resources to engage in a robust discourse on the Roman imperial ideology of his day?

18. N. T. Wright, "Paul in Current Anglophone Scholarship," *ExpT* 123 (2012): 4.

It is obvious that much of Paul's discourse engages issues pertaining to the ethnic people of Israel and the practices that define them as a covenant people of God. Less obvious, however, is how Paul perceived his gospel in relation to another gospel that was spreading like wildfire through the urban centers where communities of Jesus devotion were based. Did he find the ideology that supported the Roman imperial order simply to be innocent, harmless, and unthreatening? Or did he find it incompatible with and antagonistic to his gospel?

▲ Paul escapes Damascus in a basket (The Palatine Chapel in the Norman Palace, Palermo, Sicily, Italy).

According to Acts, Paul was a Roman citizen (Acts 22:25–29; 23:27).[19] It may not be surprising, then, that when Paul writes to Christians in Rome, he identifies Roman governance as a God-ordained instrument for order within the world (Rom 13:1–7, although the point is sometimes disputed; see below). If this is the proper reading of that passage, Paul had high praise for Roman governance, at least on this occasion.

But the question has to be asked: How "Roman" was Paul, at least during the time of his apostolic ministry? Unfortunately, the answer is not wholly clear. Some imagine that Rom 13:1–7 settles the matter in the direction of a relatively conservative stance toward the ruling authorities (in his day, Rome). Others are not so sure.

It is clear that much of what Paul advocated in his gospel ran against the grain of Roman values. A case in point is Paul's understanding of the character of his apostolic ministry. When writing to Corinthian Christians, Paul boasted in "things that show my weakness" (2 Cor 11:30), and he included in his inventory of weaknesses the following episode (2 Cor 11:32–33):

> In Damascus, the governor under King Aretas had the city of the Damascenes guarded in order to arrest me. But I was lowered in a basket from a window in the wall and slipped through his hands.

Paul does not depict himself as a great hero in this episode; in fact, he takes care to show himself in what would almost be laughable terms to his contemporaries. When judged by the values of his day, Paul's ministry looks woefully inadequate, starkly unimpressive, and pathetically non-Roman. The governor of Damascus may have played the Roman game of power and manipulation, but Paul did not. As Paul well knew, the Roman way was not to run away

---

19. Although some doubt this was the case, the portrait of Paul in Acts is most likely correct on this point.

from danger, least of all to cower in a basket so as to hide from one's adversaries. The Roman way was to stand up to those seeking to undermine one's initiatives, to preserve one's honor by outdoing one's opponents, and to meet conflict head-on in a contest of strength (physical, rhetorical, or whatever). If Paul's description of his flight from Damascus looks slightly embarrassing to our twenty-first-century eyes, it would have been all the more repulsive and distasteful to any of his contemporaries immersed in the values of the Roman imperial order.

A century before Paul, Cicero had said (*Rab. Post.* 5:16): "The very word 'cross' should be far removed not only from the person of a Roman citizen but from his thoughts, his eyes, and his ears."

Paul, of course, knew that. In highlighting the episode, Paul was playing a dangerous rhetorical game. He was using this repugnant episode to reinforce his point about the countercultural nature of his apostleship, but in doing so he ran the risk of making himself look weak and unmanly.[20] More than that, he ran the risk of making himself look non-Roman, since the Roman way was for men to avoid effeminate appearances in contexts of conflict; their task, instead, was to prove their honor through manly initiatives that heightened conflict levels.

The hidden subtext within this passage, then, is an unashamed admission on Paul's part that, as an apostle of the gospel, he did not adhere to values cherished by the Greco-Roman culture of his day. Paul boldly depicted his apostleship in ways that ran contrary to some of the foremost ideals of Roman culture, demonstrating that his identity as an apostle of Jesus involved him in patterns of life that ran contrary to the system of domination that had engulfed the Greco-Roman world.

"This union of the religious and the political was natural for Jews (including Paul), and for ancients generally, for whom politics and religion were inseparable, being two sides of one coin. The question for them was not *whether* politics and religion would mix, but only *whose* politics would shape religion and be shaped by it. For Paul the answer was the strange politics of God manifested in the crucifixion and resurrection of Jesus."[21]

We might ask, then, whether the gospel "de-Romanized" Paul? Without knowing much about his days prior to his encounter with the risen Christ, it is impossible to say. But it is fair to say (based on incidents far beyond this one example) that the gospel Paul preached included features that jarred with Roman imperial ideology.

Or perhaps it is better to speak of Roman imperial "ideologies." The plural helps to highlight the indigenous character of the **Roman imperial cult**. The cult was promulgated not primarily at the center of imperial power; instead, the imperial cult found its most aggressive promulgators in the cities spread throughout the Mediterranean basin—including the very cities where Paul based his ministry (e.g., **Philippi**, **Thessalonica**, **Corinth**, and **Ephesus**). Moreover, while imperial power was consolidated in temples to the emperor and the imperial family, it was aided all the more by its association with the many other temples dedicated to the worship of gods. The narratives of those gods often intermeshed with the

20. See too his self-depiction in Gal 4:19 and 1 Thess 2:7, where feminine characteristics are to the fore.
21. Michael Gorman, *Apostle of the Crucified Lord: A Theological Introduction to Paul and His Letters* (Grand Rapids: Eerdmans, 2003), 107.

imperial ideologies that were cherished in civic centers aligning themselves with Rome.

▲ Marble bust of Caesar Augustus

Many aspects of Paul's gospel seem to have run contrary to ideologies that intermeshed the empire to the indigenous populace. At the center of Paul's good news was the figure of one crucified on a cross. In the ancient world, crucifixion was recognized as a singularly Roman form of torture. It was reserved for those convicted (rightly or wrongly) of anti-Roman sentiment, of perverting the proper course of the Roman imperial order. Such people were the scum of Roman society. But Paul's gospel message featured just such a person ("we preach Christ crucified," 1 Cor 1:23), whose crucifixion would have implied to Greco-Roman audiences that Rome had perceived Jesus to be a miscreant, holding back the health and development of Rome's program.

Other features of Paul's gospel would have been similarly disconcerting to many within Paul's world. This is especially true in terms of commitments to the Golden Age of Augustan Rome. As outlined by the first-century poet **Virgil** (or Vergil), the Golden Age was a period of justice in which the birth of a miraculous child inaugurates a period in which the world will change, with human sins disappearing progressively from the face of the earth and a state of peace among the nations being established. That child, of course, was heralded as Caesar **Augustus**, who took the helm of the Roman empire in the last quarter of the first-century BC. Paul saw things differently, placing a wholly different individual at the point where the ages of history meet.

In Paul's day, religion and politics were intertwined phenomena; every religious commitment inevitably had a political dimension to it. When Paul's theology is registered within the political arena of the first-century world, a number of points give pause for thought in relation to the compatibility of Roman imperial ideologies and the good news preached by Paul.

1. In Roman imperial ideologies, the emperor Augustus had been heralded as "the son of God" (i.e., the adopted son of Caesar who himself had been made a god). Paul held that Jesus, the messianic "seed of David," was the true "Son of God" (Rom 1:4; 2 Cor 1:19; Gal 2:20; Eph 4:13; etc.).
2. In Roman imperial ideologies, the emperor could be heralded as the "savior" of the world. Paul held that Jesus Christ was that "Savior" (Phil 3:20; etc.).
3. In Roman imperial ideologies, the emperor was commonly thought to be a deity. Paul held that the one true God was known only through Jesus Christ, "the image of God" (2 Cor 4:4) and himself worthy to be acclaimed "Lord" (1 Cor 8:6; see also 1 Thess 1:8; 3:11; 5:28, etc.).
4. In Roman imperial ideologies, the emperor was to be worshiped. Paul held that Gentile Christians, who would previously have participated in emperor worship (along with worship of other pagan gods), had formerly been involved in idolatry (1 Thess 1:9–10; see also Gal 4:8–11, etc.).

5. In Roman imperial ideologies, Rome was favored by the gods, and all of the world was being brought under its control. Paul held that "our citizenship is in heaven" and "we eagerly await a Savior from there, the Lord Jesus Christ," under whose control everything is being brought (Phil 3:20–21).
6. In Roman imperial ideologies, the "gospel" or "good news" involved the emergence of a new era, dating back to the birth of Augustus. Paul preached a "gospel" or "good news" involving the emergence of a new era, dating back to the life, death, and resurrection of Jesus (e.g., Rom 1:2–4).
7. In Roman imperial ideologies, the new era involved the unification of the nations under the emperor's oversight. Paul (himself a Jew who had been trained in Hellenistic context and held Roman citizenship) preached the coming together of the nations within the body of Jesus Christ (e.g., Gal 3:28).
8. In Roman imperial ideologies, the Roman empire established "peace and security" throughout the world. Paul held that such assurances were illusive (1 Thess 5:3), with God alone establishing true peace (1 Thess 5:23)—himself being the "God of peace" (Rom 15:33; 16:20).
9. In Roman imperial ideologies, miscreants were expendable, through crucifixion or some other means. Paul preached that Jesus the crucified one had, in fact, been resurrected by God, thereby overturning the verdict given by the "rulers of this age" (1 Cor 2:6–9).
10. In Roman imperial ideologies, Rome's empire was sovereign, overseen by the gods (or the Fates) and having been embedded within the will of the high god Jupiter, who oversaw the historical processes leading up to its founding and its ongoing success, for all successive time. Paul preached that the God of Israel was calling people into his "kingdom" or empire (1 Thess 2:12; 2 Thess 1:5; Col 1:13).[22] Only the God of Israel was sovereign and eternal (1 Thess 1:9), and his reign would be established as such through his Son Jesus Christ, of whom the oracles of God had long ago spoken (Rom 1:2; 3:2). All other claimants to sovereignty would be eliminated (e.g., 1 Cor 15:20–28), and all the nations would become "obedient" to his eternal reign (Rom 1:5; 16:26).

▼ The Arch of Titus in Rome advertises the city's victorious reign by celebrating the destruction and plundering of Jerusalem by Roman forces in AD 70.

Bruce Longenecker

It is probably against this backdrop of contrasting "gospels" that we hear of opposition arising against Paul and of the persecution of Jesus groups that he had founded, not least the Christian communities of Macedonia (i.e., Thessalonica and Philippi). This is

22. See also Rom 14:17; 1 Cor 4:20; 6:9–10; 15:24, 50.

An Oath of Allegiance to the Roman Emperor and His Family

The following oath from Paphlagonia testifies to the burning zeal of imperial devotion that was common among urban centers of the Greco-Roman world:

> I swear by Zeus, Earth, Sun, all the gods [and] goddesses, and by Augustus himself that I will be loyal to Caesar Augustus and his children and descendants for all the time of my [life], in word, deed and thought, considering as friends whomever they consider so, and reckoning as enemies whomsoever they themselves judge to be so; and that in their interests I shall spare neither body nor soul nor life nor children, but in every way for those things that pertain to them I shall endure every danger; and that if I see or hear anything hostile to them being either said or planned or carried out, this I will reveal and shall be the enemy of [the man] who is saying or planning or doing any of these things. And whomsoever they themselves may judge to be their enemies, these I will pursue and defend them against, by land and sea, by sword and steel.
>
> But if I do anything contrary to this [oath] or do not conform to the letter with the oath I swore, I myself bring down on myself and my body, soul and life, and on my children and all my family and all that belongs to me utter and total destruction down to my every last connection [and] all my descendants. (*Inscriptiones Latinae Selectae* 8781)

probably how we are to read 1 Thess 2:2: "We had previously suffered and been treated outrageously in Philippi, as you know, but with the help of our God we dared to tell you his gospel in the face of strong opposition." In the staunchly pro-Roman context of Macedonia, Paul can speak of Christians having faced "severe suffering" (1 Thess 1:6), a "very severe trial" (2 Cor 8:2; see also 1 Thess 3:3), and "persecutions and trials" (2 Thess 1:4). Writing to Philippian Christians, Paul speaks of "those who oppose you" (Phil 1:28–30), which may refer to those who promoted the Roman program within Philippi.

This is probably how we should also interpret 1 Thess 2:14–16, where Paul speaks of Thessalonian Christians as having "suffered from your fellow citizens" in the same way that "God's churches in Judea" suffered from "the Jews who killed the Lord Jesus and the prophets and also drove us out." Paul probably does not have in mind the Jews collectively in this instance. Instead, he seems to be referring solely to the group of "elite" Jews in authority (i.e., the high priest and others in positions of leadership). It was they who exercised their influence and as collaborators with Rome (willingly or otherwise) put pressure on the civic authorities (i.e., Pilate) in order to do away with a troublemaker (Jesus) that Rome should worry about. Paul imagined much the same thing to be happening to Thessalonian Christians, with local Thessalonian keepers of the system conspiring against Christians, just as the elite in Judea had conspired against Jesus.[23]

---

23. In this way, the phrase "who killed the Lord Jesus" should not be preceded by a comma, as if qualifying the whole of "the Jews"; instead, Paul has in mind a subgroup of the Judean Jews—that is, "the Jews who [in their role as collaborators with Rome] killed the Lord Jesus." The canonical Gospels register warnings about persecution coming against Christians by local authorities: Matt 10:17–20; Mark 13:9–11; Luke 12:10–11; John 15:18–27. Nero's scapegoating of Christians (in the aftermath of the burning of Rome in AD 64) is suggestive of a general suspicion (at least) about Christians in relation to the goals of the Roman imperial order.

Rightly or wrongly, it is probable that many of Paul's contemporaries heard his gospel as peddling anti-Roman sentiment, a view articulated within the Acts narrative as well.[24] If Paul did not intend this to be the case, we might have expected him to express himself with a bit more caution.

Such a note is probably what we do see when Paul deals with the issue of "the governing authorities" in Rom 13:1–7. There, he emphasizes the need for Jesus-followers in Rome to submit to the authorities. These verses are usually thought to adopt a "conservative" posture toward the "governing authorities," and there have been unfortunately times in Christian history when the passage has been used to prop up morally corrupt regimes.

Some have seen the passage to be so problematic that they imagine it was inserted into Romans by a later scribe, seeking to enlist Paul in the task of relieving tensions between Christians and their imperial oppressors. But there is no textual basis for such a view.

"The Roman Empire does not seem to me much like an organic entity, unless it is an epidemic spreading throughout a host population feeding off the energies of the infected until it burns itself out.

"The essence of empire is the assertion of a great pattern at the expense of smaller ones. That pattern is typically less equal and more hierarchical than what went before. New levels of complexity mean some of the rich becoming richer, some of the poor being subject to harsher discipline, although the social mobility that empire stirs up means there are winners and losers at every level."[26]

Still others have attempted to infuse the passage with **anti-imperial** polemic by reading it with a heavy note of irony from start to finish. So, for instance, it is possible to play up the theme of submission in this passage, since the Roman imperial order did not ideally imagine that its subjects needed to submit to it; their allegiance to Rome should instead be freely and enthusiastically given. Or perhaps irony can be imported into the motif of the civic authorities wielding the sword against wrongdoers, since it was common to imagine the ideal world as one where the sword would have become a thing of the past; to say that the authorities are still having to wield the sword is to say that the ideal age has not transpired under Roman rule.[25]

As valiant as such attempts might be, they are not ultimately convincing. Even importing ironic readings into the passage is not enough to overturn the presentation of the ruling authorities as those instituted by God and to whom taxes and proper deference should be paid.

But that is not to say that a "conservative" reading of Rom 13:1–7 is the final word regarding Paul's view of the Roman imperial order. This passage has all too often been used to legitimate the perpetuation of social injustice and despotic domination, all in the name of God. What Paul has in mind, however, is the legiti-

24. See, e.g., Acts 17:1–10, where the Jesus movement proved itself an easy target for anti-imperial slander, and Acts 19:23–41, where the proclamation of the Jesus movement's message is recognized as having dire implications for artisan business in the service of the deities.

25. Further still, Paul speaks about fearing the Roman authorities, which might be taken to undermine the Roman preference to be respected for their governance rather than feared for their power.

26. Both quotes from Greg Woolf, *Rome: An Empire's Story* (Oxford: Oxford University Press, 2012), x.

macy of governance that falls in line with the "righteousness of God," as God seeks to rectify the whole of the created order in patterns of right relationship. To this end, legitimate "governing authorities" play a role of keeping moral chaos at bay, and in this way they are properly instruments of the creator God.

Paul does not, of course, discuss the issue of when governing authorities go wrong, when their definitions of justice and rightness fall beyond the scope of God's own righteousness — as Christians in Rome would themselves experience through **Nero**'s pogroms against them within seven or so years after receiving Paul's letter. With those situations in view, Paul's application of the gospel may well have taken on features of a different kind than those evident in Rom 13:1 – 7.

Wikimedia Commons

▲ A bust of Emperor Claudius

Paul may have had several reasons for including this discussion in this letter to Roman Christians in particular. His addressees lived in imperial Rome, of course, the center of political power of the day, so the issue may naturally have been of special interest to them. But beyond that, two other factors may have contributed to his reasoning in this instance.

1. Jews had been expelled from Rome by the emperor Claudius in AD 49 for their part in civil unrest within the city, and among that expulsion had been Jewish Jesus-followers, such as Prisca and Aquila. If some drifted back to Rome after the death of Claudius in 54, Paul knew how the displeasure of the civic authorities could disadvantage Jesus groups (and in fact had disadvantaged them). When writing to these same Jesus-groups in 57 or so, Paul saw it as prudent to encourage them to keep their heads below the political parapet.
2. The burden of Roman taxation had resulted in several instances of revolt (as recently as AD 49), sometimes resulting in the death of those who revolted. Paul would likely have known of the fruitlessness of such occurrences and perhaps wanted to ensure that the potentially counter-imperial gospel of Jesus Christ was not used to stir up trouble of that kind.

Even if instances such as these may have helped to feed Paul's preference for a conservative posture in Rom 13:1 – 7, he does not present his ideas simply as prudent advice in view of recent localized events. Romans 13:1 – 7 seems to emerge less in relation to his readers' own needs and more in relation to what he had written within the letter to Roman Christians itself. That is, Paul's own letter may have set up the rhetorical context that required him to address the issue of the governing authorities.

In the preceding chapters of the letter, for instance, Paul presented a vision in which the God of Israel is sovereign over the whole of creation and the whole of history, in a clash with all forces that compete for sovereignty. Already in Rom 1:1 – 17 Paul presented a claim about the "gospel" that has its roots in divine prophecies (contrast the divine prophecies about Rome's eternal glory in Virgil's *Aeneid*). Those prophecies speak of the arrival of a powerful and kingly (or Davidic) "Son of God" to whom the nations of the world will exhibit obedience, as participants in divine "peace," "power," and "justice/righteousness" that marks out their "salvation." Could Paul really have expected the first 275 words or so of his letter to be heard without any relevance to Roman imperial ideologies?

Toward the end of his letter, Paul allows his discourse to culminate in an affirmation drawn from the prophet Isaiah that would not comfort pro-Roman sympathizers: "The Root of Jesse will spring up, one who will arise to rule over the nations; in him the Gentiles [or nations] will hope" (Rom 15:12, citing Isa 11:10). If Paul was seeking to promote a politically innocent gospel, claims of this kind are imprudent.

Paul and Subjection to Rome

According to Neil Elliott, the most interesting question to ask is not "Why did Paul enjoin subjection to Rome?" but instead "What enabled Paul to speak, in the same letter, of an alternative?" Elliott writes: "To invoke the Spirit of God as a force striving against the bondage of the present order, to try to articulate the Spirit's unutterable yearnings for liberation—these aspects of Romans should give us pause."[27]

Perhaps it is precisely these theological features of his letter that required him to incorporate his comments about the governing authorities into his letter, in order to squash a misapplication of his politically charged discourse. Knowing full well that his discourse had often been "overinterpreted" with disastrous results (e.g., by the Corinthians), Paul may have included 13:1–7 in order to prevent a politicized "overreading" of his letter. The gospel does, in fact, make its way into the unmasking of ideologies supporting the Roman imperial order, but that fact alone cannot be used to support an anarchic agenda. Paul's gospel both erodes the power base of those who would usurp the divine narrative for their own purposes and leaves open a space to include those whose legitimate use of power can "coinhere" with the divine narrative.

In this scenario, Paul's discussion of the "governing authorities" serves to restrict his audience's imagination about their own responsibilities. In a context where the imperial propaganda machine was making claims for the divine and eternal sovereignty of Rome, Paul's gospel about God's righteousness taking over the world and defeating God's opponents might all too easily have been misheard as an injunction to unrestrained civil disobedience.

Paul was probably not at all averse to unmasking the underbelly of Roman imperial ideologies as deceptive and deficient. We see something along these lines in 1 Thess 5:1–11, for instance. There he provides resources for interpreting Rome's claim to provide "peace and security" throughout the empire—a claim that propped up the machinery of Roman propaganda as the instantiation of divine rule throughout the world. But Paul reworks the interpretive frame surrounding this claim, placing advocacy of the Roman program on the wrong side in the apocalyptic confrontation between the forces of light and darkness (5:4–5). Those whose lives serve the elusive program of Roman "peace and security" will ironically meet "sudden destruction" (5:3). The sole but sufficient resources for battle on the

27. Neil Elliott, *The Arrogance of Nations: Reading Romans in the Shadow of Empire* (Minneapolis: Fortress, 2008), 57.

side of light are the resources wielded by Jesus-followers: faith, love, and hope (5:8). Unlike the urban Macedonian elite, Paul did not equate the goal of all of history with Roman imperialism; for him, salvation history centers on "our Lord Jesus Christ . . . [who] died for us"—his death, of course, having been on a Roman cross (5:9–10). Evidently, then, speaking truth to and about power was embedded within the heart of Paul's gospel.

In this light, Rom 13:1–7 may serve to put the brakes on any interpretation of Paul's gospel that might lead to anarchic activism in the name of God. When fulfilling their God-given role, the governing authorities maintain order and restrain chaos; when fulfilling their God-given role, Jesus-followers embody the gospel that, as God's power in the world, overthrows chaos and instills right-relationed order. That the two spheres can overlap in harmonious relationship is Paul's point here, even if elsewhere he might also recognize that they can easily diverge.

Perhaps, then, what we find in Paul with regard to the Roman imperial order is less a "theology of church-state relations" and more "theologizing" about the gospel's configuration in different contexts. His reflections on the Roman imperial order might best be seen to involve malleable "hybridity," with counter-imperial ingredients rising to prominence in some contexts, remaining obscure in others, and being relatively denuded in still others.

Although Paul does not explicitly target Roman imperial ideologies in his letters, at various points in his theologizing Roman imperial ideologies are offset from the central and totalizing place that they normally expected and required, being substituted with an alternative totalizing narrative about what God has done in the death and resurrection of Christ.[29] If Paul was more supra-imperial than anti-imperial, his supra-imperialism could at times include a staunch critique of imperial ideologies. Paul's message was a gospel that set out a viable alternative to the way of life advertised by imperial ideologies. It was a gospel of inculturation into a way of life that often transgressed the gospel of Roman imperialism.

"The powerless rarely puncture the public version of reality with direct challenge. Rather, what we would expect [from the powerless who challenge the public version of reality] is discourse that is both accommodating and contestive, borrowing imperial terms and frameworks to present an alternative (and in part imitative) reality. What we would expect is discourse that variously sustained dignity, imagined a world-upside-down, made competitive claims, employed disguise, metaphor, euphemism, ambiguity, and anonymity, ensured cooperation, asserted ritual gestures, and outlined different social practices, worldview, and structures among a subordinate and publicly compliant group. What we would expect is what we get in Paul's letters."[28]

28. Warren Carter, "The Question of the State and the State of the Question: The Roman Empire and New Testament Theologies," in *Interpretation and the Claim of the Text: Resourcing New Testament Theology* (ed. Jason Whitlark; Waco, TX: Baylor University Press, 2014), 205 (197–211).

29. We might compare this to Philo of Alexandria's strategy of subtly opposing Roman imperial claims in his work *Embassy to Gaius*, without ever explicitly saying what he was doing.

A CASE STUDY IN IMPERIAL IDEOLOGY: PEACE, PROSPERITY, AND THE TOWN OF HERCULANEUM

In his book *Herculaneum Past and Future*, the classicist Andrew Wallace-Hadrill registers an interesting comment regarding the structural layout of the town of **Herculaneum**. This was a town about 130 miles south of Rome, and a town that died when Mount Vesuvius erupted a few miles away from it in the year AD 79, wiping it out through a series of pyroclastic blasts of volcanic debris. Now uncovered by a series of archaeological digs, much of the town lies like a time capsule of what life was like in a small urban context of the first century.

New Testament texts "will not deliver a monolithic 'how to' strategy for negotiating imperial power. Rather, contemporary readers will overhear a multi-voiced conversation that exhibits the complexity of negotiating it. They will encounter a range of perspectives and a variety of strategies spanning cooption and dissent, whose usefulness they will discern only in the midst of negotiating the particular circumstances of contemporary imperial powers."[30]

Wallace-Hadrill notes that Herculaneum underwent extensive renovations during the Augustan age, and he suggests that an alignment with the Roman imperial ideologies of peace and prosperity lay behind the changes in the town's layout. Whereas the town's waterfront had earlier been dominated by a military garrison advertising its strength and impregnability, just prior to the first century AD the waterfront was completely renovated to advertise two cherished characteristics of Augustan ideology—peace and prosperity. This comprehensive transformation of the town's waterfront profile was probably carried out under the direction of an influential local resident, Nonius Balbus, a strong supporter and friend of Augustus. Central to this project was the construction of at least two magnificent dwellings (one being Nonius Balbus's residence) at either end of the town's seafront limits and a tower connected to some of the town's baths.

Here's the point, made by several quotations from Wallace-Hadrill:[31] "At both the western and eastern corners were large private properties with tower- or pavilion-like structures that defined the limits of the town. In both cases, public baths with 'samovar' pools lay immediately adjacent." The consequence of this? Instead of presenting itself as a highly fortified city to deter attackers, the city of Herculaneum had "transform[ed] its defenses into a display of luxury." In the last decades of Herculaneum's existence,

> rich houses occupy the place of the garrison and the tower protruding over the shore, and the rooms faced with porticoes terraced down to the sea give the appearance of one of those rich villas captured in the landscape paintings of the time. In place of military force, Augustan peace and prosperity is on display. It is exactly the sort of message this loyal supporter of the emperor [i.e., Nonius Balbus] wanted to give, and it makes sense that his own property played part of it.

If Wallace-Hadrill is right, the extensive and expensive task of first demolishing and then reconstructing the waterfront profile of this Greco-Roman town was prompted by

30. Carter, "The Question of the State," 211.
31. Quotations are from Andrew Wallace-Hadrill, *Herculaneum Past and Future* (London: Francis Lincoln, 2011), 252–53.

the eagerness of the civic elite to align Herculaneum with Augustan ideology and to be an embodied advertisement of that ideology.

What would Paul have thought if he had visited that town and spotted the ideology that dictated its architectural design? Perhaps we can speculate by taking our cues from Paul's letter to Christians in Rome — itself a text written against a backdrop of an imperial gospel of peace and prosperity. In that letter, Paul spoke not of peace and prosperity filling creation through Augustan efforts; instead, he spoke of creation being in "bondage to decay," of its subjection "to futility," and of its "groaning in labor pains," claiming that creation "waits with eager longing" for God's "peace and prosperity" (in a sense) to take hold once and for all (Rom 8:19–23). Whereas Nonius Balbus wanted to advertise that Roman peace and prosperity had already established itself within Herculaneum through the divine initiatives of Augustus the son of God, Paul maintained that divine abundance overflows throughout the whole of creation in relation to "the one man, Jesus Christ" (Rom 5:17), who was himself the true Son of God (Rom 1:4).

Bruce Longenecker

▲▼ The statue of Nonius Balbus stands in a grand town courtyard above the seafront storage bays, looking out to (what would have been) the sea. To his left are the town's suburban baths, as well as one of the most impressive residences of Herculaneum — probably owned by Balbus himself.

SUMMARY REFLECTION

Paul's narrative of divine triumph through the suffering and resurrection of Jesus Christ had direct impact on the two most compelling "metanarratives" of divine triumph that circulated in his world. Restructuring his theology of divine sovereignty in light of the death and resurrection of Jesus Christ caused Paul's gospel to be placed on a collision course with established ideologies of divine sovereignty.

Because the early Jesus movement developed from within Judaism, circumstances required Paul to articulate his vision of divine sovereignty in relation to traditional expectations of mainstream Judaism — in which divine sovereignty was closely associated with the identity of the Jewish people. But because the early Jesus movement was spreading throughout the Greco-Roman world, Paul seems to have reflected somewhat on how his vision of divine sovereignty impacted on the claims of Roman imperial ideology — in which divine sovereignty was closely associated with Rome and its supporters.

Bruce Longenecker

What emerges, it seems, is a Paul who managed to affirm much within these macro-narratives while at the same time challenging them and offsetting their dominance in relation to a new understanding of what good news entails. Paul might have seen implications both for mainstream forms of Judaism and for the Roman imperial order in the words of Isa 52:7, which speaks of "those who bring good news, who proclaim peace, who bring good tidings, who proclaim salvation, who say to Zion, 'Your God reigns!'"

» KEY PEOPLE, PLACES, AND TERMS «

Abraham
Anti-imperial
Augustan era
Augustus
Corinth
Covenant
Covenantal nomism
Ephesus
Herculaneum
Judaism
Nero
Philippi
Roman imperial cult
Roman imperial ideology
Roman imperial order
Thessalonica
Torah
Virgil

» QUESTIONS FOR REVIEW AND DISCUSSION «

1. Regarding God's covenant with Israel, in what ways does Paul show himself to be a "thoroughly Jewish" thinker, and in what ways was his thinking new?
2. On the issue of how Paul's gospel pertains to ethnic Israel, describe the "two ways" and "replacement" views. Do you find passages in Paul's letters that problematize each of these views?
3. Describe the "new perspective." On this view, what is the purpose of the law?
4. Outline the strengths and weaknesses of the "traditional perspective" and the "new perspective." Is one of them more persuasive? In what way(s) might they be complementary?
5. In what ways did Paul's gospel run against Roman values? Give a few examples.
6. How did Paul "check" the tendency for readers to take anti-Roman sentiments too far?

» CONTEMPORARY THEOLOGICAL REFLECTION «

1. Why does God's commitment to ethnic Israel matter for Gentile believers? Why might "replacement theology" be problematic for contemporary Christian life? What historical circumstances have shown the gravity of this issue?
2. In what ways is Christian ethical behavior similar to "law-keeping," and in what ways is it different? How might Paul's perspective on the law help today's Christians navigate the relationship between the Bible and ethical practice?
3. Are there political institutions or policies that should be subverted by Christians today? Practically, what does it look like to respect the governing authorities while resisting unethical or unjust policies and institutions? Give examples.

4. How prescriptive should Paul's description of governing authorities be for Christians in general? Can that question be answered apart from consideration of specific historical contexts?

» GOING FURTHER «

Paul, Judaism, the Law, and "Works of the Law"

Dunn, James D. G. *The New Perspective on Paul.* Grand Rapids: Eerdmans, 2007.

Piper, John. *The Future of Justification: A Response to N. T. Wright.* Wheaton, IL: Crossway, 2007.

Westerholm, Stephen. *Perspectives Old and New on Paul: The "Lutheran" Paul and His Critics.* Grand Rapids: Eerdmans, 2003.

Wright, N. T. *Justification: God's Plan and Paul's Vision.* Downers Grove, IL: InterVarsity Press, 2009.

Yinger, Kent L. *The New Perspective on Paul.* Eugene, OR: Cascade, 2010.

Paul and the Roman Imperial Order

Elliott, Neil. "Imperium: Empire and the 'Obedience of Faith.'" Pages 25–57 in idem, *The Arrogance of Nations: Reading Romans in the Shadow of Empire.* Minneapolis: Fortress, 2008.

Georgi, Dieter. *Theocracy in Paul's Praxis and Theology.* Minneapolis: Fortress, 1991.

Harink, Douglas. "Politics: Yoder's Pauline Theology." Pages 105–49 in idem, *Paul among the Postliberals: Pauline Theology beyond Christendom and Modernity.* Grand Rapids: Brazos, 2003.

Still, Todd D. *Conflict at Thessalonica: A Pauline Church and Its Neighbours.* Sheffield: Sheffield Academic, 1999 (esp. ch. 9).

Wright, N. T. "Gospel and Empire." Pages 59–82 in idem, *Paul in Fresh Perspective.* Minneapolis: Fortress, 2009.

CHAPTER 13

PAUL'S THEOLOGICAL NARRATIVE AND THE MICRO-NARRATIVES OF JESUS GROUPS

CHAPTER GOALS

The goal of this chapter is to make connections between Paul's grand theological narrative and issues pertaining to everyday life within communities of Jesus-followers.

CHAPTER OVERVIEW

1. Freedom, Responsibility, and Self-Giving
2. Wise Interpretation of Scripture at "the Culmination of the Ages"
3. Moral Pageantry as Satan's Undermining of Ethical Balance
4. Care for the Poor among Communities of Jesus Devotion
5. Problematizing Violence
6. Summary Reflection
7. Key People, Places, and Terms
8. Questions for Review and Discussion
9. Contemporary Theological Reflection
10. Going Further

Paul's theological discourse is intricately connected to his attempts to influence the character of Jesus groups and the Jesus-followers within those groups. For Paul, theologizing on the grand scale is never an end in itself, but it serves to inform the kind of people Christians should be and the kind of decisions that they should make in their individual and corporate lives.

Consequently, this chapter probes issues pertaining to the moral ethos that Paul's theological discourse was meant to inspire within groups of Jesus-followers. The focus is less on "ethics" (prescriptions or stipulations about specific ethical topics) and more on "ethos." Ethics and ethos overlap, of course, but they are also distinct at times. Ethics operates on the basis of stipulations about what should or should not be done in particular situations or with regard to a particular ethical issue. Ethos is more about the atmosphere that operates within a group, informing the character of its corporate life, from which ethical decisions are made. In a nutshell, the ethos of a community informs the ethical decision-making that goes on within that community and, consequently, shapes the actions of Christians who participate within that community.

An example might suffice to demonstrate the point. Growing up in Toronto, Canada, one of the authors of this book witnessed an incident in which a man dropped a wrapper onto the sidewalk of a city street. A woman standing nearby walked over and picked up the wrapper, then went to the man and held it out to him and said something like, "You must not be from Toronto, because we don't drop litter here."

There is an ethical dimension to this statement, in that a particular practice is being evaluated for its rightness or wrongness. But the woman's statement is more about ethos than ethics, since it focuses primarily on the "ethos" of what it means to be from Toronto and on the character of Torontonian life from which specific practices emerge. In essence, the woman was suggesting that the corporate identity (or ethos) of Torontonians sets up the context out of which their actions (or ethics) emerge and against which their actions can be assessed.

Something similar is evident in Paul's theological discourse on the **Lord's Supper** in 1 Cor 11:17–34, for instance. Although Paul's discourse there includes a stipulation or two toward the end of his deliberations (see 1 Cor 11:33–34), the real "heavy lifting" of his comments is accomplished when he sets out the corporate ethos of Jesus groups through the recounting of the story of Jesus' Last Supper; that story establishes the parameters of the group's ethos, and from that ethos emerge the behavioral options (or ethics) that are legitimate for Christians.

Consequently, it is important to say what this chapter does not seek to accomplish. It is not, for instance, a complete discussion of Paul's comments on sexual ethics, social ethics, and the like. Handling those issues requires a much fuller theological and interpretive canvas than an introductory textbook allows. It is not always the case that Paul's texts are easily and readily applicable to life two millennia removed from their original situation. What does one do with the fact, for instance, that Paul expected that Jesus would be returning in the near future (see Rom 13:11–12; 1 Cor 7:26–31; 1 Thess 4:17; possibly Phil 4:5)? Did this expectation impact on Paul's view about the relationship between Jesus groups and the structures of corporate ethos beyond those groups? If Paul had known that at least two millennia would come and go before his expectations were to be fulfilled, would his perceptions on some matters have been shaped differently?[1]

What this chapter offers, then, are five case studies that foreground selected features of what emerges from Paul's letters regarding the corporate ethos of Jesus groups. These five case studies have been selected on triple criteria:

1. These are issues that appear in an assortment of Paul's extant texts, so that we are able to "triangulate" his comments.
2. These are issues that appear to be stable in that triangulation process, with the texts speaking with a constant voice, in a sense.
3. These are issues that seem relatively untouched by the "eschatological imminence" of Paul's theological expectations.

Issues that Paul dealt with that do not meet these three criteria will not be considered, since they would require a larger canvas than we have to paint on here. For example, what about "women in ministry" (to speak anachronistically)? Several of Paul's texts deal with the issue of women in communities of Jesus-followers, but those texts are not wholly stable in their content (see, e.g., 1 Cor 11:1–17 and 14:35–37, discussed in chapter 4 above). This issue, then, meets the first criterion (appearing in an assortment of texts) but not the second (speaking with a constant voice). As such, this important issue is better left to publications that can engage with it in much greater depth than would be the case here.

The five case studies regarding Paul's vision of the moral ethos of Jesus groups that meet the triple criteria set out above include the following: freedom in Christ and responsibility to others; Christian interpretation of Scripture; the dangers of moral pageantry; the urgency of caring for the poor; and the devaluing of violence. From Paul's statements on and handling of these issues, we can perceive something of the ethos he expected to animate communities of Christians in their various indigenous settings.

1. It is the case, of course, that Paul could imagine himself dying prior to Jesus' coming, as in Phil 1:21–23. This is a later letter, of course, but a foothold for this conviction might already be evident in 1 Thessalonians (5:10), Paul's earliest extant letter.

FREEDOM, RESPONSIBILITY, AND SELF-GIVING

Is it a good thing that Jesus-followers have "freedom" in Jesus Christ? And does the freedom of Jesus-followers have anything to do with the grand apocalyptic narrative that undergirds much of Paul's theological discourse?

That Jesus-worshipers enjoy freedom is a theme that appears in several of Paul's letters. In Rom 8:21 it seems almost an afterthought when Paul is speaking about creation being in bondage to decay and how it "will obtain the freedom of the glory of the children of God." In 2 Cor 3:17 Paul asserts boldly that "where the Spirit of the Lord is, there is freedom."

> "If we want to know how 'being in Christ' was embodied and experienced in Paul's world, we cannot overlook the fact that participation in the body of Christ provided the setting in which Paul's soteriology took shape and made sense."[2]

But the notion of freedom comes into play especially in Galatians 5, after Paul's depiction of slavery in earlier parts of the Galatian letter. In his allegory of **Abraham**'s offspring in Galatians 4, for instance, Paul compares Jesus-followers to offspring of the "free woman" (**Sarah**) instead of the "slave woman" (**Hagar**), concluding the allegory with the claim, "It is for freedom that Christ has set us free" (5:1). The sentence might look somewhat awkward, verging on redundancy. But Paul has constructed it in this way for a particular purpose, as will become evident from the following paragraphs.

For now, it is enough to note that Paul uses the notion of freedom as a kind of shorthand for the conviction that Gentile Jesus-followers need not "enslave" themselves to **Torah** observance. When Gentile Jesus-followers were told that they should be circumcised, Paul understood this to be a way of undermining "the freedom we have in Christ Jesus" and to be a way of "mak[ing] us slaves" (Gal 2:4). So too, Paul's claim that "it is for freedom that Christ has set us free" is followed by the exhortation to "stand firm" against those who inspire Gentile Jesus-followers to be circumcised, lest the Galatians "be burdened . . . by a yoke of slavery" (5:1). For Paul, then, the "freedom" of Christians could be used as a shorthand slogan for "salvation has nothing to do with observing the rules of the Torah"—or with anything other than Jesus Christ, for that matter.

> The Spirit is, in a sense, the immanent initiative of God within his own creation. C. K. Barrett speaks of this when he writes: "God's initiative means that he is taking in hand his final acts in putting his world to rights. In a word, Spirit is, in Paul's usage, an eschatological factor, in the sense that the Spirit is the divine agent who begins to bring the future into the present."[3]

But Paul's discourse of freedom was vulnerable to misinterpretation. This became all too clear to Paul himself when dealing with Christians in **Corinth**. If Jesus-followers are not required to observe the Torah, could it be that they really have no moral constraints

2. Richard B. Hays, "What Is 'Real Participation in Christ'? A Dialogue with E. P. Sanders on Pauline Soteriology," in *Redefining First-Century Jewish and Christian Identities: Essays in Honor of Ed Parish Sanders* (ed. Fabian E. Udoh; Notre Dame, IN: University of Notre Dame Press, 2008), 345.
3. C. K. Barrett, *Freedom and Obligation: A Study of the Epistle to the Galatians* (Philadelphia: Westminster, 1985), 66.

on their behavior? Based on Paul's gospel of "freedom," some Corinthian Christians began to imagine that they had "the right to do anything" (1 Cor 6:12; 10:23). Paul had gained a reputation among some people for promoting a moral "**libertinism**," in which one could live without any kind of moral restraint, and all to the glory of God (see, e.g., Rom 3:8; 6:1, 15). After all, if grace is freely given "apart from law" (Rom 3:21), perhaps those who have faith in Jesus can live in any way they want, without worrying about being condemned as sinners. This might even be thought to enhance God's reputation as a gracious God, who does not hold sin against those who have put their faith in Jesus.[4]

Paul cannot countenance such thinking (cf. his harsh words in Rom 3:8). Instead, he makes it clear that freedom among Christians requires careful handling, lest it become a means for their own moral servitude.

This is evident in Gal 5:13 (which will serve as a key verse at two further points further down in this discussion). Whereas the first sentence of Gal 5:13 calls Christians "to be free," in the second sentence Paul gives this critical stipulation: "But do not use your freedom to indulge the flesh." Paul often uses the word "flesh" to refer to something like "the reinforced proclivity towards sinful living" rather than "the sinful nature," as it is sometimes mistranslated). Here Paul warns against the misuse of the freedom that Jesus-followers enjoy in Jesus Christ.

> "Paul's central concern was to use the narrative [of his gospel] to form a moral community. That story imperiously rewrote the story that his own life must follow. When Paul writes to the various communities he founded, it is invariably to suggest, cajole, argue, threaten, shame, and encourage those communities into behaving, in their specific situations, in ways somehow homologous to that fundamental story."[5]

Paul's discourse of "freedom from" cannot be fully accounted for without immersing it in the soil of the apocalyptic narrative highlighted in chapter 11 above. In particular, we do well to remind ourselves of the theological contours of Paul's discourse in Romans 5 through 8. There, Paul depicts the cosmos as being held in the grip of suprahuman powers, with human sinfulness and death resulting as a consequence. Paul imagines the cosmos and everything within it suffering from the same fundamental problem—the forces of chaos seem to reign supreme, that is, the powers of Sin and Death. For Paul, what God has done in the death and resurrection of Jesus introduces a new situation, one that guarantees freedom from those forces of chaos.

In his discourse on baptism in Romans, Paul makes the point forcefully. Followers of Jesus have been baptized into Christ Jesus and have been united with him in death. As a consequence, the power of Sin is prevented from getting a foothold in their lives. Moreover, although the forces of chaos can get no traction in the lives of those who are already dead, God can reach into places where there is nothing and bring life out of them. He did precisely this in the moment of creation, and he did the same when he raised Jesus from the dead. So too those who have "died with Christ" cannot be used as instruments of the powers of chaos, but come alive as instruments of God's grace and righteousness. Those who

4. A theology of this sort was seemingly embraced and espoused by Grigori Rasputin (1869–1916), a Russian Orthodox Christian frequently referred to as the "mad monk."
5. Wayne A. Meeks, *The Origins of Christian Morality* (New Haven, CT: Yale University Press, 1993), 196.

Christ Appearing to the Apostles after the Resurrection, Blake, William/Yale Center for British Art, Yale Art Gallery Collection/The Bridgeman Art Library

▲ "Christ Appearing to the Apostles after the Resurrection" by William Blake. According to Paul, God can reach into places where there is nothing and bring life out of them.

are in Christ have been set free from the power of Sin (6:7; see also 6:18, 20, 22) and have become participants in God's eschatological life-bringing drama over against the forces of chaos.

Paul's assurances that Christians have "freedom from the Torah" play a part within this larger context of Paul's "apocalyptic" narrative. In Rom 7:1–6 Paul observes that dead persons (like those who have died with Christ) are not bound to laws that bind others, and he draws from this the view that there is no salvific necessity to observe the **Mosaic law**. In fact, Rom 7:7–25 outlines how the power of Sin hijacks even the God-given law, so that the law itself serves the chaotic purposes of the power of Sin. That allows Paul to designate the Mosaic law in Rom 8:2 as "the law of sin and death"—connoting the God-given Mosaic law itself has become unwillingly engulfed within the program of the powers of Sin and Death. It is this law in its association with powers of Sin and Death from which Paul says followers of Jesus have been "set free."

According to Romans 7, what the power of Sin induces is a character of covetousness. Whereas the law commands "You shall not covet," the power of Sin seized "the opportunity afforded by the commandment" and "produced in me every kind of coveting" (Rom 7:7–8). If we can uncover what "every kind of coveting" looks like to Paul, we can unmask what it is that the power of Sin promotes within enslaved humanity.

To discover what "every kind of coveting" looks like, we only need to expose its opposite within Paul's thinking. Later in Romans Paul encourages Christians to be debtors to each other in love, adding "for whoever loves others has fulfilled the law" and noting that "love is the fulfillment of the law" (Rom 13:8, 10). This resonates with 8:4, where Paul speaks of the "righteous requirement of the law" having been "fulfilled in us" by means of the Spirit. Although observing the law is not necessary for salvation, there is a sense in which the law itself is fulfilled in Jesus-followers through the loving patterns of life that transpire by the power of the Spirit. For the one who is "sold as a slave to [the power of] sin" (7:14), the law is a law in association with Sin and Death (8:2). Conversely, for the one who is "enslaved to righteousness" (6:18), the law finds its true fulfillment, not in the doing of its commandments but as Christians live empowered by the Spirit, who inspires patterns of love, whereby the law is inadvertently fulfilled. It is in this matrix that we find the converse of "every kind of coveting."

We are now in a position to return again to our selected passage in order to see another of its complex layers. Whereas the first sentence of Gal 5:13 calls Christians to "be free," and whereas the second sentence warns against allowing freedom to promote sinfulness, the same verse concludes with the exhortation to "serve one another humbly in love." Freedom, for Paul, is ultimately defined as freedom to serve, through love. Once again, Paul immediately brings the Torah into this, giving an assurance similar to that of Rom 13:8–10: "For the entire law is fulfilled in keeping this one command: 'Love your neighbor as yourself.'"

Paul says more about what love looks like throughout Galatians, but note here how he contrasts it with what might be thought of as a corollary of the phrase "every kind of coveting" in Rom 7:8: "If you keep on biting and devouring each other, watch out or you will be destroyed by each other" (Gal 5:14). If we unwrapped more of what this impetus of biting and devouring looks like throughout Galatians, we would find it to be little more than brute self-interestedness, a self-interestedness that results only in chaotic relationships (i.e., "you will be destroyed by each other"). In essence, Paul's gospel of freedom translates into the moral character of self-giving, in contrast to the epidemic of self-interestedness that has engulfed the course of human history. For Paul, then, the bottom line is that the gospel frees Christians from the chaos that results from enslavement to unbridled self-interestedness.

"Christians . . . are engrafted into Christ, by whose grace they are freed from the curse of the Law, and by whose Spirit they have the Law written in their hearts."[6]

Rampant self-interestedness drives competitiveness and conflict in a world where "the survival of the fittest" is the ideological presupposition shaping moral values. For Paul, what flows from such a world is moral chaos. And moral chaos is precisely what Paul thought he had found among some of the practices of Corinthian Christians. Over and over, they interpreted their freedom in Christ along individualistic lines, without regard to the health of the community of Jesus-followers.

The fact that freedom is not individualistically configured for Paul is evident, for instance, when he discusses the eating of meat that may previously have been used in a sacrifice on an altar to a pagan deity. When considering that matter, Paul does not simply make ethical pronouncements. Instead, while he affirms the liberty of individual Christians to eat freely, he spends much more time and effort crafting out what freedom looks like when it is wielded responsibly within a Christian community. Properly understood, liberty within Jesus groups is constrained by attentiveness toward others (e.g., 1 Cor 8:1–13).[8]

"The gospel that Paul preaches deals not merely with forgiveness but with *transformation.* This notion of effective transformation through union with Christ is fundamental to Paul's theological ethics."[7]

6. John Calvin, *Institutes of the Christian Religion*, 2.5.57.
7. Richard B. Hays, *The Moral Vision of the New Testament: A Contemporary Introduction to New Testament Ethics* (San Francisco: HarperSanFrancisco, 1996), 38.
8. The issue of spiritual gifts offers another example of Paul yoking freedom to corporate attentiveness. Although the Spirit has gifted all Christians in different ways, those whose gift was tongues found that their gift could so easily be used to enhance their own status within the community, promoting them over against others whose gifts were of a different kind. Despite their impressive spiritual speech, such people are merely like "a resounding gong or a clanging cymbal" when viewed through the prism of moral character within the community of Jesus-followers (1 Cor 13:1).

Behind all this is Paul's conviction that a Jesus group is to function as "the body of Christ," with each member of the community playing an essential part (whether large or small) to enhance the community (see Rom 12:3–5; 1 Cor 12:4–26).

Undergirding all this is the way of life that Jesus embodied. For Paul, the moral character of Jesus' own life was sacrificial self-giving. This feature of Jesus' life is recounted in virtually every one of Paul's letters. In particular, it stands out in glowing colors in the "kenotic hymn" of Phil 2:6–11, with its emphasis on Jesus having "made himself nothing" and "humbled himself" (2:7–8). To track the motif of Jesus' self-giving throughout the Pauline letters would be a lengthy exercise in itself, but it is enough for our purposes simply to note that christocentric cruciformity (i.e., a cross-shaped life of self-giving) lies at the heart of Paul's discourse on freedom and lashes Paul's soteriological and moral discourse together in an inseparable union.

"A Christian is the most free lord of all, and subject to none; a Christian is the most dutiful servant of all, and subject to everyone."[9]

This union of salvation and moral character is likely to explain the otherwise "intolerable" claim (as noted above) that "it is for freedom that Christ has set us free" (Gal 5:1). The phrase "Christ has set us free" pertains to the salvation of Jesus' followers, while "for freedom" pertains to the moral character of Jesus-followers. In essence, Jesus-followers have been set free from the enslavement of chaos-inducing self-interestedness in order that their self-giving Lord might become incarnate within their own lives.

All this transpires as Jesus-worshipers become participants in the drama of what God has done in Jesus Christ, through their incorporation into Christ. That story comes to life within them, as they "clothe themselves with Christ" (Gal 3:27), and as Christ becomes "formed" in them (4:19) and lives in them (2:19–20). It is a story of freedom, to be sure, but a freedom constrained by its christological basis and its corporate and relational contours.

It is also a freedom that is fundamentally apocalyptic in its configuration. That is, the self-giving one came "to rescue us from [the bondage of] the present evil age" (Gal 1:4) as his self-giving becomes embodied within his followers. The freedom that God empowers "in Christ" through the Spirit involves the shattering of the cosmically ingrained power (bifurcated in terms of "Sin and Death")—a power that embeds itself within the insatiable drive for self-advancement at the cost of others. God, in Christ and through the Spirit, is smashing all permutations of the suprahuman force that animates human self-interestedness and fosters moral chaos. In this way, Jesus' followers are being restored to "right relationship" with him and, as a consequence, with all other components of God's creation. In the process, enslavement to cosmic forces of moral chaos has been undermined; the freedom that results, however, is little other than the occasion to be enslaved to others, in the love that the Spirit inspires within those who are enslaved to God.

We return one final time to Gal 5:13. Although Christians are "called to be free," Paul exhorts his audience not simply to "*serve* one another humbly in love" (as in most translations); instead, the verb Paul uses is "enslave" (*douleuō*). Literally, Paul exhorts Jesus-followers to "enslave themselves" to each other in humble, practical love.

Paul was no doubt aware of how jarring this exhortation must have sounded within its immediate context. In the seven instances in Galatians when Paul employs the notion of

9. Martin Luther, *The Freedom of the Christian* (1520).

slavery prior to this verse, that notion functions to depict the condition from which Christians have already been freed and should not return (4:3, 7–9, 24–25; 5:1). As one whose gospel advocated "freedom" from nonessentials (Torah observance) and from the cosmic power that translates into chaotic self-interestedness, Paul's choice of verb in the phrase "*enslave yourselves* to one another humbly in love" was no doubt as intentional as it was ironic.

▲ Illuminated manuscript showing Paul holding a scroll. Even if righteousness does not come through observing the stipulations of the law, Paul nonetheless thought it wholly appropriate for Jesus-groups to learn about their relationship with God by immersing themselves in the scriptural stories about God's relationship with Israel.

Werner Forman Archive/National Library, Athens/GlowImages

WISE INTERPRETATION OF SCRIPTURE AT "THE CULMINATION OF THE AGES"

Does freedom have anything to do with the interpretation of Scripture? If the "oracles of God" have been entrusted to the ethnic people of Israel (Rom 3:2), can Scripture rightly be applied to audiences of predominantly Gentile Jesus-followers who feed on it to inform their lives and understanding?

When it comes to interpreting Scripture, we might find it within ourselves to have some sympathy for Galatian Christians. Although they found themselves in a quandary about whether the scriptural prescriptions given to Israel applied to them also, their intentions seem to have been sincere in determining how to align themselves with the Scriptures entrusted to Israel. When considering the issue of **circumcision**, for instance, it may well have seemed to them that the "plain meaning" of Scripture is relatively clear: God expects the males among his people to be circumcised on the foreskins of their penis (Gen 17:13, where circumcision is the sign of God's "everlasting covenant" with Abraham's physical descendants [through Isaac]). On what grounds, then, might the scriptural command to "circumcise" be deemed by Paul as inapplicable to Gentile Jesus-followers who consider themselves to be God's people?

Unfortunately, Paul does not offer a recipe or a set of rules for guiding communities on how to interpret the Scriptures. One thing is sure, however; even if righteousness does not come through observing the law, Paul nonetheless thought it wholly appropriate for communities of Jesus devotion to learn about their relationship with God by immersing themselves in the scriptural stories about God's relationship with Israel. So in 1 Cor 10:11 Paul states that events in Israel's history "happened to them as examples and were written down as warnings for us, on whom the culmination of the ages has come" (1 Cor 10:11; so too 10:6; Rom 15:4).

At times Paul expects his audience to understand his use of a scriptural quotation with the fuller scriptural context resonating in their ears. This must be the case, for instance, in 1 Cor 10:7, where Paul quotes from Exod 32:6 with the words, "The people sat down to eat and drink and got up to indulge in revelry." In the Exodus story this revelry is clearly not just "good clean fun"; rather, it is an expression of perverse sinfulness. But without this narrative backdrop, Paul's quotation could be read almost as if the people of Israel were enjoying a fun and healthy picnic in the park. Evidently, then, Paul assumed that his audience knew something of the scriptural story and were able to catch the import of that story and its significance for them as Jesus-followers.[10]

If in 1 Cor 10:7 Paul harnesses scriptural resources by means of direct quotations, there may be other times when he harnesses them in a more subtle fashion. For instance, when he cites Hab 2:4 in Rom 1:17 as a means to introduce his gospel, is the "informed reader" to appreciate the scriptural context in which the claim "the righteous will live by faith" is embedded? Habakkuk 1 establishes the theological context for the claim of Hab 2:4 by posing a thorny theological question: Since the world is seemingly out of joint, is it really true that the God who gave the law to Israel is also the righteous Creator who stands as sovereign over his creation?

Although Paul does not explicitly draw his audience's attention to the fact, the theological context out of which Hab 2:4 arises (i.e., the issue of theodicy) fits perfectly with the apocalyptic discourse that animates so much of Paul's letter. How should this be understood? At one end of the spectrum, it might be argued that this intertwining of scriptural context with the letter's content is simply a matter of coincidence; at the other end, it might be argued that Paul crafted his letter in such a way that theological dimensions are ready for activation, in a sense, even though he does not explicitly denote them to his audience.

"Of course Paul knows that 'seed' [in Gal 3:16] is a collective noun, but it was necessary for him first to break down the old collectivity of race in order to establish the new collectivity which is coming into being, in an inconceivable unity, with and in Christ. The curious verbal trick proves to be the key to the whole argument."[11]

Although Paul frequently embedded Scripture within his discourse, he well knew that being immersed in Scripture does not necessarily guard against the dangers of unwisely interpreting and applying Scripture to the lives of Christians. For Paul, wise readings of Scripture among Jesus-followers presupposed the transforming working of the Spirit within the interpreter and the community of believers. He knew all too well that Scripture can be interpreted to bolster the interests of virtually anyone, and he seems to have imagined a legitimate reading of Scripture among Jesus-followers that emerges from a prior and continuing transformation of the Spirit.

But legitimate readings of Scripture can emerge from various kinds of reading strategies. For instance, at times Paul seems virtually to make a text say "Pauline" things by imposing meaning onto the text that is not readily evident in the text's original context. The Abrahamic "seed" of Gal 3:16 is a case in point. Interpreting the notion of Abraham's seed with reference to Christ in exclusion to Abraham's physical offspring takes the scriptural verse

10. There may have been Jewish Jesus-followers at Corinth to assist in educating others about the scriptural stories on which Paul was building; see 1 Cor 7:18.

11. Barrett, *Freedom and Obligation*, 38.

in a direction different from what the Genesis narrative seems to suggest (see, e.g., Gen 13:15; 17:8). This is an instance in which Paul seems to assume that the scriptural text does not always coincide with the gospel in a "literal" or "straightforward" fashion.

▲ In Gal 4:21–31 Paul interprets the Abraham narrative pertaining to Sarah and Hagar.

Elsewhere, Paul evidences a different attitude toward scriptural passages, in which passages that seem to run contrary to the gospel are moved to the periphery. The passages cited in Gal 3:11–12 are particularly interesting in this regard. There, Paul sets out two passages from Scripture and allows them to stand in opposition to each other. They both seem to promise life, but they both base that promise on different premises. So Hab 2:4 promises that "the righteous will live by faith," whereas Lev 18:5 promises that "whoever does these things [i.e., the stipulations of the law] will live by them." For Paul, these two passages of Scripture advertise two opposing ways of life. Although he might have tried to align Lev 18:5 with his gospel in some fashion (as he did with the Abrahamic "seed" in Gal 3:16), Paul simply disqualifies Lev 18:5 from consideration when configuring the shape of Christian lifestyle. With the coming of the eschatological age, when Jesus-followers live at "the culmination of the ages," some passages of Scripture are no longer seen to have instructive value.[12]

Paul seems cognizant, then, that not all of Scripture coincides with his gospel. But this does not throw him off his stride, since he recognizes that the eschatological divide that separates the epochs of salvation history also runs throughout the Scriptures themselves. "Counter-gospel" Scriptures are not theological anomalies; instead, with the hindsight provided by their eschatological advantage, Jesus-followers are enabled to hear two voices within Scripture, only one of which addresses their situation. The scriptural voice that matters speaks to Christians not about things that used to matter (i.e., circumcision versus uncircumcision, etc.), but about "new creation" (Gal 6:15), as faith works practically in love (Gal 5:6).

A different reading strategy is evident in Gal 4:21–31, where Paul interprets the Abraham narrative pertaining to Sarah and Hagar. Paul draws meaning from the scriptural text in a way that coincides with the gospel and encourages the Galatian Christians to hear what Scripture "says" (4:21, 30), since he found Scripture to have "preached the gospel beforehand" (3:9). But what Scripture said and says emerges from interpretative factors beyond a

12. That this is not just some interpretive rarity is demonstrated by the fact that Paul does much the same thing with Lev 18:5 in Rom 10:5–8.

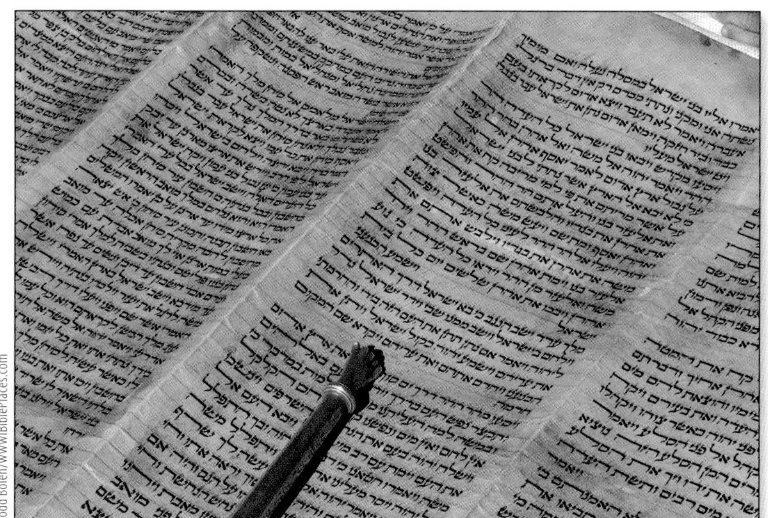

Todd Bolen/www.BiblePlaces.com

▲ Paul finds gospel within Scripture as a result of his transforming encounter with the risen Lord. In the wake of that experience, the process of interpreting Scripture underwent radical redefinition.

concern for the "literal meaning" of the Genesis story of Abraham and his progeny. The voice that Paul wants his audience to hear from Scripture speaks in harmony with his gospel only when this part of the Abraham narrative is interpreted in ways that diverge from its original narrative context.

Paul knows what he is doing here, as indicated by the fact that he identifies his interpretive method in this instance as a form of "allegory" (Gal 4:24). He knows that what the Scripture says for Jesus-followers does not follow the literal meaning of the Genesis narrative, with its undeniable connection between Abraham's offspring and the requirement of literal circumcision of the male penis (as in Gen 17). But as an allegorical exercise, he draws new meaning from the scriptural text in a manner that enhances the gospel.

The allegory of Hagar and Sarah, then, involves interpreting a scriptural text in relation to a preestablished point of view. As a consequence of reading Scripture in light of the gospel, some texts acquire new meaning, even bypassing their "literal meaning" in their original contexts. In Paul's allegory, the scriptural voice comes alive afresh only when the text is interpreted in relation to a point of view that derives beyond that text.

It seems, then, that Paul makes use of various strategies when interpreting scriptural texts. But this raises an important issue, and one that Paul's letters help to answer: What makes a particular reading of Scripture legitimate? If we were Galatian Christians, why should we have found Paul's interpretations preferable to the kinds of interpretations presented by others, especially when the interpretations of others may at times have been more in tune with the "literal meaning" of scriptural texts?

Although a full discussion of interpretation of Old Testament Scripture among Christians cannot be entertained here, it is enough to note that Paul offers some essential resources for addressing this important issue.

First, we must recognize that Paul's gospel does not ultimately derive from Scripture. He never imagines that his gospel could be assembled on the basis of stringing a few texts together in a package. Paul finds gospel within Scripture as a result of his transforming encounter with the risen Lord, an "apocalyptic" revelation from God (Gal 1:15–16; see also 1:1, 11–12). In the wake of that experience, the process of interpreting Scripture underwent radical redefinition.

Second, Paul seems to assume that Scripture is read appropriately by Jesus-followers when read in conformity with a cruciform moral character. Presumably Paul would point to this feature as providing the legitimacy to his own interpretations of Scripture. Because the self-giving

Christ has come alive in Paul, his own scriptural interpretations are valid, precisely because they help to preserve self-giving Christlikeness within Jesus groups, whereas other interpretations do not. It is not incidental, then, that Paul's outline of his own life in Galatians 1–2 precedes his interpretation of Scripture in Galatians 3–4; his readings of Scripture emerge from the embodiment of Christ within his own life, through the transforming power of God.

Paul thus sees the problems that arose among Galatian Christians, for instance, as involving a character deficiency that was compromising their ability to hear the voice of Scripture aright. A deficit in Christlike character caused the gospel to be undermined, not least through an unwise handling of Scripture. The "agitators" known to us from Galatians were interpreting Scripture incorrectly not simply because they prioritized certain passages of Scripture and Paul prioritized others. For Paul, their defective interpretation arose from a defective character (see Gal 4:17; 6:12–13). Once Christlike character is compromised, the result is that wise readings of Scripture for the edification of Christ-followers becomes jeopardized, with Scripture itself becoming an instrument for the endorsement of things that run contrary to Christlike character. Fundamentally, then, the issue at Galatia is less about circumcision and the observance of the law and is more about how Scripture is to be read in conjunction with Christlike character.

Accordingly, scriptural interpretation is not about "proof-texting the gospel out of Scripture." Instead, as a result of Christlike character infusing the hearts and minds of Christ-followers, the voice of Scripture can be heard in accordance with the gospel through a variety of interpretive strategies. The interpretations that emerge from this matrix are legitimate to the extent that they enhance the gospel as it inspires further patterns of Christlikeness within communities of Jesus devotion. In this way, there is a direct connection between Paul's approach to scriptural interpretation and his conviction that God's power is embodied within the gospel, as Jesus-followers are transformed by the Spirit to conform to the likeness of God's Son. All this may be evident within Paul's brief claim in 2 Cor 3:17 that "where the Spirit of the Lord is, there is freedom."

"No reading of scripture can be legitimate . . . if it fails to shape the readers into a community that embodies the love of God as shown forth in Christ. This criterion slashes away all frivolous or self-serving readings, all readings that aggrandize the interpreter, all merely clever readings. True interpretation of Scripture leads us into unqualified giving of our lives in service within the community whose vocation is to reenact the obedience of the Son of God who loved us and gave himself for us. Community in the likeness of Christ is cruciform; therefore right interpretation must be cruciform."[13]

MORAL PAGEANTRY AS SATAN'S UNDERMINING OF ETHICAL BALANCE

If Paul has differing strategies with regard to scriptural interpretation, he similarly advocates the use of differing strategies with regard to the maintenance of healthy relationships among

13. Richard B. Hays, *Echoes of Scripture in the Letters of Paul* (New Haven, CT: Yale University Press, 1989), 191.

Christians. In essence, what is right for one situation is not necessarily right for another, and when ethical pronouncements are applied in a formulaic or cookie-cutter fashion, opportunities arise to bolster the interests of Satan rather than to enhance communities of Christlikeness.

"The interpretation of Scripture as an activity of communal discernment — the conversation in 'the good' which is both formative and transformative and involves both destruction and construction of identities — is enabled by the Holy Spirit through Christ's resurrection."[14]

"All actions, however ostensibly spiritual, must meet the criterion of constructive impact on the church community. The task of community-building, which was originally Paul's apostolic work, is transferred to the community itself; thus, the purpose of corporate worship becomes community formation. It is crucial, however, that the work of community-building be a shared, participatory enterprise; the worship assembly is not to be monopolized by any one member. Thus, the gathered community's worship reflects and symbolizes the interdependence of the body of Christ."[15]

This is evident, for instance, in Paul's exhortations to Corinthian Christians regarding the man who first appears in the Corinthian correspondence in 1 Corinthians 5, where he is shown to be living with his stepmother. In that context, Paul exhorted Corinthian Christians to force him out of the Corinthian Jesus groups so that they could avoid the contagion of sinfulness that he was infecting them with, and with the hope that the man would decide to change his ways.

As noted in the overview of 2 Corinthians above, it is possible that this is the same man (in conjunction with some "super-apostles") who caused trouble for Paul after that point; when Paul wrote the "tearful letter" (2 Corinthians 10–13), the other Corinthian Christians had flouted his instructions by failing to oust the man from among them. When next writing to the Corinthians, however, Paul knew that they had finally demonstrated their "obedience" to his instructions (see 2:5–10). But with the man's expulsion from their communities, Paul goes on to propose that the Corinthians adopt a change in their procedures (or better, perhaps, that they take the initial procedure to its next stage). So he instructs Corinthian Christians that the man's punishment has now been "sufficient" and that they should now "forgive and comfort him" (2:7), allowing him to be received back into their midst so that they can reaffirm their love for him.

In this, Paul demonstrates his concern not only for the man but also for the moral character animating the Corinthian groups of Jesus devotion. Having exercised some corporate power through the expulsion of the man, Corinthian Jesus groups are now in danger of allowing that power to go to their head, in a sense. Having gotten a taste for that sort of thing, some members of Corinthian Jesus groups may start to imagine themselves as the moral supervisors of others, setting themselves above others in relationships of power that ultimately contravene the gospel.

14. Stephen E. Fowl and L. Gregory Jones, *Reading in Communion: Scripture and Ethics in Christian Life* (London: SPCK, 1991), 35.
15. Hays, *The Moral Vision of the New Testament*, 34.

Paul is walking an ethical tightrope here in an effort to pull off a difficult balancing act regarding the moral character of Jesus-followers. He initially had to correct a spirit of tolerant acceptance among the Corinthians; now he has to ward off a harshly judgmental spirit among them. He is aware that, in this new phase of Corinthian relationships with this man, an attitude of moral pomposity might take root among some of them. Having countered Corinthian attitudes of self-importance and superiority at virtually every turn, Paul recognizes how "Satan might . . . outwit us" inadvertently through a new strategy of moral pageantry among the Corinthians, "for we are not unaware of his schemes" (2 Cor 2:11).

"If ever he [Paul] appears dictatorial, it is at the expense of the dogmatists, whether at Galatia, Corinth, or Colossae, i.e., those who are making extravagant demands on their fellow Christians or imposing unnecessary conditions upon them. His own, more relaxed attitude to the ordinary believer . . . arises out of his confidence in God; for he was convinced that, provided his friends adhered to the primacy of God's grace, no matter what heterodox ideas they might hold about other matters, God would in due course reveal the truth to them (Phil. 3:15)."[16]

Paul captures these same dynamics of moral character when writing to Galatian Christians. Toward the close of that letter (Gal 6:1), Paul instructs them on matters pertaining to both sides of the moral coin. On the one hand, he instructs them to correct any person who is ensnared in a sin, saying "you who live by the Spirit should restore that person gently." Presumably this should happen before things get out of order, as in the case of 1 Corinthians 5, when restoring the person gently was no longer an option; in that instance, the sin was so foul that serious steps had to be taken (i.e., expulsion, at least temporarily).

On the other hand, Paul instructs Galatian Christians against the dangers involved in playing the moral watchdog: "But watch yourselves, or you also may be tempted" (Gal 6:1). The "temptation" that Paul speaks of here may be precisely what Paul entertains in 2 Cor 2:11—the temptation of enjoying the moment too much as an indication of one's own importance within the community. In the imagery of 2:11, to allow this dynamic to enter into one's moral character would provide Satan with the foothold to "outwit" the Jesus-follower through one of "his schemes." Imagining that one is doing what is "spiritual" sometimes can play directly into Satan's game of promoting self-interestedness.

"Commissioned as ministers of God's redemptive Word, we are required, in politics and private life, in work and play, in commerce and scholarship, to practice and foster that word-caring, that meticulous and conscientious concern for the quality of conversation and the truthfulness of memory, which is the first casualty of sin. The church, accordingly, is or should be a school of philology, an academy of word-care."[17]

It is probably for this reason that Paul adds the next sentence to his instructions: "Carry each other's burdens, and in this way you will fulfill the law of Christ"

16. George B. Caird, *New Testament Theology* (Oxford: Oxford University Press, 1994), 8.
17. Nicholas Lash, "Ministry of the Word or Comedy and Philology," *New Blackfriars* 68 (1987): 476–77.

(Gal 6:2). With this, Paul puts the focus on self-giving, even in the context of intracommunal correction. It is probably not too much to claim, then, that for Paul the fundamental bedrock undergirding the corporate balance and integrity of a Jesus group is the moral character of Jesus-followers, in their imitation of the one "who gave himself for our sins to rescue us from the present evil age" (1:4). That cruciform character is a defense against the self-interestedness that can all too easily begin to permeate even one's own spirituality, in Satan's game of outwitting God's people.

CARE FOR THE POOR AMONG COMMUNITIES OF JESUS DEVOTION

According to Roman imperial ideologies, the Augustan age had ushered in a new era that had taken hold of the world, an era in which concord would exist among peoples and the earth would render bountiful plenty to benefit all.

And yet, the poor were everywhere in the cities that Paul used as bases for his ministry. Recent studies have estimated that at least half of the urban population of Paul's day was embedded in poverty in one form or another. Vast swaths of people lived at subsistence level, and similar numbers of people fell below the subsistence level.

Did Paul demonstrate any interest in considering how his gospel pertained to the widespread poverty of his world? There has been a long-standing assumption that Paul's theologizing ran along lines in which there is little foothold for things like caring for the poor. This assumption has taken two predominant forms.

- For some, Paul had little care for the poor because his gospel was about enlivening human hearts to the mercies of God as a manifestation of the glory of God's righteous and eternal reign.
- For others, Paul had little care for the poor because he expected Jesus to return at any point, making poverty an issue that required no theologizing on Paul's part.

At times, these two views about Paul can easily reinforce each other.

Views of this kind are problematic, if only because they draw the wrong conclusions from things that are otherwise true. It is true that for Paul the gospel enlivens human hearts to the mercies of God as a manifestation of the glory of God's righteous and eternal reign. Moreover, it seems true that Paul imagined that Jesus might return at any point (see 1 Cor 7:29–31). But neither of these necessarily entails that care for the poor had no foothold within Paul's gospel. Paul worked hard to ensure that Jesus-followers were characterized by righteousness in their relationships with God, with other Jesus-followers, and with others beyond Jesus groups. What mattered to him was whether Jesus-followers were exhibiting the characteristics of God's righteousness, advertising and embodying God's transforming grace even in the present.

But even if there's a reason to think that care for the poor could well fit within Paul's theologizing, what evidence is there that this was indeed the case? Paul's "collection" efforts of the mid-50s might be considered in this regard. This project was intended to offset the adverse conditions of poverty of other Jesus-followers in Jerusalem. That Paul put tremendous effort into making this a success is demonstrated by a few texts in which he links his apostolic credentials to the accomplishing of this initiative (1 Cor 16:1–4; 2 Corinthians 8–9; Rom 15:25–33).

There might well be mixed signals in this initiative, however. Since the legitimacy of Paul's apostleship was questioned by some who seem to have connections with the all-important Jesus groups in Jerusalem (see, e.g., Rom 15:30–31), Paul's collection efforts likely played a role in his attempt to counter suspicion about his apostleship in the city that formed the earliest hub of the emergent Jesus movement. It is possible to argue, then, that Paul's collection effort had nothing to do with caring for the poor and everything with bolstering his own apostolic credentials. By delivering money to Jerusalem Jesus-followers, Paul was doing nothing other than buying off his critics.

Even after applying suspicion to Paul's motivations for the collection, however, something still remains unexplained. If there is a sense in which Paul was buying off his critics, he nonetheless chose to do so through a demonstration of the moral transformation of the Christians whom his gospel had nurtured. He did not demonstrate transformation by number charts of congregational growth, for instance, or by any other indicator that might be imagined. Instead, he demonstrated their transformation by the gospel in terms of their willingness to contribute from their own resources for the benefit of others. And for many of those who contributed to Paul's collection efforts, resources were already in short supply. In other words, in Paul's view, precisely the willingness of Gentile Jesus-followers to contribute to the offsetting of the needs of others was proof of the transforming power of the gospel within the Jesus groups that he had established.

This is a strong indicator that concern for the poor, although not the gospel in itself, was nonetheless one component of that gospel. This is further suggested by Paul's discussion about the collection in 2 Corinthians 8–9. There, as we have seen, Paul seeks to motivate Corinthian Christians to participate by

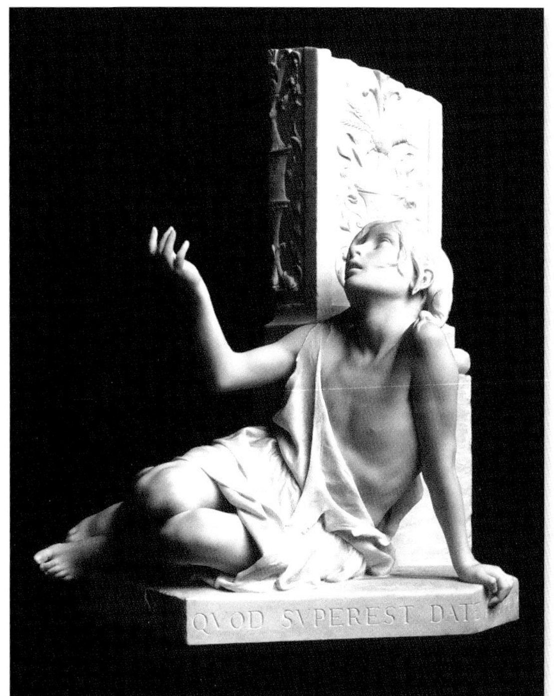

© Alinari Archives/The Image Works

▲ The poor were everywhere to be seen in the cities that Paul used as bases for his ministry.

▼ Sixth-century mosaic of the miracle of the loaves and fishes. In Paul's collection efforts, he chose to demonstrate the transformation of the Jesus-followers in terms of their willingness to contribute from their own resources for the benefit of others.

Public Domain

Jesus' Incarnation and the Roman System of Patronage

The model of Jesus becoming "poor" (i.e., in his incarnation) so that his followers might become "rich" (i.e., blessed by him) resonates in interesting ways (some comparable, some contrastive) with the system of patronage that lay at the heart of Greco-Roman urbanism. Patronage involved two people, being unequal in status, entering into a mutually enriching relationship. The patron, who was superior in status, provided financial and material support to the client, who was inferior in status. In return, the client was expected to augment the public prestige of the patron through public expressions of gratitude or in some other fashion.

Publicly advertising the beneficence of one's patron was an enterprise that clients vigorously carried out, in fulfillment of their duties within the patronage relationship. For this reason, numerous inscriptions have been found in which clients praise their patron's "goodwill" (*eunoia*) and "grace" or "gift" (*charis*). Clients sometimes followed their patron through the urban streets as an entourage, loudly acclaiming his greatness and generosity. Or they were frequently seen clustered at the entryway or within the central atrium of their patron's house, allowing passers by to catch a glimpse of the influence of the patron in generous support of his clients. In such ways, notoriety and enrichment were at the hub of the patronal relationship, to the benefit of both parties. (For a challenge to this system, see Luke 14:12–14 and 22:25–26.)

reminding them of their position within the unfolding apocalyptic story of God and their place within the story of Jesus' own self-giving. He articulates their participation in terms usually reserved for articulating the gospel—terms such as "grace," "gift," "obedience," "service," and "righteousness." If Paul's collection initiative was a hard copy of the gospel he proclaimed, it was so not because the gospel was a means to benefit Paul's own reputation and stature, but because the gospel, like the collection initiative itself, was beneficial to those in need.

It is hardly surprising, then, that at the heart of his discussion of the collection, Paul calls to mind the story of the self-giving Jesus—a story that is to drive the self-identity of Jesus-followers: "For you know the grace of our Lord Jesus Christ, that though he was rich, yet for your sake he became poor, so that you through his poverty might become rich" (2 Cor 8:9).

When read in this light, certain passages from Paul's texts emerge in fresh light. For instance, it is hardly surprising that in his general exhortations to live in a manner worthy of God, Paul's instructions to do good to the needy often have strong economic connotations. This would include passages such as Rom 12:13, 16; 2 Cor 9:13; Gal 6:9–10; Eph 4:28; 1 Thess 5:14–15; 2 Thess 3:6–13; 1 Tim 5:3–16 (see also 6:9–10, 17–18); Titus 3:14. If some of these texts were written by those seeking to preserve Paul's voice in new situations after his death, this only reinforces the point that Paul was known to articulate such concerns on a regular basis.[18]

In light of all this, it should come as no surprise to find Paul speaking harsh words to Corinthian Christians when relationships within their groups were being skewed along

18. In Acts 20:18–35, Paul gives his farewell speech to Christians, with that speech concluding in this fashion: "we must help the weak, remembering the words the Lord Jesus himself said: 'It is more blessed to give than to receive'" (20:35). As the context makes clear, the phrase "we must help the weak" involves using material resources as a means of offsetting the economic needs of others (see 20:33–34).

economic lines. When the Lord's Supper was observed in such a fashion as to reinforce economic differences at the expense of the poorer members, Paul vehemently objects. According to Paul, the Corinthian offense was so heinous that "many among you are weak and sick, and a number of you have fallen asleep" (1 Cor 11:30). Offending the Lord's Supper in their treatment of the poor has resulted in the Corinthian Christians compromising the proclamation of "the Lord's death until he comes" (11:26), a proclamation that is little else than the gospel itself.

"Paul is very much aware of the urban fact that cash and creed are intimately interrelated."[19]

Behind all this lies a verse that has been largely neglected—that is, Gal 2:10. In 2:1–10 Paul recounts discussions among leading figures of the early Jesus movement regarding whether circumcision was essential to all Jesus-followers or whether Gentile Jesus-followers could be absolved from becoming circumcised. In their discussions about "the truth of the gospel" (2:5), the leaders agreed that circumcision was not essential to the identity of Jesus-followers across the board. But they also agreed that Gentile Jesus-followers should "remember the poor" (2:10).

Rightly, then, did Peter and James and John give their right hand of fellowship to Paul, and agree on such a division of their work, as that Paul should go to the heathen, and themselves to the circumcision. Their agreement, also, "to remember the poor" was in complete conformity with the law of the Creator, which cherished the poor and needy. (Tertullian, *Against Marcion* 5.3)

Although commentators regularly imagine this to stipulate that Gentile Christians should send money to "the poor *in Jerusalem*," it is better to interpret the phrase in its most natural sense.[20] The call was for Gentile Jesus-followers to support the poor in their local contexts. The apostles of the Jesus movement seem to have imagined that Jewish Jesus-followers would naturally be supportive of the poor in their local contexts, because Jews had deeply entrenched traditions encouraging care for the poor; but since Gentiles had few traditions along these lines, the apostles deemed it appropriate to draw attention to caring for the poor as an essential feature of all Jesus groups, not just those comprised predominantly of Jewish members.

In essence, then, the leaders of the early Jesus movement had decided that

▼ When the Lord's Supper was observed in such a fashion as to reinforce economic differences at the expense of the poorer members, Paul vehemently objects.

Ms 364 fol.111 Scene of excommunication, from 'Decretales' by Jean Andre, 13th – 14th century, French School/Bibliotheque Municipale, Laon, France/Giraudon/The Bridgeman Art Library

19. Dieter Georgi, *The City in the Valley: Biblical Interpretation and Urban Theology* (Atlanta: Society of Biblical Literature, 2005), 283.
20. This is argued in Bruce W. Longenecker, *Remember the Poor: Paul, Poverty, and the Greco-Roman World* (Grand Rapids: Eerdmans, 2010).

Care for the poor was a key characteristic for many Jesus groups, to the extent that by the fourth century, Emperor Julian (emperor from 361 – 363) feared that Christianity would take over the whole world because of the "stealth of their good deeds." He wrote:

> We must pay special attention to this point, and by this means effect a cure [i.e., for the "disease" of Christianity]. For when it came about that the poor were neglected and overlooked by the [pagan] priests, then I think the impious Galileans [Jesus-followers] observed this fact and devoted themselves to philanthropy. The result is that they have led very many into atheism [i.e., Christianity because Christians denied the existence of pagan gods]."[21]

Later, insisting that the pagan temples across the empire must establish a welfare system similar to that of the Christians, Emperor Julian funded initiatives for the poor. When writing to the high priest of Galatia, he noted that Christian "benevolence to strangers" and "care for the graves of the dead" and "the pretended holiness of their lives" had been instrumental in the increase of what he called "atheism" in the empire. He noted:

> I believe that we ought really and truly to practise every one of these virtues. And it is not enough for you alone to practise them, but so must all the priests in Galatia, without exception. Either shame or persuade them into righteousness or else remove them from their priestly office. In every city establish frequent hostels in order that strangers may profit by our benevolence; I do not mean for our own people only, but for others also who are in need of money. I have but now made a plan by which you may be well provided for this; for I have given directions that 30,000 modii of corn shall be assigned every year for the whole of Galatia, and 60,000 sextarii of wine. I order that one-fifth of this be used for the poor who serve the priests, and the remainder be distributed by us to strangers and beggars. For it is disgraceful that, when no Jew ever has to beg, and the impious Galileans support not only their own poor but ours as well, all men see that our people lack aid from us.[22]

communities of Jesus devotion, regardless of their ethnicity, did not need to be identical in the practice of circumcision but, instead, in their mutual faith and their acts of generosity toward the poor. In view of the evidence presented in the preceding paragraphs, it is not surprising to hear Paul say that remembering the poor was "the very thing I had been eager to do all along" (Gal 2:10) — that is, the very thing that he had earnestly devoted himself to when taking the gospel to the Gentiles.

It is likely, then, that Paul expected the "remembrance of the poor" to be embedded within the moral identity of the Jesus groups he had founded, being integrally related to the proclamation of the good news. Caring for the poor was not something that could simply wait until God's eschatological age was fully implemented. For Paul, Jesus groups that worshiped the one who gave himself for others should be caring for the poor in the present, as they experience something of the eschatological age within their midst "until he comes"

21. Emperor Julian, "Fragment of a Letter to a Priest," in *The Works of the Emperor Julian* (trans. W. C. Wright; LCL 29), 2:337 – 38.
22. Emperor Julian, "Letter 22, To Arcacius, High-Priest of Galatia," in ibid., 3:67 – 73.

(1 Cor 11:26). In the meantime, Paul expected the ethos of Jesus groups to conform to the character of "the historical Jesus," who himself was remembered as having been concerned about the well-being of the poor.

PROBLEMATIZING VIOLENCE

In Matthew's gospel, Jesus is remembered as saying things like this: "If anyone slaps you on the right cheek, turn to them the other cheek also" (Matt 5:39), and, "Love your enemies and pray for those who persecute you" (5:44). Luke's gospel has the same kind of remembrances of Jesus, recording words like the following :

> Love your enemies, do good to those who hate you, bless those who curse you, pray for those who mistreat you. If someone slaps you on one cheek, turn the other also. If someone takes your coat, do not withhold your shirt. Give to everyone who asks you, and if anyone takes what belongs to you, do not demand it back. (Luke 6:27–30)

> Paul's moral impulse was "derived in its shape and in its meaning, and even in its language, from the novelty of the teaching and the work and the triumph of Jesus."[24]

Rightly or wrongly, these passages are frequently thought to depict Jesus' advocacy of nonviolence (albeit, nonviolent resistance).[23] But the question naturally arises, if Jesus was remembered in these terms, does the issue of violence and nonviolence have any foothold within Paul's letters?

In the early years of the twenty-first century, interpreters began to ask precisely this kind of question with rigor. In an evermore dangerous world, interpreters began to discuss whether Paul's letters contain a "residue" that is indicative of a general attitude toward violence. Is there within his letters a trace of theological DNA from which to reconstruct Paul's inclination regarding violence and the life of the Jesus-follower?

There are, in fact, resources that allow this discussion to gain some traction. It is noticeable, for instance, that all the data point in one direction regarding Paul's life immediately prior to his **christophany** on the **Damascus Road**. That is, Paul was engaged in violent activity, as we have seen in chapter 1. Although that violent activity was directed against the early Jesus movement, we cannot be sure what form it took. It was probably comprised of much more than simply making life a bit uncomfortable for Christians, making them feel ashamed of their commitment to Jesus. But we cannot tell whether it involved physically restraining them in some fashion, imprisoning them, or murdering them (the latter is improbable). But the data generally point in the direction of Paul having exercised some form of physical violence against early Christians.

The foothold for this comes from a passage like Gal 1:13, where Paul talks about his "previous way of life in Judaism" and how he intensely "persecuted the church of God and tried to destroy it" (see also Gal 1:23; 1 Cor 15:9; Phil 3:6). In 1 Tim 1:13 this persecution is listed in association with violence. The Acts narrative similarly amplifies Paul's violent persecution of Christians on seven occasions:

23. See, e.g., Hays, *The Moral Vision of the New Testament*, 319–29.
24. John Howard Yoder, *The Politics of Jesus* (2nd ed.; Grand Rapids: Eerdmans 1994), 10.

1. Paul goes "from house to house" to drag off "both men and women and put them in prison" (8:3).
2. Paul breathes out "murderous threats against the Lord's disciples" and has himself authorized to "take them as prisoners" (9:1–2).
3. **Ananias** (who restores Paul's vision after his blinding encounter with the risen Christ) speaks of "all the harm" Paul has done to God's people, seeking "to arrest all" who belong to the Jesus movement (9:13–14).
4. Jews from Damascus recognize Paul as "the man who raised havoc in Jerusalem" among Jesus-followers in Jerusalem, and the one who came to Damascus "to take them as prisoners" (9:21).
5. Paul claims that he "persecuted the followers of this Way to their death, arresting both men and women and throwing them into prison," and that he had gone to Damascus in order to bring Christians there "as prisoners to Jerusalem to be punished" (22:4–5).
6. Paul speaks of how he had imprisoned and beaten Christians, having also given approval to the shedding of Stephen's blood (22:19–20; see 7:58 and 8:1).
7. Paul remembers how he had "put many of the Lord's people in prison," and he cast his "vote against them" so that "they were put to death"; and he recalls how he tried to have them "punished" and "to force them to blaspheme," illustrating that he "was so obsessed with persecuting them" (26:10–11).

Of course, Paul ceased from his violent persecution of the Jesus movement after his christophany on the road to Damascus. And it has long been assumed that Paul's abandonment of violence was simply because of the "social" implications of that christophany. Clearly it would have been senseless for Paul to have continued his vehement harassment of Jesus-followers once he became a Jesus-follower himself.

▼ Twelfth-century fresco of the stoning of Stephen. Paul speaks of how he had imprisoned and beaten Jesus-followers, including his approval of the stoning of Stephen.

Convent of St. John, Mustair, Switzerland/Hirmer Fotoarchiv/The Bridgeman Art Library

But interpreters have begun to ask whether in fact there is more to the story than that. It is notable, for instance, that in a variety of letters Paul alludes to Jesus' words advocating nonviolence (albeit nonviolent resistance). As noted in chapter 11 above, Jesus' ethic of turning the other cheek when someone is violent toward you and of loving one's enemies shines through Rom 12:17–21. There Paul instructs his audience not to "repay anyone evil for evil," to "live at peace with everyone," not to take revenge, to "overcome evil with good," and to feed the hungry enemy and give refreshment to the thirsty enemy.

The impression that Jesus' social ethic lies behind these exhortations is reinforced when 1 Cor 4:12–13 is considered. There, Paul's words sound much like those of Jesus: "when we are cursed, we bless; when we are persecuted, we endure it; when we are slandered, we answer kindly." Further still, in what is likely to be his earliest surviving letter, Paul poses the following challenge to his audience, in words not unlike those of Jesus: "Make sure that nobody pays back wrong for wrong" (1 Thess 5:15).

While passages such as these echo the ethical sentiments of Jesus, they run contrary to the sentiments of the violent Paul who, prior to his christophany, directed intense efforts against the Jesus movement. It is questionable how frequently the pre-christophanic Paul would have advocated the attitude proposed in Phil 4:5: "Let your gentleness be evident to all."

Are passages such as these simply the outcome of "social realignment," with Paul joining the movement that he had previously persecuted? Or might they indicate something of a "theological realignment" within Paul?

Some are now of the view that what we see in evidence of this kind is the result not simply of Paul's realignment in his associations with others (i.e., from persecutor of the Jesus movement to apostle within the Jesus movement) but of Paul's theological transformation (i.e., from advocating violence to abandoning violence). The reasons for thinking so are both historical and theological.

Historically, Jesus' advocacy of nonviolence seems to have had widespread currency within the early Jesus movement. This is indicated by the way Paul can echo Jesus' words in his letters to Jesus groups in **Thessalonica** (written from Corinth), Corinth (written from **Ephesus**), and **Rome** (written from Corinth). Evidently these echoes were to carry some weight among Paul's audiences, even though Paul does not explicitly cite them as having

Regarding Paul's instruction in Rom 12:17–21 not to return evil for evil and to allow God to be the one to "repay" those who commit evil, Peter Oakes writes this: "It is very difficult for us to imagine how radical a change of behavior was called for by teaching such as this by Paul, or in Jesus' injunction to 'turn the other cheek.' Relatively few of us will have depended on violent retribution as our standard means of defence. We have been used to the idea of picking up the phone to call the police instead. In [the ancient world] . . . you were on your own — or, rather, you were part of whatever group you belonged to that might defend you. For us, renunciation of violent revenge costs little (at personal, if not necessarily at national level). For the members of a craftworker house church in first-century Rome, it cost their lives. We may baulk at Paul's appeal to God's vengeance. We would rather have a world in which defence was not needed: in which no one, even God, needed to carry out vengeance on our behalf. But neither Paul nor his hearers is in that world."[25]

25. Peter Oakes, *Reading Romans in Pompeii: Paul's Letter at Ground Level* (Minneapolis: Fortress, 2009), 125.

been uttered by Jesus. Arguably, Paul did not need to make the point explicitly because he assumed that enough people among his audiences would recognize them as echoes of Jesus' own position.

"There is not a syllable in the Pauline letters that can be cited in support of Christians employing violence."[26]

Moreover, the letter recipients were not the only ones to appreciate the echoes of Jesus; presumably some Christians in the city where Paul wrote each letter may well also have been acquainted with the contents of his letters.[27] Perhaps, then, we can draw the conclusion that Christians who knew of Jesus' advocacy of nonviolence resided not only in the cities of Thessalonica, Corinth, and Rome, but also in Ephesus, from where Paul wrote 1 Corinthians.

Further still, the fact that Paul seems to assume that audiences in Rome will hear the echo is most notable. Although Paul had not founded the Jesus groups there, he nonetheless errs on the side of taking it for granted that Christians in Rome would be able to hear those echoes. That assumption alone testifies to the widespread knowledge about Jesus' advocacy of nonviolence throughout Jesus groups of the Mediterranean basin. It is little wonder that such a Jesus emerges in both the Matthean and Lukan Gospels (Matt 5:39, 44; Luke 6:27–30).

"Paul needed a conversion from violence via a divine vindication of nonviolence — the resurrection — to conclude that nonviolence is the way of God and therefore also of the covenant people. It is those who live between the past and the future — in the overlap of the ages — who can live without violence because they trust in God's *future* victory/resurrection guaranteed by God's *past* victory/resurrection."[28]

This historical scenario plays an important role in relation to theological aspects of this issue. If Jesus groups told stories about Jesus in which his advocacy of nonviolence was part of the storytelling process, to what extent should this feature play a role in our understanding of Paul's emphasis on "Christ in me"? For instance, when Paul writes, "I have been crucified with Christ and I no longer live, but Christ lives in me" (Gal 2:20), is this claim to be divorced from Paul's earlier discussion in Galatians 1 about when Christ did not live in him? Paul describes his life then as a time when intentional violence characterized his efforts and his understanding of God's will. Does the flow of Paul's autobiographical narrative within Galatians 1–2 intimate that the "apocalyptic revelation" of God's nonviolent Son "in me" (*apokalypsai . . . en emoi*, 1:16) involved the destruction of the Paul who had prided himself on his violent initiatives in the name of God? When Jesus Christ comes alive in Paul, does the nonviolence of Jesus "apocalyptically" trounce the violence of the pre-christophanic Paul, who had been

26. Hays, *The Moral Vision of the New Testament*, 331.
27. This could have happened either by reading a letter before it was sent to its destination, or after it was sent, since we must imagine that Paul's letter-writer made a copy of a letter before it was sent (this being standard practice in the ancient world whenever texts contained substantial content).
28. Michael Gorman, *Inhabiting the Cruciform God: Kenosis, Justification, and Theosis in Paul's Narrative Soteriology* (Grand Rapids: Eerdmans, 2009), 153, 155.

immersed in "the present evil age" (1:4)? Does Paul himself become an incarnation of Jesus' nonviolent engagement with others, as the one who "loved me and gave himself for me" (2:20; see also 1:4)?

If this is feasible, there is even more to Paul's case in Galatians than might otherwise meet the eye. In outlining the biography of Galatian Christians who are entertaining the prospect of observing the law to enhance their status before God, Paul entertains the prospect of them moving from self-giving (as in Gal 4:12–15) to violence. So, when listing the kind of the acts that derive from the human enslavement to the power of Sin, Paul includes not only acts of sexual immorality, drunkenness, and idolatry, but also various entries that seem to target violent attitudes and activities. These eight entries from 5:20–21 demonstrate the point, with six of them being listed in the plural, as if to speak of not simply attitudes (e.g., hatred) but actions undergirded by those attitudes (e.g., acts of hatred):

- acts that induce hatred between people;
- competitive strife between people;
- envious jealousy between people;
- acts that incite anger between people;
- acts that promote rivalry between people;
- acts that promote division between people;
- acts that induce schisms between people; and
- acts of selfish envy.[29]

That violence is at the heart of this complex of attitudes and behaviors is indicated further by other things Paul says about it elsewhere in Galatians. In 5:26, "conceit" is shown to result in precisely the same violence-ridden entries listed in 5:20–21: "provoking and envying each other." This couples well with what Paul had already said in 5:15, where he proposes that the Galatians will be "biting and devouring each other" until they have been completely "destroyed by each other." In these cases, the attribute of competitiveness that results in "mutually assured destruction" is precisely the opposite of the moral character that becomes incarnated when "Christ is born in you" (4:19).

Is there reason to think that Paul may have wanted his own violent past to represent a possible future scenario for the Galatian Christians, should they fail to align themselves with his gospel? Was he implying that his own character of violence that he previously manifested is waiting at the gate for Galatian Christians unless they heed his warnings?

The fact that Paul is "looking over his shoulder" at his past life of violence even when addressing the Galatian situation is suggested by Gal 4:29. There he contrasts identity that comes "by the power of the Spirit" with identity that comes "by human effort," noting that the latter is characterized by the "persecution" of others. The word he uses there is precisely the same as the one he used of himself to characterize his previous life of violent persecution (1:13, 23). A life of violence and mutual destruction awaits the Galatian Christians should they fail to align themselves with the Spirit who induces the moral character that involves

29. These entries are translated in a way that diverges from the NIV and other translations, in order to bring out the sense of the plurals that Paul uses, which correspond to the word "acts" in this translation.

"Paul's most profound bequest to subsequent Christian discourse was his transformation of the reported crucifixion and resurrection of Jesus Christ into a multipurpose metaphor with vast generative and transformative power — not least for moral perceptions."[30]

"love, joy, peace, forbearance, kindness, goodness, faithfulness, gentleness and self-control" (5:22–23).

There is scope for thinking, then, that (1) Paul imagined his past to be characterized by violence, and (2) he came to understand the moral character of the Jesus-follower to involve nonviolent self-giving induced by the Spirit. What we might be seeing in a text like Galatians is Paul's assumption that violence arises out of the self-interestedness that is evident everywhere throughout "the present evil age," as well as the expectation that violence has been destroyed for those who have been "crucified with Christ" and in whom Christ is now living.

SUMMARY REFLECTION

The moral disposition Paul expects to find within communities of Jesus devotion is one defined by the cruciform character of the life of his Lord. While self-giving is not the only distinctive of Christian discipleship, Paul nonetheless finds it to be one essential distinctive that, when compromised, threatens to decouple communities from the source of their inner strength and their outward testimony.

In the matrix of cruciform self-giving, Paul expects communities to find resources for interpreting who they are in their indigenous placements and what they are called to do in their ongoing life together. Perhaps this is what he means when he speaks of "the renewing of your mind" as the means by which Jesus-followers "will be able to test and approve what God's will is — his good, pleasing and perfect will" (Rom 12:1–2).

30. Meeks, *The Origins of Christian Morality,* 196.

» KEY PEOPLE, PLACES, AND TERMS «

Abraham	Corinth	Libertinism	Sarah
Ananias	Damascus Road	Lord's Supper	Thessalonica
Christophany	Ephesus	Mosaic Law	Torah
Circumcision	Hagar	Rome	

» QUESTIONS FOR REVIEW AND DISCUSSION «

1. What is the relationship between ethics and ethos, and how does each figure in Pauline thought?
2. Define "freedom" according to Paul.
3. How did Paul's emphasis on freedom become distorted among some early Christians?
4. What does Paul mean by "the flesh"?
5. Describe the various strategies employed in Paul's reading of Scripture. Is there a criterion for legitimate interpretation?
6. What for Paul determines the moral ethos of Christian communities? Why is this so important to him?
7. How did concern for the poor figure into Paul's ministry? What is the relationship between the gospel and concern for the poor according to Paul?
8. Describe the "theological realignment" of Paul with regard to violence.

» CONTEMPORARY THEOLOGICAL REFLECTION «

1. Why might modern Christians prefer to focus on "ethics" rather than "ethos"? What are the dangers in neglecting to attend to the ethos of a Christian community?
2. In what ways do you think modern Christians might misinterpret "freedom"?
3. In his essay entitled *On Liberty*, the philosopher John Stuart Mill wrote the following: "The only freedom which deserves the name is that of pursuing our own good in our own way, so long as we do not attempt to deprive others of theirs or impede their efforts to obtain it."[31] In what ways might Paul's view differ from Mill's view?

---

31. John Stuart Mill, *Three Essays: On Liberty; Representative Government; The Subjection of Women* (Oxford: Oxford University Press, 1975), 18.

4. Reading the Old Testament can still be troublesome for Christians. Why might that be? What can Christians in the twenty-first century learn from Paul's approach to Scripture?
5. How often do you see a wealthy person sitting next to a poor person in a Christian church today? What would Paul think about that?

» GOING FURTHER «

Personal Freedom and Corporate Responsibility

Horrell, David G. *Solidarity and Difference: A Contemporary Reading of Paul's Ethics*. London: T&T Clark, 2005.

Martin, Dale B. *Slavery as Salvation: The Metaphor of Slavery in Pauline Christianity*. New Haven, CT: Yale University Press, 1990.

Paul's Interpretation of Scripture

Aageson, James W. *Written Also for Our Sake: Paul and the Art of Biblical Interpretation*. Louisville: Westminster John Knox, 1993.

Hays, Richard B. *Echoes of Scripture in the Letters of Paul*. New Haven, CT: Yale University Press, 1989.

———. *The Conversion of the Imagination: Paul as Interpreter of Israel's Scripture*. Grand Rapids: Eerdmans, 2005.

Stanley, Christopher D. *Arguing with Scripture: The Rhetoric of Quotations in the Letters of Paul*. New York: T&T Clark, 2004.

Paul's Collection for the Poor in Jerusalem; Paul and the Poor in General

Downs, David J. *The Offering of the Gentiles*. Tübingen: Mohr Siebeck, 2008.

Longenecker, Bruce W. *Remember the Poor: Paul, Poverty, and the Greco-Roman World*. Grand Rapids: Eerdmans, 2010.

Meggitt, Justin J. *Paul, Poverty and Survival*. Edinburgh: T&T Clark, 1998.

Problematizing Violence in Paul

Gabrielson, Jeremy. *Paul's Non-Violent Gospel: The Theological Politics of Peace in Paul's Life and Letters*. Eugene, OR: Pickwick, 2013.

Gorman, Michael. "While We Were Enemies: Paul, the Resurrection, and the End of Violence." Pages 129–59 in idem, *Inhabiting the Cruciform God: Kenosis, Justification, and Theosis in Paul's Narrative Soteriology*. Grand Rapids: Eerdmans, 2009.

Hays, Richard B. *The Moral Vision of the New Testament: Community, Cross, New Creation*. San Francisco: HarperOne, 1996 (esp. pp. 313–45).

Swartley, Willard M. *Covenant of Peace: The Missing Peace in New Testament Theology and Ethics*. Grand Rapids: Eerdmans, 2006 (esp. pp. 189–253).

A VERY SHORT CONCLUSION

In the words of Claude Lévi-Strauss, Paul is "good to think with."[1] In the preceding chapters, we have been "thinking through Paul"—a phrase that signals both thinking "about him" and thinking "by means of his thoughts" or "in a Pauline manner."

If it is "good to think with" Paul, it is also challenging. In the process of considering his eventful life, his canonical letters, and his theological discourse, we have found Paul to be a multidimensional individual, akin to E. M. Forster's "round character."[2] Perhaps this is one reason why "thinking through Paul" can at times complicate what we might have previously regarded as relatively simple and straightforward.

If it is "good to think with" Paul, it is also exciting. Paul consistently offers fresh angles of vision to inspire remarkable practices within communities of Jesus devotion. As Jerome Murphy-O'Connor has perceptively noted, if Paul's theology is foreign to many today, it is not that his "version of Christianity has failed, [but that] it has never been seriously tried."[3] Perhaps Paul's "version of Christianity" is deserving of further consideration, better articulation, and embodied practice within the lives of individuals and Christian communities today, some twenty centuries after Paul ministered in the service of his Lord.

If it is "good to think with" Paul, it may also be life-changing. Although this introductory textbook may be at its end, the process of "thinking through Paul" (in both senses) is not one that is ever fully completed. If Paul would encourage us to continue that process, he would expect us to do so in and on behalf of communities inspired by the Spirit of the One whom he worshiped as Lord, who gave himself to deliver us, "so that with one mind and one voice [we might] glorify the God and Father of our Lord Jesus Christ" (Rom 15:6).

1. Claude Lévi-Strauss, *Totemism* (Boston: Beacon, 1963), 89.
2. See E. M. Forster, *Aspects of the Novel* (London: E. Arnold, 1927).
3. Jerome Murphy-O'Connor, *Paul: His Story* (Oxford: Oxford University Press, 2006), 239.

GLOSSARY

Abraham: A patriarch of Israel whose story is recounted throughout much of the book of Genesis in the Old Testament. God promised to give him many descendants and a land, and gave circumcision as a sign of the covenant (Genesis 15–17). Jews traced their ethnic identity to him as the father of their nation. Although past the age of childbearing, his wife, Sarah, gave birth to a son named Isaac, after his slave, Hagar, gave birth to a son named Ishmael; see Paul's use of this story in Gal 4:21–5:1.

Achaicus: One of three people Paul mentions in 1 Cor 16:17 as having come to him from Corinth. They brought news about Corinthian Jesus groups to Paul, causing him to write 1 Corinthians.

Acrocorinth: A huge outcrop of rock that stands high above the ancient city of Corinth.

Adam: The first created human being in Genesis 1–3. Along with his wife, Eve, he ate from the tree of knowledge of good and evil and was cast out of the garden of Eden. Paul makes a theological comparison between Adam and Christ in Romans 5 and 1 Corinthians 15.

Agitators: This term is applied especially to those whom Paul felt were "agitating" the Jesus groups in Galatia. See especially Paul's use of the term in Gal 5:12.

Alexandria: The leading city of Egypt.

Amanuensis: A "secretary." One employed to take dictation or to copy a manuscript. It appears that Paul routinely used an amanuensis. He clearly did when writing Romans: "I, Tertius, who wrote down this letter, greet you in the Lord" (16:22).

Ananias: The man from Damascus mentioned in Acts 9 and 22, who is said to have restored Paul's vision after his blinding encounter with the risen Christ.

Andronicus: Paul greets him in Rom 16:7. He is probably the husband of Junia, with Paul referring to them as "outstanding among the apostles" (although this is sometimes disputed). He was a Jesus-follower prior to Paul and was in prison with Paul.

Antinomian (i.e., "anti" and "nomian," from *nomos* or "law"): This view supposes that Christians, having been freed from the law, do not have to be concerned with their behavior at all. Being freed from the law is thought to mean that one can indulge in sin and, in the process, enhance God's reputation as a gracious God who redeems sinners. Paul opposed this view. (See also "Libertinism.")

Apocalyptic: In this textbook, the term "apocalyptic" is used to denote Paul's vision of the unassailable transformation of the created order in right relationships. In this view of the triumph of Israel's God, the cosmic forces that have ensnared God's good creation in patterns of sin and death are thwarted through the death and resurrection of Jesus Christ and the power of the Spirit. See also "Jewish Apocalypticism."

Apollos: An educated Jew from Alexandria who became a powerful leader among Jesus groups. Some Corinthian Christians found him to be especially impressive. He is mentioned primarily in 1 Corinthians 1–4 and Acts 18–19.

Apostle: From the Greek term *apostolos*, which literally means "sent one." In the New Testament, the word denotes those commissioned by God to deliver the good news of the early Jesus movement. Paul employs this title as a self-designation in the nondisputed letters (Rom 1:1; 11:13; 1 Cor 1:1; 2:7; 4:9; 9:1–2; 15:9; 2 Cor 1:1; 12:12; Gal 1:1, 17; 1 Thess 2:7). In the disputed letters, the term is used to designate Paul in Eph 1:1; Col 1:1; 1 Tim 1:1; 2:7; 2 Tim 1:1, 11; and Titus 1:1.

Apphia: A member of the Colossian church. Paul refers to her as "the sister" in Philemon 2. Some scholars speculate that she was Philemon's wife.

Aquila: The husband of Prisca (also known as Priscilla); both were Paul's close fellow evangelists. They are mentioned in Acts 18, Romans 16, 1 Corinthians 16, and 2 Timothy 4. See also "Prisca/Priscilla."

Arabia: Paul reports in Gal 1:17b that after his conversion/call he went to Arabia, presumabily the Nabatean kingdom located south of Damascus and east of the Jordan River.

Archippus: A member of the Colossian church. Paul refers to him as a "fellow soldier" in Philemon 2 and admonishes him in Col 4:17 to "complete his ministry he had received in the Lord."

Ark of the covenant: Originally the chest carrying the tablets of the Ten Commandments, the ark was placed within the Most Holy Place in the temple. Once a year, on the Day of Atonement, the high priest of the Jewish people would enter the Most Holy Place to sprinkle sacrificial blood on the cover or "mercy seat" of the ark of the covenant. This probably provides the background to Paul's imagery of Jesus as the "mercy seat" in Rom 3:25.

Armor of God: Military imagery employed in 1 Thessalonians and Ephesians to call the recipients to spiritual sobriety and preparedness.

Ataktoi: A Greek term meaning "disorderly, idle, or lazy ones."

Athens: A renowned city in southern Greece. From here, Timothy traveled to Thessalonica (1 Thess 3:1). Acts 17 reports that Paul addressed the Areopagus when he was in Athens.

Atonement: The reconciliation of humanity to God through Jesus Christ.

Augustan Era: The period initiated by the Roman emperor Augustus (27 BC–AD 14) in the Imperial period of Roman rule. It was purportedly an era of peace, security, and justice brought to all the world, united under Roman rule.

Augustus: The Roman emperor from 27 BC to AD 14.

Benjamin: In both Rom 11:1 and Phil 3:5, Paul indicates that he was of the "tribe of Benjamin." Benjamin was the youngest of Jacob's twelve sons. King Saul, after whom Paul/Saul might have been named, was also a Benjamite.

Berea: After being driven from Thessalonica and before traveling to Athens, Paul and Silas visited this Macedonian city, where the Jews "were more receptive than those in Thessalonica" (Acts 17:11).

Bishop/Overseer: A leadership office in the church (Greek *episkopos*). In Paul, see Phil 1:1; 1 Tim 3:1–2; Titus 1:7; cf. Acts 20:28.

Captivity Letters: Also known as the "Prison Epistles." The label interpreters sometimes attach to Philippians, Philemon, Colossians, and Ephesians because Paul is (pictured as being) in captivity when writing these letters.

Cassander: The son of Antipater who founded Thessalonica around 315 BC. He named the city after his wife, Thessalonike, the daughter of Philip of Macedon and stepsister of Alexander the Great.

Cenchreae: A port city to the east of nearby Corinth. Phoebe, who had earned Paul's respect for her efforts on behalf of the gospel, was based there (Rom 16:1).

Cephas: An Aramaic name meaning "rock." This is the name by which Paul typically refers to Peter in his letters.

Charlatan: Someone who falsely passes himself/herself off as a specialist (in the context of this textbook, as a religious guru) by taking advantage of others, merely for financial reward.

Chloe: A woman at the head of a household in Corinth (1 Cor 1:11). She was probably a Jesus-follower herself, although we cannot be certain of that.

Chrestos: The name of someone around whom a disturbance arose among Jews in the city of Rome. The uprising resulted in the expulsions of some Jews from Rome in the year 49, under the directive of the emperor Claudius. The name in this instance might be a misunderstanding of the word Christ (or *Christos* in Greek).

Christology: Christology pertains to the claims made about the person and role of Jesus Christ.

Christophany: The appearance of Jesus Christ to the apostle Paul on the "road to Damascus."

Circular Letter: An encyclical intended for more than one audience. Ephesians is an example of a circular letter.

Circumcision: The practice of removing the foreskin of the male penis. It is deeply embedded in Jewish Scripture and tradition, as a sign of the covenant between God and the ethnic people of Israel. See especially Genesis 17.

Claudius: The Roman emperor from AD 41 to 54.

Colossae: A city that lay in the Lycus River valley roughly one hundred miles east of Ephesus. It was located in close proximity to Laodicea and Hierapolis. A one-time thriving market town, by Paul's time it had diminished in size and influence.

Colossian Philosophy: A competing spiritual movement afoot in Colossae that Paul derides as "hollow and deceptive" (Col 2:8). Although the precise nature of the "philosophy" is unknown, it apparently focused on certain Jewish religious observances, visionary experiences, asceticism linked to regulations, and "wisdom." Paul writes Colossians to combat those who were espousing such teaching.

Corinth: A leading Roman city of the first century, that sat on important transportation routes. Paul had planted Jesus groups within the city and wrote several letters to them in the mid-50s. It was from Corinth that Paul wrote his letter to the Christians in Rome.

Covenant: A legally binding relationship between two parties; in the context of Paul's letters and theology, it pertains especially to the relationship of mutual commitment between God and the people of Israel.

Covenantal Nomism: A term devised by E. P. Sanders in the 1970s in order to capture his sense that Jewish nomism (i.e., observing the law ["law" = *nomos* in Greek] is usually practiced within the context of God's loving covenant with the Jewish people.

Coworkers: People who ministered alongside Paul in spreading the gospel and caring for churches.

Crete: A Mediterranean island where the Pauline coworker Titus ministered. See Titus 1:5.

Crispus: A Corinthian Jesus-follower whom Paul baptized (1 Cor 1:14).

Damascus Road: The term commonly used to denote the place where Paul met the risen Lord, turning his life around and transforming him from persecutor of Christians to an apostle of the Christian gospel.

Day of Atonement: The day when, once a year, the sins of Israel were removed from the presence of God in the Jerusalem temple.

Deacon: A church office in at least some Pauline communities (Greek *diakonos*). See Romans 16:1; Philippians 1:1; 1 Timothy 3:8, 10, 12.

Deutero-Pauline Letters: The term used to describe letters in the Pauline corpus whose authenticity is disputed.

Diaspora: A term used to describe Jews living outside of Palestine.

Doxology: A short song of praise to God. Paul includes several doxological passages in his epistles (e.g., Gal 1:4–5; Phil 4:20; Rom 9:5; 11:33–36; 16:25–27).

Elder: A church office mentioned in 1 Tim 4:14; 5:17, 19; and Titus 1:5 (Greek *presbyteros*).

Epaphras: Paul describes him as a "fellow slave" and "faithful minister of Christ" (Col 1:7; cf. 4:12; Phlm 23). He appears to have been the founder of the church in Colossae. His interaction with Paul regarding the church seems to have spawned the letter to the Colossians.

Epaphroditus: A Philippian believer praised by Paul in Phil 2:25–30. He risked both life and limb in delivering to Paul a gift from the church in Philippi.

Ephesus: A leading seaport city of the Roman world, where Paul ministered for about three years in the mid-50s. He probably wrote some of his Corinthian letters from there, and a Pauline letter was later sent to Christians in Ephesus.

Erastus: A prominent resident of Corinth during Paul's ministry there. See especially Rom 16:23; also 2 Tim 4:20.

Eschatology: More than simply meaning "the end times," the term "eschatology" denotes the study of the final and ultimate state of the created order as it is overcome by the righteous power of God, who will "reclaim" (in a sense) his creation and its history once and for all.

Euodia and Syntyche: Two seemingly influential Philippian women who contended at Paul's side in the gospel. The apostle calls them to concord in Christ (Phil 4:2–3).

Evil Eye, the: It was commonly thought that harm could be brought against others by casting an evil glance at them in conjunction with the power of suprahuman spirits acting on behalf of the one who wielded the evil eye. Amulets for protection against the evil eye were ubiquitous in the ancient world.

Fortunatus: One of three people Paul mentions in 1 Cor 16:17 as having come to him from Corinth. They brought news about Corinthian Jesus-groups to Paul, causing him to write 1 Corinthians.

Gaius: A Christian householder in Corinth who provided hospitality for other Jesus-followers in that city. See especially Rom 16:23 and 1 Cor 1:14.

Galatia: One of the territories through which Paul passed when founding groups of Jesus-followers, and to which Paul wrote his most passionate letter, known as Galatians. See discussion of South Galatia and North Galatia in chapter 3 above.

Galilee: The region where much of Jesus' ministry was carried out, to the north of Judea and west of the Jordan River.

Gamaliel: The rabbi known in Jewish sources as Gamaliel I or Gamaliel the Elder. Acts 22:3 indicates that Paul was taught by this renowned Pharisaic teacher.

Gentile: A term used by Jews to refer to non-Jews.

Gospel: The message of "good news" proclaimed by Jesus' followers after his resurrection, being a continuation and development of Jesus' proclamation of good news during the time of his own ministry.

Hagar: The slave woman of the partriarch Abraham. She gave birth to a slave son, Ishmael; see Gen 16.

Hellenism: The rise and spread of the Greek way of life over non-Greek lands. Some Jews opposed and sought to resist its perceived negative influence.

Herculaneum: A town at the foot of Mount Vesuvius in Italy. Along with the bustling town of Pompeii, it was covered by volcanic debris in the eruption of Vesuvius in AD 79, leaving it as a wonderland for archaeologists hoping to reconstruct what it would have been like to live in the context of the first-century Greco-Roman world.

Hierapolis: A city in the Lycus River valley that lay in close proximity to Laodicea and Colossae.

Household Code: A table of household admonitions found in Col 3:18–4:1 and Eph 5:21–6:9. Cf. also 1 Pet 2:18–3:7.

Illyricum: A region on the east of the Adriatic Sea, northwest of Macedonia. It converges largely with the region Dalmatia (see 2 Tim 4:10). Paul went to Illyricum prior to writing Romans (see Rom 15:19), being the furthest he had taken the gospel at that point in his ministry.

Inaugurated Eschatology: This term denotes the belief that God's final triumph in righteousness (eschatology) has already begun with the life, death, and resurrection of Jesus Christ but is not yet completed.

Incarnation: This term refers to the belief that God himself became human in Jesus of Nazareth.

Israel: The name of the ancient kingdom (and modern state) of the Jewish people. It is also a term used to refer to the Jewish people.

Isthmian Games: The athletic competition open to athletes from all cities of Greece. The games were held in Corinth in the years before and after the Olympic Games.

Jannes and Jambres: In Jewish tradition, the names assigned to Pharoah's anonymous magicians. See Exod 7:11, 22; 2 Tim 3:8.

Jerusalem: The leading city of Judea, where Jesus was crucified and the early Jesus movement had its initial foothold.

Jerusalem Conference: A meeting between leaders in the early church concerning the Gentile mission and expectations for Gentile believers regarding the Mosaic Law. See Galatians 2 and Acts 15.

Jesus of History: The person from Nazareth whose life is remembered in various ways in the four canonical Gospels (and elsewhere).

Jewish Apocalypticism: A worldview (reflected in some of the Jewish apocalypses of early Judaism) in which the current condition of God's created order is to be set right in a cosmic rectification that involves struggle between the forces of good and evil, with God's power invading the world to uproot opposition to his powerful righteousness.

Judaism: The religion of the ethnic people of Israel, comprised of observing the commandments of God (as revealed in the five books of the Torah or the Mosaic law) in response to his gracious calling of Israel through the patriarch Abraham and his offspring.

Judea: The area to the south of Galilee and Samaria and between the Jordan River to the east and the Mediterranean Sea to the west. Jesus was crucified in its leading city, Jerusalem.

Junia: A Christian woman mentioned in Rom 16:7, probably married to Andronicus, who is also mentioned there. Both were Jesus-followers prior to Paul and earned a reputation as "outstanding among the apostles."

King Aretas IV: The ruler of the Arab kingdom of Nabatea from roughly 9 BC to AD 40.

Koinōnia: A Greek term meaning "fellowship" or "close mutual relationship."

Laodicea: A city in the Lycus River valley that lay in close proximity to Hierapolis and Colossae.

Libertinism: This view supposes that Christians, having been freed from the law, do not have to be concerned with their behavior at all. Being freed from the law is thought to mean that one can indulge in sin and, in the process, enhance God's reputation as a gracious God who redeems sinners. Paul opposed this view. (See also "Antinomian.")

Lois and Eunice: According to 2 Tim 1:5, the grandmother and mother of Timothy. Cf. Acts 16:1.

Lord's Supper: A communal meal practiced by Jesus groups in memorial of Jesus' death. Paul offers instructions on the abuse of this communal practice in 1 Cor 11:17–34.

Lydia: A "dealer in purple cloth" from Thyatira whom Paul led to belief and baptism, along with the members of her household (Acts 16:13–15).

Macedonian Vision: According to Acts 16:6–12, Paul commenced his Grecian ministry in response to this vision. He departed the seaside city of Troas in Asia and traveled to Philippi in Macedonia.

Man of Lawlessness: An antichrist figure referred to in 2 Thessalonians 2 whose identity has occasioned no small amount of discussion and debate.

Manumission: The release or setting free of a slave.

Maranatha: A transliteration of the Aramaic words *marana*, "lord," and *tha'*, "come." It is often translated as an imperative: "Our Lord, come." The term appears in the Pauline epistles in 1 Cor 16:22; it is also found in *Didache* 10:6.

Marcion: The bishop of Sinope in the second century AD who believed that the God depicted in the Old Testament was irreconcilable with the God portrayed in the New Testament. His list of canonical texts excised the entire Old Testament and included only the gospel of Luke and ten of Paul's letters.

Monotheism: The belief that only the creator God is worthy of worship, being the one from whom all things have come.

Mosaic Law: The first five books of the Old Testament, from Genesis through to Deuteronomy. The Mosaic law is very much the textual center of the Old Testament, and it is elaborated throughout the rest of the Old Testament.

Neapolis: An ancient seaport city in eastern Macedonia (contemporary Kavala). This is where Paul landed en route to Philippi (Acts 16:11).

Nero: From AD 54 to 68, Nero (ca. 38–68) was the emperor of Rome and its huge empire. He orchestrated the persecution of Christians in the Roman circus after the fire of Rome in July 64, blaming them for the onset of the fire (though the accusation was rightly thought to be baseless).

Onesimus: A slave of Philemon who became a Jesus-follower through Paul's influence. Paul writes a reconciliatory letter to Philemon on his behalf.

Onesiphorus: A supporter and encourager of Paul's in both Ephesus and Rome. See 2 Tim 1:16–18; 4:19.

Palace Guard: In Phil 1:13, Paul refers to the "whole palace [or imperial] guard" (Greek *praitōrion*; Latin *praetorium*). Although the Greek and Latin terms may refer to a palace instead of a palace guard, it appears that the apostle has in mind the elite unit of soldiers who were responsible for the safety of the Roman emperor (in this case Nero) and his family.

Paraenesis: A Greek term meaning "advice, counsel, or exhortation."

Parousia: A Greek word meaning "coming" or "arrival," often used by Paul to refer to the return or second coming of Christ.

Participationistic Eschatology: This term is used to denote the view that God's triumph of righteousness has already taken hold (although it is yet to be fully completed) and that followers of the self-giving Jesus participate in that process as they identify with their Lord (through faith and baptism) and are found "in Christ."

Pauline: An adjective referring to Paul.

Peace and Security: Arguably, a Roman imperial slogan against which Paul speaks in 1 Thess 5:3.

Pedagogue: A slave within a Greco-Roman household who played an essential role by serving as an older overseer of male offspring of the householder. The pedagogue was part custodial caregiver, part disciplinarian, part supervisory escort.

Pentecost: A Greek term that literally means "the fiftieth." It marks the Jewish festival of the Feast of Weeks, which in rabbinic thinking commemorates the giving of the law at Sinai fifty days after the exodus from Egypt. According to Acts 2:1–31, the apostles gathered in Jerusalem after Jesus' resurrection on Pentecost when the Holy Spirit descended on them.

Pharisee: A member of an ancient Jewish sect that upheld strict observance of the oral and written law.

Philadelphia: A Greek word meaning "brotherly love" (see Rom 12:10; 1 Thess 4:9).

Philemon: A believer and master of Onesimus, who was apparently led to faith by Paul in Ephesus.

Philip II of Macedon: The king of Macedon from 359 to 336 BC and father of Alexander the Great. Established Philippi around 356 BC and named it after himself.

Phoebe: A female Christian from the port city of Cenchreae near Corinth, who had assisted many Jesus-followers (probably financially) in the region (Rom 16:1–2). She probably was entrusted with delivering Paul's letter to the Jesus-followers in Rome, and she may have read the letter to them as well.

Pontius Pilate: The Roman procurator of Judea from AD 26 to 36 before whom Jesus appeared. See 1 Tim 6:13.

Porneia: A Greek word meaning "sexual immorality" or "fornication," or "unfaithfulness" (cf. *porno*graphy)

Prisca/Priscilla: A female Christian from Italy (probably Rome) referred to as "Prisca" in Paul's letters (Rom 16:3; 1 Cor 16:19; 2 Tim 4:19) and as "Priscilla" in Acts (18:2, 18–19, 26). She was married to Aquila (Acts 18:2), who is never mentioned apart from her and whose name notably appears after hers on some occasions (Acts 18:18, 26; Rom 16:3; 2 Tim 4:19). The married couple played an important role in Paul's ministry at Corinth and Ephesus, later returning to Rome, where they sponsored a group of Jesus-followers. See also "Aquila."

Pseudonymity: An ancient literary practice of authoring a document in someone else's name. Derived from *pseudonym*, meaning "false name."

Qumran: An area located near the Dead Sea where a number of scrolls were discovered in nearby caves in 1947 and in following years. Many of the scrolls testify to the life of a closely knit community of pious Jews who held views that built on common traditions within Judaism while also interpreting them in novel ways.

Redemption: Deliverance from sin and its sinister effects that has been and will be wrought by Christ.

Restraining Force/Restrainer: A figure/force mentioned in 2 Thessalonians 2. Interpretive ingenuity notwithstanding, the identity of the restraining force/restrainer remains opaque.

Roman imperial cult: The cult that sponsored the worship of the Roman emperor as divine.

Roman imperial ideology: A multifaceted ideology (subject to local permutations) that legitimated and promoted the Roman imperial order.

Roman imperial order: The rule of Rome, under the oversight of Roman emperor Augustus and his imperial successors. It was declared to be an eternal rule of justice and peace that united the whole world.

Rome: The Italian city that was the seat of political, military, and religious power over of a vast empire covering almost all of the Mediterranean basin—an empire that was expanding through military conquest during the first century. One million people resided in the bustling city of Rome.

Sarah: The wife of Abraham in Genesis who gave birth to the promised son, Isaac, even though she was past the age of childbearing (Genesis 21). Through Isaac God fulfilled the promise to make Abraham the father of many nations.

Saul: Paul's Hebrew name, a name he shared with Israel's first king.

Shema: Observant Jews of Paul's day probably prayed the Shema twice each day. Comprised of parts of Deut 6:4–9; 11:13–21; and Num 15:37–41, the prayer focuses Jewish identity on the basis of monotheistic commitment (with the opening words, "Hear, O Israel, the LORD our God, the LORD is one"). Paul reworked this prayer along Christocentric lines in 1 Cor 8:4–6.

Silas/Silvanus: A Pauline coworker, especially prominent in Paul's Grecian ministry.

Silent Years: The period of time between Paul's first visit to Jerusalem after his conversion/call (late AD 30s) and his reemergence in Antioch a number of years later (mid-40s).

Skeuos: A Greek term meaning "vessel" or "container." Sometimes employed metaphorically to refer to a person's "body" (see 1 Thess 4:4).

Socio-rhetorical: A type of literary criticism in which the reader focuses attention on the rhetoric of documents within a specific cultural, linguistic, and historical setting.

Spain: Lying to the west of Italy, this is the geographical area that Paul was eager to evangelize (see Rom 15:24, 28). Scholars are divided as to whether he ever made it there.

Splanchna: A Greek word meaning "bowels" or "guts." Metaphorically, it can refer to one's affections or heart.

Stephanas: One of three people Paul mentions in 1 Cor 16:17 as having come to him from Corinth. They brought news about Corinthian Jesus groups to Paul, causing him to write 1 Corinthians. The household of Stephanas is mentioned in 1 Cor 16:15 as having been "the first converts in Achaia," who "devoted themselves" to service, and in 1 Cor 1:16 as having been baptized by Paul himself.

Suetonius: A Roman historian (c. AD 69–125) who wrote a series of historical biographies on Roman emperors from Julius Caesar to Domitian, known as *Lives of the Caesars*.

Super-apostles: This is a term that was probably coined by Paul (2 Cor 11:5; 12:11) to highlight the character of those who were causing trouble for him among some Corinthian Jesus-followers. That is, in Paul's view these people had an inflated opinion of themselves, both as "super" and as "apostles." They probably were not apostles in the strict sense of the word, nor were they local leaders of Corinthian Jesus groups. Being pleased with their own rhetorical skill and interpretive prowess, they infiltrated Corinthian Jesus groups and sought to wean Jesus-followers there away from Paul's influence, causing the problems that are reflected in 2 Corinthians 10–13 and seem to be newly resolved in 2 Corinthians 1–9.

Systematic theology: A subdiscipline within Christian theology that seeks to organize beliefs into a formal, organized structure.

Tarsus: According to Acts, the birthplace of Paul. Located in eastern Cilicia in southeastern Asia Minor (modern-day Turkey), by the close of the first century BC it had earned a reputation as a place of culture and learning.

Tearful Letter: The letter that Paul wrote to the Corinthians after writing the letter that we refer to as 1 Corinthians; see Paul's reference to this tearful letter in 2 Cor 2:3–4.

Thessalonica: Founded by Cassander in 315 BC, this northern Grecian city, located on the Thermaic Gulf with mountains to the north and fertile land to the west, remains until now.

Timothy: A prominent Pauline coworker, regarded by Paul as a ministerial "son" (see esp. Phil 2:19–24).

Titus: A Gentile Christian who traveled with Paul (Gal 2:1, 3; 2 Cor 8:23). Paul refers to him as his partner and coworker (2 Cor 8:23), who also assisted with the collection for Jerusalem (8:6).

Torah: The first five books of the Old Testament: Genesis, Exodus, Leviticus, Numbers, and Deuteronomy. The Torah is the textual center of the Old Testament, and it is elaborated throughout the rest of the Old Testament.

Trinity: A prominent doctrine of orthodox Christian theology, which describes God as three persons in one: Father, Son, and Holy Spirit. Each of these persons is coequal and coeternal.

Troas: A Greek port city located in modern-day Turkey near the Aegean Sea. According to Acts 16:8–11 and 20:1–12, Troas served as a site for Paul's missionary endeavors and the port from which he proceeded to Macedonia (see also 2 Cor 2:12).

Tychicus: A coworker whom Paul depicts as "a dear brother, faithful minister and fellow servant in the Lord" (Col 4:7; cf. Eph 6:21–22).

Via Egnatia: A Roman road named after Gnaios Egnatios, the Roman proconsul who commissioned its construction. Begun in 146 BC, when completed in 120 BC it ran from Byzantium in the east to Dyrrachium in the west.

Virgil: Also spelt "Vergil," he was a Roman poet and epic storyteller during the time of Emperor Augustus in the late first century BC. Among his writings is the *Aeneid*, an epic story purporting to recount the history that, legitimated by the gods of Rome, paved the way for the establishment of Rome and the imperial rule initiated by Augustus.

We sections: Passages in Acts where the narrative shifts from third person to first person. See Acts 16:10–17; 20:5–15; 21:1–18; 27:1–28:16.

Zeal: (Religious) fervor. Paul employs this term in Phil 3:6 in conjunction with his persecutory activity.

SCRIPTURE INDEX

Acts

Romans

1 Corinthians

2 Corinthians

Galatians

Ephesians

Philippians

Colossians

1 Thessalonians

2 Thessalonians

1 Timothy

2 Timothy

Titus

Philemon

Hebrews

James

1 Peter

2 Peter

Revelation

SUBJECT INDEX

Note: nubers in italics point to pictures and other graphics in the text

AUTHOR INDEX